HANDBOOK OF RESEARCH ON ASIAN ENTREPRENEURSHIP

Handbook of Research on Asian Entrepreneurship

Edited by

Léo-Paul Dana

Adjunct Professor, GSCM – Montpellier Business School, on study leave from the University of Canterbury, New Zealand, Senior Advisor, World Association for Small and Medium Enterprises and Founding Editor, Journal of International Entrepreneurship *and* Journal of Enterprising Communities

Mary Han

Assistant Professor of Entrepreneurship and Strategy, Ryerson University, Canada

Vanessa Ratten

Assistant Professor, School of Business Administration, Duquesne University, USA

Isabell M. Welpe

Senior Research Fellow, Max Planck Institute of Economics, Germany

Edward Elgar
Cheltenham, UK • Northampton, MA, USA

Published by
Edward Elgar Publishing Limited
The Lypiatts
15 Lansdown Road
Cheltenham
Glos GL50 2JA
UK

Edward Elgar Publishing, Inc.
William Pratt House
9 Dewey Court
Northampton
Massachusetts 01060
USA

A catalogue record for this book
is available from the British Library

Library of Congress Control Number: 2009930866

Mixed Sources
Product group from well-managed
forests and other controlled sources
www.fsc.org Cert no. SA-COC-1565
© 1996 Forest Stewardship Council

ISBN 978 1 84720 608 4

Printed and bound by MPG Books Group, UK

Contents

Contributors

Latif Adam, Indonesian Institute of Sciences, Indonesia

Narendra M. Agrawal, Indian Institute, India

Ruta Aidis, University College London, UK

Muhammad Mahboob Ali, Atish Dipankar University, Bangladesh

Ilan Alon, Harvard University, USA

Susanne Barthmann, Siemens AG, Germany

Paul W. Beamish, University of Western Ontario, Canada

Eyal Benjamin, Swinburne University, Australia

M. Khurrum S. Bhutta, Ohio University, USA

John F. Cassidy, University of Dublin, Ireland

Ramdas Chandra, Nova Southeastern University, USA

Hsi-mei Chung, I-Shou University, Republic of China

Ruth Clarke, Nova Southeastern University, USA

Léo-Paul Dana, University of Canterbury, New Zealand and GSCM, France

Teresa E. Dana, University of Canterbury, New Zealand

Hung-bin Ding, Loyola College in Maryland, USA

Babak Fooladi, University of Ottawa, Canada

Itay Friedberg, Swinburne University, Australia

Maria Carmen Galang, University of Victoria, Canada

Wafica A. Ghoul, Davenport University, USA

Eli Gimmon, Swinburne University, Australia

Vahé Heboyan, University of Georgia, USA

Scott A. Hipsher, ZOA Refugee Care, Thailand

Ed Hopkins, Queens University of Technology, Australia

Malcolm Innes-Brown, Curtin University, Australia

Xiao Jianzhong, Kingston University, UK

Liora Katzenstein, Swinburne University, Israel

Julia Korosteleva, University College London, UK

Frank Lasch, Montpellier Business School, France

Stephen W. Litvin, College of Charleston, USA

Jane W. Lu, National University of Singapore, Singapore

Mats Lundahl, Stockholm School of Economics, Finland

Nnamdi Madichie, University of East London, UK

Gerard McElwee, University of Lincoln, UK

Tomasz Mickiewicz, University College London, UK

Bob Moore, Rollins College, USA

Mervyn J. Morris, Queens University of Technology, Australia

Adnan Omar, Southern University, USA

Sandra Pennewiss, Thames Valley University, UK

Shameen Prashantham, University of Glasgow , UK

Sudatta Ranasinghe, Open University, Sri Lanka

Vanessa Ratten, Duquesne University, USA

Tim Rogmans, Zayed University, United Arab Emirates

Nidal Rashid Sabri, Birzeit University, Palestine

Gulnoza S. Saidazimova, Radio Free Europe, Czech Republic

Elena Sannikova, University of Dublin, Ireland

Christopher Seow, University of East London, UK

Yochanan Shachmurove, University of Pennsylvania, USA

Fredrik Sjöholm, Research Institute of Industrial Economics, Sweden

David Smallbone, Kingston University, UK

Sadiq Sohail, King Fahd University, Saudi Arabia

Martine Spence, University of Ottawa, Canada

Joseph Sy-Changco, University of Macau, China

Wee-Liang Tan, Singapore Management University, Singapore

Siri Terjesen, Max Planck Institute, Germany

Mai Thi Thanh Thai, University of St Gallen, Switzerland

Sonia Tiong-Aquino, University of the Philippines, Philippines

Jay Weerawardena, University of Queensland, Australia

Isabell M. Welpe, Max Planck Institute of Economics, Germany

Richard W. Wright, Klagenfurt University, Austria and Athens University, Greece

Serkan Yalcin, Saint Louis University, USA

So-Jin Yoo, Singapore Management University, Singapore

Wenxian Zhang, Rollins College, USA

Foreword

No society can survive without entrepreneurs. The issue for researchers is to find out how in a given society entrepreneurs develop and operate. If one agrees that entrepreneurship consists in the social and individual alchemy that organizes the fusion between individual talent and opportunities then comparative entrepreneurship research will try to look at the conditions under which in particular countries such an alchemy materializes. In the majority of environments entrepreneurship is considered as equivalent to private initiative and freedom, while in others the state, or at least some inspired politician and bureaucrats, have played this role. The value of the present handbook is that it provides an exhaustive survey over 43 countries of the private and public landscape of entrepreneurial development. This work is a prolongation of Dana's original work on the subject, with a much wider scope. The landscape is extremely contrasted ranging from feudal Afghanistan to post-industrial Japan. The task is ambitious and challenging but very rewarding, and reveals a variety of paths: India's software industry for instance that emerges in a regulatory and administrative unfavourable context, while in China farmers have been the spearhead of the entrepreneurial revolution immediately after the so called 'cultural revolution'. Dana et al. in the concluding chapter provide a model that successfully gives an overall picture out of this kaleidoscope. A very useful and interesting handbook.

Philippe Lasserre
Emeritus Professor of Strategy and Asian Business
INSEAD
1 Ayer Rajah Avenue, Singapore, 138676

1 Introduction

Vanessa Ratten and Léo-Paul Dana

We are grateful to Edward Elgar for this opportunity to serve as editors of this collection of papers on international entrepreneurship in Asia. We are also thankful to the many experts who reviewed the manuscripts.

The chapter on Afghanistan is by Ruth Clarke and Ramdas Chandra (Chapter 2). They discuss how Afghanistan is one of the least developed countries in the world and how international government support is fostering entrepreneurship. They also highlight how the war-devastated country needs international entrepreneurship in the form of resources to increase infrastructure and small business activity.

The chapter on Armenia is by Vahé Heboyan (Chapter 3). This chapter explains how international entrepreneurship is important in Armenia despite being a land-locked country. The author also examines the impact of Russia on Armenia's entrepreneurial spirit.

Elena Sannikova and John F. Cassidy (Chapter 4) write about international entrepreneurship in Azerbaijan. The authors highlight how Azerbaijan's oil industry dominates most business and entrepreneurial activity in the country. The importance of oil in Azerbaijan means that more economic policy needs to be focused at developing the small business sector.

In the chapter on Bahrain (Chapter 5), Sadiq Sohail discusses how the Kingdom of Bahrain is an archipelago that has a relatively small land mass, which has affected the types of entrepreneurship occurring within the country. The author stresses the role of the large expatriate community in Bahrain that has made the country focus more on international markets particularly those in Asia. The influence of oil on Bahrain in the international economy is also highlighted.

Muhammad Mahboob Ali in writing his chapter on Bangladesh (Chapter 6) discusses how entrepreneurship has developed since the country became independent. The importance of different cultural groups in Bangladesh in increasing entrepreneurial activity is discussed. The author also stresses how entrepreneurship is critical to developing the Bangladesh economy.

The chapter on Brunei by Stephen W. Litvin (Chapter 7) examines how Brunei's international exports are primarily related to oil. The chapter discusses how the Brunei government has encouraged SMEs in the oil industry to further internationalize. In particular, the author highlights how government policy in Brunei encourages the development of SMEs through education and training.

Richard W. Wright and Malcolm Innes-Brown (Chapter 8) discuss the importance of international entrepreneurship in Cambodia as the country is amongst the least developed countries in the world. They stress the importance of culture (particularly French culture) in promoting innovation in Cambodia. Furthermore, the chapter examines how the rich history of Cambodia can be reinvigorated through proactive business policies.

David Smallbone and Xiao Jianzhong (Chapter 9) discuss how China's ability to attract foreign direct investment has increased entrepreneurship in the country. The authors highlight how small and medium-sized enterprises (SMEs) have transformed China and increased international entrepreneurial activity. The strong emphasis on planning and business development in China as being proactive in terms of their entrepreneurial orientation is stressed.

Joseph Sy-Changco (Chapter 10) discusses international entrepreneurship in the Pearl River Delta (Hong Kong, Macau and Guangdong Province). The author interestingly highlights how it is part of Chinese culture for everyone to want to be their own boss. The chapter stresses the importance of entrepreneurship in the Pearl River Delta as it is the most prosperous region in China.

Shameen Prashantham (Chapter 11) writes about how the rapid internationalization of the Indian economy has occurred. The global success of the Indian software industry that has occurred through international entrepreneurship is discussed. Furthermore, the author highlights how knowledge, intent and networks are important determinants of the internationalization process of small and new entrepreneurial firms.

Latif Adam in his chapter on Indonesia writes about how Indonesia is one of the richest countries in Southeast Asia in terms of natural and cultural resources (Chapter 12). Furthermore, the author discusses how international entrepreneneurship in the tourism and investment sector has huge potential in Indonesia.

The chapter on Iran by Babak Fooladi and Martine Spence (Chapter 13) discusses how much of the export activities of the country are around oil. However, the authors stress that the Iranian government is trying to diversify the economy through entrepreneurship. In particular, more spin-off SMEs from the manufacturing and service sector are being encouraged by the government.

Liora Katzenstein, Eli Gimmon, Eyal Benjamin and Itay Friedberg (Chapter 14) write about international entrepreneurship in Israel. The authors discuss the unique phenomenon of Israel and its rapid internationalization of its business activities in the past thirty years. The authors also highlight how Israel has achieved economic success through its internationalization policies.

Jane W. Lu and Paul W. Beamish describe in their chapter on Japan how there is little systematic investigation on the internationalization process of SMEs (Chapter 15). The authors describe the performance of Japanese SMEs' worldwide investments. The authors also highlight how foreign direct investment in Japan has created an entrepreneurial environment.

The chapter on Jordan by Vanessa Ratten examines the development of international entrepreneurship in the predominately Muslim country (Chapter 16). The history of Jordan in terms of its international growth is discussed. In addition, the attractive tax environment for fostering SMEs in Jordan is highlighted.

Sandra Pennewiss (Chapter 17) examines how Kazakhstan is the ninth biggest country in the world in terms of land mass and this fact can be harnessed to utilize the country's land mass for entrepreneurship. The author of this chapter focuses on the development of Kazakhstan as being amongst the 10 fastest growing economies in the world. However, as the author states there needs to be more international business activity in the country to further accelerate business activities.

Serkan Yalcin (Chapter 18) describes how Kyrgyzstan has developed since becoming independent from Russia. He discusses how business in Kyrgyzstan is gradually becoming more international through the privatization of state-owned enterprises. Furthermore, the chapter describes how Kyrgyzstan has quickly encouraged foreign collaboration.

Léo-Paul Dana and Susanne Barthmann discuss in the Laos chapter how it is one of Asia's most underdeveloped nations and needs to internationalize its business sector (Chapter 19). The authors highlight how communism in Laos discouraged entrepreneurship. However, the authors also state that the Chinese community in Laos is very entrepreneurially active.

Wafica A. Ghoul in the chapter on Lebanon (Chapter 20) describes how Lebanon has a strong laissez-faire commercial tradition. Moreover, the chapter discusses how the banking and tourism sector in Lebanon has encouraged internationalization. The author also highlights how for Lebanon to increase its economic growth rate it must concentrate on international entrepreneurship and in particular increase its export rate.

Nnamdi Madichie and Christopher Seow in their chapter on Malaysia (Chapter 21) discuss how Malaysia has transformed its industry to focus more on exports. The chapter describes how government support for internationalization activities in the SME sector have encouraged entrepreneurship. However, the authors also contend that as there are challenges to globalization, more focus needs to be on how Malaysia can further encourage international entrepreneurship.

Isabell M. Welpe and Teresa E. Dana discuss in the Maldives chapter how the Maldives is the smallest Asian country in terms of population but still has an international outlook (Chapter 22). The authors describe how the Maldives' geographic position has influenced their outlook on international entrepreneurship. The chapter also highlights how tourism has helped increase entrepreneurship.

The chapter on Mongolia by Malcolm Innes-Brown (Chapter 23) highlights how geography plays an important role in the development of international export rates. The impact of government policies and culture is stressed by the author in this chapter. The role of education in helping SMEs in Mongolia to internationalize is also discussed.

Léo-Paul Dana and Frank Lasch (Chapter 24) discuss the development of entrepreneurship in Myanmar despite the country's status worldwide as being secretive, and East Asia's last country to fully realize the potential of globalization. The history and development of business activities in Myanmar is investigated with a discussion on how the natural resources of the country can be utilized more to increase business activity. The role of laws and policy is also discussed in Myanmar.

Yochanan Shachmurove writes in the Oman chapter about how oil has influenced entrepreneurial activities in the country (Chapter 25). The chapter also discusses how the government is trying to foster entrepreneurship in non-oil businesses such as light manufacturing and tourism. The author also describes the government's economic reforms that are aimed at the international market.

M. Khurrum S. Bhutta and Adnan Omar (Chapter 26) write about international entrepreneurship in Pakistan. They discuss how the geographic position of Pakistan between Central and South Asia means that it is vital that the country keeps an international outlook. The authors also discuss how economic development programmes have increased attention on entrepreneurship.

The chapter on Palestine by Nidal Rashid Sabri (Chapter 27) discusses the role of education in helping developing countries like Palestine internationalize. The importance of the public sector to the Palestinian economy is examined in terms of how it affects other subsidized services like health. The contribution of the service sector and the attempts by the Palestinian government to internationalize it are discussed.

Maria Carmen Galang and Sonia Tiong-Aquino (Chapter 28) discuss local entrepreneurship and internationalization of SMEs in the Philippines. They discuss how the Philippines is the only Christian nation in Southeast Asia and how this has impacted on entrepreneurial activities. They also discuss how the legacies from the USA have impacted on the language and politics for businesses in the Philippines.

Yochanan Shachmurove describes in the chapter about Qatar (Chapter 29) its development from the oil industry. He also discusses the formation of the Qatar Petroleum Company and its entry to the Arab League. The chapter furthermore includes an examination of the increased focus on the global market and socio-political liberalization in Qatar.

Ruta Aidis, Julia Korosteleva and Tomasz Mickiewicz discuss in the chapter on Russia (Chapter 30) how it is Asia's largest country. The authors discuss the internationalization of Russia's energy resources and what this means for entrepreneurship. The impact of the private sector in Russia for international business is also examined.

Tim Rogmans (Chapter 31) examines international entrepreneurship in Saudi Arabia. The author describes how Saudi Arabia is diversifying more in the international market. The chapter also discusses how many industry sectors in Saudi Arabia are now open to foreign competition.

Wee-Liang Tan and So-Jin Yoo (Chapter 32) discuss the internationalization of the Singapore economy. The authors highlight how despite having a small land mass, Singapore is one of Asia's leading economies. Interestingly, the authors also describe how the strong emphasis on the international economy has meant that Singapore performs well in business surveys of best places to do business.

The chapter on South Korea by Ed Hopkins and Siri Terjesen (Chapter 33) examines how the country has grown significantly through export activities. The role of South Korea's international trade networks with neighbouring Asian countries is discussed. Moreover, the role of economic plans in stimulating the internationalization of SMEs is highlighted.

Sudatta Ranasinghe and Jay Weerawardena (Chapter 34) discuss Sri Lanka's international entrepreneurship outlook. The authors discuss how despite being an island nation and having some political conflict, Sri Lanka has had a relatively good economic growth rate in the past five years. The authors also stress how the economic liberalization policy of Sri Lanka has tried to encourage entrepreneurship.

Wafica A. Ghoul (Chapter 35) examines the role of the oil industry in influencing international entrepreneurship in Syria. The author discusses how the majority of exports are oil related but the government has been trying to promote a social market economy. Legislative reforms that have encouraged entrepreneurship in Syria are also discussed.

Hung-bin Ding and Hsi-mei Chung (Chapter 36) examine the success of Taiwan in achieving high export growth rates. The authors discuss how the focus on technological innovations has spurred new innovations in Taiwan. Furthermore, the authors describe how government incentives have shifted the focus of the Taiwanese economy to the international market.

The chapter on Tajikistan by Léo-Paul Dana (Chapter 37) examines one of the poorest countries in Central Asia. The role of the Soviet Union in affecting international growth rates in Tajikistan SMEs is discussed. Moreover, the role of politics and the transition to a market economy in fostering business development is stressed.

Scott A. Hipsher in the chapter on Thailand (Chapter 38) describes how politics have influenced entrepreneurship. Moreover, the free market economy in Thailand has led to a strong focus on international markets. The author also discusses the large informal entrepreneurial sector in Thailand.

Mats Lundahl and Fredrik Sjöholm (Chapter 39) discuss entrepreneurship in Timor-Leste. They examine how despite Timor-Leste being one of the poorest countries in Asia, there is still a strong entrepreneurial spirit existing in the country. Moreover, the authors describe what the government has being doing to promote entrepreneurship in Timor-Leste.

Serkan Yalcin (Chapter 40) discusses the role of entrepreneurship in Turkey, which is located at the crossroads of Europe and Asia. The role of politics and religion in promoting entrepreneurship in Turkey is examined. The author also highlights how Turkey is now classified as one of the world's top emerging markets.

The chapter on Turkmenistan by Gerard McElwee (Chapter 41) discusses the role of energy in fostering a country's international activities. The economic environment for Turkmenistan entrepreneurs is discussed that highlights the high role of government intervention. Moreover, the role of joint ventures in fostering local entrepreneurship is discussed by the author.

Mervyn J. Morris (Chapter 42) examines international entrepreneurship in the United Arab Emirates. He discusses how the strategic position of the country has influenced international business activities. The role of the Federal government in the United Arab Emirates is examined in terms of foreign policy and social affairs.

Gulnoza S. Saidazimova (Chapter 43) discusses Uzbekistan's entrepreneurial activities in the international marketplace. The historical development of Uzbekistan is examined in terms of how the country's independence has led to a renewed focus on international markets. The authors also stress how Uzbekistan has shifted its focus away from the Russian market.

Mai Thi Thanh Thai and Narendra M. Agrawal (Chapter 44) discuss international entrepreneurship in Vietnam. The authors describe how the Vietnamese people have encouraged entrepreneurship whilst complementing the political situation in the region. Furthermore, the authors describe how through remarkable policy improvements, the Vietnamese economy has achieved a strong international growth rate.

We hope readers will enjoy these as much as we did.

2 Afghanistan
Ruth Clarke and Ramdas Chandra

Introduction

By all social and economic indicators the Islamic Republic of Afghanistan is the poorest country in the Asia and Pacific region and one of the least-developed countries in the world (Asian Development Bank, 2007). Afghan authorities, with strong international support, have embarked on an ambitious program of state building, including democratic political normalization, rehabilitation of infrastructure, restoration of basic services, and institutional reform. Because of its dismal starting point however, Afghanistan will have difficulty achieving the internationally agreed Millennium Development Goals for poverty reduction by 2015 (World Bank, 2007). Statistics on each of the eight goals is very limited at this time due to the difficulty of collecting adequate data, further illustrating Afghanistan's inability to achieve advances in development.

The Afghanistan Compact, adopted at the London Conference on Afghanistan in early 2006, provides a binding agreement for engagement in the country's development over the next five years. The Compact – based on the Paris Declaration on Aid Effectiveness and the Afghanistan Government's Interim Afghanistan National Development Strategy (IANDS) – aims to consolidate institutions, curb insecurity, control the illegal narcotics trade, stimulate the economy, enforce laws, raise basic services, and protect human rights. A Joint Coordination Monitoring Board, consisting of government and development partners, oversees progress on Compact targets and benchmarks. Significant amounts of the resources coming from the world community to Afghanistan, approximately 40 percent of GNP (World Bank, 2007), target large-scale infrastructural projects to rebuild the war-devastated country. Ongoing security issues naturally make reconstruction a difficult and dangerous task, and add to the time horizon for reconstruction. The Afghanistan Compact specifically states that establishing genuine security remains a fundamental prerequisite for achieving stability and development in Afghanistan and cannot be provided by military means alone. Further, security requires good governance, justice and the rule of law, reinforced by reconstruction and development (The Afghanistan Compact, 2006).

Historically, the main industries in Afghanistan are the small-scale production of textiles (cotton), soap, furniture, shoes, fertilizer, cement, hand-woven carpets, natural gas, coal, and copper (Global Business Gateways (GBG), 2007). Agricultural products include opium, wheat, fruits, olive oil, nuts, saffron, wool, mutton, sheepskins, and lambskins. As a result of over two decades of conflict, indigenous industries including those previously engaged in exporting, such as firms in the large agricultural sector and the carpet sector, have sustained significant damage to production and markets. For example Afghanistan was at one time the leading exporter of raisins, providing 60 percent of world supply and now trails behind major producers from the USA (California), Pakistan, Turkey, and Iran (GDG, 2007). Afghanistan's major agricultural crop is the poppy, supplying approximately 93 percent of the world supply of opium. On 27 August

2007, the United Nations Office for Drugs and Crime (UNODC, 2007) released a report which indicated that opium cultivation in Afghanistan grew by 17 percent in 2007, reaching record high levels for the second straight year. While this is by far the largest export sector, the nature of the trade does not provide government with either a steady tax base or reportable foreign exchange earnings. Further this particular trade is subject to international pressure for elimination and prone to the promulgation of business outside of government control and regulation. Further comment on this follows in our discussion in the section on the environment for small and medium enterprises (SMEs).

Ricart et al. (2004) identify the importance of the effect of institutional voids in developing countries, which lead to restrictions on the growth of both domestic and foreign firms. The existence of significant institutional voids in Afghanistan occurs in both hard and soft institutions. The lack of hard or physical infrastructure such as roads, rail, air links and soft institutions such as adequate financing support, knowledge, education, and so on, drive the focus on macro developments and foreign financing for these projects. Since 2002, the World Bank has committed over US$1.45 billion for 35 reconstruction projects in Afghanistan (World Bank, 2007). A significant barrier to the development of both infrastructure and large-scale enterprises lies in a socio-political climate of opposition to privatization (Paterson et al., 2006). The confused history of government and regulation in Afghanistan has left a situation where even obtaining the correct number of state-owned enterprises (SOEs) is impossible, and where actual ownership of enterprises cannot be definitely established. Theoretically the Ministry of Finance is the owner of record of SOEs, but in effect if an SOE is privatized the sale proceeds may go to other owners. The cultural history of collectivism also leads to resistance to privatization and suspicion of competition, supported by entrenched personal interests.

The lack of a sophisticated system of business intermediaries results in continual difficulty in doing business in Afghanistan. The market is typically subject to the constraints of a poorly regulated and informal trading system under which individual small and medium enterprises must barter for single contracts. The inability of the majority of SMEs to establish consistent production and marketing schedules reduces their growth opportunities. Combined with multiple levels of payment requirements, both formal in terms of licenses and informal in terms of bribes, the ability to conduct business efficiently and effectively is considerably curtailed. In this environment where government is highly reliant on foreign partnerships, Afghanistan must simultaneously begin to build its economy at both the infrastructural and institutional level and at the individual business level. The latter effort is likely to prove a more intransient problem given the level of insecurity and ongoing physical destruction caused by the fighting between insurgents and the North Atlantic Treaty Organization (NATO) allies.

On the bright side, individual entrepreneurs do provide models of success and are responsible for some significant advances in creating infrastructure, such as wireless networks, which set the stage for the growth of SMEs, and are in themselves profitable businesses. We present this example in the third section.

In this chapter we report on the nascent development of micro, small and medium enterprises (MSMEs), fostered by a combination of domestic and international, public and private agents, who aim to support government policy towards MSMEs. Our presentation of the state of small business in Afghanistan discusses the important role of women in MSME development and the incipient renaissance of the rural sector. We examine the environment for entrepreneurship and report on the level of internationalization of entrepreneurship and initiatives to increase international expansion. We conclude with suggestions for future government initiatives for SMEs and suggestions for SMEs and entrepreneurs.

Government policy on SMEs and entrepreneurship in Afghanistan
Building on the Interim Afghanistan Development Strategy (IANDS), the Ministry of Commerce and Investment (MoCI) focuses on different aspects of development at the level of legislative infrastructure and at the level of business promotion. The Afghan government has pledged to simplify and harmonize all legislation relating to investment by the end of 2006 and to implement this legislation by the end of 2007. The focus of Afghan government policy on SMEs and entrepreneurship relates to the emphasis on overall business development and a lack of large established companies. Business development in Afghanistan is by default focused on starting and growing smaller businesses. Private sector development (PSD) falls under the PSD Directorate within the Ministry of Commerce and Industry, with the main task of the Directorate to provide PSD policy development, implementation and monitoring within the Ministry. The MoCI, in turn, has responsibility for guiding and coordinating PSD policy across government ministries and agencies, in order to encourage the development of a flourishing private sector delivering economic growth and reducing poverty. The PSD Directorate has five key areas of responsibility: enabling private sector investment by making the regulatory system more effective and efficient; promoting formalization of the economy; encouraging innovation and competitiveness; developing functioning markets; and promoting a shared stakeholder vision for PSD.

The Afghan Investment Support Agency (AISA) has been created with the responsibility for registration, licensing and promotion of all new investments in Afghanistan and has significantly simplified the bureaucratic procedures entailed (AISA, 2007). MoCI also hosts the executive agency for export development, the Export Promotion Agency of Afghanistan (EPAA). Exports seem to be increasing in 2007 with 12 percent growth reported in the first quarter. The agency offers individual consulting on exporting, although currently the website is not completely functioning for some services, such as country information. The Ministry for Women's Affairs takes a broader approach to national development, supporting the opportunities for women in general and for women entrepreneurs to some extent. In addition to direct government institutions, the Afghan government has relationships with private companies in order to execute initiatives, such as Global Business Gateways which hosts a comprehensive website for information on Afghanistan business.

Supranational institutions such as the Asian Development Bank, FINCA (a global microcredit agency) and the International Finance Corporation (IFC, the private sector arm of the World Bank) focus on providing financing for projects. A full list of lending institutions is provided by the Afghanistan Investment and Reconstruction Task Force (2007). Foreign national organizations such as the US Trade and Development Agency, which promised $500 000 in 2006 to train entrepreneurs, are also part of the global effort to improve the economy. Bilateral agreements with other countries have led to the first US–Afghanistan Council on Trade and Investment, a bilateral mechanism established under a Trade and Investment Framework Agreement (TIFA). The Afghanistan Small and Medium-sized Enterprise Development (ASMED) program is a three-year USAID-funded national programme that began in late 2006 providing technical assistance to Afghan SMEs through Development Alternatives, Inc. (DAI), a private company. The SME assistance program has an overarching goal of increasing opportunities for trade, employment, and investment in Afghanistan.

Other SME development within Afghanistan is promoted by private groups such as the All Afghan Women's Union, which offers workshops on entrepreneurship for females and has now trained over 10000 women (Montero, 2006). In this scenario it is extremely interesting to note that groups of Afghan expatriates and the diaspora in general, which numbers over 300000 in the US, are working together with in-country colleagues to develop managerial and entrepreneurial skills. One example of this effort is the Society for Afghan Engineers, which specifically works to foster international support and to encourage financial and technical assistance for the reconstruction and prosperity of Afghanistan, and collaborates with the University of Kabul to offer seminars in small business development and entrepreneurship (Society of Afghan Engineers, 2007).

Environment for entrepreneurship and the state of small business in Afghanistan
Currently the environment for foreign investment in Afghanistan as well as for indigenous entrepreneurs is extremely disheartening. Bureaucratic red tape, endemic corruption, lack of banking facilities and general lack of legal enforcements mean that foreign investment has been marginal, and even getting into the country is quite difficult given the lack of air links. Afghanistan is a country in which the economy is estimated to be 90 percent informal (World Bank, 2007) and approximately 80 percent of citizens live in rural areas. The economy is dominated by the opium trade, which is estimated to account for 30 percent of economic activity and is partially informally integrated into the economy through an informal financial transfer system referred to as 'hawala'. The hawala system facilitates the transfer of drug-related funds in Afghanistan, while at the same time serving as a vehicle for licit commercial transactions, aid flows, and remittances. By integrating the informal economy with the formal banking system in surrounding countries it is hoped that continual pressure from partners will lead to the implementation of taxation provisions and formal registration of businesses. The World Bank emphasizes that too much pressure at an early stage of economic development on the hawala system, in an effort to introduce anti-money laundering provisions, will foster distrust of foreign institutions and the banking system, and be counter-productive to development.

The exception to this general situation lies with the Afghan diaspora which has been actively engaged with developing new business. For example, Afghan Wireless Communication Company (AWCC) is a very successful joint venture between Telephone Systems International, Inc. and the Ministry of Communications (afghan-wireless.org; Scimitar Global Ventures, 2004). Telephone Systems International, Inc. is owned by Afghan/American Ehsan Bayat, President and chief executive officer (CEO), whose family has also established an educational television network. Together with the introduction of the Telecom Development Company Afghanistan Ltd., trading as Roshan, and partially funded by the Agha Khan Development Fund (Scimitar Global Ventures, 2004), Afghan Wireless has led to the establishment of access to communication for many people who had not previously had any telephone system. In 2006, 43 out of 1000 people had access to telephone service, either land or wireless (World Bank, 2007).

Entrepreneurship in Afghanistan is still very limited in nature, and will face a difficult development if the legal environment and general hard infrastructure do not change. Many burgeoning businesses are small in nature and provide income for individuals who would otherwise not be employed. These micro enterprises do have the potential to grow with the presence of adequate credit and the ongoing support of foreign aid agencies.

Since 2002, when schools reopened in Afghanistan and the normalization of the country began hesitantly to occur, Afghanis have been trying to go back to work in order to support themselves, or have turned to micro enterprises. This presents an ideal climate for the development of female entrepreneurs. Given evidence from other developing countries supporting the ability of women to succeed with a fairly small amount of assistance, the support of indigenous women entrepreneurs is vital to the success of a functioning Afghan economy. Certain sectors of the economy such as carpet-making and farming are dependent on female (and child) labor but are still under male dominance in terms of control of earnings. This is also true for commonly started micro businesses such as beauty parlors, tailoring shops and bakeries. *Microfinance Times* reports that 79 percent of micro loans go to women-owned businesses (MISFA, 2005), including loans from FINCA and Microfinance Investment and Support Facility for Afghanistan (MISFA) (PBS, 2007).

A more pressing concern for women in Afghanistan is that starting a business in a life endangering society (for women) may be more limiting than the access to money for startup costs. Adapting from Boros (2008), women entrepreneurs in Afghanistan can be categorized as a virtual 'female enclave' similar to the concept of 'ethnic enclaves' which are widely discussed by academics (Bonacich and Modell, 1980). Boros points to the fact that domains of activity in Afghanistan (Pathan) are dominated by three institutions: melmastia is hospitality, and the honorable uses of material goods; jirga are councils, and the honorable pursuit of public affairs; and finally, purdahk is seclusion, and the honorable organization of domestic life (Barth, 1969).

Women face a cultural situation where in general they have not been allowed to function as free agents for many years. Even in earlier times up to 1973, during the reign of King Muhammed Zahir, when women were able to attain a higher education and professional work status, most women remained subject to the existing patriarchal, authoritarian and restrictive societal pressures to work in the home only. Although the Soviet-backed People's Democratic Party of Afghanistan (1978) and then the occupying Soviet forces (1979–92) did support the empowerment of women, the years of the communist government (1989–92) and then the devastating years of Taliban rule until 2001–2002 removed women from the paid workforce outside the home except in a few cases for professional women. Given both the level of poverty and the length of time over which societal changes occur, it is fair to say that women will continue to struggle to take control of their own lives for some time.

At the same time as micro businesses are developing to provide basic life-support income, the revitalization of medium-sized pre-existing enterprises can start to revive and improve the overall economy. Revitalization faces several obstacles, in addition to infrastructural difficulties, including the necessity to make payments (bribes) at each stage of contact, pre-existing onerous tariffs bands which restrict smooth importation of goods to supply business, and the fragmented nature of the internal market. The Doing Business Project of the World Bank ranks 178 countries in terms of level of difficulty

Table 2.1   *Doing business in Afghanistan: ranking of Afghanistan out of a total of 178 countries (1 = best, 178 = worst)*

Starting a business	Dealing with licenses	Employing labor	Registering property	Getting credit	Protecting investors	Paying taxes	Trading across borders	Enforcing contracts	Closing a business
24	141	24	169	177	178	38	174	160	178

Source: Adapted from Doing Business Project (2008).

and cost of doing business on 10 dimensions (Table 2.1). Actually setting up a business in Afghanistan only takes four steps, which gives it a rank of 24th in the world for best practices, however the report then goes on to give the example of licensing requirements for building a manufacturing facility, which are sufficiently onerous to move Afghanistan to a rank of 141st. The brightest news is the ranking of the labor force at 24th, indicating the availability of workers. Registering property is ranked at 169th, getting access to credit at 177th, and protecting investors at 178th. Paying taxes is 38th, another potential benefit for SMEs but a negative for government programs, and trading across borders is 174th. Enforcing contracts is 160th, bankruptcy or closing business is 178th.

This picture is not encouraging overall but efforts to improve, such as programs to train entrepreneurs, do provide some hope. We turn to the issue of growing businesses in the following section dealing with internationalization.

Internationalization of SMEs
Afghanistan is naturally very interested in pursuing international markets in an effort grow its own businesses and improve the foreign exchange situation. The country was thus granted Observer status at the World Trade Organization (WTO) in 2004 (Ministry of Commerce and Industry, 2007). Accession to the WTO requires a wide-ranging commitment from both government and industry related to the mastery and implementation of a wide range of technical standards and procedures. While Afghanistan's goal is to integrate into both the regional and global economy, in particular the government is focusing on developing its status as the land bridge between the Central and Southeast Asian regions. Historically, Afghanistan was central to the Silk Road between the West and East, and now aims to be a dependable part of the route to access the preponderance of natural resources in the region and potentially to be a key player in the development of an oil pipeline from Iran to India (Scimitar Global Ventures, 2004). Naturally this ambitious goal is thwarted by the security situation and lack of adequate NATO troops to police the highways and borders of the country and prevent disruptions caused by Taliban insurgents.

In the past three years, the Ministry of Commerce and Industry has actively participated in regional economic initiatives including the Economic Cooperation Organization (ECO) as well as bilateral negotiations with neighboring countries including Iran, India, Pakistan, Kazakhstan, Kyrgyzstan, Tajikistan, Turkmenistan, and Uzbekistan. Current trading patterns in the region tend to depress selling prices in Afghanistan to the benefit of foreign trading partners. The introduction of cooperative border management and other multilateral or bilateral trade and transit agreements depends on the agreement of regional partners, some of whom have a vested interest in the current terms of regional trade, and even in the unsettled conditions in Afghanistan. Concrete progress on 'win–win' trade facilitation steps, as recommended by the World Bank, could include the creation and extension of cross-border zones allowing people and goods to move more easily across these borders and border zone bazaars, encouraging informal traders to use formal routes. Attracting new buyers to a more organized internal market should lead to the ability of Afghan traders to capture more value-added in country (Paterson, 2006). Key to this is the focus on regulated and systematic markets where products can be sold without the current inefficient and detrimental under cutting of prices discussed earlier in this chapter.

Afghanistan is currently eligible for preferential import duties under the European Union's (EU) 'Everything but Arms' initiative (EBA), the United States' Generalized System of Preferences (GSP) program as well as LDC preferences granted by Canada and Japan. These initiatives create the framework for private businesses to develop trading relationships worldwide and in particular to the developed economies directly, rather than through countries in the region (especially Pakistan) to which value added is transferred. This is particularly true in the case of the carpet industry, where prices are depressed inside Afghanistan but considerably raised for external buyers once the product has reached Pakistan.

The Afghan government continues to focus on increasing exporting by SMEs in the effort to improve the dismal balance of payments picture and help jump start the economy. The Export Promotion Agency of Afghanistan (EPAA), an executive agency of the Ministry of Commerce and Industry, accessible online, offers news and advice to exporters. The government of President Hamid Karzai recently dropped the 2 percent export tariff (EPAA, 2007) to assist in this effort. First quarter exports reached US$106.78 million, compared to US$93.81 million for the same quarter last year: a year-on-year increase of 12 percent (EPAA). Firms can find limited access to foreign buyers and suppliers at the website www.go4afghanistanbusiness.com, as well as through the EPAA.

The export sector has the potential for expansion at this time of internal country development. The large number of international programs does help develop knowledge of international resources available and may encourage firms to take the first step in international business through exporting. The potentially two largest industries for exporting are carpets and raisins. Hand-woven carpets are already a well-known product internationally and the promotion of these via trade fairs attracts foreign buyers. In August 2007, the first Afghanistan International Carpet Fair was held in Kabul attracting 5000 foreign visitors to deal with 65 Afghani exhibitors and generating US$4 million in sales (EPAA, 2007). Raisin products are also exported, although the fragmentation of production and marketing has destroyed the ability of the Afghan raisin to compete in the global market. As more products are identified that can be developed and exported, the learning curve for entrepreneurs will lead to further and perhaps more ambitious efforts to reach foreign markets.

Of greatest importance for the development of products of high enough quality to reach foreign markets is the development and enforcement of consistent quality. Standards are of vital importance for Afghan producers and exporters in order to gain access to markets that demand high quality. The example of the process for the certification of raisin quality given here provides an illustration of the difficulties facing producers.

The testing of raisins for export is conducted at two levels of in-country government. The first is the Afghan Raisin Export and Other Dry Fruit Export Promotion Institute, in the MoC, which has a small laboratory and issues a certificate of 'quality control', a procedure for which it charges 50 Afs/mt. Secondly, provincial departments of the Ministry of Food, Agriculture and Animal Husbandry also provide a certification service to exporters of raisins. A representative of the ministry checks the quality of produce in the consignment and issues a phyto-sanitary certificate at a supposed cost of 50 Afs. (in reality this cost will probably be higher). There is a combination here of poor capacity to deliver thorough testing and certification and institutional overlap in the delivery of this service. Afghan traders are currently unable to certify their product with international food safety bodies such as the Hazard Analysis and Critical Control Points, which is part of the International Standards Organization 9000, and EurepGAP, the Euro-Retailer Produce Working Group certification of Good Agricultural Practices. This is partly due to lack of thorough planting and processing information required for certification (Lister et al., 2004).

In the carpet market, the establishment and application of quality standards through labeling and certification could reinforce the traditional Afghan brand if it is linked with a strategy to deliberately position Afghan carpets in a niche upper-market segment. Such labeling could support the use of high-quality raw materials (such as hand-spun *qaraqol* wool) and the development of traditional designs (Pain and Moharram, 2004).

In summation, the future for Afghanistan is fraught with potential difficulty and the development of a functioning economy will greatly depend on the government's ability to retain control of the country. Motivation for change is naturally troublesome when security and survival on a daily basis is a top priority, particularly in the rural areas outside of Kabul, where 80 percent of the population live. The BBC reports that a coffee shop named Starbucks (no relation to the US company) has been started in Kandahar, but this is a significantly more developed area than the country as a whole (BBC, 2006). The Taliban opposition has gained territorial control over parts of Afghanistan and continues to fight the international coalition defending the government. International investment is naturally cautious of a situation where security and ownership are highly pertinent issues. Domestic MSMEs will have difficulty growing in size as well, given that internal markets function poorly and business is unable to capture value-added in house.

The development of controlled markets would be one way in which Afghanis could be guaranteed a fair market and potentially could lead to establishing a system which becomes entrenched over time. Individual micro-business owners do not have power in the market to set consistent prices that cover the amount of time spent producing the product, at a cost acceptable as a living wage. In turn, they are not able to grow their business and make more significant contributions to the economy. As long as value-added is taken outside of Afghanistan, the economy cannot grow itself sufficiently to combat the problems facing development. The privatization of SOEs is another key issue that must be addressed in order that existing, but not utilized, facilities can be overhauled and business restarted. As infrastructure development continues this should help business to begin the long climb back to economic health, which (to bowdlerize author Eric Newby, 1998) is still a very long walk in the Hindu Kush. Keeping the rest of the world focused on events on Afghanistan is a vital component of the reconstruction effort in attempts to attract monetary and military support. Continuing to keep the spotlight on Afghanistan and its strategic position in relation to the stability of Central Asia emphasizes this point and may eventually serve to bring the country into stability.

References

Afghanistan Investment and Reconstruction Task Force (2007), 'main page', retrieved 12 November 2007 from http://www.export.gov/afghanistan/.
Afghanistan Investment Support Agency (AISA) (2007), 'main page', retrieved 11 November 2007 from www.aisa.org.af.
Asian Development Bank (2007), 'ADB annual report, 2007', retrieved 12 October 2007 from http://www.adb.org/Afghanistan/.
Barth, Frederik (1969), *Ethnic Groups and Boundaries, Pathan Identity and its Maintenance*, Series in Anthropology, Boston, MA: Little Brown and Co.
Bonacich, Edna and John Modell (1980), *The Economic Basis of Ethnic Solidarity*, Los Angeles, CA: University of California Press.
Boros, Ruxandra (2008), 'Afghan women entrepreneurs: at the crossroads between globalization and local traditions', *International Journal of Business and Globalization*, **2**(4), 373–40.
British Broadcasting Corporation (BBC) (2006), '"Starbucks" in Kabul', retrieved 13 December from news.bbc.co.uk/2/hi/south_asia.
Doing Business Project, World Bank (2008), 'Doing business report, 2007: Afghanistan highlights', retrieved 11 December 2007 from http://www.doingbusiness.org/Documents/CountryProfiles/.
Export Promotion Agency of Afghanistan (EPAA) (2007), 'main page', retrieved 12 December 2007 from http://www.epaa.org.af.
Global Business Gateways (GBG) (2007), 'main page', retrieved 11 November 2007, from www.globalbusinessgateways.com.
Lister, Sarah, Tom Brown and Zainiddin Karaev (2004), 'Understanding markets in Afghanistan: a case study of the raisin market', Afghanistan Research and Evaluation Unit, Working Paper Series, June, retrieved 11 November 2007 from http://www.globalbusinessgateways.com/images/AREU.
Microfinance Investment Support Facility for Afghanistan (MISFA) (2005), *Microfinance Times*, **1:3**, December, retrieved 11 November 2007 from http://www.microfinancegateway.org.
Ministry of Commerce and Industry (2007), 'main page', retrieved 11 November 2007 from http://www.commerce.gov.af.
Montero, David (2006), *Christian Science Monitor*, May 08, retrieved 12 December 2007 from http://www.csmonitor.com.
Newby, Eric (1998), *A Short Walk in the Hindu Kush*, London: Lonely Planet.
Pain, Adam and Ali Moharram (2004), 'Understanding markets in Afghanistan: a case study of markets and the Andkhoy carpet market', Afghanistan Research and Evaluation Unit, Working Paper Series, June, retrieved 11 November 2007 from http://www.areu.org.af.
Paterson, Anna (2006), 'Going to market: trade and traders in six Afghan sectors', Afghanistan Research and Evaluation Unit, Working Paper Series, June, retrieved 12 November 2007 from http://www.globalbusinessgateways.com/images/Afghan.
Public Broadcasting Service (2007), *Handbook: Women in Afghanistan*, Wide Angle page, retrieved 11 November 2007 from http://www.pbs.org/wnet/wideangle/shows/afghanistan2.
Ricart, Joan Enric, Michael J. Enright, Pankaj Ghemawat, Stuart L. Hart and Tarun Khanna (2004), 'New frontiers in international strategy', *Journal of International Business Studies*, **35**, 175–200.
Scimitar Global Ventures (2004), 'Afghanistan: a critical land bridge for regional economic cooperation', background paper for Working Group I, Afghanistan's Regional Economic Cooperation, Central Asia, Iran and Pakistan, Bishkek, Kyrgyz Republic, 10–12 May 2004, retrieved 12 December 2007 from Scimitar%20Paper%20on%20Afghanistan-%20A%20Critical%20Land%20Bridge.pdf.
Society of Afghan Engineers (2007), 'main page', retrieved 1 October 2007 from http://www.afghan-engineers.org.
The Afghanistan Compact (2006), retrieved 12 October 2007 from http://www.fco.gov.uk.
World Bank (2007), retrieved 11 November 2007 from http://www.worldbank.org.af.
United Nations Office for Drugs and Crime (UNODC) (2007), retrieved 11 November 2007, from http://www.unodc.org.

3 Armenia
Vahé Heboyan

1. Introduction

The Republic of Armenia is a small, land-locked country situated on the south-eastern edge of Europe – in the Caucasus. Armenia is one of the oldest nations and the first Christian nation in the world (AD 301). It has an area of 29 800 square kilometers and borders with Georgia (north), Azerbaijan (east), Iran (south), and Turkey (west). Armenia is a homogenous country with a population of 3.1 million of which 98 percent are ethnic Armenians. Armenia's head of state is the President who is elected by the popular vote for a maximum of two five-year terms. The National Assembly is the highest legislative body and has 131 legislators. The Constitution Court is the highest judicial body. The capital of Armenia is Yerevan which is founded in 782 BC. Armenia has 11 administrative divisions, Marzes, including Yerevan (Gevorgyan et al., 2005; CIA, 2008).

Over centuries Armenia has been under occupation of various empires including the Roman, Byzantine, Arab, Persian, and Ottoman empires (CIA, 2008). During the World War I (WWI), Armenians living under Ottoman Turkey's occupation were subject to mass deportation and mass killings planned and carried out by the Ottoman Turkish government. More than one and half million Armenians were killed and many more were deported from their homes. The events are viewed by international genocide scholars as the first genocide of the twentieth century (IAGS, 2008; Center for Holocaust and Genocide Studies, 2008). The first Armenian Republic was established at the end of the WWI in 1918 but had a short life and Armenia became part of the Soviet Union in 1920 (CIA, 2008).

For over seventy years Armenia has been part of the Soviet Union and was one of the most industrialized republics of the Soviet Union. Armenia was strong in education,[1] science, mining, and manufacturing of chemicals, textiles, and machine tools. Armenia's scientific institutes were among the best in the entire Soviet block, supporting some of the highly recognized Soviet high-technology and military developments. Its collective farms, *kolkhozes* and *sovkhozes*, vineyards, and factories produced some of the highest quality foods and consumer goods for a market of 286 million people. Viviano (2004) observes: 'Armenia was the California of Soviet high technology, the Italy of Soviet shoe manufacturing, the France of Soviet-made cognac'.

Starting 1988, Armenia started to experience major internal and external economic, social, and political developments. A devastating earthquake hit Armenia on 7 December 1988. As a result, vast parts of the economy were paralyzed and at least 50 000 people were killed, 130 000 were injured, and about half million people were left homeless. Several large and strategic cities were damaged or destroyed, including second largest city Leninakan (currently Gyumri) (Brand, 1988). The international community and the Armenian diaspora have been instrumental in providing assistance to Armenia by pouring enormous financial, technical, and human resources into rebuilding cities and villages affected by the earthquake.

In 1991, the Republic of Armenia declared independence from the Soviet Union and the Third Armenian Republic was born and joined the international community of independent and sovereign nations. The collapse of the Soviet Union brought new challenges for Armenia. The inherited governmental and legal infrastructures were bureaucratic, corrupt, and full of nepotism. The centrally planned economy was destroyed, the majority of trade links and networks ceased to exist, major factories and manufacturing facilities were destroyed as a result of the 1988 earthquake and input shortages, the conflict with Azerbaijan, and Turkey's decision to close its border with Armenia in solidarity with Azerbaijan, left Armenia in isolation and de facto an economic embargo (Nathan Associates Inc., 2004). In addition, internal political instability in the Republic of Georgia undermined Armenia's ability to reach to its main trading markets in Russia and Europe via the Georgian Black Sea ports and inland routes. Armenia's nuclear power plant, which produced about 40 percent of Armenia's energy, was shut down in 1988 following the earthquake[2] (CIA, 2008). As a result, Armenia's economic and social crisis deepened and the depression hit the country.

Since independence Armenia has adopted the policy of complementarity in its foreign relations. It is based on the historical developments and current geopolitical realities in the world and the Caucasus region. Armenia lacks diplomatic relations with its eastern neighbor Azerbaijan due to the longstanding conflict over Nagorno-Karabakh. In early 1988, a deadly conflict erupted between Armenia and Azerbaijan over Nagorno-Karabakh, an Armenian-populated territory within the borders of the Soviet Azerbaijan. As a result, tens of thousands of people died and hundreds of thousands were displaced on both sides. A ceasefire, brokered in 1994, remains in effect and the sides are currently negotiating over the future of the Nagorno-Karabakh within the auspices of the Organization for Security and Co-operation in Europe (OSCE) Minsk Group (CIA, 2008).

Despite Turkey being one of the first countries to recognize Armenia's independence in 1991, it has been reluctant to establish diplomatic relations with Armenia because of the conflict between Armenia and Azerbaijan, and closed its border with Armenia in 1993. Officially there is no direct trade between Armenia and Turkey, but the two countries trade freely through Georgia and Iran, at a higher cost. Both nations emphasize that opening the border will create real economic opportunities for the region and both economies, however political considerations prevent the establishment of diplomatic and economic relations between two neighbors (Kyureghian and Heboyan, 2004). Armenian–Turkish relations are further complicated by Turkey's objection towards labeling the mass deportation and killings of Armenians in Ottoman Turkey at the beginning of the twentieth century as a genocide.

Armenia maintains mutually beneficial relations with its southern neighbor Iran, which since 1991 has developed from purely trade relations into multi-dimensional political, economic, and social relations. Gresh (2006) summarizes the objectives of Iran's warm policy towards neighboring, predominantly Christian, Armenia based on: (a) national interests of preserving its sovereignty by calming ethnic Azerbaijanis living in Northern Iran who called for the unification of a 'greater' Azerbaijan; (b) sustaining its economic regional and global dominance, Iran sees development of relations with Armenia and Russia as a counterbalance to Azerbaijan's pro-western policies; (c) Russia's unreliability as a secure Iranian ally in the region, which forced Iran to improve its relations with Armenia; and (d) the possibility of an increasing imbalance in the region and the possibility of another regional conflict that could potentially be more devastating than that of the previously contained Nagorno-Karabakh conflict forces Iran to adopt a pro-Armenian policy in the region. Overall, Iran–Armenia relations are based on mutual foreign policy considerations and regional and world geopolitics.

Owing to the closed border with Turkey, Georgia remains the only transit route for Armenian trade with its two biggest partners: Russia and the European Union. Armenia's relations with Georgia are also conditioned with a large Armenian minority population in Georgia and have remained limited solely in the economic area due to Georgia's orientation towards the West and regional projects with Turkey and Azerbaijan that excluded Armenia.

Armenia has sustained and further developed its partnership with its main strategic partner, Russia, which to date maintains a military base in Armenia to counter possible Turkish aggression towards Armenia. The relations are also conditioned by a growing pro-Western orientation in Georgia and Azerbaijan, and Russia views Armenia as its most reliable political ally in the region. Although in the recent years Armenia has diversified its energy resources by building a natural gas pipeline with Iran, Russia still accounts for the bulk of energy and nuclear fuel imports. Russian economic presence in Armenia increased further after the conclusion of the 2003 US$94 million debt-for-equity agreement between Armenia and Russia (EIU, 2008).

Armenia's foreign policy is balanced by close ties with European Union and United States. Armenia is a member of the North Atlantic Treaty Organization's (NATO's) Partnership for Peace plan and maintains a small but symbolic non-combat force in Iraq. Additionally, the sizable Armenian diaspora in the United States and Europe has been instrumental in developing cooperation with the West. As a result, Armenia receives substantial US foreign aid, including the Millennium Challenge Corporation's $236 million program to develop rural infrastructure in Armenia. Together with Georgia and Azerbaijan, Armenia is a participant in the EU's European Neighborhood Policy, which provides substantial assistance for developing economic and political cooperation with EU (EIU, 2008).

Fueled by liberal market and economic reforms that promoted investor confidence and boosted exports, Armenia was quick to recover from the economic decline of the early 1990s experienced by all transition countries of the former Soviet Union (FSU) and Central and Eastern Europe (CEE). Armenia's economic recovery started in 1994 along with the countries of CEE while the rest in the FSU (except Latvia) were still experiencing negative growth. Armenia's economy has registered double digit economic growth averaging 12.26 percent annually during 2001–06 (World Bank, 2007; Roland, 2000; Iradian, 2007). Its exports grew by an average of 20.83 percent annually during 2000–05 surpassing all countries in the FSU and CEE. Since the economic recovery started, the structure of Armenia's economy has changed significantly. During the early years of transition, agriculture has been the dominating sector averaging about 40 percent of the gross domestic product (GDP) in mid-1990s, compared to its current share of about 20 percent (World Bank, 2007). Increased investments by Russian and Western companies into Armenia's mining and metallurgy sectors have contributed towards revitalization of the once highly developed sector. Growth of export-oriented diamond processing[3] has increased foreign direct investments (FDI) in Armenia and speeded up the growth process. However, recent negative trends in raw diamond supply and global demand have altered the sector's performance (EIU, 2008).

During the 2000s Armenia's economy has witnessed significant developments in the construction and services sectors, mainly concentrated in the capital city of Yerevan. The construction boom is primarily financed by grants from diaspora-connected humanitarian organizations (Lincy Foundation, Hayastan All Armenia Fund) and credits from international organizations, such as the World Bank (WB) and the European Bank for Reconstruction and Development (EBRD). In 2006 and 2007, construction alone accounted for the major share of economic growth in Armenia, 8 percent and 4.3 percent respectively (13.3 percent in 2006 and 13.7 percent in 2007) (EIU, 2008).

The adoption of responsible monetary and fiscal policies in the late 1990s further stabilized financial markets and recorded low levels of inflation averaging 2.6 percent annually during 2000–05, lower than other FSU and CEE countries, except Lithuania (0.9 percent), Czech Republic (2.5 percent), and Poland (2.5 percent) (World Bank, 2007; Iradian, 2007; Mitra et al., 2007).

Impressive economic performance in the 2000s has been accompanied with a rapid appreciation of the national currency, the dram. During 2003–07, dram appreciated by 46, 27, and 29 percent with respect to US dollar, euro, and Russian ruble respectively (IMF, 2008). Its long run impact is not yet known, but exporters and recipients of remittances have already felt the impact of the appreciation. Banaian and Roberts (2007) estimate that remittances account for 80 percent of the total income in the households that receive them. However, the Central Bank of Armenia (CBA) has mainly ignored the concerns and claims that dependence on remittances is exaggerated as they account for only about 25 percent of income in Armenia. CBA also argues that dram appreciation helped to prevent complete pass-through of increasing world oil prices to the domestic market and that the appreciation creates unique opportunity for local businesses to boost their competitiveness through acquiring new foreign technologies as AMD appreciation makes foreign technologies cheaper in local currency (Emerging Markets Monitor, 2006).

Exports of goods and services grew from 21 percent in 1995–99 to about 27 percent in 2000–05 (World Bank, 2007). The structure of exports has been altered as well. Exports of diamonds and other precious stones have accounted for about 50 percent of total export in 2002–03, significant increase from 24 percent in 1998. However, since 2004, exports of diamonds and precious stones have been hit by the global trends. Base metals, benefited by major foreign investments, have become the leading export item and accounted for about 32 percent of the exports in 2005–07 (EIU, 2008).

According to the World Bank review, economic recovery and growth have increased the consumption of the poor. Data show that poverty fell from over 50 percent to 30 percent between 1998 and 2004, and extreme poverty fell from over 20 percent to just 6 percent during the same period.

Despite impressive growth and developments, unemployment is still high. The World Bank estimates the rate to be around one-fifth of the total labor force and relates employment's weak response to investments and growth to the inefficient business climate that has discouraged flexible use of labor and to the inadequate skills among the unemployed (Mitra et al., 2007).

2. Government policy on SMEs and entrepreneurship in Armenia
The government of Armenia views the SME development as a key contributor for developing its economy, reducing unemployment, improving social welfare and living standards, encouraging establishment of the middle class, and achieving social and economic stability (Government of Armenia, 2006).

On 19 March 2002 the Armenian government decreed (No. 282-N) to establish the Small and Medium Entrepreneurship Development National Center (SME DNC) to provide assistance at the state level for SME development in Armenia (OSCE, 2006). Additionally, to provide direct assistance to regional SMEs, the government of Armenia has established subsidiaries of the SME DNC in all regions during 2003–05 (Government of Armenia, 2006). The primary goals of the Center are to (SME DNC, 2008):

- provide support to start-up and operating SMEs
- enhance the efficiency and competitiveness of SMEs
- ensure the availability of business development services to SMEs
- expand financing opportunities for SMEs
- promote innovations and support the introduction of new technologies
- support the establishment of start-up businesses
- stimulate the economic activity of SMEs in the international marketplace
- develop more business opportunities in Armenia.

In 2007, the government of Armenia expanded its Project for Provision of Loan Guarantees to the SMEs to improve SME access to financial resources by guaranteeing the collateral for a maximum period of three years and for up to 70 percent of the total loan amount with priority given to SMEs located in remote and border regions. Five local and international banks are involved in this project. As a result, a decrease in interest rates and improved credit opportunities for SMEs are expected.

To promote market access opportunities government provides financial and technical support to the start-ups and assists SMEs with promotion of their products and services in local and international markets. More specifically, support is provided to SMEs for application to quality management (ISO 9000 series) and hazard analysis and critical control points (HACCP) standards. Support is also provided to enhance networking opportunities with foreign partners, access advanced technologies, and improve financial, accounting, and managerial practices (Government of Armenia, 2006).

Following pressure from International Monetary Fund (IMF), in 2008 the Armenian government stopped provision of certain tax exemptions to foreign investors that they have been enjoying for more than a decade. Additionally, starting in 2008, a new tax law will close the loopholes that allowed medium and large companies to qualify for the simplified tax that was introduced in the late 1990s to prompt small business development in Armenia (EIU, 2008).

3. The environment for entrepreneurship and the state of small business in Armenia
The Armenian government claims that due to the implemented measures, including enacted necessary legal framework to support the development of the entrepreneurial activity in the country, the SME sector has been dynamically developing during the past few years. In particular, an increasing trend of the number of newly established SMEs

in Armenia and newly created jobs is recorded. During 2003–05 about 25 000 new SMEs were established, creating over 23 000 new jobs. Data show that SME contribution to the GDP has almost doubled in 2005 over 2000, and accounted for about 40 percent of the GDP. In 2005, SMEs accounted for about 97 percent of total number of individual entrepreneurs and legal entities, 9.2 percent of the total FDI, and 27.9 percent of taxes and duties paid to the state budget. The United Nation's SME development index in 2005 for Armenia has improved from 58.1 in 2002 to 171.9 (Gevorgyan et al., 2005; CIA, 2008).

The entrepreneurial environment has improved in the 2000s, however several issues still remain. Lending rates are decreasing in Armenia but they still remain high compared to other transition economies. In December 2007 the weighted average rate has been 16.45 percent. Relatively high rates have reduced banks' role in the financial and credit sectors as businesses have been reluctant to borrow at such high rates (EIU, 2008). Armenia is improving its position of Heritage Foundation's economic freedom ranking. Its ranking[4] has improved from average score of 51.6 during 1996–2000 to 70.2 during 2004–08 (Heritage Foundation, 2008). Business surveys reveal that the time and cost of registering and licensing a company in Armenia has improved due to reduced bureaucracy and red tape. According to the World Bank's 'Doing Business 2008' (World Bank, 2008) businesses in Armenia have better access to credit and trade internationally and Armenia has the second highest score of the ease of registering property in terms of number of procedures, time, and cost. However, despite legislative improvements, SMEs still face several challenges and obstacles at the implementation process and the overall business climate is uncompetitive (EIU, 2008).

In 2006, the Armenian government started an ambitious program aimed at improvement of economic and business activity in the regions of Armenia. It aimed to introduce a loan guarantee program for regional SMEs, conduct business training, assist with market promotion, provide informational and consulting support to start-ups and over 4500 existing SMEs throughout Armenia, and facilitate collaboration between regional SMEs and foreign private and public organizations (Gevorgyan et al., 2005; CIA, 2008).

Despite considerable improvements and efforts to assist SME development, several obstacles still remain for effective SME development. An Armenian government study has classified those obstacles into three broad categories: legislative, financial, and infrastructural (Government of Armenia, 2006). Small and medium enterprises' access to credit is still a challenge, especially in the agricultural sector, as banks are eager to invest in more profitable and less risky sectors. However, an improvement can now be seen in Armenia's agricultural credit system with the establishment of farm credit organizations associated with local and international organizations.

Access to business information, consultation, professional business and managerial training, and market promotion still remain underprovided despite government efforts to improve these services. Additionally, provision of government services and assistance differs depending upon business location and unsatisfactory cooperation between various levels of government branches (Government of Armenia, 2006).

4.   Internationalization of entrepreneurs and SMEs from Armenia
The IMF reports show little evidence for internationalization of entrepreneurs from Armenia. Armenia's direct investments abroad were $3.1 million per year in average or

just 0.06 percent of GDP during 2003–06. Meanwhile, FDI in Armenia was $265 million per year in average or 5.9 percent of GDP for the same period (IMF, 2008). International involvement of Armenian businessmen and SMEs is primarily limited to trading in goods and services. The only notable documented investment abroad by an Armenia company has been the acquisition of the Emporiki Bank – Georgia S.A., based in the Republic of Georgia, by Cascade Capital Holdings in 2006 (Armenian Reporter, 2006).

Meanwhile, it should be noted that since independence, an estimated 800 000 Armenians have migrated to other countries, primarily due to social and economic hardship (EIU, 2008). Many of them became successful businessmen and entrepreneurs abroad and contributed towards economic development of their 'host' countries while remaining Armenian citizens. Additionally, since the declaration of independence by Nagorno-Karabakh, the Armenian government and the private sector have invested heavily in its economy. However, documentation and data on these investment activities do not exist publicly.

5. Conclusion

Armenia's economic recovery and development has been impressive. There have been significant changes towards transition into market economy and recovering from the economic and social hardship imposed by the collapse of the Soviet Union. Armenia has registered double-digit economic growth and low inflation since 2001, and has improved its business climate. The government of Armenia recognizes the importance of SME sector and its role in Armenia's long-term economic and social development, and has undertaken various measures to support SME activities in the country, even though bureaucracy and red tape still challenge businesses and hinder their effective development.

Recent domestic and international developments pose significant challenges for its future development. More specifically, appreciating national currency reduces competitiveness of the local industry, but also creates genuine opportunities to invest in advanced technologies to improve productivity and efficiency. Scarcity of natural resources, continuing economic embargo imposed by Azerbaijan and Turkey, rising energy prices, and global demand for food deepen problems that the Armenian economy will face in the decades to come. Given its vulnerable position, the Armenian government and the private sector should undertake measures aimed at offsetting external and internal pressure on the economy. In particular, investing in innovations, alternative energy, and human capital can prove to be an efficient remedy for the long-run success.

Public policy and economic research can play a significant role in this adjustment process. The input of academia and scientific community is valuable and critical in the policy-making process. (Re)examination of the causes and effects of internal and external shocks, as well as benefits of development scenarios can be one of the important contributors for the economic and social progress in the future.

Notes

1. Armenia's literacy rate is among the highest in the world; 99.4 percent of the population is literate according to the World Bank (2007) and CIA (2008).
2. One of the two blocks of the nuclear power plant was re-started in 1995, but the Armenian government is under international pressure to shut down the power plant (CIA, 2008). However, the Armenian government has made it clear that the plant will be shut down only after a new modern nuclear plant is built

instead. Currently, Armenia negotiates with several countries over building a new nuclear power plant (EIU, 2008).
3. Armenia processes raw diamonds imported from Russia and Israel and exports back to the countries of origin. It does not produce diamonds on its own.
4. The Heritage Foundation uses a scale of 0 to 100 percent to calculate the Economic Freedom Index , where 80–100 score means economy is free, 70–79.9 means it is mostly free, 60–69.9 means it is moderately free, 50–59.9 means mostly unfree, and 0–49.9 means the economy is repressed. More information is available at www.heritage.org.

References

Armenian Reporter (2006), 'Cascade Bank, CJSC, finalizes acquisition of Emporiki Bank – Georgia S.A.', *Armenian Reporter,* 14 January.
Banaian, K. and B. Roberts (2007), 'Remittances in Armenia II: the Impact of remittances on the economy and measures to enhance their contribution to development', *Armenian Journal of Public Policy*, 2, 229–57.
Brand, D. (1988), 'Soviet Union vision of horror', *Time Magazine*, 132, http://www.time.com/time/magazine/article/0,9171,956602,00.html.
Center for Holocaust and Genocide Studies (2008), 'The Armenian genocide', University of Minnesota, http://chgs.umn.edu/ (accessed 20 April 2008).
CIA (2008), CIA – The World Factbook – Armenia, Washington, DC: CIA, available at https://www.cia.gov/library/publications/the-world-factbook/geos/am.html.
EIU (2008), *Armenia: Country Profile 2008*, London: Economist Intelligence Unit.
Emerging Markets Monitor (2006), 'Armenia: is AMD strength starting to hurt?', *Emerging Markets Monitor*, 12, 1–3.
Gevorgyan, A., I. Karapetyan and A. Petrosyan (2005), 'Development of entrepreneurship and SME sector in the Republic of Armenia' Annual Forum – After Fifteen Years of Market Reforms in Transition Economies: New Challenges and Perspectives for the Industrial Sector: UNECE Trade Industry and Enterprise Development Week, UNECE Palais des Nations, Geneva.
Government of Armenia (2006), *Annex for Decree N1768-N of the Government of RA, Program for Small and Medium Entrepreneurship State Support*, Yerevan: Ministry of Economy of the Republic of Armenia, http://www.minted.am/upload/file/pdfs/Small/2007eng.pdf (accessed 19 April 2008).
Gresh, G. (2006), 'Coddling the Caucasus: Iran's strategic relationship with Azerbaijan and Armenia', *Caucasian Review of International Affairs*, 1(1), 1–13.
Heritage Foundation (2008), '2008 Index of Economic Freedom Online', Heritage Foundation, http://www.heritage.org/index/ (accessed 19 April 2008).
IAGS (2008), 'Resolution on the Armenian Genocide 5 October 2007', International Association of Genocide Scholars, http://www.genocidescholars.org/ (accessed 20 April 2008).
IMF (2008), *International Finance Statistics*, Washington, DC: International Monetary Fund.
Iradian, G. (2007), 'Rapid growth in transition economies: growth-accounting approach', *International Monetary Fund Working Paper*.
Kyureghian, G. and V. Heboyan (2004), 'Opening Armenia–Turkey border: measuring the economic impact', 14th Annual World Food and Agribusiness Forum & Symposium, International Food and Agribusiness Management Association, 12–15 June, Montreux, Switzerland.
Mitra, S., D. Andrew, G. Gyulumyan, P. Holden, B. Kaminski, Y. Kuznetsov and E. Vashakmadze (2007), *The Caucasian Tiger: Sustaining Economic Growth in Armenia*, Washington, DC: World Bank.
Nathan Associates Inc. (2004), *Armenian Competitiveness Assessment*, Yerevan, Armenia: United States Agency for International Development (USAID), http://armenia.usaid.gov/upload/File/armenia_competitiveness_assessment.pdf (accessed 29 March 2007).
OSCE (2006), *Small & Medium Enterpreneurship Sphere in Armenia 2004–2005* Yerevan: Organization for Security and Co-operation in Europe.
Roland, G. (2000), *Transition and Economics: Politics, Markets, and Firms*, Cambridge, MA: Massachusetts Institute of Technology.
SME DNC (2008), 'About us. Official webpage of Small and Medium Entrepreneurship Development National Center of Armenia', www.smednc.am (accessed 18 April 2008).
Viviano, F. (2004), 'The rebirth of Armenia', *The National Geographic*, March, 28–49.
World Bank (2007), World Development Indicators 2007, CD-ROM, Washington, DC: World Bank.
World Bank (2008), 'Doing Business 2008 Online', World Bank Group, http://www.doingbusiness.org/ (accessed 19 April 2008).

4   Azerbaijan

Elena Sannikova and John F. Cassidy

Introduction

Azerbaijan is located in the South Caucasus region on the western shore of the Caspian Sea, with the Russian republic of Dagestan to the north, Georgia and Armenia to the north and west and Iran to the south. This region lies to the south of the principal Caucasian mountain range, and is situated on the crossroads between Europe and Asia, bridging the Caspian and Black Seas. In terms of religion, Azerbaijan is nominally Islamic, whilst Armenia and Georgia are Christian Orthodox. After 1917 all three countries became part of the Soviet Union. Together with the other republics they gained independence in 1991. Since 1995, political and economic stability has been restored to Azerbaijan. It is primarily an oil-based economy. Whilst still characterized as a low income economy, gross domestic product (GDP) has quadrupled since 2000 amounting to US$19.9 billion in 2006. With the coming on stream of the Baku–Tbilisi–Ceyhan pipeline (BTC pipeline), GDP is expected to double by 2010. In 2006, Azerbaijan was growing at the fastest rates of all emerging markets at 34.5 percent, and in terms of gross national income (GNI) at purchasing power parity (PPP), per capita income in Azerbaijan was US$5430, compared with Armenia with US$1920 and Georgia US$1580 (World Bank, 2008).[1]

Azerbaijan's oil industry dominates all other sectors; in 2007, the oil sector accounted for circa 54 percent of GDP and 75 percent of industry.[2] The non-oil sector also grew by about 12 percent on average in the past two years partly reflecting spill over effects from oil and gas, especially in the machinery, chemical industry, construction, and telecommunication sectors.[3] Azerbaijan's low age profile (54.2 percent of the population is under 30 years of age) and high literacy rate (98.8 percent) are also other positive developmental factors. Other formerly large economic sectors, such as agriculture, have become dwarfed in value added terms by the primacy of the oil industry which only accounts for 2 percent of national employment. From the perspective of developing and internationalizing its indigenous enterprise system, Azerbaijan needs to manage its oil wealth by putting in place the appropriate policy and institutional infrastructure.

The end of communism and the collapse of the USSR has had a profound economic in Azerbaijan, where the level of GDP is only 50 percent of the pre-transition level. The figure is 60 percent for Armenia, and 30 percent for Georgia.[4] The economic transition process in the South Caucasus region has affected women more deeply than men. As with the population as a whole, women in the South Caucasus are well educated and represent an important part of labour forces. Nevertheless, their economic potential remains under-utilised. This is primarily due to social, cultural and economic perceptions of a women's role.

Government policy on SMEs and entrepreneurship

In regard to entrepreneurship and SME development, the South Caucasus as a region is making slow progress with varying levels of commitment from their governments towards SME sector development.

The respective governments of Azerbaijan embarked on economic reform in consultation with the main international financial institutions (the World Bank and the International Monetary Fund, IMF) with the aim of establishing strong, market-oriented economies with a leading role for the private sector, including foreign direct investment. Privatization was initiated in 1995. However, the government has revised this policy since 2005. Whilst wide-scale privatization has taken place in Azerbaijan, this has been primarily in regard to the small-scale sector in activities such as retail, trade and services (UNECE, 2006).

In Azerbaijan, SMEs have increasingly come to play an important role in the 'non-oil' sector of economy. Since 1993, government development programs have been aimed at SMEs. United Nations (UN) data suggests that the share of SMEs in Azerbaijan's GDP was 41.3 percent in 2003 with SME employment amounting to 60.0 percent. However, there has been a decline in the number of incorporated new enterprises between 1999 and 2002 from 3300 to 3100 with an increase in the number of enterprises that were liquidated in the same period.

Regionally, Azerbaijan is characterised by a core periphery model of spatial economic development with over 70 percent of SMEs concentrated in Baku, the capital city. Given the pivotal economic role of the oil sector, the development of local linkages in the form of local subcontractors and suppliers would be seen as an important goal. BP has suggested that there excellent opportunities for the development of local forward and backward linkages in the oil sector – not least based on their local needs. But thus far there has been limited linkage development (UNECE, 2006)

Table 4.1 lists the Azerbaijan government legislation to support SMEs in the period 1992–2003. This legislation demonstrates that much updating of state policy in regard to SMEs has been achieved and that a system of state support for SMEs is in existence. Government policy differentiates between the oil and non-oil sectors of economy.

Theoretically, this legislation has improved the mechanisms for the regulation of entrepreneurship, has provided assistance in improving the quality of human resources for SMEs, has expanded technical and financial support for SMEs, and has strengthened judicial protection of entrepreneurship and emphasized regional economic development factors. The key components of these policies are: improvements in the registration; licensing and certification of SMEs; improvements in the external communications for SMEs; the provision of assistance in the formation of sound investment mechanisms; the development of systems of cooperation between SMEs; the development of incentives for technological development of SMEs; and the development of a system for the protection of the rights of entrepreneurs.

The environment for entrepreneurship and the state of small business
The World Bank Indicators on the environment for business across 178 countries are based on 10 business regulation indicators that track the time and cost to meet government requirements in business start-up, operation, trade, taxation, and closure. Overall Azerbaijan's global ranking is number 96 (Georgia ranks 18 and Armenia 34). Azerbaijan is particularly lowly ranked in regard to licences, trading, investor protection, and paying taxes. All of these latter factors impact negatively on the entrepreneurial environment and SMEs.

Table 4.1 *Azerbaijan government legislation to support SMEs*

No.	Name of document	Status	Year of acceptance	Accepting body
1	Law on Entrepreneurial Activity	Law	1992	Parliament
2	Concept for Basic Directions of State Policy in the Field of Entrepreneurship Development	Concept	1993	Parliament
3	State Program of Development of c . . . (1993–95)	Programme	1993	Parliament
4	Decree on Urgent Activities on Development of Small Entrepreneurship	Decree	1993	President
5	Law on Enterprises. Since 2000 the Civil Code	Law	1994	Parliament
6	Law on Leasing	Law	1994	Parliament
7	Law on joint-stock companies	Law	1996	Parliament
8	Law on registration of juridical persons	Law	1996	Parliament
9	Law on Enterprises of Limited Liability	Law	1998	Parliament
10	Law on State Support for Small Entrepreneurship	Law	1999	Parliament
11	Provision on Control Books	Provision	1999	Cabinet of Ministers
12	Law on Income Tax from Physical Persons	Law	1999	Parliament
13	Law on Tax from Property	Law	1999	Parliament
14	Decree on Improvement of System of the State Control and Elimination of Artificial Obstacles for Entrepreneurship Development	Decree	1999	President
15	Law on Book Keeping	Law	2000	Parliament
16	Provision on the Ministry of Economic Development	Provision	2001	President
17	State Program of SME Development 2002–05	Programme	2002	President
18	Decree on Foundation of the Council of Entrepreneurs Under the President of Republic	Decree	2002	President
19	Provision on the National Fund for Support of Entrepreneurship	Provision	2002	President
20	Decree on Perfection of Licensing of Some Forms of Entrepreneurial Activities	Decree	2002	President
21	Decree on Additional Actions in the Field of State Protection for Entrepreneurship Development	Decree	2002	President
22	Decree on Prevention of the Interventions Interfering Entrepreneurship Development	Decree	2002	President
23	Provision on the Council of Entrepreneurs Under the President of the Republic	Provision	2003	President
24	Decree on Some Aspects of Regulation of Entrepreneurial Activity	Decree	2003	President

Source: UNECE (2006).

Table 4.2   Index of SME development in Caucasus, 2003: Azerbaijan, Armenia and Georgia compared

Variables	Azerbaijan	Armenia	Georgia
Share of the private sector in total Economy (percent)	60%	70%	65%
Share of the SME sector in GDP (percent)	41.3%	35%	29.4%
Share of number of employees in all SMEs compared to total number of employees in the economy as a whole (percent)	60%	31.0%	79%
GDP [USD/capita]	US$864	US$896	US$854
Index of SME Development	127.5	68.1	127.2

Source: UNECE SME Databank, 2003.

Table 4.2 provides comparative economic data on the Index of SME Development in the South Caucasus 2003 based on UNECE data, with Azerbaijan scoring the highest at 127.5. Armenia with 70 percent has the largest share of the private sector in the total economy, and Azerbaijan with 60 percent the smallest. In the Azerbaijan Republic, the SME share of GDP is relatively high at 41.3 percent compared with the other two Caucasian countries. The share of employees in SMEs is lower than Georgia but considerably higher than Armenia.

For Azerbaijan, as a transition economy, the concept of entrepreneurship is a relatively new career choice. The necessary enterprise infrastructure that is a given in advanced capitalist countries is still lacking. Official statistics on SMEs are scarce and often conflicting. Research on SMEs in Azerbaijan is very limited and where it does exist, it emphasizes the gender side of the equation. Given this lack of general research and data on SMEs, in this section we will look at the gender side as a proxy for understanding the underlying issues relating to SMEs in Azerbaijan.

A lack of financial and social capital, relevant knowledge and skills account for the limited development of SMEs in Azerbaijan (UNDP, 2007) In response to the lack of access to finance for SMEs, the European Bank for Reconstruction and Development (EBRD), the International Finance Corporation (IFC, World Bank) and Foundation for International Community Assistance, Azerbaijan (FINCA) have been actively involved in the provision of finance (Box 4.1).

The government of the Azerbaijan Republic has a vision concerning the import of entrepreneurship for the economy. At the policy level, entrepreneurship promotion and small business development is viewed as an effective approach for the creation of new jobs, unemployment reduction, and income generation. As is well documented, small businesses are an important and integral sector of any market economy and indeed pivotal to the capitalist development of transition economies. The institutional capacity environment is being improved in Azerbaijan. As mentioned above, laws necessary to form an entrepreneurial environment have been adopted.[5] Documents necessary for stimulating entrepreneurial activities have been prepared. The State Committee on Antimonopoly Policy and Support of SMEs manages this process. However, it is still not fully enforced (UNECE, 2006), Nonetheless, Table 4.3 paints

---

BOX 4.1   INTERNATIONAL ORGANIZATION FINANCIAL SUPPORT FOR SMES IN AZERBAIJAN

The EBRD has supported the Business Advisory Services (BAS) operations in Azerbaijan since 2003. This has put in place 330 plus projects, funded by the EBRD Early Transition Countries Fund (ETCF) and previously by EuropeAid with a total of over €1.9 million utilized. There has been an emphasis on women entrepreneurial support. The TurnAround Management (TAM) Programme, supporting larger enterprises, has undertaken 21 projects in Azerbaijan since 1998, utilizing over €1.4 million from various bilateral donors and the ETCF. The EBRD highlight environment problems such as the complex tax and customs system, bureaucratic delays and corruption continuing to be major obstacles to the development of private enterprises. According to its future strategy, the EBRD plans to help SMEs and micro enterprises in the provision of direct equity for local enterprises and non-bank micro-finance institutions, credit lines via local banks and the trade facilitation, and support medium-size enterprises together with local banks through co-financing. The SME sector will be further strengthened through the TAM and BAS programmes.

In general, the IFC's strategy in Central Asia has focused on supporting micro, small, and medium enterprises. In Azerbaijan, the IFC has helped expand availability of credit lines for small businesses and worked to establish the Micro Finance Bank of Azerbaijan, the first commercial microfinance bank in the country. In addition, the IFC has invested in a regional equity investment fund, the Central Asia Small Enterprise Fund (SEAF), which provides equity, quasi-equity, and debt financing to growth-oriented enterprises in the Central Asia region. The IFC will continue to support local companies by building the capacity of financial institutions that serve SMEs (IFC, 2008). One particular project that the IFC is involved in is the establishment of a supplier finance credit facility (SFF) of approximately $15.0 million funded by IFC, BP and Micro Finance Bank of Azerbaijan (the Bank, or MFBA). This project provides financing to small and medium-sized contractors to BP and its affiliates in Azerbaijan, the goal of which is to aid BP and its joint venture partners increase local content by expanding the participation of local Azeri enterprises in the supply chain.

FINCA provides micro-finance globally to the lowest income entrepreneurs. FINCA Azerbaijan focuses on finance to the key family breadwinners: they may be involved in trade (for example, kiosks in bazaars), services (for example, hair dressing and shoe repair), farming and other production. The Asian Development Bank is involved in trade financing in Azerbaijan.

---

a positive picture with respect to an increase in the number of enterprises set up and a greatly increased number of SMEs with fewer than 40 employees being set up. Whether this increase is because of – or in spite of – new policies, demands further research.

Table 4.3   Number of incorporated SMEs in Azerbaijan at the end of 2000–04

Country: Azerbaijan	Total number of enterprises in the country	Small and medium enterprises with number of employees	
		0–40 people	50–249 people
2000	55850	32980	22870
2004	65109	47211	17898

Source: Department of Entrepreneurship Development, Ministry of Economic Development, enterprise, Azerbaijan.

A field survey on entrepreneurship in Azerbaijan – a gender focus
In 2005 women represented 2 percent of all entrepreneurs in Azerbaijan.[6] A field survey was undertaken in the southern regions of Azerbaijan namely Masalli and Jalilabad, in the North (Guba, Gusar, Khachmaz), and in the western region – Mingechaur, and Baku. It was based on a sample of 65 women which was followed up by an in-depth study of a smaller group of 15 women entrepreneurs to identify the needs and major issues hampering the more successful performance of women in small and medium enterprises. Our field survey was conducted in sectors dominated mostly by women: food processing, textile, agriculture, beauty care, and handicrafts. It reviewed what is already known about women entrepreneurs and their experience, and highlighted some critical issues.

In our study we did not differentiate among the terms 'self-employed', 'owners', 'micro-enterprise', 'small-enterprise' and 'entrepreneur' because of the absence of precise and defined terms in Azerbaijan. The questions posed to the women entrepreneurs may be subdivided under the following headings: Policy coordination and leadership, Access to financing, Training and mentoring, Business support and information, and Access to premises, and our findings are summarized below.

Policy coordination and leadership   In Azerbaijan, between 1998 and 2004 various documents were produced supporting entrepreneurship in the country, but there were no documents produced specifically to support women entrepreneurs' equal access to ownership, finance and other resources. In terms of recommendations the government of Azerbaijan and the National Confederation of Entrepreneurs should establish focal points for women-owned SMEs, which would address all aspects of the development of women's enterprise. It is quite likely that there are no focal points/help desks for SMEs in general.

Access to financing   As mentioned above, access to finance is critical for all enterprises in Azerbaijan. A number of international organisations are involved in improving this aspect of the business environment (Box 4.1). Whilst men and women have equal property rights and equal access to their property under the constitution, in reality 90 percent of new 'privatized' property is owned by men. Women accordingly with limited or no property rights in regard to housing are without collateral when it comes to borrowing for an entrepreneurial activity. The development of property ownership, and its bedding down in legal terms in transition economies, is a principal requirement for the utilization of collateral in borrowing. The privatization process in Azerbaijan has not favoured women: privatization of housing generally results in ownership by men not women. In addition, women lack 'track records' and are often unable to meet the bank's collateral security requirements. For the period 1999–2005, only 2 percent of all micro credits have been allocated specifically to women entrepreneurs.[7] Banks in general are reluctant to provide financing for SMEs due to high transactions costs and perceived higher risk, plus they generally lack experience in SME lending.

Training and mentoring   The findings of our survey confirmed that the level of entrepreneurial training in the country is quite low despite the fact that in the last few years, a number of international organizations, such as the Academy of Educational Development (United States Agency for International Development, USAID), The Initiative for Social Action and Renewal in Eurasia (ISAR) Oxfam UK, United Nations Development Programme (UNDP), United Nations Development Fund for Women (UNIFEM), International Labour Organization (ILO), The George Soros Foundation (SOROS) have provided entrepreneurship training. In most cases, training is not demand oriented, there are no targeted programmes, and when programmes run their course there is no continuity. One of the problems is the low level of interest from local bodies and municipality officials. As a result there is insufficient knowledge of entrepreneurship rights and opportunities among women in spite of their higher education. There is a dearth of experienced leaders and a lack of finance for their organizational work. Part of the problem arises from the overall weak capacity of the training infrastructure in Azerbaijan to meet the demands for training in the general SME sector.

Business support and information   A low awareness of business development services (BDS) as well as low levels of access to these services was found during the study in Azerbaijan. The availability of BDS in some parts of each of the countries in the Caucasus is quite variable, and in many cases deficient in rural areas. Even where BDS is available at a local level, many women entrepreneurs are unable to afford to pay for commercial professional services delivered by the private sector.

Access to premises   A lack of available business premises is reported by women entrepreneurs as one of the top barriers to the growth of their enterprises. Without adequate business premises, women's access to markets is severely restricted and their production capacity limited. Women report that they have difficulty affording the rents charged for existing premises. Furthermore, many women-owned SMEs lack the necessary skills to negotiate with landlords. Incubators and technology centres specifically designed for women producers would be beneficial for them, but they are not evident in Azerbaijan. There is a plan to build an industrial park near Baku, where incubators may be located.

Internationalization of entrepreneurs and SMEs
The internationalization of SMEs is a key policy priority of advanced, transition and developing markets, yet in reality difficult to realize. For example, 8 percent of European Union (EU) 27 SMEs export and only 12 percent of the inputs of an average EU SME are imported. A lack of financial resources and skilled labour are highlighted as the key problems.[8] Furthermore, the level of internationalization is closely related to company size; the greater the scale, the more likely the firm is to internationalize.[9]

As an emerging and transition economy, the process of internationalization of SMEs in Azerbaijan is at a very elemental level. It was a republic of the highly centralized USSR where internationalization was characterized by large state-owned enterprises. Statistically we may examine Azerbaijan international relations through trade and investment data. Its key trading partners are Italy, Israel, Russia, France, Turkey, Germany, the United Kingdom, Iran, Greece and Ukraine which account for 82.3 percent of total trade. Exports are dominated by oil (91.3 percent) with some residual exports in food products (2.4 percent), machinery (1.6 percent), and textiles (0.8 percent). Imports are equally distributed among petroleum products, machinery and food.[10] In regard to investment, given its primacy as an oil exporter in former times, and with the collapse of the USSR, large amounts of FDI have flowed into Azerbaijan in recent years. In 2006, total inward foreign direct investment (FDI) stock amounted to US$13.3 billion, with outward FDI stock amounting to UD$4.3 billion (UNCTAD, 2007). Inward FDI was predominantly oil-related with disaggregated data unavailable for outward stock. There is a lack of data on the trade and investment patterns of SMEs in Azerbaijan.

The internationalization interface with SMEs in Azerbaijan is at the level of the provision of financing and training. The role of international organizations in the provision of finance in Azerbaijan such as the EBRD, the IFC, FINCA and the Asian Development Bank has been mentioned above. Furthermore, the Academy of Educational Development (USAID), ISAR, Oxfam UK, UNDP, UNIFEM, ILO, SOROS have provided entrepreneurship training. All of the above may act as catalysts, but it is important to recognize the shortcomings of these programmes – they are not demand driven and tend to lack continuity. These may catalyse and/or facilitate the internationalization of small-scale entrepreneurs in the medium term but the process is most likely generational.

The European Commission highlights the key drivers in the internationalization of SMEs as follows: the international orientation of decision-maker, the education system, access to international market information and awareness thereof, importance of language acquisition and openness to other cultures, role of government policies focused on internationalization, access to know how and technology, increased efficiency and economies of scale, increased competence through entering difficult markets, and developing innovation. On the other hand, the key barriers in the internationalization of SMEs are lack of capital to finance expansion/FDI/or exports, being able to identify foreign opportunities, limited opportunity to locate and analyse new/foreign markets, and inability to contact overseas customers.

Where does Azerbaijan fit in regard to drivers and barriers to the internationalization of SMEs? In terms of drivers, Azerbaijan has high literacy levels, its trade profile is geographically Central Asia and the former Soviet Union, the Russian language is still widely spoken – but giving way to English among the younger generation, government policies on internationalization of SMEs are not in place, access to know how and technology still needs more prioritization, and SMEs in general need to become more competitive and innovative – a challenge for SMEs globally. With regard to barriers, the provision of finance by various international donors will help to a certain degree, but it will continue to be a big problem; and identifying foreign opportunities and accessing market information should be focused on traditional regional trading partners – as is the global spatial pattern. Fundamentally, the government needs to address the development of a more supportive and proactive policy environment to promote and facilitate the internationalization of SMEs in Azerbaijan. Furthermore, the development of an international trade board to provide access to information on foreign markets would act as a springboard for SMEs wanting to internationalize.

Conclusion

This chapter was an overview on SMEs and Entrepreneurship in Azerbaijan highlighting government policy, business environment, and the internationalization of SMEs. Given the absence of any available general research on SMEs in Azerbaijan, the authors utilized a survey on women entrepreneurs as a proxy.

Azerbaijan is currently running a large current account surplus as a result of oil exports and inflows of foreign investment. The government has the available finance to invest in a non-oil sector such as the SME sector and the internationalization thereof. In examining government policy, it is apparent that Azerbaijan has put in place the appropriate policy environment to facilitate entrepreneurship and SMEs. Whilst the number of new start ups has increased, the point was raised that the policy environment needs more acting upon. The general regulatory environment for business in Azerbaijan needs improvement. One of the key problems facing SMEs is access to finance and there are a number of international organizations actively involved in providing these supports. However, these programmes must be long term and demand driven.

The survey on women entrepreneurs highlights a number of salient points with regard to the SMEs in general in Azerbaijan. Whilst SME policies are in place, there are no focal points/help desks for women entrepreneurs, and this is most likely the case for all entrepreneurs regardless of gender. The issue of access to finance is also critical to all SMEs; the issue for women relates to traditional patriarchal societies and lack of access to collateral due to male ownership of property. Small and medium enterprises are more likely to have access to finance in the city rather than the regions. Training and mentoring is sparse but various international organizations are involved – again such programmes are short term and not demand driven. Many international programmes are focused on women entrepreneurs rather than men – hence the availability of research on this topic. International donors should be gender sensitive not gender blind. Business support systems exist for SMEs – but focused on urban areas. A low awareness of these programmes may be a problem for some SMEs. Difficulty of access to premises due to high rents is also a problem for SMEs.

In understanding the determinants of the internationalization of SMEs in Azerbaijan, research and data are sparse. Azerbaijan is a young, high literacy, multilingual emerging market. In terms of trade and investment contiguous countries, Central Asia and the former Soviet Union are the current export destinations and import origins. Government policies on internationalization of SMEs are not in place and SMEs in general need to become more competitive and innovative. Key barriers to the success in developing internationalization strategies for SMEs are access to finance and access to international market information. The Azerbaijan government needs to address the development of a more supportive and proactive policy environment to promote and facilitate the internationalization of SMEs in Azerbaijan.

Acknowledgement
The authors would like to thank the International Labor Organization and the United Nations Economic Commission for Europe for their help as the background to this chapter is based on reports previously done by the first author for both organizations.

Notes
1. World Bank (2008) online.
2. Inogate Programme, http://www.inogate.org/en/participating/azerbaijani
3. Ibid.
4. UNECE Statistic Office, *Databank, 2005.*
5. In 1997 and 2000, by the Decree of the President of the Azerbaijan Republic, the 'Program for state support of small and medium enterprises in Azerbaijan Republic (1997–2000, 2000–05)' was ratified. 'Law on enterprising activities', 'Law on enterprises', 'Law on joint-stock companies', 'Law on unfair competition', 'Law on commodity exchange', 'Law on leasing', and other laws ensuring the development of a legal system for the market economy.
6. Data of International Labor Organization, 2005
7. Data of Ministry of Economic Development of Azerbaijan Republic, 2005.
8. European Commission (2007).
9. Ibid.
10. Based on 2001 data in Azerbaijan Trade and Trade Facilitation Review, Asian Development Bank.

References
Asian Development Bank (2001), *Azerbaijan Trade and Trade Facilitation Review*, ADB.
European Commission (2007), *Final Report of the Expert Group on Supporting the Internationalisation of SMEs*, December.
Inogate Programme, 'Gas and oil in Azerbaijan', http://www.inogate.org/en/participating/azerbaijani (accessed online May 2008).
International Finance Corporation (IFC) (2008), *Azerbaijan Business Enabling Environment Project 2008*, http://www.ifc.org/ifcext/eca.nsf/Content/Azerbaijan_AdvisoryProjects#Azerbaijan%20Business%20Enabling%20Envi (accessed May 2008).
International Labor Organization (2005), *Gender Mainstreaming in Entrepreneurial Training and MSME Development*, Moscow: ILO Office.
United Nations Conference on Trade and Development (UNCTAD) (2007), *World Investment Report 2007 Transnational Corporations, Extractive Industries and Development*, New York and Geneva: United Nations.
United Nations Development Programme (UNDP) (2007), *Azerbaijan Human Development Report 2007 – Gender Attitudes in Azerbaijan: Trends and Challenges*, Azerbaijan: UNDP.
United Nations Economic Commission for Europe (UNECE) (2003), *SME Databank 2003*, http://w3.unece.org/pxweb/Dialog/ (accessed May 2008).
United Nations Economic Commission for Europe (UNECE) (2006) *Series: Entrepreneurship and SMEs, Small and Medium-sized Enterprises in the Caucasian Countries in Transition*, New York and Geneva: United Nations.
UNECE Statistic Office, *Databank, 2005*, http://w3.unece.org/pxweb/Dialog/ (accessed May 2008).
World Bank (2008), http://www.worldbank.org (accessed May 2008).

5 Bahrain
Sadiq Sohail

Introduction

The Kingdom of Bahrain is an archipelago of 33 islands nestled between the Qatar peninsula and the coast of Saudi Arabia. Taking its name from the Arabic word which means 'two seas', the islands for the most part are level expanses of sand and rock. Bahrain shares no land borders, but despite its small land area that measures 48 km long and 16 km wide, it has 161 km of coastline. The islands are composed of limestone and saline sand, which is particularly noticeable on the southern side of the main island, an area characterized by desert and oil fields. Historical records show that the islands were once abundant in lush vegetation, and various ancient myths have been connected with them, including that of the Garden of Eden.

Bahrain has a recorded history dating back 5000 years, when the Sumerians knew it as Dilmun, the first great civilization of the Middle East. Since then it remained an important trading and commercial center throughout, visited and at times occupied by Babylonians, Assyrians, Greeks, Romans, Persians, Portuguese, and British.

In 1783, the al-Khalifa family captured Bahrain from the Persians. In order to secure these holdings, it entered into a series of treaties with the UK during the nineteenth century that made Bahrain a British protectorate. In 1968 the British announced their intention to withdraw military forces from the Gulf area. Bahrain attained independence in 1971.

Modern Bahrain is a small and reasonably prosperous economy. In 2007, the population was estimated at 698 585. This figure includes around 235 000 non-Bahrainis who are mostly expatriate workers, largely from Asia, making up some 60 percent of the economically active population. This proportion may seem high, but Gulf nations generally have a high percentage of expatriate workers and their families. Eighty-five percent of Bahrainis are Muslim; the remainder is mostly Christians or Parsees. Bahrain is a highly urbanized nation, with a majority living in the capital of Manama or Muharraq. The per capita gross domestic product (GDP) stands at US$ 25 300 and annual rate of inflation is estimated at about 3.5 percent. Unemployment figures are a staggering 15 percent of the population.

Bahrain was the first Gulf country to discover petroleum in 1932 and export its oil wealth. Oil provided the ruling family with an independent source of income, with which they developed a modern state administration, and given its location, Bahrain became strategically and commercially a more important country. However, the size of its oil reserves has been relatively less. Facing declining oil reserves, Bahrain has initially turned to petroleum processing and refining. Petroleum production and processing accounts for about 60 percent of exports, earns 60 percent of government revenues, and 11 percent of GDP (exclusive of allied industries).

To further diversify its economy, Bahrain has focused on developing infrastructure facilities. With its highly developed communication and transport facilities, Bahrain has attracted numerous multinational firms with business in the Gulf region. The manufacturing industry in Bahrain has also witnessed robust growth in recent years. Aluminum is Bahrain's second major export after oil. Bahrain is actively pursuing the diversification and privatization of its economy to reduce the country's dependence on oil.

Bahrain has also become an increasingly important financial services centre. The financial sector is divided between investment banks, which either are headquartered or have representative offices in Bahrain, and offshore banking units, which use Bahrain as a base. Bahrain is also focusing on Islamic banking segment and is competing on an international scale with Malaysia as a worldwide banking center.

Further diversification has been on promoting inbound tourism. Bahrain has been an attractive destination for a large number of residents particularly from Saudi Arabia. Bahrain is connected to Saudi Arabia by 24-km causeway, which opened in November 1986. A major attraction for Saudi residents is the liberal slant Bahrain has on entertainment and alcohol. But, the Bahraini government at the same time is doing a balancing act on maintaining its tourism image. However, Bahrain has not been able to attract the same numbers of high-spending European visitors that Dubai has been successful in attracting. This is a potential that Bahrain must attempt to exploit.

Diversification of the economy opens up opportunities for the economic development of Bahrain. However, given the limited size of the market, long-term prospects are linked to wider Gulf markets, particularly Saudi Arabia. The prospects for Bahrain appear to be bright as the already established financial sector is well positioned to take advantage of the economic liberalization and reforms taking place in Saudi Arabia in the wake of its accession to the World Trade Organization (WTO). The continuing development of the Bahrain Financial Harbour is a key element of the government's strategy. Unemployment, especially among the young, and the depletion of oil and underground water resources continue to remain the long-term economic problems.

Government policy on SMEs and entrepreneurship
Bahrain is a small, diversified and a reasonably prosperous nation. Despite the presence of a large expatriate workforce, about 15 percent of its citizens are unemployed. The policy of 'Bahrainization' (provide jobs to Bahrainis), employed by industry and government in the past 20 years, has not been very effective. During the past few years, the importance of SMEs to economic development has been realized and the Ministry of Industry and Commerce has prepared a policy statement for the development of SMEs in Bahrain in 2006.

Small and medium enterprises are seen as a dynamic and vibrant sector of Bahrain's economy, with the sector accounting for a substantial part of industrial output. Small and medium enterprises and entrepreneurship development programs have also significantly contributed to employment generation.

A primary objective of the government's policy on SME development is to impart more vitality and growth impetus to this sector to enable it to contribute its full potential to the economy, particularly in terms of growth of output, employment as well as exports. To this end, the policy is directed at creating an enabling environment for the small and medium enterprises to stay competitive in the face of intense global competition. The SME policy emphasizes creating a business friendly environment with minimum red tape to promote growth potential to produce young entrepreneurs who can emerge as strong and viable entities in global arena.

To achieve these objectives, the policy lays importance on providing technical, managerial and marketing skills that are needed for the growth and expansion of these enterprises.

The thrust of government policy on SME and entrepreneurship development have been in the following areas:

1. Encourage first-generation entrepreneurs. The government through the Ministry of Industry and Commerce provides support to first generation entrepreneurs through training and other measures. The targets are educated unemployed youth, who are encouraged to set up their own business ventures and be employment creators rather than employment seekers.
2. Providing access to institutional credit. Recognizing the difficulty of SMEs to access institutional credit and the importance of adequate credit delivery as necessary for the survival of SMEs, the Ministry has taken measures to improve SMEs' access to credit through facilitation of innovative financial services. Assistance has been provided to SMEs in developing appropriate business plans to leverage improved credit limits from financial institutions. The Ministry also encouraged development of a venture fund industry to boost high-technology startups.
3. Assistance in technology access and upgradation. Small and medium enterprises have limited capacity for technology management and knowledge acquisition. Further, with competitiveness being increasingly determined by leading edge technologies, the Ministry recognizes that SMEs in Bahrain develop their capacity to adopt and adapt new technologies and provides assistance in technology assessment, adaptation, product design, application of new materials, and so on. This is done by the Ministry in coordination with various external agencies as Gulf Organization for Industrial Consulting (GOIC), United Nations Industrial Development Organization (UNIDO) and others.
4. Creation of industrial infrastructure. The Ministry has been encouraging clustering of SMEs in industrial estates in order to facilitate rendering of common services and provide common facilities. In addition, the Ministry has also been exploring construction of multistoried factory blocks to house small and medium enterprises.
5. Human resources development. Recognizing the problems faced by SMEs in finding skilled manpower in critical areas, the government of Bahrain through its various agencies has been identifying training needs to continuously update the skills and competencies of persons employed in small and medium enterprises. Further, the Ministry of Industry and Commerce has from time to time recommended increase in capacity to train new manpower in specific trades. It has also worked in coordination with the Ministry of Labour to provide increased funding for industrial training and vocational institutes to take up dedicated skill upgrading programmes for entrepreneurial development.
6. Simplification of rules and procedures. Rules and procedures have been further simplified and paperwork reduced to a minimum to provide a business-friendly environment for SMEs. Best practices prevalent in other successful similar economies such as credit guarantee fund, venture capital assistance, market development assistance and so on are also being studied for incorporation.

7. Upgrading the crafts sector. Recognizing the importance of traditional arts and crafts, the Ministry has set up a business incubator for craft persons. The Craft Center boasts of a common production and testing facilities to artisans to improve their productivity and acceptance of their products. The Ministry also proposes to conduct special training programmes in traditional arts and crafts for women to upgrade their skills. As a further commitment, the Ministry proposes to provide showrooms and marketing outlets for handicraft products at important tourist places.

The environment for entrepreneurship and the state of small business in Bahrain
Bahrain has a long history as a trading nation; its comparatively liberal trade policies have made it an attractive destination, particularly for neighboring countries like Saudi Arabia. The environment for entrepreneurship development is conducive as development, diversification and privatization has been a key policy of the government. Although the GDP per capita is quite high, income distribution is increasingly inequitable and standard of living indicators fail to reflect Bahrain's significant wealth.

Issues in SME development in Bahrain
In a globalized economy, SMEs face different kinds of problem. Environmental factors however alter the relative importance. In Bahrain, financing is not as severe problem as in the European countries. The more severe problem SMEs face in Bahrain relates to technology transfer, technical know-how, establishing linkages and counseling. Supporting institutions are lesser in Bahrain as compared to developed Western countries. Even where support services exist, they are not up to the standard. Functioning of business incubators was also an issue. Past experience of setting business incubators indicated that these were not functioning effectively; they were mere infrastructures not giving any technical support. Clearly, adaptations of Western models were not useful in the Bahrain environment.

With the government committed to support and develop small and medium enterprises, a model was specifically developed, known as the Bahrain Model of Entrepreneurship Development.

Bahrain Model of Entrepreneurship Development
Bahrain's strategy to support new entrepreneurs has been lauded in the entire Middle East and North Africa (MENA) region. At the initiative of government, the Arab Regional Center for Entrepreneurship and Investment Training (ARCEIT), which is a UNIDO set-up, has set a unique program named as the Bahrain Model for Entrepreneurship Development and Enterprise Creation in Bahrain. Based on an assessment of Bahrain's environmental forces, the Bahrain Model is a formal structured network in which the entrepreneur is at the center and various ministries, chambers of commerce, supporting institutions, universities and financial institutions, are a part of the network of institutions and actors, each of them with a specific role in supporting and fostering entrepreneurship.

Based on this model, ARCEIT aims to cover two points: supporting institutions and supporting entrepreneurship. On the first point, people from the Ministry of Industry, commerce, chambers, associations, whomever the entrepreneur will have to deal with to set up a company are identified. These intermediaries are then trained on how to deal with entrepreneurs and SMEs. They are also trained on how to provide entrepreneurs with required services.

The second point covers entrepreneur development. These cover the areas on a collective front as well as the personal front of the entrepreneur through one-to-one business counseling. It is often noticed worldwide that chambers of commerce and private sector associations often target the big and wealthy companies. Small and medium enterprises do not get noticed and recognized. To overcome this neglect, the model provides for developing an association, which is named as Bahrain Young Entrepreneurs Association. This association provides an avenue to put forward their needs, concerns and even lobby with the government.

One of the issues we faced was the financial issue. We had the Bahrain Development Bank (BDB) which gives loans. We had the Kuwait Finance House (KFH) which manages venture capital funds. We have linked both of them together and now they are developing a venture capital fund. The BDB will rely on the KFH's experience in how to do it. What we have done, as UNIDO, is go to the Bahrain Development Bank and do the restructuring in order for them to be able to better suit the needs and requirements of SMEs.

State of small business in Bahrain – an evaluation
The government of Bahrain has shown a firm commitment to developing or providing the right environment. The Bahrain Business Incubator Center (BBIC) facility which was set up in 2003 on a 4000 sqm space has been regularly increased and is planned to reach 22 000 sqm. Not only this, plans are afoot to have three or four more incubators.

Bahrain is fast developing a strong reputation for its support of SMEs. Even the World Bank has recognized the Bahrain Model as the most effective mechanism. Bahrain's strategy to support new entrepreneurs has been held up as an example to the entire Middle East and North Africa region. In recognition of this, Bahrain has been named as the headquarters of the MENA Network for Business Incubation.

Despite all this, there are some concerns from the perspective of entrepreneurs. A concern relates to lack of a proper financing structure. While entrepreneurs admit that there is cash available from banks, a clear mechanism for approvals is what is lacking. Entrepreneurs have generally observed that commercial banks focus their activities either on large corporations or on retail and consumer lending, rather than on small business loans. A regulatory environment needs to be put in place.

Internationalization of entrepreneurs and SMEs
The small market size of Bahrain is a major drawback to marketing their products. A population of just 800 000 means this problem is unavoidable. However, growing integration between members of the Gulf Co-operation Council (GCC), particularly Saudi Arabia, gives scope for SMEs to internationalize.

The Ministry of Industry and Commerce in its policy statement for the development of SMEs in Bahrain in 2006 outlined the importance of export development for SMEs operating in Bahrain.

The government's policy on SME and entrepreneurship development has been to assist SMEs in the marketing efforts and export development. The government recognizes that marketing remains a problem area for most small and medium enterprises. While multilateral and regional trade policies have made markets more accessible, they have also made competition more intense. The Ministry provides SMEs with timely market intelligence, online information and advisory services for SMEs to capitalize on new trade opportunities.

Further, the Ministry has encouraged and assisted SMEs to use e-commerce to gain access to international markets and reduce transaction costs. To remain competitive in the limited local market, SMEs have been encouraged to focus on international markets. Small and medium enterprises have also been encouraged to form marketing consortia to bid for bulk orders from international markets. The Ministry also provides assistance for participation in regional and international trade fairs and franchising events. Chamber of commerce have also been encouraged to organize and facilitate franchising events in Bahrain on a regular basis.

The Bahrain Model developed to assist SMEs and young entrepreneurs also provides assistance to SMEs to go international through the growth programs. Training and counseling is provided to entrepreneurs on requirements, regulations and procedures to deal in the business and product of the entrepreneur.

Conclusion

Small and medium enterprise development is vital for the economic development of Bahrain. The government has realized the importance to Bahrain of SMEs and has played a very positive role in creating a favorable environment for SMEs to stay competitive in the wake of intense global competition. Policy initiatives have been undertaken on creating a business friendly environment with minimum red tape and produce young entrepreneurs who can emerge as strong business contenders in Bahrain. The government of Bahrain has also recognized a need for a local institution to develop and strengthen the indigenous capacities of entrepreneurship development and investment promotion, and has been successfully encouraging this. A further area that will need close examination will be the effectiveness of measures being adopted by the government and the Bahrain Model.

The Bahrain Model of Entrepreneurship Development has been internationally lauded and even the World Bank has recognized it as the most effective mechanism for entrepreneur development. Within the Middle East and North Africa region Bahrain has set an example in entrepreneurship development efforts. Even the United Arab Emirates, a more prosperous country, which initiated its own model for entrepreneurship development called the Khalifa Fund last year with a capital of 300 million dirhams (BD 30.7 million), drew inspiration from the success of the Bahrain Model.

6 Bangladesh
Muhammad Mahboob Ali

Introduction

Bangladesh became independent in the year 1971.When the country was independent, entrepreneurship among local people was limited to only 2 percent of the total population. It was ironic that at that time non-Bangalis largely controlled entrepreneurship. But Bangladesh has a magnificent model of entrepreneurial activity from ancient times to the seventeenth century. At that time it had small and cottage industries, shipping industries, gold and silver smithies, milk products, the making of combs and buttons from animal bones, treatment of raw hides, papermaking, sugar, salt industries, and so on. The then Bengal was enriched by shipping commodities to various parts of the world. After the seventeenth century these entrepreneurial activities almost ceased. Local people in the country declined to work at entrepreneurial activities due to political and historical reasons. Unequal exchange worked at that time. As a result, in this geographical location, entrepreneurship developed by the local people was almost destroyed.

Although British rulers left this area in 1947, a second colonial era started. This second colonial era continued till 1971 before the birth of independent Bangladesh. During this period West Pakistan ruled the country. At that time entrepreneurship was developed mainly by West Pakistan in different industrial sectors, but especially the jute sector. But capital flowed out from this region to the then West Pakistan. Lack of capital and lack of farsightedness by the local people, and an anti-entrepreneurial attitude, meant the local people did not become entrepreneurs. Almost 98 percent of owners of industry, mills, banks and so on during the Pakistan period were West Pakistanis and foreigners.

The country passed through three economic systems after its independence: 1972–75, socialistic attitude; 1976–89, mixed economy; 1990 to now, moving towards a free market economy. After independence, the government nationalized commercial banks, industries, mills, and factories. As saving and investment is very low, to channel saving and investment through the formal sector and to expand banking services in the remote areas of the country, nationalization of the banking sector was one of the major objectives at that time. The numbers of bank branches have now expanded, particularly in the rural areas.

Although the industrial process started after independence, because of the damage from the liberation war there was a transitory situation during 1972–75. However, under state patronage, industrial activities started. From 1976, greater emphasis was given to the private sector and was greatly expedited after 1990. Entrepreneurs also started working in different types of innovative business ventures. An extraordinary cluster of entrepreneurs, creators of innovative endeavors, produced new products and processes within large and small businesses.

Latif and Chowdhury (1997) observe that in Bangladesh at the time of initiating enterprise, an entrepreneur faced many problems, such as shortage of skilled workers and infrastructure. Akhtaruddin (2000) observed in the selection of industry, the influence of demand for product and availability of raw materials were important. Khan (2000) argued that in Bangladesh lack of political commitments and absence of creation of the healthy environment required for entrepreneurial growth are the limiting factors in the process of adequate supply of a reasonable number of entrepreneurs.

Entrepreneurship is the main way to develop the country's economy. Half of the total population is women. But they are yet to get the equal opportunity and social empowerment, although over the past 37 years there has been some progress. Chowdhury (2001) argues, in relation to Bangladesh, that the importance of women's entrepreneurship development focuses on women's development in general and their participation in income-generating activities in particular, which deserves special consideration in rational development planning on two counts. Chowdhury's comment is justified, as the country cannot develop its economy without the empowerment of women on a larger scale.

The Bangladesh economy suffers from the problems on both the supply and demand sides. Bangladesh is one of the least developed countries in the world as it suffers from poverty, imperfection in both factor and product markets, continuous disequilibria in the economy, a defective administrative structure, an inappropriate tax structure, a heavy dependence on the external sector, lack of capital stock and massive unemployment. Rate of economic growth is now rising at around 6 percent. The markets in Bangladesh are too small, in economic terms, and the size of population is too numerous. The purchasing power of the large majority of the population is minimal and around one-fifth of the total population is outside the market. Besides the formal money market the informal money market plays an important role in Bangladesh, especially in the rural sector. The government also borrows heavily from the banking channel. The Bangladesh Bank cannot still independently determine monetary policy.

The financial sector was controlled under the strict directives of the government and the Bangladesh Bank till December 1989. Financial repression syndrome was created in the economy. A financial sector reform program was started in 1990. However, a floating exchange rate system was started in 2003.

After independence the Bangladesh government faced an industrialization problem. The capital market was not active. Developed financial institutions like Bangladesh Shilpa Bank, Bangladesh Shilpa Rin Sangstha and Investment Corporation of Bangladesh worked towards industrialization of the country. The Bangladesh Small and Cottage Industries Corporation and Export processing zone worked towards entrepreneurship development. Moreover, nationalized commercial banks also took special initiatives to provide industrial credit. A capital market again started working from 1976, but cannot work properly. Fry (1995) argues that in Germany, the banking system was the primary source of both capital and entrepreneurship. Moreover, a debacle in the capital market of Bangladesh in 1996–97 was the result of widespread manipulation and irregularities in the Dhaka Stock Exchange and the Chittagong Stock Exchange. According to Ali and Wise (2007) the securities market in Bangladesh is very small. During 1994 the total number of initial public offerings reported by the Dhaka Stock Exchange was 23, and the average has only been 13 per year across the 12-year period 1994–2005. The most intense period of activity occurred in the 'bull' market of 1994–96 with an average of 22 initial public offerings (IPOs) per year. The data from the Dhaka Stock Exchange show that, on average, IPOs across the period 1994–2005 were oversubscribed by 494 percent. Moreover, oversubscription also occurred in the Chittagong market showing significant underpricing

(1111 percent on average between 2003 and 2005) in this market, and that there was a very real shortage of primary stock investment opportunities.

Bangladesh is heavily dependent on foreign aid and loan and foreign remittances. A huge deficit is prevailing in the balance of trade position of Bangladesh. It has few exportable commodities and most of these are primary products. The taxation system has little impact on the economic development policy. The tax: GDP ratio is very low, which indicates that the tax collection system is inefficient. In Bangladesh, indirect tax is still higher than direct tax. Although the value-added tax was introduced in July 1991, its objectives have not been fulfilled and its network is relatively small.

Even now a stable political atmosphere, infrastructural development and diversified exportable commodities cannot be produced. Moreover, Bangladesh is mainly a supplier of primary products, and prices of those products regularly face deterioration of terms of trade. During 2005–06, the income from total export is USD10 526 million, out of which readymade garments and knitwear supplies earns USD7901 million. This is around 75.06 percent of the total export earnings (*Bangladesh Arthanaitic Samikhya*, 2007). But forward linkage industries or backward linkage industries in the ready-made garments (RMG) sectors are not properly created. To import accessories for the garments industry from foreign countries, a huge amount of foreign exchange cost has to be incurred.

According to the Industrial Policy 2005 of Bangladesh, definitions of industries in the manufacturing sector are mentioned below:

> (a) 'Large Industry' means an industry in which the value/replacement cost of durable resources other than land and factory buildings is above 100 million taka; (b) 'Medium Industry' means an industry in which the value/replacement cost of durable resources other than land and factory buildings is between 15 million and 100 million taka; (c) 'Small Industry' means an industry in which the value/replacement cost of durable resources other than land and factory buildings is under 15 million taka; (d) 'Cottage industry' means an industry in which members of a family are engaged part-time or full-time in production and service-oriented activities.

The Industrial Policy 2005 of Bangladesh goes on to define industries in the non-manufacturing sector (trading and other services) as follows:

> (a) 'Large Industry' means an industry in which more than 100 workers work; (b) 'Medium Industry' means an industry in which 25 to 100 workers work; (c) 'Small Industry' means an industry in which fewer than 25 workers work (unlike family members in a cottage industry) (http://www.fbcci-bd.org/policy/Industrial_Policy_2005.htm)

One of the obstacles to entrepreneurship development in Bangladesh is that after such a long gap, most of the local entrepreneurs have been taking initiatives elsewhere since 1972. As a result, the country lacks the entrepreneurial habit and is passing through a second or third generation of entrepreneurship development. However, within the next 15 to 20 years the behavioral and psychological pattern of the country will change, entrepreneurial activities can have an input in the economic development process of the country.

Government policy on SMEs and entrepreneurship in Bangladesh
The government of Bangladesh has undertaken a number of initiatives in terms of monetary and fiscal related approaches and tried to implement plans to promote small and medium enterprises so that this may lead to economical advancement of the country.

Das et al. (2007) reported that a focus group of Bangladesh Bank argued that a small enterprise in Bangladesh is an entity, ideally not a public limited company, which does not employ more than 60 persons if it is a manufacturing concern, 20 persons if it is a trading concern, and 30 persons if it is a service concern, and which also fulfils the following criteria: (a) a service concern with total assets at cost excluding land and buildings, investing from BDT 50 000 to BDT 3 000 000; (b) a trading concern with total assets at cost excluding land and buildings, investing from BDT 50 000 to BDT 5 000 000; (c) a manufacturing concern with total assets at cost, excluding land and buildings, investing from BDT 50 000 to BDT 10 000 000.

The Bangladesh Bank has initiated factoring to ease the working capital crisis to ensure the process of the project undertaken by SMEs to enjoy consistent cash flow, lower management costs, and reduced credit risks. The Bangladesh Bank has acknowledged the following actions for SMEs' development.

In Bangladesh, an entrepreneurs' equity fund has been established in 2000, which provides equity to SMEs in agriculture-based industry and information and communication technology (ICT) sector through the commercial banks.

As the prime public sector institution for the promotion and development of small and cottage industries in the country, the Bangladesh Small and Cottage Industries Corporation (BSCIC) is involved in lending programs from own resources in association with the Bangladesh Shilpa Bank (BSB) and in association with consortium of commercial banks. Most of its policies are based on government experience in this sector. However, Hoque (2004) observed that as a development bank, the Bangladesh Shilpa Bank delivered industrial credit but this was not accompanied by adequate and efficient entrepreneurial guidance, supervision and direction.

The Bangladesh Small Industries and Commerce (BASIC) Bank Limited was set up in 1988 with the objective of financing small and cottage industries and it is envisaged that at least 50 percent of its loanable funds should be invested in small-scale industries. This bank offers lower lending rates to SMEs compared with those of other banks. At present, the development of the SME sector is increasingly promoted through the involvement of private agencies, such as MIDAS. MIDAS has recently increased its lending limit up to Tk 100 million. Moreover, an export promotion zone is also playing a vital role to develop export-oriented industries.

In Table 6.1 we show summary information on SMEs' refinancing.

Moazzem (2006) argued that government has to adequately distribute its resources through different budgetary measures in different sectors, preferably on SME-related and employment-enhancing activities. Considering the extent of importance of various sectors, priority is usually given to some important sectors, such as RMG, agriculture, livestock, agriculture-based industries, textiles, jute industry, and so on. His observation is very important as simply making an appropriate plan is not sufficient for the country but there should also be a bridge between planning and implementation of the policy.

Sarder (1999) found that all government agencies are overly bureaucratic in their functioning unlike private support agencies. He suggested that some sort of institutional networking, which currently is totally absent, is necessary to ensure effective support to the SME sector in the context of Bangladesh. Sarder's observation is partially true as most of the government agencies of the country are overly bureaucratic but the private

Table 6.1   Summary information on SMEs' refinancing (up to June 2007)

Name of banks/FIs refinanced	Amount refinanced (in million Taka)				No. of beneficiary enterprise			
Bangladesh	Working capital	Mid term loan	Long term loan	Total loan	Industrial loan	Commercial loan	Service	Total
Bank	45.75	125.83	79.67	251.25	672	2015	586	3273
IDA	34.98	53.13	37.17	125.28	569	698	179	1446
ADB	32.77	25.31	19.30	77.38	199	333	160	692
Total	113.50	204.27	136.14	453.91	1440	3046	925	5411

Source: Hossain (2008).

sector is also functioning under too much red tape and is as inefficient and corrupt as the government sector.

The sector should support a joint partnership approach between the public and private sectors to boost investment, creation and innovation of new products, minimizing risk and maximizing profit, and to accelerate job opportunities. Small and medium enterprises in Bangladesh should generate more inputs towards sustainable economic development. They should take initiatives to assist poor groups of people to progress their business skills, marketing and financial management. Dependency syndrome should be removed through arranging access to capital and creation of wealth.

The environment for entrepreneurship and the state of small business in Bangladesh
To develop the environment of entrepreneurship in Bangladesh, small business ventures should get priority. Non-farm activities have been initiated by different non-government organizations. The government is also trying to develop an infrastructure for small business organization. Financial institutions are also trying to provide loans to small business ventures. According to *Bangladesh Arthanaitic Samikhya* (2007), in the small and cottage industries sector – during the financial year 2005–06, different banks and financial institutions provided lending, and total investment from the owners of Taka (Tk) 211 10.73 crore[1] was made out of which long-term loan is Tk 701.43 crore. According to Khan and Hyder (2006) small enterprises are the lifeblood of any economy and are at the forefront of government efforts to promote entrepreneurial activities, innovation and increased productivity. Khan and Hyder's comment should be injected with the initiatives from the private sector also. Actually, the country faces huge unemployment, so labour-intensive industrial processes may get more emphasis. The behavioral pattern of the financial institutions should be changed. They should not only provide lending but also work as a facilitator, that is, be involved in the process of creation of a value chain. Jahur and Azad (2004) mentioned that in Bangladesh, small business enterprises are believed to have employed 87 percent of the total workforce and to produce large number of goods and services. Khanka (2006) argued that creation of infrastructural facilities involves huge funds which small entrepreneurs lack. As depicted by *Bangladesh Arthanaitic Samikhya* (2007), the percentage contribution of large and small industries to the GDP in Bangladesh is given in Table 6.2.

Table 6.2   Contribution of small to large industries as a percentage of GDP

Industry	1999–00	2000–01	2001–02	2002–03	2003–04	2004–05	2005–06	2006–07 (provisional)
Small and cottage industry	5.80	6.60	7.70	7.20	7.45	7.93	9.21	10.28
Middle to large industry	4.40	7.00	4.60	6.60	6.95	8.30	11.41	11.56
Total	4.80	6.70	5.50	6.80	7.10	8.19	10.77	11.19

Source: Bangladesh Arthanaitic Samikhya (2007: 83).

The contribution of small and cottage industries in Bangladesh as a percentage of GDP is very significant, although middle to large industry is also contributing.

Micro-credit programs that the non-government organizations (NGOs) operate are otherwise aimed at alleviating poverty but the rate of interest, which many NGOs charge, is too high. Absence of corporate social responsibility is one of the causes for the recent violent movement in the garments sector of Bangladesh. According to Muhammad (2006) studies in Bangladesh reveal that only 5 percent of the borrowers showed improvement in their situation with the help of micro credit, and those have other sources of income. Many of them could not bear the burden and fled their village with many liabilities on their head. Muhammad's observation is also partially true. In a real sense, the success of people who use micro credit for removing poverty is very limited. Only those who have alternative sources of fundings may overcome their poverty.

In both rural and urban areas of Bangladesh, there are large numbers of moneylenders, pawnbrokers, mahajans, and so on. Patrick (1980) depicted that in underdeveloped countries, a considerable portion of the funding is used relatively unproductively by large numbers of relatively poor people. Patrick's observation is still applicable for Bangladesh. The country had not a great deal of success in eliminating such traditional financing institutions by attempting to substitute new financial institutions. Success stories of NGOs are very few.

Solaiman and Sohel (2007) observed that there is a bright future for rural women entrepreneurship development, especially in the dry fish sector of Bangladesh. However, the presence of women in the formal sector in Bangladesh is not significant. The government is acting as the catalyst for encouraging women in all areas. Yet women entrepreneurs are mostly concentrated in the low-productivity and low-profit margin sectors. Solaiman and Sohel's comment very much applies in the real economic scenario of the country.

Women entrepreneurship is not widespread. Women must be encouraged to get the assistance of banks so that small business enterprises can be developed. Moreover, collateral is also required to take a loan from a bank, which hampers access to bank credit. Excess liquidity and a relatively high spread between deposit and lending rates in the banking sector is also prevailing. The Bangladesh Bank has a 'laissez-faire policy' and does not take the required steps against commercial banks. Owing to this, good entrepreneurs are difficult to encourage.

Table 6.3   FDI as a percentage of GDP

Year	1970	1975	1980	1985	1990	1995	2000	2003
Foreign direct investment as a percentage of GDP	0.00	0.00	0.05	0.00	0.01	0.00	0.59	0.20

Source: http://globalis.gvu.unu.edu/.

Internationalization of entrepreneurs and SMEs from Bangladesh
The government of Bangladesh has been trying to attract foreign investment in Bangladesh, but this has been insignificant. Moreover, since 1997, sector wise FDI inflow has taken a new turn, with renewed interest of multinational companies (MNCs) in gas, electricity, and telecommunications becoming visible. Foreign investors are essentially out of the capital market, no private mutual funds have been established and the role of the stock market in financing new industrial investments has declined sharply. As per Industrial Policy 2005, foreign direct investment will be encouraged in all industries in Bangladesh except those on the reserved lists, banking, insurance and other financial institutions. This type of investment can be made in local public and private sectors individually or jointly. The capital market will be open for 'portfolio' investments (Industrial Policy 2005). The inward–outward globalization process is considerable in wealth creation for a country like Bangladesh as textile and apparel SMEs can be expanded into higher-value added through worldwide services. Table 6.3 indicates foreign direct investment as a percentage of GDP. The table reveals that foreign direct investment in Bangladesh declined in 2003.

Globalization's modus operandi ensures many potential opportunities. Entrepreneurs are the most significant players who can make prudent use of other resources and can add value themselves as an enormous provider for the economic development of the country. If internationalization of entrepreneurs can be applied properly in the country then it may create success in Bangladesh. Because SMEs may be developed from low value-added 'blue-collar' work to higher value-added 'white-collar' work this may be added to the value chain of invention bounded by the SMEs scheme. Abdullah (1996) argued that as the globalization of the world economy is taking place, acquisition of modern technology has become indispensable rather than a choice for a developing country to ensure the economy has the competitive edge. His argument is justified, as without superior technology sustainable economic development is not feasible. Although Bangladesh has a huge amount of labour, most of it is unskilled. As such, the creation of core competency through conversion of human capital is required. This may be done with the help of international cooperation. Moreover, structural alliances among domestic and multinational corporations may be encouraged to attain excellent outcomes.

Bangladesh's accession into the WTO and the globalization process provide simultaneous opportunities as well as threats in international business. To increase its export capability, it will have to face tough challenges from developed countries, which are technologically superior. Bangladesh appears to be at a lower level of globalization compared with a number of countries, evaluated by a recently formulated index of globalization.

The index is intended to reflect the extent to which a country is involved in international transactions, that is trade, capital flow, movements of people, and transmission of information, ideas, and technology.

According to United Nations Conference on Trade and Development (2006) experts recognized the useful role of international development organizations in building productive capacities and delivering technical assistance to many developing countries. While recognizing the unique role of each programme, there should be a response based on a common set of principles. Representatives of international organizations and agencies agreed to the principle of better coordination and enhanced partnership. Some overlap might occur in technical assistance at the country level, particularly with bilateral aid programmes. Recipient countries have a vital role to play in coordinating the work of a range of multilateral and bilateral agencies that supply them with technical support. Policy-makers as well as the private sector of the country should consider the UNCTAD guidelines for entrepreneurship development.

When one non-resident Bangladeshi (NRB) established a software company in Dhaka for exporting of software and information technology (IT) services to Volvo Motor Company in Sweden in 1988, Bangladesh entered the global market. Unfortunately, NRBs do not get proper guidance and help from public or private initiatives. Financial institutions fail to perform any sort of active advocacy and promotional activities to encourage NRBs to invest in Bangladesh.

The export sector of Bangladesh is now facing more competition in the international market due to the expiry of the multifiber agreement (MFA). Further, the strengthening role of the globalization process of trade and investment, and the advent of post-MFA, are creating problems for Bangladesh, which is facing a highly competitive situation in the global environment. Ali (2003) mentioned that price should be fixed on the basis of analyzing the international market properly. Costing requires a promotional campaign to get wider recognition. When an international contract is made information regarding the legal, ethical, and sociocultural background of the investing country should also be collected.

Bangladesh should also encourage entrepreneurship in the tourism sector. There is a lot of potential to develop the tourism sector. Historically, tourists from foreign countries used to visit ancient Bengal. At that time Bengal was well known for its beauty as well as its ancient industrial base. But after English rule and later Pakistani rule, Bengal lost its own image. The independence of Bangladesh cannot provide any positive image to create tourism, but if the tourism sector can be explored, it will have positive impact on gross domestic product. The World Travel and Tourism Council (WTTC) estimates that in 2002 travel, tourism and related activities will contribute 11 percent to the world's GDP. As such, Bangladesh can also increase its GDP by taking appropriate steps from the development of entrepreneurship in the tourism sector.

Information and communication technology is the key strength in the twenty-first century. This technology helps to attain the internationalization of entrepreneurs and their investment in diversified sectors. Foreign investment may be made in composite textile, telecommunications, pharmaceuticals, power and energy, manufacturing, the capital market and financial services of Bangladesh. Business process reengineering is also mandatory, especially in the jute sector, for which international cooperation is required.

Conclusion

Entrepreneurs in Bangladesh mostly aim to earn huge profits, which ultimately hampers the growth of their business. Owing to market distortion, entrepreneurs can sometimes be guided only by the policy of earning a huge profit. Moreover, middlemen also suck a large portion of profit, resulting in customers being deprived of getting the product at a reasonable cost. Under a free market economy, only those firms which are competitive may survive, using economies of scale. The Bangladesh Bank advised different banks to provide loans in the ICT sector, and agriculture-processing industries as a growth sector, but lack of entrepreneurial development failed to attain any positive impact. The Bangladesh Bank is also emphasizing on women's entrepreneurship. But if the country only offers the policy framework but does not execute it then how can it develop entrepreneurship?

To attain competitiveness, both internal and external factors should be properly arranged. Starting with removing red tape, ensuring the electricity supply, political stability, the removal of corruption, eradication of rent seeking, collateral-free lending, minimizing business and financial risk, and so on are required. Young people, especially females, on a large scale should be encouraged to take initiatives to start entrepreneurship through establishing small and medium enterprises. Moreover, mid- and high-tech industries also should be established under a joint venture project with the cooperation of a foreign nation so that industries may be established. Monetary and fiscal policies of the country should be properly frameworked and implemented.

The private sector of the country has gone through a paradigm shift. Development of legal frameworks and proper fiscal and monetary policies, modern banking mechanism and adequate power generation are essential. Moreover, public and private partnership should be developed so that entrepreneurs can contribute to economic development.

The problem lies with the psychological and behavioral mindset of society. Society itself is not able to encourage the entrepreneurs in true sense. Moreover, human nature is naturally individualistic. Real corporate social responsibility in this country is still not practised. The service sector requires information about current and prospective customers' needs and demands. As such the behavioral and psychological mindset of society should be changed.

A corruption-free society is most welcome for the nation but at the same time policymakers should be aware that in any transitional period there might be problems, especially for the poorer section of the country. Steps should be taken so that there is no adverse impact on employment or a decline in purchasing power. If this cannot be done then this may create a vicious circle of poverty and lead to a low-level equilibrium trap, and marginal social benefit will be outweighed.

However, let us hope that by trial and error, the country can develop entrepreneurs. They will be able to contribute to the economic progress of the country with vision and mission, and add value in society through their dynamism and innovativeness and by minimizing risk and maximizing return.

Note

1. Crore = 10 million.

References

Abdullah, M. (1996), 'Entrepreneurship development in light engineering industries in Bangladesh:problems and policies', *Management Development*, **9**(1&2), 34–48.

Akhtaruddin, M. (2000), 'Socio-economic profile of industrial entrepreneurs: a study on northern region of Bangladesh', *Bank Parikrama*, **25**(4), 39–52.

Ali, Muhammad Mahboob (2003), 'Software marketing in Bangladesh: problems and prospects', *The AIUB Journal of Business and Economics*, **1**(3), 107–11.

Ali, Muhammad Mahboob and Victoria Wise (2007), 'Equity funding through initial public offerings: the case of Bangladesh', accepted for publication in the blindly refereed *Global Business & Economics Anthology*, a volume of selected papers from the 2007 Business & Economics Society International (B&ESI) Conference that took place in Antibes – French Riviera / France at the Hotel Ambassadeur, 16–20 July.

Bangladesh Arthanaitic Samikhya (2007), Ministry of Finance, The Government of the People's Republic of Bangladesh, Dhaka, June, pp. 83–94.

Chowdhury, Masuda M. Rashid (2001), 'The emerging women entrepreneurs of Bangladesh', *FBCCI Journal*, **2**(5–6), 2–4.

Das, Bhagaban, Nikhil Chandra Shil, Alok Kumar Pramanik (2007), 'Strengthening SMEs to make export competitive', *Journal of Business and Technology [Dhaka]*, **2**(01 & 02), 55.

Fry, Maxwell J. (1995), *Money, Interest, and Banking in Economic Development*, London: Johns Hopkins University Press.

Hoque, Mohammad Ziaul (2004), *Industrial Loan Default–The Case of Bangladesh*, Dhaka: The University Press.

Hossain, Syed Yusuf (2008), 'Economic condition of Bangladesh and commodity price' (in Bengali), paper presented at the seminar on Economic Condition of Bangladesh and Commodity Price organized by Bangladesh Economic Association on 26 April at Planning and Development Academy, Dhaka, Bangladesh, 9.

http://globalis.gvu.unu.edu/ (accessed 2 January 2007).

http://www.katalystbd.com/admin/downloads/20060925122428.pdf (accessed 10 January 2007).

Industrial Policy 2005, http://www.fbcci-bd.org/policy/Industrial_Policy_2005.htm (accessed 15 January 2007).

Khan, A.R.(2000), *Entrepreneurship-Small Business and Lives of Successful Entrepreneurs*, Bangladesh: Ruby Publishers.

Khan, Jahangir H. and Hyder, Akmal S. (2006), 'Towards a matrix for small enterprise development: from a developing economies institutional perspective', *The AIUB Journal of Business and Economics*, **5**(2), 111–36.

Khanka, S.S. (2006), *Entrepreneurial Development*, New Delhi: S. Chand and Co.

Jahur, Mohammad Saleh and A.S.M.Sohel Azad (2004), 'A study on small business enterprises in Bangladesh – searching for growth factors and obstacles', *Journal of Institute of Bankers Bangladesh*, **51**(1), 73–89.

Latif, Ehsan and Md Hedayet Ullah Chowdhury (1997), 'Socio-economic profile of entrepreneurs: a study on selected enterprise of Dholai Khal', *Bank Parikrama*, **22**(3&4), 57–65.

Moazzem, Dr Khondaker Golam (2006), 'Meeting the challenges in SME development in Bangladesh: special reference to government's budgetary measures', report prepared for KATALYST, Bangladesh, 9 September, p. 30.

Muhammad, Anu (2006), 'Monga, micro credit and the Nobel Prize', http://www.countercurrents.org/gl-muhammad041206.htm (accessed 8 January 2007).

Patrick, Hugh T. (1980), 'Financial development and economic growth in underdeveloped countries', W.L. Coats Jr and D.R. Khatkhate (eds), *Money and Monetary policy in less Developed Countries: Survey of Issues and Evidence*, Oxford and New York: Pergamon Press, pp. 37–54.

Solaiman, Mohammad and Mir Hossain Sohel (2007), 'Innovation in dry fish industry: a study on women entrepreneurs', paper presented in the ninth South Asian Management Forum hosted by North South University, Dhaka, Bangladesh held on 24 and 25 February, pp. 39–46.

Sarder, Jahangir H. (1999), 'The profile of small enterprise support: agencies in Bangladesh', *Finance and Banking*, **5**(1 & 2), 21–42.

United Nations Conference on Trade and Development (2006), http://www.unctad.org/en/docs/c3em28d3_en.pdf, 22 December.

7 Brunei
Stephen W. Litvin

Introduction

Brunei Darussalam, generally referred to as Brunei, is located 4 degrees north of the Equator, snuggled within the confines of the Malaysian state of Sarawak on the northern shore of the island of Borneo. The nation, a remnant of the British Empire, is a small petroleum-rich Malay-Islamic-Monarchy. At 5765 km^2, Brunei is virtually the same size as Canada's smallest province, Prince Edward Island, and just smaller than USA's state of Delaware. Interestingly, the Brunei government owns a cattle ranch in Australia considerably larger than the entire nation itself (United States Department of State, 2008)!

In 1963, the British territories on the Malaysian peninsula, including Singapore, as well as the British North Borneo territories of Sabah, Sarawak, and Brunei were offered independence – and the nation of Malaysia was born. The lone abstainer from the new federation was the Sultanate of Brunei. (Singapore joined, but was expelled two years later and became an independent state.) Brunei's royal family opted not to join due to concern that its vast oil reserves would be nationalized by the new Malaysian government. Following this decision to pursue its independence, Brunei held initial elections. However, when the winner was a socialist party running on an anti-Malaysia and anti-British platform, the Sultan invalidated the results and the nation remained a British protectorate until 1984, when formal independence was finally obtained. Brunei is still ruled by the royal family, with the current Sultan the twenty-ninth in his family line.

Today, Brunei's population approximates 380000, with, due to declining birthrates, a projected annual growth rate of less than 1 percent (APEC, 2006). The population is culturally diverse. Malays, virtually all Muslim, constitute 67 percent. There is a large Chinese minority (15 percent). The balance, classified as 'Other,' includes the 3 percent indigenous tribes people that inhabit the interior portions of the nation.

The 2007/08 United Nation's Human Development Index, a composite measure of three dimensions of human development: life expectancy, education levels, and standard-of-living, placed Brunei thirtieth in the world (UNDP, 2008), very high for what is generally considered a developing nation. Brunei's 2007 per capita gross domestic product (GDP) of US$32167 ranks twenty-fourth worldwide, third in Asia, behind Singapore's US$35163 and Japan's US$34312 (IMF, 2008).

One of the interesting features of Brunei is Kampung Ayer, translated as Water Village. Kampung Ayer is home to 30000 residents and is built entirely on stilts above the Brunei River. The community, complete with homes, shops, and schools, is an intriguing mixture of old and modern, with people living over water as they have for centuries, but in homes that today feature running water, electricity, satellite dishes, and Internet connections.

For many years, *Forbes Magazine* listed Brunei's Sultan as the world's richest person. The most current list (2008) finds his wealth surpassed by others, falling to seventeenth place, with a personal net worth of US$23 billion. What has not fallen, however, is the claim that the Sultan's Palace is the world's largest home, with 1788 rooms, 257 bathrooms, and a floor area of 200000 m². Numerous stories note that the Sultan is the world's number one car collector, with a garage that contains between 3000 and 5000 classic and luxury automobiles.

Solely among the Malay-speaking states, Brunei uses Arabic script, known as *Jawi*, although most signs are written both in Jawi and Roman letters. Dobbs-Higginson (1994: 353) noted, Brunei is the region's 'odd man out; a small wealthy sultanate which seems like a bit of the Middle East stuck in the centre of Southeast Asia'.

Economics

Crude oil and natural gas production account for just over half of Brunei's GDP, and more than 90 percent of its exports. Oil revenues also account for 90 percent of government revenues. Oil was discovered in 1929, but revenues were modest until offshore deposits were found in the late 1950s, from which time petroleum has remained the nation's dominant economic sector. Use of the nation's petro-revenues has allowed Brunei to become a virtual welfare state (often referred to as 'Shellfare' in recognition of the overarching influence of Shell Oil, the government's partner in the local oil industry). All Bruneians receive free education from primary school through university, free medical care, and subsidized rice, housing, and retirement account contributions (Anaman, 2004; Anaman and Kassim, 2006). However, many of these benefits accrue only to Brunei citizens, basically limited to the Malay Muslim segment of the population. Others, to include the nation's significant Chinese population, are classified as 'Stateless Permanent Residents' and are excluded from many of these programs.

It is also important to note that the majority of work performed in Brunei is by foreign workers who hold short-term work permits. It is estimated that a rotating cohort of 100000 foreign workers reside in Brunei, a sizable portion of its 180400 workforce (United States Department of State, 2008).

Brunei has no personal income tax. There are also no export, sales, payroll or manufacturing taxes. The corporate tax rate was recently lowered from 30 percent to 27.5 percent. All companies contribute 10 percent of employee salaries to the Employees Provident Fund, the nation's equivalent of the USA's Social Security.

In recognition of the fact that the nation's oil production has begun to fall, and that its finite oil reserves are projected to last only 25 more years (natural gas will last for 40 years), recent five-year National Development Plans have called for an expansion and diversification of the economy's non-petroleum sectors. It is hoped that encouraging Bruneians to engage in entrepreneurial endeavors will play a significant part in this diversification. In a country where the government employs 80 percent of the workforce, such diversification would seem highly prudent.

Entrepreneurship in Brunei

Entrepreneurship in Brunei is today in its infancy. Of those small businesses that do exist, 90 percent are micro enterprises, which on average, employ between one and five workers (Brunei Government, 2008).

In a nation where so much is provided simply as a function of being born a citizen, and with what has been a near-promise of life-time employment in the government sector, there has historically been little motivation to embark upon an entrepreneurial path. An article in the *Brunei Times* (Ng, 2007), the government controlled newspaper, quoted a recent university graduate as saying: 'I'm still waiting for the government to give me a job . . . My friends say, it's better to work with the government, because it is more stable. I think so too.'

Emphasizing a need for change of such a mindset, a *Brunei Times* editorial stated:

> A small country like Brunei can only provide limited posts for government officers, which is now the most favoured destination of university graduates. But the leader of this country has already given a clue that entrepreneurship must start now. His Majesty cannot be more right when prioritising SMEs [small and medium enterprises]. This is a sector that must be forged, developed, given attention. Young talented people of Brunei must start to think of 'selling their individual capabilities' to be outsourced by international companies, and work from right here in the country. Or, they can initiate a new business that one day can play a global role. The world is flat. It has no boundaries . . . If we do not adapt to this kind of world by improving our capacity and strengthening our entrepreneurship, we will be left behind. (Syah, 2007)

While achieving this goal will not be easy, the nation has embarked upon numerous training programs to provide skills and inculcate an entrepreneurial spirit. Among these are 'Start your own Business' and 'Manage your own Business' courses offered by the University of Brunei Darussalam (UBD), 'Skills Development' and 'Personal Development' courses by the Ministry of Industries and Primary Resources, and intensive entrepreneurial courses offered through the Institute of Technology Brunei Darussalam. However, as per Khan (2004: 9) these programs have suffered from lack of integration among providers and have yet to 'generate a strong stimulation primarily to the young generation for an entrepreneurial career'. Providing support for Khan's concern, a posting on the Brunei Government website (2008) announcing this year's 'Entrepreneurship Week' training programs read: 'Since its formation twelve years ago, the Youth Development Centre has produced a number of youths who are committed and confident in setting up their own businesses. About twenty former trainees have opened up businesses with the skills they obtained from the centre.'

The most telling comment was that 'about twenty former trainees' had opened their own businesses, which would seem a low return for 12 years of entrepreneurial training. As Rosli (2007) commented:

> Innovation in business has yet to take root in Brunei's growing business community. Doing a careful market research and putting ideas on a business plan help an entrepreneur gain a sharp perspective of the venture as well as the creativity to give birth to something fresh. Alas, a business plan is a term that has yet to gain popularity among [Brunei's] small enterprises.

The difficulty of getting financing is a complaint heard by small businesses the world over. Brunei is no exception (Lai, 2008). To counter this, the government offers financing for 'good business plans' through the Enterprise Facilitation Scheme, with an emphasis upon the development of the nation's agriculture, fisheries, manufacturing and tourism sectors, each deemed to be strong entrepreneurial opportunities.

Two other challenges face the country's quest to grow their entrepreneurial sector. The first is cultural, as, per Khan (2004), a UBD professor, the Malay majority have generally not embraced entrepreneurship, leaving this to the Chinese minority.

The other issue is gender related. As observed by another UBD professor, Mona

Kassim (2006), entrepreneurial opportunities within Brunei's 'masculine society' have generally been limited to non-growth women-oriented industries such as health and beauty and food services. The government is working to overcome gender inequity, with noted successes such as the rapid increase of women in the workplace (13 percent in 1971 versus 33 percent in 2006) and university enrollment of women, now in 2006 65 percent of incoming students. But challenges remain, Kassim notes, for women wishing to venture beyond the limited sectors that have been open to women and as they strive to be taken seriously in the marketplace.

Conclusion
Brunei is a nation that understands the need to broaden its economic foundation as it nears the end of a century of good fortune funded by oil, and it is wisely investing funds and energies into programs designed to create an expanded entrepreneurial class. The challenge will be the need to develop the skills and change the mindset of a people that have not been entrepreneurial by nature, that are used to having foreign workers do most of the work, where the employer of choice has long been the government, and overcoming the otherwise nice problem of a citizen-class that has been treated so well by their government that perhaps their motivation for risk has been diminished. But the nation of Brunei seems to understand these challenges, and hopefully will find effective answers before the wells run dry.

References
Anaman, K.A. (2004), 'Determinants of economic growth in Brunei Darassalam', *Journal of Asian Economics*, **15**, 777–96.
Anaman, K.A. and Kassim, H.M. (2006), 'Marriage and female labour supply in Brunei Darussalam: a case study of urban women in Bandar Seri Begawan', *The Journal of Socio-Economics*, **35**, 797–812.
APEC (2006), 'Brunei Darussalam energy demand and supply outlook 2006', http://www.ieej.or.jp/aperc/2006 (accessed August 2008).
Brunei Government (2008), 'Success of entrepreneurship week needs involvement of all Parties', http://www.brunei.gov (accessed August 2008).
Dobbs-Higginson, M.S. (1994), *Asia Pacific, Its Role in the New World Disorder*, London: Mandarin.
International Monetary Fund (IMF) (2008), http://www.imf.org (accessed 25 December 2007).
Kassim, M. (2006), 'Women entrepreneurs in Brunei', http://www.revver.com/video/40487/women-entrepreneurs-in-brunei/ (accessed August 2008).
Khan, G.M. (2004), 'Encouraging entrepreneurship in Brunei Darussalam', http://www.sbaer.uca.edu/research/1998/ICSB/f007.htm (accessed August 2008).
Lai, A. (2008), 'Help for Brunei's small businesses', *ASIA INC*, http://www.asia-inc.com (accessed August 2008).
Ng, B. (2007), 'Unemployment woes', *Brunei Times*, 19 July.
Rosli, S. (2007), 'Homework is key to success in charting their paths to success', *Brunei Times*, 14 December.
Syah, S. (2007), 'Entrepreneurship key to future success', *Brunei Times*, 21 July.
UNDP (2008), 'Human Development Report', http://www.undp.org/ (accessed August 2008).
United States Department of State (2008), 'Background note: Brunei Darussalam', http://www.state.gov (accessed August 2008).

8   Cambodia[1]
Richard W. Wright and Malcolm Innes-Brown

Introduction to Cambodia: origins of a post-traumatic society
Cambodia is one of the countries (the other two being Laos and Vietnam) formerly referred
to as Indochine Française – French Indochina. Covering 181 035 square kilometres, it lies
on the Gulf of Thailand bordering Laos, Thailand, and Vietnam. Its population, one
of the fastest growing in Southeast (SE) Asia, is about 14.4 million. Although there has
been migration from rural areas to urban centers over the past 10 years (principally to
the capital Phnom Penh and the tourist city of Siem Reap), approximately 85 percent of
Cambodians live in rural villages cultivating rice. Cambodia is among the least developed
countries (LDC) in the world. Its most recent Human Development Index ranking is 130
out of 177 countries rated (World Bank, 2006a). Gross national income (GNI) per capita
is US\$ 480.00. The adult literacy rate is 81 percent for males and 59 percent for females.
Life expectancy is 55 for males and 60 for females (World Bank, 2007).

The first advanced civilizations in present-day Cambodia appeared in the first millennium AD. During the third, fourth, and fifth centuries, the Indianized states of Funan
and Chenla coalesced in what is now Cambodia and southwestern Vietnam. These states
had close relations with China and India. Their collapse was followed by the rise of the
Khmer Empire, a civilization which flourished from the ninth century to the thirteenth
century. The Khmer Empire declined yet remained powerful in the region until the
fifteenth century. The empire's center of power was Angkor, where a series of capitals
were constructed during the empire's zenith. Angkor Wat, the most famous and best-
preserved religious temple, is a reminder of Cambodia's past as a major regional power.

After a long series of battles with neighbours, Angkor was sacked and abandoned in
1432. The Angkorian court moved the capital to Lovek where the kingdom sought to
regain its glory through maritime trade. The attempt was short-lived as continued wars
with the Thai and Vietnamese resulted in the loss of territory and the conquest of Lovek
in 1594. During the next three centuries, the Khmer kingdom alternated as a vassal state
of the Thai and Vietnamese kings, with short-lived periods of relative independence
between (Osbourne, 2000).

In 1863 King Norodom, who had been installed by Thailand, sought the protection
of France. By 1867, the Thai king signed a treaty with France, renouncing suzerainty
over Cambodia in exchange for the control of Battambang and Siem Reap provinces
which officially became part of Thailand. The provinces were ceded back to Cambodia
by a border treaty between France and Thailand in 1906. Cambodia continued as a
protectorate of France from 1863 to 1953, administered as part of the French colony of
Indochina. Osbourne (2000) gives a comprehensive account of how after war-time occupation by the Japanese from 1941 to 1945, Cambodia gained independence from France
on 9 November, 1953 and became a constitutional monarchy under King Norodom
Sihanouk.

In 1955, Sihanouk abdicated in favor of his father in order to be elected prime minister.

Upon his father's death in 1960, Sihanouk again became head of state, taking the title of Prince. As the Vietnam War progressed, Sihanouk adopted an official policy of neutrality until ousted, in 1970 while on a trip abroad, by a military coup led by Prime Minister General Lon Nol and Prince Sisowath Sirik Matak. From Beijing, Sihanouk realigned himself with the communist Khmer Rouge rebels who had been slowly gaining territory in the remote western and northern hillside provinces and urged his followers to help in overthrowing the pro-United States government of Lon Nol. This hastened the onset of unrest and a state of civil war which lasted for the next 30 years (Vickery, 1994).

Operation Menu, a series of secret B-52 bombing raids by the United States on alleged Viet Cong bases and supply routes along the Ho Chi Minh Trail running through Laos and Cambodia, was acknowledged after Lon Nol assumed power; US forces briefly invaded in a further effort to disrupt the Viet Cong. Carpet bombing continued and, as the Cambodian communists began gaining ground, eventually included strikes on suspected Khmer Rouge sites until halted in 1973 (Chandler, 1992).

Some two million Cambodians were made refugees by the bombing and fighting and fled to Phnom Penh. Estimates of the number of Cambodians killed during the bombing campaigns vary widely, as do views of the effects of the bombing. In fact no one quite knows for sure how many innocent Laotian and Cambodian civilians were killed in what Hun Sen later called 'Kissinger's dirty little secret war'. Estimates suggest up to 500 000 people perished (Documentation Centre of Cambodia, 1994). Large craters from the US bombing of Laos and Cambodia are still visible in the landscape of Rattanakiri bordering Laos and Vietnam in northern Cambodia. A cogent argument mounted by Hun Sen – widely accepted today among Cambodians – is that Henry Kissinger and others from the Nixon administration should be put on trial for war crimes alongside leaders of the Pol Pot regime (Fawthrop and Jarvis, 2005). This has been a sticking point in the long-delayed establishment of a Khmer Rouge Trial. A second sticking point is that many former members of the Khmer Rouge Army (including Hun Sen) currently hold positions of importance in the present-day Cambodian government. Any hint of destabilization or any faint possibility of return to civil unrest by bringing to trial standing members of the Khmer Rouge is rigorously resisted in modern-day Cambodia. At the time in the early 1970s, the US Seventh Air Force argued that the bombing prevented the fall of Phnom Penh in 1973 by killing 16 000 of 25 500 Khmer Rouge fighters besieging the city. Other observers argued that the bombing drove peasants to join the Khmer Rouge. David Chandler writes that the bombing provided 'the psychological ingredients of a violent, vengeful and unrelenting social revolution' (Chandler, 1999). By 1973, if anything, the situation in Phnom Penh was worse than in Saigon. Everywhere the beleaguered city had the appearance of ruination. Unable to be defended, the bridge over the Tonle Sap River connecting the suburbs of the city hung broken, breeched and impassable in the water; roads potholed and unsealed under clouds of dust thrown up by the thin bouze of old motorbikes coursing the sparsely trafficked boulevards and avenues; unkempt groups of soldiers wandering around offering each other marihuana; naked street-urchins, encrusted with dirt and grime, running about begging, stealing, surviving; the saffron-robed monks, mostly young noviciates, returning with little in the way of alms to their pagodas; an enervating pall of dense humidity hanging over the city making the inhabitants wan and listless.

Any form of attempted entrepreneurship of small business at this time was in a token hiatus, a bottomed-out enterprise aimed solely towards keeping body and soul together while waiting for the besieged city to fall. In 1973 the country faced devastation and widespread famine, and when liberation finally did come in the form of leading elements of the Khmer Rouge Army marching down the main avenue of Mongivong Boulevard on 17 April 1975, there was widespread welcome relief. Yet in one of the great reversals of modern times, the liberation of Phnom Penh within hours turned from relief to the beginning of three years, nine months and twelve days of extreme agrarian Maoism, genocide and total loss of national identity. In what was to be the greatest transmigration in world history, Phnom Penh, a city of about one million people was emptied within two weeks, sending the entire population out on forced marches to work in the countryside. The regime's leaders declared Year Zero; abolished money; blew up the central bank and shut down all other banks; threw out the civil service; stopped all postal services; closed hospitals practicing Western medicine; vanquished any form of private ownership; established a cadre dictatorship of mutual suspicion, mistrust and internal denunciation; turned educational institutions into animal byres; expelled all foreigners; destroyed the monkhood; dethroned the king; broke up families and imposed eugenics. The regime eliminated intellectuals, landlords, entrepreneurs and the business sector. Market activities were banned and all commercial transactions were outlawed. Having gained control the Khmer rouge leaders pronounced Democratic Kampuchea the new nomenclature of the country. By the time Polpotism was done, only six lawyers, seven doctors and virtually no teachers were left alive. Vickery (1994), Chandler (1992), Osbourne (2000), Kiernan (1996), the present deputy prime minister Sok An (2008) and other Cambodians who have documented Democratic Kampuchea under Pol Pot, have given various estimates ranging from 1.7 to over 3 million of the country's then population of between 6 and 7 million, disappeared. This human tragedy was due to the regime's imposition of forced labor, malnutrition and murder during one of the worst episodes of genocide in the last century.

What made this execrable experiment in social engineering madness was a fatal irony of miscalculation in the organization and implementation of what might otherwise have been a rational ideology for a rice-growing country like Cambodia. Michael Vickery (1994), a long-time resident of Cambodia since the early 1960s and fluent in Khmer (the language), has argued that purity in the communist ideology of Saloth Sar (Pol Pot), Khiev Samphan, Ieng Sary and others of the Khmer diaspora living on the Left Bank Paris in the 1960s, was reasonable in the light of colonial power and privilege. After all, on the back of peasant-grown high-yield rice of exceptional exportable quality, Cambodia from the mid-1950s through to mid-1960s was the wealthiest nation in Southeast Asia and Phnom Penh the 'jewel of Asia'. Disparity in access to this wealth between rich and poor – especially against the wider background of geopolitical power-play between super powers in the Cold War – fomented aggressive socialism. Saloth Sar returned to Cambodia determined to level disparity in wealth and power and saw ultra-left wing radicalism as the country's only course. In effect, what was planned paralleled China's Cultural Revolution, and, in its Cambodian manifestation, the Chinese played a key role in the implementation of Khmer Maoism. Not only did the Khmer Rouge seek to recreate Kampuchea (the historical name) by rebuilding the country's agriculture on the model of the eleventh century, they accepted Chinese communal version of rice cultivation thereby destroying traditional village Cambodia. This was a fatal error, and its Chinese-led imposition on the totality of Khmer people via mass relocation, tearing apart families, clothing everyone in anonymous black pyjama-style garments, wrecking village Cambodia, forcing rice-field labor even among the sick and elderly and conscripting young, immature, 12- to 14-year-old boy-soldiers into the service of a fanatical regime, created a broken, utterly worn-out country. In effect, Pol Pot ended up with the complete opposite of his dreamed agrarian utopia.

From fear of Chinese-supported expansionism of Vietnam, neighboring Thailand found reason to offer tacit recognition and even support for the Khmer Rouge cause, especially along the Cambodian–Thai border. The Thais wanted a buffer protecting their neutrality. In a ridiculous attempt to regain what they considered Kampuchean territory, the Khmer Rouge invaded the Southern Mekong Delta in Tonkinese Vietnam. To the consternation of Thailand, the Vietnamese responded by mobilizing their armed forces. The Vietnamese were also concerned to stop genocide of ethnic Vietnamese living in Cambodia. At the time, Hun Sen was one of many who had deserted the Khmer Rouge Army to organize a nationalist resistance movement from inside Vietnam. In November 1978, the Vietnamese Army and the Cambodian Nationalist Army invaded Cambodia. Hun Sen was one of those to lead Cambodian forces back down Monivong Boulevard on 7 January 1979, to liberate Phnom Penh. For 10 years between 1979 and 1989, the Vietnamese occupied Cambodia. During this time, Hun Sen (whose wife is Vietnamese) steadily built his power base. Civil war between the liberation government and Khmer Rouge continued throughout the 1980s. Peace efforts began in Paris in 1989, culminating two years later in October 1991 in a comprehensive peace settlement. A United Nations Tactical Administration Commission (UNTAC) was given a mandate to enforce a ceasefire, deal with refugees, disarmament and create a new constitution. Insurgency of one kind or another continued until 1996 when the Khmer Rouge finally surrendered and 30 years of civil strife at last ended. Pol Pot died in the remote Khmer Rouge enclave of Anlong Veng near the Thai border in 1997 under suspicion that he was poisoned by Ta Mok, his deputy, former field commander and brother-in-law. After 27 years of legal and political wrangling, the Khmer Rouge Tribunal is at last in the process of indicting Khiev Samphan, Ieng Sary, and other leaders of the Khmer Rouge (now all aged in their eighties) for crimes against humanity.

After the brutality of the 1970s and the 1980s, and the destruction of the cultural, economic, social and political life of Cambodia, it is only in recent years that reconstruction efforts have begun and some political stability has finally returned to Cambodia. The stability established following the conflict was shaken in 1997 during a *coup d'état*, but has otherwise remained in place. Cambodia has been aided by a number of more developed nations like Japan, France, Canada, Australia and the United States, primarily economically. Money raised in schools and community groups in these countries has gone towards the rebuilding of infrastructure and housing.

Designing renewal: government policy for SME and opportunity for entrepreneurship
Cambodia is a quintessential Buddhist country. Traditionally, the people of Cambodia – known as Khmers – were not inclined to become entrepreneurs, as enterprise was not seen as contributing to Buddhist society. A merchant class developed after independence from France in the mid-1950s, but of course was subsequently extinguished under the Khmer Rouge (McIntyre, 1996).

With the Vietnamese occupation came some restoration of public life and private enterprise. Trade resumed but, in the absence of a national currency, commerce relied on barter or foreign money. Only in March 1980 was the currency (the 'riel') reintroduced, and then only within the context of a domestic socialist economy. The local currency has continued to the present time, but with over 4000 riel to the US dollar, the Cambodian currency has never been floated on international money markets. Indeed the dollar economy, as with many LDCs, is extensively used both domestically and internationally (Vutha et al., 2005). Micro enterprise, usually single or family businesses, slowly began to emerge as people started drifting back into Phnom Penh and other regional towns and cities such as Battambang, Siem Reap, Prey Vang (Innes-Brown, 2003). Cigarettes, condensed milk, kerosene, rice, soap and sugar were subsidized by the state but started to become traded goods in markets controlled by the state. For the 10 years of Vietnamese occupation, a limited-reference Cambodian government operated within a Marxist-Leninist centrally planned economy strictly controlled by the occupying Vietnamese. Among local Khmers during this time, there was considerable resentment against the Vietnamese, a sentiment that continues among Cambodians to the present time. However the Occupation brought a measure of social, political and economic restoration clearly contrasted from the total devastation of Polpotism. Government policy to restore the private sector did not begin until after the Vietnamese withdrawal in 1989. In the meantime, it can be argued that an incremental decade-long shift had begun with present-day emergence of a robust market economy being more or less patterned on successive political regimes (Godfrey et al., 2001: 19ff). The enormous strain put on the economy during the 1970s and 1980s, has meant a long-extended recovery, with the emergence of SMEs being a relatively recent phenomenon.

After the 1989 withdrawal of the Vietnamese, reforms enhanced the economic environment for entrepreneurs to operate in the private sector. The local authorities divided farmland and distributed it to those living on it. In the urban areas, the Law of Private Ownership allowed persons to claim title to property occupied, and even to sell it. This was somewhat problematic because people drifting back into Phnom Penh in 1979 found their houses being lived in by other families. There were no title deeds of ownership nor any mechanism to establish previous ownership. Everything – quite literally – had to be re-started: education, health, infrastructure, governance, law and order, local markets to buy food and clothes, water, electricity, all of it during the Occupation (Sok An, 2008). When the Vietnamese left in 1989, the country (now renamed Cambodia), still fighting civil war, at least had its own precarious government and nascent economy.

Things began to move quickly. The monarchy, now restored and Sihanouk on the throne as king, laid out pathways for social and economic development. The government shared the view of international aid donor nations that the avenue for development lay in the private sector with the sector itself characterized by SME growth (World Bank, 2004). Given Cambodia's high percentage of rural population (85 percent), the government steered the economy towards decentralized enterprise in which local income generation would provide a basis for accrual of disposable income. This in turn would provide the government with a source of taxable revenue to provide services and ultimately to build infrastructure. The government was given sound advice and technical assistance by international consultants along the lines that privatization also establishes a resource base for improving current account figures through supply-side trading, gaining a credit rating for enhanced FDI and ultimately confidence in floating local companies on domestic and foreign stock markets (World Bank, 2003b). These long-term objectives aimed to back the local currency in order to establish hedge-funding measured against world-dollar values. All this seemed ambitious at the time, but given the country's decimation, the situation was seen as one in which a 'leap forward' into modern technological and economic environments could be achieved. These measures were predicated upon rapid development of both public and private sector management, stability in prices, a demo-cratic government and the separation of powers, particularly an independent judiciary. As with most LDCs, the young Cambodian government saw 'economic' rights above 'political' rights arguing that earning personal income is a greater liberating factor in the fight against poverty than unaffordable freedoms normally granted systemically through democratic governance (Carpenter and Chandarany, 2005; Interview, HE Sok Sophanna, 2003; Perez, 1998).

Despite this view, in seeking to generate wealth via SMEs and to consolidate a private sector, the government saw considerable scope for supposing that the distribution of resources would in no small way contribute to democracy (Interview, HE Om Yentieng, 2001). In this stance, Sihanouk, Hun Sen, Sok An, Om Yentieng, Prince Ranaraddh, Prince Sirivudth and others in the government like Sam Rainsy (subsequently opposi-tion leader), saw democracy as much about protecting the rights of minorities as about respecting the views of majorities (Interview, HE Sam Rainsy, 2001). All in Cambodia at the time were understandably concerned that when wealth is generated among decentral-ized minorities, then the sort of class distinctions which gave agency to the Khmer Rouge would be greatly mitigated (Interview, HE Stephen Bridges, 2003).

By 1992, three-quarters of the economy was in private hands. Some entrepreneurs operated from their homes, while others lived in their shops. Smaller-scale vendors set up impromptu stalls. Petrol was sold on roadsides, in used soda-pop bottles. Entrepreneurs were required to pay a signage tax and, therefore, many merchants – including promi-nent retailers in Phnom Penh – opted to have no sign (Kato et al., 1998).

The new constitution introduced the Royal Cambodian Model in 1993. Article 56 specified that the kingdom would have a market economy. In August 1994, liberal laws were implemented to encourage entrepreneurship in the kingdom (Sen, 2004). A problem, however, was that a very lenient implementation of public policy allowed latent corruption to persist (Heineman and Heineman, 2006; Innes-Brown, 2001a). Also in 1994, special zoning laws were introduced to limit development in the area of Siem Reap; only small-scale ventures were allowed near Angkor Wat, and large hotels were required to be 4 kilometers away. Nevertheless, entrepreneurs could bribe officials and obtain exemptions. The French daily paper, *Figaro*, once dubbed Cambodia the 'Kingdom of Corruption'. The essential underpinnings of a democracy – the above-mentioned separa-tion of powers – although earnestly intended, in practice unfortunately has been even more earnestly ignored (Innes-Brown, 2002). The World Bank (2007) estimates that 81 percent of small businesses pay bribes in order to 'get things done', and that over 30 percent is routinely added to Cambodian import and export costs by corrupt customs officials and at least a similar figure during international-aid procurement.

Although the government has on paper plans to reduce poverty, in reality this is not happening. Poverty remains stubbornly high with 39 percent of the population living on less than US$1 per day (World Bank, 2003a). One explanation is that not enough local provincial income-generation is actually occurring (Interview, HE Sok Sophanna,

Table 8.1   Challenges

Indicator	Cambodia	Region	OECD
Procedures (number)	10.0	8.7	6.0
Duration (days)	86.0	46.5	14.9
Cost (% GNI per capita)	190.3	34.9	5.1
Paid in min. capital (% of GNI per capita)	50.8	50.0	32.5

2003). This in turn is related to an absence of micro-management and micro-finance. Politicization and corruption at all levels of village and urban life, make normal con-course of decentralization in full measure impossible (Innes-Brown, 2001a). Poverty remains an entrenched and intractable issue, becoming even more so by growing divisions between rich and poor (Interview, HE Stephen Bridges, 2003). Rural Cambodia is a structural problem with its roots in executive failure to implement National Assembly (the Cambodian parliament) pro-poor legislation and overall failure to ensure efficacy in infrastructure development mostly funded by donor aid. It is anticipated that infra-structure may improve with Chinese entry into donor aid due to strong emphasis on non-conditional tied aid in all respects, including non-conditional human rights com-pliance. In 2005 Chinese aid was US$600 million, an interesting figure given that the total of Western foreign-aid was also US$600 million. In a constant effort to ease donor dependence and encourage SMEs, the government has implemented initiatives such as the Socio-Economic Development Plan (2001–05), the National Poverty Reduction Strategy, and the Governance in Action Plan, known in combination as the Rectangular Strategy (Sen, 2004).

The challenges currently facing entrepreneurs seeking to launch new businesses in Cambodia remain formidable. World Bank data for 2007, shown in Table 8.1, include: the number of steps entrepreneurs can expect to go through to launch; the time it takes on average; and the cost and minimum capital required as a percentage of gross national income (GNI) per capita.

The broader results of the government policies on SMEs and entrepreneurship are to some extent reflected in the country's scores in the Doing Business rankings, compiled by the World Bank and the International Finance Corporation. Cambodia's rankings, out of 178 countries, are as in Table 8.2.

Environment for entrepreneurship, the state of SME and economic potential
Until interrupted by apotheosis of the 1970s, entrepreneurship in Cambodia developed rapidly after independence from France. In 1955, there were 650 small and medium-scale factories in Cambodia. By 1968, there were almost 4000. Most entrepreneurs, however, were not industrialists. Many were speculators who tried to make fast money in alcohol, beef, gold, land, tobacco, salt and other commodities. These people also contributed to economic instability, wealth disparity and political unrest which in turn gave impetus to the radical 1970s and 1980s upheavals.

Today, Cambodia is described as a 'pre-emerging market' (World Bank, 2007). Reports (Murshid and Ballard, 2006) substantiate a high degree of covert economic activity in the

Table 8.2   Rankings with regards to ease

Ease of . . .	2008 rank	2007 rank	Change in rank
Starting a business	162	164	+ 2
Dealing with licenses	144	145	+ 1
Employing workers	133	135	+ 2
Registering property	98	98	0
Getting credit	177	177	0
Protecting investors	64	62	−2
Paying taxes	21	21	0
Trading across borders	139	136	−3
Enforcing contracts	134	134	0
Closing a business	178	178	0

Source: World Bank (2007).

entrepreneurial and small-business sectors. Since the attempted coup in 1997, there has been macroeconomic stability accompanied by relatively high growth factors, including GDP growth running at 6 percent in the early 2000s to a massive 13.7 percent in 2006, over 10 percent in 2007 and currently around 9 percent this year. In 2003–04, the economy suffered due to SARS and drought, with GDP growth falling to 4.6 percent. The bourgeoning Cambodian economy is largely due to the vibrant garment, construction and tourist industries. Cambodia is one of the fastest growing economies in SE Asia. In 2006, textile exports increased by 40 percent and tourism by 20 percent, with inflation running at 5.1 percent (*Phnom Penh Post*, November 2006). These figures are second only to China in GDP growth, a fact which comes as a surprise to many. Cambodia now shares with many other SE Asian countries, a rapid growth pattern based upon economic integration and liberalization characteristic of emergent economies in which the SME sector is dominant (Limao and Olorreage, 2006). Even so, only 4 percent of GDP filters down to the agricultural sector where 85 percent of the population live (Innes-Brown, 2001b). In other words there is no transference of wealth generation in SMEs from a spin-off in GDP nor is there achievement towards government aspiration to gain social equity or to reduce poverty. In addition, inflation is running at high levels – 5.1 percent in 2006 – and rising. The cost of petrol, food and rent have greatly increased. Along with many other LDCs, Cambodian rice has doubled in price over the past 18 months, causing hunger and distress. Along the same lines, the vast oil and natural gas reserves in the Gulf of Thailand (estimated revenue of US$5 billion per year) along with large-scale exploration by BHP-Billiton and Mitsubishi for mineral resources, has caused concern that 'a Nigerian effect' of corruption and mismanagement will not benefit the people of Cambodia nor lead to progress in national development (Ear, 2006).

Against this background small and micro business is in fact making a contribution to the country's economic growth. Most SMEs are either self-operated or have between three and ten employees, usually members of an extended family on a rotational basis. Tourist companies invariably employ fewer than ten people; hotels, restaurants, guided tours, transport in the thriving tourist area of Siem Reap (the service center for Angkor Wat) also operate as small or micro businesses. A new international airport has been

Table 8.3   Statistics on small industrial establishments, 1999–2006

	1999	2002	2003	2004	2005	2006
Manufacturing	24 227	26 920	25 985	28 131	29 297	31 149
Manufacture of food, beverage and tobacco	19 147	21 568	20 869	22 712	23 727	25 455
Textile and wearing apparel	396	1 417	1 406	1 672	1 665	1 689
Wood and wood products	814	13	13	16	2	–
Paper and paper products	23	15	21	25	31	33
Chemical, rubber and plastic products	67	275	96	120	153	159
Non metallic mineral products	777	757	681	680	719	797
Manufacture of basic metals	24	–	–	–	–	–
Fabricated metal products	1 623	1 899	1 850	2 239	2 334	2 380
Other manufacturing industries	1 356	976	1 049	667	666	636

Source: SME Secretariat (2007: 7).

recently opened at Siem Reap adding a network of ancillary transit, service and retail SMEs. The average time tourists spend in Phnom Penh is two days and four days in Siem Reap, including the boat trip along the Tonle Sap River and across Tonle Sap Lake (the most popular tour excursion in Cambodia) between Phnom Penh and Siem Reap. Increasingly tourists are beginning to discover and appreciate beautiful French architecture among the standing colonial buildings of Battambang.

As national economic settings have recovered over the past decade, so too SMEs, particularly in the capital and provincial centers, are growing. The data in Table 8.3 gives a picture of growth from the late 1990s onwards.

The figures in Table 8.4 summarize the total of SMEs which are now established in Cambodia. What is interesting about these figures are the number not licensed and therefore operating outside the formal economy – that is, not paying taxes, not subject to any regulatory statutes governing health, safety or environmental impact, nor indeed operating on land or in premises actually owned or leased. There is no protection under law nor any compliance obligation recognized. What is quite remarkable about all this is that the actual quality of goods and services produced is exceptionally high. Khmer people work hard and establish a reputation for their self- or family-operated businesses solely on word of mouth in their local neighborhood. Khmer crafts and architecture – especially in wood and stone – have great artistry and their music, dance and theater segue in exquisite Angkorian cultural heritage. Garments made in the sweat-shops of Cambodia are of world-class quality in material and manufacture. Khmer tourist guides are usually multilingual graduates of the Royal University of Fine Arts having qualified with a five-year degree in anthropology, Khmer heritage studies or architecture. Even though there is economic immaturity underlying the scenario of SMEs in Cambodia, the quality of service, goods and products distills from hundreds of years of applied Khmer culture in which Buddhist notions of not doing things to annoy people, and of peace and harmony, resonate in their personal and working lives.

Table 8.4   Total of small industrial establishments as of 2007

Sector	Total	Total licensed	% of licensed est.
Manufacture of food, beverage and tobacco	25 455	12 350	49
Rice milling	23 103	10 922	47
Textile and wearing apparel and leather industries	1 689	167	10
Woods and wood products	–	–	–
Paper product, printing and publishing	33	25	76
Chemicals	159	155	97
Non-metallic mineral products except product of petroleum and coal	797	652	82
Basic metal industries	–	–	–
Fabricated metal product, machinery and equipment	2 380	1 613	68
Other manufacturing industries	636	435	68
Total	54 252	26 319	49

Source: SME Secretariat (2007: 4).

Because of a weak judiciary and corruption in the police and government ministries, many SMEs do not operate legally and in fact contribute substantially to the breakdown in civil society. Many entrepreneurs deal in contraband goods smuggled to Cambodia from Thailand and Vietnam; others illegally export gems or rare animals from Cambodia. Well known anti-human trafficking protagonist, Somaly Mam (2008) reports that prostitution is Phnom Penh's leading industry, with 15 000 women and girls – more often than not sold into sexual slavery – working in Phnom Penh and another 10 000 elsewhere in the country. It is impossible to get exact figures, but Somaly thinks that the sex industry in Cambodia has a turnover of many millions of dollars – a graphic, sad and staggering statistic. The NGO which Somaly founded, Agir Pour les Femmes en Situation Preccaire (AFISIP) (translated: Acting for Women in Distressing Circumstances), has gained a worldwide reputation, attracting large additional funding which has been used to establish the Somaly Mam Foundation, an organization which combats trafficking of girls and women beyond Cambodia. It is a profoundly abject situation that Cambodia's largest business enterprises are the sex industry, human trafficking and, increasingly, manufacture and cross-border smuggling of illicit drugs, particularly amphetamines. To a lesser extent the same is true of child labor. Entrepreneurs – both Khmer and foreigners – have been accused of making children as young as six years old work in garment-making sweat-shops. Other children become entrepreneurs themselves, taking advantage of arbitrary opportunities, selling food and drinks to long-distance travellers on boats, buses and trains.

Yet for all of this, Cambodia is making progress as a fast-growing emergent nation rediscovering its national identity. There are a growing number of young professionals returning from postgraduate study in North America, Europe, Australasia, Japan, other ASEAN countries and China, with world-class skills and knowledge in vital areas such as ICT, management, marketing, banking and finance, international trade, commercial and civil law, human resource management and good governance in the public sector (Innes-Brown and Chhuon, 2003). The older generation of mostly Khmer Rouge survivors and Francophile administrators holding positions of leadership in government, resent, yet recognize, new-order skilling and technological application – even though both are mysterious to them and, as victims of a deeply excoriating history in their lifetimes, they are understandably wary of any sort of tectonic shift in Khmer destiny in the future.

Internationalization of entrepreneurs and SMEs
The Chinese have always had a pervasive impact on the economy in Cambodia. Gold, silver and coins were introduced to Cambodia by the Chinese, and Chinese traders flourished at Angkor. Immigrants from China came to dominate the realm of business, especially in entrepreneurship.

Traditionally, the ethnic Khmers tended to be attracted to occupations related to agriculture, government service, and monastic life; commerce and industry were occupations that were left to ethnic minorities. Muslims (Khmer Cham) controlled the cattle trade, commercial fisheries and the weaving industry; while the ethnic Chinese engaged in international trade and in retailing.

Abercrombie reported on the situation during 1964:

> Nearly a third of Phnom Penh's population of 403 500 are Chinese. Together with Vietnamese importers, shopkeepers, and moneylenders, they dominate the city's – and the country's – commerce. In the shops strange goods caught my eye: dogmeat sausages, incense sticks, begging bowls, silver elephants, betel leaves, Chinese comic books, brass hongs, and bamboo flutes. (1964: 518)

Notice that the above account does not mention Khmer entrepreneurs. Elaborating on the ethnic Chinese in Cambodia, Abercrombie explained, 'Rarely holding citizenship, they maintain their own language, customs, and schools' (1964: 526).

Today, Cambodia is among the most homogeneous countries in Asia; however, small but influential minority groups persist. Micro, small businesses and entrepreneurial activity are concentrated largely in the hands of the ethnic Chinese community, while the Vietnamese community is often associated with fishing-related occupations. Although both of these minorities have suffered persecution in Cambodia – especially the Vietnamese – the Chinese are emerging as an important economic force. As mentioned earlier, Chinese aid is now crucial to the well-being of the current regime and ethnic Chinese Khmers are the main players in contemporary Cambodian SMEs. Many have sophisticated *guanxi* networks and *gei mian zi* business relationships in Mainland China, Taiwan, Singapore, Vietnam and Thailand. King Sihanouk (now retired and known as the Father King) normally spends half his time in Beijing and Pyongyang and the other half in Cambodia. When in Cambodia it is not unusual for him to bring his somewhat eccentric North Korean bodyguard of highly efficient female martial-arts exponents.

In 2001, Cambodia chaired ASEAN, is now an active member of the ASEAN-China Free Trade Area and has consolidated bilateral relations with the European Union (EU), North America, New Zealand and Australia. In 2004, Cambodia became the first LDC to gain accession to the World Trade Organization (WTO), thus entering the world stage with both opportunities and responsibilities outside the protected quota system previously prevailing, particularly in the garment industry. The country is vulnerable to external change in international trading patterns. Although Cambodia maintains an open-door policy across mutual borders with Vietnam and Thailand, relative advantage in production costs from start-up to market favors the larger neighbors, particularly Vietnam. Cambodia relies heavily on imports from Thailand, with a considerable trade imbalance weighted towards Thailand. China is now Cambodia's major trading partner and investor, a situation which is both postitive and negative for Cambodia; negative particularly in the sense that China's purchasing power pushes up local prices in land and property values. For the rich this is a good thing; for the vast majority of Khmers, they are left without capital to purchase land, without disposable income to buy raw materials or have in their possession enough wealth to purchase investment portfolios. The competition from China is simply too great. In the manufacturing sector, Chinese investors are in position to buy raw materials which are subsequently manufactured into garments using Khmer labor and sold in offshore markets benefiting the Chinese much more than the Cambodians. This has caused Khmer workers to push for wage rises, a push that merely results in investors turning to Vietnam to manufacture with consequent job losses in Cambodia. The same push has caused companies (with the support of the government) to crush an embryonic Khmer labor movement and ban workers' activism (Godfrey et al., 2001; Phnom Penh Post, November 2006).

Conclusion: what does peace bring?
Cambodia is now required to comply with WTO commitments, which is proving difficult. For example, there is a requirement under WTO membership for countries to develop a sound legal system conducive to fair determinations, especially in commercial transactions. Associated with this is a requirement to have a predictable business environment in which SMEs can occur (Fitzgerald and Strange, 2004). Without these fundamentals in place, achieving most favored nation (MFN) status within WTO, is problematic.

Nevertheless, compared to China, its ASEAN neighbors, and to other emergent economies, Cambodia ranks relatively high in economic freedom (Fitzgerald and Strange, 2004). Average tariff rates are lower than in China and elsewhere. There is less official government intervention than in many other countries. Comparing the fiscal burden of governments, Cambodia scores very low on the list.

Yet, as suggested during this chapter, an optimistic picture for SMEs lies squarely in the private sector rather than in action taken by government. For example, as one observer put it: 'Tax burden is low because of the inability to tax and not because of the willingness not to burden the tax payers; tariff is low because room must be left for corruption . . . and the official government intervention is less but corruption – a form of unofficial government intervention – is pervasive' (Dana, 2007, p. 62).

Although most enterprises in Cambodia are privately held, entrepreneurship in the kingdom is concentrated largely in grey- or black-market areas. One explanation is that the historical experience of Cambodia makes immediate gains more attractive than waiting for an uncertain future. All middle-aged Cambodians can remember the day money was made useless; the result is a predisposition to reject currency as a medium for savings. For large purchases, Cambodians often use the damleung (1.2 ounces of gold) to buy property, and the chi (0.13 ounces of gold) for items such as televisions.

Entrepreneurship in Cambodia is largely short-term in nature, due to high risks and uncertainty. People use a young tree for firewood, as they are too impatient to wait seven years for it to produce rubber. A more long-term orientation would be desirable in the future. In Cambodia, however, institutions are weak and traditions are strong.

The long-term development of the economy remains a daunting challenge. The Cambodian government is working with bilateral and multilateral donors, including the World Bank and the International Monetary Fund (IMF), to address the country's many pressing needs. The major economic challenge for Cambodia over the next decade will be fashioning an economic environment in which the private sector can create enough jobs to handle Cambodia's demographic imbalance (more than 50 percent of the population is under 21 years old). The population lacks education and productive skills, particularly in the poverty-ridden countryside where the majority of Khmers live. An administration which is corrupt, does not engage representative government, is careless with its mandate to govern, on one the hand, leaves avenues open to be filled by private enterprise while, on the other, making impossible a reliable legal framework, an entrusted currency, or a validated fiscal responsibility necessary for equitable, non-speculative SMEs. With settings put right, this situation could well reverse.

Note

1. This chapter includes material published in Dana (2007).

References

Abercrombie, Thomas J. (1964), 'Cambodia, Indochina's "neutral" corner', *National Geographic*, **126**(4), 514–51.

Carpenter, Keith and Ouch Chandarany (2006), 'Financing SMEs in Cambodia: why do banks find it so difficult?', *Cambodia Development Review*, **10**(2), 9–11.

Chandler, David (1992), *Brother Number One: A Political Biography of Pol Pot*, Boulder, CO: Westview Press.

Chandler, David P. (1999), *A History of Cambodia*, Boulder, CO: Westview Press.

Dana, Léo-Paul (2007), *Asian Models of Entrepreneurship – From the Indian Union and the Kingdom of Nepal to the Japanese Archipelago: Context, Policy and Practice*, Singapore and London: World Scientific.

Documentation Center of Cambodia (1994), *Yale University Genocide Program*, Phnom Penh.

Ear, Sophal (2006), 'The political economy of aid, governance and policy-making: Cambodia in global, national and sectoral perspectives', doctoral dissertation, University of California, Berkeley.

Fawthrop, Thomas and Helen Jarvis (2005), *Getting Away with Genocide: Elusive Justice and the Khmer Rouge Tribunal*, Sydney: NSW University Press.

Fitzgerald, Stephen and Larry Strange (2004), 'Capacity-building practices of Cambodia's external partners', *Council of Administrative Reform*, Phnom Penh: CDRI.

Godfrey, Martin, So Sovannarith, Tep Saravy, Pon Dorina, Claude Katz, Sarith Acharya, Sisowath Chinto and Hing Thoraxy (2001), 'A study into the Cambodian labor market: reference to poverty reduction, growth and adjustment to crisis', *Development Analysis Network*, Phnom Penh: CDRI.

Heineman, Ben and Fitz Heineman (2006), 'The long war against corruption', *Foreign Affairs*, June.

Innes-Brown, Malcolm (2001a), 'What could you do with $5000000 per year?', *Phnom Penh Post*, December.

Innes-Brown, Malcolm (200b), 'Research on student learning in the context of renewal in Khmer higher education', International Development Program Conference on Regional Progress and Unity, Phnom Penh.

Innes-Brown, Malcolm (2002), 'Re-thinking Cambodia's aid agenda', *Phnom Penh Post*, March.

Innes-Brown, Malcolm (2003), 'Stability and diversity: educational, economic and political potential in Cambodia leading up to and following the 1998 CPP-FUNCINPEC alliance in Cambodia', Seventh Annual Conference on International Managements and Global Business, Bangkok.

Innes-Brown, Malcolm and Chan Than Chhuon (2003), 'Value-laden priorities in higher education for Cambodian private sector-led development', Neth Barom (ed.), *Sixth Socio-Cultural Research Congress*, Bonn: Heinrich-Bell Foundation.

Interview, HE Om Yentieng, Advisor to the Prime Minister on Cambodian Human Rights, 2001.

Interview, HE Sam Rainsy, Leader of the Opposition, Phnom Penh, November, 2001.

Interview, HE Sok Sophanna, Secretary of State, Ministry of Commerce, Phnom Penh, May, 2003.

Interview, HE Stephen Bridges, British Ambassador to Cambodia, Phnom Penh, June, 2003.

Kato, Toshitasu, Chan Sophal and Long Von Psieth (1998), 'Regional economic integration for sustainable development in Cambodia', *CDRI Working Papers*, no. 5, Phnom Penh.

Kiernan, Ben (1996), *The Pol Pot Regime: Race, Power and Genocide under the Khmer Rouge*, New Haven, CT: Yale University Press.

Limao, Nuno and Marcelo Olorreage (2006), 'Trade preferences to small developing countries and the welfare costs of lost multilateral liberalization', *The World Bank Economic Review*, **20**(2), 217–40.

Mam, Somaly (2008), *The Road to Lost Innocence*, New York: Random House.

McIntyre, Kevin (1996), 'Geography as destiny: cities, villages and Khmer Rouge orientalism', *Comparative Studies in Society and History*, **38**(4), 730–58.

Murshid, Klass and Brett Ballard (eds) (2006), *Annual Development Review, 2004–2005*, Phnom Penh: Cambodian Development Research Institute (CDRI).

Osbourne, Milton (2000), *The Mekong: Turbulent Past, Uncertain Future*, Princeton, NJ: Atlantic.

Perez, Andres (1998), 'The International Center for Human rights and democratic Development: a new approach to politics and democracy in developing countries', in Robert Millar (ed.), *Aid as Peacemaker*, Ottawa: Carleton University Press.

Phnom Penh Post, fortnightly broadsheet English-medium newspaper, ed. Michael Haynes.

Sen, Hun (2004), 'Rectangular strategy for growth, employment, equity and efficiency', speech to the Council of Ministers, Phnom Penh.

SME Secretariat, Government of Cambodia (2007), *Technical Report: SME Statistics in Cambodia*, Phnom Penh.

Sok An (2008), 'Cambodia's past', *Council of Ministers Working Paper*, Phnom Penh.

Vickery, Michael (1994), *Cambodia, 1975–1992*, Boston, MA: South End.

Vutha, Hing, Larry Strange and Klass Murshid (2005), 'Trade research institutions in Asia-Pacific: capacity-building needs in developing countries', *Asia Pacific Research and Training Network on Trade*, Phnom Penh: CDRI.

World Bank (2003a), *World Bank in Cambodia: Working for a Cambodia free of Poverty*, Washington, DC: World Bank.

World Bank (2003b), *Cambodia Environment Monitor*, Washington, DC: World Bank.

World Bank (2004), 'Cambodia at the cross-roads', *East Asia and the Pacific Region*, Washington, DC: World Bank.

World Bank (2006a), *Cambodia's Poverty Assessment*, Phnom Penh: World Bank.

World Bank (2007), *Country Report: Cambodia*, Phnom Penh: World Bank.

9 China
David Smallbone and Xiao Jianzhong

Introduction

China is the fastest growing economy in the world, reflected in a dramatic increase in GDP per head of about 300 percent over the past 10 years. This has been achieved through China's success along a number of dimensions, including attracting foreign direct investment, as part of its 'open door' policy; restructuring and reforming its state-owned enterprises; building up a selected number of large enterprises to become globally competitive 'national champions'; investing in science and technology infrastructure; and allowing a private enterprise sector to emerge.

It is well documented that small and medium-sized enterprises (SMEs) have been a major driving force in China's transformation from a relatively closed, stagnating economy to one based on rapid growth and dynamic industrial expansion. At the same time, the nature of the SME sector in China contains some distinctive features, reflecting the relatively short period of transition to date and some specific features of the Chinese context, which have shaped the development path of private sector development in the country.

Previous writers have identified a number of phases in the development of China's SMEs. For example, IFC (2000) identified three phases:

1. Phase 1: 1978–83

The Third Plenum of the Chinese Communist Party's Eleventh Central Committee is said to mark the beginning of market-oriented reforms in China. Although no specific announcement was made with respect to the development of private business, the Plenum's emphasis on economic development and individualistic incentives gave an impetus to the development of private business in the country. At the outset, the private sector was limited to individual businesses (*getihu*), which developed initially in a regulatory vacuum. At the time, the private sector's role was seen to focus on filling gaps in the economy left by state-owned enterprises (SOEs), focusing particularly on the distribution of consumer goods and services. Such thinking led to restrictions being placed on the types of enterprise that could be created, with the number of employees being limited to eight.

The boom in non-state enterprises began in rural areas, where township and village enterprises (TVEs) emerged as a leading force. Township and village enterprises provided a mechanism for the transfer of surplus rural labour into non-agricultural activity and for raising farmer's incomes. They also provided a foundation for the accomplishment of gradual reforms and economic development in the countryside. In the period between 1978 and 2003, the number of TVEs is reported to have increased by around 20 percent per annum, to reach 21.85 million in number, employing 135.7 million people and contributing 30 percent of national gross domestic product (GDP) (Xue Liang, 2006). At the same time, by the beginning of the twenty-first century, it had become clear that TVEs

Table 9.1   Private enterprise development in China

Year	Firms		Employment	
	Number (10 000)	Growth rate (%)	number (10 000)	Growth rate (%)
1990	9.8	8.3	170.3	3.8
1991	10.8	9.9	183.9	8.0
1992	14.0	28.8	231.9	26.0
1993	23.8	70.4	372.6	60.7
1994	43.2	81.7	648.4	74.0
1995	65.6	51.6	956.0	47.4
1996	81.9	25.2	1171.1	22.5
1997	96.1	17.3	1349.3	15.2
1998	120.1	25.0	1709.1	26.7
1999	150.9	20.5	2021.6	18.3
2000	176.2	16.8	2406.5	19.0
2001	202.8	15.1	2713.9	12.0
2003	300.7	16.4	4299.3	14.7
2004	365.3	21.5	5017.5	16.7
2005	429.9	17.7	5823.9	16.1
2006	494.7	15.1	6395.5	10.0

Source: China Statistical Yearbook (2000–2006).

were facing new challenges as the Chinese market became increasingly open to domestic and foreign competition. Few TVEs had adopted modern management systems and an increasing number were restructured into other forms of non-state ownership.

2.   *Phase 2: 1984–92*
This phase is characterized by the rise of the privately run enterprise (*siying qiye*), employing more than eight people. This type of enterprise started to emerge after 1981 but did not come under regulation until 1988. Some larger enterprises emerged from the leasing of state or collective enterprises to individuals. In this model, the private entrepreneur paid a fixed rent to the state or collective organization and operated the firm as if it were their own. By accumulating assets in this way, the entrepreneur was able to reduce the collective ownership share and gradually transform the enterprise into a solely owned firm.

3.   *Phase 3: 1993 to date*
While experimentation continued, a coherent strategy of transition to a market system began to emerge after 1993, with an emphasis on creating a rule-based system to provide a level playing field for the development of private enterprises and to build market supporting institutions. From 1992 to 2002, the emphasis was on the reform of state-owned SMEs to reduce the level of state ownership and on the development of privately owned enterprises. As Table 9.1 shows, the period 1992–95 saw the most rapid development of private firms, encouraged by Deng Xiaoping's call for further market-oriented reforms. Entrepreneurs emerging during this period included more highly educated individuals, who were often engineers or managers from SOEs. There were also some small SOEs

that were taken over by entrepreneurs through subcontracting or management buyout. Since 2002, China's entrepreneurial class has included foreign-educated Chinese returning to China to start businesses.

Because of the Chinese emphasis on decentralization and local experimentation with reforms, private sector development has been greatly influenced by local conditions, which includes the attitudes of local government towards the role of the market. More generally, the experimental nature of initial private sector development, in an environment of legal and regulatory uncertainty, is a distinctive feature of the Chinese model. It means that for most of the reform period, private enterprise has developed without clearly defined property rights, using a particularistic approach rather than one based on universal rules, leading to collusion between local governments and enterprises, including the use of rent-seeking behaviour.

Entrepreneurship and government policy
In China, national policy in support of SME development is relatively recent, having been approved by the State Council in 2000, in recognition of the potential contribution of SMEs as job generators. As a result, all provinces, autonomous regions, municipal governments directly under central government and ministries were urged to take: 'Effective measures to strengthen SME support especially high-tech SMEs and those innovative SMEs, which can develop new products, improve products quality and fill gaps in the market'.[1] The main policy response of the government of China was to provide the legal basis for government involvement in SME promotion, through the Law on Promoting SMEs, which was introduced in 2003.

Since then, one of the main policy initiatives by central government has been to create a network of some 2000 loan guarantee agencies, which the National Development and Reform Commission (NDRC) oversees and provides guarantees for. This initiative aims to address the finance gap faced by SMEs, which is affected by the reluctance of the large state-owned banks to finance them compared with large SOEs. The SME Promotion Law also made provision for state intervention in the field of business development services (BDS), although actions in this area have so far been rather limited. Current national SME policy objectives in China are to improve the environment for SME development and seek to increase employment in SMEs, as well as their wider contribution to China's economic and social development.

The SME Law is important because it provides a legal basis for policy interventions at different levels of government. In practice, support for SMEs varies considerably between cities, as local governments vary in their commitment to supporting SMEs and in their ability to generate resources to pay for such support. For example, in Chengdu, a mid-size city which is the capital of Sichuan Province, SME support is organized through Chengdu SME Bureau, which currently offers training programmes and some advisory support for SMEs, funded through a combination of local, provincial and NDRC funding. In Lanzhou, capital of Gansu Province, SME support is the responsibility of the Lanzhou Economic Commission (LEC). At the same time, the number of entrepreneurs assisted is very small, with some 30–40 reported to be trained annually on a 'start-your-own-business' programme run by the LECs SME Service Centre and a handful of businesses receiving intensive consultancy support (three in 2006 and five in 2007), in a city of 3.2 million people.

A number of recent policies in China have focused on research and development (R&D) and science and technology themes, aiming to facilitate high-technology development, technology transfer and the diffusion of research results. A key element in this approach has been the science and technology parks aiming to incubate China's R&D capability and drive its high-technology policy. Once a firm located on a Science Park qualifies as a high-technology enterprise, a newly established firm receives a moratorium on taxes and a 50 percent reduction for a further five years (Wright et al., 2008). At the same time, a lack of entrepreneurship and management skills in firms located on science parks has been identified as a weakness, together with insufficient intellectual property rights (IPR) and patent protection, and a lack of access to venture capital (Watkins-Mathys and Foster, 2006).

It is important to note that the definition of SME used in China is different from that understood in most of the developed world, with size definitions varying between sectors. For example, in manufacturing, even a small enterprise may employ up to 300 people, with assets of up to RMB40 million and annual sales of up to RMB30 million. In construction, the upper size limit is 600 employees for a small firm and 3000 for a medium-sized enterprise. This is much higher than the upper limit of 249 employees used in the European Union (EU) to define an SME, or 500 employees in the USA and Canada. Clearly, an SME in China can be a rather different entity from the targets of SME policy in Western countries, because of these definitional differences.

Another feature of China's SMEs sector is the multiplicity of legal forms with different ownership characteristics, including state, collective, as well as privately owned. This is a common characteristic of SMEs in transition economies, where a private sector is still emerging. However, survey evidence from Chengdu, Lanzhou and Shenzhen referring to the 2005–06 period, showed privately owned enterprises to consistently outperform firms in mixed, state or collective forms of ownership, in terms of both sales and employment change (Smallbone and Xiao, 2006).

The environment for entrepreneurship and the state of small business
One of the consistent findings of research on entrepreneurship in transition economies is the role of the institutional environment in influencing entrepreneurial behaviour (Peng 2000; Peng and Heath 1996; Welter and Smallbone, 2003) and China is no exception. For example, in a survey of 500 SMEs conducted by the authors in Central China in 2003, the most commonly identified external barrier by surveyed entrepreneurs was the burden of taxation and administrative costs (identified by 52 percent of responding firms). Significantly, however, 'increasing competition in the market place' was ranked second (by 43 percent of firms), as market reforms contribute to the development of the private enterprise sector. Less positively, 28 percent of firms pointed to the lack of a business support infrastructure as an external barrier; and 16 percent to other infrastructural deficiencies.

At the same time, Chinese entrepreneurs have found creative ways around formal institutional deficiencies. For example, in some rural areas, private enterprises have been able to obtain a collective licence to operate by paying an 'administration fee' to a state or local government organization to receive its stamp on their application for registration. Such firms were known as 'red hat' firms, because they were registered as having collective ownership when in fact they were privately owned. The so-called 'red hat' enabled them to avoid the prohibition of private firms and ideological harassment by

Table 9.2   Regional variations in private enterprise development: number of enterprises and employment

Year	Eastern				Central				Western			
	Firm No % (0000s)		Employment No. %		Firm No. %		Employment No. %		Firm No. %		Employment No. %	
1991	9.54	68	175.4	68	2.45	18	45.3	18	1.97	14	38.1	15
1993	15.9	67	235.1	63	4.5	19	76.9	21	3.4	14	60.6	16
1994	28.5	66	405.5	63	9.1	21	147.8	23	5.6	13	95.2	15
1995	43.3	66	599.8	63	13.8	21	218.2	23	8.4	13	137.9	14
1996	53.0	65	723.1	62	17.8	22	274.2	23	11.2	14	173.7	15
1997	61.1	64	821.1	61	21.1	22	318.9	24	14.0	15	209.3	16
1998	75.9	63	1036.5	61	25.0	21	383.5	22	19.3	16	289.2	17
1999	93.3	64	1245.3	62	27.6	19	423.7	21	24.0	17	352.7	17
2000	118.5	67	1577.4	66	29.3	17	416.0	17	28.4	16	413.2	17
2001	136.4	67	1768.5	65	33.0	16	459.3	17	33.4	17	486.0	18
2003	205.0	68	2852.7	66	48.0	16	734.8	17	47.7	16	711.8	17
2004	247.7	68	3248.6	65	60.6	17	937.8	19	57.0	16	831.1	17
2005	289.2	67	3815.8	66	72.4	17	1027.0	18	68.3	16	981.1	17

Notes:
Eastern China: Liaoning, Hebei, Beijing, Tianjin, Shandong, Jiangsu, Shanghai, Zhejiang, Fujian, Guangdong, and Hainan.
Central China: Heilongjiang, Jilin, Shanxi, Henan, Hubei, Anhui, Jiangxi, and Hunan.
Western China: Inner Mongolia, Shaanxi, Ningxia, Gansu, Qinghai, Xinjiang, Tibet, Sichuan, Chongqing (from 1998 on), Guizhou, Yunnan, and Guangxi.

Source: China State Bureau of Statistics (2000–2006).

government. In Shunde, Guangdong, almost all firms at the village level were 'red hat' firms before the enterprise ownership reform programme took place in 1992, encouraged by some local government officials. More recently, private entrepreneurs throughout China have created a system of 'back-street banks' (Tsai, 2002) to finance ventures in response to inadequate credit system and China's informal network of private sector capital has grown rapidly, particularly in the Eastern region of the country. The value of informal capital is estimated to be between 2 and 5 percent of the country's GDP, or about RMB950 billion (China Peoples Bank, 2005) and China's private sector would grind to a halt without it.

With a population of 1.3 billion, spread over 23 provinces and five autonomous regions, China is an enormous country. As a result, it is not surprising that there is considerable variation in levels of development between regions, with fast growing regions showing the highest levels of entrepreneurship. Table 9.2 summarizes the distribution of private enterprises and private sector employment across three broad regions: Eastern China, Central China and Western China. The table emphasises the domination of Eastern China in private sector development, accounting for 67.3 percent of all private firms in 2005 and 65.5 percent of private sector employment. Whilst the total number of private firms has increased by more than 30 times since 1991, and private sector employment by almost 23 times, the regional shares have remained fairly constant. Within the Eastern region, private enterprises are particularly concentrated in the five provinces, or municipalities, of Jiangsu, Zhejiang, Guangdong, Shanghai and Shandong, which accounted for 48.9 percent of the number of enterprises and 47.5 percent of private sector employment in 2005. People in these regions are said to have a strong sense of entrepreneurship and willingness to start a business (Kanamori and Zhao, 2004). These are all relatively developed areas with business traditions, access to foreign markets and preferential policies to promote entrepreneurship. By contrast, in Western China, levels of business ownership are very much lower and economic development a national government priority.

The contemporary period has seen the emergence of a new breed of entrepreneurs, who differ from entrepreneurs prominent during the initial stages of economic reform. They are innovative and more likely to be found in high-technology and modern service firms than in traditional sectors. Prior to 1993, entrepreneurs in China originated mainly from the lower occupational classes, such as unemployed workers, farmers and craftsmen driven by survival pressure. By 2006, entrepreneurs were increasingly drawn from occupational groups that included professionals, former managers and officials.

SMEs internationalization
China is currently the most active internationalizing economy among developing countries. In 2006, for example, it was the largest recipient of foreign direct investment (FDI) (with US$78.3 billion); the third largest exporter (about US$969.1 billion) (World Bank, 2007). Another trend is the expansion of outward FDI, which has grown to fifth among developing economies with the total of US$46.3 billion in 2005 (UNCTAD, 2006). These trends are testimony to China's open-door policy, which has increasingly encouraged free trade, with a step-by-step abolition of trade restrictions. Since 1978, China has changed its policy from the administration of foreign trade by central government to giving much greater autonomy in foreign trade to provincial governments and allowing private enterprises to engage in foreign trade (Chow, 2006).

Most exports come from SMEs. Official Chinese estimates of the contribution of SMEs to exports are shown in Table 9.3. The table shows that SMEs are contributing more than two-thirds of all exports by value, and a growing contribution at that. It means that Chinese SMEs contribute more than their counterparts in mature economies, such as the USA and the EU (Hall, 2003), although part of the explanation for this lies

Table 9.3   Chinese SMEs export in US$ (billion)

	SMEs export	Total export	Percentage
2001	134.6	266.2	50.6
2002	182.4	325.6	56.0
2003	272.5	438.4	62.2
2004	390.4	593.4	65.8
2005	518.2	762.5	68.0

Sources: Data on total exports are extracted from World Bank (2007); data on SME exports are drawn from NDRC (2006).

in the breadth of the definition of SME used in China. The main target markets include North America, European, Hongkong, Japan and Korea. Most of the exporting SMEs are located in the east of the country, in Shandong, Liaoning, Shanghai, Zhejiang, Jiangsu, Guangdong and Fujian.

There is also evidence that FDI has played a major role in China's transformation to a market-based economy, contributing to building technological capacity and the acquisition of management knowledge. Foreign direct investment is highly concentrated in the coastal provinces, with manufacturing accounting for 60 percent. Since the Chinese government launched its open-door policy, the inflow of FDI has been encouraged by a variety of government initiatives, including Special Economic Zones, Open Coastal Cities, Economic and Technological Development Zones, and Open Coastal Areas, tax breaks for joint venture, and tax rebates for enterprise exporting and free trade zones. Initially, foreign firms were required to have Chinese joint venture partners (mostly SOEs) and all of their production had to be re-exported. But in 1986, the government made provision for wholly owned foreign enterprises to operate in China, as well as passing other legislation designed to create a more attractive environment for FDI (Breslin, 2004). Since economic reform started in 1978, China's policy concerning foreign investment has made a 180-degree turn, from treating it as a form of exploitation by foreigners to welcoming it for China's economic development (Chow, 2006). As a result, the inflow of FDI into China has remained strong over this period and foreign enterprises have been a major driving force for China's export performance.

Furthermore, forming a joint venture with a foreign enterprise is an important route to internationalization for SMEs in China, where many act as original equipment manufacturers (OEMs) for foreign companies. Numerous overseas purchasing offices have been set up in Hong Kong (to concentrate on consumer products companies in Guangdong Province) and in Shanghai (to mainly cover Jiangsu and Zhejiang provinces with their industrial products manufacturing complexes) (*Purchasing Magazine*, 2005). As a result, an important part of China's rapid export growth has depended on foreign investment and processing materials supplied by or purchased from foreign firms. Total processed exports grew from US$57 billion in 1994 to US$416.5 billion in 2005, representing 54.7 percent of China's total exports.

Facing strong competition, while possessing limited material and human resources, an alliance may offer Chinese SMEs an opportunity to initiate distribution channels with foreign companies (Chen Hsiu Li, 2004), in order to capitalize on the abundant supply of cheap labour and low manufacturing cost and exploit their leading position as a global supplier of mass-produced goods (Ihrcke, 2005). In recent years, the Chinese authorities have favoured international joint ventures as a means of transferring technology and expertise to Chinese firms (Peng, 2000), as part of a wider strategic push to nurture technology development in China. Members of the Chinese diaspora, who are Western educated and familiar with Chinese culture, have been encouraged to return in recent decades to set up international businesses in China.

Huawei is an example of how the joint venture route strengthened a Chinese company's international competitive capabilities. A collective enterprise founded by a former army officer in 1988, Huawei is now challenging the global market in the field of network equipment such as Cisco Systems. It has entered into a number of joint ventures, for example, to develop and make 3G phones with NEC and Siemens, and with the Electronic Data Systems Corporation to market Huawei's equipment in the USA. In 1999 it established a software development centre in Bangalore (*Business Week*, 2003).

At the same time, outward FDI by Chinese firms has also grown markedly in recent years, reaching a value of US$21.16 billion in 2006. More than 30 000 Chinese enterprises have invested around the world and 80 percent of investors are small and medium-sized enterprises (China Ministry of Commerce, 2006). The Chinese government's internationalization policy for SME development aims to lead Chinese SMEs to the world. A foreign exchange and cooperation programme fosters exchange between Chinese SMEs and foreign firms, assisting SMEs to participate in international exhibitions and fairs.

The international competitiveness of Chinese production has hitherto been mainly based on a combination of low production costs and a favourable exchange rate, although there is evidence that the costs of doing business in China are rising. While labour costs for unskilled employees had remained virtually unchanged for the past decade, these costs are now rising, particularly after the revised Labour Law in 2007. In addition, as central government proceeds with reforming the public utilities sector, the cost of oil, gas, water and electricity are expected to rise in the future and industrial land prices are likely to continue to rise. Policies to promote environmental protection and currency appreciation would add further upward pressure on operating costs in China.

The upward pressure on production costs in some regions of China (for example, Shenzhen, Guangdong) is already contributing to some shift in the pattern of production, with lower cost locations in Western China and Eastern Europe proving attractive. For example, in the shoe sector in Donguan, Guangdong Province, there is evidence of several hundred SMEs closing or relocating in the last two years (*Southern Daily*, 2008).

Conclusions
The ongoing transformation of the Chinese economy from central planning to a socialist market system is impressive by any standards and a fascinating contrast to the chaotic effects of the system collapse, which affected most of the former Soviet republics. In this context, entrepreneurship and small business development is playing an important role in driving China's current wave of economic growth, released by facilitating economic policies and a decentralized policy approach allowing local experimentation through the activities of what some have termed the local entrepreneurial state (Li Jun and Matlay, 2006). This refers to the emergence of collective enterprises and TVEs, which were dominant change agents at a certain stage in the development of the non-state owned enterprise sector in China. The model involved local government coordinating economic activities within their territories, as if they were diversified business corporations. Fiscal decentralization reforms provided a foundation for local government led economic growth by giving local officials both the incentive and the investment funds to promote localized entrepreneurship.

However, despite the proactive role of some local governments in facilitating entrepreneurship in China in the 1980s and 1990s, there is evidence that the institutional environment contains certain deficiencies from a private sector perspective, which includes political interference in market activities. As a result, the influence of institutional factors on entrepreneurship development in China contains both positive and negative features. On the one hand, conditions of ambiguity and uncertainty can create entrepreneurial opportunities as a result of regulatory or organizational gaps (Yang, 2004), but on the other hand, exploiting what have been termed 'institutional holes' is often risky, encouraging entrepreneurs to adopt a short-term, exploitative approach to business opportunities. Implicit in this view, is the idea that the sources and characteristics of entrepreneurship in China are evolving over time, shaped by the development of the (formal) institutional environment. Although the process in China is distinctive, the institutional environment is a recurrent influence on the nature and extent of entrepreneurship in all transition economies and a key element in the social context for entrepreneurship in such conditions.

Note

1. General Office of the State Council, 2000.

References

Breslin, S. (2004), 'Capitalism with Chinese characteristics: the public, private and the international', Working Paper No. 104, Asia Research Centre and Murdoch University, Canberra: National Library of Australia.

Business Week (2003), 'Jumping the hurdles at Huawei', 22 December, http://www.businessweek.com/magazine (accessed 16 November 2007).

Chen Hsiu Li , Y.H. (2004), 'The establishment of global marketing strategic alliances by small and medium enterprises', *Small Business Economics*, **22**(5), 365–77.

China Ministry of Commerce (2006), *China FDI Statistics Report, 2006*, http://www.mofcom.gov.cn (accessed 19 November 2007).

China Peoples Bank (2005), 'Informal credit reaches 950 billion', *China Business News*, 26 July.

China State Bureau of Statistics (2000–2006), *China Statistical Yearbook*, Beijing: China Statistical Press.

China Statistical Yearbook (2000–2006), *Yearbook of China, 1992–2006*, Beijing; China: Statistics Press.

Chow, G.C. (2006), 'Globalization and China's economic development', *Pacific Economic Review*, **11**(3), 271–85.

General Office of the State Council (2000), 'Opinion of the State Economic and Trade Commission on policies to promote the development of SMEs', document no. 59, General Office of the State Council.

Hall, C. (2003), 'The profile of SMEs and SME issues in APEC 1990–2000', *Journal of Enterprising Culture*, **11**, 167–337.

IFC (2000), *China's Emerging Private Enterprises: Prospects for the New Century*, Washington, DC: International Finance Corporation.

Ihrcke, K.B. (2005), *Study on the Future Opportunities and Challenges of EU–China Trade and Investment Relations*, Brussels: Commission of the European Communities.

Kanamori, J. and Z. Zhao (2004), *Private Sector Development in the People's Republic of China*, Tokyo: Japan: Asia Development Bank Institute.

Li Jun and H. Matlay (2006), 'Chinese entrepreneurship and small business development: an overview and research agenda', *Journal of Small Business and Enterprise Development*, **13**(2), 246–62.

NDRC (2006), 'Summary of exporting SMEs in China', *SME Briefing*, **352**.

Peng, M. (2000), *Business Strategies in Transition Economies*, Thousand Oaks, CA: Sage Publications.

Peng, M. and P.H. Heath (1996), 'The growth of the firm in planned economies in transition: institutions, organizations, and strategic choice', *Academy of Management Review*, **21**(2), 492–528.

Purchasing Magazine (2005), ' Buyers look toward China – but with a degree of caution', 13 January, http://www.purchasing.com/article (accessed 9 October 2007).

Smallbone, D. and Jianzhong Xiao (2006), 'Researching the BDS markets in Chengdu, Lanzhou and Shenzhen', a report to DFID and the NDRC, Coffey International Development Ltd, Reading.

Southern Daily (Nanfang Daily) (2008), 'Thousands of shoe manufacturing prepares to exit', 22 January http://www.nddaily.com/headlines.

Tsai, K.S. (2002), *Back-Alley Banking: Private Entrepreneurs in China*, Ithaca, NY: Cornell University Press.

UNCTAD (2006), *World Investment Report 2006: FDI from Developing and Transition Economies*, New York: United Nations. www.unctad.org/wir (accessed 1 November 2007).

Watkins-Mathys L. and J. Foster (2006), 'Entrepreneurship: the missing ingredient in China's STIPs?', *Entrepreneurship and Regional Development*, **18**, 249–71.

Welter, F. and D. Smallbone (2003), 'Entrepreneurship and enterprise strategies in transition economies:

an institutional perspective' in D. Kirby and A. Watson (eds), *Small Firms and Economic Development in Developed and Transition Economies: A Reader*. Aldershot: Ashgate, pp. 95–114.

World Bank (2007), *China Data and Statistics*, http://web.worldbank.org/wesite/external/datastatistics (accessed 22 December 2007).

Wright, M., Liu Xiaohui, T. Buck and I. Filatochev (2008), 'Returnee entrepreneurs, science park, location choice and performance: an analysis of high technology SMEs in China', *Entrepreneurship Theory and Practice*, **32**(1), 131–56.

Xue Liang (2006), 'The evolution of township and village enterprises (TVEs) in China', *Journal of Small Business and Enterprise Development*, **13**(2), 235–41.

Yang, K. (2004), 'Institutional holes and entrepreneurship in China', *The Sociological Review*, **52**(3), 371–89.

10 China, part 2
Joseph Sy-Changco

I. Introduction

For the Chinese, the pertinence of entrepreneurship is particularly relevant in the proverb: 'It is better to be a chicken's head than a phoenix's tail.' There is a large consensus on the belief that every Chinese person wants to be his own boss (Liao and Sohmen, 2001, p. 27).

The Pearl River Delta is the most economically prosperous and dynamic region in the People's Republic of China (PRC). Located in Southern China, it covers the Guangdong Province and the two Special Administrative Regions of Hong Kong and Macau. It is also the location of two of the original four Special Economic Zones (Shenzhen and Zhuhai) of the PRC. This chapter will cover the state of entrepreneurship in Guangdong Province, Hong Kong and Macau.

Hong Kong

Hong Kong (HK) is located at the eastern side of the Pearl River Delta, beside the Guangdong province in the north and fronting the South China Sea in the east, west and south directions. It was occupied by the British in 1841. In the early 1950s, Hong Kong embarked on its export-led industrialization which grew rapidly in the 1960s. By 1970, it eventually emerged as a major financial center and one of the richest economies in Asia. On 1 July 1997, it became the Hong Kong Special Administrative Region (SAR). In this set-up, China's socialist economic system is not imposed on Hong Kong and thus Hong Kong enjoys a high degree of autonomy in all matters except foreign and defense affairs for the next 50 years (Dana, 2007).

Currently, the majority of Hong Kong's entrepreneurs engage in small and medium-sized enterprises (SMEs). Their 290 000 SMEs account for 98 percent of the local enterprises employing more than 1.36 million people or 60 percent of private sector employees. Most of the SMEs are concentrated in the services sector with the majority of activities taking place in the import and export trades, wholesale and retail, and restaurants and hotels (Chua, 2003a). Their vitality and business performance are of crucial importance to the development of their economy.

Macau

Macau is a territory located in southeast China, 61 kilometers west of Hong Kong and 105 kilometers away from Guangzhou. With a population of only 531 400, Chinese represent 96 percent of its total population while Portuguese and foreigners account for 2.5 percent and 1.5 percent respectively (Macau SME website).

Macau was the first and last European settlement in the Far East, with over 400 years of Portuguese rule ending on December 1999 when it became the Macau Special Administrative Region (SAR) of China (Dana, 1999). Like Hong Kong, it continues to enjoy a high degree of autonomy in all matters except foreign and defense affairs and retains its own government, passports, visas, tariff, postal system and currency.

With a capitalistic system, Macau is an open city of commerce and trade. It is strategically located and has a well developed infrastructure. Raw materials and capital goods are free from import tariff; foreign exchange and movement of capital are unrestricted. Macau also has very low levels of taxation, the lowest in the region. With these advantages in a competitive business environment, it also functions as a bridge to facilitate regional economic cooperation.

With gaming and tourism as their leading sector, Macau is turning into a tourism gaming center, a Meetings, Incentives, Conventions, and Exhibitions (MICE) center and a trading service center. Furthermore, the government is striving to construct Macau into a business service platform in three respects: (1) the Service Platform for the Economic Cooperation between China and Portuguese Speaking Countries, (2) the Economic Cooperation Platform for Western-Guangdong, and (3) the Global Chinese Entrepreneurs Networking and Co-operation Platform.

Receiving 22 million visitors in 2006, new hotels, casinos and entertainment facilities will be gradually put into use. In 2006, gross domestic product (GDP) grew 16.6 percent, where the number of new start-up companies also increased by 1.2 percent (3110 companies). In the first quarter of 2007, the economic growth rate increased by 25.6 percent and is expected to remain high.

The Mainland and Macau Closer Economic Partnership Arrangement (CEPA) is seen to further promote economic and trade cooperation and development between the two. The CEPA is composed of three main areas: (1) trade in goods, (2) trade in services, and (3) trade and investment facilitation. On the other hand, the Economic and Trade Cooperation Action Plan between China and Portuguese-Speaking Countries serves to strengthen Macau's role as the Service Platform for the Economic Cooperation between China and Portuguese Speaking Countries.[1]

Guangdong
Guangdong province is located on the southern coast of China with a total of 79 million registered permanent residents and 31 million migrants. With its provincial capital Guangzhou and economic hub Shenzhen, Guangdong is the country's richest province having the highest total GDP among all provinces, reaching US$422 billion in 2007 and contributing approximately 12.5 percent of national economic output. It hosts the largest import and export fair in China called the Canton Fair.[2]

From an economic backwater, the Guangdong prospered as it began its open-door policy, taking advantage of its access to the ocean, proximity to Hong Kong, historical links to overseas Chinese, and low rate of taxation (Zhang and Kang, 1997). Its economic boom exemplifies the reality of the vast labor-intensive manufacturing powerhouse China has become (Leung, 1996). Based mainly on manufacturing and export, its foreign trade in 2007 is by far the largest of all of China, accounting for 29 percent of China's US$2.17 trillion foreign trade (roughly US$634 billion).

In 1980, Shenzhen, Zhuhai and Shantou Special Economic Zones (SEZs) were established to attract technology transfer.[3] The affluence of Guangdong, however, remains very much concentrated near the Pearl River Delta.

Guangdong officially became the most populous province in January 2005. The massive influx of migrants from other provinces, dubbed the 'floating population', is due to Guangdong's booming economy and high demand for labor. Guangdong is also the ancestral home of large numbers of overseas Chinese. Emigration in recent years has slowed with economic prosperity, but this province is still a major source of immigrants to North America and elsewhere in the world.[4]

II. Government policy on SMEs and entrepreneurship in Hong Kong, Macau and Guangdong Province

Hong Kong

Comprising mostly small and medium business enterprises (98 percent), Hong Kong's government facilitates and creates a favorable business environment by providing legal, social and institutional frameworks necessary for the effective operation of markets (Yu, 1998).

In manufacturing development, the government motivates the people to exercise their entrepreneurial spirit. They are not provided any subsidy nor the industry protected. Rather, they are furnished with consultancy facilities such as the Hong Kong Productivity Centre and the Trade Development Council to assist entrepreneurs to pick the 'right' industries (Yu, 1998).

For an economy that 'imports practically everything that it consumes, processes, or re-exports' pegging the Hong Kong dollar to the US currency provides a predictable and conducive business environment for an economy. The government continues to do this despite debate on the matter (Chua, 2003a).

Simplified procedures and responsive government administration has been identified as one of the strengths that promotes entrepreneurship by Global Entrepreneurship Monitor (GEM). The HKSAR enables people to start up business in Hong Kong in a simple way (Chua, 2003b). The Trade and Industry Department through the Small and Medium Enterprises Information Centre (SMEIC) acts as a 'first stop' service center for business starters and provides SMEs with information about business licenses, SME support services and other matters related to running businesses (Chua, 2003a).

Hong Kong's tax system, which enables people to acquire high levels of personal saving that can be used to finance new businesses, is the most business friendly in the world. Currently, taxes are levied on three types of income – profits, salaries and property (Chua, 2003a).

Hong Kong has a sound and efficient legal system that strictly adheres to the rule of law. Rated as one of the 'least-corrupt' places in Asia, the Independent Commission Against Corruption (ICAC) ensures that the Hong Kong government and firms deal honestly and fairly (Chua, 2003a).

Legislation on the protection of intellectual property rights has been firmly established and promoted by the Intellectual Property Department, which deals with intellectual property issues, law and public education (Chua, 2003a). The Customs and Excise Department takes vigorous action against copyright piracy and trademark counterfeiting. Hong Kong's anti-piracy laws and enforcement programs have been praised by the Business Software Alliance (BSA) as the best in Asia.

The Mainland and Hong Kong Closer Economic Partnership Arrangement (CEPA) opens up huge markets for Hong Kong goods and services and investment, while Hong Kong serves as a springboard for Mainland enterprises. The key steps taken to smooth the way for SMEs to start and operate businesses in China are the following: (1)

reduction and elimination of tariff and non-tariff measures; and (2) lowering of business costs and promotion of trade and investment between the mainland and Hong Kong (Chua, 2003a).

On the other hand, foreign investors are welcome to establish businesses in Hong Kong to tap the vast opportunities of the Mainland market. The CEPA benefits them in three broad areas: (1) trade in goods, (2) trade in services and (3) trade and investment facilitation.[5]

In addition, the HKSAR takes the lead in providing a physical infrastructure for business and industry development such as excellent telecommunications, efficient and international airport, and good transport and road systems, one of the largest container terminals in the world. The Hong Kong Science and Technology Park provides a 'one-stop' infrastructure support service for technology-based companies.[6] Business advisory services are provided by the Hong Kong Applied Science and Technology Research Institute Company Ltd, the Hong Kong Productivity Council, the Trade Development Council, and the Vocational Training Council (Chua, 2003b).

Various kinds of funding schemes were set up to encourage entrepreneurship: Special Finance Scheme for Small and Medium Enterprises (SMEs), Applied Research Fund and Innovation and Technology Fund.

Hong Kong puts value on education, research and development. It aims to have a productive and adaptable workforce with continual investment in higher education and capitalizing on the robust research culture in universities through the Trade and Industry Bureau (Mok, 2005).[7]

It promotes international student exchange programs and organizing cross-cultural learning schemes or tours, giving more choices in courses and freedom for students to develop their own study plan (Mok, 2005).

Through the Vocational Training Council, the New Technology Training Scheme, and the Industrial Support Fund, the government is able to develop and offer grants and subsidized training courses with global market trends.

The state-funded Hong Kong Industrial Technology Centre Corporation promotes innovations and applications of new technology, while the Cooperative Applied Research and Development Scheme offers equity investment or preferential loans to fund projects with commercial potential.

Macau
The medium and small-sized companies represent 95 percent of the local business enterprises in Macau. They play an important role in developing international trade and invigorating Macau's domestic economy. Their success acts as a booster for their sustained economic growth and social stability (Macau SME website).

Groups of enthusiasts have teamed up to encourage local medium and small enterprises, and thus accelerate Macau's economic development. They formed the 'Small and Medium Enterprises Association of Macau' to improve operation conditions and increase business opportunities for medium and small companies. This association strives to identify Macau's future development plans while it explores overseas markets and solves the problem of their limited resources with the objectives of energizing corporate and individual spirits and creating a new foundation for producing more quality products and services for Macau (Macau SME website).

The Small Medium Enterprise Service Center (SMEC) together with Macao Business Support Center (MBSC) and the Institute for the Promotion of Investment in Macau (IPIM) launched multi-faceted facilities and services for Macau's SMEs, such as:

- the One-stop Service for Macao Economic and Trade Consultation (includes information on investment environment, business opportunities and business matching)
- the Mainland China Business Advisory Service
- SME's Consultation Scheme (includes Credit Guarantee Scheme)
- assisting in the participation of economic and trade fairs (includes information on local and global fairs and exhibitions)
- assisting in fair and exhibitions events held in Macao
- application for convention and exhibition activities organized by IPIM
- application for financial incentives provided to SMEs allowing them to participate in exhibition activities
- application for the special package provided to local SMEs for business promotion
- organize workshop, business and information exchange activities.

Guangdong
The Chinese government aspires to make China a leader in high-technology where modernization and innovation will be necessary conditions for development. As a result, it has been particularly promoting high-technology entrepreneurship, establishing many high-technology parks throughout the country. Tax incentives, monetary grants, and relaxed laws have engendered a more welcoming environment for growing technology enterprises (Liao and Sohmen, 2001). While funding is perhaps less of a problem for Internet entrepreneurs, labor supply is inadequate with the exodus of technical graduates who move abroad and never return.

III.   The economic and sociocultural environment for entrepreneurship and the state of small business

Hong Kong
There has long been an enterprising culture in Hong Kong (Dana, 1995). It is believed that the more educated and richer a person is, the greater the chance he or she will start a business in order to take advantage of opportunities.[8] However, these days, the vast majority of young entrepreneurs are no longer risk-takers, in contrast to generations back in the 1950s and 1960s. They would rather startup companies utilizing standard technologies, selling existing products and services, and tapping into the competitive markets. This may be attributed to various factors such as Hong Kong's high cost base, lack of entrepreneurial education and the relatively wealthy environment of modern Hong Kong, which does not motivate youth the way poverty motivated the older generation.

On the other hand, Hong Kong's economic success is mainly attributable to the dynamics of adaptive entrepreneurs who are alert to opportunities and exploit them. They discover, exploit and take advantage of situations where they can sell for high prices that which they can buy for low prices (Yu, 1998).

When the companies find themselves in volatile situations, they respond quickly to business opportunities, making quick decisions, acting promptly, and maintaining a high degree of flexibility and adaptability (Chau, 1993: 25).

For small firms, with small overhead, machinery and personnel costs, the opportunity cost of shifting to other sectors is low making it easy for small firms to switch to new kinds of production to get out of a declining sector (Yu, 1998).

Many entrepreneurs have left Hong Kong and returned (Dana, 1996). These are called Boomerang Entrepreneurs.

Macau
In Macau, SMEs are struggling in the aftermath of the gaming industry's liberalization. With casinos needing much manpower and offering higher wages, SMEs are currently facing labor shortages and difficulties in hiring foreign workers.

High turnover is a problem with qualified professionals who stay only a few months at a small company before they are lured to the casinos where they can, on average, earn up to MOP13000, from salaries average between MOP7000 to MOP10000 per month at an SME. A banking industry source told *Macau Business* (Pina, 2007a) that when new casinos like Wynn and the Venetian opened, many bank employees shifted jobs, lured by higher salaries and a new working experience.

Since local residents number roughly half a million, and more than a third are still teenagers, it is easy to see why there are labour shortages. The gaming sector absorbs more than 50 percent of able-bodied local adults. And they still cannot fill all vacancies.

According to the Macao SME Association, 30 of its 300 members declared bankruptcy in a year: 'These companies had clients but no employees' (Pina, 2007b, p. 3). But another reason for business difficulties is the rising rents of office and commercial spaces.

Albano Martins, an economist, has forecast that importation of foreign workers would help balance the situation. Another solution is for workers who left their SME bosses in recent years to let go of their 'casino fever' and, in doing so, restore balance to the local labour market and keep more small businesses open. 'The SMEs will survive if there are no strangling measures imposed [such as] ridiculously high rents and restrictions on importing foreign labour' (Pina, 2007b, p. 6).

Guangdong
Compared to Hong Kong companies, Shenzhen companies are more willing to pursue opportunities, regardless of resource constraints, and are more focused on rapid growth (GEM, 2004). In Guangdong, the four main growth barriers were identified: aversion to risk and failure, taxes, lack of resources and little readiness to change and adapt (Accenture, 2002).

In starting-up and running successful business, the first problem is to face political and legal uncertainty. Another obstacle is the lack of access to resources, in particular funding, labor and technology. The third barrier is the low social status attributed to private business in China. To overcome the barriers, they focused on the Confucian values of persistence, diligence, thrift, and the strong role played by the family as key supporting factors for entrepreneurial development (Liao and Sohmen, 2001).

Another often quoted characteristic universal to successful entrepreneurship is business acumen. It is a key to successful entrepreneurship along with hard work, luck and fate, but such trust in fate may also partially explain (1) the reliance on opportunism over long-term strategy and (2) the emphasis of short-term profits and opportunism instead of long-term strategy (Liao and Sohmen, 2001).

The two major characteristics unique to entrepreneurs in China are political nimbleness and interpersonal harmony, while hard work and liquidity are factors Chinese entrepreneurs use to hedge for an unpredictable environment (Liao and Sohmen, 2001). Additionally, interpersonal harmony and *guanxi* are important factors for further reducing risk. To accelerate growth, the Chinese find it important to maintain good business contacts even if there are illegal measures involved (Liao and Sohmen, 2001).

Resembling Chinese overseas, China's start-ups are controlled by families since they are more trusted and accept minimal compensation in return for future gains. In contrast, young graduates would leave immediately if wages are delayed. Both the low availability of funds in China and the importance of capital in initial stages indicate how important this benefit from kin can be to a growing business (Liao and Sohmen, 2001).

IV. Internationalization of entrepreneurs

Hong Kong

Hong Kong entrepreneurs tap foreign countries, mainly North America and Europe, as their major markets. With China now a member of the World Trade Organization, Hong Kong's preferred market has moved closer. Its proximity to China and its status as a Special Administrative Region of the mainland is one of the most unique aspects of its entrepreneurial experience and growth (Chua, 2003a). By employing what they learn from capitalist nations, Hong Kong can compete in world markets and catch up with the economically more developed nations (Yu, 1998).

Hong Kong's SMEs abundant experience in global business trade will put them in the world market. This will expand in the form of partnerships with overseas companies, as well as with mainland companies (Chua, 2003a).

Macau

With more than 200 million total population of Portuguese-speaking countries, there are many potential markets to be developed. At present, China exports machinery and provides technical labor to these nations, giving Chinese-made products an excellent competitive advantage. Given the language, culture and intimate relationships, Macao has been in contact with the countries for a long time. This can be reflected in the International Commercial Conference for Portuguese-speaking countries, which is held annually in Macao.

To strengthen the economic cooperation and development between China and Portuguese-speaking countries, and to improve the international status of Macao SAR, the first 'Economic Co-operation Forum between China and Portuguese-speaking Countries' was held, and the 'Economic and Trade Cooperation Action Plan' was signed, establishing the mode of cooperation between the participating countries.[9]

Guangdong

Due to its geographic location, Guangdong has benefited most from foreign investments, the majority of which come from Hong Kong. Many of the SMEs in Guangdong service the requirements of larger companies especially in original equipment manufacturers (OEMs). Through international exhibitions and in particular, through the bi-yearly Canton Fair, SMEs in the province are able to reach foreign clients.

V.   Conclusion with regard to academia and public policy and opportunities for future research

The Pearl River Delta Region continues to be an economically thriving region and a source of growth of PRC. For the entrepreneurs in SME, the different parts of the region offer them a variety of opportunities besides the peculiar challenges inherent in these different areas.

Hong Kong

Hong Kong's reputation as a major financial center – and one of the richest economies of Asia – contribute to its perception as a place where entrepreneurship thrives and the entrepreneur is well respected. Its location, facilities and infrastructures, government policy on SMEs and entrepreneurship, and economic and social environment (Chua, 2003a) provide a good ground for economic growth.

The Hong Kong government remains a firm advocate of developing an environment that is conducive for SMEs to grow and improve in the areas of technology application and innovation (Chua, 2003a). It sets out policy framework in bringing the various sectors, including the university sector, the business and the industry, together for exploring and developing entrepreneurial opportunities (Mok, 2005).

Macau

The present unprecedented economic boom in Macau has been a mixed blessing to Macau's SMEs. Although the government supports the development of SMEs, the existing labor shortage and the increasing cost of doing business, especially with the spiraling rental costs, make the present condition a truly challenging one for the entrepreneurs. More than ever, Macau's entrepreneurs must seek ways and means to reinvent their businesses in order to take advantage of the new opportunities offered by the boom in Macau tourism as well as the foreign market linkages provided by the Macau government.

Guangdong

A large amount of structural reform has already taken place in the China economy. As these changes take place, there will be increasing opportunities for organizations to unleash greater entrepreneurial spirit, but the organizations cannot sit back and wait for the government to provide an entrepreneurial culture. Leaders need to be proactive and take the measures to encourage entrepreneurship and innovation throughout their organizations.

On a microeconomics level, entrepreneurs continue to face the issues of finding and retaining skilled workers, lack of infrastructure and efficient credit system. Increasing education and greater understanding about entrepreneurship will hopefully alleviate this problem (Liao and Sohmen, 2001).

With accelerating reform and increased exposures to the West, values in China are also changing, successful entrepreneurs are upheld as role models and idols. The Internet is changing the nature of entrepreneurship by introducing stronger foreign involvement through foreign-educated entrepreneurs and foreign funding (Liao and Sohmen, 2001).

Overseas-invested businesses that are on the move are increasing. More small and medium-sized enterprises are expected to leave the Pearl River Delta because of poor operation, dwindling profit, rising labor and environmental costs and a lack of competitiveness. To address this, Chinese authorities have emphasized quality over speed in future economic development across the country. Guangdong is determined to drop its extensive development pattern and will follow stringent regulations regarding environmental protection and higher standards for innovation and construction of modern enterprises system. Governor Huang Huahua lays out 10 key missions to be fulfilled this year, with the adjustment of industrial structure at the core of the tasks.

Local governments in the Guangdong have been trying hard to adjust industrial structure with new urban development plans. Conventional overseas ventures that are quick to make timely adjustments according to the changed business operating environment continue to prosper. On the other hand, a company's money-losing spree stopped in 2006 when it adjusted its business expansion strategy and spent more on research and development while vigorously opening up the China domestic market.

Notes

1. http://www.ipim.gov.mo/en/subpage.asp?include=macauenv/index.asp.
2. http://www.en.wikipedia.org/wiki/Guangdong#cite_note-1#cite_note-1.
3. http://tradelinephil.dti.gov.ph/dti/downloads/appendix_a.pdf.
4. http://en.wikipedia.org/wiki/Guangdong.
5. Mainland and Hong Kong Closer Economic Partnership Agreement, http://www.tid.gov.hk/english/cepa/cepa_overview.html.
6. http://www.atip.org.
7. http://www.info.gov.hktib/roles/first/chap4.
8. Global Entrepreneurship Monitor, Hong Kong and Shenzhen (2004).
9. http://www.ipim.gov.mo.

References

Accenture (2002), 'Liberating the entrepreneurial spirit in China', http://www.accenture.com/Global/Research_and_Insights/Policy_And_Corporate_Affairs/LiberatingChina.htm (accessed 18 March 2008).
Asian Technology Information Program, http://www.atip.org (accessed 5 March 2008).
Chau, L.L.C. (1993), *Hong Kong: A Unique Case of Development*, Washington, DC: World Bank.
Chua, B.-L. (2003a), 'A status report of entrepreneurship in Hong Kong' proceedings of Entrepreneurship in Asia, Mansfield Center for Pacific Asia, April.
Chua, B.L. (2003b), 'Research Report: Entrepreneurship in Hong Kong: Revitalizing Entrepreneurship', New York: The Mansfield Center for Pacific Affairs.
Dana, Léo-Paul (1995), 'Enterprising culture in Hong Kong', *Journal of Enterprising Culture*, 3(4), 497–510.
Dana, Léo-Paul (1996), 'Boomerang Entrepreneurs: Hong Kong to Canada and Return', *Journal of Small Business Management*, 34(2), 79–83.
Dana, Léo-Paul (1999), 'The development of entrepreneurship in Macao and Hong Kong: a comparative study', *Public Administration and Policy*, 8(1), 61–72.
Dana, Léo-Paul (2007), *Asian Models of Entrepreneurship – From the Indian Union and the Kingdom of Nepal to the Japanese Archipelago: Context, Policy and Practice*, Singapore and London: World Scientific.
Global Entrepreneurship Monitor, Hong Kong and Shenzhen (GEM) (2004), The Chinese University of Hong Kong.
Leung, C.K. (1996), 'Foreign Manufacturing Investment and Regional Industrial Growth in Guangdong Province, China', *Environment and Planning*, 28(3), 513–36.
Liao, Debbie and Philip Sohmen (2001), 'The development of modern entrepreneurship in China', *Stanford Journal of East Asian Affairs*, 1, 27–32.
Macau SME Website, http://www.ipim.gov.mo/sme_resources_list.php?type_id=18 (accessed 24 April 2008).

Mok, Ka Ho (2005), 'Fostering entrepreneurship: changing role of government and higher education govern-
ance in Hong Kong', *Research Policy*, **34**(4) 537–54.
Pina, Joyce (2007a), 'Bad days to come', *Macau Business*, http://www.macaubusiness.com/index.php?id=1007
(accessed 24 April 2008).
Pina, Joyce (2007b), 'MB Report: Macau Business', *Macau Business*, http://www.macaubusiness.com/index.
php?id=1007 (accessed 6 February 2008).
Sit, V. and S.L. Wong (1989), *Small and Medium Industries in an Export-Oriented Economy: The Case of Hong
Kong*, Hong Kong: Centre of Asian Studies, University of Hong Kong.
Yu, Tony Fu-Lai (1998), 'Adaptive entrepreneurship and the economic development of Hong Kong', *World
Development*, **26**(5), 897–911.
Zhang, Z. and C. Kang (1997), 'China: A Rapidly Emerging Light-Manufacturing Base in Guangdong
Province', in W. Dobson and S.Y. Chia (eds), *Multinationals and East Asian Integration*, Canada and
Singapore: International Development Centre, Canada and Institute of Southeast Asian Studies.

11 India

Shameen Prashantham

Introduction

Internationalization among small and new firms, notably in knowledge-intensive sectors, can be remarkably rapid (Oviatt and McDougall, 2005). This phenomenon is often driven by three factors: knowledge, intent and networks. These factors operate at the level of both the firm and the individual entrepreneur. However, international entrepreneurship can be hampered by macroeconomic disincentives or a hostile environment (Zahra, 2005). This often tends to be the case in emerging economies such as India (Dana, 2000). The global success of the Indian software industry therefore acquires significance as an exception and exemplar which has symbolized India's rise as an economic power. This chapter explores some findings about international entrepreneurship in India with special reference to the software industry.

Key influences

A synthesis of the literature on international entrepreneurship suggests that three interdependent factors, often embodied by the entrepreneur himself or herself (at least initially), play an important role in the internationalization of small and new entrepreneurial firms: knowledge, intent and networks.

First, the importance of market and technological knowledge in driving international entrepreneurship is well documented in the literature (Jones and Coviello, 2005). Innovation is a key goal for small entrepreneurial firms and knowledge is the chief preoccupation of knowledge-intensive firms (Hitt et al., 2001). Domains of specialized knowledge of the entrepreneur often determine the firm's main offerings and therefore the prior experience (including education) of the entrepreneur is crucial, and may have a bearing on his or her strategic and international orientation, innovativeness and network relationships (Ibeh and Young, 2001). The innovative behaviour of entrepreneurial firms can have a positive impact on their performance in international markets (Kundu and Katz, 2003). Central to such innovative behaviour is adeptness at accumulating and leveraging knowledge in the internationalization process (Sapienza et al., 2006). Developing and using knowledge relevant to internationalization can be a challenge to small and new firms in emerging economies in the absence of adequate infrastructure and exposure overseas.

Second, the entrepreneurial firm's international orientation or intent is vital to successful internationalization (Dimitratos and Plakoyiannaki, 2003). It may, for instance, have a bearing on decisions such as market selection and changes in entry mode (Lu and Beamish, 2001). Related to this, the firm's strategic orientation has a bearing on how well the technology strategy of the firm is integrated with the overall corporate strategy of the firm (Kundu and Katz, 2003). The apparent tension in the literature as to whether successful small entrepreneurial firms adopt a formal or informal approach to capability development is indicative of the heightened need for a strategic orientation that is flexible.

Third, research has emphasized the role of interorganizational relationships. Internationalization scholars have drawn on social capital theory to conceptualize and study this phenomenon (McNaughton and Bell, 1999). As Coviello (2006) has pointed out, new ventures have certain network relationships that can play a significant role in initial market entry. It would seem likely that such founding relationships can have path-dependent consequences in terms of the subsequent development of the firm. Initial network relationships are often directly attributable to the entrepreneur and/or top management team (Coviello and Munro, 1997). Oviatt and McDougall (2005) argue that initially strong ties are important to ventures but over time a set of weak ties are more likely to provide information and opportunities that facilitate accelerated internationalization. As the portfolio of network relationships expands, and especially as the ventures' confidence and capabilities grow, international growth accrues (Johanson and Vahlne, 2006).

International entrepreneurship in India

The evolution of the Indian economy as a global player has been slower than China's but nonetheless remarkable. Yet the macroenvironment in emerging economies such as India is not always conducive to international entrepreneurship. Disincentives may take the form of institutional barriers or a lack of 'soft infrastructure' such as efficient product, capital and labour markets as well as regulatory mechanisms (Khanna and Palepu, 1999: 126). Small and new firms may be hampered by an unstable political climate, low technology level, poor local infrastructure, unstable exchange rate and inconsistent implementation of government policy (Ibeh and Young, 2001). Calof and Vivier (1995) found that internationalizing emerging economy small and medium enterprises (SMEs) may face problems related to domestic and international politics (for example, the dismantling of sanctions) and trade policy (for example, the General Agreement on Tariffs and Trade – GATT). Other disincentives include elaborate procedures (Jain and Kapoor, 1996) and complex bureaucracy (Naidu et al., 1997).

Public policy in emerging economies generally reflects the politicoeconomic philosophy, which for example may have socialist leanings, as was historically the case in post-British India (Vachani, 1997). The underlying philosophy of the initial economic development activities after India gained independence from the British in 1947 was that the government was best placed to act as the key driver of business activities. As a consequence, Indian entrepreneurs had to become adept at playing the 'game' of obtaining requisite licences, which involved using a combination of lobbying strength and political connections. In such a scenario, primarily large businesses had the financial and political influence to succeed in the long term. Smaller firms were often hampered by government control. In relation to exports, the Indian government was initially not very encouraging, especially after an acute balance-of-payments crisis in the 1970s. Public policy at the time tended to be inward looking, with the emphasis being on import substitution, rather than exports. A key objective was to limit the use of valuable foreign exchange by Indian firms (Vachani, 1997) and as Naidu et al. (1997: 119) note, 'high levels of government interface has effectively inhibited international entrepreneurship'.

The economic liberalization efforts initiated by the government of India from 1991 onwards have considerable changed this situation (Vachani 1997). Although it has been suggested that the caste system has suppressed entrepreneurship among Indians, studies have demonstrated innovative abilities among Indian entrepreneurs (Dana, 2000;

Kundu and Katz, 2003). Policy measures to encourage entrepreneurship have come in various forms such as, among many others, the National Institute for Entrepreneurship and Small Business Development and Entrepreneurship Development Institute of India (Dana, 2000). Jain and Kapoor (1996: 80–81) suggest that economic liberalization appears to have fostered positive attitudes towards international entrepreneurship: 'the surveyed Indian firms viewed exporting as . . . an activity worth the efforts as it enhances firm stability and entails greater growth and profit potential'. In similar vein, Naidu et al. (1997: 124) observe that

> India has the potential of being a major player in world exports. It has the ingredients for success – entrepreneurial spirit of business people, ingenuity and motivation, and a wealth of resources . . . Recent liberalization of the Indian economy creates opportunities for Indian enterprises to successfully break into foreign markets.

Perhaps nowhere has their prediction been truer than in the Indian software industry.

The software industry in India: an exception and exemplar

The case of the Indian software industry is significant in that it has transcended difficulties associated with entrepreneurship in India (Dana, 2000). According to Correa (1996: 177), 'India is the most successful software exporter among developing economies'. The origins of the Indian software industry, notable particularly because of its strong export focus, can be seen in the early 1970s when the government promoted software exports (Correa, 1996). This was also a period when stringent regulations saw international information technology (IT) majors such as IBM pulling out of the country, thus creating a void that domestic hardware vendors rushed in to fill. The early 1980s saw the personal computer (PC) revolution enhancing the international demand for software, as well as the beginnings of liberalization policies in the Indian economy. Software exports from India began to grow.

Most Indian software companies adopted a remarkably simple and uniform strategy. It entailed exploiting the low labour costs for software programming talent in India, compared to the West, especially the US, through the provision of software developers for on-site work at client sites (often referred to as 'body-shopping'), supplemented by off-shore software development in India.

The historical basis for India's pool of technical talent lies partially in the establishment of educational institutions and public sector undertakings in fields such as aeronautics, notably in the southern Indian city of Bangalore (referred to as the Silicon Valley of India). Also, a unique impetus to the Indian software industry came from multinational enterprises that established local subsidiaries following the liberalization initiatives of 1991. Notable in this regard are Motorola and Texas Instruments, which were instrumental in attracting talent. Several other technology multinationals such as IBM, Intel, Microsoft, Oracle and Sun Microsystems have since set up development centres, many dealing with state-of-the-art technology.

What are the factors that have led to the success of the Indian industry? Kundu and Katz (2003) suggest that managerial characteristics such as entrepreneurs' educational background, technological innovativeness and strategic orientation have played a vital role. According to Correa (1996), factors such as the widespread use of the English language, apart from programmers' skill and quick response to demand, have contributed to success; he warns other developing economies that some of these factors (such as the use of the English language) have a historical basis that other countries (for example, China) will find difficult to easily emulate. Although the widespread availability of technical education in India is often mentioned, the supply still falls well short of demand. The competencies of software professionals, stemming from their training and experience, professional treatment of employees and network relationships with Indian software entrepreneurs in Silicon Valley in the US have been other success factors. Government policy became increasingly supportive of this successful industry (Correa, 1996). Apart from a tax holiday, the government upgraded the Department of Electronics into the Ministry of Information Technology. But one of the key challenges remains the creation of suitable infrastructure.

Indian software international entrepreneurs: four examples
The success of the Indian software industry has encouraged many entrepreneurs to launch their own software start-ups. The following is a brief account of four such entrepreneurs and their firms in Bangalore, in relation to their knowledge, intent and networks (for further details, see Prashantham, 2008). These examples are indicative of the diverse routes that may lead to founding and growing a software firm in India.

Vikas
Vikas was founded by an engineer following his graduation in 1995 because of the 'fire in [his] belly', despite pressure from his parents to study further and become the first postgraduate in the family. He is neither from a prestigious Indian university nor foreign trained, yet his passion to be innovative led him to pursue aggressively his entrepreneurial dreams. His knowledge base is constantly evolving, guided by market trends; having begun in software services he is leading the company to diversify into call centres. His intent, in terms of internationalization, has been to avoid popular and highly competitive markets such as the US. Instead, he has focused on Australia, recently setting up a one-man marketing team there; his next targets are the 'virgin territories' of South Africa and Zimbabwe. His networks have mainly been domestic, with only recently proactive measures being taken to acquire and cultivate network relationships overseas. The government, according to him, has failed to make life easier for entrepreneurs and he has experienced many instances of running from pillar to post in order to get things done for the business. Policy measures are often half-baked according to him; for instance, the government may improve roads but 'forget that power also is essential'.

New Creation
New Creation (NC) was founded by a computer professional trained at Rutgers University, after spending 10 years in the US. Although he harboured the occasional desire to become an entrepreneur at some point, his decision to start NC was precipitated by a family crisis which forced him to return to his home town of Bangalore in 2000. He was given a project to work on by a former American client. His knowledge base is a function of his more recent work in the US and deals primarily with e-commerce. His intent appears to be to remain fully focused on international business, as he feels he has a long way to go before establishing himself in India. Towards this end, he relied heavily on the Internet for international business development in non-American markets. His

networks primarily stem from professional contacts in the US, and he is trying to expand these by engaging business development contractors who, for a commission, canvas the wares of Indian firms in foreign markets. In his experience, the government can be very bureaucratic. While seeking to move premises, he found the paperwork and formalities to be cumbersome. But he acknowledges the support provided by initiatives such as the Software Technology Parks of India.

Ekomate

Ekomate was founded by a computer professional who studied at the University of Texas in Austin and stayed on in the US for a brief professional stint. At Austin he had also attended entrepreneurship classes at the business school, clearly indicating an interest in starting up his own firm, which he did upon his return to India in 1996 after calculating that that could be more remunerative than a salaried job at an IT firm. His knowledge was chiefly Internet oriented, based on his training and professional experience in the US. Accordingly, his firm's chief mandate has been 'to help firms get on to the Net'. However his knowledge base has evolved over time, expanding with client needs – especially those of loyal customers. To that extent, he feels that he has ceased to be a specialist and has become more of a generalist. His intent in terms of geographic focus has been flexible and it took three years before he received his first international contract – an unsolicited order from a British firm who located him through the firm's website and were impressed thereafter by his speed of response to requests for information and proposals. His networks today seem to primarily comprise of existing clients, although a few orders did come as a consequence of professional contacts in the US. In terms of government-related bodies, he has mainly dealt with the Software Technology Parks of India (STPI), and has found his association with them beneficial.

Mitoken

Mitoken was spun off from Motorola's Indian operations and is unique in terms of its focus on being a 'pure product player'; in other words, it offers packaged solutions rather than the customary software services offered by most Indian software firms (including the three discussed above). The directors of the firm are graduates of prestigious business and engineering schools in India and abroad; the chief executive officer (CEO) is an alumnus of the Indian Institute of Managament in Bangalore, India's premier business school. The timing of the directors' decision to successfully propose the spin-off coincides – rather significantly – with the craze for Internet start-ups. Not surprisingly, the company offers a software product for software companies that it describes as 'Web-native'. Nonetheless, the relevance of the offering has remained undiminished even after the collapse of most dot-coms. The knowledge of the CEO and his core team follows from the work carried out initially at Motorola and from prior education. The intent has been to target software firms across the world in a cluster-by-cluster approach after initially operating in India, with a view to refining the product before launching overseas. It is envisaged, however, that in less than five years the vast majority of business will be from abroad. The networks, to which much attention is paid, emanate from Motorola and business school contacts, as well as venture capitalists and senior IT and business professionals who have been formally inducted as company advisers. While Mitoken's CEO did not voice any strong reservation about government policy, he felt that product-oriented firms did not receive quite the impetus or supportive industry forums that they needed.

The last-mentioned case holds interest because it reflects a growing desire for small and new firms in the Indian software industry to move up the value chain. One manifestation of this desire is the emergence of a small but growing number of Indian software ventures as product, rather than services, companies. These firms seek to operate primarily on the basis of intellectual capital, not cost advantage. Recent research has begun to profile some of them and indicates that these firms also bring to bear their knowledge, intent and networks to foster accelerated internationalization. For example, Prashantham and Balachandran (2009) identify the case of Skelta, a venture that has successfully utilized a link with Microsoft India to enhance technological innovation and gain global visibility. Prashantham et al. (2009) describe the case of Liqvid Krystal, founded by a returnee from Silicon Valley, with an offering in the area of computer science education. It is interesting that alongside efforts to promote its offering in international markets, this venture perceives a significant opportunity in the domestic market as well, which is testimony to India's thriving economy in the first decade of the twenty-first century.

Insights from international entrepreneurship research in India
Limited international entrepreneurship research has been undertaken in the Indian software industry. But insights have already begun to emerge. Further to Kundu and Katz's (2003) work, some research has examined the role of network relationships in facilitating the internationalization of small and new Indian software firms. Social capital can be especially valuable in an emerging economy setting where small and new firms' resource poverty may be magnified. Commenting on the Bangalore cluster within the Indian software industry, Prashantham (2008: 12) observes:

> This empirical setting has certain unique features that emphasize resourcefulness. There are accentuated resource constraints. In a developing economy context, there are greater challenges to overcome, and hence highly entrepreneurial behaviour is required given the limited size of the domestic market and the environmental hostility manifested through frustrations with infrastructural shortcomings and bureaucratic red tape. This challenge, in turn, accentuates the resource constraint . . . Consequently, reliance on network relationships is likely to be particularly high.

At least three ideas emerge in relation to the leverage of network relationships that have relevance to contexts beyond the Indian setting.

Leveraging networks actively
Prashantham's (2008) exploratory case study research among Bangalore software ventures suggests that network relationships are more likely to yield valuable internationalization outcomes when leveraged proactively. He finds that small and new firms that develop greater stocks of social capital, in both international markets and the local milieu, increase their odds of attaining growth through accelerated internationalization. But this research also indicates that the endowment of network ties per se does not guarantee success when social capital is not actively utilized. Indeed, one of Prashantham's findings (2008) is that some Bangalore firms have been remiss in taking full advantage

of their social capital in that they have used local network resources relatively passively. This is consistent with the work of scholars who identify the leverage of interfirm relationships as a vital organizational capability (Coviello and Munro, 1997).

Leveraging networks discerningly
Prashantham and Zahra (2006) have argued, based on a survey of 96 internationalizing Indian software SMEs, that different types of network relationships will affect internationalization outcomes in different ways. They found that coethnic ties overseas, that is, network relationships with firms run or managed by fellow-Indians abroad, had a greater bearing on the focal SME's entry mode commitment. The greater the extent of coethnic ties, the more likely was an SME to go beyond exporting and establish a presence (for example, through a strategic alliance) in its lead international market. They found also that non-coethnic or mainstream network ties were more influential on another aspect of internationalization, namely, international revenues as a proportion of total revenues. These differential effects of network types indicate that realistically, not all networks are good for everything. Therefore discernment in their utilization is called for. Small and new firms could perhaps also benefit from monitoring their portfolio of network relationships and replenishing those ties in which they are deficient.

Leveraging networks reflectively
Prashantham's (2006) three-year longitudinal research on four Bangalore firms suggests that successful internationalization is associated with leveraging networks relationships for knowledge, not merely new business opportunities. Over time, owing to limits of direct benefits that can be extracted, initial ties may yield fewer revenue opportunities. However, other benefits could still be extracted, notably learning outcomes (Yli-Renko et al., 2002). Knowledge accumulated about new international markets could, for example, be applied by the focal firm in its pursuit of further international revenues. However, such learning does not occur automatically. Of vital importance is a reflective attitude on the part of internationalizing firms – chiefly of the entrepreneur – that results in attention being devoted to learning prospects even when interfirm ties do not translate directly into international revenues. Prashantham's (2006) research shows that firms which retain a single-minded focus on extracting revenue-related benefits miss the opportunity of attaining valuable learning over time.

Future directions
Implicit in the idea that knowledge, intent and networks drive international entrepreneurship is the notion that being resourceful is crucial to the success of internationalizing small and new firms. As argued above, the need for resourcefulness is accentuated in an emerging economy such as India. This provides an interesting opportunity for researchers to study phenomena concerning the resourceful use of knowledge and networks by entrepreneurial firms possessing the intent to grow internationally. The opportunity exists for research on international entrepreneurship in India in a number of directions. Three are briefly outlined below.

First, research on the temporal aspects of internationalization could be considered more deeply (Jones and Coviello, 2005). Given India's rapid economic growth in a number of sectors, a range of phenomena could potentially be observed within high-velocity environments through longitudinal quantitative and qualitative research, providing further insight into extant understanding of the speed of internationalization (Oviatt and McDougall, 2005). Another useful area of research relating to the temporality of internationalization concerns network dynamics (Coviello, 2006). Issues meriting attention include the evolution of the stock of social capital and its effects on growth performance outcomes (Prashantham, 2006).

Second, light could be shed on the role of economic geography in international entrepreneurship (Zahra, 2005). For example, research in the Indian software industry is suitable for enquiry into how location within a regional cluster (for example, Bangalore) facilitates or constrains internationalization-seeking behaviours of the entrepreneur and firm (McNaughton and Bell, 1999). The Indian context is also promising in relation to investigating how inter-milieu links – for example, between Bangalore and Silicon Valley – may be developed and institutionalized, which in turn creates opportunities and challenges for internationalizing small and new firms (Prashantham et al., 2009).

Third, research in India could be effectively incorporated in comparative studies of international entrepreneurship. Interesting comparators potentially exist in both advanced economies and other emerging economy contexts. To illustrate, Prashantham and Balachandran (2009) engage in an exploratory comparison of international entrepreneurship in Bangalore and Cambridge, UK, while Prashantham et al. (2009) attempt a similar exercise in relation to Bangalore and Lahore, Pakistan. Theoretical insights emerge in relation to issues of wider research interest such as the nature of tie embeddedness and inter-milieu linkages, respectively.

The first decade of the twenty-first century has seen an upward surge in the attention being paid to India by business practitioners, academia and the media. Research on international entrepreneurship is only beginning to take advantage of the great opportunity that India represents. India appears poised to remain a fascinating and insightful setting in which to engage in international entrepreneurship research in the years to come.

References

Calof, J.L. and W. Vivier (1995), 'Adapting to foreign markets: explaining internationalization', *Journal of Small Business Management*, **33**(4), 71–9.
Correa, C.M. (1996), 'Strategies for software exports from developing countries', *World Development*, **24**, 171–82.
Coviello, N.E. (2006), 'Network dynamics of international new ventures', *Journal of International Business Studies*, **37**, 713–31.
Coviello, N.E. and H.J. Munro (1997), 'Network relationships and the internationalization process of small software firms', *International Business Review*, **6**, 361–86.
Dana, L.P. (2000), 'Creating entrepreneurs in India', *Journal of Small Business Management*, **38**(1), 86–91.
Dimitratos, P. and E. Plakoyiannaki (2003), 'Theoretical foundations of an international entrepreneurial culture', *Journal of International Entrepreneurship*, **1**, 187–215.
Hitt, M.A., R.D. Ireland, S.M. Camp and D.L. Sexton (2001), 'Strategic entrepreneurship: entrepreneurial strategies for wealth creation', *Strategic Management Journal*, **22**, 479–91
Ibeh, K.I.N. and S. Young (2001), 'Exporting as an entrepreneurial act: an empirical study of Nigerian firms', *European Journal of Marketing*, **35**, 566–86.
Jain, S.K. and M.C. Kapoor (1996), 'Export attitudes and behaviour in India: a pilot study', *Journal of Global Marketing*, **10**(2), 75–95.
Johanson, J. and J.-E. Vahlne (2006), 'Commitment and opportunity development in the internationalization process: a note on the Uppsala internationalization process model', *Management International Review*, **46**, 165–78.
Jones, M.V. and N.E. Coviello (2005), 'Internationalisation: conceptualising an entrepreneurial process of behaviour in time', *Journal of International Business Studies*, **36**, 284–303.

Khanna, T. and K. Palepu (1999), 'The right way to restructure conglomerates in emerging markets', *Harvard Business Review*, **77**(4), 125–34.
Kundu, S.K. and J.A. Katz (2003), 'Born-international SMEs: BI-level impacts of resources and intentions', *Small Business Economics*, **20**, 25–57.
Lu, J.W. and P.W. Beamish (2001), 'The internationalization and performance of SMEs', *Strategic Management Journal*, **22**, 565–86.
McNaughton, R.B. and J.D. Bell (1999), 'Brokering networks of small firms to generate social capital for growth and internationalization', *Research in Global Strategic Management*, **7**, 63–82.
Naidu, G.M., S.T. Cavusgil, B.K. Murthy and M. Sarkar (1997), 'An export promotion model for India: implications for public policy', *International Business Review*, **6**, 113–25.
Oviatt, B.M. and P.P. McDougall (2005), 'Defining international entrepreneurship and modeling the speed of internationalization', *Entrepreneurship Theory and Practice*, **29**, 537–54.
Prashantham, S. (2006), 'Social capital and the international growth of new technology-based firms: temporal effects and limits', AIM working paper no. 43.
Prashantham, S. (2008), *The Internationalization of Small Firms: A Strategic Entrepreneurship Perspective*, London: Routledge.
Prashantham, S. and G. Balachandran (2009), 'Local bridging ties and new venture internationalization: exploratory studies in Bangalore and Cambridge', in M.V. Jones, M.E. Fletcher, P. Dimitratos and S. Young (eds), *Internationalization, Entrepreneurship & the Smaller Firm*, Cheltenham, UK and Northampton, MA, USA: Edward Elgar.
Prashantham, S. and S.A. Zahra (2006), 'Social capital types and internationalization: a study of Indian software SMEs', AIM working paper no. 45.
Prashantham, S., A. Qureshi and S. Young (2009), 'Comparative international entrepreneurship: the software industry in the Indian subcontinent', in M. Feldman and G.D. Santangelo (eds.), *Progress in International Business Research*, Bingley: Emerald.
Sapienza, H.J., E. Autio, G. George and S.A Zahra (2006), 'A capabilities perspective of early internationalization on firm survival and growth', *Academy of Management Review*, **30**, 914–33.
Vachani, S. (1997), 'Economic liberalization's effect on sources of competitive advantage of different groups of companies: the case of India', *International Business Review*, **6**, 165–84.
Yli-Renko, H., E. Autio and V. Tontti (2002), 'Social capital, knowledge and the international growth of technology-based new firms', *International Business Review*, **11**, 279–304.
Zahra, S.A. (2005), 'A theory of international new ventures: a decade of research', *Journal of International Business Studies*, **36**, 20–28.

12 Indonesia
Latif Adam

1. Introduction

Indonesia, a sprawling archipelago of around 17 000 islands, is one of South East Asia's rich countries, in terms of both natural and cultural resources. With a total area of 1 919 440 square kilometers, its landscape contains varied natural resources, ranging from timber, oil, gas, copper, to gold. Like its natural landscape, the Indonesian population consists of various ethic groups (see Dana, 1999). There are 350 languages spoken throughout the country. Although 90 percent of Indonesia's 235 million population are Muslims, other religious influences are present in the country, including Christianity, Hinduism, and Buddhism. With such rich cultural and natural resources combined with a large population, Indonesia should be attractive for both tourism and investment.

Unfortunately, due to such problems as unreliable infrastructure, poor contract enforcement, bad labor regulations, complicated customs and tax administration, and massive corruption (World Bank, 2005), Indonesia is not as attractive as its South East Asian neighbors in attracting foreign investors. This may be because these problems force investors to pay extra costs to what investors usually pay for investing in other South East Asian countries. Indeed, as James et al. (2003) pointed out, the cost of doing business in Indonesia is much higher than in the other countries. Accordingly, during 2000–2006, the growth rate of investment in Indonesia was less than 7 percent per year, lower than those in Vietnam, Thailand, Malaysia, and China (World Bank, 2005), and lower than in the pre-crisis years of the 1990s.

The low level of investment has reduced the competitiveness of Indonesian products in either domestic or export markets. For example, in the manufacturing sector, Sambodo et al. (2007) found that between 1993 and 2005 the competitiveness of 32 out of 64 industries investigated steadily declined. This may be because without a sufficient level of investment it would be difficult for enterprises to maintain and improve their competitiveness, because they may face difficulties to improve the quality of their products, intensify their efforts to innovate and create new products, and to replace ageing machineries to improve efficiency in the production process (Lindblad and Thee, 2007).

The decline in the competitiveness of many of Indonesia's manufacturing industries has led to this sector's slow growth. During 2005–07, the manufacturing sector grew by only a sluggish 5.3 percent a year – lower than the government's initial target of 8 percent a year for the period 2005–09. Consequently, the contribution of the manufacturing sector to the Indonesian economy (gross domestic product – GDP) declined slightly from 28 percent in 2005 to 27.6 percent in 2007.

The low level of investment contributed to slow economic growth. Although over the last two years the Indonesian economy grew by more than 6 percent, during 2000–2007, annual growth of the Indonesian economy, on average, was still less than 6 percent per annum. This growth rate was too low to increase employment and reduce poverty. Accordingly, a high unemployment rate and a high incidence of poverty still characterized the Indonesian economy. In 2007, the number of open unemployed persons was 10.5 million (9.75 percent of Indonesian the total labor force), while the number of people who live under poverty line was 37.17 million (17.1 percent of total population).

The high rate of unemployment and poverty may result in socio-economic instability. Therefore, since the economy is still growing slowly, Indonesia's commitment to reduce unemployment and poverty should be continued as this commitment may have a beneficial impact on overcoming socio-economic instability. To this end, the government needs to find an alternative solution to boost economic growth by promoting small and medium enterprises (SMEs).

There are many reasons why SMEs could be relied on as an alternative sector to drive economic growth. Firstly, SMEs play a significant economic role during both good and bad times (Sandee et al., 2000). During the crisis, many studies (for example, Berry et al., 2001; Sandee, 2002; Sandee et al., 2000) found that SMEs had weathered the crisis better than large enterprises (LEs). Those studies pointed out that like LEs, in general, SMEs also suffered from the crisis. However, unlike LEs, many SMEs have not been very dependent on formal markets and formal credit, so that they were able to survive and succeeded in adapting to the sudden shock more quickly and flexibly than their larger counterparts. Accordingly, during the crisis, SMEs played an important role as a buffer by creating employment and generating incomes for those belonging to the lower socio-economic class (Berry et al., 2001; Hill, 2002; Yamamoto, 2001).

Furthermore, statistical evidence confirmed the argument that SMEs play a vital role in the Indonesian economy and potentially in its future sustainable economic development. In 2005, 99.9 percent of all enterprises were SMEs. They approximately produced 60 percent of Indonesia's GDP and absorbed more than 99 percent of Indonesia's labor force (Thee, 2006). Small and medium enterprises also play an important role in the efforts to increase non-oil exports. In 1999, 18 percent of total exports were produced by SMEs (Berry et al., 2001). Moreover, SMEs are located throughout the country (Firdausy, 2005) and are less likely to be foreign- or government-owned than LEs (Hill, 2002). Thus, they can be harnessed as an important vehicle to support regional economic development (Yamamoto, 2001) and redistribute assets along ethnic lines (Hill, 2002).

However, despite playing an important economic role, SMEs also suffer from a number of problems. Four basic problems are commonly faced by the majority of SMEs, namely, limited technology, a small market, capital constraints, and information constraints. These four basic problems, partially or jointly, adversely affect the ability of SMEs to improve their productivity. Accordingly, the majority of studies (for example, Berry et al., 2001; Yamamoto, 2001) conclude that a low level of productivity is a salient characteristic of SMEs.

The problem of low productivity reduces the ability of SMEs to create employment, generate income, support regional economic development, and reinforce the structure of exports (Yamamoto, 2001). Moreover, Berry et al. (2001) emphasized that productivity growth is an important requirement for SMEs to maintain or increase their competitiveness. Hence, the lower productivity of SMEs, the more likely they are to fail to maintain or improve their competitive position in the markets. This is particularly true when there is an increase in the level of wages.

By using value added per worker as a proxy for labor productivity, Adam (2007) calculated that value added per worker of SMEs is indeed much lower than that of LEs. In

1975, value added per worker of SMEs was 39.7 percent that of LEs, while in 2001 it was 33.2 percent. However, Adam (2007) also found that although value added per worker of SMEs is still much lower than that of LEs, the growth rate of value added per worker of SMEs has continued to increase. Between 1975 and 2001, while value added per worker of LEs grew by 2.8 percent per year, value added per worker of SMEs rose by 2.1 percent per year. As van Diermen (1997), Berry et al. (2001), and Yamamoto (2001) previously concluded, this finding suggests that despite having lower productivity, small and medium industrial enterprises (SMIEs) are not evenly stagnant, but some of them have a capability to grow and develop.

2.   Government policy on SMEs and entrepreneurship in Indonesia
Conceptually, the development of SMEs has always been a government top priority in Indonesia. This is emphasized in almost all of key government documents, like the Five-Year Development Plans (Repelita), the Grand Outlines of Government Policy (GBHN), and many other official statements (Hill, 2002). To implement these official statements, the government has launched numerous policies to assist and improve the operations of SMEs (Box 12.1). These have been the responsibility of various ministries and the banking system (Firdausy, 2005; Hill, 2002).

Nevertheless, there has never been a comprehensive official evaluation of these policies and their effectiveness (Hill, 2002). However, almost all empirical studies (for example, Adam, 2007; Firdausy, 2005; Sandee et al., 1994; van Diermen, 1997) conclude that these numerous policies have been largely ineffective in assisting and improving the operations of SMEs. For example, by comparing SMEs that did and did not enjoy direct financial assistance, Sandee et al. (1994) and Adam (2007) mentioned that they have a similar pattern of development, suggesting that the effectiveness of direct financial assistance provided by the government in enhancing the entrepreneurship of SMEs is questionable.

Various explanations have been given of why the policies designed to support SMEs have rarely been effective. One view is of the government's basic approach to developing SMEs. The government tends to set SMEs as unable to adapt to the operations of the market mechanism. Accordingly, many policy instruments for SMEs have been designed on the basis of political and social considerations rather than economic motivations (Hill, 2002; Sandee, 2002; van Diermen, 1997).

Strong emphasis on the provision of direct assistance is a manifestation that Indonesia's policy instruments for SMEs have been designed on the assumption that SMEs will be affected adversely by the unfettered operation of the market mechanism (Boomgard et al., 1992). Such an assumption leads the government to provide its direct assistance on the basis of a strong welfare orientation rather than consider economic incentives. Hence, many empirical studies (for example, van Diermen, 1997; Sato, 2001; Adam 2007) found that the government's direct assistance programs failed to provide economic incentives to stimulate SMEs to become dynamic.

Moreover, policy instruments for SMEs tend to be supply driven (Berry et al., 2001; Hill, 2002). The inability of the government officials to understand completely the characteristics, the problems, and the needs of SMEs is the main reason why the policies for SMEs have tended to be supply driven rather than demand or market driven (Hill, 2002; Thee, 2002). The problem is that, because policy instruments for SMEs tend to be supply

---

BOX 12.1 SEVERAL IMPORTANT PROGRAMS TO PROMOTE SMES IN INDONESIA

Period
Soeharto government
1. Direct Financial Assistance
   - Nation wide subsidized program (KIK/KMKP) program (1972–90) aimed at small indigenous enterprises. Terminated in 1990 because of high default rate (more than 27 percent).
   - General rural credit (KUPEDES) program, aimed at small business development in rural areas.
   - Small enterprise credit (KUK) program (1990) under which commercial banks had to allocate 20 percent of their loan portfolio to small enterprises.
2. Direct Technical Assistance
   - Small industries development (BIPIK) program aimed to coordinate program of input provision for SMEs, under which technical assistance was provided to clusters of SMEs.
3. Indirect Assistance
   - Foster Father-Business Partner (Bapak Angkat) program aimed at developing business partnerships under which large private enterprises and state-owned enterprises (SOEs) were pressured to develop and assist their business partner (small enterprise) in management, marketing, technology, and accessing finance.
   - Requirement that SOEs had to allocate 1 to 5 percent of their profits to SMEs to assist them in improving their performance.

Megawati government
   - Improvement in land certification to enable SMEs to get better access to credit.

SBY government
   - Commitment to improve business climate for SMEs and provide credit to SMEs.

Sources: Thee (2006: 2–7).

---

driven, they fail to provide sufficient means either to overcome the problems or promote the interests of SMEs (Berry et al., 2001; Sato, 2001).

In addition to the weaknesses of policies directly targeting SMEs, SMEs also suffer from other economic policies. Although the government has designated the development of SMEs as a top economic policy priority, paradoxically many other policies have tended to discriminate against SMEs (Hill, 2002; Sandee, 2002; Sandee et al., 2000). For example, Indonesian trade policies still maintained a protective regime to provide preferential treatment to LEs (Hill, 2002; Sandee, 2002). Moreover, although Indonesia has implemented Anti-Monopoly Law since 2001, this law has several shortcomings, including vague provisions in its some articles and exemptions for certain kinds of enterprises (Thee, 2002), both of which open the possibilities for several LEs to maintain their monopolistic practices. The problem is that many LEs which enjoy high protection from the government and continue to engage in monopolistic practices are those producing several important commodities which are major inputs for many SMEs (Adam, 2007).

Fiscal and monetary policies, on several counts, also often work against SMEs. For instance, in relation to fiscal policy, the government frequently offered fiscal incentives, like tax concessions, for specific investments in particular regions. The problem is that almost all fiscal incentives offered by the government are frequently related to a certain minimum size which excludes SMEs. Similarly, in relation to monetary policy, several regulations, such as the imposition of a ceiling on lending rates or collateral requirements, have made banks reluctant to lend to SMEs (Hill, 2002; Sandee, 2002).

3.   The environment for entrepreneurship and the state of small business

The preceding discussion suggests that to meet its commitment to give priority to the development of SMEs, the Indonesian government has to take various actions to improve the entrepreneurship of SMEs. The first important action that the government should take is to reassess its preference for providing direct assistance on the basis of political and social considerations. Besides requiring huge financial support and much involvement of government officials (Boomgard et al., 1992), there has been little evidence that these government direct assistance programs have contributed significantly to the improvement in the performance of SMEs (Adam, 2007; Sandee et al., 1994). Rather, as many empirical studies found (Adam, 2007; Cole, 1998; Sato, 2001), SMEs which grow and develop are those that are able to adapt to and interact with the operation of the market mechanism. Hence, instead of launching interventionist welfare-oriented policies, the government should pay more attention to the creation of a competitive business environment that provide incentives for SMEs to grow and develop. To this end, first, the government should be able to manage and stabilize macroeconomic conditions.

In regard to macroeconomic conditions, in recent times, controlling and slowing down the rate of inflation has been the highest government priority. Indeed, over the last seven years, the decision of the Indonesian government to increase the price of electricity, fuel, and diesel several times due to high world oil price pressure resulted in a sharp increase in the rate of inflation. The high rate of inflation was also driven by a considerable increase in the price of foods, such as rice, soybean, corn, and wheat. Thus, although the government sets its target for the inflation rate to be 6.5 percent for 2008, in January and February 2008 the rate of inflation has already reached 2.42 percent. This high rate of inflation may reduce the demand for SMEs' products in the domestic market and hamper improvement in the competitiveness of SMEs (also LEs) in export markets.

Another important action that the government could take to create a conducive economic environment is to ensure that SMEs and LEs are able to compete fairly. As discussed previously, the Indonesian government introduced several regulations that discriminated against SMEs. These discriminatory regulations constrained SMEs in their access to several important resources and burdened them in dealing with the bureaucracy. Therefore, eliminating discriminatory policy against SMEs and strengthening the implementation of the Anti-Monopoly Law are other important government policies that can facilitate improvement in the entrepreneurship of SMEs.

Remedying various supply-side problems may also provide a conducive environment for SMEs to improve their entrepreneurships. First, SMEs suffer from the lack of new investment. Because of the lack of new investment, the machinery and other equipment of SMEs has aged. The use of old machines and other equipment contribute to high production costs (Adam, 2007).

The decision of the Indonesian government to launch several labor policy measures, such increasing UMR (regional minimum wages), extending severance pay coverage to workers leaving voluntarily and workers dismissed for criminal activity, and requiring producers to continue paying salaries to workers on strike, also contribute to rises in production (labor) costs. Moreover, the increasing militancy of the labor unions has resulted in numerous labor disputes and disruption in production activities. Disruption in production activities is also due to frequent conflicts between competing unions in the workplace (James et al., 2003).

Indonesia's decentralization policy, which has enabled local governments to have more power, authority, and responsibility in managing their own local economies has also to some extent been detrimental to SMEs. In an attempt to increase their own revenues, local governments frequently levy new taxes and charges. Some of these new taxes and charges, have little or no legal basis and are nothing more than nuisance taxes. Others overlap with similar charges imposed by the central government. These nuisance taxes and overlapping charges add unnecessarily to the costs of doing business in Indonesia (James et al., 2003).

The decision of the Indonesian government to maintain high tariffs on high-quality imported raw materials is another problem that hampers the improvement of SMEs. Such a decision not only increases production costs, but also limits the ability of SMEs to improve the quality of their products (Adam, 2007).

From a policy point of view, addressing the aforementioned supply-side problems is also an important step that the government of Indonesia should take to help SMEs to improve their entrepreneurship. This suggests that the government should maintain and intensify its efforts to go further in reforming its industrial policy so to create a more competitive and open economic environment. The government could also help SMEs to reduce their production costs by eliminating taxes and tariffs on inputs, providing efficient port and custom clearance, and getting rid of nuisance charges (James et al., 2003). Also, the government should provide more access for SMEs to sources of capital (for example, bank/finance) so that they can invest in replacing their obsolete machines and other equipment.

4. Internationalization of entrepreneurs and SMEs from Indonesia

Although the majority of SMEs remain local market oriented, some of them have penetrated international markets for many years. Indeed, as many studies (for example, Berry et al., 2001; Hill, 1998; Sandee and van Diermen, 2004; Urata, 2000) found, SMEs play a growing role in increasing Indonesia's manufactured exports. For example, over the period 1983 to 1992, Hill (1998) showed that direct exports from Indonesia's SMEs went up from $133 million to $2.1 billion. Accordingly, the share of SMEs' exports in the total Indonesia's industrial exports increased from 10 percent in 1983 to 13.2 percent in 1992. Moreover, Sandee and van Diermen (2004) estimated that during 1996–2000 exports from SMEs grew by more than 80 percent a year. Meanwhile, in 1999, Berry et al. (2001) showed that 18 percent of Indonesia's total manufactured exports originated from SMEs. The exports of SMEs consisted mainly of textiles, garments, and footwear (27 percent), wood products (22 percent), and basic machinery (16 percent).

Several factors have helped SMEs to penetrate export markets. One factor is business cooperation between SMEs and buyers of their products. Indeed as many scholars have emphasized (for example, Adam, 2007; Berry et al., 2001; Cole, 1998; Sandee and van Diermen, 2004; Yamamoto, 2001), cooperation with buyers of products, particularly foreign buyers, is an important factor that enables SMEs to market their products in the international markets.

For example, the findings of studies by Cole (1998), Sandee and van Diermen (2004) and Adam (2007) indicate that cooperation with foreign buyers benefited SMEs because the buyers are willing to provide technical and managerial assistance as well as information about current technology and market demand. This assistance enabled SMEs to adopt new designs and efficient methods of production. More importantly, this assistance also enabled SMEs to produce higher-quality and value-added products demanded by export markets. In sum, as Berry et al. (2001), and Sandee and van Diermen (2004) emphasized, cooperation with foreign buyers helps SMEs to modernize the methods of production and participation in the global market.

5.   Conclusion

Indonesian SMEs are not all static. Although improvement of their entrepreneurship is not as fast as those of LEs, some SMEs are able to improve their entrepreneurship so that they can grow and develop. The ability of some SMEs to grow and develop is remarkable because it has occurred in circumstances where various government economic policies tended to discriminate against SMEs. More importantly, the growth and the development of SMEs enable them to maintain their important role in the Indonesian economy, particularly in creating employment, generating income both for households and for the national economy.

The Indonesian SMEs have also penetrated international markets and contributed significantly to increasing Indonesia's manufactured exports. Business cooperation with foreign buyers facilitates SMEs to enable them to market their products in the international markets. Why and how foreign buyers have assisted SMEs is worth investigation.

References

Adam, L. (2007), 'The economic role of formal and informal inter-firm networks in the development of small and medium industrial enterprises: study of symbiosis in the Indonesian garment industry', unpublished PhD thesis, University of Queensland, Brisbane.

Berry, A., E. Rodriguez and H. Sandee (2001), 'Small and medium enterprise dynamic in Indonesia', *Bulletin of Indonesian Economic Studies*, **37**(3), 363–84.

Boomgard, J.J., S.P. Davies, S.J. Haggblade and D.C. Mead (1992), 'A subsector approach to small enterprise promotion and research', *World Development*, **20**(2), 199–212.

Cole, W. (1998), 'Bali's garment export industry', in H. Hill and K.W. Thee (eds), *Indonesia's Technological Challenge*, Canberra: Research School of Pacific and Asian Studies, Australian National University and Singapore: Institute of Southeast Asian Studies, pp. 255–78.

Dana, L.P. (1999), *Entrepreneurship in Pacific Asia: Past, Present & Future*, Singapore, London and Hong Kong: World Scientific.

Firdausy, C. (2005), 'Roles, problems and policies of the Indonesian small and medium enterprises in globalization', in C. Tisdell (ed.), *Globalization and World Economic Policies: Effects and Policy Responses of Nations and their Grouping*, New Delhi. Serial Publications, pp. 1–39.

Hill, H. (1998), *Indonesia's Industrial Transformation*, Sydney: Allen and Unwin.

Hill, H. (2002), 'Old policies challenges for a new administration: SMEs in Indonesia', in C. Harvie and B.C. Lee (eds), *The Role of SMEs in National Economies in East Asia*, Cheltenham, UK and Northampton, MA, USA: Edward Elgar, pp. 158–80.

James, E.W., D.J. Ray and P.J. Minor (2003), 'Indonesia's textile and apparel: the challenges ahead', *Bulletin of Indonesian Economic Studies*, **39**(1), 93–103.

Lindblad, T. and K.W. Thee (2007), 'Survey of recent developments', *Bulletin of Indonesian Economic Studies*, **43**(12), 1–33.

Sambodo, M.T., A.H. Fuady, L. Adam and Purwanto Derajat Persaingan (2007), *Merangkai Benang Kusut Daya Saing Perekonomian Indonesia (An Investigation into Determinants of Competitiveness of the Indonesian Economy)*, LIPI Press.

Sandee, H. (2002), 'SMEs in Southeast Asia: issues and constraints in the pre- and post-crisis environment' in C. Harvie and B.C. Lee (eds), *Globalization and SMEs in East Asia. Cheltenham*, Cheltenham, UK and Northampton, MA, USA Edward Elgar, pp. 61–82.

Sandee, H., and P. van Diermen (2004), 'Exports by small and mediun sized enterprises in Indonesia', in M.C. Basri and P. van der Eng (eds), *Business in Indonesia New Challenges, Old Problems*, Singapore: Institute of Southeast Asian Studies, pp. 108–21.

Sandee, H., P. Rietveld, H. Supratikno and P. Yuwono (1994), 'Promoting small-scale and cottage industries in Indonesia: an impact analysis for Central Java', *Bulletin of Indonesian Economic Studies*, **30**(3), 115–42.

Sandee, H., R.K. Andadari and S. Sulandjari (2000), 'Small firm development during good times and bad: the Jepara furniture industry', in C. Manning and P. van Diermen (eds.), *Indonesia in Transition Social Aspects of Reformasi and Crisis*, Indonesian Assessment Series, Canberra: Research School of Pacific and Asian Studies, Australian National University; Singapore: Institute of Southeast Asian Studies, pp. 184–98.

Sato, Y. (2001), 'Structure, feature and determinants of vertical inter-firm linkages in Indonesia', unpublished doctorate of philosophy, University of Indonesia.

Thee, K.W. (2002), 'Competition policy in Indonesia and the new anti-monopoly and fair competition law', *Bulletin of Indonesian Economic Studies*, **38**(3), 331–42.

Thee, K.W. (2006), 'SME promotion policies in Indonesia', *Private Sector Development in Indonesia*, Discussion Paper no. 46, Asian Development Bank Institute, Tokyo.

Urata, S. (2000), *Policy Recommendations for SME Promotion in the Republic of Indonesia*, report of JICA Senior Advisor to Coordinating Minister of Economy and Finance, and Industry, Tokyo, May

Van Diermen, P. (1997), *Small Business in Indonesia*, Aldershot: Ashgate.

World Bank (2005), *Raising Investment in Indonesia a Second Generation of Reforms*, Washington, DC: World Bank.

Yamamoto, I. (2001), 'The dynamism of small and medium enterprise and inter-firm linkage in Indonesia', *Nippon*, **5**(1), 1–23.

13 Iran
Babak Fooladi and Martine Spence

Introduction

The Islamic Republic of Iran (hereafter referred to as Iran) is the eighteenth largest country in the world in terms of area covered (1 648 195 km²). The country is in Central Eurasia, and is located on the north-eastern shore of the Persian Gulf. The country is the world's fourth largest oil exporter and most of its economic activities are based on this sector. The main goals of the country's present Ninth Government (2005–09) are to reduce unemployment and diversify the economy, thus decreasing Iran's dependency on oil. Stimulation of entrepreneurship is among the policies proposed to achieve these goals.

In 2006/07, Iran's population was 70.5 million, of which 48.2 million were located in urban areas and the remainder in the rural parts of the country. According to the Labour Force Survey published by the Statistical Center of Iran (SCI), the Iranian unemployment rate stood at 12.1 percent in the winter of 2006/07, unchanged from the same period the previous year. Broken down demographically, unemployment was 13.8 percent in urban areas and 8.8 percent in rural areas. Three reasons could account for the lower unemployment rate in the rural areas: (1) the high incidence of agricultural activities; (2) a higher population of females involved in agricultural activities than in various productive activities in urban areas; and (3) the migration of villagers to urban areas.

Iran's economy has been growing for at least the last 10 years. It continued its upward trend in 2006/07. Using 1997/98 constant price indices, gross domestic product (GDP) grew by 6.1 percent in 2006/07 over the previous year. Meanwhile growth in non-oil GDP, reached 6.6 percent over the same period. Several reasons could account for the increase in production in the review year. These reasons include, but are not limited to, spin-offs from the oil, manufacturing and mining sectors along with some services sectors such as trade, transport, storage and communications and financial services. Using the same data, the percentage of GDP increase attributable to the agriculture, oil, services, and manufacturing sectors were 0.7, 0.3, 3.4 and 1.7[1] respectively. Figure 13.1 shows the contribution of GDP growth in percentages from each individual sector of the economy.

The economic activity of the country is governed by socio-economic plans. The first of these plans covered the period 1980 to 1984 and its goal was to revive the economy. Iran is now in its Fourth Socio-economic Plan, a key objective of which is to reduce the unemployment rate from 12.1 percent to 8.4 percent by 2010. Careful and detailed government initiatives have been developed to reduce unemployment to such a level. These initiatives are as follows:

1. Incentives for the creation of employment by SMEs.
2. Technical and credit assistance to the private and cooperative sectors.
3. Loan facilities extended by banks to small and medium enterprises (SMEs).

A more detailed exploration of this last initiative follows.

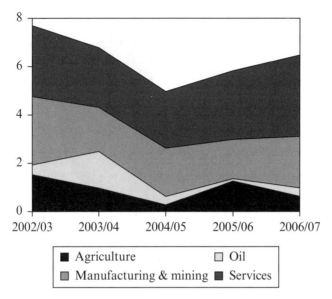

Source: *Annual Report of the Central Bank of Iran, 2006/2007.*

Figure 13.1   Contribution to GDP growth in percentages

Government policy on small and medium enterprises and entrepreneurship

Iran's classification of SMEs corresponds to what would be considered micro and small enterprises (MSE) in other countries. Micro firms are firms with fewer than 10 employees and small firms employ fewer than 50 persons. So far the Iranian government has not segregated any data that relates to enterprises which are so-called medium and employ 50 to 249 people. These data are aggregated with data pertaining to larger firms. Micro and small enterprises are mainly under the jurisdiction of two ministries, the Ministry of Industries and Mines (MIM) for industrial firms and the Ministry of Commerce (MOC) for service firms. According to information provided by the MIM, 70 000 to 74 000 industrial units are active under its supervision. Ninety-five percent of those units employ up to 50 persons, and the rest, which consists of almost 4000 units, are considered to be medium and large businesses. The MOC oversees and regulates 400 000 to 500 000 services, trade-related enterprises, and micro-level workshops which employ an average of 1.97 workers. The majority of firms in Iran are MSEs and in 2003 this sector generated about 1.3 million jobs.

Large public and quasi-public enterprises make up approximately 80 percent of the Iranian economy. This is largely due to those businesses engaged in exploiting, processing and trading crude oil, petroleum products and natural gas. Even though the vast majority of businesses in Iran are classified as micro, small, and medium enterprises, the heavy dependency of the country's economy on oil has created an environment that requires an extensive revision to diversify from a single pole commodity economy dependency. Several programs were put in place with this aim.

Article 44 of the Constitution deals with privatization. According to this Article, 80 percent of the shares of public owned enterprises should be transferred into private hands. Given the present preponderance of the public sector in the economy, increased

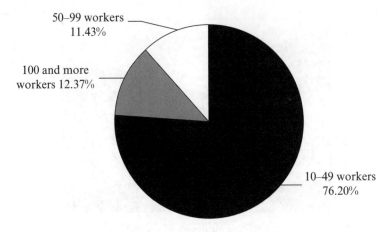

50–99 workers
11.43%

100 and more
workers 12.37%

10–49 workers
76.20%

Source: Iran Statistical Yearbook (2007).

Figure 13.2   Distribution of manufacturing establishments with 10 or more workers by size in 2006/07

participation of the private sector is expected to enhance productivity and enforce fiscal discipline. Implementing the policies set out in the Fourth Socio-economic Plan will be possible only if privatization occurs as planned. All of these in return should help to, eventually, remove economic bottlenecks, despite the international sanctions put in place by Western powers due to concerns with Iran's nuclear program. It is important to note, however, that even without various economic reforms the situation of the SME sector would greatly improve if this dispute were resolved.

Article 3 of the Executive By-law, approved in November 2005, emphasizes the development of credit facilities aimed at SMEs to support their expansion. Article 3 stated that 35 percent of the banking system credit capacity was required to be dedicated to SMEs. The banks' shares of the credits to be provided were almost $19 billion. The net worth of the projects which were submitted by the end of 2006/07 was $35 billion, of which the banks approved $14 billion. Of this amount, 48.8 percent was for enterprises with fewer than 10 employees and 51.2 percent for enterprises with 10 to 49 employees. During its course, the program resulted in the creation of 765 405 jobs, corresponding to an investment of about $12 000 per job. The manufacturing and mining sectors had the highest share of these funds, with 48.9 percent of the total. Figures 13.2 and Table 13.1 illustrate the distribution of manufacturing establishments with 10 or more workers by size and type of activities in 2006/07.

These initiatives had an impact on new firm creations and the deliverance of permits to establish new commercial entities. A total of 3194 new manufacturing facilities were established with investment of almost $5 billion. These figures show increases of 4.8 percent in number of establishments and 63.2 percent in investment compared with the previous year. Investment was highest in facilities for the production of chemical products and accounted for 33.8 percent of total investment in the establishment of new manufacturing units.

The number of permits delivered to establish new commercial entities amounted to

Table 13.1   Distribution of manufacturing establishments with 10 or more workers by type of activities

Type of activities	%
Manufacture of food products and beverages	17
Manufacture of textile	10
Manufacture of fabricated metal products, except machinery and equipment	8
Manufacture of machinery and equipment	7
Manufacture of rubber and plastic products	6
Manufacture of chemical and chemical products	6
Manufacture of basic metals	4
Manufacture of motor vehicles, trailers and semi-trailers	4
Manufacture of electrical machinery and apparatus	3
Manufacture of coke, refined petroleum products and nuclear fuel	1
Manufacture of other non-metallic mineral products	22
Other industries	12

Source: Iran Statistical Yearbook (2007).

54 300 in 2006/07, a 74 percent rise over the previous year. Investment based on these permits grew by 58 percent to $150 billion. Investments by the private sector increased by 27.7 percent in the same period, with a corresponding decrease in investment in the public sector. This is indicative of the investors' tendency toward investing in SMEs. Credits and financial aids were extended to the manufacturing and mining sectors by banks and credit institutions during 2006/07. While the trading and services industries remained one of the important pillars of a successful economy, the Iranian government made a special effort to promote development of a solid manufacturing infrastructure.

With a key part of the Iranian economy based on oil income, creating an environment that could focus on improving the situation of existing industries has been a major challenge for different governments. Overhauling, upgrading, and refurbishing the infrastructure for manufacturing-based industries remains a critical task that would benefit Iran's SME sector. Various development policies directly related to Iran's SMEs were developed using United Nations Industrial Development Organization (UNIDO) guidelines. However, these policies somehow lacked implementation due to the enormous oil income that was generated. More specifically, the funds were directed to specific regions and industrial estates, and not spread evenly across the country. These estates, nevertheless, have the potential to stimulate the operating environment of SMEs, and could be counted as a key success indicator. In addition to industrial estates, different forms of SME concentrations such as special economic zones; science, research, and technology parks; business incubation centers; and industrial clusters exist in Iran. Reducing the costs of infrastructure and logistics for the sector and thus increasing efficiency were and still are value-added benefits resulting from the concentration philosophy.

Despite all this, overall development policies and specifically SME strategies cannot be considered totally efficient mainly due to the fact that there is no particular policy of reducing the impact of the embargo on the country. Development of fundamental infrastructure for a strong economy such as building power plants, heavy industries and automobile industries were mainly in favor for specific regions and SMEs could not really play an active role in other parts of the country. Recent governments, however, have placed an emphasis on developing programs that could generate non-oil income. Providing policies and general guidelines to SMEs is considered a major path that could not only generate income but also reduce the unemployment rate. The Trade Promotion Organization (TPO) of Iran, an agency administered by the Ministry of Commerce, is actively seeking solutions that could increase exports of non-oil products. Since the majority of firms in Iran are SMEs, increasing exports will increase non-oil income significantly.

Policy formulation faced a new era in the history of Iran in 1996/97, almost eight years after the war between Iran and Iraq. It was then that many economic variables such as the exchange rate, non-controlled high inflation rate, and low per-capita income rate came under the government control through the Central Bank of Iran (CBI). It was also at that time that inflation reduced from 23.2 percent in 1996/97 to 12.6 percent in 2000/01. Having said that, increases in wage rates did not keep pace with inflation and deterioration of purchasing power ensued. Iran's ratio of total tax collected to GDP is in the order of 5–6 percent, which is low compared to countries with similar income level. Therefore, a major part of the government's revenue is still generated through oil and gas. However, a major policy reformulation is being drafted by the Ninth Government, which could bring Iran into a new economic era.

The environment for entrepreneurship and the state of small business in this country
As discussed earlier, Iran's export is heavily dependent on oil and gas products. According to available information, production of petroleum accounts for up to 80 percent of the country's export earnings and consists of 40–50 percent of the government's annual budget. The Iranian government realizes that a stronger economy relies on less oil and gas dependency and involving SMEs will in return increase the value of non-oil exports. Steps to decrease this dependency were taken in the Third Socio-economic Development Plan (2000/01–2004/05), which emphasized the reform of many of the trans-sectoral areas, all of them directly related to Iran's industrial development priorities.

These reforms touched upon: the reorganization, privatization, and management of state-owned enterprises; regulation of monopolies and promotion of competition in economic activities; employment policies specifically focused on youth and women; taxation, monetary, foreign exchange, and environmental policies; the reorganization of financial market; and, finally, the development of science and technology.

The plan's overriding aims were to eradicate poverty, specifically through employment generation; to reduce the country's economic dependence on oil revenues through the promotion of non-oil exports; and to start restructuring the institutional business framework in view of Iran's possible accession to the World Trade Organization (WTO). The International Labour Organization (ILO) puts great emphasis on job creation in small and medium enterprises in Iran since large sections of the workforce are created by this sector and hence a significant part of the employment generation would occur in MSEs. With regards to SMEs, the plan focused on self-employment, and entrepreneurial activities, especially among women. It implemented the establishment of Provincial Councils to attract private and cooperative investments.

The Fourth Socio-economic Development Plan (2005/06–2010/11) emphasizes the role of cooperatives to encourage productive employment in small and medium enterprises. More specifically, Article 39 of the Plan that relates to SMEs indicates that the government is bound to perform the following:

1. Facilitate the development of various networks and clusters between SMEs to further improve their technical knowledge and engineering background.
2. Help the SME sector to overcome its various obstacles to increase its competitiveness and further correct the economy's uni-polar structure.

In Iran, SMEs are not under the supervision of a specific government organization. Different government agencies have different responsibilities with respect to this sector of the economy, sometimes resulting in confusion when it comes to policy initiation.

As part of the employment promotion plan that was mentioned earlier, the Ministry of Industries and Mines provides loans of about $6000 without any collateral for hiring every new worker. In the 10 months after it was launched in 2002, this loan program was reported to have generated 26 000 additional jobs, and the Supreme Employment Council has extended this scheme for the creation of 100 000 extra jobs per year until 2010.

By the same token, during 2002–03 the Ministry of Labour and Social Affairs started to provide loans of about $3200 to entrepreneurs, with an attractive subsidized interest rate of 6 percent for recruiting every new individual worker. This program was called The Emergency Employment Scheme, and the CBI reviewed this program in 2005. Most of the workers interviewed by the CBI to evaluate this scheme were satisfied. It was also found that, of the 8000 units that benefited from the program, 92 percent were still in operation two to three years later.[2]

Though measuring the success of such programs at a national level requires an extensive systematic bureaucratic organization since it is important to evaluate the sustainability of the jobs created, the CBI is in favour of pursuing them. Other similar programs were also offered by the Ministry of Agriculture and the Ministry of Cooperatives to further reduce the unemployment rate. Moreover, several tax and discount incentives were offered by different organizations to promote SMEs' and MSEs' activities. These incentives are mainly designed to promote exports.

Different financial aids to small enterprises are provided via the Ministry of Commerce and the Ministry of Labour and Social Affairs. The annual national budget passed by Parliament determines the allowable amount to be distributed to these enterprises. There are also certain agreements between different banks and government organizations. Through these agreements, SMEs are introduced to various banks by different government agencies or act independently depending upon their annual revenue.

In Iran, different layers of government organizations are responsible for training skilled workers for the SME sector. The different technology universities established before 1979 were replaced by various engineering universities after the revolution. Research activities on different sectors of the industry are provided by engineering research institutes which are ruled and governed by specific universities across the country. More precisely the public vocational-technical educational system in Iran consists of four programs. Among these is a two-year package standing halfway between high school and university education. The degree sought in this program is either an Associate of Arts and/or Science degree. This program is ruled and administered by the Ministry of Education. There also exists another program that is offered through a network of public and private non-degree institutions and is administered by the Ministry of Labour. Impressively enough, an analysis that was conducted by the Technical Vocational Training Organization (TVTO) indicates that there are 456 of the latter non-degree centers offering 712 types of courses and employing 13 000 people in 22 different provinces. Furthermore, the Management and Planning Office (MPO) provides $3200 to educate youths who are interested in establishing their own enterprises. Other educational institutions such as Jehad-e-Daneshgahi provide short courses in business to young entrepreneurs.

Internationalization of entrepreneurs and SMEs
Small enterprises are mainly located within the cities since they are not harmful for the environment and the majority of these small industrial units provide the market with local goods. Lack of manufacturing networking mechanisms such as industrial clusters appears to be one of the major problems that these enterprises are currently faced with. As a result, the trade promotion organization (TPO) of Iran is developing consortia to help groups of small firms to export.

The Export Development Bank of Iran has recently launched new programs which provide SME owners who are promoting non-oil products exports with various forms of financial assistance. Furthermore, traditional financial aids could be provided to these units in accordance with Islamic banking regulations.

As stated earlier, the Iranian government has started to steer its focus towards improving the situation of non-oil products for further enhancement of the economic growth of the country. The policies of Iran's Ninth Government, which was in power when this chapter was written, reflect this focus. The non-oil Supreme Export Council Cabinet members adopted various policies in August of 2007 geared towards promoting the export of various SMEs products. A list of the most important policies follows:

1. Providing aids to SMEs that could promote export status of various non-oil products.
2. Promoting service sector exports while considering techno-engineering services as the number one priority.
3. Providing various aids for further export of value-added products.
4. Developing the country's export infrastructure.
5. Providing aid for SMEs to attend non-oil product export exhibitions held outside of the country.
6. Providing aids for the creation of different industrial clusters, establishment of export management companies, large exporting companies, and export consortia.
7. Providing partial payments of export insurance, shipping cost, and warranties that should be issued for exporting different products.

It is important to note that the TPO of Iran is developing industrial clusters to enhance and further improve the export situation of the non-oil products. Some of these clusters are still at their pilot stages and they require maturity. More importantly, creating a cooperative atmosphere will be taken as the number one priority, which the government is considering very seriously.

Conclusion

Despite the fact that Iran is categorized as a developing nation, the country is flourishing with all essential resources (human, natural, and so on) that could bring its economy into the next phase. Achieving such a goal requires substantial productivity increase within the SME sector.

Acknowledgement

Writing this book chapter would not have been possible without the help of many individuals, and organizations who all tried their best to provide an updated image of the Iranian economy and specifically the SME situation in this country. Specifically we would like to express our sincere gratitude towards Dr Mohammad Mousavi (University of Tehran, Faculty of World Studies), and Dr Kambiez Talebi (University of Tehran, Faculty of Entrepreneurship).

Notes

1. In some parts inconsistency may exist due to rounding. The authors are not responsible for any of the data generation that is reported in this report.
2. The latest available data relates to the year of 2005 and corresponds to the end of the Eighth Government era.

14 Israel

Liora Katzenstein, Eli Gimmon, Eyal Benjamin and Itay Friedberg

Introduction

Israel is a unique phenomenon among the world's nations, as it is a country built on an ideology and a religion. The country has its origins in the times of the Bible, some 3000 years ago. The 'Jewish Temple' in the land of the Bible has been destroyed several times over and its inhabitants were sent to exile in neighboring countries, from where they emigrated worldwide, creating today's 'Jewish Diaspora'.

In the 1880s Jews, seeking escape from persecution in Eastern Europe, began migrating back to their homeland, then an Arabic-speaking part of the Ottoman Empire. Following World War I (WWI), Britain replaced the Ottoman Empire as the ruler of Palestine.

In 1917, Britain issued the Balfour Declaration, stating support for a Jewish homeland in Palestine. Following the end of WWI, Zionist immigration increased, confronting increased violence from local Arab communities. As a result of the Holocaust in World War II (WWII), pressure grew for the international recognition of a Jewish state, and in 1947 the United Nations (UN) proposed the partition of the Palestine Mandate into two states, one Jewish and one Arab. The Arab states rejected partition and invaded Palestine as soon as the British withdrew, in 1948.

Following the war of independence (the first of seven more wars that plagued the country on average once a decade), the modern state of Israel was declared on 14 May 1948. This very small country, of about 20 000 square kilometers, and no land access for its goods, began the struggle of its physical and economical survival. At that time, the country numbered some 600 000 inhabitants, and its major economic activities were agriculture related, with exports of about US$500 000. Its capital was the divided city of Jerusalem, with a wall in its center.

Some 60 years later, in 2008, the country boasts more than 7 million inhabitants with exports coming close to US$60 billion, 60 percent of which were high-technology (high-tech) products and less than 3 percent were agricultural produce, and a gross domestic product (GDP) per capita of about US$22 000.

In 2007, Israel enjoyed a literacy level of over 90 percent, the highest percentage of engineers in workforce worldwide, second place in scientific publications worldwide and one of the highest levels of economic growth in the Western world, around 4 percent. Since the early 1990s, Israel enjoys a massive influx of capital into its economy and capital markets. In 2005 alone, the country enjoyed foreign direct investment of US$6 billion.

In 2006, Israel ranked 19 out of 121 countries in the global business competitiveness index of the World Economic Forum (up from its 2005 rank, which was 22) compared with a rank of 25 for Korea, 27 for India and 64 for China (Figure 14.1).

Table 14.1   Economic development in Israel through five years: 2003 to 2007

Criteria	2003	2004	2005	2006	2007
GDP (current prices in $ billion)	115.4	128.9	129.7	140.5	148.5
GDP real growth rate (%)	1.3	4.3	5.2	5.1	5.3
GDP per capita (current prices, $000)	17.3	18.2	18.9	20.1	22.5
GDP per capita growth rate (%)	−0.5	3.0	3.5	3.4	3.4
Exports of goods and services ($ billion)	43.5	52.8	57.9	62.6	61.0
Imports of goods and services ($ billion)	44.4	52.3	57.5	61.7	64.1
Unemployment rate (%)	10.7	10.4	9.0	8.4	7.3
Inflation rate (CPI, end of year, %)	−1.9	1.2	2.4	−0.1	3.4
Current account (% of GDP)	0.5	0.4	3.3	6.0	3.1

Sources: State of Israel, Ministry of Finance, International Affairs Department, Economic talking points, 6 May 2007; Central Bureau of Statistics; Bank of Israel; Ministry of Finance.

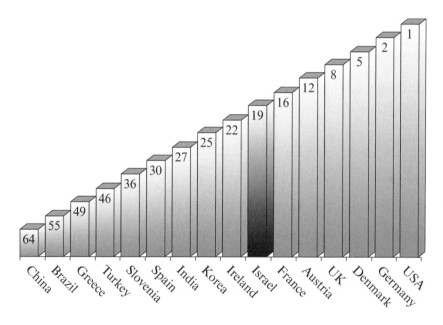

Sources: State of Israel, Ministry of Finance, International Affairs Department, Economic talking points, 6 May 2007; World Economic Forum, Global Competitiveness Index (GCI) 2006.

Figure 14.1   Business competitiveness index, 2006

Israel ranks second only to Canada, in terms of foreign presence on US stock exchanges with over 100 firms. It also has a strong presence in the stock exchanges of Europe and Asia.

This impressive growth comes with the cost of growing economic disparity. While the Israel of 1960 was a model of equality, today it is the country with the largest disparity between the haves and have nots, followed by the US.

Government policy on SMEs and entrepreneurship in Israel
Being surrounded by hostile countries, Israel had to become 'export oriented from day one'. The government has played a major role in creating the right infrastructure and atmosphere for the country's emerging SMEs and high-tech companies.

Immediately after the establishment of the state in 1948, the country has been spending a major part of the reparation money received from Germany (as compensation for life and property loss during the WWII Holocaust) on the creation of a modern infrastructure, including roads, ports, rail roads, construction plants, and so on.

One has to remember that Israel's economic profile has developed from a socialist, Eastern European-like economy in its first years to a fully fledged capitalist state today. Accordingly, the role of the government has evolved from one of regulator to that of a facilitator.

In its early years, Israel's economy was marked by large state-owned companies, such as Israel's electric company, Israel's national water company, Israel military industries, and so on, most of which still exist today, but have lost a lot of their prominence. Needless to say, small businesses were not encouraged during the early years of statehood (Dana, 1999). Rather, they were neglected and even punished by special tax rates, bureaucratic red tape and punitive levels of value added and national insurance taxation. Ideologically, small business owners were regarded as 'capitalists', who should not be appreciated as much as their 'real' pioneers who were the members of the communal agricultural settlements in the forms of 'Moshavim' and 'Kibutzim', and obviously, the revered members of the Israel Defense Force (IDF).

In order to promote export-oriented industries, the Israeli government created the Office of the Chief Scientist (OCS) at the Ministry of Industry and Trade in the early 1970s, with the role of supporting the country's nascent high-tech industry through monetary grants and tax incentives. By 2008, the ministry has added many other successful programs, such as the Incubators, Bi-national Funds, and the Export Institute. With a budget of about US$300 million, the OCS is able to co-fund hundreds of small and larger high-tech companies. While the OCS together with the Bi-National Funds provide conditional grants to high-tech companies every year, the Export Institute and its affiliates, subsidize export-related activities of SMEs and high-tech companies.

In addition, the country boasts a vibrant and vigorous venture capital industry, with over 50 funds, most of which include international participation of major foreign players, such as Benchmark, Sequoia and Apex. This industry was actually created by the Israeli government who established the first venture capital fund 'YOZMA' in 1993, with joint government and private funding, totaling US$200 million.

Israel serves as a world model in the establishment and operation of technological incubators where the government supports 100 percent of the infrastructure and operating costs for a period of two years, with a sum of US$300000. Originally established in the early 1990s to support technologically trained Russian immigrants, the 30 incubators which are spread throughout the country, supply an umbrella and nurturing environment for high-tech entrepreneurs.

In addition, since the early 1990s, Israel has enjoyed a remarkable opening to the world with newly established diplomatic relations with Asian (China, India, and so on) and North African (Morocco, Tunisia, and so on) countries. This new opening to the world also encourages major multinational companies to set up production and/or research and development (R&D) facilities in Israel. These companies, including IBM, Motorola, Intel, and Siemens, enjoy government grants and tax breaks in the country's periphery. This move was followed by important international service companies such as major law, accounting and investment banking firms.

The environment for entrepreneurship and the state of small business in the country
The Israeli economy enjoyed annual growth of 5.2 percent in 2005 and 5.1 percent in 2006, well above the average global growth of 3.5 percent and 4.1 percent in same years.

Trajtenberg (2006: 4) stated that 'the Israeli economy offers a fascinating illustration of extraordinary success in innovation, particularly in Information and Communication Technologies (ICT), which came largely as a result of a concerted, long term strategy of government support for commercial R&D, which levered the potential of a highly skilled labor force'. The Israeli military and security industry and its graduates' experience is one of the major sources for technological innovation applied in commercial products.

The entrepreneurial environment is present with various indices of the entrepreneurship activities based on launching new start-ups along with the status of new ventures, i.e. up to 42 months old. According to the Global Entrepreneurship Monitor (GEM) report of Israel (Menipaz et al., 2008) the Total Entrepreneurship Activity (TEA) in 2007 was 5.4 percent of the workforce (18 to 64 years old) which represents the prevalence rate of people who are involved in entrepreneurial activity as a nascent entrepreneur or an owner-manager of a new business. The GEM global 2007 report (Bosma et al., 2008) shows that the Israeli TEA rate is higher than that of Russia (2.7 percent) and Japan (4.3 percent), but lower than the TEA of India (8.5 percent), the US (9.6 percent), and China (16.4 percent).

In the Israeli workforce the rate of nascent entrepreneurs (planners of new business) was 3.6 percent, the rate of new firm (between 4 and 42 months old) entrepreneurs was 2.0 percent, and the rate of entrepreneurs who own and manage their established business for more than 42 months was 2.4 percent. Starting new businesses is segregated by motive of either opportunity or necessity.

In Israel, the motive of opportunity (as opposed to necessity) consisted 75 percent of the TEA, the same level as in the well developed countries. Females comprised one-third of the entrepreneurs in 2007. Some 13.3 percent of the entrepreneurs define their business as high-tech new business, and 31 percent of the entrepreneurs expect an export rate of 25 percent to 100 percent.

Some 11.4 percent of the new businesses offer a unique product with no known competition. Additionally, 28.5 percent of new businesses expect to employ at least 20 employees in the next five years.

As a result of massive immigration of close to 1 million highly educated people from the former Soviet Union, the OCS established a network of technological incubators throughout Israel. Generous grants of 85 percent of the cost of each project to a maximum of US$300000 for a period of two years were provided to eligible new ventures. Since 2003 the management and ownership of the different incubators has been partially and gradually privatized. The program is considered highly successful in encouraging technological new ventures in Israel.

Another government fund is the Magnet Program (translated abbreviation for 'R&D

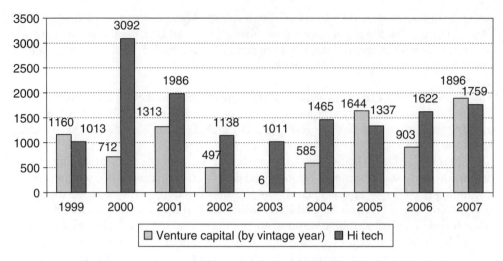

Source: Israel Venture Capital Research Centre – Year book 2008, www.ivc-online.com.

Figure 14.2   Capital raised by Israeli venture capital funds and high-tech companies (US$ million)

for Generic Technologies') which supports the formation of consortia involving cooper-ation between several academic research groups and industrial entities. Each consortium deals with a different subject mostly in the field of information technology or biotech-nology. The Magnet annual budget is US$50 million. Grants are averaged between half to US$1 million per participant and may cover up to 66 percent of the approved R&D expenses. Participants are not required to repay any royalties.

In 2008, there are about 50 venture capital funds operating in Israel. In the last 12 years the total capital raised was about US$10 billion with investments made in more than 1000 Israeli start-up companies. Since 1993, the average size of the leading Israeli venture capitalist (VC) fund, jumped from US$20 million in 1993 to more than US$250 million in 2007. Israeli VCs invest exclusively in start-up companies engaged in the devel-opment of technological innovation with global application in areas of:

- communication
- computer software
- IT
- semiconductors
- life sciences – medical devices and biotechnology
- homeland security.

In order to encourage foreign investments, Israel signed agreements of avoidance of double taxation with 42 countries worldwide, including the world's big seven economies. Foreign direct investments (FDI) in Israel fell by 32 percent in the year 2007 to US$9.7 billion, still an impressive figure considering the size of Israel's economy. In 2006, FDI reached the highest ever level of US$14.2 billion with a growth rate of close to 200 percent from 2005 (as can be seen in Figure 14.3).

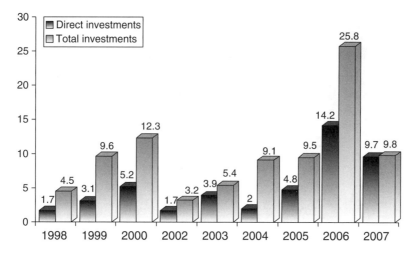

Note: The trend of buying Israeli start-up companies has continued throughout 2007.

Source: Ministry of Finance.

Figure 14.3 Foreign investments (US$ billion)

The FDI decline in 2004 can be explained by the fact that in 2004 there were important investments that were executed only in the first quarters of 2005. In the first four months of 2005 alone, FDI grew 1.5 times compared with 2004, mostly in non-publicly traded Israeli companies that grew by 227 percent (from US$637 million to US$2.1 billion) from 2004 to the first four month of 2005. These high levels of FDI are forecast (Bank of Israel, 2007) to continue in coming years due to macroeconomic stability, manpower quality, R&D formation, and the continuing process of privatization.

The above mentioned indicators signal foreign confidence in the Israeli economy and provide supportive environment for starting new businesses. Another indicator for foreign confidence in the Israeli economy is the upgrading in credit rating obtained in February 2008 from the international rating agency, Fitch, for Israel's foreign currency credit rating from A- to a stable A, and local currency credit rating from A to a stable A+. Stable A is the highest rating Israel has received from the agency since Fitch began rating it in 1995.

Traditional businesses are not eligible for the Chief Scientist grants, which are available only for high-technology SMEs. Non-technological SMEs can apply to the Authority For Small Businesses which deploys local offices around the country. Among the services are the Israel Small Medium Enterprise Association (ISMEA), with headquarters in Tel-Aviv, and close to 20 service offices called MATI, that is, 'Center for nurturing new businesses'. These centers are conceived as one-stop shops for small businesses and use a variety funds for supplying loans to the local SMEs. Usually loans under 70 000 NIS (about US$20 000) require a personal guarantee in addition to two external guarantors, while loans over 70 000 NIS require collateral. The terms of the loans offered by MATIs are better than bank loans.

In a roundtable discussion regarding high-growth entrepreneurship reported by Science Business (Hudson et al., 2007), the panellists listed the nurturing factors

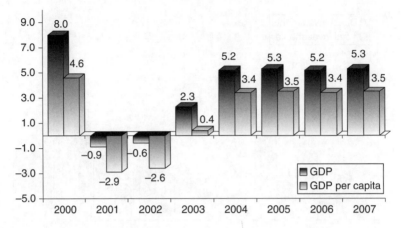

Note: Growth forecasts for 2008 suggest Israel has yet to achieve its full potential.

Source: Central Bureau of Statistics, Ministry of Finance.

Figure 14.4   GDP and GDP per capita (annual rate of change, %, in constant prices

required for high-growth entrepreneurs. Most of these factors actually exist in the Israeli environment:

- A thriving ecosystem where businesses get networks of suppliers, researchers and customers – these networks are strong in Israel.
- Financial backing – a large number of venture funds along with governmental funds (Incubators program, Tnufa, Nofar, Heznek) are available for start-ups. Agreements for industrial R&D with 19 countries facilitate funding of start-ups.
- An open market with minimal restrictions and room for manoeuver – the local Israeli market is unrestricted in most business sectors (except power and water supplies). Six free trade agreements (including USA, European Union, and the European Free Trade Association – EFTA) extend market opportunities.
- 'Big brothers' – although big sheltering corporations rarely exist in Israel, the availability of a large number of foreign corporations such as Microsoft, IBM and so on may compensate.
- A big local market – though the Israeli market is relatively small, it is compensated by abundant export opportunities.

The GDP per capita 10-year growth in Israel fell from 26.9 percent during 1987–96 to 10.9 percent during 1997–2006. However, between 2003 and 2007 the Israeli economy experienced five years of consecutive growth, as shown in the Figure 14.4. During 2007, Israel's GDP grew by 5.31 percent to US$162 billion in comparison to 3.5 percent of the world average growth. This growth is due to the improvement in national security, governmental tax and capital reforms, as well as privatization policy, exports by the high-technology sector, and global economy conditions (Landa and Even, 2007).

However, in 2008 the Israeli Ministry of Finance forecast a drop in GDP growth to 2.4 percent due to (1) the revaluation of the local currency (Shekel) in relation to foreign currency (from January 2006 to February 2008 5.3 percent against the euro and 22.8 percent against the US dollar) and to (2) the high growth in recent years and exploitation of excess resources which cyclically resulted in a reduced rate of growth (Geva, 2008).

The global competitiveness report 2006/07 of the World Economic Forum ranked Israel second (after Finland) in the world by the availability of scientists and engineers index; second in the world (after the USA) for venture capital availability; third (after New Zealand and Hong Kong) in strength of investor protection; and eighth (after Germany, Japan, Sweden, Finland, Switzerland, Denmark, France, and before the USA) in the world by the capacity of innovation. Israel's ranking in public institutions was twenty-fourth, and in the macroeconomic index it was forty-third. The overall Global Competitiveness Index (GCI) ranking of Israel was seventeenth out of 125 countries – up one place from the previous year. Measuring the ease of starting a business, Israel was ranked 40 out of 58 countries in red-tape regulations and 13 out of the same 58 countries for ease of registering a new business (Bosma et al., 2008).

Internationalization of entrepreneurs and SMEs
The acquisition of the Israeli start-up Mirabilis by America On Line (AOL) in June 1998 for US$400 million, boosted the expectations from the high-tech start-up industry to new levels. The ICQ software messenger developed by Mirabilis was aiming at Internet users worldwide. This turning point had set three base rules which later came to be the drivers for the internationalization of the Israeli start-up industry: (1) the target market has to be global, (2) the distribution should be simple and (3) the venture should appeal to international players.

The information and communications technology (ICT) market was suitable for internationalization; hence building on ICT was a classic arena for young start-ups, fuelled by fantastic exit stories, focusing their R&D efforts towards ICT. According to the Israeli Central Bureau of Statistics, the export of ICT surged from US$8 billion in 1997 to US$16 billion in 2006, representing a growth rate of 17 percent to 26 percent of total Israeli export.

This explosion of ICT technologies was noticed by global IT and communications corporations, who scanned Israel for innovation-led solutions. The result is about 110 international research centers operating in Israel, most of them as a result of international corporations (such as Intel, Microsoft, Google) acquiring Israeli companies.

According to the Israel Venture Capital (IVC) 2006 report, 76 deals, adding up to more than US$10 billion worth of mergers and acquisitions were made by international corporations in Israel during 2006. The large number of Israeli public companies in North America, Europe and Asia in relation to Israel's small number of population (about 7 million people) can explain its influence on high-technology business culture worldwide.

The focus towards international customers, as well as a potential financial exit to an international player, and large exposure to global corporations, has led Israeli start-ups to think, talk and act global from their inception.

Conclusion
High-technology entrepreneurship in Israel is successful in many aspects. When it comes to entrepreneurial infrastructure, the similarities between the Silicon Valley in California and the high-tech industrial centers in Israel are certainly striking (*The Economist*, 2008).

Some of the policies and processes initiated in Israel for fostering high-tech entrepreneurship were adopted elsewhere in Asia.

For example, the Israeli incubator model was adopted in Singapore and Korea, and the Israeli model of 'Yozma' venture capital fund was used in establishing the Korean VC industry. In addition, joint R&D funds were established between Israel and Singapore and between Israel and Taiwan.

Reviewing economic events in Israel through the last decades, the following elements may explain its out-performance of high-technology entrepreneurship:

- The fact that Israel is surrounded by hostile nations, means that it does not have nearby available export markets and must, therefore, be export oriented from day one.
- The fact that every young person must join the Israel Defense Force at the age of 18, means that the country possesses a huge supply of potential high-tech mavericks. Promising young technologists receive special advanced scientific training as well as access to large-scale state-of-the-art projects. This, in turn, fosters teamwork and leadership capabilities.
- During the last three decades, Israel has managed to successfully transfer state-of-the-art technological developments, especially in the areas of software, communications and Internet to civilian use. Additionally, a successful pattern of cooperation between military, academic and industrial R&D has been developed.
- Israel's research universities and MBA programs have been a source of excellence for the development of highly qualified scientists and managers.
- Since the early 1960s, Israel's government has put forward a large number of programs for the encouragement of capital investments (Approved Enterprise, and so on) and for scientific R&D (Office of the Chief Scientist, Incubators, Bi-national Funds, the Export Institute and so on) and initiated the local venture capital industry through the 'Yozma' fund.
- The promise for the resolution of the conflict with its Arab neighbors, coupled with the hope for 'A New Middle East' in the early 1990s, has resulted in the establishment of political and economic relations with countries in Asia (India, China, and so on), East Europe and North Africa that previously had no connection to Israel.
- The influx of close to a million highly trained scientists and engineers from the former Soviet Union into Israel in the early 1990s has supplied the country with a vast resource of technical and technological know-how at a low cost.
- The booming of technological start-up companies, who found easy access to capital markets (mostly National Association of Securities Dealers Automated Quotations – NASDAQ), afterwards being known as 'The Bubble Period' of the late 1990s, enabled tens of Israeli companies to raise considerable amounts of money internationally, mostly in the United States.
- The Free Trade Agreements that Israel enjoys with the United States and Europe, provide its products and services with preferential treatment, and hence price advantages, in these two huge marketplaces.

The situation today is that Israeli entrepreneurs tend to sell out early mostly to big foreign firms rather than to build up their companies to capacity. Therefore, Israel is currently an exporter of start-ups and an R&D center for large technology firms (*The Economist*, 2008).

References
Bank of Israel (2007), *Annual Report 2007*, Jerusalem: Bank of Israel.
Bosma, N., K. Jones, E. Autio and J. Levie (2008), *Global Entrepreneurship Monitor, 2007 Executive Report*, Wellesley, MA: Babson College and London: London Business School.
Dana, Léo-Paul (1999), 'Small business in Israel', *Journal of Small Business Management*, **37**(4), 73–9.
Geva, U. (2008), *Economic Highlights*, International Affairs Department, Ministry of Finance, Government of Israel.
Hudson, R., N. Moran and P. Wrobel (2007), *High-Growth Entrepreneurship – The Policy Challenge for Europe – Report of a Roundtable Discussion*, The Science Business Innovation Board, 20 June 2007, London: Science Business Publishing.
Landa, B. and S. Even (2007), *Israel Economy in the Era of Globalization* (in Hebrew), Tel Aviv: The Institute for National Security Studies.
Menipaz, E., Y. Avrahami and M. Lerner (2008), *Global Entrepreneurship Monitor, Israel – 2007*, Era Center for Business Technology and Society, Ben-Gurion University.
State of Israel, Ministry of Finance, International Affairs Department, Economic talking points, May 6 2007 (PPT Slide presentation pp. 1–38).
The Economist (2008), 'Land of milk and start-ups', 19 March.
Trajtenberg, M. (2006), *Innovation policy for Development: An Overview*, Haifa: Samuel Neaman Institute of the Technion – Israel Institute of Technology.

15 Japan[1]
Jane W. Lu and Paul W. Beamish

Introduction

With the decline in trade barriers and the advancement in technology, small and medium-sized enterprises (SMEs) are playing an increasingly important role in international markets (Oviatt and McDougall, 1994, 1999). As a consequence of this surge, the internationalization of SMEs began to attract greater levels of attention in both the entrepreneurship literature and the international business literature. This increased attention led to the birth of a new academic field: international entrepreneurship, which is at the intersection of the two literatures (McDougall and Oviatt, 2000).

Within this new yet fast-growing field, studies have looked at the internationalization of SMEs from a variety of countries. However, to the best of our knowledge, there is little systematic investigation on the internationalization of Japanese SMEs. Given the importance of Japan in the world economy and the dominance of SMEs in Japanese economy (Dana, 1998), such a study is much needed. In addition, most studies on the internationalization of SMEs tend to use cross-sectional data, probably due to the difficulties in locating the necessary data. As one of the first steps towards addressing these issues, this study examined 1118 foreign direct investments made by 221 Japanese SMEs during 1964–99. This longitudinal data allowed us to provide both a historical account and a detailed analysis of the internationalization process of SMEs. Specifically, we explore the characteristics and performance of Japanese SMEs' worldwide investments. We focus on Japanese SMEs' foreign direct investment (FDI) activities because Japan has been the second leading source of FDI flows, behind only the United States (UNCTAD, 2000) and because FDI entails higher risk and hence is more entrepreneurial in nature (Beamish and Lu, 2004).

In this examination, we answer questions concerning the form that Japanese SMEs' FDIs have taken, including such features as entry mode, investment size, control strategies and the sectors and regions in which investments have been made. Further, we explore questions concerning the organizational implications of these investments by looking at relationships between the characteristics of the investments and the performance of foreign subsidiaries.

We initiate our study with a description of the data and methodology for this research. We then proceed to an overview of the internationalization of Japanese SMEs in terms of the timing, the sectoral pattern and the location of Japanese SMEs' FDIs, followed by an examination of their foreign subsidiary characteristics (subsidiary age, investment size, control and entry mode) across major sectors and regions. Further, by attempting to link aspects of subsidiaries with performance, the conclusions of this study should have appeal to SME managers who have invested or are interested in making foreign investments.

Methodology

Data

We collected information on both Japanese SMEs and their international subsidiaries. The main source of Japanese parent company information is *Nikkei NEEDS* tapes, an electronic database compiled by Nihon Keizai Shinbun-sha. This database provides financial information on all Japanese firms listed on the Tokyo stock exchange. The *Nikkei NEEDS* tapes reports detailed firm-level information compiled from the firm's balance sheet and income statement and includes other supplementary data (for example, number of employees). Annual information can be traced since 1964 from this database. For this study, we used information up to the 2000 edition which provided information on more than 3000 publicly listed Japanese firms. Where required, additional parent company information was gathered from the *Analysts' Guide*, a publication by Daiwa Institute of Research, the *GlobalVantage* database and various editions of the *Japan Company Handbook*, all of which have a coverage of parent firms similar to that in the *Nikkei NEEDS* tapes.

The source of information for the foreign direct investment of Japanese firms is *Kaigai Shinshutsu Kigyou Souran, Kuni-Betsu*. This source is published by Toyo Keizai Inc., a large Japanese compiler and publisher of business-level, statistical and economic information. The data reported in *Kaigai Shinshutsu Kigyou Souran* was based on responses to questionnaires sent to all firms listed on Japanese stock exchanges, as well as to major unlisted firms. Researchers at Toyo Keizai used press releases, annual reports and telephone interviews to supplement the questionnaire data and to increase the comprehensiveness of the information reported in *Kaigai Shinshutsu Kigyou Souran*. The coverage of *Kaigai Shinshutsu Kigyou Souran* is close to the population of foreign subsidiaries for firms that responded to the survey (Yamawaki, 1991). In terms of the data in *Kaigai Shinshutsu Kigyou Souran*, it provides information on the date of establishment, the entry mode, the equity position and identity of the subsidiary's parents. It also reports the subsidiary's industry, its equity capital, sales, and total employment, the identity of joint venture partners, local and expatriate employment levels and subsidiary performance. For this study, the 1986, 1989, 1992, 1994, 1997, 1999 and 2001 editions were used to develop a relatively complete, longitudinal profile of Japanese SMEs' internationalization process. The 2001 edition of this data source provides information on more than 19 000 subsidiaries (both SMEs and large) of Japanese firms established in more than 100 countries in the world.

Sample

There is no generally accepted definition of SMEs. That most widely used in the entrepreneurship literature is the definition provided by the American Small Business Administration (SBA). The SBA defines SMEs as stand-alone enterprises with fewer than 500 employees (for example, Baird et al., 1994; Beamish and Lu, 2004; Wolff and Pett, 2000). As we use longitudinal data on Japanese firms and firm size changes over time, we need to define an SME at a specific time. We included a Japanese firm in the sample if its number of employees met the SBA's SME definition at the time of its first FDI. Please note that as number of employees can only be traced back to 1964, for firms who made FDIs prior to 1964, we used employee information of the first data year. In this way, we could make sure that our sample firms were SMEs when they started inter-nationalizing. Using these criteria, we identified 221 Japanese SMEs with 1118 overseas subsidiaries. In the analyses that follow, some of the 1118 subsidiaries were removed from the sample because of incomplete data on individual variables. On average, in the full sample, the response rate was 30 percent for the performance measure and 90 percent or higher for all other variables.

The data description that follows is primarily descriptive, utilizing charts and tables to portray a general picture of the internationalization of Japanese SMEs. The form of analysis on subsidiary characteristics and their association with performance in later sections is exploratory, and is supplemented by statistical tests to substantiate differences and relationships.

An overview of the internationalization of Japanese firms

Timing of internationalization
All foreign investments by listed Japanese SMEs in our sample were made after the Second World War. The earliest were made in 1952 as a holding company in France. The second one was in 1954 in the industrial machinery industry in Australia. The third was in 1955 in the real estate industry in the United Sates. Figure 15.1 depicts the timing and the flow of Japanese SMEs' FDIs since 1964 when the flow became continuous. It shows both the number of Japanese SMEs who made their first FDIs and the number of FDIs established by Japanese SMEs in each year. The pattern of these two lines are qualitatively consistent.

The overall pattern of these two lines shows an accelerating rate of internationaliza-tion of Japanese SMEs over time, consistent with findings in studies using non-Japanese samples (that is, Hisrich et al., 1996; Oviatt and McDougall, 1994, 1999; Zahra et al., 2000). Within this general pattern, however, there were two setbacks in the flow of Japanese firms who established their first FDIs. The rate of newly internationalizing Japanese SMEs and the number of newly established FDIs by Japanese SMEs increased slowly but steadily in the 1970s, accelerated in the 1980s and reached its first peak in 1990, when 14 Japanese SMEs made their initial FDIs and 85 FDIs were established by Japanese SMEs. The onset of the 1990s saw a rapid decline in the rate of internationali-zation by Japanese SMEs. This was followed by an increase in the number of interna-tionalizing Japanese SMEs and the number of FDIs by Japanese SMEs which reached its second peak in 1996 when 16 Japanese SMEs initiated their FDI activities and 91 FDIs were made by Japanese SMEs. This second upward trend was short as it was followed by another sharp decline in the late 1990s.

The overall pattern of the timing of Japanese SMEs' overseas investment is closely related to the development of the Japanese economy. After 1950, the Japanese economy recovered from the Second World War and experienced a period of fast economic growth. Being the backbone of the industrial sector in Japan, Japanese SMEs were encouraged to expand into foreign countries (Bird, 2002). The surge in the number of newly internationalizing Japanese SMEs and the number of FDIs by Japanese SMEs during the second half of the 1980s was reflective of the 'bubble economy' in Japan where firms were influenced by an over-heated economy and easy money. Some firms pursued expansion without much regard for their resources and capabilities. The sharp decline

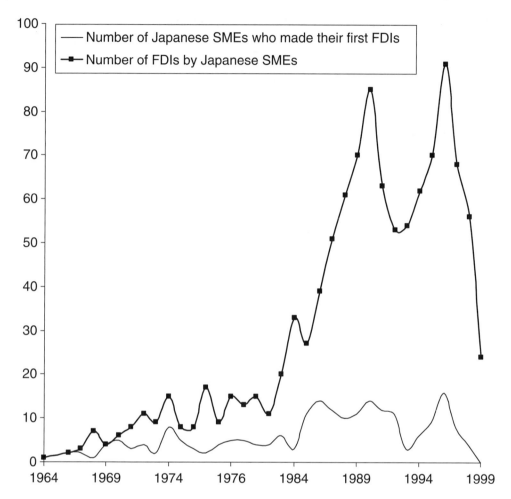

Sources: Toyo Keizai (1986, 1989, 1992, 1994, 1997, 1999, 2001).

Figure 15.1   Timing of the internationalization of Japanese SMEs

in investment in the first half of the 1990s showed the effects of the burst of the 'bubble economy' on Japanese firms in terms of their internationalization. There was another sharp investment surge in the mid-1990s which was followed by a quick decline with the onset of the 1997 Asian financial crisis.

Sectoral pattern
The Japanese SMEs' international subsidiaries in the sample were classified into one of 10 broad industry categories. Table 15.1 provides a breakdown of Japanese SMEs' FDIs by industry and by time periods. The sectoral pattern in Table 15.1 shows that investments have been made in all ten broad Standard Industrial Classification (SIC) industry categories. While Japanese SMEs' FDI had wide industry coverage, it was not evenly distributed across all sectors. Japanese SMEs' FDIs were concentrated in the manufacturing

Table 15.1   Sector of Japanese SMEs' international subsidiaries

Sector	Before 1970	1970–79	1980–89	1990–99	Total
Agriculture, forestry and fishing	0	2	7	5	14
Mining	0	0	3	2	5
Construction	0	0	3	4	7
Manufacturing	14	48	149	290	501
Transportation	0	3	4	12	19
Wholesale trade	9	41	114	177	341
Retail trade	0	3	8	25	36
Finance, insurance and real estate	3	4	25	67	99
Services	0	5	27	62	94
Total	26	106	340	644	1116

Table 15.2   Region of Japanese SMEs' international subsidiaries

Region	Before 1970	1970–79	1980–89	1990–99	Total
Asia	15	46	128	355	544
North America	9	33	116	139	297
Europe	1	11	72	120	204
South/Latin America	0	8	8	17	33
Oceania	1	7	15	11	34
Africa/Middle East	0	1	1	4	6
Total	26	106	340	646	1118

industry and wholesale trade, which respectively accounted for 45 percent and 31 percent of all Japanese SMEs' overseas subsidiaries. This pattern is consistent across different time periods. The motivations behind overseas production are well documented. For example, the establishment of production-oriented subsidiaries in foreign countries helped to circumvent trade barriers erected by the foreign governments. Japanese SMEs could also take advantage of location-specific resources, such as competitively priced labor forces, in China and Southeast Asia. The nature of the wholesale trade sector meant that the firms in this industry were at the forefront of internationalization because they had the most extensive exposure and connections to foreign markets.

Location pattern
Table 15.2 decomposes the number of entries by region over different time periods. The six regions specified in this table conform to the breakdown of regions provided in Toyo Keizai (2001). Seven regions were specified in Toyo Keizai (2001); however, because of the small numbers of entries made into Africa and the Middle East, these categories were combined in the table. When assigning countries to regions, the categorization procedure used in Toyo Keizai (2001) was followed.

A comparison across different columns in Table 15.2 indicates that overall, the most popular investment region among Japanese SMEs was Asia which was home to 49 percent of the subsidiaries in this study's database. North America and Europe were

Table 15.3   Top six host countries of Japanese SMEs' international subsidiaries

Before 1970	1970–79	1980–89	1990–99	Total
Taiwan	USA	USA	USA	USA
USA	Singapore	Taiwan	China	China
Hong Kong	Korea	United Kingdom	Hong Kong	Hong Kong
	Hong Kong	Hong Kong	Singapore	Singapore
	Brazil	Singapore	Thailand	Taiwan
	Germany	Germany	Malaysia	United Kingdom

the next two most popular regions, respectively receiving 26 percent and 18 percent of cumulative investment from Japanese SMEs by the end of 2000. Three other regions, South and Latin America, Oceania and Africa/Middle East accounted for the remaining 7 percent of Japanese SMEs' direct investment.

Another observation from Table 15.2 is that the regional preference of Japanese investors changes over time. Although Asia has been the major destination of Japanese SMEs' FDI throughout all time periods, the gap in terms of the number of FDIs between Asia and North America was minimal before 1990s. In the 1990s, Asia attracted increasingly much larger shares of Japanese SMEs' FDIs and the gap between Asia and North America as host region for Japanese SMEs' international subsidiaries widened significantly. The change in Japanese SMEs' FDI location preference is consistent with Asia's growing prominence as a major recipient region of worldwide FDI (UNCTAD, 2000).

At the country level, the ten most popular host countries to Japanese SMEs' FDIs (cumulatively) are USA, China, Hong Kong, Singapore, Taiwan, the UK, Thailand, Malaysia, Korea and Germany. The total number of subsidiaries in these 10 host countries accounted for more than 78 percent of all Japanese SMEs' international subsidiaries. Table 15.3 presents data on the top six host countries for Japanese SMEs' international subsidiaries by time period.

As can be seen from Table 15.3, Taiwan was the most popular investment location for Japanese SMEs before 1970. Although Taiwan's position was replaced by the USA after 1970, it remained as a popular investment location for Japanese SMEs along with other emerging markets in Asia. After the 1980s, China became the second most popular investment location to Japanese SMEs, just behind the USA. The popularity of China as a host country is in general a reflection of the successful institution of the 'open door policy' initiated by the Chinese government in 1979. Given its huge market growth potential and low production costs, China has been one of the most popular investment locations to foreign investors, especially Japanese investors. In a survey by Japan External Trade Organization (Jetro) 2001, 95.7 percent of the respondents (Japanese firms) named China as the primary location for their FDIs within the next three years (Lugo, 2001).

To have a better understanding of the sectoral and location patterns of FDIs by Japanese SMEs, we decomposed 2001 data by sector and by region in Table 15.4. It is clear that there were significant differences (p<0.01) in location choices across sectors. The FDIs in the manufacturing sector were heavily concentrated in Asia while other sectors such as wholesale trade, finance, insurance and real estate, and services were

Table 15.4   Distribution of Japanese SMEs' international subsidiaries, 2001 (by sector and by region)

Sector	Asia	North America	Europe	South/ Latin America	Oceania	Africa/ Middle East	Total
Agriculture, forestry and fishing	4	6	1	1	2	0	14
Mining	1	1	0	0	3	0	5
Construction	6	1	0	0	0	0	7
Manufacturing	318	99	61	9	13	1	501
Transportation	10	3	4	0	1	1	19
Wholesale trade	125	110	85	10	8	3	341
Retail trade	25	5	4	0	2	0	36
Finance, insurance and real estate	21	44	21	11	2	0	99
Services	32	28	28	2	3	1	94
Total	544	297	204	33	34	3	1118

Note: Pearson *chi*-square = 221.909, p = 0.000.

more evenly distributed across all regions. The heavy concentration of manufacturing in Asia confirms the investment motivations of Japanese SMEs, that is to capture the untapped market potential of Asian countries and/or to take advantage of competitively priced labor in Asian countries.

Characteristics of Japanese SMEs' international subsidiaries
This section examines the characteristics of individual subsidiaries of Japanese SMEs. It begins by examining the entry mode and then moves to three other subsidiary characteristics (subsidiary age, subsidiary size and Japanese control), which are in turn measured by four variables. In looking at these characteristics, a comparison is made across industrial sectors and regions to identify any differences.

Entry mode
The entry mode decision is one of the most important decisions made when undertaking a foreign investment. This is because the choice of mode can affect both the likelihood of survival of the foreign subsidiary (Li, 1995) as well as its performance such as profitability and market share (Pan et al., 1999). Four entry modes are evident in our sample. These modes include both shared and solely owned subsidiaries, as well as newly established and acquired subsidiaries (or Greenfield and Brownfield subsidiaries). Using these two dimensions (full or shared ownership, and acquired or new subsidiary), four mutually exclusive entry modes can be identified (see Table 15.5). These are:

1. Wholly owned – Greenfield operation in which 95 percent or more of the equity is possessed by one Japanese firm.
2. Joint venture – Greenfield operation in which two or more firms possess at least five percent of the subsidiary's equity.

Table 15.5   Entry mode of Japanese SMEs' international subsidiaries

Mode	Before 1970	1970–79	1980–89	1990–99	Total
Wholly owned	16	60	188	310	574
Joint venture	8	41	111	243	403
Acquisition	0	2	17	48	67
Capital participation	2	2	23	36	63
Total	26	105	339	637	1107

3.   Acquisition – the purchase of a controlling interest in an existing enterprise.
4.   Capital participation – the purchase (via an equity infusion from a Japanese firm) of a partial interest in an existing domestic firm.

As displayed in Table 15.5, the two modes that involved the acquisition (partial or full) of an existing domestic operation were rarely implemented. Eighty-eight percent of all Japanese SMEs' subsidiaries were established as Greenfield operations (52 percent wholly owned and 36 percent joint venture). This strong preference for Greenfield operations is consistent across all time periods. The prominence of Greenfield operations among all entry modes in Japanese SMEs' subsidiaries is consistent with the general conclusion of previous research that Japanese investors have a distinctive preference for new start-ups (Greenfield) over acquisitions (Beamish et al., 1997).

We also examined the impact of using a more stringent definition of joint venture (JV), as advocated by Delios and Beamish (2004) which requires the possession of at least 20 percent of the subsidiary's equity. This alternative definition reduced the number of JVs from 403 to 394. In the subsequent analyses related to entry mode, we employed both JV definitions and found qualitatively similar results. We report the results by the 5 percent or more equity level JV definition, but the discussions are applicable to the alternative JV definition.

Tables 15.6 and 15.7 provide breakdown of entry modes using 2001 data by sector and by region. Table 15.6 shows that entry mode differs significantly ($p < 0.01$) by region. Joint venture is the preferred mode in Asia, while wholly owned is more dominant in North America and Europe. Table 15.7 shows that entry mode differs significantly ($p < 0.01$) by sector. In the manufacturing sector, joint venture is the preferred mode; while in the wholesale trade, finance, insurance and real estate, and services sectors, wholly owned is a more dominant entry mode. This partly reflects the need for control in these sectors.

Given most investments in Asia by Japanese SMEs are in the manufacturing sector, this regional pattern of entry mode is actually consistent with the sectoral pattern in Table 15.7. In addition, this pattern can be partially attributed to the general trend in which joint ventures are preferred for foreign entries in developing countries in which foreign investors have little experience. On the other hand, the 'choice' of joint venture over wholly owned may not be a reflection of preference but rather the lack of availability of alternatives. Investment regulations were stringent on the ownership and control of foreign-owned enterprises, and wholly owned foreign subsidiaries were rare before 1990 in Asia.

Table 15.6   Entry mode of Japanese SMEs' international subsidiaries, 2001 (by region)

Region	Wholly owned	Joint venture	Acquisition	Capital participation	Total
Asia	200	302	11	22	535
North America	209	47	24	17	297
Europe	120	35	30	18	203
South/Latin America	19	11	0	2	32
Oceania	23	5	2	4	34
Africa/Middle East	3	3	0	0	6
Total	574	403	67	63	1107

Note: Pearson *chi*-square = 216.587, p = 0.000.

Table 15.7   Entry mode of Japanese SMEs' international subsidiaries, 2001 (by sector)

Sector	Wholly owned	Joint venture	Acquisition	Capital participation	Total
Agriculture, forestry and fishing	3	9	2	0	14
Mining	3	2	0	0	5
Construction	3	3	0	1	7
Manufacturing	166	252	39	38	495
Transportation	11	5	1	2	19
Wholesale trade	248	64	15	10	337
Retail trade	18	15	1	2	36
Finance, insurance and real estate	68	20	4	7	99
Services	54	32	5	3	94
Total	574	402	67	63	1106

Note: Pearson *chi*-square = 160.959, p = 0.000.

Subsidiary age

Subsidiary age is the first of the latter three subsidiary characteristics examined in this section (see Tables 15.8 and 15.9). Subsidiary age is defined as the operation time period of the subsidiary in the host country from the declared date of subsidiary formation. As expected, subsidiaries in the services, construction and finance, insurance and real estate sectors have the lowest age because the majority of investments by Japanese SMEs in the these sectors were made in the 1990s. In terms of region, subsidiaries established in Asia, Europe and Africa/Middle East have the lowest age because the majority of investment by Japanese SMEs in these regions were made in the 1990s. Overall, the differences in subsidiary age across sectors and regions are a reflection of the timing of entry (see Figure 15.1 and Tables 15.1 and 15.2).

Subsidiary size

Subsidiary size reflects the level of commitment that foreign investor(s) have made to their international subsidiaries. It can be measured by sales, capitalization and employment.

Table 15.8   Characteristics of Japanese SMEs' international subsidiaries, 2001 (by sector)

Sector	Subsidiary age (year)	Number of employees (count)	Japanese equity ownership (percentage)	Japanese expatriate (percentage)
Agriculture, forestry and fishing	12.59	30.67	74.75	2.22
Mining	12.77	107.00	100.00	12.98
Construction	8.25	76.40	85.00	10.60
Manufacturing	10.01	203.61	79.70	4.89
Transportation	8.67	16.29	81.09	36.96
Wholesale trade	10.57	34.40	93.36	19.55
Retail trade	8.87	65.30	70.12	7.05
Finance, insurance and real estate	8.48	32.81	93.59	30.80
Services	7.60	72.07	88.91	32.00
Total	9.81	121.99	85.69	12.74

Note: All differences significant at $p < 0.01$.

Table 15.9   Characteristics of Japanese SMEs' international subsidiaries, 2001 (by region)

Region	Subsidiary age (year)	Number of employees (count)	Japanese equity ownership (percentage)	Japanese expatriate (percentage)
Asia	9.51	161.65	79.20	8.22
North America	10.44	65.21	93.33	24.99
Europe	9.12	63.59	93.98	10.77
South/Latin America	10.21	125.50	90.86	16.72
Oceania	12.85	62.64	100.00	17.73
Africa/Middle East	9.49	21.40	80.00	26.47
Total	9.81	121.99	85.69	12.74

Note: Differences in subsidiary age significant at $p < 0.10$, all other differences significant at $p < 0.01$.

In this study, we employ the number of employees because the other two measures, sales and capitalization, were infrequently reported.

Again, as might be expected, subsidiaries in the manufacturing sector appear to be the largest, as these have the highest mean number of employees. Meanwhile, subsidiaries in the transportation, finance, insurance and real estate, and wholesale trade sector had the lowest number of employees. The differences in subsidiary size are quite dramatic. For example, the ratio of mean number of employees in Japanese SMEs' international subsidiaries in the manufacturing, wholesale trade and transportation sectors is approximately 12:2:1. In terms of region, subsidiaries in Asia have the highest mean number of employees because the majority of Japanese SMEs' investment in Asia is in the manufacturing sector.

Japanese control
Parent control in a subsidiary refers to the influences the parent has over the operation and the output of the subsidiary. The control of foreign subsidiaries is a critical issue within multinational enterprises because the parent's ability to influence systems and decisions has ramifications for both the foreign affiliate's likelihood of success (Root, 1987; Stopford and Wells, 1972; Woodcock et al., 1994) and its probability of survival (Li, 1995). There are a variety of control mechanisms that can be used by a foreign invest-ing firm. Two of the more prominent and commonly used are control through equity ownership and control through assigning parent company employees (expatriates) to overseas subsidiaries. We measured the extent of Japanese SMEs' control by looking at these two mechanisms; that is, the percentage equity ownership of Japanese investor(s) and the percentage of Japanese expatriates in total employment. The use of ratios rather than absolute numbers helps to control for the biasing effects of subsidiary size.

When we look at the extent of Japanese control across sectors, we find that the per-centage of equity holdings of Japanese SMEs are the highest in the wholesale trade and finance, insurance and real estate sectors. The higher percentage equity holdings reflect a greater prevalence of wholly owned subsidiaries in these two sectors. As shown in Table 15.6, nearly 74 percent and 69 percent of Japanese SMEs' subsidiaries in the wholesale trade and finance, insurance and real estate sectors respectively are wholly owned sub-sidiaries. Furthermore, as evidence of substantive differences in control we find that in 49 of the 64 joint ventures in the wholesale trade sector and 17 of the 20 joint ventures in the finance, insurance and real estate sector, the Japanese SMEs' equity holding is greater than 50 percent. Consistent with high Japanese equity holdings, these two sectors also have a higher percentage of Japanese expatriates, compared to manufacturing sector.

This observation is consistent with previous observations on Japanese investment in other host countries. For example, Beamish and Delios (1999) studied Japanese invest-ment in a variety of transitional economies and found that the mean equity possessed by Japanese firms in the trading sector was almost 20 percent higher than the mean for manufacturing sector subsidiaries. The use of a higher percentage of expatriates and the holding of higher equity levels in subsidiaries in the wholesale trade and finance, insur-ance and real estate sectors is indicative of the need to have more direct control over the operations of subsidiaries in these two sectors. This need stems from the high value-added activities that are performed in these subsidiaries. Direct control of the subsidiar-ies in these two sectors helps the parent firm to better integrate these high value-added activities into its global strategy (Anand and Delios, 1996).

Compared to the manufacturing sector, the service sector has a much higher percent-age of Japanese expatriates. This reflects the non-standardized and skilled labor that goes into the production of the services rendered by subsidiaries in the service sector. Hence, the need for control is greater. In the manufacturing sector, activities tend to be more routine, and once operations are established, the need for control is less intense.

In addition, we observe (Table 15.8) that in most of the sectors where the percentage of Japanese expatriates is high, the total average number of employees in the subsidiary is relatively low. This is because a higher proportion of those subsidiaries tend to be sales offices.

In term of region, the Japanese SMEs' equity holdings were the highest in North America and Europe, consistent with the prevalence of wholly owned mode in these two

Table 15.10   Performance of Japanese SMEs' international subsidiaries, 2001 (by sector)

Sector	Loss	Break-even	Profitable	Total
Agriculture, forestry and fishing	0	0	2	2
Mining	0	1	1	2
Construction	0	1	2	3
Manufacturing	37	45	132	214
Transportation	1	1	2	4
Wholesale trade	24	26	71	121
Retail trade	2	0	3	5
Finance, insurance and real estate	7	4	7	18
Services	2	4	3	9
Total	73	82	223	378

Note: Pearson *chi*-square = 14.455, p = 0.565.

regions (see Table 15.7). In contrast, the percentages of Japanese SMEs' equity holdings and Japanese expatriates were the lowest in Asia, the most popular location for subsidiaries in the manufacturing sector.

Characteristics and performance of Japanese SMEs' FDIs
This section attempts to establish links between the above subsidiary characteristics and performance. As reported earlier, subsidiary performance is given as a managerial report: subsidiary general managers reported whether the subsidiary made a loss, break-even or gain in the year of the survey (Toyo Keizai, 2001). Among the 1118 subsidiaries in our sample, there are 378 responses to the performance variable. Among these, 223 subsidiaries reported profitable operations, 82 break-even and 73 identified their subsidiary as making a loss in 2000. This section provides a general picture of the performance of Japanese SMEs' FDIs by sector, by region, by entry mode, and by subsidiary characteristics.

Sector and performance
We compare the performance of Japanese subsidiaries across sectors by comparing the percentage of profitable, breakeven and loss-making subsidiaries. As shown in Table 15.10, there seem to be differences across sectors. Among the two major sectors, manufacturing and wholesale trade, the manufacturing sector had more profitable subsidiaries in absolute numbers. However, the overall differences across sectors were not statistically significant.

Region and performance
Table 15.11 compares the performance of Japanese SMEs' subsidiaries across regions. Among the three major regions: Asia, North America and Europe, subsidiaries in Asia are the most profitable. This is consistent with the performance differences across sectors (see Table 15.10) because the majority of Japanese SMEs' manufacturing subsidiaries are located in Asia. However, as with the results in Table 15.10, the results in Table 15.11 were statistically insignificant.

Table 15.11   Performance of Japanese SMEs' international subsidiaries, 2001 (by region)

Region	Loss	Break-even	Profitable	Total
Asia	34	48	133	215
North America	18	21	50	89
Europe	13	8	26	47
South/Latin America	2	2	7	11
Oceania	5	1	6	12
Africa/Middle East	1	2	1	4
Total	73	82	223	378

Note: Pearson *chi*-square = 10.979, p = 0.359.

Table 15.12   Performance of Japanese SMEs' international subsidiaries, 2001 (by entry mode)

Mode	Loss	Break-even	Profitable	Total
Wholly owned	41	44	92	177
Joint venture	29	34	98	161
Acquisition	2	3	14	19
Capital participation	1	1	19	21
Total	73	82	223	378

Note: Pearson *chi*-square = 14.281, p = 0.027.

Entry mode and performance
The relationship between entry mode and performance has been a central focus in a number of studies of foreign direct investment. Within the present study, performance differences across entry modes were significant (see Table 15.12). Among the two most popular entry modes, wholly-owned and joint venture, joint venture have a higher percentage of profitable subsidiaries. The result is a little surprising, because it contradicts the findings by Nitsch et al. (1995) who found that wholly owned Japanese subsidiaries in Europe performed best.

There are two explanations for this. First, each entry mode has its own advantages and disadvantages. On one hand, the wholly owned mode enables the foreign investor to have complete control of the subsidiary. This eliminates the potential for conflicts between partners that exists in the case of joint ventures. However, making investments solely by themselves, foreign investors often do not have access to the potential help that local partners in joint ventures can provide, such as local knowledge. On the other hand, it is well known that joint ventures can sometimes be difficult to manage due to the potential conflicts among partners. However, when well-managed, joint ventures can be effective forms of foreign entry, with partners pooling complementary resources together. Thus the mixed results on the relationship between entry mode and perform-ance demonstrate that both modes have viable rationales for their implementation, and that other considerations may interact to tip the balance toward one mode or another.

Table 15.13 *Characteristics of Japanese SMEs' international subsidiaries, 2001 (by performance)*

Region	Subsidiary age (year)	Number of employees (count)	Japanese equity ownership (percentage)	Japanese expatriate (percentage)
Loss	11.50	118.47	87.07	9
Break-even	10.98	71.20	86.96	19
Profitable	14.07	171.47	83.95	9
Total	12.90	138.12	85.20	11

Note: Differences in Japanese expatriates not significant, all other differences significant at $p < 0.01$.

Second, there are differences in sample characteristics. While the sample for the study by Nitsch et al. (1995) was made up mainly of large Japanese firms, our study focused exclusively on Japanese SMEs. By definition, SMEs face constraints in resources and capabilities (Beamish, 1999; Jarillo, 1989). Such constraints become more prominent when SMEs start to internationalize (Zacharakis, 1997). One way to overcome this difficulty is to form joint ventures so as to have access to partners' resources (Beamish, 1999; Jarillo, 1989; Zacharakis, 1997). Taking the differences in sample characteristics into consideration, our findings actually suggest that a contingency approach (Shaver, 1998) may be required to distinguish how the performance of these two modes differs.

Subsidiary age, size, Japanese control and performance
Table 15.13 explores the basic relationships between subsidiary age, size, Japanese control and performance. It shows that subsidiary age is positively related to subsidiary performance. If we take subsidiary age to be a proxy for the foreign investor's experience in the host country, it is not surprising that more experienced foreign investors have higher performing subsidiaries. The fact that subsidiary experience is positively associated with subsidiary performance is supportive of the theories and results of prior studies (for example, Delios and Beamish, 1999; Johanson and Vahlne, 1977). In our sample of Japanese SMEs, profitable subsidiaries have operated an average age of 14 years, while unprofitable subsidiaries have operated an average age of about 11 years.

The size of the investment was likewise expected to have a relationship with performance. It is clear from Table 15.13 that profitable subsidiaries had the largest investment size in terms of the total number of employees. Investment size reflects parent firms' commitment to the subsidiaries as well as the resources available to the subsidiaries. The positive association between investment size and subsidiary performance highlights the importance of resources in undertaking foreign investments, especially for SMEs.

As shown in Table 15.13, both measures of Japanese control display observational differences across subsidiary performance categories. The percentage of Japanese equity holdings has a consistently negative relationship with subsidiary performance, while the percentage of Japanese expatriates shows a less consistent pattern. The negative relationship between Japanese equity holdings and subsidiary performance is consistent with our findings that on average, Japanese SMEs' joint ventures outperformed their wholly owned subsidiaries (Table 15.12).

The result contradicts the findings of Killing (1983), who used a small sample of joint ventures established only in developed countries, and the findings by Ding (1997), who used a sample of Sino–US joint ventures in China. However, the result provides support for Tomlinson's (1970) argument that the sharing of responsibility with local associates will lead to a greater contribution from them and, in turn, a greater return on investment. More importantly, if we consider the concentration of Japanese SMEs' international subsidiaries in Asia, our findings are consistent with Beamish's (1985) observation of a strong correlation between unsatisfactory performance and dominant foreign control in subsidiaries in less developed countries.

Discussions and conclusions
Before offering our final thoughts on these results, we suggest that interpretations of the results from this study should be tempered by limitations in our analysis. First, our sample consisted of only Japanese SMEs. Caution should be taken in generalizing the results of this study beyond the Japanese context. Further, due to the problem of data availability, this study only included publicly listed SMEs. Future studies could include unlisted SMEs to provide a more complete picture of the internationalization of SMEs.

Despite these limitations, this illustration and analysis of the characteristics and performance of Japanese SMEs' internationalization adds to the body of international business literature and entrepreneurship literature in two ways. First, it presents an overview of Japanese SMEs' internationalization, which has received sparse attention in the literature. Second, it provides insight into the links between subsidiary characteristics and performance.

Japanese SMEs' internationalization after the Second World War, had a steady but slow increase through the 1970s and the first half of 1980s, followed by a rapid surge in the late 1980s. The investments were mainly in the manufacturing and wholesale trade sectors, clustering in Asia, North America and Europe. Greenfield operations were the dominant entry mode, within which, joint ventures were implemented with the greatest frequency.

Our analysis of subsidiary characteristics reveals significant differences across sectors and investment regions. Consistent with the timing pattern of Japanese SMEs' FDIs, the subsidiary age was the lowest in the services, construction and finance, insurance and real estate sectors, and in Asia, Europe and Africa/Middle East where the majority of entries was made in the 1990s. Reflective of the nature of the sectors, manufacturing had the highest mean number of employees. Control by the Japanese in terms of both equity ownership and percentage of Japanese expatriates was highest in the wholesale trade and finance, insurance and real estate sectors, suggesting that more control was desired when high value-added activities were conducted in the foreign subsidiaries.

The associations of subsidiary performance with subsidiary characteristics were also examined. Contrary to previous findings on the relationships between sector, location and performance, there was no significant relationship between either sector and performance or location and performance. This suggests that the sector and investment location are not by themselves related to subsidiary profitability, at least for Japanese SMEs' investments.

More importantly, we observed a positive relationship between subsidiary age and performance, a positive relationship between subsidiary size and performance, and a negative relationship between Japanese control and performance. The positive relationship between subsidiary age and performance reflects the positive host country experience effect on Japanese SMEs' subsidiary performance. It also demonstrates the importance of entry timing to capture the investment opportunities at an early stage and to achieve first-mover advantages. It suggests that Japanese SMEs should internationalize as soon as they are ready.

The positive relationship between subsidiary size and performance shows the importance of resources in international expansion. Combined with the observation that Japanese SMEs' joint ventures outperformed their wholly owned subsidiaries, this suggests that Japanese SMEs use joint ventures in their international expansion to overcome their resource constraints.

Finally, the negative association of the Japanese equity holdings with subsidiary performance illustrates the importance of the participation of local partners in the management of international subsidiaries. Local partners contribute to better subsidiary performance by providing local knowledge about government regulations and about local market conditions, and by helping build local networks to circumvent the barriers which are often impenetrable to foreign investor(s). Our findings suggest that Japanese SMEs should structure their joint ventures in a way that can maximize the participation from local partners.

Acknowledgements

This research was supported by a research grant from the National University of Singapore (#R-313-000-045-112), by a Social Sciences and Humanities Research Council of Canada Grant (#410-2001-0143), and by the Asian Management Institute at the University of Western Ontario.

Note

1. A version of this paper appeared in Dana (2004).

References

Anand, Jaideep and Andrew Delios (1996), 'Competing globally: how Japanese MNEs have matched goals and strategies in India and China', *Columbia Journal of World Business*, **31**(3), 50–62.
Baird, I.S., M.A. Lytes and J.B. Orris (1994), 'The choice of international strategies by small businesses', *Journal of Small Business Management*, **32**(1), 48–59.
Beamish, Paul W. (1985), 'The characteristics of joint ventures in developed and developing countries', *Columbia Journal of World Business*, **20**(3), 13–19.
Beamish, Paul W. (1999), 'The role of alliances in international entrepreneurship', *Research in Global Strategic Management*, Greenwich, CT: JAI Press, pp. 43–61.
Beamish, Paul W. and Andrew Delios (1999), 'Japanese investment in transitional economies: characteristics and performance', in D. Denison (ed.), *Organizational Change in Transitional Economies*, Ann Arbor, MI: University of Michigan Press.
Beamish, Paul W. and Jane W. Lu (2004), 'Japanese perspectives of international entrepreneurship', in Léo-Paul Dana (ed.), *Handbook of Research on International Entrepreneurship*, Cheltenham, UK and Northampton, MA, USA: Edward Elgar, pp. 512–32.
Beamish, Paul W., Andrew Delios and D.J. Lecraw (1997), *Japanese Multinationals in the Global Economy*, Cheltenham, UK and Lyme, NH: Edward Elgar Publishing Ltd.
Bird, Allan (2002), *Encyclopedia of Japanese Business and Management*, London and New York: Routledge.
Dana, Léo-Paul (1998), 'Small but not independent: SMEs in Japan', *Journal of Small Business Management*, **36**(4), 73–76.
Dana, Léo-Paul (2004), *Handbook of Research on International Entrepreneurship*, Cheltenham, UK and Northampton, MA, USA: Edward Elgar.

Delios, Andrew and Paul W. Beamish (1999), 'Ownership strategy of Japanese firms: transactional, institutional and experience influences', *Strategic Management Journal*, **20**(10), 915–33.

Delios, Andrew and Paul W. Beamish (2004), 'Joint venture performance revisited: Japanese foreign subsidiaries worldwide', *Management International Review*, **44**(1), 69–91.

Ding, D.Z. (1997), 'Control, conflict, and performance: a study of U.S.–Chinese joint ventures', *Journal of International Marketing*, **5**(3), 31–45.

Hisrich, Robert D., Sandra Honig-Haftel, P.P. McDougall and B.M. Oviatt (1996), 'International entrepreneurship: past, present, and future', *Entrepreneurship Theory and Practice*, **20**(4), 5–11.

Jarillo, J.C. (1989), 'Entrepreneurship and growth: the strategic use of external resources', *Journal of Business Venturing*, **4**, 133–47.

Johanson, J. and J.-E. Vahlne (1977), 'The internationalization process of the firm – a model of knowledge development and increasing market commitments', *Journal of International Business Studies*, **8**(1), 23–32.

Killing, J.P. (1983), *Strategies For Joint Venture Success*, New York: Praeger.

Li, J.T. (1995), 'Foreign entry and survival: effects of strategic choices on performance in international markets', *Strategic Management Journal*, **16**(5), 333–51.

Lu, Jane W. and Paul W. Beamish (2001), 'The internationalization and performance of SMEs', *Strategic Management Journal*, **22**, 565–86.

Lugo, Letotes Marie T. (2001), 'Japan firms seen to pour more FDIs', *BusinessWorld* (Manila), 13 December.

McDougall, P.P. and B.M. Oviatt (2000), 'International entrepreneurship: the intersection of two research paths', *Academy of Management Journal*, **43**(5), 902–8.

Nitsch, D., Paul W. Beamish and S. Makino (1995), 'Characteristics and performance of Japanese foreign direct investment in Europe', *European Management Journal*, **13**(3), 276–85.

Oviatt, B.M. and P.P. McDougall (1994), 'Toward a theory of international new ventures', *Journal of International Business Studies*, **25**(1), 45–61.

Oviatt, B.M. and P.P. McDougall (1999), 'Accelerated internationalization: why are new and small ventures internationalizing in greater numbers and with increasing speed?', in Richard Wright (ed.), *Research in Global Strategic Management*, Stamford, CT: JAI Press.

Pan, Y., S. Li and David K. Tse (1999), 'The impact of order and mode of market entry on profitability and market share', *Journal of International Business Studies*, **30**(1), 81–103.

Root, F.R. (1987), *Entry Strategies for International Markets*, Lexington, MA: D.C. Heath.

Shaver, J.M. (1998), 'Accounting for endogeneity when assessing strategy performance: does entry mode choice affect FDI survival?', *Management Science*, **44**(4), 571–87.

Stopford, J.M. and L.T. Wells Jr (1972), *Managing the Multinational Enterprise,* New York, NY: Basic Books.

Tomlinson, J.W.C. (1970), *The Joint Venture Process in International Business: India and Pakistan*, Cambridge, MA: MIT Press.

Toyo Keizai (2001), *Kaigai Shinshutsu Kigyo Soran (Japanese Overseas Investment)*, Tokyo: Toyo Kauai Shinposha.

UNCTAD (2000), *World Investment Report 2000: Transnational Corporations, Market Structure and Competition Policy*, United Nations: New York and Geneva.

Wolff, A. James and Timothy L. Pett (2000), 'Internationalization of small firms: an examination of export competitive patterns, firm size, and export performance', *Journal of Small Business Management*, **38**(2), 34–47.

Woodcock, C.P., Paul W. Beamish and S. Makino (1994), 'Ownership-based entry mode strategies and international performance', *Journal of International Business Studies*, **25**(2), 253–73.

Yamawaki, Hideki (1991), 'Exports and foreign distributional activities: evidence on Japanese firms in the United States', *Review of Economics and Statistics*, **73**, 294–300.

Zacharakis Andrew L. (1997), 'Entrepreneurial entry into foreign markets: a transaction cost perspective', *Entrepreneurship Theory and Practice*, **21**(3), 23–39.

Zahra, Shaker A., R. Duane Ireland and Michael A. Hitt (2000), 'International expansion by new venture firms: international diversity, mode of market entry, technological learning and performance', *Academy of Management Journal*, **43**(5), 925–50.

16 Jordan
Vanessa Ratten[1]

Introduction

The formal conventional name of Jordan is the Hashemite Kingdom of Jordan. The kingdom covers an area of 89 300 square kilometres. Its neighbours are Iraq, Israel, Saudi Arabia, and Syria. Jordan has a strategic location as it is at the head of the Gulf of Aqaba. Arabic is the official language. The majority of the population is Sunni Muslim (Dew and Shoult, 2007). During most of its history since independence, Jordan was beset by economic difficulties. Until 1948, most of the nation's trade was carried out with its British neighbour to the west; after Israel's independence, the Arab boycott stopped this otherwise fruitful trade. Outside the Dead Sea, Jordan has few natural resources; however, peace with Israel has made possible the joint development of industry and of the Dead Sea – including the extraction of potassium salts for fertilizer.

Present-day Jordan was formerly ruled by the Greeks, the Romans, and the Byzantines. Between about 500 BC and AD 200, this land was home to the Aramaic-speaking Nabataeans – business-minded, pre-Islamic Arabs who were prosperous traders; when they were threatened by their enemies, they would dissuade the invaders by explaining that fighting was bad for business.

Situated on the cross-roads of major caravan routes linking Egypt, Arabia, and Mesopotamia, the Nabataean capital – Petra – was a hub of international trade. Here, ivory arrived from Africa, and silk from China, as well as incense from Yemen. Petra was the central storage and dispatch centre. From here, it was a month-long trip to Yemen and no other people braved the voyage; the Nabataeans hence had the monopoly on the incense trade. Herod's troops came to Petra and asked to be shown the route to Yemen, but none survived the journey.

The Nabataeans also pioneered petroleum exports. Their camel caravans trekked across the desert, carrying bitumen from the Dead Sea to Gaza and there the cargoes were transferred for shipping to Egypt. During the Byzantine period – from AD 324 to AD 632 – Jordanian entrepreneurs prospered by selling provisions to travelling caravans, which linked the Mediterranean with the Far East. During the seventh century, Muslim Arabs conquered the territory. Then came almost a century of rule by the Crusaders, who were defeated by Salah el Din, in 1187. The Mamelukes then ruled until the arrival of the Ottomans, during the early sixteenth century. In response to the disloyalty expressed by Bedouins, Sultan Abdul Hamid II decided it would be wise to relocate loyal Ottoman subjects to the Middle East. His new policy, in 1878, exempted migrants to Transjordan from 12 years of taxes, and this encouraged Circassians to move to the land east of the Jordan River. Agricultural and animal herding allowed the population to be self-sufficient.

During the Great War of 1914 – the First World War – Colonel T.E. Lawrence, also known as Lawrence of Arabia, promised the Arabs an independent kingdom, in exchange for assistance in liberating Palestine from the Ottoman Empire. Victorious

Britain subsequently divided the territory it conquered from the Ottomans. While the coastal area – west of the Jordan River – would retain the name British Palestine, the Emirate of Transjordan was created on the East Bank. Both territories remained under British mandate.

In 1921, Abdullah ibn Hussein – brother of Arab Prince Faisal who established the government in Syria – was appointed the emir of the new emirate; this entity was a self-governing territory under British mandate. Amman – known by the Romans as Philadelphia – became its capital. Thousands of people began to work for the state. When Transjordan became a kingdom, in 1946, the British made Abdullah its monarch. Transjordan enjoyed a fine friendship with Britain, which continued to subsidize its economy.

When Arab armies invaded Israel, in 1948, radio stations in neighbouring countries advised Palestinians to leave their homes 'because Arab cannons would not be able to distinguish between Jews and Arabs, when reducing the country to cinders'. The well-to-do *effendis* went abroad, and half a million came to Transjordan. This created economic problems.

In 1949, the country was re-named the Hashemite Kingdom of Jordan, and the West Bank (of the Jordan River) was annexed in 1950. When King Abdullah was assassinated, in 1951, his son Talal was allowed to rule – but only for a few months, after which he was deposed on the grounds of mental illness. Talal's son, Hussein ibn Talal succeeded him.

Often, industrialization leads to urbanization. In Jordan, urbanization was spurred by immigration, and until the 1950s, industrialization was relatively slow, allowing merchants and agents for foreign firms to dominate markets. Then, urbanization prompted industrialization. While the government operated large-scale industries, the small enterprise sector was limited, as industrial entrepreneurs were few. There was little investment in manufacturing.

In 1956, the Sinai Campaign led Jordan to break its ties with London – an expensive decision, as this meant foregoing $36 million a year in subsidies. Fearing that communism would replace British influence, the United States provided economic assistance when Britain stopped doing so. In 1958, Jordan joined Iraq to create the Arab Federal State, but this entity ended after Iraq became its own republic, in July 1958.

In 1960, Jordan offered citizenship to all Arab refugees applying for it. The population of Jordan subsequently swelled with Palestinians. In 1965, King Hussein traded land with Saudi Arabia, thereby extending the Jordanian shoreline along the Gulf of Aqaba. This would allow development of Jordan's port city.

On 5 June 1967, Jordan joined in the Six-Day War against Israel. In a counterattack by the Israelis, on 6 June, Jordan lost the West Bank, which it had annexed 17 years earlier. The next day, Jordan gave up East Jerusalem and accepted a United Nations cease-fire. Following the Six-Day War, Jordan's industrial production dropped by a fifth. The West Bank had produced 70 percent of Jordan's fruit. In 1970, Palestinian guerrillas clashed with the Jordanian army, and the following year, the prime minister of Jordan was assassinated by Palestinians in Cairo.

When Jordan did away with compulsory military service, in 1991, it was the first Arab country to do so. Less military expenditure meant more funding available for economic development.

Peace with Israel – signed in 1994 – ushered in a new era of prosperity for Jordan. The agreement opened up a new market for Jordanian products, while giving a greater range of products to Jordanian consumers. Prior to the peace agreement, tourism had been growing at an annual rate of 1 percent; since then, the tourism sector has been growing by as much as 18 percent a year. This high rate of increase in tourism is in contrast to many of Jordan's Middle East neighbours and illustrates how more focused on the international market Jordan is becoming.

King Hussein died on 7 February 1999, a day after his eldest son – Abdullah ibn Al-Hussein al Hashemi – was sworn in as regent. King Abdullah has continued the legacy of his father by promoting and encouraging good international business relations with countries outside the Middle East as well as with its neighbours. In particular, Jordan has a close relationship with the United States and sometimes acts as a negotiator in Middle East country discussions and international business negotiations. In July 2007 there were municipal elections in which 20 percent of all seats in municipal councils were designated for females (www.cia.gov/library/publications/the-world-factbook/geos/jo.html#Econ). This shift in policy is part of Jordan's international initiatives to appeal more to Western businesses and foreign direct investment. In November 2007 parliamentary elections were held in which the majority of seats went to independent pro-government supporters (http://lcweb2.loc.gov/frd/cs/jotoc.html). These supporters are influencing the further internationalization and opening up of the Jordanian economy. Following these elections King Abdullah has initiated more reforms of the social welfare system in Jordan so that the amenities available to Jordanian citizens are more like those in Western countries (Madfai and Madfai, 2007). These reforms involve developing a healthcare and housing network and improving the educational system of the country.

Government policy on SMEs and entrepreneurship in Jordan
Jordan has been creating an attractive environment for enterprise, allowing the free flow of capital and profits. To promote investment, tax rates have been reduced and capital gains and dividends are exempt from tax. Hotels, hospitals, industrial firms and mining enterprises pay income tax at the rate of 15 percent. This low rate of corporate tax has encouraged hotels to flourish and for industrial firms to move their Middle East base to Jordan. Insurance companies and banks pay 35 percent. All others are taxed at the rate of 25 percent.

In accordance with the Investment Promotion Law, agricultural projects benefit from exemptions from customs duties, social service contributions and income tax. Flexible loans are available from specialised credit institutions. In spite of its semi-arid climate, the fertile Jordan Valley produces three harvests a year; this includes citrus fruits, bananas, melons, and vegetables. The central highlands, which receive more rain, provide cereal grains as well as fruits and vegetables. Much Jordanian produce is exported. Outside shops selling green almonds, vine-leaves and mint, the scent of rose water emanates from rows of micro-scale confectioneries making *konafeh* and selling fresh *bassboussah*. Jordanians enjoy fresh and tasty foods.

Jordan has significantly improved its infrastructure during the past two decades. Beginning in 1993, the telecommunications policy evolved into the National Telecommunications Programme, raising the penetration ratio of telephone lines. The Telecommunications Corporation was commercialized and restructured into the Jordan Telecom Company, which now operates three satellite earth stations. The Telecom

Regulatory Commission was also established, to provide a transparent and fair competitive environment for service companies.

Maritime transport and railway companies benefit from full duty exemptions on fixed assets. In addition, they are entitled to a 75 percent exemption on income tax and the same on social services tax.

The environment for entrepreneurship and the state of small business in Jordan
Most small business in Jordan is in the service industry. The gross domestic production composition by sector is agriculture 3.5 percent, industry 10.3 percent and services 86.2 percent. The main industries that small business in Jordan are in are clothing, phosphate mining, fertilizers, pharmaceuticals, petroleum refining, cement, potash, inorganic chemicals, light manufacturing and tourism. Whilst many big businesses are in the petroleum refining industry, increasing numbers of small business owners are focusing on the tourism sector. There has been an increased interest on Jordan by international travellers because of the vast history and culture of the country. Thus, small hotels and tourist operators have started to enter this sector and create a culture for entrepreneurship within the hotel sector.

Entrepreneurs in Jordan are likely to have had a self-employed father. Most industrialists in Jordan have college degrees; typically, they have entered industry relatively late in life. Yet, their industrial enterprises usually employ fewer than five people.

A large proportion of entrepreneurs in Jordan, produce mostly custom-made products, made to order. Few individuals are keen to take the risk and to make something that may not sell.

To assist the small business sector, the Queen Alia Jordan Social Fund allocated funds to teach people to train entrepreneurs. The name of the fund was later changed to the Jordanian Hashemite Fund for Human Development.

In conjunction with the International Labour Organization, the Amman Chamber of Industry developed a seminar to help existing entrepreneurs. As well, the Jordan Institute of Management – an autonomous division of the Industrial Development Bank – has been training entrepreneurs and potential entrepreneurs.

In cooperation with the United Nations Industrial Development Organization (UNIDO), the Ministry of Industry has been preparing profiles of project opportunities suitable for small-scale entrepreneurs. The same ministry has also been working on developing micro-enterprise in remote areas; this project has been assisted by the German Agency for Technical Co-operation.

Special financial assistance has also been available to entrepreneurs. The Development and Employment Fund was established, to support self-employment projects. As well, the Small-Scale Industries and Handicrafts Fund – operated by the Industrial Development Bank – has been directing loans to enterprises with fewer than five employees.

The Jordanian constitution gives women equal rights as men, with regard to work. The National Charter gives women equal opportunities as men, in education, training, and employment. Women also get the same paid leave of absence for the purpose of *haj* – pilgrimage.

The Business and Professional Women's Club encourages women to become entrepreneurs, and it provides assistance to women in business. The Noor Al-Hussein Foundation – in cooperation with the General Federation of Jordanian Women and with funding from the United Nations Population Fund – initiated a Women and Development Programme to encourage entrepreneurship among Jordanian women.

Also, the Jordan River Foundation initiated income generation projects for women, including weaving and embroidery. The foundation supports micro and small enterprises, mostly for women. Focus is on sustainable micro-finance programmes for owners of micro-enterprises – mostly women, who cannot access commercial banks.

Yet, local culture views the economic independence of women as disruptive of family life. Therefore, the participation of women, in the labour force, is still low. Furthermore, unemployment is higher among women than it is among men. When asked about this, employers explained to the author that since the labour law dictates a policy of equal pay for equal work, it therefore makes economic sense to hire men rather than women: 'Women get paid leave of absence in the case of childbirth – so it is better not to hire them.'

Many women are self-employed, and official statistics are misleading, as they do not reflect those working from their home. It is common for village women to produce traditional handicrafts – including embroidered dresses and pillowcases – at their place of residence.

In the formal sector, as well, women are concentrated in the textile industry. They are also clustered in leatherworks, chemical industries, and service industries including banking, tourism and hospitality.

Data obtained from the Development and Employment Fund indicate that credits have been given to women in a variety of domains. Most of these entrepreneurs had sewing and knitting enterprises. Others were in goat-raising, poultry-raising, bee-keeping, dairy-processing and patisseries.

The Badia region of Jordan is an arid zone, which has tremendous potential in terms of providing electricity. The very intense sun and desert winds are ideal for the production of non-pollutant, renewable energy. Furthermore, ground water makes possible the cultivation of land, while the landscape could attract tourism.

In May 1992, the Royal Geographic Society of the United Kingdom launched a joint development programme with the Jordanian Secretariat of the Higher Council of Science and Technology and the Centre for Overseas Research and Development of Durham University. Known as the Jordan Badia Research and Development Programme, its objective was specified as the sustainable development of the desertified Badia environment. The programme was housed in the former complex of the H5 pumping station, along the Karuk–Haifa pipeline.

Internationalization of entrepreneurs and SMEs: drivers and roadblocks

The Jordanian government wants to further internationalize its economy (Mashhour, 2008). In 2008 the government stopped subsidizing the petroleum and other consumer good sectors (www.cia.gov/library/publications/the-world-factbook/geos/jo.html#Econ). This has meant businesses in these sectors need to focus on the international market as a driver for further domestic and international expansion activities. A previous roadblock to internationalization of the Jordan economy was its reliance on government support to fund its operations. Therefore, the shift in policy towards the international market will mean more attention will be paid to international alliances and networks. Jordan's major export partners are US 22.4 percent, Iraq 12.9 percent, India 8.3 percent,

UAE 7.8 percent, Saudi Arabia 7.5 percent and Syria 4.9 percent (www.cia.gov/library/publications/the-world-factbook/geos/jo.html#Econ).

The Investment Law No. 16 of 1995 – published in the *Official Gazette*, issue 4075, 16 October 1995 – superseded the Encouragement of Investment Law No. 11, of 1987, and the Law Regulating Arab and Foreign Investments No. 27, of 1992. The new legislation led to the creation of the Investment Promotion Corporation (IPC), an independent legal entity, responsible for marketing Jordan internationally. The IPC creates links between Jordanian firms and counterparts abroad; it assists investors and serves as liaison with the government. Among its services, it identifies opportunities for investments; it facilitates the registration and licensing of investments; and it tabulates data and technical information, for distribution to interested parties.

In 1999, the IPC opened the Investor Reception Centre, in the North Terminal of Queen Alia International Airport, in Amman. The centre welcomes prospective investors and facilitates immigration procedures. Representatives are available to help individuals plan their itinerary. On site, there are fax and Internet facilities for use by business people. The centre also provides a database on business and industry in Jordan, along with a repository of joint venture and other investment opportunities.

To enhance its role as a hub of commerce, Jordan has created Free Zones for manufacturing and storage of transient goods. Products, in such zones, are duty-exempt. Salaries of foreign employees in Free Zones are exempted from income tax and social service payments. The first public Free Zones was established in Aqaba. There are also private Free Zones in Aqaba, Qweira, and Shidieh.

The Jordan Industrial Estates Corporation provides industry parks with vocational training centres. Firms operating in these parks are permanently exempted from real estate taxes. The Sahab Estate is 3 kilometres from Amman; its 250 hectares (625 acres) accommodate about 350 firms, employing 14 000 persons. Further north is the smaller Al Hassan Industrial Estate; in 1998, the United States designated this estate as the world's first Qualifying Industrial Zone (QIZ). The Gateway Project Company's Jordan Valley Free Zone was designated as the second QIZ.

A firm with a qualifying product – produced in a QIZ – has duty-free access to the United States, and no quotas on production. In addition, fixed assets for production enter Jordan free of duty. Firms are entitled to total exemptions from income tax and social contributions, when operating in a QIZ.

To qualify for QIZ incentives, at least 35 percent of a product's appraised value must have QIZ content, with one of five options:

1. If at least 8 percent of a product's value originates in Israel, and 11.7 percent in a Jordanian QIZ, then the product is qualified for QIZ privileges provided that the remaining value added to reach 35 percent comes from any of the following: Israel, a Jordanian QIZ, Palestinian territories, or the United States. In the case of high-technology products, these qualify if at least 7 percent of the value originates in Israel, and 11.7 percent in a Jordanian QIZ, provided that the remaining value added to reach 35 percent comes from any of the following: Israel, a Jordanian QIZ, Palestinian territories, or the United States.
2. A product qualifies for QIZ incentives when produced by joint Israeli–Jordanian efforts in which Israeli and Jordanian manufacturers each maintain a minimum of

20 percent of total production costs. Raw materials, design, wages, salaries, research and development, all count toward production costs.

3. A product may qualify for QIZ incentives if it is the result of a joint Israeli–Jordanian effort in which Israelis provide at least 20 percent of the total production cost, while 11.7 percent of the content originates in a Jordanian QIZ.
4. A product may qualify for QIZ incentives if it is the result of a joint Israeli–Jordanian effort in which Jordanians provide at least 20 percent of the total production cost, while a minimum of 8 percent of the content comes from Israel.
5. A high-technology product may qualify for QIZ incentives if it is the result of a joint Israeli–Jordanian effort in which Jordanians provide at least 20 percent of the total production cost, while a minimum of 7 percent of the content comes from Israel.

Land and buildings in Qualifying Industrial Zones may be leased or purchased, via the Industrial Estates Corporation. There is no restriction on project ownership, and profits may be fully repatriated tax-free.

Organizations which promote business in Jordan include: the Amman Chamber of Commerce; the Amman Chamber of Industry; the Amman World Trade Centre; the Federation of Jordanian Chambers of Commerce; the Jordanian Businessmen Association; the Jordanian Export Development and Commercial Centres Corporation; the Jordanian National Committee of the International Chamber of Commerce; and the Jordan Trade Association.

Towards the future

In order to compete in the international market without relying heavily on government support, small and medium enterprises (SMEs) need to attract investment in order to create jobs (Dew and Shoult, 2007). In Jordan SMEs also have to reduce their independence on foreign grants. The Jordanian government needs to reduce their budget deficit and this will mean major changes in business policy so that SMEs are self-sufficient and can compete globally. Jordanian policy may be described as forward-looking. The Companies Law states that a public shareholding company must allocate at least 1 percent of its annual net profits toward supporting vocational training and scientific research. The presence of a skilled workforce, coupled with competitive wages, gives Jordan a competitive advantage in world markets. Although the concept of minimum wage was recently introduced, in Jordan, salaries are still low enough to make Jordanian industry very competitive.

Since the peace agreement with Israel, Jordan has also benefited from Israeli technology and access to the Israeli market. In addition, the QIZ concept gives Jordanian firms a great advantage, enabling further cost reductions thanks to economies of scale.

In November 1999, King Abdullah ibn Hussein launched a push for socio-economic and fiscal reforms, including modernization and accelerated privatization. In January 2000, at the World Economic Forum in Davos, he reaffirmed his commitment to the growth of the private sector.

Given the high educational level of Jordanian entrepreneurs, and the low wages expected by employees, Jordanian firms have a comparative advantage, in regional and in world markets. Jordan's market-oriented economy, coupled with a stable political environment, government incentives and a world-class infrastructure, suggest that Jordan will have very fruitful economic times ahead.

Acknowledgement
Thanks to the Amman Chamber of Industry; the Central Bank; the Ministry of Finance; the Ministry of Industry and Trade; the Ministry of Planning; the Ministry of Tourism; the Ministry of Transport; Noor Al-Hussein Foundation; and the Union of Jordanian Chambers of Commerce, for providing the information used to write this chapter. Thanks also to Mrs Kholoud Al-Khaldi, Enterprise Development Specialist, in Amman, Jordan, for comments of the first draft.

Note
1. This chapter draws on Dana (2000).

References

Dana, L.P. (2000), *Economies of the Eastern Mediterranean Region: Economic Miracles in the Making*, Singapore, London and Hong Kong: World Scientific.
Dew, P. and A. Shoult (eds) (2007), *Doing Business with Jordan*, 2nd edn, London: GMB Publishing.
Madfai, A.R.A. and A.R. Madfai (2007), *Jordan, the United States and the Middle East Peace Process, 1974–1991*, Cambridge: Cambridge University Press.
Mashhour, A. (2008), 'A framework for evaluating the effectiveness of information systems at Jordan banks: an empirical study', *Journal of Internet Banking and Commerce*, **13**(1), 1–15.
www.cia.gov/library/publications/the-world-factbook/geos/jo.html#Econ (accessed 26 July 2008).

17 Kazakhstan
Sandra Pennewiss

1. Introduction

Kazakhstan is often described as featuring lunar landscapes, for a country with an impressive 2.7 million sq km (making it the ninth biggest country in the world, larger than Western Europe) of which vast areas consist of mountains and never ending steppes, that might be a befitting term. However, the Kazakhs have always known how to prosper and make use of the lands and its riches.

Kazakhstan, in an almost reluctant move, was the last province of the former Soviet Union to break away and declare independence on 16 of December 1991. Immediately afterwards the country fell into a staggering recession. Supply and export chains crumbled, economic insecurity and political immaturity threw the country into a period of uncertainty. The country's future was so much unpredictable that *The Economist* suggested the region could turn to Islamic Fundamentalism (Dana, 2002).

Today Kazakhstan is amongst the 10 fastest growing economies in the world and has developed a custom Western-style approach to democracy and economic systems. Having introduced its own currency the Kazakh Tenge, the country joined the International Monetary Fund in July 1996, reached rank 56 in the World Economic Forum's Global Competitiveness Index (GCI) in 2006 and was admitted to the United Nations in 1992.

Aiding this runaway economic growth are the country's vast resources of fossil fuels and mineral deposits, such as the world's third largest oil reserves, amongst other scarce metals and gasfields. Also rather handy is the ownership of one of the world's biggest Cosmodrome 'Baikonur', raking in an annual lease of US$115 million from Russia.

Historically as well as economically the region has seen its share of war and peace, prosperity and hardship. Traditionally the Kazakh people were always free spirited, their livelihoods depending mostly on livestock and trading. Being nomads they typically moved from the rivers in southern Kazakhstan to the north in summer in search of pastures, trading with those passing along the Silk Road. In fact the country's approach and policies since its independence suggest that centuries of economic suppression and collectivism by Russia and the Soviet Union have done nothing to dampen that free, entrepreneurial spirit.

The area of today's Kazakhstan is believed to be inhabited since the Stone Age and Mongol tribes settled there from the first to the eighth century. Being invaded in the twelfth century by Genghis Khan many a Kazakh family now claims ancestry with the famous Mongol. As the following three centuries saw an influx of Turk-speaking tribes, assimilating the existing population and forming the Kazakh Khanate, the Kazaks began to emerge as a distinct ethnic group in the late fifteenth century.

Out of fear of being invaded by eastern Mongol tribes, the existing Khans of Kazakh turned for protection to Russia by around 1730. But the Tsarist Empire in its attempt to assimilate rather than protect Kazakhstan alienated the indigenous population, resulting in a series of uprisings that were bloodily suppressed. One of the biggest Anti-Russian Rebellions, in 1916, saw a death toll of more than 150 000 Kazakhstanis and more than double as many fleeing abroad, marking the beginning of a major decline of Kazakh indigenous population.

In the late nineteenth century the first attempt of altering the Kazakh's nation through social engineering took place when Russia force-migrated peasants into the country to make use of the vast area and bring profit to the empire. Secondary objectives included setting up enterprise and pacifying the region by generating a strong Russian dominance. By the early twentieth century an estimated 1 million Russian settlers had been relocated by the Empire to harvest the Kazakh lands, ploughing mainly in the northern part of the country and heavily engaging in agriculture while most of the Kazakh population stayed in the southern areas tending their livestock.

Just a few decades later the Russian Empire was exchanged with the Communistic Soviet Union in 1917 when the Bolsheviks began their revolutionary movement to overthrow the Tsar. The change of government, however, did nothing to better the rather dire circumstances of the Kazakh nation. On the contrary the new establishment set out to challenge the very soul and existence of Kazakhstan's native population.

When the Bolsheviks came to power they aspired to transforming the entire new-born Republic through economic and social engineering, but the independence-orientated culture of Kazakhstan presented them with a unique problem.

Kazakhs' livestock economy was ruled by clan authority and in 1926 two-thirds of the entire population was believed to be at least semi-nomadic, moving with their herds in summer. They lived in yurts that could be packed up ready to move at a day's notice.

Soviet Russia's aim was to forcefully settle the population so they would have to take up occupations in the collective Kolkhozes and engage in organized livestock-keeping and farming, an idea and lifestyle alien to the cultural and social values of the Nomad Kazakhs. As part of the scheme the Nomads were made to surrender their livestock into the Kolkhozes.

The forceful policies by the Soviet government traumatized many Kazakhs who would rather slaughter their livestock by the millions than surrender them, causing an economic crisis that was followed by starvation and mass emigration.

Conquest (1988) highlights a census showing that the number of households declined from 1 233 000 in 1929 to 565 000 in 1936. The number of cattle shrank from 7 332 000 to a meager 1 600 000 and sheep from nearly 22 million to just 1.7 million.

Today the country's agriculture only has only a small impact on the overall scale of Kazakhstan's economy, amounting to just 5.7 percent of the gross domestic production in 2006 but receives much attention from both Kazakhstan-based development organizations as well as international financial and technical support programs.

The former Kolkhozes have all but privatized in a government-operated scheme that was aided by international advisors and could be called both fair as well as unique. Farmers and workers of the Kolkhozes were all given equally proportional tickets or vouchers that entitled them to claim a percentage of the land and livestock belonging to their Kolkhozes. Most of the state-owned land was given into private hands this way. The now independent but also much smaller land and livestock owners, however, did not have the human resources or machinery to tend their newly given assets.

A temporary vacuum leading to a shortage of agricultural products due to falling production was overcome by financial and technical aid. Some farmers then resorted to reawaken the Kolkhozes in a more informal way and continued using the collective set-up of the Kolkhozes to tend their livestock and farms in a joint fashion, helping them to overcome financial and resource related shortages.

In comparison with other former Soviet states Kazakhstan is determined to use its natural wealth to move the country towards a Western-style economy. A possible contribution to Kazakhstan's openness in regard to foreign aid and advice is the country's strong ethnic diversity. The Russian Empire had used the country as a 'stowaway' for unwanted individuals, often intellectuals like the writer Dostoevsky, the famous poet Abai or the scientist Shokan Valikhanov. Those thinkers and scholars mixed with the local population and helped spawn the initial literacy rate.

Today the Kazakh population counts 16.8 million, of which the ethnic Kazakhs represent 59.2 percent of the population and ethnic Russians 25.6 percent, with a rich array of other groups represented, including Tatars, Uzbeks, and Ukrainians and some minorities such as Russian Germans (especially Volga Germans), Polish and Czechs.

2. Government policy on SMEs and entrepreneurship

Developing 'big' industry has naturally been a paramount objective for Kazakhstan and, after completing various stages of privatization, the country turned its attention to the 'smaller' businesses.

Kazakhstan features a range of government bodies and Innovation Think-Tanks for Small and Medium Sized Businesses. Key players responsible for research and development are the Kazakh Small Business Development Fund and the Agency for Small Business Support.

These agencies could be considered the key instruments in developing, regulating and overseeing the development of the SMEs. Their responsibilities include:

- drafting proposals on legal Acts
- acting as an intermediary between the central and local authorities to coordinate efforts and activities
- analyzing and monitoring small and medium enterprises (SME) tendencies
- issuing credit guarantees for SME to be used in the Commercial Banking Environment
- participating in the application and control of funds and investments channeled towards SMEs

Apart from national and regional help the government has also accepted international advice and funds from different countries and agencies to support SMEs.

Kazakhstan consulted and secured support from The European Bank for Reconstruction and Development (EBRD), which was established in 1991 when communism was crumbling in Central and Eastern Europe to nurture the developing private sector in a democratic environment.

In March 2006 the EBRD expanded its existing support program for SMEs in Kazakhstan to US$10 million which will be managed through Kazakhstan's Alliance Bank. The purpose of the loan is to assist the Alliance Bank in servicing and credit lending to privately owned businesses with fewer than 150 employees.

Alliance also became a partner in the EBRD's Kazakhstan Small Business Program umbrella with a separate US$5 million loan, signed in January 2006, to be used for financing micro and small enterprises, including rural and agricultural business.

More financial support is being given by banks especially to the agricultural sector, for example, from the World Bank and the National Bank.

However, Technical Assistance is also available, through the United States Agency for International Development (USAID), Humanist Institute for Cooperation with Developing Countries (HIVOS), the EuroAsia Foundation, the British Know-How Fund and the Peace Corps. National organizations are the Congress of Kazakh Entrepreneurs, Kazakh Training Centre and the Women Entrepreneurs of Kazakhstan.

The USAID and other institutes have repeatedly expressed their satisfaction about the policies and widespread support that Kazakhstan tries to give to SMEs. These organizations work closely with Kazakhstan authorities and strongly recommended de-centralizing support, and providing it on a smaller more regional basis.

Another very important partner in the development of SMEs is the United Nations Industrial Development Organization (UNIDO) which since 1998, has given US$1 024 000 for program support inside of Kazakhstan. The goal of the organization is to: 'Promote and support a dynamic and efficient small- and medium-scale enterprise (SME) sector that contributes increasingly to equitable economic growth, employment creation and income generation' (Anon., 1998). The UNIDO's strategy is exactly what most experts recommend, to implement the above goal by setting up small regional support offices throughout the country, which will provide business support related services. The key elements of this service include:

- information and referrals for starting or registering a business and how to obtain forms or instructions
- general business counselling on specific issues or problems of particular clients, such as marketing, market research and finance, production, taxes and governmental regulations, personnel and equipment sourcing
- loan packaging providing assistance in preparing business plans or loan applications in order to apply for financing from banks or other funding sources
- training in the form of workshops and seminars on starting and operating businesses.

The strategy seems to pay off, according to the outputs gathered from those two centers, they have generated much interest and provided numerous SMEs with support specific to their needs. The offices in Atyrau and Almaty assisted over 700 start-ups with finance management, accounting and registration issues. They also trained nearly 3000 entrepreneurs and held seminars for start-ups involving subjects such as funding, marketing and business plan writing.

Currently the government has begun to review legislations on tax breaks and cutting red tape to ease the creation and sustainability for SMEs. Free trading zones have been set up in certain areas of the country. Furthermore, import taxes have been lifted from items such as machinery and tools that are either not available in Kazakhstan or do not satisfy the quality standards necessary to guarantee optimum operation.

From the existing as well as proposed initiatives it seems clear that Kazakhstan is

Table 17.1   Transparency International's Corruption Perception Index, 2006

Country	Corruption perception ranking	Corruption perception score
Armenia	78	3.0
Kazakhstan	93	2.4
Moldova	93	2.4
Uzbekistan	93	2.4
Kyrgyz Republic	118	2.1
Azerbaijan	124	1.8
Georgia	124	1.8
Tajikistan	124	1.8
Turkmenistan	Data unavailable	1.8

Source: Transparency International (2006).

determined to boost its overall economy and create a stable environment for SMEs, who provide a large percentage of employment as well as national income.

3.   The environment for entrepreneurship and the state of small businesses
According to Jurgen Rigterink, CEO of the DSC ABN AMRO Bank Kazakhstan, corruption is one of the main impediments for investors followed by a weak institution and legislation base. According to Mr Rigterink, corruption needs to be eliminated to encourage small investors to enter the country. During an international conference on "Corporate Finances" in May 2008, he stated: 'If you want to diversify the economy, a more wide range of investors is needed. The government has already taken steps, it is a priority for the government, but at the same time it is an obligation of the citizens of Kazakhstan' (Jurgen Rigterink in Anon., 2008).

Table 17.1 is a compilation from Transparency International's Corruption Perception Index with a selection of countries whose circumstances are similar to Kazakhstan. The corruption perception score relates to perceptions of the degree of corruption as seen by business people and country analysts, and ranges between 10 (highly clean) and 0 (highly corrupt)

The list of cases and allegations against foreign companies paying off Kazakhstan officials is long and includes prominent figures, even implicating Mr Nazarbayev. The US Justice Department and judicial institutions of other countries are investigating claims against representatives of companies such as: ABB Vetco Gray and ABB Vetco Gray UK, also Baker Hughes was charged who acted as an intermediate for ExxonMobil, BP Amoco, and Phillips Petroleum.

In 2006 spokespersons from all involved organizations denied any wrongdoing. In 2007 Baker Hughes pleaded guilty as charged and agreed to pay a US$ 44 million fine, and other cases are still under investigation or have their verdicts pending (Department for International Development, 2006).

Whilst those cases involve big industrial conglomerates, they still have an indirect impact on SMEs as bribery affects all strata of society. If a political establishment fails to provide transparent financial accountability at the top of its structure, it is impossible to manage, control and prohibit corruption, in fact almost giving a silent consent to such practices in lower levels of administration, thus creating a national culture of bribery and nepotism.

The implications of corruption for SMEs most probably revolve around issues such as: access to finance might be dependent on personal contacts, registration of new businesses is hindered or furthered depending on the applicants' ability to pay the 'informal fee', thus obstructing the development of a truly free market and, of course, once corruption is firmly embedded into governmental structures and societies it is hard to overcome and will certainly inhibit foreign investments, especially SMEs who are vulnerable to corruption as they lack the financial power or personal connections to fight such structures through official channels.

Recent amendments and proposed legislative changes to the tax code indicate the country's propensity on drawing tax as much as possible from foreign investments as well as exports while easing the burden on recipients of low income and on SMEs. Taxes in connection with income as well as value added tax (VAT) have been reduced to aid middle-class development and small businesses. In his address to the people in 2008, the president expressed that the government's aim was to introduce a new tax code that would help modernize the country and diversify the economy by easing taxes for businesses in non-resource related sectors.

The VAT was reduced from 14 percent to 13 percent. Other incentives to develop the agricultural sector include tax cuts for the import of goods and machinery such as ploughs and cultivators to 0 percent and track-type tractors from 15 percent to 5 percent. At the same time custom duties on oil and mineral products were increased and the government is considering plans to introduce new duties on exports for crude and refined products. A working group has been set up to devise further plans and strategies with the aim to implement a new tax code by January 2009.

Politically the country has, since its independence, been ruled by Mr Nazarbayev. After the formation of the country, the constitution limited a presidential incumbent to two terms in office. However, close to the end of his second term Mr Nazarbayev started to make heavy amendments to the constitution. This would allow him to stay in office for an unlimited amount of terms and set the precedence for a more autocratic form of government. Of course Mr Nazarbayev won the elections that followed shortly after his amendments to the constitution in December 2005, securing him the title of President for Life if he so pleases. The entire process as well as the elections were criticized not just by his opposition but also by international observers such as the Office for Democratic Institutions and Human Rights (OSCE) who called the elections flawed and 'failing to meet international democratic standards'. Some of the raised concerns included ballot box stuffing, harassing voters, and pressurizing students to vote for the incumbent as well as intimidating the opposition. Another highlighted aspect included media bias and, given that the mainstream media is either owned by Mr Nazarbayev's daughter Dorigo or intimidated and shut down, this is hardly surprising. A thorough analysis of the country by *The Cacianalyst* finds that Mr Nazarbayev has, through subtle manipulation, put himself on a pedestal that shields him from legal prosecution and rules any criticism against him an illegal act against the state. The paper also concludes that: 'While the executive branch clearly trumps both the legislature and judiciary in Kazakhstan, the other institutions nonetheless play an important symbolic role, necessary for the country to continue to secure foreign assistance. They have also helped

Table 17.2   Vital statistics

Total	2000	2001	2002	2003	2004	1 October 2005
Registered small enterprises	76 743	98 300	113 319	128 187	195 707	209 758
Of which are operational	63 556	75 505	85 493	91 039	144 156	158 154
Employment (000s)	1001	979	1088	1210	1752.9	1788.4
Change in % of registered small enterprises		+28%	+15%	+13%	+52%	+ 7%

Source: USAID Enterprise Development Project (2005).

legitimize Nazarbayev's grabs for power' (Department for International Development, 2000).

Reading between the lines of the country's activities in and outside of the economic scope there are clear indicators that Kazakhstan is not entirely ruled by democratic process but by more or less subtle manipulation instigated by the executive branch which is exclusively controlled by the president.

One of the most accurate available sources on the state of SMEs in Kazakhstan comes from the USAID Enterprise Development Project and ranges from 2000 to 2005. The project separates small enterprises from medium-sized businesses by defining entities of small entrepreneurship to be individuals with no more than 50 employees on a yearly average basis. A special financial restriction applies to formations that constitute a legal entity (USAID Enterprise Development Project, http://en.casme.net).

Table 17.2 shows the number of registered businesses labeled as 'Small enterprises' but also the number of employees for any given year, which can be used to calculate the average number of employment for small businesses. For example in 2000 there were 63 556 operating businesses with a total number of 1 001 000 employees. Given those numbers, the average business consisted of 15.75 employees.

The significant increase of registered SMEs from 2003 and 2004 is attributed to the introduction of a 'One Stop' registration process, improved credit facilities to SMEs and other positive changes in legislation to ease the financial strain on small businesses and to cut red tape.

Together with previously mentioned plans to review the existing tax legislation in favour of diversifying the economy, SME are on the receiving end and will find excellent conditions to start new businesses and improve sustainability for existing businesses.

4.   Internationalization of entrepreneurs and SMEs

Looking at SMEs in general, they seem to have a propensity to remain un-internation-alized and trade within proximity and local market restraints depending on their individual resources. Kazakhstan's SMEs are no exception and as of yet there is little to no existing data that would suggest much activity in internationalization.

However, this fact is hardly surprising as the country is just beginning to enter a stage of stability in economic and political terms. Current programs focus on the development of a middle class, the training of entrepreneurs and support systems for SMEs. The country is taking one step at a time and so far all implemented strategies have been a huge success. As Kazakhstan is in the process of joining the World Trade Organization (WTO), the United Nations Development Program (UNDP) in conjunction with its Kazakh counterpart the CPAP have drafted a strategy with a focus on globalization issues:

> UNDP will also assist Kazakhstan in better understanding the impact of globalization on its economy and people . . . focusing on the potential positive and negative impacts. This will help to widen awareness and understanding of the full impact of WTO accession on Kazakhstan and the resultant challenges to various economic sectors and the people of Kazakhstan. (*Action Plan 2005–2009 (Government of Kazakhstan and the United Nations Development Program)*)

Currently globalization and internationalization is a topic that is increasingly being picked up by the Kazakh government, financial institutions and scholars alike, and it should only be a matter of time before the momentum reaches entrepreneurs and SMEs.

One major factor that has been identified as impeding small business to internationalize is Kazakhstan's still underdeveloped Communication Sector which is an essential tool needed for SMEs to internationalize.

According to a survey conducted by Internet World Stats (2008), in 2007 only 8.5 percent of the population had access to the Internet; while this is a sharp increase from only 2.7 percent in 2005 it still indicates a lacking infrastructure necessary for SMEs to access possible markets, build vertical alliances with other businesses and connect with peer entrepreneurs to share knowledge.

There is worldwide recognition of the importance and possibilities for small businesses to internationalize. The Organisation for Economic Co-operation and Development (OECD) has studied impediments amongst a large body of SMEs in its member countries as well as governmental policies and strategies aimed to help achieve high rates of internationalization in those countries.

The OECD has found the main contributors that impede internationalization in SMEs are factors such as lack of entrepreneurial, managerial and marketing skills, bureaucracy, missing access to information and knowledge, language barriers and cultural differences, competition of indigenous SMEs in foreign markets, lack of governmental support and incentives, and complexity of trade documentation and legislation (Marcel, 2008).

Kazakhstan is not a member of the OECD but would clearly benefit from the experience and existing support of such an organization, especially in terms of determining the exact needs amongst SMEs and entrepreneurs in respect of real and perceived barriers, and impediments. At present the available data on small businesses in Kazakhstan is at best sketchy due to a lack of reporting procedures and research projects. Wojciech Huebner describes in his *SME Development* (2000) that a report required to be submitted by 3797 organizations: only 18 percent fulfilled the task, 60 percent refrained from indicating current activities and another 22 percent did not fully complete the reporting process for various other reasons.

As it is vital for any new strategy to first conduct a thorough analysis of the situation, one hopes that Kazakhstan will expand its economic development strategies to encourage SMEs and entrepreneurs towards new markets to insure competitiveness and economic sustainability.

5. Conclusion

A fast growing and upcoming industry nation, Kazakhstan has overcome the first phase of repositioning its industry and privatizing the country's assets. This was done in phases focusing on big industry and moving on to smaller businesses, Kolkhozes and homes.

Especially during the sale of houses and land, the Kazakhstanis' approach can only be described as a role model for fairness. Local residents were given the chance to buy their formerly state-owned homes for a fraction of their actual value and Kazakhstanis were encouraged to buy up smaller businesses and portions of land belonging to their Kolkhozes.

While there are critics of the current establishment and corruption is present in all strata of Kazakhstan's governmental bodies, the country also pushes hard for social, academic and economic development.

Hopefully, with the increasing saturation of wealth amongst Kazakhstan's population and the establishment of a healthy middle class, nepotism and corruption will play a diminishing role in the country's everyday life.

Being an ethnic as well as religiously diverse nation, Kazakhstan has much talent and strength to draw upon. Government strategies to nurture the economy are as much present as programs to improve health services, reduction of unemployment and poverty rates, free quality education and women's rights. A success indicator of how well those strategies have been enacted is the fast reduction in Kazakhstan's poverty rate and a steady increase in wages. And whilst shortly after its independence there had been an exodus of skilled labour, the country has made sure it remains attractive not only to foreign workforce but also to investors.

For entrepreneurs Kazakhstan can be strongly recommended as a country of enormous opportunities, with the safety of a stable political system as long as one is willing to adapt to the 'unofficial fees and who's your contact' methodology of the system.

References

Action Plan 2005–2009 (Government of Kazakhstan and the United Nations Development Program), http://www.un.kz/img/docs/en/1105.doc (accessed 7 May 2008).

Anon. (1998), 'UNIDO Project DP/KAZ/98/009, NT/KAZ, 98/009', http://www.unido.org/datal/project/project.cfm?c=9931 (accessed 14 May 2008).

Anon. (2008), 'Basic problem for investors in Kazakhstan is corruption – head of DSC "ABN AMRO Bank Kazakhstan"', http://eng.gazeta.kz/art.asp?aid=110676 (accessed 25 May 2008).

Conquest, Robert (1988), *The Harvest of Sorrow*. London: Arrow Books.

Dana, Léo-Paul (2002), *When Economies Change Paths: Models of Transition in China, the Central Asian Republics, Myanmar, and the Nations of Former Indochine Française*, Singapore, London and Hong Kong: World Scientific.

Department for International Development (2000), 'Sultan Nazarbayev?: Central Asia's latest president-for-life', http://www.cacianalyst.org/?q=node/294 (accessed 22 May 2008).

Department for International Development (2006), 'Central Asia, South Caucasus and Moldova: regional assistance plan', http://www.dfid.gov.uk/pubs/files/rapcascm.pdf (accessed 20 May 2008).

Huebner, Wojciech (2000), 'SME development in countries of Central Asia (Kazakhstan, Kyrgyzstan and Uzbekistan): constraints, cultural aspects and role of international assistance', Vienna, http://www.unido.org/fileadmin/import/userfiles/puffk/huebner.pdf (accessed 10 May 2008).

Internet World Stats (2008), 'Internet World Stats: usage and population statistics', http://www.internetworld-stats.com/asia/kz.htm (accessed 30 May 2008).

Marcel, Roy (2008), 'AECM Seminar on Internationalization of SMEs', http://www.aecm.be/DE/documents/2_MRoypresentation.pdf (accessed 1 July 2008).
Transparency International (2006), Corruption Perception Index, http://www.transparency.org/news_room/in_focus/2006/oecd_progress/foreign_bribery_asia_pacific (accessed 27 May 2008).
USAID Enterprise Development Project (2005), 'SME Statistics – Republic of Kazakhstan', http://en.casme.net/docs/Digest_of_Kazakhstan_SME_Statistics_eng%20edit_05.pdf (accessed 2 May 2008).

18 Kyrgyzstan
Serkan Yalcin

Introduction to Kyrgyzstan

Kyrgyzstan, or Kyrgyz Republic, is located in Central Asia and borders China, Tajikistan, Uzbekistan, and Kazakhstan. Kyrgyzstan has 198 500 sq km of land, of which only 7 percent is arable as the country is very mountainous; the Tien Shan Mountains cover approximately 95 percent of Kyrgyzstan. Kyrgyzstan, known as the Switzerland of Central Asia, has many natural beauties, among which are perfect mountains, valleys, lakes, and rivers (Kyrgyz Government, 2007).

The Kyrgyz have been in Central Asia since the first millennium BC and have carried their name throughout the centuries. In the late 1800s, Kyrgyzstan joined the Russian Empire. After the socialist revolution in 1917, the Kyrgyz together with all the peoples of the former Tsarist Russia formed the Union of Soviet Socialist Republics (USSR). After the collapse of the USSR, Kyrgyzstan obtained its independence in a peaceful way on 31 August 1991, the date of the Declaration of Independence (Kyrgyz Government, 2007). In 2005, The Tulip Revolution resulted in the dismissal of the former President Askar Akayev, who had run the country since 1991. The former Prime Minister Kurmanbek Bakiyev became the new president in July 2005. Kyrgyzstan's recent concerns are privatization of state-owned enterprises, development of democracy and political freedoms, reduction of corruption, and improving inter-ethnic relations (CIA, 2007).

Kyrgyzstan has a multi-ethnic population of around 5 million people, consisting of Kyrgyz, Russians, Uzbeks, Kazakhs, Uighurs, Ukrainians, Germans, Tatars, and Tajiks. The urban population is around 65 percent and the literacy rate is 98 percent. Its main cities are Bishkek, the capital, Osh, and Jalal-Abad. The main religions are Islam and Russian Orthodox. Kyrgyzstan has a young population (mean age is 22.7) and is generally bilingual in Kyrgyz and Russian. When we consider the availability of a young and educated labour force, and the fact that there are not many jobs available and the salary level is low in Kyrgyzstan, this situation creates an attractive labour market for companies (Kyrgyz Government, 2007; US Department of State, 2007).

Although some states of the former USSR such as Uzbekistan, Tajikistan, and Georgia had social and political troubles and even interior wars after the independence, the situation in Kyrgyzstan was positive as the country was very quick to implement economic reforms and construct foreign relations; consequently, many foreign countries have helped Kyrgyzstan (Dana, 2000a). Nevertheless, Kyrgyzstan faced many economic problems after independence since the Kyrgyz economy was closely linked to that of the USSR economy. The economic system at that time was arranged in a way to allow assembly operations that were fed by supplies of components from other parts of the USSR. With the collapse of the USSR, the former production and supply chain linkages with other states of the USSR broke down and the production volume decreased severely (Chattopadhyay, 1999). Accordingly, gross domestic product (GDP) declined sharply between 1991 and 1995. All economic indicators deteriorated: hyperinflation, unemployment, real income, poverty, external borrowing (no more Soviet subsidies), depletion of assets, domestic consumption, and government expenditures. In 1993, the national currency, the Som, was introduced, prices were liberalized, and an open external trade regime was adopted. These efforts led to recoveries in the economy, beginning in 1996. However, the economy was negatively affected by the 1998 Russian financial crisis. After that, the economy began to grow with its strong sectors of agriculture (Kyrgyzstan has the world's largest natural growth walnut forests) and mining (mainly gold). In addition, construction, power, and service sectors also began to develop. This economic growth was also supported by some governmental policies such as macroeconomic and exchange rate stability, fiscal deficit reduction, tight fiscal and monetary policy, and inflation reduction. The GDP increased by 7.1 percent in 2004. However, in 2005, political upheavals led to the Tulip Revolution; the economy was affected negatively and uncertainties occurred in the economic and political environments. The economic performance is now contingent on how effectively and quickly Kyrgyzstan can achieve political stability. In 2006, the Kyrgyz GDP was US$2.8 billion and GDP per capita was US$536. Today, there are many serious challenges for Kyrgyzstan: poverty, external debt, economic diversification, strengthening governance, human development, and regional cooperation on water, energy, and trade (United Nations, 2007a; World Bank, 2007).

Government policy on SMEs and entrepreneurship in Kyrgyzstan
Government policy on small and medium-sized enterprises (SMEs) in Kyrgyzstan is based on the following institutional components: the State Commission for Small and Medium-Sized Business Support under the Government of Kyrgyzstan, the business incubator of the State Commission, the State Inspection on Standardization and Metrology, 10 micro credit organizations, the Chamber of Commerce and Industry, financial, technical, informational support to entrepreneurs and SMEs from the government (Hubner 2000; State Commission, 2006). Figure 18.1 shows the governmental establishment with respect to the SME sector.

The State Commission or Fund for SME Support is the key governmental unit that offers short-term SME credits as well as other services, and this unit is the main national counterpart of the United Nations (UN) SME project in Kyrgyzstan. The Kyrgyz government established the State Commission in 1992 to increase the effectiveness of SME policies. In 1998, the main task of formulating SME policies was given to the Ministry of Industry and Foreign Trade. However, significant contributions are still being provided by the State Commission. The State Commission provides support in forming governmental policies for SMEs and entrepreneurs, and assists the implementation of these policies especially in licensing of entrepreneurial activity and registration. In addition to the Commission, various commercial banks, German credit lines, the European Bank for Reconstruction and Development (EBRD), World Bank, Central Asian–American Enterprise Fund, and Swiss Helvetas offer credit to SMEs while the United Nations Development Programme/United Nations Industrial Development Organization (UNDP/UNIDO) SME Project KYR, the Gesellschaft für Technische Zusammenarbeit (GTZ) SME Project, the Japanese Cultural Center in Kyrgyzstan, and the Soros Foundation offer technical assistance (State Commission, 2005).

In sum, the government tries to provide as much help as possible to stimulate SMEs and entrepreneurship by establishing the legal framework and various assistance

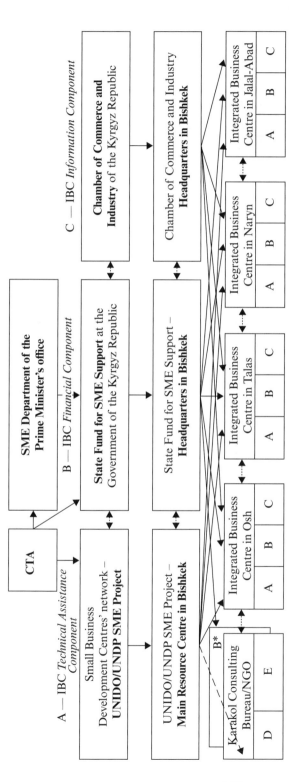

Notes:
A = Component of the Small Business Development Centres' network (UNIDO/UNDP Project).
B = Component of the network of the State Fund for SME Support at the Government of the Kyrgyz Republic (Regional Office).
C = Component of the network of the Chamber of Commerce and Industry of the Kyrgyz Republic (Regional Department).
D = SME Consulting Bureau at the local NGO, trained and supported by the SBDC network (new model).
E = NGO.
Multi-way information flows within the Integrated Business Centres' network and their parent organizations:
* B: Regional Office of the State Fund for SME Support in Karakol (the process of setting up of a fully-fledged Integrated Business Centre in Karakol has not been completed).

Source: Hubner (2000: 32).

Figure 18.1 SME policy advice and the national network of integrated business centres (IBC) in Kyrgyzstan

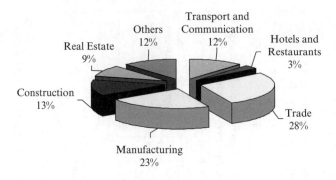

Source: National Statistical Committee of the Kyrgyz Republic (2008).

Figure 18.2 Sectoral breakdown of SMEs in Kyrgyzstan

programs. However, the transitory nature of the country sometimes postpones these programs. In my interview with the State Commission in 2004, the chairman had indicated that they were all aware of the problems facing SMEs and entrepreneurs but they were also limited in their efforts since they did not have large resources. The Information for Investment Decisions Inc. (2002) underlined that economic and especially political problems do not always allow the government to give the necessary support; many Kyrgyz officials, including the former President Akayev, stated that the problems had clearly been identified, but the problem was that solutions of these problems were not so easy because of lack of institutional environment as well as political resistance to change. Dana (2007) also pointed out the transitory nature of this and the fact that although governments throughout Asia recognize the importance of entrepreneurship, their respective promotion efforts differ greatly, reflecting national priorities, demographic factors, and cultural values. Therefore, historical, cultural, and public policy factors and social norms and education affect entrepreneurship.

The economic and sociocultural environment for entrepreneurship and the state of small business in Kyrgyzstan
Kyrgyzstan is a small country without oil and gas and it relies mainly on gold, hydro-electric power, and perhaps in the future some rare minerals. Thus, the role of SMEs is critical since economic growth prospects by big state-owned enterprises are limited as they struggle to adjust to the new economic system. Therefore, real economic growth is believed to be realized by new small companies and new-generation entrepreneurs (Hubner, 2000).

In Kyrgyzstan, businesses employing up to 50 employees in the production sector are small, whereas those with 51 to 200 employees are medium-sized businesses; the corresponding numbers in the service sector are 0–15 and 16–50 employees, respectively (United Nations Economic Commission for Europe, 2003). The sectoral dispersion of SMEs in Kyrgyzstan is shown in Figure 18.2.

The number of officially registered businesses and the number of people employed by these businesses have been growing and SMEs now account for 44.3 percent of GDP, and 60 percent of total employment (National Statistical Committee of the Kyrgyz

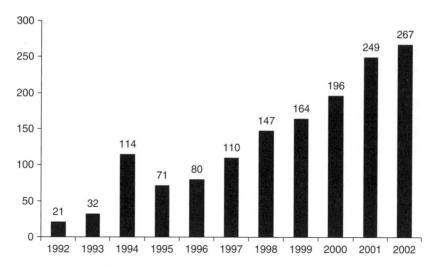

Source: National Statistical Committee of the Kyrgyz Republic (2008).

Figure 18.3 Number of SMEs in Kyrgyzstan (thousands)

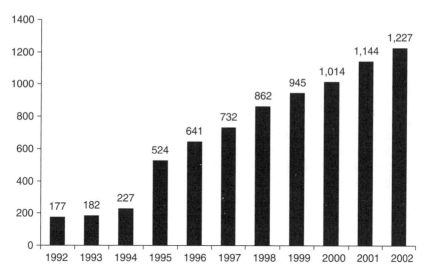

Source: National Statistical Committee of the Kyrgyz Republic (2008).

Figure 18.4 Employment in SMEs in Kyrgyzstan (thousands)

Republic, 2008). Figure 18.3 and Figure 18.4 respectively show the number of SMEs and the number of people employed by SMEs in Kyrgyzstan.

Kyrgyzstan implemented extensive small-scale privatization, but progress on large-scale privatization has proceeded more slowly. By 2000, all commercially viable small businesses had been fully privatized, and about 1300 medium- and large-scale enterprises were privatized under a mass privatization programme (Babetskii et al., 2003).

Traditional entrepreneurship among the indigenous people involves herding, 86 percent of which is pasture, and is still important (Dana, 2000a). However, rural entrepreneurship was neglected; there was no privatization in grazing pasture whereas privatization of agricultural land was quick. When cooperatives were disbanded, people obtained livestock. However, since there was uncertainty as to access to pastures, many farmers preferred to slaughter their livestock to get money (Dana, 2002).

The economic and sociocultural environment factors affecting the conception and birth of enterprises can be grouped into three in the entrepreneurship field: the person (the ability to establish a new venture), the process (the behaviour and events leading to establishing a new firm), and the rate (the experiences of incumbent companies) (Liao and Welsch, 2005). Perhaps, the second factor is more relevant than the others to Kyrgyzstan. When the USSR system was replaced by the private enterprise system, many people lost their jobs. Today, there are not many jobs available and some available jobs require skills that local people do not have; salaries are very low (GDP per capita is US$536) as well. Thus, many people may be encouraged to engage in entrepreneurship in one way or another rather than working in a company. For example, during my work at a university in Bishkek between 2003 and 2005, many of my students told me that they would rather prefer to establish their own business, no matter how small it may be, rather than work for a very low level of salary. I later saw my students together having established micro-enterprises. This example of my students perhaps shows a reality in Kyrgyzstan: why work for US$100–200 per month when a person needs at least US$400–500 per month to survive, especially in cities? Being an entrepreneur is also an option today as private property is allowed now. Although this option seems to be logical compared with being an employee especially considering job scarcity and low salary levels in Kyrgyzstan, the problems with this option are that many people do not have prior entrepreneurial skills as private enterprises were not allowed in the USSR system. In addition, people do not have capital to start a business and credit availability is limited. Therefore, the process factor as indicated by Liao and Welsch (2005) both stimulates and discourages the indigenous Kyrgyz people to engage in entrepreneurship. The rate factor is not really relevant to Kyrgyzstan as existing local companies do not have enough experience.

Economic elements are important for entrepreneurship as entrepreneurs generally, although not always, begin with such questions as 'is it desirable and is it feasible to start a business?' (Shapero and Sokol, 1982, p. 74). The financial push (US$100–200 salary versus US$400–500 living expenses) may be a logical, desirable, and perhaps the key motive behind the entrepreneurship in Kyrgyzstan. Although the person, the behaviour, and the rate framework, and the economical conditions provide valuable explanations for entrepreneurship, we need to take into account the sociocultural element as well; Dana (2000b) states that value systems and cultural norms affect acceptability and perceived utility of entrepreneurship.

There is no doubt that the USSR work culture had negatively affected entrepreneurship and employee productivity. Kaynak et al. (2006) found that the biggest problem foreign investors have in Kyrgyzstan is low productivity of local employees resulting from the USSR work culture; an employee can leave work around 2 or 3 p.m. as he thinks that he has worked enough for the day, or a street seller may not want to sell you at noon all the apples she has because 'what she will do until evening'! These are two examples I faced myself. Such logic is still dominant, especially among middle-aged and old people; however,

Table 18.1   Differences between centralized and market-oriented systems

	Environment created by the old and centralized system	Requirements of the new, market-oriented system
Organizational structure	Vertical, hierarchical structure of communication	Flat structure, horizontal communication channels
Communication	Isolated channels of communication with diversified information for selected subjects	Open channels with identical information for all participating units
	Language of communication: commands, quantities, direct allocation of resources, non-anonymous information	Language of communication: prices, anonymous information of the market
	Rigid rules of plan implementation, tasks imposed by higher authority	Entrepreneur surrounded by opportunities and competing alternatives
	Passive implementation of imposed tasks	Proactive attitudes encouraged
External relations	Closed, national economy, autarchy, self-sufficient economy	Open economy attempting integration with the world economy
	Macro philosophy: how to earn for necessary imports?	Macro philosophy: how to promote exports?
Cost	Little consideration to production cost	Cost efficiency-main condition for success
Consumer	Important but only declarative terms	Focus crucial
Marketing	Waste of resources	Information concerning choices of companies and consumers
Competition philosophy	Waste of efforts and resources	Systematic mechanism guaranteeing efficiency and best allocation of resources
Quality	Internal, domestic standards of quality	World-class, internationally competitive products
Risk	Exposure to little risk and uncertainty	Entrepreneurs functioning in the world of risk, permanent uncertainties and probabilities
Financing	Soft-budget constraint	Stringent rules of the financial system become main guideline for company strategy
Education	Formal and massive education	Pragmatic approach to training and education

Source: Hubner (2000: 18).

young people especially those with a college education do not tend to display such USSR logic. Therefore, education is important in changing the old work culture. Over 70 years of USSR rule changed lots of things in Kyrgyzstan, it is not easy to change all this in a short period of time. Table 18.1 shows the difference in the two economic systems.

When we consider the scope of change as outlined in Table 18.1, we cannot expect an instant change. The change is very big and comprehensive as it covers the government, institutions, consumers, and companies. Hubner (2000) argued that the required changes should be understood in the context of the economic system as a whole and they are rooted in the features of the centralized system of the USSR.

Therefore, it is normal to see many problems during this transition process. Among factors hindering entrepreneurship in Kyrgyzstan are administrative barriers, excessive inspections by different parties each following their own procedures, unclear and unstable tax policy, lack of financing, complexity of the licensing/permit system, multi-layer corruption, and insufficient knowledge of business and market economy rules by potential and incumbent entrepreneurs (Hubner, 2000; Suhir and Kovach, 2003).

Internationalization of entrepreneurs and SMEs from Kyrgyzstan: drivers and roadblocks
Kyrgyzstan became a World Trade Organization member in 1998; many of its neighbours are not yet WTO members. Being a WTO member helps access to the markets of other WTO member countries and the Kyrgyz food exporters have access to the European market. However, very few of the Kyrgyz food producers can meet the European Union (EU) food safety standards. Therefore, most food exports still go to Russia and CIS countries where standards are much lower. Although trade with China (a WTO member) has increased in recent years, China is not a major destination for the Kyrgyz exports (International Trade Centre, 2005). There has been an important change in the destination of Kyrgyz exports between 1988 and 2006. Germany, Russia, and Kazakhstan accounted for 70 percent of the Kyrgyz exports in 1988. Switzerland and Afghanistan became new export destinations in 2006. Kazakhstan and Russia have remained among the top four export destinations during this period. The Kyrgyz government pursues a trade policy that is outward oriented and allows better market access to improve Kyrgyzstan's integration into global markets (United Nations, 2007b).

Kyrgyz exports are composed of gold, electricity, and other commodities; technical, climatic, and world market conditions heavily determine the export volume. These factors are independent of the economic activities of the country. Therefore, export increase or decrease does not mean much for economic productivity. Gold and electricity account for more than half of the total value of exports. Since these two sectors are operated by big firms, SMEs do not much contribute to Kyrgyz foreign trade. Since the private sector is weak and lacks capital, knowledge, and experience, SMEs are guided by the government, and they are not so influential in foreign trade (International Trade Centre, 2005). Table 18.2 shows Kyrgyz exports by sectors.

Although there is no published research on the internationalization of SMEs in Kyrgyzstan, to the best of our knowledge, the mode of internationalization must be export and in live animal and animal products and agriculture sectors; electricity, mining, and machinery exports are undertaken by big firms since local SMEs do not have such capabilities nor resources to operate in these relatively capital-intensive industries. The reason for why SME exports are so limited should be sought in the poverty level of Kyrgyzstan; the problems of SMEs mentioned earlier are other roadblocks on internationalization. In sum, Kyrgyz SMEs do not have many resources, skills, and expertise that will facilitate internationalization. If the quality of products increases, then SMEs in Kyrgyzstan may have more of chance in international markets; however, this depends on

Table 18.2   Kyrgyz exports by sectors (US$ million)

Sectors	2004	2005	2006
Mineral products	94.1	96.9	177.8
Textile and fabrics	79.5	77.4	96.7
Machinery, equipment; electrical equipment and parts	35.6	32.1	51.2
Stone, gypsum, cement, asbestos, ceramics; glass and articles	37.9	46.2	43.9
Vegetable products	26.1	18.1	36.6
Prepared foodstuffs; beverages; tobacco and manufactured tobacco substitutes	42.9	37.2	28.9
Live animals, animal products	12.1	18.1	23.7

Source: National Statistical Committee of the Kyrgyz Republic (2008).

investment in technology or technology transfer. Since the governmental resources are limited, foreign companies in Kyrgyzstan can be a source of technology transfer.

Conclusion
Kyrgyzstan has realized significant reforms to improve the climate for entrepreneurs and SMEs. Nevertheless, there are still a number of barriers to entrepreneurship and SMEs. The high level of uncertainty, poverty, institutional rigidities, lack of capital accumulation and credit sources, and inefficient USSR work habits have inhibited the development of a strong entrepreneurial environment and private sector. Consequently, SMEs operate mainly in agriculture, petty trade, and the informal sector (Babetskii et al., 2003). Since Kyrgyz SMEs cannot produce high-quality products, their prospects for internationalization are also limited.

There seem to be various policy issues for the government with respect to entrepreneurship and SME development. Although the government does not have many resources as Kyrgyzstan is poor, it can decrease the burden of establishing and running enterprises. In addition, as technology transfer is needed, the government needs to find ways to increase foreign investments to Kyrgyzstan so that indigenous firms can learn from the foreign experience. When we consider the landlocked nature of the country, and thus transportation difficulties, the information technology sector may be one key sector for the economy. A government policy to develop the information technology sector could be useful. Although all these policy suggestions may be appropriate, the realities of Kyrgyzstan have prevented and will prevent the implementation of such policies. Kyrgyzstan has a high level of corruption and some political upheavals. It is hard to change old habits and established traditions. The former President Akayev was in power from 1991 to 2005; no matter how well or badly he ruled the country, a single administration cannot provide the changes needed.

With respect to academia, new venture establishment and development in Kyrgyzstan can be examined by utilizing the social capital theory, which states that network ties provide access to resources and information (Liao and Welsch, 2005). In Kyrgyzstan, the banking sector gives loans to big and loss-making state enterprises; thus, private SMEs and micro-enterprises are neglected. The indigenous entrepreneurs have to rely on their own sources and networks to raise capital; 93 percent of entrepreneurs did not use bank credit, as the 1997 Living Standards Household Survey showed (Babetskii et al., 2003). Therefore, in the absence of credit sources, skills, and experience as in the case of Kyrgyzstan, many entrepreneurs are expected to utilize their relatives and friends to establish and survive new ventures. Dana (2007) indicated that Muslims in Central Asia have constructed networks of like-minded co-ethnics in neighboring countries and this enhanced trade opportunities. Overseas business transactions are also facilitated by these ethnic networks in which members speak the same language and share similar values, influenced by the same religion. Therefore, the social capital theory may have valuable explanations for the indigenous entrepreneurship and the internationalization of SMEs in Kyrgyzstan. Other valuable research can be on institutional environment (IE). There is recent interest in IE and entrepreneurship, as evidenced by special issue initiatives by major journals such as *Entrepreneurship Theory and Practice*. As the IE in Kyrgyzstan is newly emerging and unstable, it should no doubt have implications on the entrepreneurial environment and the SME sector. Rigorous research on this subject can enrich our understanding of IE and entrepreneurship interactions in post-socialist transition economies.

References

Babetskii, Ian, Alexandre Kolev and Mathilde Maurel (2003), 'Kyrgyz labour market in the late 1990s: the challenge of formal job creation', *Comparative Economic Studies*, **45**(4): 493.
Chattopadhyay, Satya (1999), 'Assessment of quality management practice in the Republic of Kyrgyzstan', *Managerial Auditing Journal*, **14**(1/2): 62.
CIA (2007), *The World Factbook*, https://www.cia.gov/library/publications/the-world-factbook/geos/kg.html (accessed 1 November 2007).
Dana, Léo-Paul (2000a), 'Change and circumstance in Kyrgyz markets', *Qualitative Market Research*, **3**(2): 62–73.
Dana, Léo-Paul, (2000b), 'Creating entrepreneurs in India', *Journal of Small Business Management*, **38**(1): 86–91.
Dana, Léo-Paul (2002), *When Economies Change Paths, Models of Transition in China, the Central Asian Republics, Myanmar and the Nations of Former Indochine Française*, Singapore, London and Hong Kong: World Scientific.
Dana, Léo-Paul (2007), *Asian Models of Entrepreneurship, from the Indian Union and the Kingdom of the Nepal to the Japanese Archipelago, Context, Policy, and Practice*, Singapore, London and Hong Kong: World Scientific.
Hubner, Wojiech (2000), *SME Development in Countries of Central Asia (Kazakhstan, Kyrgyzstan, and Uzbekistan): Constraints, Cultural Aspects and Role of International Assistance*, Vienna: United Nations Industrial Development Organization.
Information for Investment Decisions Inc. (2002), *Attracting FDI to Kyrgyzstan Current Status, Final Report Relating to UNDP Reimbursable Loan Agreement (RLA) No. 02-001*, www.undp.kg/english/publications/2002/fdi.pdf (accessed 1 February 2007).
International Trade Centre (2005), *Evaluation of International Trade Centre, (UNCTAD/WTO), Country Reports, Kyrgyz Republic*, http://www.itcevaluation.org (accessed 1 March 2008).
Kaynak, Erdener, Serkan Yalcin and Ekrem Tatoglu (2006), 'A comparative study of foreign direct investment activities in Georgia and Kyrgyz Republic', *Multinational Business Review*, **14**(3): 29–52.
Kyrgyz Government (2007), http://www.gov.kg (accessed 17 December 2007).
Liao, Jianwen, and Harold Welsch (2005), 'Roles of social capital in venture creation: key dimensions and research implications', *Journal of Small Business Management*, **43**(4): 345–62.
National Statistical Committee of the Kyrgyz Republic (2008), http://www.stat.kg/Eng/Home/Index.html#Top1 (accessed 1 January 2008).
Shapero, Albert and Lisa Sokol (1982), 'The social dimensions of entrepreneurship', in C.A. Kent, D.L. Sexton and K.H. Vesper (eds), *Encyclopedia of Entrepreneurship*: 72-90. Englewood Cliffs, NJ: Prentice-Hall, pp. 72–90.
State Commission for Small and Medium-Sized Business Support under the Government of Kyrgyzstan (2005), www.smbusiness.kg (accessed 8 April 2005).
Suhir, Elena and Zlatko Kovach (2003), *Administrative Barriers to Entrepreneurship in Central Asia*, Washington, DC: Center for International Private Enterprise, US Department of Commerce.

United Nations Economic Commission for Europe (2003), *Small and Medium-Sized Enterprises in Countries in Transition, Series: Entrepreneurship and SMEs, United Nations*, www.unece.org/indust/sme/smepubli.pdf (accessed 12 October 2007).

United Nations, (2007a), *Country Studies*, www.unescap.org/tid/publication/tipub2437_kyrgyz.pdf (accessed 16 December 2007).

United Nations (2007b), *Traders' Manual for Landlocked Countries: Kyrgyzstan, Economic and Social Commission for Asia and the Pacific, United Nations*, www.unescap.org/tid/publication/tipub2458.pdf (accessed 17 October 2007).

US Department of State (2007), http://www.state.gov/r/pa/ei/bgn/5755.htm#people (accessed 13 November 2007).

World Bank (2007), *Kyrgyz Republic, Country Brief*, http://web.worldbank.org (accessed 24 December 2007).

19 Laos[1]
Léo-Paul Dana and Susanne Barthmann

Introduction
The Lao People's Democratic Republic – also known as Laos – is one of Asia's most undeveloped nations, and among the five poorest in the world. The landlocked country, enclosing 236 800 square kilometres, is nestled between Cambodia, China, Myanmar, Thailand and Vietnam. Laos is sparsely populated. It is among the least urbanized nations in Asia.

Traditionally, business activities in Laos were not associated with high social status. Cultural values, stemming from religious beliefs, emphasized instead the elimination of desire. Commerce, on the other hand, was perceived as a means to satisfy desire. Social forces thus discouraged enterprise, and trade was usually the role of those with inferior social standing. When Lao men refrained from doing business, women often succeeded (Dana 1997). Yet, the communist take-over further discouraged entrepreneurial spirit. As a result, Lao society is generally non-entrepreneurial. The Chinese community of 67 000 people – 1.3 percent of the population – is very active in the entrepreneurship sector. Large corporations in Thailand each earn more than the value of all the goods and services produced in all of Laos.

Government policy
During the nineteenth century, France persuaded one of the leaders to accept a French protectorate, as insurance against conquest by China or Siam. France then united all of the Lao principalities into one country. This came to be named Laos, which is the plural of Lao. France used Laos as a buffer between their Asian acquisitions and British Burma. The French imposed a Vietnamese-staffed civil service in Laos, but they did not contribute to the protectorate. When the Japanese occupied French Indochina in 1941, the Lao people obtained more autonomy than they had experienced under French protection. Following the Second World War, France tried to take back Laos; in 1949 the latter was declared an independent associate state of the French Union. The United Nations recognized Laos as a separate country, and in 1953 France allowed Laos to become a monarchy. In 1954, communists occupied areas of two Lao provinces, namely, Phong Saly and Sam Neua. In 1959, King Savang Vatthana became monarch of the Lao kingdom. By 1960, the communist-led *Pathet Lao* (Lao People's Party) forces made advances, and during a three-day period in December that year, Vientiane was ruled by four successive governments.

In 1962, the Royal Lao Government and the State of Israel embarked on a joint experimental farm, along the Mekong River. Known as the Vientiane Pilot Project, this project provided farmers with seed, fertilizer, insecticide and even irrigation. The objective was to transform subsistence farmers into market-oriented entrepreneurs. Participants prospered and by 1968, 250 families had participated in the project (White, 1968).

In December 1975, the Lao Patriotic Front – the political arm of the *Pathet Lao*

– abolished the monarchy and created a communist entity, the Lao People's Democratic Republic. All Christian seminaries were closed that year. When the Lao People Revolutionary Party took control of the Lao People's Democratic Republic, in 1975, it implemented a policy of accelerated socialisation. Harsh policies shunned entrepreneurship and co-operatives replaced private initiatives. Former royalists were sent to re-education camps where they were forced to accept communism. In 1977, Laos and Vietnam signed a treaty of friendship and co-operation.

In 1987, Laos implemented its New Economic Mechanism – a radical shift in public policy. This recognized market forces as legitimate, and began liberalizing the centralized economy. The first national election took place in 1989. Inflation reached 76 percent that year. In 1990, the state launched a drive to attract foreign investment, privatise state enterprises, develop import-substitution industries and promote exports. In 1991, a new constitution ushered in further economic reforms. New laws were subsequently introduced, governing property, labour and foreign investment. New relationships were also developed. Laos signed treaties of friendship and co-operation with Thailand in 1991, with Cambodia in 1992, with China in 1994, and with Myanmar in 1994.

In April 1994, Laos and Vietnam signed an agreement on goods in transit, which allowed these commodities to be transported across either Laos or Vietnam, on the way to the other. It was expected that this would facilitate international trade. In May 1994, Laos introduced a liberal law governing investments. This streamlined foreign investment regulations and tax structures. Legislation included tax holidays, a 1 percent import duty on capital goods associated with production, and a flat-rate corporate tax of 20 percent. This was to lead to a major influx of foreign capital to create joint ventures, as well as 100 percent foreign-owned investments in commerce, industry and services. Furthermore, the government committed itself to expedite the business application process. Japanese and Taiwanese investors expressed considerable interest. Until 1996, Laotians needed permission to change residences; then, this requirement was done away with.

On 23 July 1997, Laos joined the Association of South East Asian Nations (ASEAN). In 2000, gross domestic product (GDP) growth was 4.5 percent. Yet, GDP per capita was a mere US$272 that year, and half the nation's budget came from foreign aid. In March 2001, Laotian and Thai officials initialled an agreement to build a second bridge to link the two countries; the geographic position of Laos could help it become an important assembly and transshipment centre.

Given that three-fifths of the gross national product (GNP) comes from agricultural output, the government has instituted reforms providing incentives to farmers. The plan introduced preferential tax policies for agriculturalists, and increased investment in the sector, especially in irrigation. The plan also raised the prices of produce, and linked remuneration with output.

The environment for entrepreneurship and the state of small business
W. Robert Moore, Chief of Foreign Editorial Staff at *National Geographic*, wrote about Vientiane, the capital of Laos, 'Biggest buildings in town, except for a few government offices are the Buddhist temples' (1954: 666). Even today, religious beliefs are very important in Laos, and Laotians are noticeably influenced by folk tales, superstitions, and traditional animist beliefs – in addition to the ancient beliefs of the national religion, Theravada Buddhism. An article in the 28 August 1992 issue of *Asiaweek* explained that

it is commonly believed that the Mekong River gets 'hungry' for human souls, without which the annual rains will not arrive:

> a little girl (was) swept away by the current while picnicking with her family on a sandbank. Her mother and father made no attempt to save her. Two foreigners snatched the child from the swift water after a desperate effort. The parents were fearful because the river had been thwarted in claiming the child. (p. 63)

Across Laos, Theravada monasteries, known as wats, dominate every town, and almost every house, shop and office has a private temple. It is even common for boats cruising the Mekong River, to dock for the crew to jump ashore, light incense and pray. The Lao wats are architecturally distinct from monasteries elsewhere in Asia. In Laos, wats have large terraces, and flare symbols on the roofs. Theravada monks are highly influential in Lao society. They are consulted on virtually all matters, thereby playing a role in a diversity of spheres, ranging from private life to government policy. They have traditionally had a great impact on the educational system; it used to be that the only schools were in wats.

The official calendar used in Laos is that of the Lao Buddhist era – not to be confused with the Thai calendar; the Christian year 2010, for example, corresponds to 2648 in the Lao calendar, and 2553 in the Thai calendar.

Central to the belief system in Laos is the ultimate goal to extinguish unsatisfied desires. Its doctrine focuses on aspects of existence, including *dukkha* (suffering from unsatisfied desire), and *anicca* (impermanence). Assuming that unsatisfied desires cause suffering, suffering can be eliminated if its cause – desire – is eliminated. A respectable person, then, according to this ideology, should not work towards the satisfaction of materialistic desires, but should, rather, strive to eliminate the desire itself. A monk, for instance, is specifically prohibited by the religion, from tilling fields or raising animals.

Lao folk tales reinforce the belief that a male monk should not labour for material wealth; yet, the same folklore conditions women to accept a heavy burden in exchange for honour, protection and security. Even the Lao currency portrays agricultural work being done by women.

Numerous Lao families who farm during the wet season become self-employed gold-diggers during the dry season. The prospectors camp along the Mekong River, especially in the region of Luang Prabang. The women do the heaviest work, digging for dirt and panning it in wooden trays. The men weigh the gold, up to one gram per day.

The *Far Eastern Economic Review* quoted a London newspaper as saying that 'Lao rice farmers have a reputation in this dynamic region for lying down, closing their eyes and listening to their crops grow in fertile paddy fields' (Anon., 1994: 60). Indeed, entrepreneurial spirit is not very prevalent in the traditional Lao belief system. Dana (1995) addresses this issue in detail.

Although annual per capita rice output in Laos is 350 kilograms, some provinces experience occasional rice shortages. Many farming communities are migrational; people deforest land for a crop, and then move elsewhere.

Internationalization of entrepreneurs and SMEs
In Laos, the internationalization of entrepreneurs and SMEs tends to be inbound. Whereas American involvement in Lao business tends to be in the form of large business,

Thai investments tend to be in the medium-size category, as are Australian ventures. Even more involved in small business are French entrepreneurs.

One problem encountered by foreign entrepreneurs in the manufacturing sector is the poor infrastructure. Given the generally inadequate conditions of the roads – often flooded during the rainy season – and the lack of a railway, a quarter of all traffic in Laos uses the Mekong River. People and buffalo stand side by side, on boats or barges, for hours. Sometimes, cargo gets damaged.

A gift from the people of Australia, the US$30 million Friendship Bridge across the Mekong River between Laos and Thailand was opened in 1994. It was hoped that this would increase opportunities for trans-border entrepreneurship.

As for the Lao people, 85 percent are involved in agricultural sectors, and seldom directly involved in internationalization. Crops include coffee, corn, rice, tea, tobacco, vegetables and wheat, much of which could be exported. Opium is another important crop, of which Laos produces about 300 tons annually, much of it for export.

Conclusion

Reforms have increased the autonomy of firms, and the state no longer has the monopoly on supply, purchasing and marketing. Yet, enterprise is largely limited to women and minorities, as local culture does not encourage it. The local shortage of skilled labour limits manufacturing. Furthermore, the shortage of educated individuals limits the service sector.

Note

1.   This chapter includes material that first appeared in Dana (1995, 1999, 2002, 2007).

References

Anon. (1994), 'Indochina', *Far Eastern Economic Review*, May, p. 60.
Dana, Léo-Paul (1995), 'Small business in a non-entrepreneurial society: the case of the Lao People's Democratic Republic (Laos)', *Journal of Small Business Management*, **33**(3), 95–102.
Dana, Léo-Paul (1997), 'Vongpackdy, Laos', *Management Case Quarterly*, **2**(3), 29–32.
Dana, Léo-Paul (1999), *Entrepreneurship in Pacific Asia: Past, Present & Future*, Singapore, London and Hong Kong: World Scientific.
Dana, Léo-Paul (2002), *When Economies Change Paths: Models of Transition in China, the Central Asian Republics, Myanmar, and the Nations of Former Indochine Française*, Singapore, London and Hong Kong: World Scientific.
Dana, Léo-Paul (2007), *Asian Models of Entrepreneurship – From the Indian Union and the Kingdom of Nepal to the Japanese Archipelago: Context, Policy and Practice*, Singapore and London: World Scientific.
Moore, W. Robert (1954), 'War and quiet on the Laos Frontier', *National Geographic*, **105**(5), 665–80.
White, Peter T. (1968), 'The Mekong River of terror and hope', *National Geographic*, **134**(6), 737–87.

20 Lebanon
Wafica A. Ghoul

Introduction to Lebanon

Lebanon is strategically located on the Mediterranean Sea. It has a surface area of 10 452 km²; its natural resources are limestone and water. Its population is estimated at 4.06 million, growing at 1.2 percent, the population density is 440 per km², the active labor force is1.62 million, life expectancy at birth is 70.9, and the adult literacy rate is 87 percent. The official language is Arabic; however French and English are widely spoken.

Lebanon has a free-market service-oriented economy and a strong laissez-faire commercial tradition, where priority is given to the public sector and efforts are concentrated into one geographic area, namely, Beirut the capital. Lebanon also boasts a free and open trade regime; it is seeking to accede to the World Trade Organization (WTO) and gained observer status in 1999.

Lebanon's gross domestic product (GDP) is around US$20 billion, and GDP per capita is US$5490. Current figures for the sectors of the economy are not available, however in 2002 they were the following: industry 13 percent, services 68 percent, and public administration 13 percent of GDP, according to Gaspard (2004). It is worth mentioning that industry consists of mining, manufacturing, energy and water, whereas construction is included in services.

Lebanon has several major problems, the most serious being that its national debt is around US$40 billion = 200 percent of GDP. It suffers from a trade deficit, with exports approximately at 20 percent of imports and a very high rate of unemployment at approximately 20 percent.

Lebanon's main comparative advantages include its geographic location since most Arab countries are within a 24-hour traveling distance of Beirut, its openness to the international community, and being a meeting point where the Western and Eastern cultures interact and blend. Another advantage is Lebanon's human capital; Lebanese people are generally well educated, multi-lingual, skilled, gifted and qualified, in addition to having artistic skills which have proven to be very profitable in the areas of manufacturing clothing, footwear, jewelry, and furniture.

The Lebanese pound (Lira or LBP) has been pegged to the dollar since September 1999, US$1=1507 Lira, and the minimum wage = 300 000 liras/month or US$200/month. The fixing of the LBP with respect to the US$ has led to high interest rates, which brought additional costs to Lebanese businesses.

The economy suffered a contraction in 2006; the growth rate was –6.5 percent and inflation was 7 percent, although many prices have increased by a much higher percentage. A recent study of 18 Arab capital cities has ranked Beirut fourteenth in terms of attractiveness to investors (*Al-Mughtareb*, 2007).

Lebanon currently suffers from a volatile political situation with a constant threat of an outbreak of hostilities and a possible return of the civil war. The election of a new president scheduled in November 2007 is adding to the turmoil and inducing more Lebanese nationals to leave the country, particularly young people who are fresh out of college.

The political division originates partly from the differences in opinion about Lebanon's identity, with some people aligning themselves with Syria and Iran and others preferring the alignment with the US and France. The ongoing political conflicts are hindering the implementation of reforms to the economy and the political system. Lebanon has managed to get a pledge of about US$7.6 billion in international grants and aid as a result of the Paris III conferences in January 2007; however, the magnitude of the public debt is expected to grow. The International Monetary Fund (IMF) has projected GDP growth at 5 percent in 2007, due to an expected boost from reconstruction efforts in the amount of US$2 billion to US$3 billion, whereas the Economist Intelligence Unit expects real GDP growth to be 1.5 percent in 2008 and 2.6 percent in 2009.

Impact of the summer 2006 war
The war lasted from 12 July through 14 August 2006. It was followed by a tight naval, air and ground siege; as a result the government lost revenues from the seaports and the airport. The additional defense spending contributed to raising the budget deficit to about 4 percent of GDP in 2006. Merrill Lynch reported that the war destroyed Lebanon's infrastructure and productive capacity, causing a total estimated cost of some 30 percent of GDP, whereas Bear Stearns estimated the cost of the war at 17 percent of the GDP.

The Ministry of Agriculture reported agricultural direct and indirect losses to be US$200 million. Direct losses were the destruction of agricultural infrastructure: farms, irrigation systems, farming machinery, animal production. Indirect losses included the loss of marketing infrastructure (roads, trucks); loss of most of the agricultural labor force due to the flight of foreign workers. In the industrial sector, direct losses were US$200 million, they included damages to 142 factories (85 were completely destroyed); 99.3 percent of damaged factories were uninsured against wars and 70 percent are indebted to a bank or financial institution.

The Association of Lebanese Industrialists (ALI) reported indirect losses in the industrial sector to be US$828 million, broken down as follows: US$300 million production losses, two years will be needed to reconstruct factories; US$280 million material costs for buildings and establishments; US$140 million loss from lack of trade activities due to Israel's blockade; US$100 million loss due to the 10 percent increase in exporting costs.

In January 2007 at the Paris III conference, the Lebanese government presented a five-year plan which proposed major social, fiscal and economic reforms. The conference resulted in US$7.6 billion in soft loans and grants pledged by the international community, which were to be closely tied to the implementation of the suggested reforms.

In September 2007 Lebanon received a US$100 million loan from the World Bank to help carry out reforms in the social affairs and energy sectors. According to the *Oxford Group Newsletter* (2007b), 'the funds form part of the total US$975 million pledged by the World Bank at Paris III, the international donor conference for Lebanon held in Paris' in January 2007 where Lebanon was promised US$7 billion. The article continued to say that the European Union (EU) had pledged a total of US$2.9 billion at Paris III, of which a 74 million euro (US$100 million) loan was given to Lebanon in September 2007 to be used for financing 'six projects that focus on the rehabilitation and reconstruction

Table 20.1   Classification of Lebanese registered businesses into SMEs or large companies

	SMEs			Non-SMEs	
Number of employees	1 to 10	11 to 25	26 to 50	51 to 100	>100
Number of companies	36 400	30 400	9600	3200	400
% of total	45.50	38	12	4	0.50

Source: Ministry of Finance (2006).

of infrastructure, facilitating access to bank loans for Lebanese enterprises, reconstruction assistance, support for institutional reforms, and an EU university scholarship fund for Palestinian refugees'.

Government policy on SMEs and entrepreneurship in Lebanon
The Lebanese economy is a small business economy, with 95.5 percent of companies employing at most 50 employees. One study defined a small Lebanese business as one employing five to eight employees, and a medium business as one employing nine to 30 employees (http://www.ilo.org/public/english/protection/safework/papers/smechem/).

> About 200 000 companies are currently registered in Lebanon, of which 80 000 are active and 95 percent have less than 50 employees. (Ministry of Finance, 2006)

Other data show that about 99 percent of companies employ fewer than five people, if we consider all companies including those which are not registered. Lebanon has very few enterprises which employ more than 100 employees.

It is estimated that small businesses employ 72 percent of the work force, and contribute 48 percent to the gross national product. Small businesses in Lebanon typically show very low productivity and 'report' very modest incomes for their owners. The Ministry of Economy and Trade (MoET) is responding to this economic and social situation by working on the modernization of existing small family enterprises, as well as taking measures to stimulate new SME creation throughout the country.

The Lebanese government's efforts to help SMEs
In 2004 an Integrated SME Support Programme (ISSP) was started by three parties: the Ministry of Economy and Trade, the Ministry of Industry, and the European Union. The program aims at improving the business environment in Lebanon; it is based in the Ministry of Economy and Trade and is financed jointly by the EU and the government of Lebanon with a budget of €17.8 million. It started its operations in April 2005. The participation of the EU program ended 31 December 2007.

The ISSP has led to the creation of an SME Unit at MoET, which will aid the government in planning and implementing its efforts to assist SMEs. The SME unit will be a valuable source of information for SMEs; it will promote the collaboration between the public and private sector, by creating committees for public/private dialogue. Its staff will be trained by EU experts and through on-site visits to comparable international SME units.

The SME unit will identify obstacles which face businesses in Lebanon, followed by proposing legislation and regulatory reforms which can help ease the obstacles. The unit plans to create a Competitiveness Council for Lebanon, and to play a coordinating role with national and international fund donors who desire to aid Lebanese SMEs.

As a part of its efforts to enhance the growth and development of new and existing SMEs, the ISSP program has recently funded the establishment of four Business Development Centers (BDCs) which are spread throughout Lebanon; these were launched in 2007. The contribution of ISSP is up to €700 000 to each BDC, however, each is run by a consortium which is contributing the bulk of the budget, and providing up to 5000m² of space.

According to Declan Gordon Carroll, Senior Enterprise Development Advisor at the Lebanese Ministry of Economy and Trade,

> BDCs are models of Public Private Partnerships where key economy actors within the private sector (e.g. Chambers, Universities, and Foundations etc) join with Public entities to provide appropriate and professional services which cannot be resourced fully through either the public or private sector. Where these services are targeted at enterprise, the involvement of the Private sector ensures that the services are geared directly to the needs of the SMEs. (Personal email)

The BDCs will support SMEs by being a host and an incubator for high-potential start-up enterprises, and by providing advisory services to new and existing SMEs in the various areas of marketing, finance, and compliance with regulations, among other things. It is hoped that the BDCs will help Lebanon to start the process of recovery after 30 years of conflict by reviving its agricultural and industrial sectors, limiting the phenomenon of urban sprawl, and turning brain-drain into brain-gain. It is expected that the BDCs will become the main channel for providing support schemes and services from the government and donor agencies to the SME sector.

The economic and sociocultural environment for entrepreneurship and the state of small business in Lebanon

Focus on how environment is affecting the discovery/perception, evaluation and exploitation of opportunities
The problems that face Lebanese entrepreneurs arise from poor economic conditions, the regulatory framework as well as financial institutions' policies and practices. Businesses face hurdles which include red tape, bureaucratic corruption, arbitrary licensing decisions, complex customs procedures, archaic legislation, and a slow judicial system which is not very effective. Additional problems include high telecommunications and power charges, varying interpretations of rules and regulations, and a weak enforcement of existing intellectual property right (IPR) legislation

The hostilities which went on in the summer of 2006 have caused a huge setback and erased at least a decade's worth of progress and economic growth. Optimists might view this as an opportunity due to the massive reconstruction efforts that are currently underway. However, one cannot deny that one major impact of the war was the flight of investments and, more importantly, human capital which is difficult to replace. The BDCs which were mentioned earlier come at a time when they are really needed to assist entrepreneurs especially in the areas which were affected very negatively by the war, mainly South Lebanon, Bekaa Valley, and the southern suburb of Beirut.

Table 20.2   The ease of doing business in Lebanon

Ease of	2008 indicator rank
Doing business	85
Starting a business	132
Dealing with licenses	113
Employing workers	53
Registering property	92
Getting credit	48
Protecting investors	83
Paying taxes	33
Trading across borders	83
Enforcing contracts	121
Closing a business	117

Source: The Doing Business project.

The cost of financing is very high in Lebanon. It is well known that entrepreneurs worldwide have a hard time getting funds usually because of the lack of fixed assets which can be used as collateral. According to a World Bank study of SMEs in the Gulf Cooperation Council (GCC) countries: 'The banking sector is more often than not geared towards offering traditional, safer and shorter-term credit creation facilities to borrowers while avoiding those risks entailed in uncollateralized micro-credit to the poor' (United Nations Development Programme, 2005)

What makes getting loans harder is some entrepreneurs' lack of expertise in properly formulating projects and presenting information transparently. Additional burdens include the high cost of complying with government regulations, especially that the average entrepreneur generally has no access to policy makers.

A main goal for ISSP which was mentioned earlier, is to aid Lebanese SMEs in obtaining financing, by creating a joint guarantee scheme with Kafalat which is a financial company whose objective is to help (SMEs) gain easier access to commercial bank financing by providing them with loan guarantees if the borrowers can prove that the business is feasible. Small and medium enterprises in the following economic sectors are targeted by Kafalat: industry, agriculture, tourism, traditional crafts, and high technology. According to its website, Kafalat 'uses its capital to issue credit guarantees of 75 percent of loan funds in order to lower effective interest rates. Thus guaranteed loans have very low interest rates equivalent 2.5–3 percent a year'. By 2004 Kafalat guaranteed US$263 million in subsidized loans, with the average loan being US$77 000, distributed to over 3396 applicants. Kafalat has received a cash injection of 4 million euros to support the launching of the four new BDCs in Lebanon.

The 'ease' of doing business in Lebanon: a World Bank study
In this section we discuss the difficulties which are encountered when doing business in Lebanon, by looking at a study that was conducted by the International Finance Corporation (IFC), which is a member of the World Bank Group. The IFC conducts an annual survey that ranks 178 economies on the ease of doing business within each country.

Table 20.3 Starting a business indicator

Starting a business indicator	Lebanon	MENA	OECD
Procedures (number)	6.0	9.7	6.0
Duration (days)	46.0	38.5	14.9
Cost (% GNI per capita)	94.1	66.0	5.1
Minimum capital required (% of GNI per capita)	60.4	487.7	32.5

Note: OECD = Organisation for Economic Co-operation and Development.

Source: The Doing Business project.

Table 20.4 Dealing with licenses indicator

Dealing with licenses indicator	Lebanon	MENA	OECD
Procedures (number)	20.0	19.4	14.0
Duration (days)	211.0	201.4	153.3
Cost (% of income per capita)	229.5	445.7	62.2

Source: The Doing Business project.

The survey ranks economies from 1 to 178, with a rank of 1 being best. The rank of a given country is determined through the examination of 10 indicators which evaluate the ease of doing business, the time, cost, and complexity of meeting government requirements when starting a business. These rankings indicate the impact of regulations on businesses; they can be used to identify bottlenecks which might be constraining business investment, productivity and growth. In the 2008 survey, Lebanon had a rank of 85 in the category of the ease of doing business, which is 10 points lower than last year.

Lebanon is located in the Middle East and North Africa (MENA) region. Lebanon was comparable to other countries in the MENA region.

As demonstrated in Table 20.3, the IFC study found that when starting a new business, entrepreneurs have to go through six procedures (MENA 9.7); it takes 46 days (MENA 38.5), on average, and the cost is 94 percent of gross national income (GNI) per capita, compared to the MENA average of 66 percent.

As far as dealing with licenses, Table 20.4 shows that Lebanon has about the same number of procedures as the MENA countries; it takes 10 days longer to complete those procedures, however the good news is that the cost is lower in Lebanon.

As far as registering property, the average number of procedures is higher than the MENA average, but the length of time, and the cost are lower (Table 20.5).

According to *Oxford Group Newsletter* (2007a), in October 2007 the Lebanese government announced that it had taken major steps towards simplifying, speeding up, and reducing the cost of the business registration process by at least 50 percent. This achievement was possible through working with the International Finance Corporation (IFC), a member of the World Bank Group. Entrepreneurs will be able to register a new business by completing a single form and mailing it through Libanpost, Lebanon's official mail service network, along with the necessary fees, to a government office. In return,

Table 20.5   Registering property

Registering property indicator	Lebanon	MENA	OECD
Procedures (number)	8.0	6.8	4.9
Duration (days)	25.0	48.4	28.0
Cost (% of property value)	5.9	6.6	4.6

Source: The Doing Business project.

they will receive a registration certificate within one week through the mail, within an average time frame of a week. Libanpost will do the leg-work which used to be the responsibility of business owners, by circulating the documents between the various government agencies and 'will deliver a certificate of registration approved and stamped by the commercial registry, the tax identification number issued by the ministry of finance and all other relevant documentation to the business owner' (Oxford Group Newsletter, 2007a).

Internationalization of entrepreneurs and SMEs from Lebanon: drivers and roadblocks
Smaller companies in general cannot deal with globalization and international competition very well and usually have a limited ability to promote and sell their products beyond their local borders. It has been suggested that small companies worldwide have a fear of expanding beyond their local market (Tobin, 2006). Their concerns include the following:

1.   The differences in language, culture, and business practices.
2.   The complexity and cost of the expansion, as well as the credit risk of foreign customers.
3.   The timing of the expansion which means that companies are pre-occupied with and tend to focus on local growth before thinking about expanding overseas.
4.   The concern about the small size of the company which is mistakenly perceived to be a hindrance.

It appears that export activities and establishing subsidiaries in foreign markets are the most common methods currently used by Lebanese businesses to go international. The fact that Lebanon is mostly a small business economy makes it difficult for Lebanese SMEs to compete with multinational companies (MNCs) locally and internationally; however, some have managed to carve out their own niche markets in segments which are normally neglected by large MNCs, for example olive oil exporters, haute couture designers, and jewelry and watch exporters. Lebanese exporters are facing challenges abroad as evidenced by Lebanon's trade deficit, which was at 38.7 percent of GDP in 2004.

Next we discuss some of the current problems which face Lebanese exporters; these have been discussed by the Chamber of Commerce, Industries and Agriculture (CCIA) and Challita (2005, 2006). The Lebanese government has not made a real effort to help exporters by reducing bureaucracy and delays, simplifying administrative procedures, and easing customs formalities such as delayed clearing. A major problem which faces exporters is the uncompetitive prices due to the cost of imported raw materials, especially with the recent appreciation of the euro, and the high cost of local production (fuel, electricity, and labor, especially employer contributions to the social security fund, taxes, and so on). To add to the problem, some trade agreements such as the Greater Arab Free Trade Agreement (GAFTA) have put Lebanese products at a competitive disadvantage both locally and abroad. Another problem is the lack of subsidies or low subsidies by the Lebanese government to the manufacturing sector. To top things off, the Lebanese government has not been known to take retaliatory measures against countries which block Lebanese exports to their markets.

Some of the problems which face Lebanese exporters are self-inflicted, and could be rectified by the companies themselves. These include a lack of marketing strategies and policies in foreign markets; and a narrow focus on regional markets due to lack of expertise in remote markets, such as the CIS, Africa and South America. Thus most exporters are focusing on regional markets which are less strict, such as the Gulf Cooperation Council, instead of stimulating demand by Lebanese expatriates who are all over the world, last estimated at 15 million people. Other major hurdles include the inability to meet International Quality and Safety Standards adequately, as well as inadequate labeling as far as nutritional value and constituents or components are concerned, not to mention unattractive packaging.

Some of the problems that foreign governments have control over include administrative impediments such as customs formalities and delayed port clearing, protectionist measures, as well as the strict International Quality and Safety Standards.

There are a few organizations which are currently helping exporters in Lebanon; we list three of those below:

1. *Export Promotion Council*, whose responsibilities include helping exporters to penetrate foreign markets efficiently and effectively.
2. *Euro Info Correspondence Centre* (EICC) which has a main objective of enhancing cooperation between Lebanese and European companies.
3. *Euro-Lebanese Center for Industrial Modernization* (ELCIM) which has assisted food manufacturers in getting access to loans, conducting feasibility studies, and improving the quality of production.

Conclusion

The Integrated SME Support Programme Inception Report (2005) cites a recent study which was funded by the EU and conducted for the Economic and Social Fund in Lebanon. The study concluded that the Lebanese economy could improve if small enterprises were 'integrated in the modern segments of the economy, through various sub-contracting arrangements and linkages with larger enterprises, as is the case in all well developed economies'.

It is crucial for Lebanon to foster the creation, development and internationalization of high-potential, innovative enterprises that will become the cornerstone of its economic prosperity.

Lebanon needs to re-position itself, and diversify its mix of products and services, in terms of composition and destination. The Lebanese government needs to promote

Lebanon *again* as the business center in the Middle East, a role that it used to play before the civil war. It needs to subsidize products which require skilled labor such as manufacturing watches, jewelry, or high fashion, by giving them tax breaks or similar incentives. The focus should be shifted to high-value customized products, instead of high-volume, standardized products; an example is high-fashion custom-made clothing, especially when it comes to exports. Another method for stimulating the business environment in Lebanon is to encourage industries which use raw materials available in Lebanon, such as olive oil, wine, and agricultural crops.

Lebanon needs to develop research centers which can be a fertile ground for the collaboration between academics and industry. These centers could lead to technological advances in manufacturing, thus enhancing the competitiveness of exports.

In the next few years we would like to explore the success of the new initiatives which were started by the Lebanese government and the EU, by looking at cases of real companies which were hosted, serviced, or turned around through the assistance of the four BDCs. It would be interesting to find out if these business development centers will be able to accomplish their theoretical objectives, in a typical Third World country where bureaucracy and unethical behavior dominate the business scene.

References

Al-Akhbar (2007), 'The distribution of the Labor force in Lebanon', 10 July, http://al-akhbar.com/ar/taxonomy/term/12%2C14154 (accessed 29 July 2008).

Al-Mughtareb (2007), An Interview with Ouini, Hobeika, and Itani about Industry and Investments in Lebanon, June issue, http://64.69.89.54/articles.asp?cid=44&aid=208 (accessed 19 July 2007).

Challita, D. (2005), 'Local Cuisine goes down a treat overseas', *Lebanon Opportunities*, November, 16–19.

Challita, D. (2006), 'Made in Lebanon, industrialists relying on overseas markets to remain above water', *Lebanon Opportunities*, March, 16–19.

Gaspard, Toufic (2004), *A Political Economy of Lebanon, 1948–2002: The Limits of Laissez-faire*, Leiden: Brill.

The Integrated SME Support Programme Inception Report (2005), http://www.economy.gov.lb/NR/rdonlyres/3CO3D334-8CE3-4A97-A88C-69F326052D9F/0/InceptionReport.doc (accessed 11 March 2009).

Kafalat website, www.kafalat.com.lb (accessed 11 March 2009).

Ministry of Finance (2006), 'SME's in Lebanon', a private study conducted for the MoF, the study involves only registered companies.

Oxford Group Newsletter (2007a), 'Lebanon: making easy work of business, 8 October.

Oxford Group Newsletter (2007b), 'Lebanon: financing in a time of risk and reform', 26 September.

The Doing Business project (2008), http://www.doingbusiness.org/EconomyRankings (accessed 29 July 2008).

Tobin, M. (2006), 'Debunking the five myths of global expansion', *Financial Executive*, **22**(2), 57.

21 Malaysia

Nnamdi Madichie and Christopher Seow

Introduction to Malaysia

Malaysia consists of 13 states – Johor, Kedah, Kelantan, Melaka, Negeri Sembilan, Pahang, Perak, Perlis, Pulau Pinang, Sabah, Sarawak, Selangor, Terengganu – and one Federal Territory (*wilayah persekutuan*) with three components, the city of Kuala Lumpur, Labuan, and Putrajaya.

A middle-income country, Malaysia has transformed itself from an agrarian society into an emerging multi-sector economy with growth exclusively driven by electronics exports, manufacturing, services and tourism. The economy grew at 4.9 percent in 2003, over 7 percent in 2004 and 5 percent in 2005–06. In 2005, its currency the Ringgit (RM) was 'unpegged' relative to the US dollar – thus enabling it to appreciate by 6 percent against the US dollar in 2006. Currently the economy remains dependent on continued growth in the US, China, and Japan. In the Ninth Malaysia Plan (or 9MP) the government presented a comprehensive blueprint for the allocation of the national budget from 2006 to the year 2010 – targeting the development of value-added manufacturing and an expansion of the services sector.

However, the small to medium enterprises (SME) sector in Malaysia is neither very well reported in the academic literature nor adequately recognized by practitioners. This chapter therefore (1) highlights the contribution of the SME sector to the economic development of Malaysia; (2) discusses the level of government assistance to the sector; (3) provides some insight into the social and economic environment facing Malaysia's SMEs; and (4) highlights the challenges of globalization and the growing need for internationalization of the sector.

A nationwide census conducted in 2005 based on a preliminary assessment of 523 132 enterprises indicated that 99.2 percent of the samples were SMEs. It also reported that 86.5 percent were engaged in the services sector (mainly in retail, restaurant, wholesale, transportation and communication, and professional services businesses), 7.3 percent in the manufacturing sector (mainly in the textile and apparel, metal and mineral products, and food and beverages industries) and 6.2 percent involved in the agricultural sector (mostly in food crops, horticulture, and livestock).

Small and medium enterprises also constituted a major source of employment, providing jobs for over 3 million workers (or 65.1 percent of total employment). Indeed about 2.2 million workers were employed by SMEs in the services sector, while 740 000 and 131 000 workers were employed in the manufacturing and agriculture sectors respectively. Furthermore, SMEs generated RM154 billion (47.3 percent) of value added and RM405 billion (or 43.5 percent) of output in 2003.

Productivity levels of SMEs were also significantly lower than that of large enterprises, with about 84 percent of SMEs reliant on their internally generated funds and funds sourced from friends and family members, while 16 percent sourced their funding from financial institutions. In contrast, 50 percent of large enterprises relied on the financial institutions. Furthermore, 54011 of the 523132 enterprises indicated having difficulty accessing funding from financial institutions, mainly due to lack of collateral.

Government policy on SMEs and entrepreneurship in Malaysia
In its SME development drive, the government, through various ministries and agencies, initiated numerous programmes to support SMEs development in order to render them more competitive, resilient and thereby increase their contributions to the economy. Towards this end, three broad strategic thrusts can be identified: (1) strengthening enabling infrastructure; (2) building the capacity and capability of SMEs; and (3) enhancing access to finance.

Such financial and non-financial supports were geared toward enhancing SMEs' marketing and promotion capabilities, with assistance extending to cover areas like direct promotional activities, brand and franchise development, as well as linkages with larger organizations. To assist SMEs to expand their market, several programmes were also put in place, including the Market Development Grant (a matching grant scheme to cover expenses in promoting SMEs' products overseas), Industrial Linkage Programme (a programme to link SMEs with large companies and multinationals) and Local Market Expansion Programme (to link Bumiputera information and communication technology companies with government-linked companies (GLCs). Another important area is to assist SMEs in branding and packaging of their products. Key programmes include Grant for Enhancing Product Packaging, Design and Labelling Capabilities of SMEs; Brand Promotion Grant; and Malaysia's Best brand for agricultural products (Bank Negara, 2006).

An outline of the direction for SME development is also enshrined in the National SME Development Blueprint 2006 – where a total of 245 key programmes involving RM3.9 billion were earmarked for implementation (Bank Negara, 2006). In line with the objective of enhancing national competitiveness and economic resilience, the key priority for SME development outlined under 9MP was to develop SMEs that are equipped with strong technical and innovative capacity, as well as sound business management skills. This would ensure production of high-quality goods and services at competitive prices and integration into the international supply chain (Bank Negara, 2006).

In a publication of the Small and Medium Industries Development Corporation (SMIDEC) entitled *Policies, Incentives, Programmes and Financial Assistance for SMEs*, a comprehensive information on the policies, incentives, support programmes and financial assistance available for SMEs by both the government and private sectors was highlighted. As the leading organization in SME development, SMIDEC initiated this inaugural publication to provide a comprehensive information resource on available assistance for SMEs' reference which includes:

- *SME development initiatives* – formulated in accordance with the policies and strategies outlined in 9MP and the Third Industrial Master Plan (IMP3)
- *tax incentives* (direct and indirect) – direct tax incentives are available through partial or total relief from income tax payment for a specified period, while indirect tax incentives are provided in the form of exemptions from import duty, sales tax and excise duty

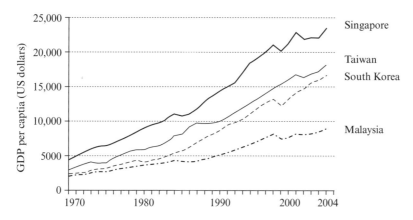

Source: World Bank (2005).

Figure 21.1   Malaysia's rising gap – GDP per capita (1970–2004)

- Various *support and capacity building programmes* – these assistance programmes address five main areas (access to markets; technology adoption; skills upgrading; information; and infrastructure support, including industrial sites and incubator centres)
- *financial assistance* for SMEs is available through various channels and instrumentations, including the credit guarantee scheme (see Boocock, 2005).

However, there seems very little direct help by the government in the development of the SME sector, despite the effort and attention paid to the eradication of poverty and restructuring of society since *Merdeka* (Independence) and the introduction of the New Economic Policy (NEP) in the 1970s (Omar, 2002; Yunus, 1994, 1998). This is in addition to the billions spent on infrastructure development, economic aid, and improvement of social services for national and rural areas, including education and basic health services (SERU, 1993), which resulted in a decline in the incidence of rural poverty from 58.7 percent in 1970 to 19.3 percent by 1990 (Kasim, 1991; Ministry of Agriculture, 1992). Poverty nonetheless persists in various parts of the country to the extent that local critics have questioned the effectiveness of the government's rural development programmes – with poor credit ranking high on the agenda (Bank Negara, 2006; Boocock, 2005; Chan, 2005; Daly et al., 2006; Gibbons and Kasim, 1990).

There is also a lack of agencies/programmes supplying credit to the poor on reasonable terms for income-generating activities (Gibbons, 1988). It seems that the challenge of tackling extreme poverty had neither been fully understood nor acknowledged (see Figure 21.1) – let alone addressed – by the responsible institutions and policies until the replication of the Grameen Bank Approach (GBA) identified by Chan (2005).

Although Malaysia's modern financial system has a range of public and private institutions, including the Islamic Bank, Credit Guarantee Corporation (CGC) and Agricultural Bank (Bank Pertanian), the institutions engaging in micro-finance are mostly non-governmental organizations (NGOs) such as the (1) Amanah Ikhtiar Malaysia (AIM), (2)Yayasan Usaha Maju (YUM), (3) Koperasi Kredit Rakyat (KKR) and (4) Partners in Enterprise Malaysia (PIE). Among these, AIM and YUM are modelled after the GBA, targeting the very poor. Koperasi Kredit Rakyat targets low-income plantation workers, while PIE targets the urban poor and low-income families.

In the special case of AIM, the initiative was modelled after the Grameen Bank of Bangladesh and adjusted to suit the Malaysian local context, *Projek Ikhtiar*, as an innovative approach to rural poverty eradication (AIM, 1989; Omar, 2002; Yunus, 1998). Ikhtiar provided small loans on reasonable terms to members of poor rural households to finance income-generating activities, through a specialized delivery system taking credit to their villages (AIM, 1989; Chan, 2005; Gibbons and Kasim, 1990). However, although strongly supported by the government, AIM legally remains an NGO, whose funds are channelled through the Islamic Economic Development Foundation (YPEIM), and any operating costs not covered by borrowers have to be met by the federal and state government.

The economic and sociocultural environment for Malaysian SMEs

Malaysia has integrated commitments to poverty elimination into an economic development strategy. Frameworks such as the NEP and New Development Policy (NDP) were introduced in 1970 and 1991, respectively, to reduce poverty and income disparities between ethnic groups, and particularly to improve the position of the Bumiputera – Malays and indigenous people, who constitute majority of the poor population. Poverty tends to be rural, although the incidence of urban and rural poverty increased in the 1990s (Henderson et al., 2002) compared with the 1970s and 1980s (Yusoff et al., 2000).

Instituted in 1970 as a response to the growing discontent about the economic inequalities between the Malays and other races who were still gaining economic ascendancy, the two-pronged objective of the NEP was to eradicate poverty, as well as to obliterate the strict lines identifying a particular ethnic group with a particular economic activity or occupation. Under the NEP, emphasis was put on increasing effective 'Bumiputera' ownership and participation in the corporate sector, improving participation in high-income occupations, as well as narrowing income inequality and eradicating poverty.

Embedded within these larger policies is the issue of creating a Bumiputera Commercial and Industrial Community (BCIC), which involves fostering Bumiputera entrepreneurs, professionals and creating a Bumiputera middleclass (Government of Malaysia, 2001). This became the backbone of Malaysia's strategy for strengthening national entrepreneurship – which was not undertaken to the exclusion of the non-Bumiputera entrepreneurs – with resulting impressive economic performance relative to other developing countries.

Malaysia has, nonetheless, managed to sustain a relatively high level of growth such as the average growth of 4.7 percent per annum during the period 1996–2000. Real GDP expanded at an average rate of 8.7 percent per annum, before registering a negative growth rate of 7.4 percent in 1998 and an average growth of 7.2 percent in the period 1999–2000. However this growth had declined to about 6 percent by the second quarter of 2006 (Figure 21.2) (Government of Malaysia, 2001).

In 2001, both the unemployment and inflation rates remained low at 3.9 percent and 1.3 percent respectively (Bank Negara, 2005). Moreover the Malaysian experience with financial sector reforms has undergone continuous transformation (Siddiquee, 2006) in the last decade driven by financial liberalization and consolidation, economic transformation (Zamani, 2006) technological advancements and more discerning consumers.

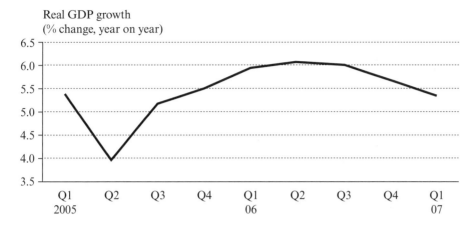

Real GDP growth
(% change, year on year)

Source: Economist Intelligence Unit, *The Economist* (2007).

Figure 21.2   Malaysia: real GDP growth (2005–07)

Table 21.1   Origins and components of Malaysian GDP, 2006

Origins of GDP 2006	% of total	Components of GDP 2006	% of total
Agriculture	9.1	Private consumption	43.7
Mining	15.7	Public consumption	12.9
Manufacturing	30.5	Gross fixed capital formation	20.2
Construction	2.8	Stock building	0.5
Services	45.7	Exports of goods and services	122.2
Others	−3.8	Imports of goods and services	−98.8
Principal exports (fob) 2006	US$ bn(a)	Principal imports (CIF) 2006	US$bn (a)
Electronics	37.6	Intermediate goods	69.8
Electrical machinery	13.5	Capital goods	13.6
Chemicals and chemical products	5.6	Re-exports	6.8
Crude oil	5.2	Consumption goods	5.8
Palm oil	3.7	Dual-use goods	2.5

Source: *The Economist* (2007).

As a result, the Malaysian financial system has emerged stronger and more diversi-fied and competitive since the Asian financial crisis (Zamani, 2006). The banking sector is now stable as domestic banks boast low levels of non-performing loans. Real GDP growth will bolster the debt-servicing capability of consumers and firms (see Table 21.1); the Malaysian Ringgit is set to strengthen against the US dollar as the recent relaxation of rules governing foreign-exchange accounts increases demand for the Ringgit; and owing to dependence on exports as the main economic driver, the vulnerability to a slow-down in world economic growth is imminent.

However, Malaysia's large foreign-exchange reserves provide it with a cushion in the event of regional economic and financial shocks (see Table 21.2). In certain industries

Table 21.2   Malaysia: economic structure

	2002(a)	2003(a)	2004(a)	2005(a)	2006(a)
GDP at market prices RM bn	362.0	395.0	450.2	495.2	546.3
GDP US$ bn	95.3	104.0	118.5	130.8	148.9
Real GDP growth (%)	5.4	5.8	6.8	5.0	5.9
Consumer price inflation (Av; %)	1.8	1.0	1.5	3.0	3.6
Population (m)	24.5	25.1	25.6	26.1	26.6
Exports of goods fob (US$ m)	93 383	104 999	126 642	141 808	160 540(b)
Imports of goods fob (US$ m)	−75 248	−79 289	−99 149	−108 653	−126 237(b)
Current-account balance (US$ m)	7 190	13 381	14 872	19 980	23 072(b)
Foreign-exchange reserves excl gold (US$ m)	33 361	43 822	65 881	69 850	82 133
Total external debt (US$ bn)	48.3	48.6	52.2	51.0	50.9(b)
Debt-service ratio, paid (%)	7.1	7.8	6.2	5.6	4.9(b)
Exchange rate (Av) M$:US$	3.80	3.80	3.80	3.79	3.67

Notes:
(a) actual.
(b) Economist Intelligence Unit estimates.

Source: The Economist (2007).

where specific jobs are in short supply, manufacturing firms tend to lose workers since the labour turnover is rapid and continuous in this sector. Generally, losing a highly skilled worker seems to hurt SMEs more than large manufacturing firms.

Likewise, Malaysia's industrial sector has experienced an increasing number of large firms 'poaching' the low paid and experienced workers from the SMEs by offering higher wages. Indeed as Anuwar (1992) suggested, while SMEs tend to bear the cost of training of labour, larger manufacturing firms enjoy the benefits.

Another initiative set by the Malaysian government was the formation of the Industrial Technical Assistance Fund (ITAF) in the 1990 budget (Anuwar, 1992) for the provision of RM50 million annually to increase research and development (R&D) activities among SMEs. The ITAF was supposed to match-fund the total project costs incurred by SMEs undertaking feasibility studies, quality and productivity improvements, product and design development, and market development. Although targeted to assist SMEs, ITAF did not have major impact on SMEs, which could not even avail themselves of the requisite start-up funds for R&D activities (Chan, 2005). Indeed, the so-called policies favouring SMEs have been 'weak, uncoordinated, unsustained, and uneven' (Chan and Lau, 2005).

The government attempted to implement industrialization policies through a series of five-year master plans (see Table 21.3) – from 1966 through to 2010. Interestingly 6MP concentrated on 12 major industry sectors that were considered central to Malaysia's industrialization, but these industries mainly produced low-technology products at best.

The 6MP concentrated on technology development within domestic industries in relation to market development and product improvement to meet the export standards

Table 21.3 Public expenditure on poverty (percentage of overall development budget)

Malaysia Plan	Period	Percentage
1MP	1966–70	27
2MP	1971–75	31
3MP	1976–80	30
4MP	1981–85	24
5MP	1986–90	26
6MP	1991–95	27
7MP	1996–2000	22
8MP	2001–05	NA
9MP	2006–10	NA

Sources: Adapted from Yusoff et al. (2000); Government of Malaysia (2001).

– especially for rubber products (tyres and latex-dipped goods); palm oil products; electronics and electrical products; and iron and steel industry.

The government acknowledges that its main strategic planning is targeted towards the agricultural sector rather than the industrial sector and that the main aim of IMP is not R&D – a high-risk activity with lagging technical expertise – thus, the private sector's reluctance to pursue it. Again, the problem is manifested even more in SMEs since they have even less technical expertise and financial resources for R&D (Anuwar, 1992).

It can be argued that on an individual level, attitudes toward enterprise creation in Malaysia have been previously split along racial lines – due to the identification of race with economic activity. Historically, the Chinese (and the Indian-Muslim community) have had a long tradition of entrepreneurship, and their community members have had less resistance to the whole notion of entrepreneurship. In fact, the handing over of family businesses from father to son was the norm for these groups. This was in contrast to the Bumiputera community which, as a whole, did not have a tradition of entrepreneurship, but were used to being either employed in the government service, or self-employed as agricultural farmers or smallholders.

Also, encouraging SME development was mainly aimed at creating a large pool of genuine medium-scale entrepreneurs who are able to compete in the global marketplace. This stance is echoed in the research works of a variety of scholars who point to the SME sector as a spawning ground for entrepreneurship, which provides opportunities for value-added employment creation, income distribution, training and skill development, which completes the supply chain links with big industries and MNCs (Harper, 1999).

Internationalization of Malaysian SMEs: drivers and roadblocks
There are a range of SME internationalization frameworks available in the literature: from the 'stage of development' or 'Uppsala' models through the strategy/resource-based approach (Bell et al., 2003) to the network approach (Bell and Young, 1998; Caviello and McCauley, 1999; Madichie and Ibeh, 2006). In his review, Ibeh (2001) noted the importance of the contribution made by the Uppsala internationalization model to the understanding of the process which suggests that firms adopt an incremental, evolutionary

Table 21.4   Evidence of the limitations of psychic distance

Main destinations of exports 2006	% of total	Main origins of imports 2006	% of total
US	18.8	Japan	13.2
Singapore	15.4	US	12.5
Japan	8.9	China	12.1
China	7.2	Singapore	11.7
Thailand	5.9	Thailand	5.4
Total	56.2		54.9

Source: Adapted from *The Economist* (2007).

approach to foreign markets (see Doole and Lowe, 2004), gradually deepening their commitment and investment as they acquired market knowledge and experience.

However, many studies on firms with small domestic markets, service firms, high-technology firms, entrepreneurial firms, subcontractors, and international new ventures have reported evidence that counter the incremental model. The psychic distance model has also been increasingly questioned (see Table 21.4) in the face of vast improvements in global communications and transportation infrastructures, and the resulting increasing market convergence.

On the one hand, the remarks by Bell and Young (1998; 2004) that the incremental internationalization models 'merely identify the internationalisation patterns of certain firms – but not of others – and . . . they fail to adequately explain the processes involved' (1998: 15) would appear to reflect the consensus position on the topic. It has been argued, on the other hand, that successful entry into new foreign markets depended more on a firm's links with its current markets, both domestic and international than on the chosen market and its cultural traits.

The specific resources which are likely to be important would include decision maker(s)' international orientation and experience, product quality and technology, networking/relationships, finance (including access to credit facilities) and foreign market information; however, SMEs need not possess all these specific resources in order to internationalize or perform well in the international market. What is rather more crucial is the skill and vision with which they are guided by their decision makers toward deploying internal capabilities, while leveraging external resources in lagging areas.

As the drivers of globalization remove barriers that traditionally segmented the competitive environments of small and large firms, firms of all sizes are beginning to share the same competitive space. Symbiotic arrangements are evolving through which smaller firms enter the value chains of larger firms, to the benefit of both sides (Etemad et al., 2001).

In Malaysia, there are many government assistance plans, including financial assistance, tax incentives and business advisory assistance, among others. The privatization and SME development policies are evidence of the government's encouraging attitude toward enterprise creation, based on the premise that it encourages other national objectives such as those embodied within the NEP. In general terms, however, some of the factors that act as internationalization drivers include changes in:

- the global socio-economic environment
- government attitude towards and involvement in enterprise development, and more importantly
- the interplay of market forces epitomized by shifts from the primary to the secondary and tertiary sectors

While the first two points have been covered previously, the latter point deserves some commentary here. Manufacturing seems the most important sub-sector of the Malaysian economy, contributing 24 percent to GDP and 48 percent to total export earnings. However, most industrial manufacturing firms are very small and more labour than skill intensive, meaning that any technology diffusion policy initiated by the government has not reached the SMEs. This presents major road blocks to their internationalization aspirations.

There are, however, a variety of roadblocks facing Malaysian SMEs; the lack of managerial and technical expertise is one major problem, which is manifested in the low amount of technical and managerial expertise from the existing post-secondary institutions of learning going into large manufacturing industries. Even then, the exports often cannot meet the growing needs of the industrial sector. Although, the lack of managerial expertise impairs the whole industrialization process and this ultimately hurts their technology diffusion and innovative capabilities of SMEs (Anuwar, 1992).

Although not unique to Malaysia, the lack of means to obtain loans is another problem. In Malaysia the financial institutions are neither set up to – nor fully developed for – assisting SMEs. Instead they tend to provide loans to large manufacturing firms, which are perceived as more long-term and comprehensive projects – consistent with national industrialization policy goals, including mainly exports of high-technology manufacturing products.

Conclusions

Malaysia's road to industrialization very well depends on a healthy sub-sector of SMEs – a significant percentage of the labour force in the industry is concentrated in this sector. Indeed it is persuasive to argue that SMEs will either play a major role in the industrialization process or their limitations will hurt Malaysia's economy. Furthermore, with transforming SMEs low-technology and low value-added products into high-technology and high value-added products, Malaysia can increase its export capacity greatly and even compete more with the industrialized world. But, as evident from the state of the SMEs in Malaysia, this sub-sector is in need of great assistance.

The government has formulated and attempted to implement a series of policies to assist SMEs – with limited impact. The government, therefore, needs to embark on an aggressive education policy targeted at post-secondary institutions to educate managerial and technical experts that are dedicated to work in the industry. It also needs to train these experts to better understand the contribution of SMEs to the economy in general.

There is also a need to set policies providing incentives to SMEs for investment in R&D (not only matching funds but grants based on performance) and financial institutions to give loans to SMEs. One way to tackle this dilemma is to convince all sub-sectors of the industry (SMEs and large industries) along with the research universities and financial institutions that as part of a national goal, they have to work together for the benefit of the country (in other words, government should set common goals for all parties involved in the economy).

In conclusion, the success of SMEs and their contribution to the industrialization process depends on direct assistance from the government with a set of effective policies.

A major culprit is the country's attempts at heavy industrialization and reliance on the foreign-owned, export-oriented industrialization of the 1970s, which not only created a series of 'white elephants' that soaked up government investment and remained relatively unproductive but also exacerbated uneven development, compounding pre-existing regional inequalities to the detriment of the rural states on the eastern peninsula (Dana, 1987).

Arguably the funds poured into heavy industrialization would have been far better spent on 'Chinese-style' rural industrialization to increase agricultural productivity; and attending to the long-standing and serious structural weakness in the economy's industrial base – the under-development of an SME sector capable of linking with the transnationals (especially in the electronics industry) via the supply of high-value products and services. Indeed, the diversion of funds from rural areas has been one of the triggers of civil unrest in the country – also a reason for the rise of the Islamic Party of Malaysia (PAS) opposition in the eastern peninsular states.

Henderson et al. (2002: 30) concluded that:

> Although Malaysia's record on reducing poverty has been good by regional and world standards, it arguably could have been better. On the one hand, misdirected development policies (for example, heavy industrialisation in steel, cement, petrochemicals) were clearly a significant factor which stunted the nation's poverty reduction effort by taking up large amounts of government investment and exacerbating uneven development in the rural states. Arguably, the development funds channelled into heavy industrialisation would have been better spent on other pro-poor forms of economic development (for example rural industrialisation, agricultural productivity, and SMEs).

This is worrying given the extent to which Malaysian development strategies emphasise 'projects' over 'policies' – the latter having changed relatively little since the early innovations of the NEP and the former representing the operationalization of long-standing policy tenets of the latter – thus making project implementation the core element of bureaucratic efforts.

References

Amanah Ikhtiar Malaysia (AIM) (1989) *Amanah Ikhtiar Malaysia Annual Report 1989*, Penang: Jutaprint.
Anuwar, A. (1992), *Malaysia's Industrialization: The Quest for Technology*, Singapore: Oxford University Press.
Bank Negara (2005), *Definitions for Small and Medium Enterprises in Malaysia*, 13 September, Malaysia: Secretariat to National SME Development Council.
Bank Negara (2006) *Small and Medium Enterprise Annual Report 2005*, Bank Negara, Central Bank of Malaysia, 7 August.
Bell, J. and S. Young (1998), 'Towards an integrative framework of the internationalization of the firm', in G. Hooley, R. Loveridge and D. Wilson (eds), *Internationalization: Process, Context and Markets*, London: Macmillan.
Bell, J., D. Crick and S. Young (2004), 'Small firm internationalization and business strategy: an exploratory study of "knowledge-intensive" and "traditional" manufacturing firms in the UK', *International Small Business Journal*, **22**(1), 23–56.

Bell, J., R. McNaughton, S. Young and D. Crick (2003), 'Towards an integrative model of small firm internationalization', *Journal of International Entrepreneurship*, **1**, 339–62.

Boocock, G. (2005), 'Measuring effectiveness of credit guarantee schemes: evidence from Malaysia', *International Small Business Journal*, **23**(4), 427–40.

Caviello, N. and A. McCauley (1999), 'Internationalization processes and the smaller firm: a review of contemporary empirical research', *Management International Review*, **39**(3), 223–56.

Chan, S.H. (2005), 'An exploratory study using micro-credit to encourage the setting up of small businesses in the rural sector of Malaysia', *Asian Business and Management*, (14), 455–79.

Chan, K. and T. Lau (2005), 'Assessing technology incubator programs in the science park: the good, the bad and the ugly', *Technovation*, **25**, 1215–28.

Daly, T., D. Kaye and N. Sutorius-Lavoie (2006), 'Malaysia: rich pickings with little risk', *Chemical Week*, **168**(13), 31–42.

Dana, Léo-Paul (1987), 'Industrial development efforts in Malaysia and Singapore', *Journal of Small Business Management*, **25**(3), 74–6.

Doole, I. and R. Lowe (2004), *International Marketing Strategy: Analysis, Development and Implementation*, 4th edn, London: Thomson Learning.

Etemad, H., R.W. Wright and L.P. Dana (2001), 'Symbiotic international business networks: collaboration between small and large firms', *Thunderbird International Business Review*, **43**(4), 481–99.

Gibbons, D.S. (1988), *The Grameen Reader*, Malaysia: Amanah Ikhtiar Malaysia.

Gibbons, D.S. and Kasim, S. (1990), *Banking on the Poor*, Penang: AIM.

Government of Malaysia (2001), *Eighth Malaysia Plan, 2001–2005*, Kuala Lumpur: National Printing Department.

Harper, T.N. (1999), *The End of Empire and the Making of Malaya*, Cambridge: Cambridge University Press.

Henderson, J., D. Hulme, R. Philips and N. Nur (2002), 'Economic governance and poverty reduction in Malaysia', http://www.gapresearch.org/governance/MalaysiaReportMay2002.pdf (accessed 14 October 2006).

Ibeh, K.I.N. (2001), 'On the resource-based, integrative view of small firm internationalization', in J. Taggart, M.M.J. Berry and M. McDermott (eds), *The Multinational in the New Era*, Academy of International Business Series, Vol. 8, Palgrave, pp. 72–87.

Kasim, S. (1991), 'Poverty reduction under the National Agricultural Policy: on the role of credit', paper presented at National Seminar on National Agricultural Policy (NAP): An Agenda for Change, Serdang, Selangor, 3–4 September.

Madichie, N. and K. Ibeh (2006), 'A commentary on the internationalisation of the Nigerian movie industry', paper presented at the 29th Institute for Small Business and Entrepreneurship (ISBE) Conference, 29 October–2 November, Cardiff, UK.

Ministry of Agriculture (1992), 'Malaysia: country paper on rural poverty', International Workshop on Rural Poverty and Ways and Means to Alleviate it, 21–27 January, Melaka.

Omar, M.Z. (2002), 'Towards the reduction of rural poverty in Malaysia: lessons from the innovative scheme of the Amanah Ikhtiar Malaysia', *Borneo Review*, **13**(1): 13–35.

Siddiquee, N. (2006), 'Public management reform in Malaysia: recent initiatives and experiences', *International Journal of Public Sector Management*, **19**(4), 339–58.

Socio-economic Research Unit (SERU) (1993), *Laporan Kajian Impak Projek Ikhtiar*, Unit Penyelidikan Sosioekonomi, Jabatan Perdana Menteri (Mei).

The Economist (2007), 'Malaysia: Economic structure', Economist Intelligence Unit (EIU), June, http://www.eiu.com (accessed 10 July 2007).

World Bank (2005), *World Development Indicators 2005*, Washington, DC: World Bank.

Yunus, M. (1994), *Banking on the Poor*, Dhaka: Grameen Bank.

Yunus, M. (1998), 'Poverty alleviation: is economics any help? Lessons from the Grameen Bank experience', *Journal of International Affairs*, **52**(1), 47–57.

Yusoff, M., F.A. Hasan and S.A. Jalil (2000), 'Globalisation, economic policy, and equity: the case of Malaysia', paper presented at OECD workshop on Poverty and Income Inequality in Developing Countries: A Policy Dialogue on the Effects of Globalisation, 30 November–1 December, Paris.

Zamani, A. G. (2006), 'Re-engineering the Malaysian financial system to promote sustainable growth', BIS Papers No 28, pp. 269–76, August, Monetary and Economic Department, Basel, Switzerland: Bank of International Settlements.

22 Maldives
Isabell M. Welpe and Teresa E. Dana

Introduction

The Republic of Maldives is the smallest Asian country with regard to population. The country is an island nation consisting of a grouping of 1192 coral islands, with a total land mass of 115 square miles (that is, 298 square kilometres) in the Indian Ocean. The Republic of Maldives is located south of India's Lakshadweep islands, and south-west of Sri Lanka.

Situated in the Indian Ocean and scattered on both sides of the Equator, this archipelago is divided into 26 ring-shaped clusters (Dana, 2007). Until the twelfth century, Buddhism was the dominant religion of the people of the Maldives. Visitors, sailors and traders have influenced culture, society and economy of the Maldive islands over the years. From 1153 until 1968 the Maldives were governed as an Islamic sultanate. The Maldives were under the influence of Portugal since 1558 and the Netherlands since 1654. In 1887 the Maldives became a British protectorate and gained independence from Britain in 1965. Since 1968 the Maldives have been a republic. Tourism began to be developed by the beginning of the 1970s.

The first settlers on the Maldives probably came from the south-west coasts of the Indian subcontinent and the western shores of Sri Lanka. Dhivehi, which belongs to the Indo-Iranian group, with strong Arabic influence is the unique language of the Maldives. The 263 000 islanders call themselves Dhivehis. They share a mixed ethnic ancestry of Arab, Aryan, Dravidian, Negroid and Sinhalese origin. The Dhivehi society is homogeneous, with one language, one culture and one religion. The national religion is Islam; all citizens are Sunni Muslims. The weekend lasts from Friday to Saturday. It is unlawful to enter the country with an idol of worship. Except on designated tourist islands, alcoholic beverages and pork are illegal, as are dogs (Dana, 2007). Each island is enclosed by a coral reef and surrounded by a shallow lagoon. None of the islands rises beyond 10 feet (3 metres) above sea level. Agricultural production is limited as most of the islands have poor, sandy soil.

This chapter is the result of ethnographic research, conducted by one of the authors, in the Republic of Maldives (Teresa Dana). Despite the fact that the literacy rate in this country is higher than that of neighbouring countries, many people, especially those over 45 years of age, cannot read; consequently, all participants in this study were interviewed orally. Dhivehi entrepreneurs were asked to describe their business activities, their motives for being entrepreneurs, and their constraints – as they perceived them – in their own words. In addition, several questions attempted to identify financial issues. In order to gain an understanding of local values, a qualitative approach was chosen for this study.

In addition to Dhivehi entrepreneurs themselves, several non-entrepreneurs were also interviewed. Among them were the Ministry of Finance and Treasury; the Ministry of Fisheries and Agriculture; the Ministry of Planning, Human Resources and Environment;

the Ministry of Tourism; the Ministry of Trade and Industries (including its Foreign Investment Services Bureau); and the Ministry of Transport and Communications. Para-statal entities were also consulted, including the Maldives Industrial Fisheries Company Limited, the Maldives National Ship Management Limited, and the State Trade Organization. Others were approached, as well, including the Maldivian National Chamber of Commerce and Industry and the Maldivian Traders Association. Banks were also sources of insight, namely the Bank of Ceylon, the Bank of Maldives, the Habib Bank, and the State Bank of India.

The Maldives have a mixed economy which rests on the following three activities: tourism, fishing and shipping. Tourism is by far the most important and largest industry in the Maldives, accounting for around 20 percent of gross domestic product (GDP), more than 60 percent of the Maldives' foreign exchange and over 90 percent of government tax revenues flow in from import duties and tourism-related taxes. The beautiful, unpolluted beaches on small coral islands, blue waters and glorious sunsets attract tourists worldwide, bringing in about US$325 million a year. Tourism and other services in the tertiary sector contributed 33 percent to the GDP in 2000. Since the establishment of the first resort in 1972, over 84 islands have been developed as tourist resorts, with a total capacity of over 16 000 beds. It is recorded that over 500 000 tourists visited the islands in 2003 (Ministry of Trade and Industries).

Tourism as an industry is followed by the fishing industry. In an attempt to liberalize regulations to allow foreign investment the government has started economic reform programmes in 1989 and lifted import quotas and opened some exports to the private sector.

The fishing sector employs about 20 percent of the labour force and contributes 10 percent of GDP. All fishing is done by line as the use of nets is illegal. About 50 percent of fish is exported, especially to Sri Lanka, Germany, the UK, Thailand, Japan, and Singapore. Total exports of fish reached about US$40 million in 2000 (Ministry of Fisheries and Agriculture).

Finally, agriculture and manufacturing also play a role in the economy of the Maldives. Agriculture is, however, constrained by the limited availability of cultivable land and shortage of domestic labour. Due to the availability of poor soil and scarceness of arable land in the islands, agriculture is limited to only a few subsistence crops, such as coconut, banana, breadfruit, papayas, mangoes, taro, betel, chillies, sweet potatoes, and onions. Agriculture contributes about 6 percent of GDP (Ministry of Fisheries and Agriculture).

In addition to tourism, fishing and agriculture, industrial activities include garment production, boat building, and handicrafts. The industrial sector provides only about 7 percent of GDP. There are no Patent Laws in the Malvides. The population of the islands is scattered with the greatest number of people living on the capital island, Malé. Limitations on potable water and arable land, plus the added difficulty of congestion, are some of the problems faced by the economy in Malé. Development of the infrastructure is mainly dependent on the tourism industry and its complementary tertiary sectors, transport, distribution, real estate, construction, and government. Taxes on the tourist industry have been plowed into infrastructure and it is used to improve technology in the agricultural sector.

There is growing concern towards the coral reef and marine life due to coral mining, sand dredging, solid waste pollution and oil spills from boats. Mining of sand and coral has destroyed the natural coral reef that once protected several important islands, now making them highly susceptible to the erosive effects of the sea. The destruction of large coral beds due to heat is also a growing concern. Maldivian authorities are concerned about the impact of erosion and possible global warming in the low-lying country.

Government expenditure on education was 18 percent of the budget in 1999. Both public and private schools have made remarkable progress in the last decade. Further, there are private institutions that are staffed by community-paid teachers without formal training who provide basic literacy skills in addition to religious knowledge.

The Maldives has experienced relatively low inflation throughout the recent years (around 3–6 percent). In 2005, as a result of the tsunami, the GDP contracted by about 5.5 percent; however, the economy rebounded in 2006 with a 13 percent increase. In 2005 GDP was US$ 817 million. Major import partners are Singapore, India, Sri Lanka, Japan, and Canada.

The Maldives has been running a merchandise trade deficit in the range of US$200 to US$260 million since 1997. In 2004 it was US$444 million. Over the years, the Maldives have received economic assistance from multilateral development organizations, including the United Nations Development Programme, the Asian Development Bank, and the World Bank. Individual donors, including Japan, India, Australia, and European and Arab countries (such as the Islamic Development Bank and the Kuwaiti Fund) also have contributed (Ministry of Finance and Treasury).

Government policy on SMEs and entrepreneurship
Legal institutions for commerce in the Maldives have existed since 1932 but are still underdeveloped as exemplified by the lack of comprehensive commercial laws. Only in 1988 was the Decree on Limited Companies instituted and in 1989 the Law on Foreign Investments in the Republic of Maldives (Law No. 25/79) was implemented. Today, on the Maldives there are no restrictions on the ownership of equity and there is no income tax, no tax on corporate profit, no capital gains tax, no value added tax (VAT), no sales tax, and no property tax (World Bank Group, 2007).

The majority of entrepreneurs in the Maldives operate their businesses as sole proprietorships and they manage the firms themselves. Only a few have private limited liability companies with a small number of shareholders; however, even these enterprises are managed by the owners rather than by professional managers. Certain limited liability companies have a mix of directors, some of whom are foreigners. Among non-natives, enterprises often take the form of joint ventures with local participation; other firms are registered, with the Registrar of Capital Companies, as wholly owned foreign companies (Ministry of Trade and Industries).

Interestingly, registered partnerships appear to be uncommon in the Maldives. When asked why this is so, entrepreneurs explained that in the Dhivehi culture it is not necessary to formalize a partnership between individuals who trust one another; among those who do not trust one another, a partnership is avoided altogether.

Dhivehis inhabit 199 of the 1192 islands that comprise the Maldives and 88 islands are set aside for tourism developments. Although the government provides electricity to some communities, all the resorts and several other islands that do not have access to public electricity rely on privately owned generators, of which there are hundreds.

The telecommunication (telecom) infrastructure is relatively well developed. The telecom monopoly belongs to Dhiraagu, which supplies mobile phones as well as Internet services. It is an affiliate of the British Cable and Wireless Company. Almost all of the islands in the south have facilities. Although telephones are less common in the north, the Maldives have more telephones per capita than any other member of South Asian Association for Regional Cooperation (SAARC) (Ministry of Transport and Communications). The Dhivehis also have more televisions per capita than any other SAARC member (Dana, 2007).

However, financial services are very limited in the Maldives. The Bank of Maldives is the only local, commercial bank. It saw its beginnings as a joint venture between the state and a Bangladesh-based firm, the International Finance and Investment Company Limited. The other three commercial banks are foreign, namely, the Bank of Ceylon, the Habib Bank, and the State Bank of India. These are all open from Sunday to Thursday.

Lending rates are determined on the basis of the London Interbank rate (LIBOR) plus a margin. More capital is lent to the tourism industry than to any other sector. The second largest recipient of loans is commerce (Bank of Maldives). Banks are the only firms required to pay a tax on profits (Ministry of Finance and Treasury). There are no finance companies, investment banks or trading banks in the Maldives. Neither does this country have a stock market. Yet, the apparent lack of capital markets is not reported as being a constraint for entrepreneurs (Dana, 2002).

There are neither buses nor trains in the Maldives. In the capital, which has cars, motorcycles and taxis, the most common means of transportation is to ride a bicycle. Between the islands, boats come and go depending on local needs, produce, the weather and the vessel's owner. There are only five airports in the Maldives, that is, one per 2384 islands. Many planes are equipped with floats, in order to land and take-off from the sea.

The most important island is Malé, formerly known as the Sultan's island. This island is the sole political capital and economic centre of the Maldives. It is about 1 kilometre wide, 2 kilometres long, and home to one-quarter of the nation's 264000 people. There are also foreign workers from Egypt, Sri Lanka, and elsewhere. In addition, traders come here to conduct business, so the number of people on the island is said to swell to 100000 on some days (Ministry of Planning, Human Resources and Environment). Yet, Malé is rather clean and tidy for the crowded capital of a nation. The town boasts 20 mosques, numerous small shops and very busy markets. It also offers many small tea-houses, where Dhivehi men enjoy small snacks, such as fish balls, curry, breads, cakes, and samosa. To wash it all down, a cup of black tea, loaded with sugar, is the popular choice. Although men spend many hours in tea-houses, chatting about business and smoking, cultural norms make it unacceptable for women to frequent such establish-ments. Important institutions include the firewood market, the fish market, the wet market and the Singapore Bazaar, which is a conglomeration of shops selling handicrafts mostly to tourists.

A short boat-ride away is the island of Hulule, where Malé International Airport is situated. From here, turbo-props go back and forth to Colombo (Sri Lanka), while jets link the island republic to Dubai, Kuala Lumpur, Singapore and Trivandrum (India). Charter flights bring in tourists from Europe. In addition, Air Maldives, Hummingbird Island Airways Pvt. Ltd., and Maldivian Air Taxi provide air services to other islands.

Yet, most of entrepreneurs arrive here from outlying islands, aboard dhonis, traditional Maldivian vessels, which travel at an average speed of 7 knots. These are wide-based boats with deep bottoms. They have high curved hulls like those of Viking ships and a structure upon which a sail could be mounted, but none are attached. There are a few planks of wood on each side of the vessel and a couple in the middle. Passengers sit, stand and lie on these planks during their voyage at sea. At night, they stretch out and sleep on cargo, separated from each other by produce and merchandise. For some, the journey to and from the central trading area takes several days. While dhonis are used for short trips, larger vessels known as vedi are employed for trips to other islands.

The economic environment for entrepreneurship and the state of small business
The distribution sector of the economy contributes more to the GDP than does any other sector and the most popular form of small business activity in the Maldives is commerce. The distribution function is fragmented among a multitude of merchants. Traders identify opportunities for arbitrage, and transport goods from areas of low cost to markets where the same goods are worth more. In Ukulhas, for instance, a kilo of tuna costs only 3.5 rufiya (Dana, 2002). After a two-day journey, the same can be sold in Malé for 23 rufiya. (The currency has been steady at 11.72 rufiya per US dollar, even during the Asian crisis.)

These businessmen are not clad in suits and ties but rather, most wear cotton sarongs that are constantly being hiked up above the knees and then lowered to the ground. Shirts are often in checkered, plain and modern designs with short sleeves and collars. A few of these men sport pants, but no one wears socks. All have some variety of flip-flops on their feet. A look into their glass-like hazel eyes reveals tenderness tempered by the sea. These people are at one with nature and they emit warm personalities. At night, many lie on their boats and on concrete blocks awaiting departure back home, where they will head to pick up more produce from their island, only to return once again.

In some cases, a dhoni may be too big to dock at the pier of an island. In such cases, all the merchandise and bags as well as passengers are ferried aboard a small, wooden, motorboat that navigated back and forth in the dead of night. The men pile the boat high with coconuts, melons, barrels and boxes. A flashlight is used on the dhoni to alert the small boat of its location. Aside from distribution, the economic sectors that contribute the most to the country's GDP are tourism, fisheries, and agriculture.

In contrast to other countries that have encouraged industrialization, the economic policies of the Maldives were designed to promote tourism and fisheries. Tourism, contributing one-fifth of GDP, is the largest provider of foreign exchange. Fishing is also important as Dhivehis catch over 100000 metric tonnes annually (Ministry of Fishery and Agriculture), more than half of which is exported (Ministry of Trade and Industries). Over two-thirds of the nation's exports are fish and fish products. According to the census, more people work in fisheries than any other sector.

A few entrepreneurs introduced commercial tourism here, in 1972. That year, the first of the resorts in the Maldives was established. Soon, several resorts began setting up, but never more than one per island. Tourism is perceived as disruptive to traditional lifestyle, and for this reason, it is strictly regulated. Tourists are encouraged to stay together, and away from the Dhivehis. An Inter Atoll Travel Permit is required outside the tourist zone. This is issued by the Ministry of Atolls Administration, only if sponsored by a resident.

At first, most of the tourists to the Maldives came from Western Europe, causing the industry to be seasonal. During the 1990s, an increasing number of tourists arrived from East Asia and Australia (Ministry of Tourism). This continued until 1997, when several Asian currencies were devalued, making the Maldives relatively expensive to visit.

Nevertheless, the annual number of tourists visiting the Maldives exceeds the national population. Most visitors stay at resorts. Each resort is on its own island. In addition to over 10 000 beds at the resorts, there are also guesthouses and hotels. Several sea vessels also provide accommodations. The *MV Coral Princess*, for instance, was custom-built for 45 guests. Despite opportunities for entrepreneurship in the tourism industry, few local entrepreneurs take notice of these. About half of the resorts are owned and managed by foreign firms.

In contrast, fishing is a sector to which the Dhivehis have long been attracted. Fishing is the traditional occupation of Maldivian men and commercial fishing continues to use the traditional line and pole method. It is the people's principal means of livelihood and is the second most important source of foreign exchange. Each year, on 10 December, the nation celebrates Fisherman's Day, to highlight the importance of the role of fishing in the economy.

Until the 1970s, fishing was done from sailboats. Since then, the state has encouraged the modernisation of the country's fishing fleet, through the addition of motors. One man pumps the fuel, four men pull in the anchors, one starts the engine and two others shout directions. After these procedures take place, they navigate slowly amidst other boats. Bumping into a few does not seem to disturb the other vessels' crew. There are no lifejackets on board.

The principal catch is skipjack. Yellow fin tuna, red snapper, mackerel and barracuda are also important. Fishermen use the pole and line method to catch skipjack and trolling for surface fish such as jacks, little tuna, mackerel, and wahoo. Net fishing, coral mining and the use of harpoons have been banned as such techniques are harmful to the aqua culture. Since 1980, lobsters have been protected and since 1993 the same has been true for dolphins, giant clams and whales. Other protected marine life includes black coral, conch, turtles and whale sharks.

Much activity takes place in Malé's fish market. Local fishermen bring the day's catch here to sell to other Dhivehis. Fishing dhonis arrive in an orderly fashion and young men carry the fish to the market. The fish are placed in tidy rows on the floor and are then available for sale. Prices are reflective of the day's supply. There is never any fish remaining. Tuna is the popular choice.

It used to be that the industry's main exports were dried and smoked tuna to Sri Lanka. Now, exports have expanded to include canned, frozen and salted fish. Such products are now shipped to the Far East as well as to Europe. In order to tap marine resources, the government established a 200-mile Exclusive Economic Zone (which encloses 900 000 square kilometres of sea).

Although the government allows people to cultivate state property, some islands have minimal amounts of fertile terrain, limiting the ability to grow crops. Many islands are nevertheless able to use their arable land in order to grow produce for supplementary income. Main crops include bananas, breadfruits, coconuts and papayas. Some islands grow bamboo, banyans, betel nut, chilli, mangoes, millet, pandanus, taro, sweet potatoes and yams. On very few islands it is possible to grow citrus fruits and pineapples.

The island of Thoddu, at the top of the Ari atoll, grows most of the watermelons and pumpkins for the region. Most of the vegetables grown on this island are sold, rather than consumed locally. Each watermelon can earn up to US$5, especially during the month of Ramadan. The lack of availability of green vegetables on this island, and on many others, is problematic, and many children are iron-deficient as a result. People eat tuna and rice, every day. The only livestock on the island are chickens, which are eaten on special occasions. Surplus may be transported to Malé where a hen is worth 40 rufiyaa. Bats, cats, and rats are the only mammals on Thoddu. On other islands, people raise goats for special occasions. Malé and the tourist resorts are the main markets for agricultural produce. Since production is less than demand, it is necessary to import large quantities of fruits, vegetables, meat and poultry. Such imports are draining foreign exchange reserves.

The traditional industries of the Maldives are still very much alive, employing about 25 percent of the workforce. It is not uncommon to see a self-employed fisherman making his own boat. Women are often seen weaving mats, or making ropes. Blacksmiths are usually men. Other cottage industries supply souvenirs to the tourist trade.

Modernization has also given rise to a new industrial sector. Fish is now being packaged at processing plants such as the canning facility operated by Mifco, the Maldives Industrial Fisheries Company Limited, in Malé. Also, soft drinks are bottled locally. Light manufacturing includes the production of garments, bricks, detergents and pipes. Yet, the government is careful not to encourage rapid industrialization. At the Asia-Pacific Ministers' Conference on Tourism and Environment, in 1997, His Excellency Mr Maumoon Abdul Gayoom, President of the Republic of Maldives, declared, 'Past experience has shown that rapid modernization is accompanied, more often than not, by enormous damage to the environment.'

The lack of self-sufficiency makes the Maldives rely greatly on imports, almost half of which originate in Singapore (Ministry of Trade and Industries). Their main trading partner since the 1970s, Singapore exports to the Maldives goods worth approximately US$10 million monthly (Ministry of Foreign Affairs). Import duty, based on cost, insurance and freight (CIF) value, is a sufficient source of revenue for the Republic of Maldives (Ministry of Finance and Treasury).

Almost one-quarter of all exports from the Maldives go to Sri Lanka, and about one-fifth to the UK. During the late 1990s, the SAARC announced plans to encourage preferential trading accords among its member countries, the total population of which exceeds 1 billion people. This includes about 400 million middle-class consumers, a considerable market to tap and a possible opportunity for Dhivehi entrepreneurs (Dana, 2002, 2007).

Internationalization of entrepreneurs and SMEs from the Republic of Maldives
Much entrepreneurship literature associates entrepreneurs with an affinity for, or at least a tolerance of, calculated risk. Indeed, small business usually involves some degree of risk (Dana, 2007). Also, financing is often a central issue for entrepreneurs, as reflected in literature. However, the Dhivehis do not associate risk with business activities, nor do they feel constrained by the lack of financing, despite the absence of capital markets

and the limited banking facilities in this archipelago (Dana, 2002). A few products are exported, such as tuna, but there is little perceived need for internationalization at the moment.

Conclusion

In the absence of abundant resources, Dhivehi entrepreneurs view entrepreneurship as the function of acting upon arbitrage opportunities. With little formal education, they appear as unskilled people using simple technology. Yet, they perform important economic functions. They do not perceive the lack of formal infrastructure nor the lack of capital as a constraint. Nor are they concerned with risk. They associate risk with global warming causing the sea level, thereby drowning their islands, the average of which is a mere 10 feet above sea level. While the islands thrive on a subsistence market economy, the capital is a town of small enterprises. Unemployment never exceeds 1 percent, and the people are on average, the richest in the region.

References

Dana, Léo-Paul (2002), 'Sustainable development in the Maldives: the Dhivehi context of entrepreneurship', *International Journal of Entrepreneurship and Innovation Management*, **2**(6), 557–65.

Dana, Teresa E. (2007), 'The Dhivehis of the Maldives', in Léo-Paul Dana and Robert B. Anderson (eds), *International Handbook of Research on Indigenous Entrepreneurship*, Cheltenham, UK and Northampton, MA, USA: Edward Elgar, pp. 181–92.

World Bank Group (2007), *Doing Business in the Maldives*, The World Bank, The International Finance Corporation and Palgrave Macmillan, http://doingbusiness.org/.

23 Mongolia
Malcolm Innes-Brown

Introducing Mongolia: political antecedence to present day SME potential

With the fall of the Manchu Dynasty in 1911, having been earlier deposed by China, the last of the Great Khaans in Mongolia – Jebtsun Damba Khutukhtu (the living Buddha of Urga) – was reinstated. By 1919 the country was re-occupied by China until 1921 when a ferocious battle in the streets of Urga (the present day Ulaanbaatar) between the Chinese occupiers and a force of White Russians liberated the city. The victory was far from fortuitous as the Russians, who were led by Baron von Ungern-Sternberg (the 'mad Baron') proved to be an extravagant, quixotic and cruel leader, inflicting gross abuse not only upon the Great Khaan and his people, but also upon his own soldiers. In 1924 the Great Khaan died, the same year as a second brief but monumental battle between remnant von Ungern-Sternberg forces and an uprising led by a popular nationalist named Sukhbaatar (Mongolians tend to use only one name). The uprising was supported by a detachment of the Red Army and the victory established Mongolia as the second country after Bolshevik Russia itself – and the first in Asia – to become a communist state. A Moscow-scripted constitution was formally adopted in 1924, although Sukhbaatar negotiated Mongolian independence under the new constitution.

During the battles, the traditional Tibetan-style wooden buildings of the city were largely destroyed, Urga was renamed Ulaanbaatar. Sovietization of the city's architecture – still very much evident in the somber, gaunt, public buildings today – began. Closer ties with Russia formed in 1936 when the two countries signed a mutual-aid pact with a re-written constitution which consolidated power of the communist regime by 1940. A plebiscite in 1945 voted overwhelmingly to maintain Russian suzerainty including the continued use of Cyrillic script rather than a return to traditional Mongolian written language. Marshall Choibalsan, victorious in the Russo-Mongolian 1938 defense of the western border against an eastern advance of the Imperial Japanese Army from Manchuria, became prime minister in 1938 until 1952. From 1952, the year when Tsedenbal began his long term of office, extension of Russian consolidation into all aspects of Mongolian political, economic and cultural life continued for the next 30 years.

Until the break-up of the Soviet Union, Mongolia remained a client-state. An alliance of democratic parties won government from the ruling Mongolian Peoples' Revolutionary Party (MPRP) in 1996. From 1924 to 1996, the MPRP had remained in power for 75 years and in doing so became historically the longest single party to hold government in world history. For much of that time, Mongolia was influenced by hegemonic alignment with Moscow, an alignment which included appointment from Moscow of the Mongolian president. During the late 1930s, Stalinist purges in Mongolia resulted in the destruction of over 700 monasteries and the disappearance of between 50000 and 70000 people, including virtually all lamas and shamanist priests. In a twist of history, as well as being the first country after Russia to become communist, during

December 1989 and January 1990, when Mongolia had its own democratic Revolution, the country was the first Soviet-aligned nation to embrace democratic reform and a market economy.

Throughout the 75 years of socialist rule, the main thrust of industry and commerce centered upon inefficient, over-capitalized and hidden full-employment state-owned enterprises. Although nomadic herdspeople cultivated their own peripatetic means of survival on vast open steppelands, no private sector existed, including no individual ownership of land or property, nor did the means of production – including material supply, manufacturing inputs or product distribution – reside in private hands. Instead, Moscow's interest in Mongolia lay primarily in cautious geo-politics of Sino-Russian relations under which much of Mongolia was heavily and secretly fortified by the Soviets in return for a largely Russian supply-side Mongolian economy. In effect the client-status of Mongolia meant that for over seven decades small industry and medium-sized commercial activity, which might have otherwise been realized in cross-border trade or in developed domestic markets, did not exist. The most that can be said is that the state allocated production quotas in dairy and animal products for which the families of herdspeople were paid cost recovery by government.

Mongolia is a landlocked country lying strategically between China on the east, Russia and Kazakhstan on the west, Siberia to the north and Tibet in the south. Mongolia is a unique and fragile country. Its population of 2.7 million is vulnerable to any transmissible endemic disease and its natural environment is easily at risk from altered balance in eco-systems. With a population density of 1.4 persons per square kilometer, Mongolia is one of the most sparsely inhabited regions on earth. There is astounding natural diversity. In the eastern Altai mountains bordering Kazakhstan, Tabun Bogdo, at 15 266 feet (4653 meters), is the country's highest peak. In the southern wilderness of the Gobi Desert, continental climatic extremes include summers of plus 50-degees Celsius and winter temperatures of minus 50 degrees Celsius. In the capital, Ulaanbaatar, it is not uncommon for winter temperatures to fall below minus 20 Celsius. The average annual temperature for the capital is minus 1 degree Celsius, making it the world's coldest capital city. It is also the world's most isolated capital, while Mongolia itself, at an average height above sea level of 5100 feet, (1554 meters), is one of the highest plateau countries in the world. Mongolia has an ancient tradition of monochromatic steppeland communities living in a natural environment not propitious to small and medium enterprise (SME) in the sense that non-pastoral economies would know. Livestock – principally horses, sheep, yak, camels and goats – far outnumber people, making products produced by animal husbandry the main basis for SMEs. The population is predominantly Khalkha Mongol (80 percent) with minority ethnic groups including Oirat Mongols, Kazakhs, Chinese and Russians. Two-thirds of the population is under 30 years of age and 28.5 percent are under 14 years old. Compared with Mongolia's population of 2.7 million, some 18.5 million ethnic Mongolians live in the Chinese province of Inner Mongolia.

Despite the long decades of Russian influence, Mongolians have always strenuously sought to hold their independence extant. Throughout its colorful history, Mongolian independence has not only been a question of pan-Mongol activism, but a complex set of circumstances surrounding successive Manchu, Sino-Japanese, Tsarist and Soviet aspirations. Each of these have extended forward principally from a mighty thirteenth-century land empire stretching from the western borders of Europe to include all of what is now modern Russia and China. In the sixteenth-century, an intense tradition of profound Mongol culture enshrined in Sonan Gyatso lamaism (a parallel to Tibetan Buddhism) formed across Mongolia. Mongol religion, art and music survived the cultural crucible of Marxist-Leninism, and even to this day, the atavistic mysteries of shamanism, the teachings of Buddhism and life in monastic orders enters into everyday life in modern Mongolia.

Against this background, in an attempt to elevate local industry, Soviet organization of Mongolia into a modern socialist state replicated Russian collectivization during the 1950s, which, as far as Mongolia was concerned, resulted in futile moves to marshal nomadic herders into communes. Mongolia then, as now, remains one of few places on earth where is it possible to see genuine nomadic lifestyle, differing little since the time of Ghingiss Khaan. Even so, collectivization caused great disruption with a shift of population that was 78 percent rural in the 1950s to 58 percent urban by the time of the democratic revolution in 1990 (Innes-Brown, 2001: 78). This trend has continued with the population of Ulaanbaatar growing from about 500 000 in the early 1990s to over 800 000 at the present time. Rapid democratization simultaneously with a move from central planning to a market economy in 1990, together with ongoing urbanization has brought heightened opportunity for SMEs to emerge and to gain a foothold. Analysis of this foothold is given below along with concomitant development of the nation's banking and financial systems, progress in representative government, democratic elections, an independent judiciary, a professional civil service and international trading arrangements. There has been considerable progress, but equally considerable setbacks. Along the same lines, a vital aspect of Mongolian potential is the Soviet legacy of universal free education. At the time of the democratic revolution in 1990, the literacy rate was 98 percent, one of the world's highest, and an achievement which won the country an international United Nations Educational, Scientific, and Cultural Organization (UNESCO) award. Since the arrival of democratization this figure fell to 83 percent by the end of the 1990s (Innes-Brown, 2001: 79). The high regard for education results in an intellectually agile and professionally flexible population, especially among a nascent, but now emergent, middle class. There is strong priming in the urban workforce for SME engagement.

Events in Mongolia at the time of the country's democratic revolution were unprecedented, and have had a profound influence on both strengths and weaknesses relating to SME. The question of how political reform leads to economic reform is fundamental to Mongolia's emergence as a democracy with a market economy. Both have now replaced Marxist-Leninism and central planning. Transition is both political and economic with the emergence of SME radically affected by the break-up of the Soviet Union. Along with former Soviet republics, Mongolia suffered a dramatic decline in subsidy (which ran at 32 percent of GDP in 1990) (*The Economist*, 1990). The sudden withdrawal of economic support caused desperate times in Mongolia during 1991 and 1992 until international aid programs from the West began trickling in by 1993. Even so, in 1992 a stock exchange was optimistically opened (in the old cinema building on Sukhbaatar Square) and President Ochirbat, running as a non-communist, won the country's first free elections in 1993. Poverty increased from 15 percent in 1990 to 36 percent by 2000 (MOSTEC, 2000: 5 – based upon United Nations (UN), Asian Development Bank (ADB) and World Bank (WB) figures). Bilateral and multilateral capacity-building aid programs were seen by the Mongolian government as priorities greater than private sector development during the early 1990s (Batchimeg et al., 2005). Likewise, the international donor-aid community placed human development in the struggle against poverty as an imperative of more immediate importance than SME-led private sector growth. The argument that defunct and decrepit remnant Soviet state industries could be handed to an embryonic, over-enthusiastic and largely reckless group of inexperienced entrepreneurs liberated into private enterprise, was wisely tempered by the measured advice of international transitional market economy experts from whom the MPRP (which re-invented itself into a democratic socialist party) were quick to learn. At the same time, residual mistrust of the former communist party grew during the early 1990s, together with increasing cross-border China trade at bottom-end local markets selling in Ulaanbaatar, gave momentum to the voice of democratic alliance parties. Although the multi-party alliance message was immature and confusing to international observers, for a nation so fervently embracing democracy, Mongolians went to the polls in 1996 giving the democratic alliance a landslide victory and in so doing made history in ending the 75 years of unbroken MPRP mandate. As a sign of the fresh wind blowing through the nation, Bagabandi, a democratic political activist, was elected by the Great Hural (the national parliament) as prime minister. However, after four years of chaotic, rambling, inept and corrupt democratic government, in the December 2000 election, the day following a mass rally of 30000 gathered all night in Sukhbaatar Square – when temperatures fell to minus 22 degrees Celsius – the people put the MPRP overwhelmingly back into power. At the time, the assumption was that after more than 75 years in the job, unlike the hapless democratic alliance, at least the MPRP had experience in governing the country. At the recent July elections this year, the MPRP led by Prime Minister Enkhbold attracted violent riots in the streets of Ulaanbaatar, again the main problem seeming to rest with corruption and Members of Parliament (MPs) doing more to use their positions in parliament to benefit themselves as distinct from representing their constituents. Six people were killed in the riots and the MPRP Headquarters were set alight and razed to the ground. As the time of publication, the situation remains in confusion.

Business environment for SME and entrepreneurship

During the seven decades of client-status with the Soviet Union, Mongolia operated within the Council for Mutual Economic Assistance (COMECON) bloc. Virtually no private ownership of land, property or the means of production existed. The cogent embrace of democracy and a market economy in 1990 took place against a long history of entrenched central planning and state-owned enterprises. Production and sequestration of raw materials were held for repatriation to the Soviet Union in return for massive domestic subsidization. That the private sector has grown exponentially over the last decade is perhaps testament to the reversal of moribund enterprise, massive over-state capitalization, jejune foreign investment, stringent political control and enforced detachment from international trade during the Soviet era.

With these thoughts in mind, since the democratic revolution in 1990 the Mongolian commercial climate has altered in favor of SME, initially in conjunction with South Korean joint ventures. Increasingly, the early 1990s border trading with China in bottom-end local markets has given way since the early 2000s to value-added service enterprise. For example the information and communication technology sector now contributes 8 percent to GDP, employing 11 500 people in some 140 companies (FIFTA,

2008). Mongolia presents as a small country with an inexpensive, well-qualified and educated workforce able to support ICT. By 2002, voice (fixed phone) companies generated $US20 million while cellular and data/Internet companies such as Micom, MCS Electronics and Bodicom generated $US22 million. Three local players in software development – Grape City Mongolia, Engineersoft and Interactive – whilst young, inexperienced and operating in a somewhat fragmented environment (including outsourcing), have nevertheless achieved global standards with individual company annual turnovers of $US3 million. Within the economic spectrum of SME, about 60 percent of Mongolia's telecom is government-owned and Japan has a 12 percent stake in cellular and Internet connectivity, with the remainder held by local private companies.

Mongolia has vast reserves of copper and is rich in other mineral resources and precious metals such as gold, uranium, coal, molybdenum and oil against which ancillary SMEs continue to emerge. Some 80 percent of the country remains unexplored, holding the possibility of huge resources potential. In the past, mining has been problematic because of fluctuations in world commodity prices, remoteness, transport difficulties and environmental considerations (*Chicago Tribune*, 2007). There is no road link west to China or south to Tibet. With ADB support, the road between Ulaanbaatar and Irkutsk in Russian Siberia was sealed in the early 2000s. The southern arm of the trans-Siberian railway links Ulaanbaatar with Beijing to the east and Moscow to the east. Effectively, Mongolia's only seaport is Tianjin just south of Beijing. Air China and MIAT (Mongolia's airline) operate services between Ulaanbaatar and Beijing.

Apart from logistics, the notion that domestic consumerism underscores SME does not necessarily hold good for transitional nations. The features which characterize globalization bear heavily on consumers in poor countries, especially the flow-on welfare effects of globalization in the developed world leaving developing nations prone to uncertainty (James, 2000). This has been the case in Mongolia where demand-side economics cannot really be said to reliably depend on informed preference formed exogenously over product cycles (Lal, 2000). Likewise, the argument that Western-based organizational theory applies to entrepreneurial activity in less developed countries (LDCs) assumes that isomorphic trends in Western economies underlying SME are necessarily consistent with enterprise opportunity in transitional and emergent economies (Farashahi and Hafsi, 2005) is problematic in a nascent market economy such as Mongolia.

Despite such generic scenarios, the World Bank's *Country Reports* have consistently pointed to a number of elements in the commercial environment conducive to doing business in Mongolia. They draw attention to the country's solid commitment to both democratic government and to a market economy. Inherent within these twin SME environments, comparison with other Asian countries reveals some interesting features. In the wake of long decades of socialist rule and a centrally planned economy, and despite the ups and downs since 1990, Mongolia is essentially politically stable, has an accountable civil service and an independent judiciary. Details of these three key factors are outlined in figures 23.1, 23.2 and 23.3.

It is clear from figures 23.1–23.3 that transition to a market economy with underlying SME causality is highly plausible. Since 1990, the first SMEs to emerge were in the tourist industry. Starting with just two companies that offered adventure tours into the Gobi Desert, by 2008 more than a dozen companies specialize in eco-tourism, visits to cashmere and leather factories, horse and camel expeditions, holiday accommodation in

Source: World Bank.

Figure 23.1 Political stability and absence of violence (percentile rank 1–100)

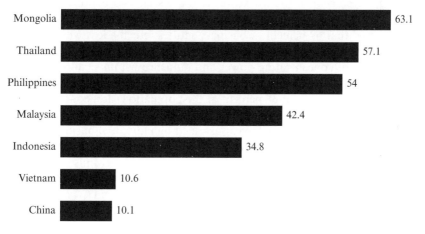

Source: World Bank.

Figure 23.2 Voice and accountability (percentile rank 1–100)

soum (often remote countryside settlements), community *gers* (the traditional round felt tents of the nomads) and guided tours during *Naadam* (the annual Mongolian summer festival of horse racing, wrestling and archery) (Ministry of Transport and Tourism, 2008). In addition, as Ulaanbaatar has grown to almost twice its size since 1990 (now over 800 000 people – 40 percent of the country's population) so too have SMEs multiplied. From virtually none during the socialist era, there are now more than 30 000 registered businesses operating in the capital, for example: over 250 hair salons, about 100 cosmetic retailers, 60 tailors' shops, more than 100 cobblers, more than 30 laundries, 700 vehicle repairers and about 800 pawnbrokers and much more in hospitality, ICT, animal products and service industries. Small and medium enterprises in Mongolia now

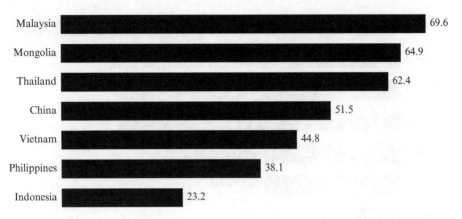

Source: World Bank.

Figure 23.3   Rule of law (percentile rank 1–100)

employ about 80 percent of the workforce and are seen as a major contributor to job creation and to reducing poverty (Prime Minister's Reports, 2008). At the same time, it should be noted that 67 percent of business entities return a loss with only 33 percent achieving profit margins. Franchising in Mongolia is not common mainly due to the communist legacy of concentrating power and influence within a cadre system (Vozikis and Castrogiovanni, 2000). Private urbanized SME currently outweighs livestock and herding (still the occupation of 38 percent of the population) as a contribution to GDP. The private sector has grown remarkably since Mongolia's move to democracy and a market economy in 1990. Despite losses sustained by individual businesses (above), the private sector now accounts for approximately 80 percent of GDP (Dashtseren, 2006: 8). In 2007 GDP was $US8.448 billion–$US2,900 per capita (Ministry of Finance and Economics, 2008). The dreadful *zuds* (extremely severe winters) of 2000–2001, resulted in massive livestock losses and anemic GDP growth of 1.1 percent (*Xinhua News Agency*, 2001). This was made worse by falling prices for primary industry products. The situation improved to 4 percent in 2002, 5.5 percent in 2003, 10.6 percent in 2004, 6.2 percent in 2005, 7.55 percent in 2006, and 9.9 percent in 2007 (US Department of State, 2008). Overall, livestock and herding contribute 20.6 percent to GDP, mining 27.4 percent, transportation, storage and communications 12.2 percent and trade and service some 24.8 percent, with SMEs embedded into all these sectors. Despite these figures, it is hard to make accurate estimations regarding Mongolia's GDP as about one-third is a cash economy not passing through the banks or taxation system. Tax reforms enacted in January 2007 have now significantly expanded the country's tax base helping government revenue in 2008 jump by 33 percent largely on the back of SME productivity (US Department of State, 2008). The outline shown in Box 23.1 indicates examples of SMEs in Ulaanbaatar and four sample *aimags* (provinces).

Government policy on and assistance for SME and local business enterprise
Mongolia's national government is a multi-party democracy in a republic with a presidential head of state. Each *aimag* has a *hural* (centre of provincial government). The

---

BOX 23.1 EXAMPLES OF SMES IN ULAANBAATAR AND FOUR SAMPLE PROVINCES

- Tourist retailing: paintings, carvings, sculptures, souvenirs, decorative plants, writing services on gifts and presents
- Repairing: home equipment, tools, various devices, televisions radios watches and clocks
- Crafting: working with gold and silver, precious metals, ceramics, jewellery, woodwork, garment making, saddle making (for both horses and camels)
- Teaching: training for local maintenance and repair jobs, house painting and decorating
- Commercial: photocopying, internet cafes, videotaping, video-renting, audio reproduction
- Shoe and clothing repairs: leather work, fabric repair, sewing and mending, shoe polishing, shoe repairs
- Vehicles: car washing and detailing, vehicle servicing and routine maintenance, garaging, passenger and trade vehicle repair
- Transport: carriage service, freight unpacking and freight forwarding, courier services, taxis, warehousing
- Hospitality: guesthouses and *ger* accommodation, kiosks, cafés and restaurants, catering
- Retail: street-side shops, shop counters in supermarkets (milk, bread, yoghurt, meat, vegetables), sidestreet newspaper stands, confectionery and ice-cream vendors (even in winter!), stalls in local markets (small goods, cross-border traded items such as toys, stationery), currency exchange services
- Production of raw materials: cashmere, leather

Source: Dashtseren (2006).

---

national parliament in Ulaanbaatar is known as the Great Hural and is made up of elected members of parliament with a ministerial cabinet headed by the prime minister. There are 21 *aimags* and numerous *soums* (small, isolated settlements) spread across each *aimag.* As of mid-2008, the Mongolian government has taken on board key focus areas throughout the country to activate support, resources, advice and millennium development goals into robust strengthening of SME and private entrepreneurship. The aim is to enhance existing SMEs and create new enterprises by offering education and training in micro-financing and business development. For Mongolia the situation is related closely to the government's intention to reduce poverty by private income generation, create jobs and establish better connectivity in domestic logistics. Around 62 percent of private economic entities have up to five employees, 32 percent have between five and 20 with 6.5 percent of private enterprises employing more than 20 persons (Regzenbal, 2008). Some

70 percent of private companies are in Ulaanbaatar and 30 percent in regional centers, particularly in Erdenet, the second largest urban center in the country. Specifically the government has adopted three guiding principals for promoting SME:

- to promote strong intra and inter-sector partnership for pro-poverty reduction through human development
- to develop/implement strategies through institutions and networks for sustainability and capacity-building
- to create self-reliant and competitive rural and urban communities to compete in domestic and international markets (UNDP, 2008).

To achieve these objectives, the government has continued assistance to local business development under a government initiative called 'One Village, One Product'. The aim is to encourage *soums* within each *aimag* to concentrate on eight identified marketable items such as cashmere garments, wool, cheese/yoghurt, leather goods, jewellery, meat and animal products. Value-adding from raw materials obtained from sheep, goats, yak, cattle and precious metals through to manufacture and distribution is being achieved by overcoming obstactals such as minimal collateral access to micro-finance. In addition, lack of credit facilities which have previously forced clients to try and run businesses without the necessary capital or take out informal loans at excessive rates, have been mitigated by government establishing Business Development Centres (BDCs) in regional *aimag* hubs coordinated from Ulaanbaatar. Since 1990, the Mongolian central banking system has gradually strengthened to underwrite a diversified financial infrastructure of competitive commercial institutions now able to protect SME loans via commercially viable loan guarantee schemes. Much of this has been achieved in conjunction with intensive training in business skills such as writing business proposals, undertaking feasibility analyses, and designing market products to meet client demand before micro-development loans are issued. Part of this commercial education has also centered upon helping entrepreneurs engaged in micro and small enterprises to link local poverty alleviation through networking to identify and expand market opportunities, increase the chances of sustainability and replicate SME models for business development throughout Mongolia.

With the assistance of UNESCO, the Mongolian government has organized concentrated training programs in SME. In particular the University of Meiji has collaborated with the National University of Mongolia to deliver training on Japanese entrepreneurship in practical areas such as human resource management (HRM), marketing strategies, banking and finance, international trade negotiation, writing business plans, accounting and taxation, investment project research and consumer behavior (UNESCO, 2006).

In 1996 Mongolia was first among transitional nations to accede to the World Trade Organization (WTO). Since then, the government has made much progress in redressing areas of weakness in order to meet WTO requirements. In particular, as with many recently acceded countries, Mongolia has concentrated upon legislation covering intellectual property rights (IPR) and upon protecting SMEs from violation of IPR. This protection has been aimed at securing effective competition from product development to product design and delivery to market. The protection also extends to raising financial backing and the inclusion of expanded business to the point of export, licensing and

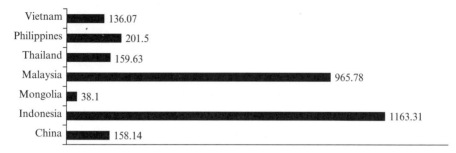

Note: The figure above summarizes the costs to register a firm in a foreign country.

Source: FIFTA (2008).

Figure 23.4   Cost of starting a business

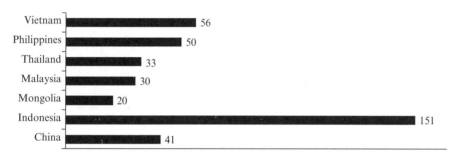

Source: FIFTA (2008).

Figure 23.5   Number of days for starting a business

franchising (Regzenbal, 2008). Much of this has been implemented by the Mongolian National Chamber of Commerce and Industry (MNCCI) which has coordinated IPR via the Chamber's Patent and Trademark Bureau.

The Mongolian National Chamber of Commerce and Industry is housed in an impressive Tsarist St Petersburg-style building close to Sukhbaatar Square and the Great Hural (Government House, a large, forbidding-looking building constructed in prototypical Soviet-style monolithic architecture). The Chamber is active and successful in promoting SMEs. There is realistic and well-placed assessment of business conditions and relative potential. Figures 23.4–23.8, put out by the Chamber, show general business conditions in Mongolia and emphasize Mongolian comparative advantage achieved during the last decade.

Within the general parameters outlined in figures 23.4–23.8, on a micro level the cashmere industry is a key element in small and medium enterprise and offers a potent example of how government has attempted to protect and assist a vital national interest. Leveraging relative purchasing advantage, Chinese companies have been buying the greater part of Mongolian cashmere fibers and subsequently use these resources as raw material for tertiary production of high-end woolen garments successfully marketed

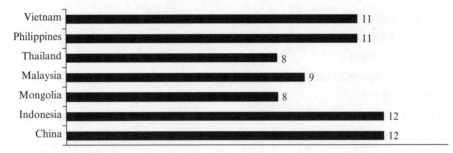

Note: Political stability combines several indicators which measure perceptions of the likelihood that the government in power will be destabilized or overthrown by possibly unconstitutional and/or violent means, including domestic violence and terrorism.

Source: FIFTA (2008).

Figure 23.6   Number of procedures for starting a business

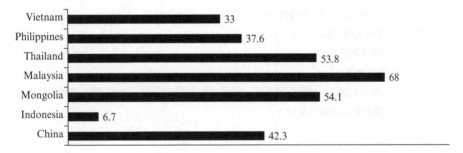

Note: Control of corruption measures perceptions of corruption, conventionally defined as the exercise of public power for private gain.

Source: FIFTA (2008).

Figure 23.7   Control of corruption (percentage rank 1–100)

globally. The government has sought expert foreign industry advice and used Mongolian traditional skill in fiber-blending specifications attractive to international buyers. This has acted to counterbalance Chinese dominance. The government has taken these steps in order to establish greater control over value-chain in fiber production at source. Some government measures outlined by Lecraw et al. (2005: 5) have been taken:

- no changes in FDI law to allow backward integration by brand name holders of processes (that is, Chinese companies) into the herding sector
- no government assistance extended to induce processors in Mongolia to integrate forward into international channels of distribution in top brand names
- the Mongolian fiber mark will be promoted only if it is accompanied by strict quality control, thus attracting FDI only into high-quality fibers which Mongolia is exclusively capable of excelling

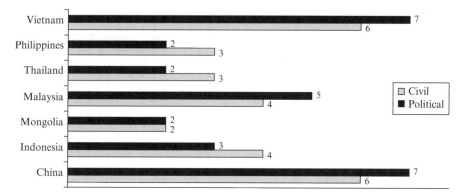

Note: Measures levels of civil and political rights defined as those unable to be exercised due to direct government policy and indirect insider power structures.

Source: FIFTA (2008).

Figure 23.8 Civil and political rights

The results have been effective in demonstrating that the Mongolian government is capable of sophisticated statutory and technical provision in relation to its core commercial enterprises. In this case the aim was not to compete in final product distribution internationally, but to maintain focus on what the industry is best at: producing the world's highest quality blended cashmere fiber.

International trade and economic cooperation supporting SME
Like all transitional nations, Mongolia has both multilateral and bilateral relations. As well as accession to WTO (mentioned earlier) the country is a member of many world bodies such as most agencies of the UN, the International Labor Organization, the Asian Development Bank, the International Monetary Fund, the World Health Organization, and so on. Within the framework of the Doha multilateral trade negotiations, Mongolia has been primarily interested in protection of small and vulnerable industry in landlocked countries. With this in mind, the inherent problems associated with lack of transport infrastructure has seen constant support from the ADB and more recently a 'Transit Transport Framework Agreement' with China and Russia. The clear intention would be to upgrade the southern arm of the Trans-Siberian Railway running through Mongolia, and, more importantly, create a road link across the vastnesses of steppelands and Gobi Desert east to Beijing. There are currently no overland roads links between Mongolia and China. Building roads north and east would greatly enhance international competitiveness.

Attracting FDI has been of considerable importance in supporting Mongolian SMEs. Foreign investment in private companies has continued to grow, particularly from China and Canada.

Table 23.1 indicates FDI among some of Mongolia's major trading partners.

At present Mongolia has more than 30 bilateral trade and economic cooperation agreements with Russia, China, South Korea, Japan, Canada, the US, the EU, ASEAN

Table 23.1   Foreign direct investment into Mongolia (US$ million)

By major countries	Total (1990– 2004)	%	2000	2001	2002	2003	2004	2005
China	457.7	40.7	33.0	47.3	135.3	46.3	126.0	228.1
Canada	184.0	16.3	–	–	6.0	120.1	51.5	154.2
South Korea	85.4	7.6	11.0	23.4	15.8	6.0	6.5	18.9
Japan	66.0	5.9	17.1	1.5	2.8	6.9	5.4	5.9
USA	39.2	3.5	7.8	2.4	2.6	0.4	3.2	5.5
Russian Federation	36.2	3.2	2.4	5.7	1.6	2.7	2.3	7.45
By sector								
Geological prospecting and exploration	483.8	43.0	16.8	57.0	38.5	151.5	147.6	183.9
Trade and catering service	166.5	14.8	5.5	5.7	89.5	7.0	37.5	54.4
Light industry	86.6	7.7	27.1	4.9	2.9	4.6	3.4	1.9
Banking financial service	66.1	5.9	0.7	19.7	4.0	0.2	21.0	9.6
Processing of livestock raw material	55.7	4.9	11.6	6.3	0.3	2.8	3.0	1.1
Engineering construction of building material	51.5	4.6	8.1	8.1	6.0	2.6	1.8	0.7

Source: MNCCI (2004).

nations and others. Mongolia and the People's Republic of China signed the first post-1990 trade agreement in 1991 followed by an Economic and Technical Cooperation Agreement in 1994. Under these agreements, Mongolian exports to China consist 90 percent of raw materials from livestock and semi-possessed mineral products. The main imports from China include foodstuffs, consumer goods and construction materials. Trade with Russia declined sharply after transition to a market economy but still represents about 20 percent of overall trade turnover (MNCCI, 2005).

Conclusion
The remarkable thing about Mongolia is that in world consciousness the country still somehow remains 'the forgotten land'. Yet its importance as Asia's first transitional nation and therefore harbinger of political and economic transitional success elsewhere, particularly in the Commonwealth of Independent States (CIS – the former Soviet republics), cannot be overstated. What makes this important is that a remote Central Asian country, having robustly taken up democratic governance and flung itself enthusiastically into market economics, now has over 30 000 small private enterprises from a starting point of zero in 1990. Along with this have come supporting networks of government, WTO accession, central and merchant banking, international trade agreements, fiscal and regulatory legislation, protection measures of key enterprises within industry-specific policies and a commercial environment attracting sustained FDI.

At the same time it must be said that poverty has remained stubbornly at 39 percent, communicable disease endemic and fragile eco-systems supporting traditional herding under threat. English has replaced Russian as the second language and the country moved into the information technology age. The people have embraced privatization and small business enterprise, yet remain per capita the most heavily subsidized recipients of international aid in the world. The nexus between democratic revolution, the adoption of a market economy and the legacy of Soviet dependence is redolent of past and present mixed personal feelings and confused national identity. Portraits of Ghingiss Khaan hang on every wall. The Great Khaan is embossed onto the national currency (the *tugrit*). Present sentiment in Mongol consciousness is one of quiddity stretching 800 years from the once great empire. This consciousness now gives agency to Mongolian individual endeavor, but the country overall is still finding its way. Indeed, some people question whether liberal democracy and capitalist enterprise are what will ultimately sustain a small, vulnerable landlocked country set strategically between an increasingly hegemonic Russian Federation and a surge in Sino-pantheonism. Bearing in mind that entrepreneurship less than a generation ago was totally unknown, Mongolian SME is agile, explorative and gaining in acumen, technical know-how, due diligence and reliable risk management. It is now rapidly moving from lower market-entry products to more sophisticated value-added goods and services delivered domestically and internationally.

References

Batchimeg Namsraidorj, Enkhjargal Adiya and Rosalind Chew (2005), 'Indigenous small and medium enterprises in Mongolia', in Léo-Paul Dana (ed.), *Handbook of Research on Ethnic Minority Entrepreneurship: A Co-evolutionary View on Resource Management*, Cheltenham, UK and Northampton, MA, USA: Edward Elgar, pp. 168–74.
Chicago Tribune (2007), 'Mongolia's gold rush: blessing or curse', 13 May.
Dashtseren, Tsetsen (2006), *Easing the Barriers of Formality: A Study on the Regulatory Framework Affecting Mongolian Micro and Small Businesses*, Bangkok: International Labor Office.
Farashahi, Mehdi and Taibb Hafsi (2005), 'Applicability of management theories to developing countries: a synthesis', *Management International Review*, 45(4), October, 483–511.
Foreign Investment and Foreign Trade Agency (FIFTA) (2008), *Steppes in the Right Direction: Top Reasons for Investing in Mongolia*, Ulaanbaatar: Mongolian–Russian Business Forum.
Innes-Brown, Malcolm (2001), 'Democracy, education and reform in Mongolia: transition to a new order', in Mark Bray and W.O. Lee (eds), *Education and Political Transition: Themes and Experiences in East Asia*, Singapore: Oxford University Press.
James, Jeffrey (2000), 'Do consumers in developing countries gain or lose from globalization', *Journal of Economic Issues*, 34(3), 537–57.
Lal, Deepak (2000), *The Poverty of Development Economics*, 2nd edn, Cambridge, MA: MIT Press.
Lecraw, Donald, Philip Eddleston and Alene McMahon (2005), *A Value-chain Analysis of the Mongolian Cashmere Industry*, Ulaanbaatar: Mongolia Economic Policy and Competitive Project, USAID.
Ministry of Economics and Finance (2008), *Annual Report*, Ulaanbaatar: Government of Mongolia.
Ministry of Science, Technology, Education and Culture (MOSTEC) (2005), *Annual Report*, Ulaanbaatar: Government of Mongolia.
Ministry of Transport and Tourism (2008), *Annual Report*, Ulaanbaatar: Government of Mongolia.
Mongolian National Chamber of Commerce and Industry (MNCCI) (2004), *Business to Mongolia: Foreign Investment*, Ulaanbaatar: MNCCI.
Mongolian National Chamber of Commerce and Industry (MNCCI) (2005), *Annual Report*, Ulaanbaatar: MNCCI.
Prime Minister's Reports (2008), *Mongolia Development Gateway*, Ulaanbaatar.
Regzenbal, Mishigdorj (2008), 'IP awareness and capacity of SMEs in Mongolia', address to the Mongolian National Chamber of Commerce and Industry, Ulaanbaatar.
The Economist (1990), 'Batmonh's last Hural?', 27 January.
UNDP (2008), *Enterprise Mongolia*, SME Promotion Program, Ulaanbaatar.
UNESCO (2006), Progress report, *Small and Medium Sized Enterprise Project of Japan*, Beijing.
US Department of State (2008), *Bureau of East Asian Affairs,* Washington, DC.
Vozikis, Georg and Gary Castrogiovanni (2000), 'Foreign franchisor entry into developing countries: influences on entry choices and economic growth', *New England Journal of Entrepreneurship*, 3(2), 9–19.
Xinhua News Agency (2001), 'Mongolian foreign investment growth at ten-year low', 5 January.

24 Myanmar[1]
Léo-Paul Dana and Frank Lasch

1. Introduction

Myanmar covers 678 500 square kilometres, and borders Bangladesh, China, India, Laos, Thailand, the Bay of Bengal and the Andaman Sea. Kipling (1890) reported about Burma, that it was quite unlike any land. Several other authors confirmed the specific character of the former Union of Burma as 'virtually unknown to the outside world' (Garrett, 1971: 343); 'most reclusive country of mainland Southeast Asia' (Hodgson, 1984: 90); 'the secretive nation' (Swerdlow, 1995: 73); and 'East Asia's last frontier' (Hirsh and Moreau, 1995: 10).

Until the 1950s, Burma was the world's most important rice exporter. In 1988, after an era of socialism, a market-oriented economy was introduced. Since then, many of Myanmar's social indicators (literacy rate, the doctor:population ratio, and so on) have compared favourably with those of its richer neighbours (Thein, 1996). Yet, although the country is generously endowed with hardwood forests, oil, precious gems, silver and other minerals, its people have not prospered.

The earliest people known to have flourished in this region are known as the Pyu (a people who used the Sanskrit script and observed Buddhism with some elements of Hinduism). They were defeated by ancestors of today's Burmese. In 1287, the Mongols destroyed the empire of the Pagan dynasty. The region was then ruled in the form of small states. Three ethnic groups (the Burmese, the Mons, and the Shans) governed this region until the sixteenth century, when a second Burmese empire was created. A third empire was established in 1752 and lasted until the arrival of the British (traders from England arrived previously, in the seventeenth century). Border troubles between Burma and British India led to a succession of conflicts (wars of 1824–26, 1852–54, and 1885) that finally made the former Kingdom of Burma a province of British India. In the following years (1890s), Burma became an important exporter of oil. Uprisings and claims for independence resulted in the India Act of 1935 and Burma was separated from India.

Before World War II, the annual rice exports exceeded 3 million tons and Burma was considered the predominant rice exporter in the world (Swerdlow, 1995). Other sources confirm this positive economic development of Burma, especially its agricultural performance: 'Burma is one of the few countries in Asia that have a considerable exportable surplus of food' (Christian, 1942: 3).

The Japanese invasion in 1941 forced the British to withdraw in 1942. The following year, in 1943, Japan declared Burma independent and set up a pro-Japanese government. Allied troops finally defeated the Japanese in 1945 and the Union of Burma came into existence in 1948, but civil war raged until 1952. In 1962, military rule was established, chasing Burma's elected prime minister and the 'Burmese way to Socialism' – a mix of Buddhism, central planning and isolationism. English was banned as 'representative of a degenerate and decadent culture' (Maung, 1991: 222) and reinforced the rupture with the

Western democracy model. The only legal political party (Burma Socialist Programme Party) nationalized the banks, the transportation system, wholesale trade, retail trade, and foreign-owned companies. The state-controlled planned sector dominated the national economy; the lack of foreign capital and technology caused limited growth during the 1960s. The single-party socialist state, and the one-party constitution, led to a progressive breakdown of the formal firm-type sector of the economy, annihilating the environment for entrepreneurship and small business.

In 1974, the country was renamed the Socialist Republic of the Union of Burma, committed to self-reliance, state control, isolation, and strict neutrality. Steinberg (1982) gave an account of the times. Strong economic recession caused by declining trade marked the mid-1980s, and per capita income decreased while inflation escalated. Formerly among the most prosperous economies of Asia, Burma was designated by the United Nations in 1987 as one of the least developed nations in the world. Falling living standards and political frustration fuelled widespread riots during the first half of 1988.

Finally, in 1988, tens of thousands of demonstrators removed the dictatorship, but in the absence of an entrepreneurial class, a new leadership arose from the military. Following a *coup d'état*, in 1988, the 'State Law and Order Restoration Council' took over the country and adopted a market-oriented policy. Central planning was officially discarded. One year later, the government changed the English version of the country's name to the Union of Myanmar. During the following years, the manufacturing sector produced about 6 percent of gross domestic product (GDP). To obtain foreign exchange, exports were encouraged causing local shortages and pushing domestic prices up. The mid-1990s met rampant inflation. In 1997, the United States declared economic sanctions against new investments in Myanmar. In 1997, Myanmar joined the Association of South East Asian Nations (ASEAN), but as Asia entered its financial crisis, the market rate of Myanmar's currency fell by nearly 100 percent in the same year, and the dollar traded at more than 300 kyat[2] (the official exchange rate stood at about 6 kyat per US dollar). In 1998, new import restrictions were imposed and in 1999, approvals for foreign direct investment fell by 96 percent. During the 1990s, the annual inflation averaged 27.13 percent.

2. Government policy on SMEs and entrepreneurship

Historically, colonial policy in Burma is said to have obstructed the development of local entrepreneurship as the colonial government gave preferential treatment to those it favoured (for example, British India Steamship Navigation Company, British Overseas Airways Corporation – BOAC, Burma Match Co. Ltd, Bombay Burmah Trading Corporation, Ltd, and so on, as discussed by Furnivall, 1957, and Macaulay, 1934).

Nevertheless, there appears to have been an entrepreneurial spirit, despite colonial policy. Despite European and Indian immigrants occupying major entrepreneurial roles, the Burmese displayed considerable entrepreneurship in a Schumpeterian sense in that they put into effect new combinations in the means of production and credit (Adas, 1974: 210). Successful entrepreneurship was recorded in the motion picture industry (Christian, 1943; Sein, 1950), the printing industry (Swe, 1972), and rice milling (Hla, 1975). Wai (1955) described Burmese financiers as prosperous moneylenders, like the Chettyars, who traced their origins to southern India. Burmese entrepreneurs were also successful middlemen in the rice business (Christian, 1942; Steinberg, 1982) despite the fact that elsewhere in the region middleman occupations were habitually dominated by the Chinese.

The predominant economic policy model in Burma after independence focused on import substitution, self-reliance, tight state control, isolation and regulatory mechanisms to discourage importation of goods. Instead of specialization in sectors of competitive advantage, this policy resulted in over-diversification and the creation of a highly protected, low-quality, high-cost, and inefficient industrial sector.

In 1988, the Burmese Socialist Programme Party started to reform the economy such that the 'state would retain monopoly in commodities, broadcasting, the oil industry and gems and jade mining, but private enterprise would be allowed in transport, all kinds of industry and services, fishing, publishing and trade' (*Herald Tribune*, 1988: 2). In the same year the State Law and Order Restoration Council initiated a market-oriented system, and private entrepreneurship was resumed that year. Foreign investment manufacturing, tourism and transportation were also allowed in 1988. Other important reforms included the state-owned Enterprises Law of 1989. A strong political sign was the revocation of the 1965 Law for the Establishment of a Socialist Economic System.

In 1990, a number of liberalization measures promoted a market economy. The Commercial Tax Law was introduced that year and the agricultural sector profited from the reduction of controls and regulations (for cultivation, milling, storage, transport, and marketing of agricultural products). According to the Planning Department of the Ministry of National Planning and Economic Development, during the 1989–90 and 1990–91 periods the economy grew by 3.7 percent and 2.8 percent respectively. The Short-term Plan of 1992–96 intended to pursue an export drive and to achieve an average annual growth rate of 5.1 percent. These efforts resulted in actual growth rates – of 9.7 percent the first year, 5.9 percent the second year, and 6.8 percent the third year (Khup, 1996). However, these figures are somewhat distorted by the fact that inflation is underestimated.

3.   The environment for entrepreneurship and the state of small business

The bazaar

Christian described bazaars in Burma: 'Rubies, spinels, garnets . . . are bought and sold in open market . . . next to a bazaar selling potatoes, garlic, and Chinese radishes' (Christian, 1943: 501–2). Shops are clustered according to products or services: jewellery shops stand adjacent to other jewellery shops, fruit-sellers are clustered with other fruit-sellers, rice comes in many varieties and different grades; some is damaged from poorly maintained husking machines. Cleaning, sorting and packing rice is for some women a social activity. Food is plentiful; there are also dried fruits, and baked goods. Lemon-barley is a favourite, as is green-coloured cream soda. Chickens, ducks, goats, hogs, quail and sheep are sold alive, lined up in a row, children are selling dry fish carefully laid out on the pavement. As is the case with traditional merchandise, modern items are also clustered. Moneychangers use the same exchange rates, buying and selling currency as if it were a commodity. Nobody has any competitive advantage and there is no product differentiation. Although it is seemingly not possible to differentiate among them, each has own, loyal clientele. The focus here is not merely on transactions, but on the relationship between buyers and sellers.

Family entrepreneurship

In 1857, King Mindon moved his capital to Mandalay and its Zegyo Bazaar became a principal distribution centre, the town prospered and artisans made it the handicraft centre of Myanmar. An example of family entrepreneurship in Mandalay is *shwe saing* (the making of gold leaf). This is occupation is found nowhere else in Myanmar (May, 1996). The skills are propagated from father to son, and non-family members are excluded. *Shwe saing* is restricted to a few families and transmitted from one generation to the other. Instead of competing with one another, entrepreneurs join forces in a symbiotic manner. This type of co-ordination facilitates an otherwise complicated process of production and marketing.

The first stage involves melting gold blocks; five households are involved in this initial phase of production. Thirty households are involved in the later stages of production. Molten gold is poured into a conical vessel, producing finger-shaped bullions. Rollers flatten these bullions, which are beaten by skilled craftsmen to obtain thin sheets of gold. Another household is in charge for further processing. The golden is further cut up, into pieces and placed between sheets of bamboo paper made only for the purpose of producing gold leaf. The golden is beaten again, to become film-thin. Finally, the strips of gold are joined with one another, to form quadrangles (about 25cm^2).

Elephant labour

Myanmar has up to 7000^3 domesticated elephants (Gray, 2001). About 2700 elephants are employed by the Myanmar Timber Enterprise which has a monopoly on teak extraction. Elephant labour is crucial in areas where vehicles cannot penetrate without causing major ecological damage. Teak production is a 30-year cycle and only trees of a certain girth are felled within a special area. Given this selection process, trained elephants outmatch machinery. An elephant starts education and training at the age of three and can learn one command every two days. Training completed, a bull elephant works five to eight hours per day, and the animals use their tusks, forehead and trunks to move tons of logs at a time. A labour elephant retires at the age of 55.

4. Internationalization of entrepreneurs and SMEs

In 1994 and 1995 the government policy focused on foreign investment and trade. A number of price controls and subsidies were phased out, taxes were streamlined, banking was restructured, and international business was facilitated. Foreign capital was attracted into Myanmar by the Foreign Investment Law. Foreign-owned enterprises and joint ventures with local enterprises were permitted (income tax holidays, further tax relief for exporters, and so on). The Foreign Investment Law guaranteed repatriation of profits and stated that investments would not be nationalized. Entrepreneurs arrived from Singapore, South Korea and Thailand. But the state did not succeed in mobilizing domestic capital for investment and exchange constraint hampered to some extent this measures of internationalization.

In 1998, new import restrictions were established, causing a boom in the parallel economy. Myanmar's economic objectives of the 1990s stressed the development of agriculture as the base sector of the economy and the evolution of the market-oriented economic system. Yet, the initiative to shape the national economy was intended to be kept in the 'hands of the State and the national peoples'.

In 2008, the price of rice doubled between January and May. Then, Cyclone Nargis devastated the rice bowl region of Myanmar. Nevertheless, the state – which had a monopoly on rice exports at the time – announced it would meet all contractual commitments. Meanwhile, covert exports also flourished. Myanmar is responsible for 23.4 percent of the 4653 tonnes of opium produced around the world each year (according to sources at the United Nations Office for Drug Control and Crime Prevention (UNODCCP), destined mainly for the production of heroin. According to *The Economist*, the wholesale price per kilogramme of heroin in New York has reached about US$80 000; at 40 percent purity, the retail price is US$290 000. Inexpensive production and a huge profit margin go hand in hand. Its profitability encourages bribery of law enforcement officials and makes this international trade hard to control.

5.   Conclusion

The liberalization of the agriculture sector started in 1988, legalizing border trade, and encouraging foreign investment. Entrepreneurs in Myanmar are involved in agricultural processing, light manufacturing, production of footwear, pharmaceuticals and textiles, export markets include China, India, Singapore and Thailand. But managers complain about labour shortages and the lack of loyalty among employees (as reported by Speece and Sann, 1998). As a consequence, most large companies have a minimal presence in the capital of Yangon, and most investments are small scale. Operating at subsistence level is characteristic for many local enterprises. The observer of the everyday life finds many examples of self-employed individuals pursuing all kinds of activity: selling air for vehicle tyres; fixing umbrellas on a street corner; barbers setting up impromptu stalls to shave tourists for the price of a coconut; micro-scale merchants selling flashlights and lighters; vendors weighing nails; women walking to the station to sell food to passengers on the train; women selling sparrows (to worshippers who will free them for good luck) and catching them again as soon as they are let loose.

Meanwhile, the parallel economy focuses on consumer goods and pirated intellectual property. Retailers include Mister Donut (the sign of which uses the font of Dunkin' Donuts), and merchants selling photocopies of the book *Burmese Days* (Orwell, 1930). A Ronald McDonald look-alike promotes Mac Burger, a fast-food outlet serving MacHam, MacChicken, and MacBurgers.

The government's objective has been mainly focused on improving agricultural output, increasing the production of land, but Myanmar is still to be considered as among the less developed countries. Yet absolute poverty is limited due to the abundance of inexpensive food and other essentials.

Notes

1.   Different sources were used for this country study of entrepreneurship in Myanmar: various field interviews contributed to the chapter as well as government information obtained from the Ministry of Agriculture and Irrigation, the Ministry of Commerce, the Ministry of Co-operatives, the Ministry of Finance and Economy, the Ministry of Industry, the Ministry of Information, the Ministry of National Planning and Development, the Ministry of Rail Transportation, the Myanmar Timber Enterprise, the Union of Myanmar Chamber of Commerce and Industry, and the University for the Development of the National Races of the Union. The chapter includes also material that first appeared in Dana (2002; 2007).
2.   The unit of currency, spelled kyat, is pronounced 'chat'.
3.   This is a significant number, given that there is a total of 15 000 Asian elephants in captivity (Chadwick, 2005).

References

Adas, Michael P. (1974), *The Burma Delta: Economic Development and Local Change on an Asian Rice Frontier 1852–1941*, Madison, WI: University of Wisconsin.

Chadwick, Douglas H. (2005), 'Thailand's urban giants', *National Geographic*, **208**(4), 98–117.

Christian, John LeRoy (1942), *Modern Burma: A Survey of Political and Economic Development*, Berkeley, CA: University of California Press.

Christian, John LeRoy (1943), 'Burma: where India and China meet', *National Geographic*, **84**(4), 489–512.

Dana, Léo-Paul (2002), *When Economies Change Paths: Models of Transition in China, the Central Asian Republics, Myanmar, and the Nations of Former Indochine Française*, Singapore, London and Hong Kong: World Scientific.

Dana, Léo-Paul (2007), *Asian Models of Entrepreneurship – From the Indian Union and the Kingdom of Nepal to the Japanese Archipelago: Context, Policy and Practice*, Singapore and London: World Scientific.

Furnivall, John Sydenham (1957), *A Study of the Social and Economic History of Burma*, Rangoon: People's Literature Committee and House.

Garrett, W.E. (1971), 'Pagan, on the road to Mandalay', *National Geographic*, **139**(3), 343–65.

Gray, Denis D. (2001), 'Working elephants make last stand in Myanmar', *The Jerusalem Post*, 13 March, p. 7.

Herald Tribune (1988), 'U Ne Win is removed from office in Burma', 26 July, p. 2.

Hirsh, Michael and Ron Moreau (1995), 'Risky Business', *Newsweek*, 19 June, p. 10.

Hla, Lludu U. (1975), *Rice*, Mandalay: Kyipwaye Press.

Hodgson, Bryan (1984), 'Time and again in Burma', *National Geographic*, **166**(1), 90–121.

Khup, San (1996), 'Macroeconomic policies with special emphasis on infrastructural development,' in Tan Teck Meng, Low Aik Meng, John J. Williams, and Ivan P. Polunin (eds), *Business Opportunities in Myanmar*, Singapore: Prentice Hall, pp. 69–79.

Kipling, Rudyard (1890), *Letters from the East*, New York: Frank F. Lovell.

Macaulay, R.H. (1934), *History of the Bombay Burmah Trading Corporation, Ltd., 1864–1910*, Colchester, London and Eton: Spottiswoode, Ballantyne and Co.

Maung, Mya (1991), *The Burma Road to Poverty*, New York: Praeger.

May, Daw Khin San (1996), 'Mandalay: the handicraft centre of Myanmar', in Tan Teck Meng, Low Aik Meng, John J. Williams, and Ivan P. Polunin (eds), *Business Opportunities in Myanmar*, Singapore: Prentice Hall, pp. 47–52.

Orwell, George (1930), *Burmese Days*, New York: Harcourt-Brace.

Sein, Thaung (1950), *Problems of the Burmese Film*, Rangoon: Bamakhit Press.

Speece, Mark, and Phyu Phyu Sann (1998), 'Problems and conflicts in manufacturing joint ventures in Myanmar', *Journal of Euro-Asian Management*, **4**(3), 19–43.

Steinberg, David I. (1982), *Burma: A Socialist Nation of Southeast Asia*, Boulder, CO: Westview Press.

Swe, Myint (1972), *History of Burmese Printed Books*, Rangoon: Kayathuka Press.

Swerdlow, Joel L. (1995), 'Burma: the richest of poor countries', *National Geographic*, **188**(1), 70–97.

Thein, Myat (1996), 'Socio-economic and cultural background of Myanmar', in Tan Teck Meng, Low Aik Meng, John J. Williams, and Ivan P. Polunin (eds), *Business Opportunities in Myanmar*, Singapore: Prentice Hall, pp. 17–24.

Wai, U Tun (1955), *Burma's Currency and Credit*, Calcutta: Orient Longmans.

25 Oman

Yochanan Shachmurove

1 Introduction

Although Oman is not as rich in oil as some of its Arabic neighbors, oil production has been a major component of Oman's gross domestic product (GDP) since commercial export of oil began in 1967. During the 1980s and 1990s, the Omani economy was highly susceptible to fluctuating oil prices. In response to diminishing oil reserves, the Omani government has taken serious measures to enhance its natural gas resource facilities and related businesses, as well as to expand non-oil and non-energy related industries such as light manufacturing, agriculture, fisheries, and tourism.

The current stable period of growth in Oman is being driven by strong oil prices, increasing volumes of liquefied natural gas (LNG) sales and investments in downstream industries like power, telecoms and tourism.[1] Real GDP growth is estimated to have reached 6.6 percent in 2006 due to strong growth in LNG production and domestic spending increases from high oil revenue, although crude oil output eased in 2006 and is expected to continue to fall over 2007 and 2008 because of the effects of enhanced oil recovery projects, which are unlikely to be fully felt before 2010.[2] Recently, Oman invited international oil firms to sign production sharing deals early next year as part of a US$10 billion plan to boost oil output to 1 million barrels per day, up from the current 770 000 barrels (hydrocarbons account for 40 percent of Omani revenues).[3] High oil prices and strong LNG exports are likely to offset the negative effects of decreased oil production on government revenues. Business Monitor Online, in its Q4 2007 Oman Economic Outlook, sees overall industrial growth reaching 6.3 percent this year, before slipping slightly back to 5.2 percent in 2008, with petrochemicals, aluminum and ports being critical components of Oman's non-oil economy. The Muscat Securities Market continues to forge new all-time highs, and, coupled with the several new listings expected this year, reflects good growth and delivery of financial results in the private sector.[4]

The recent economic reform program of the government is primarily designed to meet the growing demand for jobs caused by rapid growth in the young adult population.[5] A critical part of this program is the development of the services sector, in particular the tourism sector, which is expected to grow by 19 percent; current development projects for villas, hotels, apartments, and retail facilities are slated to accommodate 250 000 people, resulting in an expected increase of 2 million tourists a year.[6] Consequently, the construction industry will also experience a boost from tourism-related spending.

The remainder of the chapter is organized as follows. Section 2 describes government policies with regard to small and medium enterprises (SMEs) and entrepreneurship in Oman. Section 3 details the environment for entrepreneurship and the state of small business in Oman. Section 4 describes government policies towards foreign investors. Finally, section 5 briefly concludes.

2 Government policy on SMEs and entrepreneurship in Oman

Oman is a tax haven, with no levies on personal income, capital gains or housing; for-eigners are permitted to own property and take out local mortgages without the spon-sorship of developers within the nation, a privilege once offered only to Omani nationals and other members of the Gulf Cooperation Council (GCC).[7] Businesses also benefit from a relatively transparent and clear legal system; there is no history of investment disputes involving foreign investors. However, some sectors of the economy have had a legacy of poor regulation, such as the banking sector.[8]

A summit was held by the Omani Chamber of Commerce and Industry for SMEs on 12 November 2007. This summit discussed various types of SMEs, their financial chal-lenges, and the importance of maintaining cooperation among SMEs funding bodies.[9] The Minister of Commerce and Industry announced the formation of a committee that comprises officials of the Ministry of Commerce and Industry and the SMEs' funding and supporting bodies to offer recommendations and proposals that may later on be discussed at future meetings to be organized by the Directorate General for Small Enterprises at the Ministry of Commerce and Industry.[10]

The process of starting and registering a business in Oman follows these steps:

1. Check uniqueness of the company's name and pick-up registration forms from the Ministry of Commerce (1 day).
2. Application for grant of a specific license (30 days).
3. Deposit the legally required initial capital in a bank and obtain deposit evidence (1 day – simultaneous with previous procedure).
4. Registration with the commercial registry at the Ministry of Commerce and Industry (15 days – simultaneous with previous procedure).
5. Registration with the Oman Chamber of Commerce and Industry (7 days).
6. Registration with Muscat Municipality and approval of Limited Liability Company (LLC's) name plate (5 days).
7. Make a company seal (2 days).
8. Notification of the Tax Department of the Finance Ministry (1 day).
9. Register Employees for Social Insurance (1 day).

3 The environment for entrepreneurship and the state of small business in Oman

Economic freedom within Oman

According to the Index of Economic Freedom, which measures ten specific freedoms across over 160 countries worldwide, Oman's economy is the world's forty-second freest economy, and is third freest amongst the 17 countries in the Middle East/North Africa region.[11] This index takes a holistic approach to measuring the level of freedom to busi-nesses within a country, using 10 metrics as its guide:[12]

- Business freedom
- Trade freedom
- Fiscal freedom
- Government size
- Monetary freedom

- Investment freedom
- Financial freedom
- Property rights
- Freedom from corruption
- Labor freedom.

Amongst these ten categories, Oman exceeds the world average in eight, showing significant opportunity for economic growth and stabilization within the region. Oman has shown the most significant promise within the categories of fiscal freedom, trade freedom, labor freedom, and freedom from corruption.[13] These categories are most representative of the strength of the market in terms of financing opportunities and the ability to reap the benefits of trade.

Fiscal freedom – 98.5 percent 'Oman has low tax rates. There is no income tax on individuals, and the top corporate tax rate is 12 percent. There is no consumption tax or value-added tax (VAT). In the most recent year, overall tax revenue as a percentage of GDP was 2.8 percent.'[14]

One factor strongly driving the flexibility within the economy of Oman is the low level of taxation on income generated through the business environment. Within this nation, private income is not taxed, and the highest corporate tax rate is 12 percent, a significantly lower number than the tax rates used in most first-world nations across the globe. By allowing entrepreneurs to more effectively retain their businesses' earnings, the nation has created an environment with incentives to execute new business ideas.

Trade freedom – 83.6 percent 'Oman's weighted average tariff rate was 3.2 percent in 2005. Prohibitive tariffs, import bans and restrictions, burdensome licensing requirements, subsidies, and protectionist government procurement policies add to the cost of trade. An additional 10 percentage points is deducted from Oman's trade freedom score to account for non-tariff barriers.'[15]

With much more lenient tariff rates than its counterparts within the Middle East/ North Africa region, Oman has continued to stimulate business transactions for its entrepreneurs. Compared to its neighboring nations, Oman has been extremely successful in cultivating an environment that fosters innovation and trade within the region.

Labor freedom – 77.2 percent 'Relatively flexible employment regulations could be further improved to enhance employment opportunities and productivity growth. The non-salary cost of employing a worker is low, and dismissing a redundant employee is not difficult. The labor laws enforce the "Omanization" policy that requires private-sector firms to meet quotas for hiring native Omani workers.'[16]

Labor is relatively flexible in Oman, allowing great opportunities for employment productivity. With low hiring and firing costs, labor flexibility tends to be high. Combining this lateral freedom with low non-salary costs, such as health benefits, medical insurance and other forms of employee attraction, the entrepreneurial environment of Oman is able to flourish.

Freedom from corruption – 54 percent 'Corruption is perceived as present. Oman ranks 39th out of 163 countries in Transparency International's Corruption Perceptions Index for 2006. In 2005, several high-ranking government officials, including a member of the State Council, were sentenced to between three and five years in prison for bribery, misuse of public office, and breach of trust.'[17]

The role of corruption within the society of Oman is hindering the opportunity for entrepreneurs to fully utilize the economic incentives from creating new ventures. With relatively high corruption within the economy, the misuse of power continues to destabilize the economy of Oman and prevents entrepreneurial activities.

The entrepreneurial environment in Oman is most enhanced by the ease of starting new businesses in this environment relative to the rest of the world. By allowing for the easier set-up of businesses through more comprehensive and flexible implementation systems, Oman has allowed for greater entrepreneurial activity.

Sector opportunities

The state of small business in Oman can be inferred from the most relevant economic opportunities in the Sultanate. With 43 percent of the population living beneath the age of 20, the demand for services will only increase in the next couple of years, which has led the government to turn to the private sector to provide services.[18] The push towards private services has been observed in the education sector, where Oman recently issued new licenses for universities, as well as in the provision of public utilities (power and water). Additionally, the privatization of the postal service is also under consideration.[19]

Improving communications infrastructure has a positive impact on any small business. In late November, Oman's Telecommunications Regulatory Authority (TRA) announced that it is inviting applications to bid for licenses to re-sell basic public mobile communications services in the country, which is expected to bring cheaper calls to the mobile user, but unlikely to lead to a significant increase in the number of mobile phone subscribers as the number of mobile phones per capita reaches 100.7 per 100 people in 2008.[20]

Oman's strategic location in the Gulf has made ports an integral part of the diversification from its hydrocarbon economy. For example, the Salalah transshipment port not only moves goods to and from inland, but also shifts containers between vessels following different routes.[21] The port is midway between the Red Sea and the Arabian Gulf and well located to connect eastern and southern Africa and the Indian subcontinent to the main east–west trade route between China and Europe, handling 2.5 million 20 ft equivalent containers annually, with a capacity to hold 400 meter long container carriers.[22]

With approximately 90 percent of Omani hospitals government owned and expatriates only being allowed to use them in cases of emergencies, private medical services targeted towards middle-income expatriates will address the growing low-paid expatriate worker demand. Additionally, specialized healthcare services should see an increase in demand as well.[23]

The Omani Center for Investment Promotion and Export Development (OCIPED) recently announced the creation of a fund to provide services for SMEs. With an estimated 80 million jobs needed in the next 12 years in the Middle East and North Africa (MENA) region alone to keep the current unemployment rate at 20 percent, the Oman Venture Capital Fund aims to create employment opportunities for young Omanis and develop a new middle class of entrepreneurs by providing comprehensive services to address the needs of SMEs. Access to financing, appropriate technology, and mentoring of owners of small and medium-sized enterprises and fostering the emergence of ventures run by women are some of these pressing needs.[24] This increase in employment will help stimulate significant opportunities for entrepreneurs.

Some of the major infrastructure projects on the anvil in the country include the expansion of the Seeb International Airport and Salalah Airport, and the construction of three new airports at a cost of US$3 billion, construction of a port complex in Oman at a cost of US$490 million, and a US$1.34 billion project for the construction of a 252-km long pipeline in the country.[25] Tourism will most likely create opportunities for local small business to satisfy the needs of visitors, as has been the case in other touristic developing countries. With a more significant infrastructure in place, Oman's business leaders will have the opportunity to establish strong business models because of the resources they will have at their disposal.

Increases in tourism, foreign investment and a regional boom in air travel have caused Muscat's Seeb International Airport (MCT) to approach its capacity of 5 million. Passenger numbers have soared by an unprecedented 26 percent in 2006.[26] Increasing levels of tourism have provided, and will continue to provide, significant revenue for the economy.

Business Monitor International forecasts that the construction industry in Oman will grow at an average annual rate of 8.7 percent over 2008–12.[27] The recently signed Free Trade pact with the US is also likely to impact the tourism and consequently construction industry. Oman's real estate development industry is focused on tourism, seeking to attract a quality of tourist which prefers low-key, traditional, less flashy environments, unlike its neighbor Dubai.

The current real estate development project in Oman is the Blue City Project. It is a planned, self-contained metropolis that will not only include leisure and tourist facilities but also hopes to open two hospitals and a university within the 34 sq km of coastal land, with its development split into several phases due to be put in place over a 20-year period and cost up to US$20 billion. 'The Wave' in Muscat, is a US$805 million project, backed by the Omani government, spread over 260 hectares of land along 6 km of beachfront; designed around a series of neighborhoods containing 4000 villas and apartments, it will feature a golf course, a 300-berth marina, shops, hotels, offices and parks, all 5 km from the capital's Seeb International Airport.[28] The Salam Mountain Beach Resort and Spa is a US$1 billion project with luxury hotels, villas and apartments, golf courses, an eco-marina centre and Dubai-esque man-made canals set against the mountains, with stunning views of the Gulf of Oman.[29]

The recent construction boom has led to the development of complex financial products and investment schemes such as real estate funds (the legal structures of which have yet to be tested), which shows potential growth in the legal market as more investors recognize the financial potential of Oman's real estate sector.[30]

4   Internationalization of entrepreneurs

Sultani Decree No 12/2006 permits non-Omanis to own land in Oman for the purpose of residence or investment, provided the land is part of a designated 'integrated tourist resort', causing a surge in residential and commercial land demand – and consequently increasing prices – as well as in the infrastructure projects (utilities) required to sustain the construction boom.[31]

Since WTO accession in 2000, automatic approval of foreign investment in a venture of up to 70 percent has been available, and anything above this level requires Ministry of Commerce and Industry approval; non-Omanis need a ministry license to conduct commercial, industrial, or tourism businesses and face the following regulatory environment: (1) in 2003, the government extended national tax treatment to all registered companies regardless of percentage of foreign ownership, (2) new majority foreign-owned entrants are restricted from most professional service areas, such as engineering, legal services and accountancy, and (3) Oman has no restrictions or reporting requirements on private capital movements.[32]

In terms of FDI, Oman offers a set of incentives to attract investors. For the industrial sector, they offer: (1) no restrictions on reporting requirements or private capital movements, (2) five-year tax holidays, renewable by another five years, (3) low-interest loans from the Oman Development Bank (limited) and the Ministry of Commerce and Industry, (4) subsidized plant facilities and utilities at industrial estates, and (5) exemptions from custom duties on equipment and raw materials during the first 10 years of a project.[33] The Sultanate of Oman's policy of 'Omanization' – the training of Omani personnel capable of replacing the expatriate workforce, is likely to affect foreign entrepreneurs in the future.[34]

5 Conclusion

The Omani tourism-oriented economic development presents the largest opportunities for small businesses and entrepreneurs. Businesses need to be developed to support the demands from the visiting tourists, be it in retail, real estate, or entertainment. The government realizes that foreign direct investment will play a large role in the development of the tourism infrastructure, making tourism the most attractive area for international entrepreneurs to find opportunities. The hydrocarbon industry will continue to finance the Sultanate's development projects, which coupled with foreign direct investment will continue to diversify the country's economic base. The political environment in Oman is favorable towards long-term investments due to its political and economic instability.

Acknowledgment

The research leading to this paper has been partially supported by the Shwager Fund at The City College of the City University of New York.

Notes

1. Economic Outlook – Q4 2007 (2007, October). Business Monitor International Online. Retrieved 27 November 2007, from http://www.businessmonitor.com/cgi-bin/request.pl?view=articleviewer&article=149443&SessionID=332956053855926&iso=OM.
2. Oman economy: Business climate overview (2007, February). EIU ViewsWire. Retrieved 27 November 2007, from ABI/INFORM Global database (Document ID: 1227335501).
3. Economic Alert – Oil Sector Boost Only Short – Term Solution (2007, November). Business Monitor International Online. Retrieved 27 November 2007, from http://www.businessmonitor.com/cgi-bin/request.pl?view=articleviewer&article=156663&SessionID=332956053855926&iso=OM.
4. Ratings Update – Oman (2007, June). Business Monitor International Online. Retrieved 28 November 2007 from http://www.businessmonitor.com/cgi-bin/request.pl?view=articleviewer&article=134563&SessionID=364094511679471&iso=OM.
5. Oman (2006, August). *Country Monitor*, **14**(32), 9. Retrieved 27 November 2007, from ABI/INFORM Global database (Document ID: 1126906191).
6. Economic Outlook – Q4 2007.

7. Ben West (2007, 11 August). Avoiding the 'al-bling' environment Oman is drawing on long-established traditions to attract buyers to its new developments, says Ben West: [Surveys edition]. *Financial Times*, p. 4. Retrieved 30 November 2007, from ABI/INFORM Global database (Document ID: 1318537161).
8. Business Environment Outlook – Q4 2007 (2007, October). Business Monitor International Online. Retrieved 27 November 2007, from http://www.businessmonitor.com/cgi-bin/request.pl?view=articlevie wer&article=149444&SessionID=332956053855926&iso=OM.
9. Minister of Commerce and Industry Meeting (2007, November). Factiva. Retrieved on 28 November 2007, from the IPR Strategic Information Database, document ID Document IPRSID0020071112e3bc0001e.
10. Minister of Commerce and Industry Meeting.
11. http://www.heritage.org/index/countryFiles/pdfs/Oman.pdf.
12. http://www.heritage.org/research/features/index/index.cfm.
13. http://www.heritage.org/index/countryFiles/pdfs/Oman.pdf.
14. http://www.heritage.org/index/countryFiles/pdfs/Oman.pdf.
15. http://www.heritage.org/index/countryFiles/pdfs/Oman.pdf.
16. http://www.heritage.org/index/countryFiles/pdfs/Oman.pdf.
17. http://www.heritage.org/index/countryFiles/pdfs/Oman.pdf.
18. Oman economy: Ringing the changes (2007, September). EIU ViewsWire. Retrieved 30 November 2007, from ABI/INFORM Global database (Document ID: 1367788001).
19. Oman economy: Ringing the changes.
20. Regulatory Development – Oman to Issue Resale Mobile Licences (2007, November). Business Monitor International Online. Retrieved 28 November 2007 from http://www.businessmonitor.com/cgibin/ request.pl?view=articleviewer&article=156673&SessionID=364094511679471&iso=OM.
21. Robert Wright (2007, 7 February). Desert town that became a port at crossroads of world trade Oman's Salalah port has answered a need for a trans-shipment hub, but it is not all plain sailing for its operators, writes Robert Wright: [Asia edition]. *Financial Times*, p. 3. Retrieved 1 December 2007, from ABI/ INFORM Global database (Document ID: 1212220031).
22. Robert Wright (2007, 7 February).
23. Oman economy: Ringing the changes.
24. OCIPED announces creation of first venture capital fund to establish knowledge-based economy in Oman. AME Info. Retrieved 20 August 2007 from http://www.ameinfo.com/images/news/0/44290-ocipedlogo.jpg.
25. BMI Industry View – Oman – 2008 (2007, November). Business Monitor International. Retrieved 30 November 2007 from http://www.businessmonitor.com/cgi-bin/request.pl?view=articleviewer&article=1 57132&SessionID=876244385567591&iso=OM.
26. Anne Paylor (2007, September). Booming Tourism, Regional Focus Boost Muscat. *Air Transport World*, **44**(9), 51. Retrieved 30 November 2007, from ABI/INFORM Global database (Document ID: 1370922841).
27. BMI Industry View – Oman – 2008.
28. Ben West (2007, 11 August). Avoiding the 'al-bling' environment Oman is drawing on long- established traditions to attract buyers to its new developments, says Ben West: [Surveys edition]. *Financial Times*, p. 4. Retrieved 1 December 2007, from ABI/INFORM Global database (Document ID: 1318537161).
29. Ben West (2007, 11 August).
30. Middle East: Omania. (2007, May). The Lawyer, 29. Retrieved 27 November 2007, from ABI/INFORM Global database (Document ID: 1279050911).
31. Middle East: Omania.
32. Business Environment Outlook – Q4 2007.
33. Business Environment Outlook – Q4 2007.
34. Salma M. Al-Lamki (2005), 'The role of the private sector in Omanization: the case of the banking industry in the Sultanate of Oman', *International Journal of Management*, **22**(2), 176–88. Retrieved 1 December 2007, from ABI/INFORM Global database (Document ID: 866572681).

Appendix

Table 25A.1   Starting a business

Year	Ease of doing business rank	Rank	Procedures (number)	Time (days)	Cost (% of income per capita)	Min. capital (% of income per capita)
2004	–	–	9	34	4.9	667.1
2005	–	–	9	34	4.9	667.1
2006	–	–	9	34	4.8	648.9
2007	43	98	9	34	4.5	564.5
2008	49	107	9	34	4.3	541.8

Table 25A.2   Dealing with licenses

Year	Rank	Procedures (number)	Time (days)	Cost (% of income per capita)
2004	–	–	–	–
2005	–	–	–	–
2006	–	16	242	883.1
2007	126	16	242	883.1
2008	130	16	242	847.6

Table 25A.3   Employing workers

Year	Rank	Difficulty of Hiring Index	Rigidity of Hours Index	Difficulty of Firing Index	Rigidity of Employment Index	Non-wage labor cost (% of salary)	Firing costs (weeks of wages)
2004	–	44	40	0	28	–	4
2005	–	44	40	0	28	–	4
2006	–	44	40	0	28	10	4
2007	25	33	40	0	24	10	4
2008	26	33	40	0	24	11	4

Table 25A.4   Registering property

Year	Rank	Procedures (number)	Time (days)	Cost (% of property value)
2004	–	–	–	–
2005	–	2	16	3
2006	–	2	16	3
2007	15	2	16	3
2008	15	2	16	3

Table 25A.5   Getting credit

Year	Rank	Legal Rights Index	Credit Information Index	Public registry coverage (% adults)	Private bureau coverage (% adults)
2004	–	–	2	N/A	0
2005	–	4	2	N/A	0
2006	–	4	2	N/A	0
2007	94	4	2	17.5	0
2008	97	4	2	12.4	0

Table 25A.6   Protecting investors

Year	Rank	Disclosure Index	Director Liability Index	Shareholder Suits Index	Investor Protection Index
2004	–	–	–	–	–
2005	–	–	–	–	–
2006	–	8	5	3	5.3
2007	62	8	5	3	5.3
2008	64	8	5	3	5.3

Table 25A.7   Paying taxes

Year	Rank	Payments (number)	Time (hours)	Profit tax (%)	Labor tax and contributions (%)	Other taxes (%)	Total tax rate (% profit)
2004	–	–	–	–	–	–	–
2005	–	–	–	–	–	–	–
2006	–	14	52	–	–	–	20.3
2007	5	14	52	–	–	–	20.3
2008	5	14	62	9.7	11.8	0.1	21.6

Table 25A.8   Trading across borders

Year	Rank	Documents for export (number)	Time for export (days)	Cost to export (US$ per container)	Documents for import (number)	Time for import (days)	Cost to import (US$ per container)
2004	–	–	–	–	–	–	–
2005	–	–	–	–	–	–	–
2006	–	10	22	665	10	26	824
2007	95	10	22	665	10	26	824
2008	104	10	22	665	10	26	824

Table 25A.9   *Enforcing contracts*

Year	Rank	Procedures (number)	Time (days)	Cost (% of debt)
2004	–	51	598	13.5
2005	–	51	598	13.5
2006	–	51	598	13.5
2007	109	51	598	13.5
2008	110	51	598	13.5

Table 25A.10   *Closing a business*

Year	Rank	Time (years)	Cost (% of estate)	Recovery rate (cents on the dollar)
2004	–	4.1	4	32
2005	–	4.1	4	33
2006	–	4.1	4	34
2007	61	4.1	4	35
2008	59	4	4	35.5

26 Pakistan

M. Khurrum S. Bhutta and Adnan Omar

Introduction

Pakistan is a vital crossroads between Central and South Asia. With a population of 165 million and a gross domestic product (GDP) of US$437.5 billion (CIA, 2006), it has a significant role to play in the global economy. Pakistan is better placed than ever before for a significant boost in its economic outlook. Several economic development programs have been launched in the past few years and, equally importantly, have been complemented by external support including debt rescheduling and financial incentives at a concessional rate. These measures if allowed to continue unhindered could well see a GDP growth increase not seen in Pakistan's history. This of course is not a foregone conclusion; to realize this progress Pakistan will have to continue on its recent road of fiscal and monetary policies and build on this business-friendly environment. However, there seems to be a realization that Pakistan has performed far below its potential in the 1990s and needs to play catch-up with its neighbours who are doing a lot better.

Research has often likened Pakistan's economy to its small and medium enterprise (SME) sector. The significant role played by SMEs in Pakistan's economy is clear from research and statistics (Bhutta et al. 2007; Khawaja 2006). According to the 2005 Economic Census of Pakistan, there are 3.2 million business enterprises nation-wide and SMEs constitute over 99 percent of them. They employ 78 percent of the industrial employment and by value contribute nearly 35 percent. Pakistan exports are estimated to be US$16.1 billion primarily in textiles, rice, leather goods, sports goods, chemicals, manufactures, carpets and rugs, and imports at US$22.1 billion primarily in petroleum and petroleum products, machinery, plastics, transportation equipment, edible oils, paper and paperboard, iron and steel, tea. (Government of Pakistan, 2005).

Different countries and organisations define SMEs in a number of ways. In Pakistan, the Small and Medium Enterprise Development Authority (SMEDA) has defined the SMEs in terms of employment generated as well as investment in productive assets. The SMEDA's definition of SMEs is primarily based on the number of personnel employed in the enterprise (Table 26.1). The secondary criterion for classification of SMEs, is the value of productive assets employed in the enterprise.

The SME sector in Pakistan is primarily a less formally organized sector; more than 96 percent businesses are owned and managed by an individual as a sole proprietary concern. While 2 percent are partnerships, there are hardly any corporate entities in the SME sector, implying that the inclusion of professional people in business management process is yet to be seen. Among the SMEs involved in retail, wholesale and so on, 98 percent employ fewer than five people and 99 percent fewer than 10 people. Even within the manufacturing sector the trend is no different and nearly 87 percent employ fewer than five people and 98 percent fewer than 10 people. Similar patterns of employment distribution can be traced among other sectors, except for mining where SMEs tend to employ more people. The mining sector averages around 56 percent employing between

Table 26.1   Definition of SMEs

	Employment	Productive assets (Rs millions)
Small	Between 10–35 people	2–20
Medium	Between 36–99 people	20–40

Source: http://www.smeda.org.

Table 26.2   SME sectors in Pakistan

Sectors	Number of firms
Food and beverage	1 241
Textiles	6 932
Leather, footwear, sports, handicraft	1 514
Chemical, plastic, rubber, paper, non-metals, industrial, printing	3 345
Metals	4 366
Others	3 152
Total	20 550

Source: Rana and Asad (2007).

6 and 50 people. On the whole, the percentage of large firms is very small. These characteristics of the SME sector suggest that most of the businesses are in a low-growth trap, dealing in traditional products and unable to climb up the technology ladder. They often become vulnerable to economic and social shocks, and disappear from the scene. This view gets credence from the fact that 19 percent of SMEs are less than five years old and only 4 percent are able to survive beyond 25 years. The encouraging sign, however, is their mushroom growth, which makes it imperative that there should be a mechanism through which they could get support in terms of resources such as capital, finance, trained human resource, or services like advice on technology up-gradation, marketing, or quality management (Khawaja, 2006).

A breakdown by sector of SMEs is given in Table 26.2.

Government policies on SMEs and entrepreneurship
More recently research and policy papers (Bhutta et al., 2007; Khawaja, 2006; World Bank Report) have depicted the SMEs sector as a vehicle for employment generation and poverty eradication. Furthermore, as the global business environment for SMEs constantly changes, SME policies within a particular socio-economic development strategy cannot be static; rather they have to be continuously changed and dynamically adapt to the business conditions. The government has played a crucial role and devised policies to develop this sector. Some of the initiatives include The Khushali bank and the Tawana Pakistan program which were measures promoted to reduce poverty. Other initiatives include the Pakistan Poverty Alleviation Fund (PPAF), Rural Support Programmes (RSPs), the First Women Bank (FWB) and the Agricultural Development Bank (ADB).

Small and medium enterprises can be affected by changes in laws and policies adopted by a government, for example labour law, financial law, export regulations, banking system regulations, tax regulation. Thus the SME sector comes close to being a cross-cutting issue. The role of government as a facilitator of business has to ensure the promotion of SMEs in all its departments and central offices, along with ensuring that the provincial and local governments also take their share of this responsibility. This translates into coordination and regular information exchange mechanisms among institutions which constrains their collective ability to deliver in the SME development process. The Ten Year Perspective Development Plan 2001–2011 was developed to take notice of the numerous zoning and other regulations imposed by the federal, provincial and local governments and public sector utilities which negatively affect SMEs, and legislation based on the US Small Business Regulatory Enforcement Act of 1996 was enacted which includes a Regional Small Business Ombudsman, as a first step to 'level playing field' for these firms (SMEDA, 2005: 5)

Some policy measures that play a critical role in SME development in Pakistan, as identified by SMEDA, are discussed below.

Tax and labour issues
Taxation policies are of great importance to businesses but become critical to SMEs. They are often cited as one of the major reasons that SMEs drift into the informal economy. The size-related disadvantage of SMEs is especially felt as these firms cannot in most cases afford professionals to help them understand and navigate through the morass of taxation issues. Small and medium enterprises in Pakistan have to stumble through an increasingly complex legal and taxation environment, from their inception all the way through growth and development phases.

Perhaps developing economies such as Pakistan can take a leaf out of Japanese taxation history, where in 1949 they replaced their taxation system with a new system that allowed certain tax merits using 'certain formula of quick bookkeeping', thereby especially helping a burgeoning SME environment by simplifying the reporting requirements as well as simplifying the tax code.

Labour laws are another very important set of regulations that impact SMEs. The labour law in Pakistan is considered to be one of the most complicated areas that any business enterprise deals with. There are 56 labour laws, some of them being industry specific, that firms have to weave through. In addition to this, there are numerous labour inspections under these laws, which are yet another impediment in the growth of SMEs.

Taking this in view, in 2002 the Government of Pakistan introduced a new set of regulations that aimed at providing a higher degree of flexibility in the labour market, including protection against arbitrary loss of employment, reductions in income and unhealthy work practices, while simultaneously creating a favourable environment for facilitating industrial promotion. The Government of Pakistan has developed a number of strategies for socio-economic development. Salient among these initiatives are:

- a poverty reduction strategy paper
- a micro finance sector development program
- an SME sector development program
- reforms in the education sector, the financial sector and tax administration.

Pakistan has started to play catch-up with its neighbours, having finally realized the importance of SMEs. Some of the recent changes include the creation of a single entity to interact with SMEs and another to help in the financing of SMEs. These two entities are briefly discussed below.

Small and Medium Enterprises Development Agency   Perhaps the most important resource that the government helped create was the Small and Medium Enterprises Development Agency in 1998 to help contribute towards the growth and development of SMEs in Pakistan. The SMEDA provides necessary services to help SMEs overcome the weaknesses that are endogenous to their very nature. 'The objectives of this organization include the creation of a conducive and enabling regulatory environment; development of industrial clusters; and the provision of Business Development Services to SMEs in all areas of business management' (SMEDA). This is a one-stop shop for SMEs and entrepreneurs, and acts as a clearing house of information and policy development on virtually all the issues affecting these firms.

Small Business Finance Corporation   The SBFC is a Development Finance Institution (DFI) established by the Government of Pakistan in 1972, primarily to assist entre-preneurs in setting up cottage industries. It provides financial and technical services on a sustainable basis to enable them to contribute to economic development through exports, to promote entrepreneurship and to create employment opportunities (Small and Medium Enterprise Bank).

   Another important aspect of developing the SME sector is the human resource com-ponent. Innovative skills along with entrepreneurial spirit are vital to the success of any firm. The low literacy rate of Pakistani population is an immense challenge to its compet-itiveness. The Government of Pakistan has adopted a strategy to strengthen non-formal skills and entrepreneurship development, and to improve the population's general capac-ity for self-employment. It has established a number of institutions that impart training and skill development. These include the Institute of Management Sciences and the Technical Training and Vocational Authority. Provincial vocational training councils, government universities and various other support institutions have, however, remained rather passive regarding the shaping of human resource development for SMEs.

   All these initiatives and programs have greatly enhanced the position of SMEs in Pakistan and helped focus attention on this critical sector of the economy.

Economic and sociocultural issues
Pakistan's geography, strategic location, rich cultural heritage and its economic variety and potential, offer Pakistan a unique position in the global economy. Pakistan has brought about great change in its economic position since its independence when it had virtually no industrial base. This has been supported by growth in the telecommunication industry, infrastructural development and fiscal reforms, to name a few. These develop-ments have brought Pakistan into the league of developing nations, gradually moving from a low-income to middle-income economy. The per capita income has increased from US$492 in 2002–03 to US$720 in 2005–06 (Government of Pakistan, 2005).

   Pakistan has been leveraging its resources and population to further its aims for this purpose. Recently significant growth in SME financing and other sectors has helped stimulate the economy. In fiscal year 2006 the private credit stood at Rs400 billion up from Rs20 billion just a few years ago.

On the economic front several changes have opened up that provide opportunities for entrepreneurs and SMEs to leverage their position. Akhtar (2006) listed a few of these opportunities:

> *Liberalization of the foreign investment regime and trade.* Foreigners and overseas Pakistanis have been allowed 100 percent equity in all sectors and foreign investment is treated at par with domestic investment. Moving from import substitution industrial strategy, Pakistan has adopted a conducive trade policy supported by tariff restructuring, rationalization and reduction; withdrawal of import quotas, import surcharges and the regulatory duties; and foreign exchange liberalization.
>
> *Restructuring of the financial markets.* The banking industry in Pakistan is perhaps one of the most healthy and vibrant sectors of the economy. The State Bank of Pakistan has managed to discourage segmentation of credit markets, reduce high intermediation cost stemming from overstaffing and inefficiencies, and the accumulation of non-performing loans.
>
> *Strengthening of governance structure.* Pakistan has developed a robust regulatory framework for businesses, and has backed this with strong regulators, who operate on the basis of modern and transparent set of economic regulations consistent with international standards.
>
> *Privatization.* Reversing the 1970s nationalization of industry and banking system, Pakistan since 1990 has privatized 161 firms.

On the social and cultural front, opportunities have been exploited that have led to a huge increase in entrepreneurial concerns. For example, the Sialkot district has developed tremendously through the sporting goods industry as well as surgical instruments. The development in the infrastructure has improved the locales to the point that cottage industries and entrepreneurs working from homes has grown several fold. All this has helped achieve a large increase in per capita income of the individuals and families involved. In the 1970s migration of families to the UK and Europe had drained manpower from this region; now more and more people are involved in the local economy and contribute to either family concerns or firms that are being run professionally. Similar experiences are seen in other industrial zones, such as those near Karachi, Lahore, Gujranwala, and Faisalabad.

A major roadblock in the development of SMEs is the caste/family system role. Approximately 85 percent of the firms are operated by 12–13 castes/families. This may be a hang on from the pre-independence era, when the caste system in India played a major role in the occupations of individuals. As the caste system or family ownership stronghold weakens, this will open up more avenues for entrepreneurs.

Yet another issue in the success of SMEs in Pakistan is the high rate of employee turnover. On the average there is a 20–25 percent turnover rate in the various sectors of SMEs, the highest being in the leather and sport goods sector, at 44 percent, and the lowest being in the food and beverage industry, at 19 percent. This level of turnover proves to be costly and SMEs do not get the benefit of organizational development and continuity.

In short, SMEs in Pakistan have a key role to play in providing additional employment and facilitating the transformation of the economy. They help in distributing resources such as manpower, finances and technologies to develop society more equitably. They facilitate a large number of entrepreneurs and self-employed to survive and exist. It is widely agreed that there could be no successful economic development without an active and robust SME sector, but in Pakistan several obstacles have to be overcome before this sector can contribute to its full potential.

Drivers and roadblocks to internationalization
Much research and policy development on entrepreneurship and SMEs is internally focused and generally domestic in nature. It is relatively easy to gain insights to a domestic market and needs, but success in internationalization requires acquisition of a range of types of knowledge, for example, market identification and segmentation, global marketing and a committed attitude to internationalization and a global vision.

Among the major obstacles/barriers to the international growth of Pakistan's SMEs are the failures of SMEs to monitor external changes and prioritize market opportunities, and they have little or no production orientation nor an ability to access required financial resources.

Also the removal of subsidies and tariffs under the World Trade Organization (WTO) rules has created new challenges to SMEs while simultaneously opening up new export markets. The adjustment process is difficult with significant employment implications. However, where clusters or industry associations have been active, these adjustments have been overcome; for example, the experience of the surgical instruments industry of Sialkot.

The foreign trade policies of a nation have both direct and indirect effects on the indigenous capacity, which influences the performance of SMEs. Pakistan trade policy, in the recent past has certainly stimulated SME development and has led to innovation in products because of the industrial environment it has helped foster.

Regional economic cooperation is in fact a key to the promotion of regional economic integration which enables countries to benefit from the global trading flows arising from unhindered investment and transfer of technology. As the trend of regional trade becomes even more dominant, the South Asian Association for Regional Cooperation (SAARC) area countries plan to set up a South Asia Free Trade Area (SAFTA) by 2013. This is aimed at reviving regional trade and economic growth in the region. In addition to these regional efforts, bilateral conditions have also been improving; for example, the fan and bicycle industries in Pakistan and India have coordinated with each other. Another example is the gas pipeline currently under construction from Iran through Pakistan into India. The opening up of new markets and a better understanding of older markets have helped create an environment conducive to the development of SMEs, especially those manufacturing firms with export potential. As recently noted:

> there are also indirect benefits of the enlarged trading market: the SMEs can serve as subcontractors to the larger firms, and ultimately may become exporters themselves. Their minimum gain is the SMEs growth associated with dynamic benefits of inter-firm linkages. This evidence reaffirms the positive benefits of trading blocks for the SMEs of the member countries. (Khalid)

As discussed in previous sections the roadblocks to internationalization of SMEs and entrepreneurs include government policy issues, financial issues, employee turnover issues, caste/family influence issues, and education issues. However, as discussed in this chapter, the Pakistan government has made tremendous strides in trying to overcome these issues.

In addition to government efforts, industry organizations also play their part and actively help promote their members. Approximately 54 percent of Pakistan SMEs belong to a business or industry association. These associations play an important role in helping these firms gain access to market and industry information. In addition, other countries such as China, Singapore, Indonesia, and Sri Lanka share their expertise with Pakistani associations. By associating with like institutions in foreign countries, the associations are able to establish links and obtain information on foreign markets. However, many SMEs feel that these associations are waste of time or that they do not have the resources to take advantage of the information that these associations provide. Overcoming these stereotypical responses remains a big challenge.

Conclusion

Pakistan's economy has often been referred to as an economy of SMEs. Policies in the past have given little general perspective or direction in defining parameters of activity within the macroeconomic framework, but more recently efforts have been more focused on this critical sector. Pakistan SMEs suffer from several constraints and weaknesses and this has affected their ability to adapt to the changes in the global economic markets. However, the importance and contribution of SMEs in the economic growth of Pakistan, suggests that there is a significant potential to enhance their growth through appropriate regulations and promotion.

The measures adopted in the past few years are not sufficiently prioritized to create a coherent SME policy. More recently, the government has given the responsibility for developing SME policies to SMEDA, in an attempt to coordinate and create efficacy in the policies. Several broad areas have been identified for intervention, including, linkages between macroeconomic and microeconomic polices, business environment, provision of credit, training human resources and developing an effective legal system.

Creating a favourable business environment for SMEs in Pakistan's economy and eliminating unnecessary obstacles which obstruct their development is perhaps the most important aspect, and while it involves dealing with other sectors of the economy the relationship between the government and SMEs is also being addressed. Another area that is being addressed is the improvement of the delivery mechanisms for assistance and access to resources for SMEs in Pakistan, for example, finance, business development services, qualified human resources, and technology. Market-driven support programs are important to attain sustainability, maximize the potential for cooperation with the private sector, and minimize distortions in the economy. Yet the structures for such a system still need to be mutually agreed and implemented in Pakistan. Last but not least, the establishment of a sound mechanism by which the development of the SME sector and the effectiveness of the assistance provided can be monitored is crucial. There is also ample scope to make use of SME promotion channels to achieve major aims related to equitable and sustainable socio-economic development which Pakistan has not yet fully exploited. Cases in point are gender development and environmental issues.

Implementing change requires the formulation of a policy for SME development and assigning specific responsibilities for its implementation and continuous improvement.

Opportunities for further research include studying the characteristics that are present in successful entrepreneurial/SMEs firms, to identify these characteristics and try to emulate them in the other firms. A better understanding of the ownership structure of SMEs will help in the development of this sector and will help target the policies to those areas that need them the most. Another crucial area to address is the supply chain. The concept of value addition and at what point value is being created needs to be appreciated and resources expanded in that direction. Another point worth researching is the impact of industry clusters and whether they play a role in the development and promotion of SMEs.

Pakistan has come a long way in the development of SMEs in the past few years but a lot of work still remains to be done. Pakistan will have to continue on its recent road of fiscal and monetary policies and build on this business-friendly environment. However, there seems to be a realization that Pakistan has performed far below its potential and needs to play catch-up with its neighbours.

Acknowledgement

The authors would like to express their thanks to Thomas Delassue for his help with research for this chapter.

References

Akhtar, Shamshad (2006), Governor of the State Bank of Pakistan, at the International Conference of Young Presidents Organization, 4 November, Lahore, Pakistan.

Bhutta, Khurrum, A. Rana and U. Asad (2007), 'SCM practices and the health of SMEs in Pakistan', *Supply Chain Management: An International Journal*, 12(6), 412–22.

CIA (2006), *World Fact Book*, www.cia.gov/library/publications/the-world-factbook/index.html (accessed: 5 December 2007).

Government of Pakistan (2005), 'Economic Survey of Pakistan 2005–06', www.finance.gov.pk/survey/home. htm (accessed 25 December 2007).

Khalid, Aftab, 'SME development in Pakistan, issues and remedies', Government College University, Lahore Pakistan, www.gcu.edu.pk/Publications/VC-SME.pdf (accessed 5 December 2007).

Khawaja, Shahab (2006), 'Unleashing the potential of the SME sector, with a focus on productivity improvements', Pakistan Development Forum – SMEDA, www.pakistan.gov.pk/divisions/economicaffairs-division/media/S-III-AN-OVERVIEW-OF-SME-SMEDA.pdf. (accessed 5 December 2007).

Rana, Arif I. and Usman Asad (eds) (2007), 'A survey report on the health of the small and medium manufacturing enterprises in Pakistan', Entrepreneurship & Small and Medium Enterprise Centre SME PULSE LUMS, University Press, Pakistan.

Small and Medium Enterprise Bank, www.smebank.org (accessed 5 December 2007).

Small and Medium Enterprise Development Authority (SMEDA), www.smeda.org (accessed 5 December 2007).

SMEDA (2005), 'Developing SME policy in Pakistan', www.smepolicy.net.pk (accessed 5 December 2007).

World Bank Report, 'Pakistan Country Assistance Strategy', Annex II, www.worldbank.org/ (accessed 5 December 2007).

27 Palestine
Nidal Rashid Sabri

1 Introduction

Palestine is located between the south-eastern part of the Mediterranean Sea and the Jordan River. Because of the strategic location of Palestine and it being sacred to various religions, it has been a place of conflict throughout history. In 1918 Palestine which used to be an Arab home for a period of 14 centuries, came under the British mandate when the Ottoman Empire was defeated in the World War I.

Today, the majority of Palestinians are living in parts of the historical Palestine known as West Bank, East Jerusalem, Gaza Strip and inside the green line of Palestine. The Palestinian population is almost 10 million, of whom half are living in Palestine, while the other half is living in exile in neighbouring Arab states and all over the world. In spite of the political situation, the human development index in Palestine is moderate as expressed by education, health and income per capita, due mainly to the significance of workers' remittances who are working abroad mainly in Arab Gulf states and Northern America, which formed about 16 percent of gross domestic product (GDP) (AMF, 2006; UNCTAD, 2004). Exporting labour is considered a positive aspect due to the substantial received cash inflow from abroad. For example, the human development index in Palestine is about 0.736 and ranks at 100 out of 170 states, which is higher than the average of Arab states and higher than the medium human development index, and it is about the average of the world human development index. The life expectancy at birth for Palestinian is about 72.9 years, ranking at 64 among the 170 world states; their adult literacy rate of 92.4 percent ranks 48 out of 170 states. The average size of the Palestinian family is about 5.8 persons, with 3.3 rooms comprising the average Palestinian housing unit (PCBS, 2008; UNDP, 2006, 2008). In addition, Palestinian women are relatively well educated in comparison to other developing countries and have a high status compared with most Arab states in terms of literacy rate, education, work opportunities as well as having a significant share in advanced professions including dentists, journalists, lawyers, chemists, and civil engineers, while their share in self-employed business was about 17 percent of the total businesses in Palestine (PCBS, 2006).

The Palestinian economy is affiliated to the emerging economies but it has distinguishing characteristics, which may be summarized as follows.

1. The Palestinian National Authority (PNA) has no national currency. This situation resulted in using three currencies for different purposes such as exchange transactions, saving and wealth measurement. Having multi-currency circulations reduces the efficiency of the Palestinian economy and denying the benefits which may be accomplished from the revenues associated with the use of national currencies such as the seigniorage process.
2. The increasing role of public sector in the Palestinian economy. This is pointed out by the increasing share of the public sector in total consumption, investments, GDP,

Table 27.1   Summary of the Palestinian economy in 2007

Economic activity	US$ million
Agriculture and fishing	341
Mining, manufacturing, electricity and water	527
Construction	104
Wholesale and retail trade	415
Transport	479
Financial intermediation	192
Services	915
Public administration	599
Other sectors	564
Total gross domestic product (GDP)	4136
Gross national income (GNI)	4499
Final consumption expenditure	5376
Gross capital formation	1127

Source: PCBS (2008).

in hiring employees and in channelling external cash inflows, which ranged between 22 and 65 percent compared with the private sector (Sabri, 2003). The public services in Palestine are run by three major groups: the Palestinian National Authority through central budget allocations, the United Nations Relief and Works Agency (UNRWA), which offers free goods and services to the Palestinian refugees, and the non-governmental organizations (NGOs) which have a significant role in offering social, health and educational subsidized services. The total government budget expenditures of the PNA reached about US$2 billion in 2007.

3. The Palestinian economy is mainly a service economy. The contribution of the service sector is more than 67 percent of the Palestinian GDP compared with 8 percent for agriculture and 13 percent for the industry sector (PCBS, 2008). The service sector includes government, hotels, restaurants, storages, financial, communication, transportation, education, health sectors and other sectors. The total contribution of the service sector reached about US$2749 million as presented in Table 27.1. The total gross domestic product of the Palestinian economy reached US$4136 million, while the final consumption expenditures of the Palestinian economy reached about US$5376 million in 2007.

4. The role of the financial sector in the Palestinian economy saw a significant development since the advent of the Palestinian National Authority. The financial sector includes 32 banks with 135 branches, 9 insurance corporations, and 270 money change firms, a stock market of 25 listed Palestinian corporations and 6 brokerage corporations (Sabri, 2003; Sabri and Jaber, 2006). The total deposits of Palestinian residents increased by 11 percent during the year 2007, raising the deposits value in banks located in Palestine to about US$6645 million (IMF, 2008; MAS, 2008).

5. Moderate inflation rate. The inflation rate in the Palestinian economy is relatively low and ranged between 3 percent and 5 percent in the last five years (PCBS, 2008).

Table 27.2   Summary of taxes prevailing in Palestine as in June, 2008

Taxes	Rates
Income tax	
1. Self-employed income	5% to 15%
2. Payroll income	5% to 15%
3. Corporate income	15%
Indirect tax	
4. VAT on all goods and services	14%
5. Customs duties (based on goods and source)	0% to 200%
6. Excise on some produced goods	30% in average of sale value
7. Fees in petroleum products	20% to 60% plus 14%
8. Excise on tobacco, wine	Average rate 50% of value
9. Local taxes (property and education tax)	17% and 7% of rent

Source: Compiled by the author.

However, it is expected to increase significantly during the year 2008 due to the international increase of the prices of basic foods, up by 11 percent (IMF, 2008).

6.   The Palestinian economy has relatively three types of taxes; including income taxes, value added tax (VAT) and local taxes. However, the income taxes rates are low compared with those of other countries; they ranged progressively between 5 percent and 15 percent according to specified brackets and the ratio of income taxes imposed on corporations is a fixed rate of 15 percent, while the main tax is VAT, which is a comprehensive tax imposed on all transactions related to goods or services including medical services and basic needs. The VAT is the main internal source of revenues for the Palestinian economy (Sabri, 2004). The VAT rate in June 2008 was 14 percent of the total sales value of goods or services, the collection of VAT is the responsibility of the supplier of the goods or the services. Customs are imposed in all exported goods between 0 and 200 percent besides the VAT taxes. Table 27.2 summarizes the tax status in Palestine as existed in June, 2008.

2.   Government policy on small and medium enterprises and entrepreneurship

The issue of small-scale firm against large-scale firm is one of the most debatable issues in the world economic context, and the argument among the policy-makers to compare between the advantages and disadvantages of both alternatives is continued. Both sizes of firms have advantages and disadvantages regarding job opportunities for skilled and unskilled labour, varieties of locations, cost of production, economy of scale, ownership structure and the allocated invested capital. For the Palestinian economy, a survey study was carried out to compare between the two alternatives, to answer the question whether the Palestinian policy-makers in the new emerged states should emphasize enhancing the SMEs over large-scale firms or visa versa. The study (Sabri, 1998) indicated that there are some advantages in favour of small-scale industry, such as small-scale firms have higher labour productivity than large-scale firms, and have higher ratio of assets turnover as well as in inventory turnover than large-scale industry, in spite of the large-scale firms having better opportunity in getting external financing.

Table 27.3   Initiation of entrepreneurship forms in the Palestinian industries

Ratio	Initiation of present manufacturing ventures
26%	1. Investor 'Entrepreneurs' invested money without previous experience
28%	2. Investors 'Entrepreneur' invested money with experiences
17%	3. Working in trade and expanded to industry 'Backward integration'
16%	4. Expansion of workshops to a factory
9%	5. Employee entrepreneurship
4%	6. Other forms of ventures
100%	Total

Source: Sabri (1999).

To understand the entrepreneurship initiation in the Palestinian economy, we find that the majority of the Palestinian entrepreneurship is initiated based on individual or family saving with little support from the official agencies. However, the main motivation for establishing new SMEs is different from one venture to another. A study conducted to examine the background of initiations in the Palestinian economy found that 53 percent of ventures established by individuals were based on their savings and experience to start a new venture. A quarter of the added ventures were established in the Palestinian economy by entrepreneurs without previous experience in the field. The motivation was just to invest available savings in order to find a self-employed job. While other ventures were established and emerged from small projects more were developed projects, as a backward integration or expansion from small workshops to more advanced factories, as shown in Table 27.3.

The role of the Palestinian government in enhancing SMEs is relatively limited, due to the fact that official policy prefers large-scale firms in order to have more job opportunities and to use more advanced technology. There are many statements mentioned in the economic development plans issued by the Palestinian Ministry of Planning (MoP) between 2005 and 2008 about supporting Palestinian small and medium-sized enterprises who have difficulties in financing their operations, and in all development plans for enhancing SMEs as one of the Palestinian economic strategies (PNA- MOP, 2005, 2006, 2007). However, in reality there is no favourite policy adopted by the Palestinian National Authority regarding SMEs' taxes exemptions or business regulations, nor is there any allocated fund to offer special financing programmes for such sector. In addition, The Palestinian Law of Investment Promotion Number 1 of 1998 (PNA, 1998) gives tax exemptions in three aspects: exemption from customs and other taxes, income tax exemptions of zero taxes for five years regarding new established firms, and exemption of furniture and electronic equipment from customs fees. However, such privileges are granted only to new established large firms with minimum capital of US$150 000 and not for small-scale firms, as stated in Article 22 and 23 and article 35; other aspects of the promotion investment law do not apply to SMEs (PNA, 1998). On the other hand, the SMEs receive attention from groups other than the central government, which can be summarized as follows:

Table 27.4   Summary of microfinance in Palestine directed to SMEs

Indicators	Values
Number of active borrowers	26 900
Outstanding balance (US$ million) in 2005	44.5
Average outstanding balance per loan (US$) in 2005	2905
Number of loan officers for all firms	179
Number of offices for all firms	72
Number of firms – institutes including UNRWA and PBC in 2007	11
Accumulated value of loans awarded by UNRWA in US$ million up to end of 2007	129.8
Number of accumulated loans awarded by UNRWA in Palestine up to 2007	119 979
Number of accumulated loans awarded by PBC (1996–2006)	2976
Accumulated loans awarded by PBC (1996–2006) in US$ million	98.1

Sources: Khaled et al. (2006); UNRWA (2008); PBC (2008).

1. Palestinian SMEs receive substantial support from the microfinance programmes run by the UNRWA. For example, the mission statement of UNRWA Micro-enterprise Programme aims to improve small business and micro entrepreneurs, sustain jobs, decrease unemployment, empower women and provide income-generating opportunities to Palestine refugees (UNRWA, 2005). The UNRWA granted about 130 000 loans for SMEs since it operated this programmes to a value of US$120 million up to 2007. One-third of the total granted microfinance loans were directed to small firms operated by women (UNRWA, 2008).
2. The SMEs receive also financing services from specialized NGOs: some of these organizations work with firms operated by women only, while others work with all small firms regardless of type of business and gender of ownership. Currently, the major NGOs institutions working as microfinance institutions offering loans to SMEs and members in PNSMF are: Palestinian Businesswomen's Association; Palestine for Credit and Development – FATEN; Palestinian Agriculture Relief Committee – PARC; Arab Centre for Agricultural Development – ACAD; American Near East Refugees Aid – ANERA; Corporative Housing Foundation – CHF; Young Men's Christian Association – YMCA; Caritas – Jerusalem (associate member) (PNSMF, 2008). The above NGOs include local and international firms offered about 26 900 loans, with an outstanding balance of about US$45 million (Khaled et al., 2006) up to 2005.
3. There is one institute, as the Palestine Development Fund, which offers microfinance services to SMEs. It is considered as a semi-government institute and offers both small as well as large firms loans to establish new firms. The fund offered about US$98 million to 3000 Palestinian borrowers, mainly medium-scale firms (PBC, 2008). Table 27.4 summarizes the microfinancing loans offered by all groups to SMEs in Palestine during the last ten years.

3.   The environment for entrepreneurship and the state of small business

1. The business environment in the Palestinian SMEs. The Arab business environment has relatively adverse practices due to some aspects of Arab culture and social

Table 27.5   Examples of management disputes and succession issue in the Palestinian family

Business	Level of generations	Main dispute reason	The end
Clothes	First generation	Relationship to contractors	Partners left the business to one owner
A chocolate company	First and second generation	Marketing and management strategies	Sold to outsiders
A food company	Second generations	To rehabilitate the factory	Transferred the business to another country
A hotel	Second generation	Distribution of work among partners	Sold to other owners
A furniture company	Second generation	Marketing and management strategies	Sold to other owners
Wholesaling	Second generation	Over withdrawals of profits	Closed the business

Source: Sabri (2008b).

habits, and this may complicate the advancement of Arab business (Sabri, 1996). The Arab business firm is mainly a family business, thus we have to consider the issues facing family business in general to understand the major merits of Arab business environment. A family business firm, as mentioned in the international literature, may face various issues such as continuing under future generations, reduced performance in managing a family business firm, the need for training family managers who inherited their businesses from first or second generations and, finally, the conflict in management between family members (Sabri, 2008a). Examples of management disputes and succession issues found in family business firms in a recent study are presented in Table 27.5 (Sabri, 2008b). Small and medium business enterprise disputes among management occur mainly in sole ownerships and partnerships instead of private and public corporations. However, almost all SMEs are organized mainly as sole ownerships, partnerships or private corporations, and rarely as public corporations, which separate between management and ownership to avoid the issue of succession and dispute among management teams.

2. Ease of starting business. Far from the political situation in Palestine, we may find that doing business in Palestine is relatively easy due to simple regulations stated by the related Palestinian agencies and municipalities. This conclusion is supported by the World Bank survey which assesses the various aspects of doing business, including starting a new business and getting credit. For example, in a 2006 survey conducted by the World Bank, Palestine was ranked 127 among 170 world states regarding easiness of doing business, while it ranked 117 out of 170 regarding getting credit financing, as shown in Table 27.6, which places it in the middle among the Arab states according to the World Bank assessment.

3. A substantial number of Palestinian SMEs work in the informal sector, run by individuals who have little education and are financed by family savings with low worker productivity (Malki et al., 2004).

Table 27.6   Rank of doing business in Palestine in 2006 among the 170 world states

Economy	Ease of doing business	Starting a business	Getting credit
Saudi Arabia	38	156	65
UAE	77	155	117
Jordan	78	133	83
Algeria	116	120	117
Palestine	127	142	117
Iraq	145	136	159
Sudan	154	82	143
Djibouti	161	157	117
Egypt	165	125	159

Source: World Bank (2007b).

Table 27.7   Summary of the Palestinian small-scale firms

Economic sector	Number of units	Five or fewer workers	Sole ownership	Single branch	Capital share
Agriculture	5 539	94%	93%	98.8%	0.7%
Mining, manufacturing	13 177	77%	78%	92%	20.0%
Wholesale, retailing, repair, restaurants, hotels	55 048	97%	88%	94.9%	35.4%
Construction	704	59%	55%	87.6%	1.6%
Transportation, communications	873	63%	58%	82.5%	9.3%
Other services; education, health, finance, electricity, etc.	21 938				33.0%
Total economic units	97 279	90.7%	85.0%	93.8%	100.0%

Sources: PCBS (2005, 2006).

4. About 91 percent of Palestinian economic units are considered to be small firms (four employees or fewer) which accounted for 88 489 units out of the total 97 279 economic units for the whole Palestinian economy. The majority (85 percent) of the small firms work as sole ownerships and are not organized in any of the four legal forms of companies existing in Palestine. Only a small percentage of SMEs is organized either as partnerships or a private corporations. The firms organized as private corporations are mainly working in manufacturing, real estate and wholesaling, while sole ownership and partnerships firms work mainly in retailing, repair, and restaurants, as expressed by amount of labour and allocated capital investments presented in Table 27.7. The number of firms classified as medium-scale firms with employees numbering between 5 and 19 account for 8 percent of the total economic units working in both service and manufacturing sectors. The majority of employees in SMEs working in manufacturing (91 percent), construction (94 percent), wholesaling and retailing (93 percent) are male, while the majority of females work in

Table 27.8 Employment status in Palestine

	Partial (%)	Total (%)
1. Employers		4.1
2. Self-employed; distributed as		26.5
Legislator, senior officials	3.8	
Professionals	23.6	
Services and market workers	18.2	
Skilled agriculture and fishery workers	14.2	
Craft workers	17.1	
Machine operators	8.8	
Elementary occupation	14.3	
3. Wage employees; distributed in		58.3
Agriculture	16	
Industry	13	
Construction	12	
Services	59	
4. Unpaid family		11.1

Source: PHDR (2005).

education (54 percent), health firms (41 percent) and social firms (31 percent). The small-scale firms working in retailing and wholesaling with less than four employees accomplished higher value added to the GDP compared with other sizes of business firms, while the large-scale firms with 10 employees or more work in transportation, communications and storage businesses (PCBS, 2005, 2006, 2007).

5. Employment status in SMEs in Palestine. In the private sector we find that about 27 percent of total employment in the Palestinian economy is working as self-employed and distributed as professionals, operators, skilled and craft workers. The self-employed group is organized mainly in small-scale business firms. On the other hand, about 58 percent of the total labour in the Palestinian economy is working as employees within four economic sectors, but are mainly working in SME service firms, as shown in Table 27.8. In addition, about 11 percent of all Palestinian workers are working in small family firms as unpaid workers (PHDR, 2005), mainly in retailing, restaurants, repairs shops and on agricultural farms.

6. Main operational and financial features in the Palestinian SMEs. The main operational and financial features of the Palestinian SMEs are summarized in Table 27.9. It indicates that about 96 percent of the SMEs in Palestine are family businesses, with a quarter of the firms facing conflict in management. The SMEs in Palestine have limited marketing polices and a high percentage of idle capacity, and the majority of business firms have no brand names for their products and sell from their locations with no special distributors. On the other hand, Palestinian SMEs have good profit ratios and rates of return as well as a high turnover ratio of assets. The higher idle capacity ratio for manufacturing firms is mainly due to the political situation and many barriers exist which hinder the movement of people and goods among different parts of Palestine. The majority of the Palestinian manufacturing firms are subcontracted to large firms, and located in rented buildings. Finally, Palestinian SMEs working in other sectors

Table 27.9   Major operational and financial features in the Palestinian SMEs

Operational and financial features	Value (%)
1. Family business (ownership-management)	96
2. Conflict in management	23
3. Subcontracted firms for other large-scale firms	30
4. Firms located in rented building	45
5. Selling from the business location outlets	63
6. Selling through exclusive agents	18
7. Firms use own products' brand	26
8. Idle capacity ratio (8 hours per day)	60
9. Rate of return on investments	34
10. Leverage ratio (debt to assets)	14
11. Net profit margin	16
12. Assets turnover ratio (times a year)	2.2
13. Inventory turnover ratio (times a year)	10.7
14. Labour productivity per % of $ sales value	24 550
15. A job creation by $ value of capital	13 750

Sources: Sabri (1998, 1999).

may have similar features to some aspects of the manufacturing sector but have differences in other aspects. For example, the idle capacity does not exist in the construction, service or retailing sectors, but does exist in the hotel sector.

4.   Internationalization of Palestinian SMEs
The Word Bank report (Word Bank, 2007a) stated in a recent report that the Palestinian investment climate is good with a relatively efficient bureaucracy and well developed financial markets. However, Palestinian enterprises have not invested enough to maintain their international competitiveness, despite the fact that Palestinian development plans considered promoting strategic partnerships between local and international as one of the government plan strategies (PNA-MOP, 2005, 2006, 2007, 2008).

5.   Conclusion
The Palestinian nation is considered to be an emerging economy with moderate-level human development and a relatively high advancement level in education, including women. About 97 percent of the economic units in Palestine are organized as SMEs units working with 10 employees or fewer (2008). The small- and medium-scale firms operating in Palestine are mainly family businesses in the service sector and retailing businesses financed by individual and family savings. In spite of the nominal support mentioned in the economic plans issued by the Palestinian National Authority, nothing has materialized to support SMEs, and no single regulation or tax or customs exemptions issued to enhance the sector were offered. However, the only support coming to this sector is that related to the microfinance programmes run by the UNRWA and about 10 specialized NGOs, which offer reasonable support for the SME sector mainly through short-term loans with simple collateral instruments.

References

AMF (2006), *Unified Arab Economic Report: 2006* (League of Arab State, Arab Monetary Fund, Arab Fund for Economic and social Development and AOPEC, September 2006, UAE).

IMF (2008), *Macroeconomic And Fiscal Framework; For The West Bank And Gaza* (First Review of Progress, Staff Report for the Meeting of the Ad-Hoc Liaison Committee, May).

Khaled, Mohammed, Kate Lauer and Xavier Reille (2006), 'Meeting the demand for microfinance in the West Bank and Gaza' (CGAP, World Bank working paper).

Malki, Majdi, Yasser Shalabi, Hassan Ladadweh, Omar Abdel Razeq and Shaker Sarsour (2004), *Social and Economic Characteristics of the Informal Sector in the West Bank and Gaza Strip* (Palestine Economic Policy Research Institute, MAS, Ramallah, Palestine).

MAS (2008), *Quarterly Economic and Social Monitor*, **11** (Palestine Economic Policy Research Institute (MAS), PMA, and PCBS) Palestine.

PBC (2008), Palestinian Banking Corporation (Ramallaha, Palestine), http://www.palbanking.com (accessed March 2008).

PCBS (2005), *Establishment Census 2004 Main Findings* (PNA, Palestinian Central Bureau of Statistics, Ramallah, Palestine).

PCBS (2006), *Characteristics of Establishment in the Palestinian Territory Establishment Census 2004* (PNA, Palestinian Central Bureau of Statistics, Ramallah, Palestine).

PCBS (2007), *Characteristics of Services Activities; Economic Survey Series 2005* (PNA, Palestinian Central Bureau of Statistics, Ramallah, Palestine).

PCBS (2008), *Palestine in Figures 2007* (PNA, Palestinian Central Bureau of Statistics, Ramallah, Palestine).

PHDR (2005), *Human Development Report of Palestine 2004* (Birzeit University, Palestine).

PNA (1998), *Palestinian Investment Promotion Law No. 1 of 1998* (Palestinian National Authority, Palestine).

PNA-MOP (2008), *Building a Palestinian State; Towards Peace and Prosperity* (Ramallah, Palestine).

PNA-MOP (2005), *Medium Term Development Plan 2005–2007* (Ramallaha. Palestine).

PNA-MOP (2006), *Medium Term Development Plan 2006–2008* (Ramallaha. Palestine, January 2006).

PNA-MOP (2007), *Quick Recovery Program July–December 2007* (Ramallaha, Palestine).

PNSMF (2008), 'Microfinance' *Palestine Newsletter* (Palestinian Network for Small & Microfinance), **1** (March).

Sabri, Nidal Rashid (1996), 'Applying feasibility studies techniques to Arab business environment', *Middle East Business Review*, **2**, 44–56.

Sabri, Nidal Rashid (1998), 'Financial analysis of the Palestinian industry', *Small Business Economics*, **11**, 293–301.

Sabri, Nidal Rashid (1999), 'General features of the Palestinian industry', *International Management*, **3**, 33–42.

Sabri, Nidal Rashid (2003), *Public Sector and the Palestinian Economy* (Ramallah, Palestine: Moaten Publishing Institute).

Sabri, Nidal Rashid (2004), *Tax Policies in Palestine* (HDIP, Palestine).

Sabri, Nidal Rashid (2008a), *Financial Markets and Institutions in the Arab Economy* (Nova Science Publishers, New York).

Sabri, Nidal Rashid (2008b), 'Performance and succession in Palestinian family businesses', in *Culturally-Sensitive Models of Family Business in Middle East* (India: ICFAI University Press) pp. 112–33.

Sabri, Nidal Rashid and Rania Jaber (2006), 'Financial Policies Issues', in Nidal Rashid Sabri (ed.) *Palestine Country Profile* (Cairo and France: Economic Research Forum, and Institut de La Méditerranée).

UNCTAD (2004), *Development and Globalization: Facts and Figures* (United Nations, United Nations Conference on Trade and Development, New York and Geneva).

UNDP (2006), *Human Development Report* (United Nations Development Program, New York).

UNDP (2008), *Human Development Report 2007–2008* (United Nations Development Program, New York).

UNRWA (2005), *UNRWA Medium Term Plan 2005–2009* (United Nations Relief and Works Agency for Palestine Refugees, Gaza, Palestine).

UNRWA (2008), *UNRWA in Figures* (Public Information office, United Nations Relief and Works Agency for Palestine Refugees Headquarter, Gaza, Palestine, February).

World Bank (2007a), 'WEST BANK and GAZA investment climate assessment: unlocking the potential of the private sector', (Social and Economic Development Department Middle East and North Africa Region, Report No. 39109 – GZ).

World Bank (2007b), 'Doing Business 2006', http://www.doingbusiness.org (accessed March 2008).

28 Philippines
Maria Carmen Galang and Sonia Tiong-Aquino

1 Introduction

Named after Prince Felipe who later became King Philip II of Spain, the Republic of the Philippines is an archipelago of 7107 islands in Southeast Asia, with the capital, Quezon City, located in the largest island of Luzon. Total population is projected to reach over 91 million by 2007, with around 34 percent under the age of 15 years.[1] With a gross domestic product (GDP) per capita of US$3300 (2007 est.), a population below the poverty line at 30 percent (2003 est.) and unemployment rate at 7.4 percent (2007), the country is currently classified by the World Bank as one of the 55 lower middle-income economies. Nonetheless, the adult literacy rate is at 92.6 percent, and the country is the third largest English-speaking country in the world. The Philippines is also the only Christian nation in Asia, with more than 80 percent of the people Catholic. Culturally, the Philippines is a mix of Malay, Chinese, Spanish and American influences.

Prior to the arrival of the Spaniards in 1521, the Philippines was first populated by Malays, followed by Chinese and Arab merchants and traders. The Catholic religion and feudalistic land ownership were the legacies of Spain, which occupied the Philippines for over 300 years. The Philippine revolution against Spain, Asia's first nationalist revolution, coincided with the Spanish–American War. However, the declaration of independence by Filipino revolutionaries on 12 June 1898 was not recognized, as the Philippines was ceded to the United States by Spain in the Treaty of Paris that same year. Japan occupied the country during World War II, and the US granted independence to the Philippines on 4 July 1946 after the fall of Japan. In 1964, the Philippine government deemed the date of Philippine independence to be 12 June 1898.

The legacies of the US include public education, the English language and a democratic political system. From World War II, the people elected the President for a term of four years, with a possibility of re-election for a second term. After World War II, the country was seen to be the most advanced in East Asia (after Japan), but by the 1980s it was considered as the 'sick man of Asia' (Villegas, 1999, p. 2).

In 1972, the then President, Ferdinand Marcos, who was elected in 1965 and could not run for a third term, declared martial law on the grounds of national security against a Communist movement. He was toppled in 1986 by Corazon Aquino in a surprise 'snap election' followed by the non-violent People Power revolution (EDSA 1). Aquino survived the new six-year term of office, despite numerous coup attempts.

Aquino was succeeded by Fidel Ramos in 1992, then by Joseph Estrada in 1998, both through general elections. Estrada, however, was later impeached on corruption charges, and was succeeded by his Vice President, Gloria Macapagal-Arroyo, after a second People Power revolution (EDSA 2). Macapagal-Arroyo was subsequently elected in 2004. Under the presidency of Ramos, with political stability, the economy started to enjoy a resurgence, and proved to be resilient through the Asian financial crisis of the 1990s. The real GDP growth is expected to exceed 7 percent in 2007, its fastest in 25 years.

Small and medium enterprises (SMEs) are defined in the Philippines to be business enterprises having fewer than 200 employees or not more than PhP[2] 100 million in assets (excluding land) (SMED Council, 2006). In 2003, SMEs comprised 99.6 percent of the 810 362 establishments in the country (Bureau of Small and Medium Enterprise Development, 2005). Of these, 92.1 percent are classified as micro enterprises having fewer than 10 employees or with assets of PhP 3 million or less; 7.5 percent as small enterprises (10–99 employees or with assets of PhP 15 000 000 or less), and 0.4 percent as medium enterprises (100–199 employees or with assets of PhP 100 000 000 or less). Small and medium enterprises employed 3 877 369 persons, representing 67.9 percent of the country's labor force, with most (89.6 percent) in micro and small enterprises. Most SMEs are engaged in wholesale and retail trade (53.8 percent), followed by manufacturing (15.1 percent) and hotels and restaurants (11.0 percent).

While SMEs outnumber large firms 9:1, the bulk of the revenue earnings and value-added output are contributed by the large enterprises. Small and medium enterprises account for only 28 percent of the total revenues of PhP 1019 million and 26.5 percent of total value-added in production of PhP 408 million (Aquino, 1999). They also contribute to the country's effort to promote exports. However, while it is estimated that 60 percent of exporters are SMEs, they account for only 25 percent of the total revenue from exports, and most of these firms are small exporters with yearly average exports of US$100 000 (Aquino, 1999).

2 Government policy on SMEs and entrepreneurship

The promotion of SMEs, as a strategy for economic development and poverty alleviation, was first given emphasis by the Philippine government in the 1970s during the worldwide oil crisis (SMED Council, 2006). Key legislation, however, did not come until later: specifically, the Magna Carta for Small Enterprises[3] in 1991 and later amended in 1997, and the Barangay[4] Micro Business Enterprise (BMBE) Act in 2002 (SMED Council, 2006). There are also numerous[5] legislations providing special incentives to promote business activities in general. The central provisions of the Magna Carta for Small Enterprises include the definition of SMEs; the creation of the Small and Medium Enterprises Development (SMED) Council and the Small Business Guarantee and Finance Corporation (SBGFC), the latter providing an alternative mode of financing; entitling SMEs to 10 percent of government procurement; and, mandating a lending quota for financial institutions. The Barangay Micro Business Enterprise (BMBE) Act supports micro-enterprises and informal sectors through incentives to local government registered barangay micro-enterprises, exemption from income taxes, reduction in local taxes, exemption from payment of minimum wages, financial support from government financial institutions, and technology assistance from government agencies.

The SME Development Plan 2004–2010 formulated by the SMED Council, with the support of the Japan International Cooperation Agency (JICA), and Macapagal-Arroyo's Ten-Point Agenda have as goals the increase of small and medium enterprises from 8.7 to 12 percent, or a total of 32 000 new small and medium enterprises; the increase of the SME sector's gross value-added contribution to 40 percent from 32 percent; an annual growth rate of 16 percent in exports sales by exporting SMEs; the creation of 6–10 million jobs through more opportunities to entrepreneurs; tripling of loans available to SMEs; and development of 1–2 million hectares of land for agri-business. The Plan sets down the following strategies:

- To enhance the operations of the individual SME through
  - providing comprehensive and focused support to enhance managerial and technological capability; and
  - providing support in identifying business opportunities;
- To assist priority industries[6] by
  - strengthening support to growth industries active in international markets; and
  - providing support for industrial linkages of SMEs with leading industries;
- To improve the SME operational environment through
  - developing SME financing support programs and strengthening financial institutions;
  - streamlining systems that provide programs and incentives to SMEs;
  - streamlining implementation of SME policies and regulations; and
  - strengthening and building the capability of institutions that generate and implement programs for SME development.

The Department of Trade and Industry (DTI) is the government agency responsible for developing and regulating business enterprises, large and small. Within the DTI, SME services are provided by the Bureau of Small and Medium Enterprise Development (initiating and coordinating specific SME programs and projects), Small Business Guarantee and Finance Corporation, Philippine Trade Training Center, Product Development and Design Center of the Philippines, and Cottage Industries Technology Center. Numerous other government organizations at both national and local level are also involved in the promotion of SMEs, such as the Department of Science and Technology, Department of Labor and Employment, and Department of Interior and Local Governments, as well as non-government organizations (NGOs) such as the Small Enterprises Research and Development Foundation, Inc. (SERDEF), and the Philippine Center for Entrepreneurship. Together, these organizations provide support to SMEs through advocacy and promotion; financing; entrepreneurship management training; technical/product development assistance; marketing/distribution assistance; business information assistance; regulations, and skills training (Pineda, 2003).

3   The environment for entrepreneurship and the state of small business
From 1999 to 2006, the number of micro, small and medium-sized enterprises (MSMEs) declined a very slight average of 0.76 percent per year (see Table 28.1), despite new business names being issued on yearly average of around 190 000 from 2000 to 2004 (see Table 28.2).

These figures do not include the informal sector, examples of which include street vending or other unrecorded cash sales (Dana, 2007), as they are not registered with either DTI or SEC, or are operating without a Mayor's Permit or a City/Municipal Business License (Tecson, 2004). Tecson (2004) cites estimates that the informal economy in the Philippines represents about 40 percent of the country's gross national product (GNP), which would translate into hundreds of thousands of micro enterprises.

Table 28.1 Number of establishments by firm size

Year	Micro	Small	Medium	Total MSMEs	% change	Total establishments	% of MSMEs to total
1999	751 556	68 781	3 239	823 576			
2000	747 740	67 166	3 070	817 976	−0.68	810 960	99.6
2001	743 949	61 759	2 923	808 631	−1.14	809 460	99.7
2002	743 426	60 566	2 874	806 866	−0.22	811 960	99.6
2003	743 628	60 785	2 922	807 335	0.06	820 960	99.6
2004	713 566	64 501	2 980	781 047	−3.25	783 923	99.6
2005	714 675	62 811	2 851	780 337	−0.09	782 980	99.7
2006	720 191	57 439	2 839	780 469	0.02	783 065	99.7

Sources: Bureau of Small and Medium Enterprise Development (2005); *1999–2006 List of Establishments*, National Statistics Office.

Table 28.2 Number of business names issued* to MSMEs, 2000–2004

Year	Micro	Small	Medium	Total	% change
2000	166 224	5 482	72	171 778	
2001	162 330	5 362	49	167 696	−2.38
2002	157 759	5 885	88	163 732	−2.36
2003	198 906	7 186	66	206 158	25.91
2004	243 704	3 656	1 128	248 488	20.53

Note: * Business establishments apply for business names with the Department of Trade and Industry (DTI), except those partnerships and corporations that are already registered with the Securities and Exchange Commission (SEC). The sharp increase of micro enterprises in 2004 could be partly due to the change in definition of micro enterprises, as well as the increase in SEC-registered corporations registering with the DTI.

Source: Bureau of Small and Medium Enterprise Development (2005).

Despite the BMBE Act introduced in 2002 to incorporate these informal sector micro enterprises into the formal sector by offering incentives, only 4048 had approved applications as of March 2007. Analysis done by Tecson (2004), together with feedback from a focus group of 68 representatives from the MSME sector, indicates that the low BMBE registration is attributed to the onerous process and costs of registration that outweighs the benefits of registration, benefits which they are already enjoying by remaining in the informal sector (particularly exemption from or reduction of income taxes and local fees, and payment of minimum wage). Access to credit would not play a major factor in decisions to register, as most of these enterprises probably do not go to banks, as they lack the required collateral (Dana, 2007), and financing may come from relatives or the local '5–6 lender'[7] (Tecson, 2004). Business registration under the Magna Carta is deemed as cumbersome as under the BMBE Act (Tecson, 2004).

Under the Magna Carta, financial institutions are required to set aside loans for MSMEs. The 1991 law required banks to set aside 5 percent of their net loan portfolio

Table 28.3   Compliance of banks to mandatory credit allocation loans, 1991–2004 (million Pesos)

Year*	Total net portfolio	Total compliance**	% to net loan portfolio
1991	201 564	16 836	8.35
1992	187 594	20 804	11.09
1993	276 462	34 218	12.38
1994	385 316	53 559	13.90
1995	560 213	88 041	15.72
1996	791 568	113 844	14.38
1997	886 844	219 005	24.69
1998	1 027 845	240 764	23.42
1999	1 001 567	248 193	24.78
2000	986 427	231 629	23.48
2001	992 243	248 543	25.05
2002	943 850	272 030	28.82
2003	1 046 551	234 370	22.39
2004	1 065 401	237 385	22.28

Notes:
*   As of 31 December every year, except 2004 (as of 30 September).
**   Total compliance includes both direct loans and indirect compliance, which means alternative modes such as cash on hand, unavailable committed credit lines, holdings of SBGFC notes, and so on. On average from 1991 to 2004, percentage of direct compliance of total net portfolio is 17.24 percent, and indirect compliance is 2.10 percent.

Source: Bureau of Small and Medium Enterprise Development (2005).

for small enterprises; this was revised in 1997 to 6 percent for small and 2 percent for medium-sized enterprises. Table 28.3 shows that the percentage mandated has been exceeded every year since its introduction. Nonetheless, proposed amendments to the Magna Carta include a total increase to 10 percent, with 8 percent to be allocated to micro and small enterprises, and the remaining 2 percent to medium-sized enterprises.

In addition to mandatory financing from private banks, the Small Business Guarantee and Finance Corporation (SBGFC) launched the SME Unified Lending Opportunities for National Growth (SULONG) program. Through this program, SMEs can avail of loans at lower interest rates, using forms of collateral other than land-based ones, and a shorter standardized application form that can be used by all government financing institutions participating in the program (Tecson, 2004). Microfinancing, especially to enterprises in the informal sector, is also available through cooperatives such as credit unions (Dana, 2007), and NGOs such as the Center for Agricultural and Rural Development, Tulay sa Pag-unlad, Inc. and the Negro Women for Tomorrow Foundation (Tecson, 2004). The size of loans of these three NGOs average PhP 5000. In addition, families can be a source of funding, as dollar remittances from overseas Filipinos are estimated to reach US$14 billion in 2006 (Madarang, 2006). Thus, access to financing does not seem to be problematic for Philippine SMEs (Dana, 2007), despite the country's low savings rate and absence of business angels (Madarang, 2006).

Tecson's (2004) review of the regulatory framework advises adjustments in existing policies, and their implementation, as they have inadvertently created disincentives to SMEs. Another area needing improvement is in the unnecessary duplication of the many government agencies involved in promoting SME development in the Philippines (Pineda, 2003).

Government policies also address the cognitive, social and normative environments that are important influences on entrepreneurship behaviors (Baughn et al., 2006; Dreisler et al., 2003; Spencer and Gómez, 2004). Most of the policies, stipulated in the SME Development Plan and key legislation, seem to target those with a positive attitude towards entrepreneurship but may or may not yet be engaged in entrepreneurial activity. However, some of those already engaged in entrepreneurial activity do not necessarily have a positive attitude towards entrepreneurship, but may have engaged in the activity due to lack of a better alternative in the form of employment or employment that pays sufficient income. Thus, proposed amendments to the Magna Carta include initiatives that directly address negative attitudes: celebration of the MSMED Week in July, and Presidential Awards for Outstanding MSMEs and Good MSME Practices. Some of the existing initiatives aimed at the cognitive and social environment contribute to the success of entrepreneurs, which will likely develop positive attitudes as well (Begley and Tan, 2001). The efforts of the non-profit Philippine Center for Entrepreneurship, such as a weekly television show, weekly newspaper column, quarterly magazine (*SME Insight*), online mentoring program (www.gonegosyo.net), and books on inspiring stories of top Filipino entrepreneurs, should not go unmentioned.

Nonetheless, a country summary report on the Philippines written for the Global Entrepreneurship Monitor (GEM) Project by Madarang (2006) indicates that the normative environment for entrepreneurship is positive, based on a survey of 2000 adults: more than 80 percent of respondents accord successful entrepreneurs respect and high status and believe entrepreneurship to be a desirable career choice; 45.8 percent expect to start their own business within the next three years; 54 percent of the early-stage entrepreneurs report that their businesses are opportunity based, versus the 46 percent who report being forced into starting a business by necessity.

While this country report is quite optimistic about the state of entrepreneurship in the Philippines, there is still room for improvement. One indication that the normative environment may not be as conducive as it can be is that only 120 higher education institutions out of the 2036 in the directory of the Commission on Higher Education (CHED)[8] offered a four-year undergraduate Bachelor's program in Entrepreneurship, and only one had a Master's program. There were more degree programs in Business Administration, the most popular undergraduate program, with 22 percent of the undergraduate students during the academic year 2004–2005 (CHED, 2007). At the Master's level, Business Administration was the second most popular (27 percent), after teacher-training (43 percent). Most Business Administration graduates however are geared towards becoming employed in business rather than becoming entrepreneurs. This may change, as those offering elective subjects are mandated to convert to a Bachelor's degree in Entrepreneurship within three to five years. Also, two private-sector institutions that focus solely on entrepreneurship were established.

At the secondary levels, the Department of Education introduced the Youth Entrepreneurship and Cooperativism in Schools (YECS) Program in 1997 (Sibayan and Guanzon, 2003). It was hoped that given the high unemployment rate and the increasing cost of higher education, high school graduates, instead of seeking employment, would be able to create jobs for themselves, and perhaps even for others, eventually to finance their education, through such simple forms of entrepreneurial activity as variety stores, mini-canteens, selling school supplies, souvenir or seasonal items, or poultry raising.

Nonetheless, Madarang's (2006) report indicates that 72.8 percent of the 2000 adults surveyed felt confident that they had the skills and knowledge required to start a business, and 68.1 percent perceived that they had good opportunities for starting a business. Indeed, there are other means of improving entrepreneurial and managerial capabilities outside the formal educational system.

4   Internationalization of entrepreneurs and SMEs from the Philippines

Tecson (2004) estimates that over 70 percent of SMEs are either not oriented to growth or do not succeed in growing and have no international activity. Part of the thrust of developing SMEs is to take advantage of globalization (Alfonso, 2001), if only in terms of subcontracting with larger foreign multinationals. This latter type comprise only a very few SMEs, but they tend to employ more people and use more sophisticated technology (Tecson, 2004).

Tecson (2001) noted that in 1994, micro-enterprises exported 0.44 percent of their total output, whereas small and medium-sized enterprises exported 18 percent of their output, which compares favorably with the average of 19 percent for the entire manufacturing sector. The subsectors in the manufacturing industry where SMEs account for a fairly large share of industry output and total exports, are food, wearing apparel, wood and cork products, furniture/fixtures, and professional and scientific equipment. There are other subsectors where SMEs also show a high degree of export orientation, but the subsector itself may not be export oriented or are dominated by larger firms. Tecson (2004) estimates that 20–25 percent of manufacturing SMEs are engaged in exporting, whether indirectly through subcontracting networks, or directly through intermediaries such as trading companies.

Various laws and regulations provide all exporting firms, regardless of size, with several tax incentives, subsidies, assistance in facilitation of exports/imports, special locations. Most of the needs expressed by the MSME focus group, however, were in government assistance to attend international trade fairs and exhibits, information about foreign markets, and assistance by commercial attaches in Philippine embassies in promoting local businesses to foreign customers or potential business partners (Tecson, 2004).

Inflows of foreign direct investment (FDI) to the Philippines exceed outflows: from 2002–07, FDI inflows amount to an average of US$1.4 billion per year, representing 1.35 percent of GDP, and outflows US$0.27 billion, which is 0.27 percent of GDP (The Economist Intelligence Unit, 2007). However, no data on the share of SMEs in FDI were accessible. Nevertheless, this is an area that can be leveraged by the Philippine government to promote the internationalization of SMEs (Oviatt and McDougall, 2005; Wattanapruttipaisan, 2005). Linkages with foreign business partners can help improve SME productivity and technological capabilities, which are recognized problems in the Philippines. Also, foreign linkages can be directed more specifically towards the high-technology sectors or sectors with high value-added, in order to make the Philippine economy much more competitive in this era of globalization. Many of the fast-growth SMEs, engaged in restructuring existing industries or generating new industries, are internationalized, but they are only a small proportion (5–25 percent) (Tecson, 2004).

5 Conclusion

Clearly, the importance of SMEs to the Philippine economy has been recognized by the Philippine government, indicated by the numerous policies and initiatives that have been introduced to support their development, such as financing, training, market access, technical assistance, and networking. However, more needs to be done as SMEs, while more numerous than large enterprises, are mostly in wholesale and retail trade, and contribute less in terms of revenues, value-added, and decent employment. The overall vision of the SME Development Plan 2004–2010 is to create globally competitive SMEs in the new economic environment. Studies, similar to the analytical review of Tecson (2004) and Pineda (2003) of the regulatory framework, and gathering of feedback from entrepreneurs themselves and potential entrepreneurs through such means as focus groups (Tecson, 2004) or general surveys (Madarang, 2006), will support this objective, by ensuring the effectiveness and efficiency of the policies and initiatives of the government. Resources of the government however are limited, and the support of the private sector, as well as international development agencies, will be needed.

Notes

1. Source of most statistical information in this section comes from the CIA World Factbook (entries for the Philippines were last updated 12 February 2008) and the official website of the Philippine government.
2. Philippine Pesos; US$1.00 = PhP 46.48 (at 22 August 2007).
3. This Act is currently undergoing amendment through SB 1646, which was passed on second reading by the Senate on 3 October 2007, and HB 1754, which is going through the House of Representatives.
4. Barangay refers to the smallest political unit in the country's system of government.
5. Tecson (2004) notes that a study in the 1980s identified 278 laws and regulations affecting SMEs in the manufacturing and processing sectors, and that the Department of Trade and Industry had identified 107 laws and regulations as of May 2003.
6. The 11 priority industries for which the Philippine SMEs have competitive potentials, as well as those with growth prospects because of high export possibilities and strong domestic demand are the food industry, organic and natural products, marine products, wearables, leather goods, home furnishings, construction materials, micro-electronics, information technology (IT) services, and motor vehicle parts and components.
7. Usurious money lending, at 20 percent interest per week.
8. www.ched.gov.ph.

References

Alfonso, O. (ed) (2001), *Bridging the Gap: Philippine SMEs and Globalization*, Quezon City: SERDEF, Inc.
Aquino, S.T. (1999), 'A Study on Women Entrepreneurs in SMEs in the APEC Region: Philippines', unpublished study.
Baughn, C.C., J.S.R. Cao, L.T.M. Le, V.A. Lim and K.E. Neupert (2006), 'Normative, social and cognitive predictors of entrepreneurial interest in China, Vietnam and the Philippines', *Journal of Developmental Entrepreneurship*, **11**(1), 57–77.
Begley, T.M. and W.L. Tan (2001), 'The socio-cultural environment for entrepreneurship: A comparison between East Asian and Anglo-Saxon countries', *Journal of International Business Studies*, **32**(3), 537–53.
Bureau of Small and Medium Enterprise Development (2005), *Small and Medium Enterprises Statistical Report*, Philippines: Department of Trade and Industry.
Commission on Higher Education (CHED) (2007), *Medium-term Development Plan for Higher Education, 2005–2010*, Manila, Philippines: Office of Policy, Planning, Research and Information.
Dana, L.P. (2007), *Asian Models of Entrepreneurship*, NJ: World Scientific.
Dreisler, P., P. Blenker and K. Nielsen (2003), 'Promoting entrepreneurship – changing attitudes or behaviour?', *Journal of Small Business and Enterprise Development*, **10**(4), 383–92.

Madarang, I.J. (2006), *Philippines*, GEM Global Summary 2006, Global Entrepreneurship Monitor, www. gemconsortium.org (accessed 5 March 2008).
Oviatt, B.M. and P.P. McDougall (2005), 'Defining international entrepreneurship and modeling the speed of internationalization', *Entrepreneurship Theory and Practice*, **29**(5), 537–53.
Pineda, E.P. (2003), 'The role of SME promotion agencies in entrepreneurial development: an assessment', *Philippine Management Review*, **10**, 119–36.
Sibayan, S.I. and J.S. Guanzon Jr (2003), 'Can public high schools develop entrepreneurial characteristics among their students?', a research activity funded by the Small Enterprises and Development Foundation (SERDEF) and Institute for Small Scale Industries (ISSI), University of the Philippines.
SMED Council (2006), *SME Development Plan 2004–2010*, Philippines: Bureau of Small and Medium Enterprise Development, Department of Trade and Industry.
Spencer, J.W. and C. Gómez (2004), 'The relationship among national institutional structures, economic factors, and entrepreneurial activity: a multi-country study', *Journal of Business Research*, **57**(10), 1098–107.
Tecson, G.R. (2001), 'When the things you planned need a helping hand', support environment for SMEs, in O. Alfonso (ed.), *Bridging the Gap: Philippine SMEs and Globalization*, Quezon City: SERDEF, Inc.
Tecson, G.R. (2004), 'Review of existing policies affecting micro, small and medium scale enterprises in the Philippines', report submitted to the Department of Trade and Industry.
The Economist Intelligence Unit, with The Columbia Program on International Investment (2007), *World Investment Prospects to 2011*, www.cpii.columbia.edu (accessed 15 March 2008).
Villegas, B.M. (1999), 'Economic prospects under the Estrada administration', in L.Y.C. Lim, F. Ching and B.M. Villegas (eds), *The Asian Economic Crisis: Policy Choices, Social Consequences and the Philippine Case*, www.asiasociety.org (accessed 13 February 2008).
Wattanapruttipaisan, T. (2005), 'SME development and internationalization in the knowledge-based and innovation-driven global economy: mapping the agenda ahead', paper presented at the International Expert Seminar on 'Mapping Policy Experience for SMEs', Phuket, Thailand, 19–20 May.

29 Qatar
Yochanan Shachmurove

Introduction

The Qatari peninsula extends 100 miles from Saudi Arabia into the Persian Gulf and is slight smaller than the state of Connecticut. Because of its great vantage point en route to India, the British initially sought out Qatar for colonial interests. But the discovery of oil and other hydrocarbons in the early twentieth century later changed their interests.

In 1935, a 75-year concession was granted to Qatar Petroleum Company, which was owned by Anglo-Dutch, French and US interests.[1] High-quality oil was discovered in 1940 at Dukhan, but because of the start of World War II oil exports did not begin until 1949. During the 1950s and 1960s increasing oil reserves brought prosperity, rapid immigration, and substantial social progress.[2]

In 1971, the United Arab Emirates, Bahrain and Qatar planned on forming a union of Arab Emirates. However, by mid-1971 they still had not settled on the terms of the agreement and the end of the year termination date of the British treaty relationship was approaching.[3] Thus, Qatar sought full independence as a separate entity and became autonomous on 3 September 1971. Qatar was quickly recognized as an independent state and gained admittance to the United Nations and the Arab League.

Since 1995, Emir Hamad bin Khalifa Al-Thani has ruled Qatar after seizing control of the country when his father Khalifa bin Hamad Al Thani was out of the country.[4] Emir Hamad has been very open to global markets and the country has experienced a notable amount of sociopolitical liberalization, including the enfranchisement of women, a new constitution, and the launch of the Al Jazeera news source.

The Qatari wealth of hydrocarbon resources is the driving force behind the country's tremendous economic growth in recent years. The increase in the production and cost of oil and gas during the last five years has doubled the gross domestic product (GDP) of Qatar keeping its GDP per capita as the ninth highest in the world. Its nominal growth levels averaged 15.6 percent between the years 1995 and 2005.[5] Qatar has the third largest reserve of natural gas in the world that is estimated to last for over 200 years at current production levels.[6] By 2010 the amount of natural gas that Qatar exports is expected to triple, making the country the largest natural gas exporter in the world.[7] In addition to Qatar's bounty of natural gas, Qatar has the largest reserve of crude oil in the world, estimated to be 14.5 billion barrels.[8]

With 62 percent of Qatar's GDP coming from the oil sector the government is heavily dependent on its oil reserves.[9] Qatar hopes to diversify its income sources by enhancing its industrial sector by developing the north gas field, iron and steel, petrochemical, and refining industries. Finance, insurance, real estate, manufacturing industry, building and construction, government services, and social services are some of the other sectors into which Qatar hopes to diversify. By setting high standards and producing quality products that are cost-efficient, Qatar has become one of the most industrially developed economies in the region.

Government policy on small and medium enterprises (SMEs) and entrepreneurship
Like all countries, Qatar has its own guidelines for foreigners interested in doing business in Qatar. Foreign investors must appoint an agent or sponsor in order to do business *with* Qatar. There are two types of agents: a service agent and a commercial agent. In the case of a foreign investor planning to undertake a project which is to be executed for Qatari private entities and leave the country upon completion, a service agent is required to take care of all administrative work with the government.[10] If the business intends to import to Qatar, a commercial agent is required to act as a sales or distributor representative.[11] Experts believe that the requirement for a service agent in Qatar is becoming more lenient, and may be abolished in the years to come.[12]

If foreign investors wish to *do* business in Qatar it has become common practice to establish a Limited Liability Company. In this case foreign ownership cannot exceed 49 percent of the capital, with a Qatari partner owning at least 51 percent.[13] Qatar has also developed a common law framework based on Western law to be implemented in the new Qatari Civil and Commercial Court, as well as in the Qatari Financial Center (QFC) and Regulatory Authority (QFCRA). The Qatar Financial Center (QFC) was established in 2005 to provide a financial and business center in Doha to attract international financial services institutions and multinational corporations wishing to participate in Qatar's rapidly growing economy as well as a platform to provide services elsewhere in the region.[14] New Qatari laws also allow foreigners to earn up to 80 percent or more of the company's profits if the foreigner is the main person involved in the venture.[15] The joint venture company does not require a service agent or sponsor to conduct business. This new regulatory framework will most likely increase applications for Qatari business licenses.

Foreign companies wishing to *invest* in the Qatari agriculture, manufacturing, health, education, tourism, power, or mining sectors are allowed to establish up to a 100 percent foreign-owned branch office pending approval from the government.[16] These types of companies do not require an agent.

In Qatar there are no personal taxes, social insurances, or other statuary deductions from salaries and wages paid in the country.[17] Qatari and Gulf Corporation Council (GCC) nationals are not subject to income tax in Qatar. This may seem misleading because Qatar is not a tax-free zone. Foreign investors, partnerships and companies operating in Qatar must pay a tax on corporate business. By law, all occupations, professions, service trades, contract executions or any other businesses are subject to these terms.[18] Certain tax exemptions are allowed in Qatar, depending on whether the activities of the foreign firms are directly benefiting Qatar, incorporating modern technology, and/or fulfilling a strategic goal for the government.[19]

The banking sector has undergone substantial growth in the past decade. Banks are increasingly marketing their services to wealthy individuals, both expatriate and local. In the past five years, total outstanding personal loans and credit lines have more than tripled.[20] The quick growth of lending programs draws attention to the sizable amount of liquidity in Qatari bank accounts, although the easy availability of retail credit lines is causing problems as a growing number of citizens have never dealt with credit before and are finding themselves overextended.[21] The Qatar Development Bank, a major financial arm of the government, has recently been restructured in order to encourage Qatari nationals to establish small businesses.

The Qatar Development Bank (QIDB) was founded in 1997 and specializes in the promotion and financing of small and medium enterprises. The objectives of QIDB are to: (1) provide industrial loans and finance imports of raw material, machinery, and technical equipment, (2) provide loans for export of industrial products, (3) undertake studies, provide advisory services and promote sound projects identified through a comprehensive development strategy, and (4) promote small and industrial projects and monitor their implementation phase.[22] In this way, Doha hopes to build the number of local business owners in the country and consequently improve needed competition to various sectors.

The environment for entrepreneurship and the state of small business
Qatar has established a sense of credibility among the business community by developing high standards in quality management and cost-efficiency making Qatar one of the most industrially developed countries in the region.[23] In the last five years, Qatar has taken steps to improve its trade and investment climate in line with its World Trade Organization (WTO) standards by reducing tariffs, removing unnecessary restrictions and barriers to trade, creating better access to world markets, providing investors more opportunities and incentives, and enhancing trade cooperation by signing bilateral economic, commercial and technical cooperation agreements.[24] As the largest trading partner of Qatar, the United States is working with the Qatari government to establish a free trade agreement along with Singapore and the EU.[25]

Qatar is trying to improve its efficiency in the goods market. Qatar's poor ranking contributes to insufficient domestic competition, a small base of local suppliers, and low incidence of foreign ownership.[26] Qatar's ranking on foreign ownership has improved from 2000 to 2005 showing that the initiatives to relax the rules and restrictions for foreign investment and ownership are beginning to show positive effects.

Emir Hamad recognizes the need for education to ensure Qatar's future prosperity and has established a very modern school system. His wife, Sheikha Mozah, founded and leads the Supreme Education Council (SEC). This is the country's leading authority on education policy for primary schools and is responsible for the complete overhaul of the traditional Qatari school system into a more western style. The SEC's major initiative has been the shift from public schools to a government-funded independent school system.[27] The Supreme Education Council also supports Qatari teachers by providing training and a curriculum, developing and conducting standardized tests, monitoring student's progress and evaluating school performance.[28] Qatar is currently looking for primarily US, German, British and New Zealand school management firms to help in the training of teachers, with 40 schools already undergoing major reforms. Qatar is also seeking to improve its higher education. With an enrollment rate of less than 20 percent, tertiary education in Qatar is insufficiently developed.[29] The Qatar Foundation for Education (QF), also founded by Sheikha Mozah, has established 'Education City', a 2500-acre campus on the outskirts of Doha. 'Education City' aims to provide world-class education from kindergarten to the postgraduate level, notably through partnerships with Western universities such as Weill Cornell Medical Center, Carnegie Mellon, Virginia Commonwealth University and Texas A&M. The project aims at enhancing the capacity for innovation, fostering collaboration between the university and the private sector, and reducing the shortage of scientists and engineers. These are three areas in which Qatar does relatively poorly.

Weill Cornell Medical Center is currently working with the Qatari government to build a cutting-edge teaching hospital that will mainly concentrate on women's and children's health.[30] Since the establishment of this medical school, Qatar has developed a strong appreciation for US medicine and many of the Qatari medical professionals are US trained. In Qatar, there are four government hospitals, 23 primary health care centers, and at least 12 private medical and dental facilities.[31] Of the most respected medical centers, Hamad Medical Corporation provides modern diagnostic and disease treatment care, and is the country's leading non-profit healthcare provider. Foreign investment in the health care sector in Qatar is very promising especially since Qatari law allows for 100 percent foreign investment in the health care sector, pending approval from the government.[32]

A housing boom in Qatar is taking place due to the influx of foreigners. This has put upward pressure on real estate prices, causing inflation. Nevertheless, the demand for luxury goods and leisure activities is likely to increase over the coming years due to the excess of liquid assets – particularly from Qatari nationals. This demographic, which is growing steadily, wants to purchase luxury goods and the retail industry is only too happy to supply them. High-class brands, which accounted for only a very small percentage of the total market 10 years ago, now represent a considerable income stream.[33]

High demand for commercial, residential and industrial space is pushing prices up and real estate investors are reaping the benefits.[34] Analysts have questioned whether or not supply can keep up with demand, especially in the residential market. In response, the government has initiated several major housing projects. This has catalyzed the building of many shopping centers. Several housing developments already in place will bring restaurants, marinas, and shops into the area, presenting a wealth of opportunities for entrepreneurs. The major problem for Qatar, however, is that most of the new residential developments in Qatar are aimed at the upper middle class. This is cause for concern for lower- and middle-class families, many of whom face rising rents and increased taxes.[35]

Until recently, foreigners were not allowed to buy or own any property in Qatar. Owing the quick growth of the expatriate population in recent years, this law has been changed to allow foreign ownership of certain properties.[36]

Qatar is a country with a population of less than a million people, of which just over 200 000 are Qatari citizens.[37] Qatar has a labor force consisting primarily of expatriate workers making up most of the population of the country. The largest group of foreign workers comes from India, Pakistan, the Philippines and South Asia.[38] There is also a significant number of Arab, European and American experts and professionals in the area. Although the dependence of Qatar on a foreign workforce is high given the severe shortage of Qatari labor, the policy of the government is to ensure the employment of its citizens. The government, however, facilitates the recruitment of foreign labor by instituting liberal immigration and employment laws.[39]

Barwa Real Estate Company is constructing a residential area for laborers, known as Barwas Al Baraha (Workers City), in the outskirts of Qatar's capital city of Doha. The project was launched after a recent scandal in Dubai's labor 'slave' camps. This project aims to provide a reasonable standard for living as defined by the new human rights legislation. 'Workers City' will cost around US $1.1 billion and will be a completely integrated city in the industrial area of Doha.[40] Along with living space, the residential project will provide parks, recreational areas, malls, and shops for laborers. Phase one of the project is set to be complete by the end of 2008, with the full completion scheduled for mid-2010.[41]

Internationalization of entrepreneurs and SMEs from Qatar
Qatar's tourism industry, nonexistent 10 years ago, is beginning to get serious about promoting the country as a luxurious travel destination. Qatar has already hosted a tennis competition that is part of the Association of Tennis Professionals (ATP) Tour, and was the site for the 2006 Asian Games, which is the second largest sporting event after the Olympics. The government considers boosting the tourism industry vitally important to the future of Qatar and is planning to invest US $15 billion for tourist attractions and related projects in the coming years.[42] To further boost the sector, the government has formed a new body, the Qatar Tourism Authority, which has identified five major tourist attractions to be developed. In addition, visa restrictions were relaxed in early 2002 and nationals of 33 countries can now obtain visas on arrival.[43]

Much of Qatar's current infrastructure development is meant to eventually support a substantial jump in tourist numbers. Just fewer than 1 million visitors came to the country in 2006, 90 percent of them on business trips.[44] The Qatar Tourism Authority hopes to attract 1.5 million individuals per year by 2010 and the tourism industry has already started preparing for these numbers.[45] Eight new hotels with 2550 rooms will be added in the next two years. Occupancy rates in star hotels in the country have currently peaked at between 80 and 90 percent and are set to triple by 2010.[46] Other plans of the tourism authority include the state-of-the-art US $5 billion Doha International Airport, which is due for completion in 2015 and will bring the capacity of passengers from the current 12.5 million to 50 million in 2020.[47] Also in the coming years Qatar will build a US $2.5 billion artificial island called the 'Pearl of the Gulf', which will be a tourist hotspot.[48] Additionally, Qatar is pursuing niche tourism in various areas, including the sports, medical convention and exhibition markets.

Many Qatari companies have partnerships with overseas firms. A major partner is Exxon Mobil, which owns shares in Qatar's two liquefied natural gas (LNG) companies; Qatargas and Rasgas, while Total and ConocoPhillips have shares in Qatargas.[49] Exxon Mobil has also partnered with URS Qatar to carry out research on LNG safety, sulfur, and environmental management.[50]

Qatar's imports were US $4 billion in 2002. Import growth in 2003 was about 30 percent year on year, with 2003 imports exceeding US $5 billion.[51] Capital goods associated with oil and LNG-related projects dominate Qatar's imports. Other key imports include motor vehicles, foodstuffs, luxury items, electronics and a range of manufactured goods. The customs duty for general cargo entering Qatar is 15 percent.[52] But commodities required for the development of infrastructure, including food and personal effects, are exempt from custom duties. A minimal tariff of 5 percent is levied on most other goods, and a protection tax duty of up to 20 percent is charged for products such as imported steel and cement that compete against similar locally produced goods.[53] Goods manufactured in GCC countries are exempt from customs duties. Temporary imports in Qatar require permission from the General Director of Qatari Customs, as well as a check or bank guarantee for the Customs Department for the amount of the duty to permanently ship the goods to Qatar. This is refunded with proof of export from Qatar. Normal customs clearance by air is one to two days and by sea is two to four days.[54]

In 2003, Qatar's exports were US $12 billion. Japan, China and India buy most of Qatar's exports of crude oil and LNG.[55] Qatar Petrochemical Company (QAPCO) exports a range of petrochemicals to the GCC countries as well as to India, Pakistan and Australia. The products of Qatar Fertilizer Company (QAFCO) go to India and China and the products of Qatar Steel Company (QASCO) are sold mainly to the other GCC member states. Qatar has also become vulnerable to energy price fluctuations. Since Qatar's economy is so highly dependent on natural gas, the country has been trying to diversify its sources of income by further development of the natural gas industry, which already represents one-third of its exports.

Qatar's recent economic boom has created serious challenges in the transport and infrastructure sectors. Record levels of imports and exports have placed a major strain on the port system and Doha International Airport. The country's most important ports are Ras Laffan and Messaieed, respectively located to the north and south of Doha.[56] Both are struggling to keep up with an influx of container traffic due to a number of factors, including slow customs processes and a serious shortage of cranes. Port upgrades are planned and a brand new port, soon to be built on reclaimed land off the coast of Doha, will help to speed up shipping. This new port will function as a free-trade zone and will share land with Doha International Airport.[57] In addition, the US $5 billion, 40-kilometer long Qatar–Bahrain Bridge should be completed by 2010, linking Qatar with the rest of the region and should contribute to furthering regional economic integration and mobility.[58]

Conclusion

Qatar is a dynamic market with excellent growth potential. By transferring reliance on oil profits to modern health facilities, tourism infrastructure, and Western-style education institutions, the Qatari government aims to establish a forward-looking and highly skilled population. However, with the fast-paced growing markets, the Qatari government is not always able to establish necessary laws and procedures which business requires. Sometimes regulations are not widely published and are at times enforced with little or no consultation with the private sector.

Acknowledgment

The research leading to this paper has been partially supported by the Shwager Fund at The City College of The City University of New York.

Notes

1. Wikipedia Foundation Inc. (2008).
2. Wikipedia Foundation Inc. (2008).
3. Wikipedia Foundation Inc. (2008).
4. Wikipedia Foundation Inc. (2008).
5. Kerbaj (2006).
6. Kerbaj (2006).
7. Kerbaj (2006).
8. Kerbaj (2006).
9. Kerbaj (2006).

10. Kerbaj (2006).
11. Wallace, D. (n.d.).
12. Wallace, D. (n.d.).
13. Kerbaj (2006).
14. Clinton (2006).
15. Wallace (n.d.).
16. Wallace (n.d.).
17. Kerbaj (2006).
18. Wallace (n.d.).
19. Wallace (n.d.).
20. Oxford Business Group (2007).
21. Oxford Business Group (2007).
22. Clinton (2006).
23. Kerbaj (2006).
24. US Department of Commerce (2004).
25. US Department of Commerce (2004).
26. Geiger (2005).
27. Wallace (n.d.).
28. Wallace (n.d.).
29. Geiger (n.d.).
30. Wallace (n.d.).
31. Wallace (n.d.).
32. Wallace (n.d.).
33. Oxford Business Group (2007).
34. Oxford Business Group (2007).
35. Oxford Business Group (2007).
36. Oxford Business Group (2007).
37. Stewart (2004).
38. Kerbaj (2006).
39. Kerbaj (2006).
40. Bowman (2008).
41. Bowman (2008).
42. Kerbaj (2006).
43. Stewart (2004).
44. Oxford Business Group (2007).
45. Oxford Business Group (2007).
46. Kerbaj (2006).
47. Geiger (2005).
48. Stewart (2004).
49. Wallace (n.d.).
50. Wallace (n.d.).
51. Stewart (2004).
52. Wallace (n.d.).
53. Wallace (n.d.).
54. Wallace (n.d.).
55. Stewart (n.d.).
56. Oxford Business Group (2007).
57. Oxford Business Group (2007).
58. Geiger (2005).

References

Bowman, D. (2008), 'Qatar to build $1.1 bn labourer city. *Arabian Business*, 2 March, http://www.arabianbusi-ness.com/512568-qatar-to-build-11bn-labourer-city.

Clinton, S. (2006), *Doing Business in the Qatar Financial Centre*, Clifford Chance.

Geiger, T. (2005), '*Qatar: successful policies bode well for the future*' World Economic Forum, pp. 189-9, http://www.weforum/pdf/Global_Competitiveness_Reports/Profiles/Qatar.pdf.

Kerbaj, R.N. (2006), *Doing Business in Qatar*, Doha: MGI International.

Oxford Business Group (2007), *The Report: Emerging Qatar*, London: Oxford Business Group.

Stewart, B. (2004), *Doing Business with Qatar*, Council for Australian–Arab Relations, Australia: Bayliss Associates.

US Department of Commerce (2004), *Doing Business in Qatar: A Country Commercial Guide for U.S. Companies*, Washington, DC: US Department of State.
Wallace, D. (no date), *Consider Qatar*, Doha: American Embassy in Doha.
Wikipedia Foundation Inc. (2008), *Qatar*, 23 April, http://en.wikipedia.org/wiki/Qatar (accessed 24 April 2008).

30 Russia
Ruta Aidis, Julia Korosteleva and Tomasz Mickiewicz

1. Introduction to Russia

Russia is the world's largest country, a nuclear superpower with unsurpassed energy resources. It is also a country which finds itself at the crossroads of possible development paths. Market-oriented mechanisms have been introduced but Soviet era laws remain on the books. Corruption has become a way of life and freedom of the press has been gradually eliminated in the early 2000s. Within this backdrop, private entrepreneurship has emerged, albeit in a distorted way.

As the heart of the Soviet empire, Russia had tremendous control of enormous amounts of natural resources and human capital. Yet, 20 years ago, in the late 1980s, it was a country where entrepreneurship was marginal, the economy was stagnant and the ruling communist hierarchy had no clear formula for solving the deepening crisis. Unfortunately the reforms characterizing Russia's attempts at rebuilding statehood after the collapse of the Soviet Union in the 1990s, first under Mikhail Gorbachev and then Boris Y'eltsin, were inconsistent and did not foster macroeconomic stabilization.

However, since 2000, under Vladimir Putin's leadership, macroeconomic stabilization as well as institutional stability has been achieved. In addition, an unprecedented increase in the price and demand for oil and gas resources has resulted in a rapid growth of Russia's gross domestic product (GDP). Russia now has a large private sector, though not without its limitations. At first glance, 'de jure' regulations often seem reasonable, yet it is the selective and arbitrary manner by which they are enforced that results in a lack of consistency or stability for firms (Aidis and Adachi, 2007; Aidis et al., 2008). In addition, the inadequacies of the Soviet system resulted in Russians becoming accustomed to a corrupt and malfunctioning legal environment (Gel'man, 2004). Unfortunately, this negative legacy continues to characterize the business environment today. As a result, large, politically connected enterprises dominate Russia's business landscape. Moreover, the lack of universal property rights is reflected by the uneven distribution of income, and Russia is plagued by some of the most extreme social differences and pockets of dire poverty (Buccellato and Mickiewicz, 2008; Gerry et al., 2008; Glaeser et al., 2003).

2. Government policy on SMEs and entrepreneurship

Similar to most other economies emerging from the Soviet system, the creation of the private sector and the development of entrepreneurship was a new phenomenon in Russia. The first resolution of the Council of Ministers on 'Primary measures on development and state support of small entrepreneurship in Russia' was issued in 1993 and was followed by the Russian Federation Federal Law in 1995 which approved state support for small enterprises. There have been numerous governmental resolutions and programmes all aimed at creating better legal conditions for small entrepreneurship. However, in practice, the vast majority failed to be implemented. A study evaluating the effectiveness of the 1995 Federal Law on small and medium enterprises (SME) support indicated that nearly 80 percent of this law was never implemented (OECD, 2000: 50).

In a study of barriers to Russian SMEs, Radaev (2003) identified the uncertainty of federal SME policy and the lack of policy coordination at both the federal and regional levels, among the main reasons for the breakdown in Russian SME policy in the late 1990s. In addition, the 1998 financial crisis had a significant negative impact on both SME support and development. In the aftermath of the crisis, the state largely curtailed its support programmes.

Interestingly, until recently, small enterprises were the only legally qualified private entities explicitly defined in Russian legislation. The definition for medium-sized enterprise was missing. This situation changed in 2007 with the Russian Federation Federal Law 'On Development of Small and Medium Entrepreneurship in Russian Federation', which for the first time provided a clear definition of different types of SMEs including micro- (less than 15 employees), small (between 16 and 100 employees) and medium-sized (between 101 and 250 employees) enterprises. The law further differentiates between the following categories of SMEs: legal entities, individual entrepreneurs[1] and farmers.

The 2007 law on SME development envisaged the following primary support policy measures: special taxation regimes, simplified accounting, financial support, business infrastructure development, including the creation of business incubators and provision of counselling services, transfer of state and regional property to start-ups at favoured conditions, and allocation of state orders to SMEs. This is truly an admirable list of support that the government has identified, yet it is too early to declare if this new initiative will be successfully implemented and have a more substantial impact on SMEs as compared with the previous efforts.

2.1   Tax policy

According to the World Bank's (2007) 'Doing Business 2008' survey, Russia is ranked 130 out of the 178 participating countries in terms of the quality of its tax regime. The total tax rate as a proportion of profit that a medium-sized business would normally pay has been steady at the level of 51.4 percent over 2006–08.

A large number of SMEs pay taxes in accordance with special tax regimes, namely, a simplified tax system (UNS), and a single tax on businesses' imputed income (ENVD).[2] Whereas entrepreneurs have discretion over the adoption of a simplified tax system, a single tax (ENVD) is compulsory for a number of business activities subject to regional law.

Many entrepreneurs find the ENVD system to be inefficient since it is based not on actual income but on imputed income.[3] (Zlobin et al., 2005). However, in light of the mandatory nature of the ENVD, businesses do not have the freedom to transfer to a simplified or standard tax system. Prior to 2003, regional authorities set a base yield for various types of business activities, subject to an ENVD. Consequentially, this gave them significant power over the calculation of the ENVD providing ample opportunities for corrupt behaviour to flourish.

Furthermore, following the tax code amendments in January 2002, social tax was excluded from the single tax, significantly increasing the overall tax burden. This caused many small firms to partly move to the shadow economy, leading to an overall drop in tax collection. As a result, regional authorities raised the base yield in the vain hope of

Table 30.1   Russian entrepreneurs' awareness of state support programmes

SME programmes	I am aware of these programmes and I believe that many can benefit from them (%)	I am aware of these programmes, but I believe they will not work and there is no benefit from them (%)	I am not aware of these programmes (%)
Creation of business incubators	10	11	79
Micro credit schemes	17	14	69
Subsidizing of loan interest fee	16	14	70
Partial guarantee schemes	18	13	69
Export support	12	10	78
Creation of venture capital funds	6	8	86

Source: OPORA Russia (2006).

compensating for the losses, which only increased the incentives for businesses to retreat further into the shadows.

A new tax policy, which was introduced on 1 January 2003 and revised in 2006, aimed at addressing some of the aforementioned deficiencies, in particular freeing small businesses from the social tax, simplifying accounting, and centralizing the setting of a base yield used in calculation of the imputed income. Thus, the regional authorities were no longer allowed to set a base yield. However, in spite of this improvement, municipal authorities have gained some discretionary power to regulate a coefficient which is used to correct a base yield, taking into consideration some particularities of businesses such as the range of goods sold, seasonality of operations and location.[4] The declared objective was to create opportunities to reduce the tax burden for businesses facing the least favourable conditions. However, in reality, this approach has allowed municipal authorities to pursue a differential policy towards SMEs favouring well-connected business owners.

According to OPORA's 2006 survey data,[5] 61 percent of the interviewed entrepreneurs paid the ENVD. Half of these respondents believed that the overall tax burden had increased since the municipalities obtained some discretionary power over the ENVD. A similar percentage of entrepreneurs stated that if given the option, they would transfer to a simplified tax system.[6]

2.2   State financial support

Though state financial support for SMEs exists, the 2003 OPORA survey of Russian SMEs found that 42 percent indicated that one of the main obstacles preventing businesses from accessing state finance was lack of information about these programmes (see also Table 30.1).

The 2007 Federal Law set provisions for financial support of SMEs primarily in the form of state subsidies and state and municipal guarantee schemes. The federal budget funds are provided to Russian regions through tender schemes.

Currently based on the 2005 Resolution,[7] state subsidies are largely allocated to support export-oriented SMEs, in particular to subsidise up to 50 per cent of their

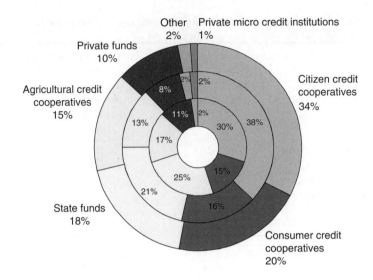

Note: The inner circle – 2003; the middle circle – 2004; the outer circle – 2005.

Source: RCSME (2007: 14).

Figure 30.1   *The typology of micro credit organizations by market share, 2003–05*

interest fees on loans issued to finance the production of goods and services for export; to subsidise up to 50 percent of costs related to certification of exported goods and so on.

Apart from case-by-case financial support, the new state policy sets provisions for developing infrastructure for SME financial support, namely, providing guarantee schemes and creating investment funds which attract venture capital to finance SMEs, and, finally, facilitating micro credit financing. The state participates in micro credit schemes through providing subsidies to regional and municipal funds, and subsidizing micro credit institutions such as consumer and agricultural credit cooperatives. However, as Figure 30.1 shows, alongside the dynamic development of the financial sector in Russia, the direct provision of funds by the government has shrunk over recent years, which paradoxically, is probably a good sign: given the largely unchecked discretionary power of officials coupled with corruption, state intervention is more likely to distort the competitive environment than provide real assistance to entrepreneurs that display a genuine potential for success.

Overall, the state policy towards SMEs can be regarded as largely declarative in nature, inefficient, lacking coordination and poorly implemented. Where implemented, these policies tend to be used to favour the businesses that have close ties to government officials to the detriment of businesses that do not. In addition, the legacy of corruption and favouritism inherited from the Soviet period results in many Russians simply accepting the lack of 'level playing field' for business development as the norm.[8]

3.   The environment for entrepreneurship and the state of SMEs
Similarly to many other transition economies, SMEs mushroomed in Russia at the beginning of 1990s. This development was a result of both the response to the availability

Table 30.2 Small and medium-sized enterprises in Russia, 2002–05

SME indicators	2002	2003	2004	2005
Number of SMEs (000s)	8000	8441	6212	6891
Share of SMEs as a % of total number of enterprises	93	94	92	92
Market share, as a % of total annual turnover	39	47	51	46

Note: SMEs are defined according to the standard EU employment size criterion.

Source: RCSME (2006).

of new market opportunities as well as the lack of governmental regulations. This growth stagnated in the second half of the 1990s due to increasing economic entry barriers, as the initial division of markets was finalized (Radaev, 2003).

Indeed, Broadman (2002) identifies an unprecedented degree of concentration of industrial output in Russia. He suggests that at the oblast level this figure could be well over 95 percent while in comparison, the average national four-firm concentration ratio is approximately 60 percent. This dominance of large vertically integrated enterprises poses a real threat to the further growth and development of Russian SMEs not only on a purely competitive sense but, perhaps even more importantly, through the preferential treatment (both legal and illegal) given to large enterprises by local authorities (see OPORA Russia, 2006).

A decrease in the number of SMEs in 2004 (see Table 30.2) can also be partly attributed to the fact that many individual entrepreneurs failed to re-register their businesses that year.[9] The contribution of Russian SMEs to the total annual turnover is moderately high and it is likely to be underestimated, given that there is a large proportion of small enterprises and individual entrepreneurs who operate in the shadow economy.

However, SMEs are not evenly distributed across Russia. In general, they are largely concentrated in the Central and North Western districts, whereas individual entrepreneurs and farmers prevail in the Southern district (see Figure 30.2). The uneven distribution for regions ranges from a mere 50 in the Republic of Ingushetiya to 186 in Moscow city, when measured per thousand of economically active population (RCSME, 2006).

3.1 Environment for entrepreneurship

In March 2005 OPORA together with VTsIOM, Russia's public opinion research centre, conducted a survey to study the conditions and factors affecting the development of small entrepreneurship (summarised in Table 30.3).

On the basis of the results of the survey, OPORA's experts constructed an aggregate index for each of the key indicator variables, characterizing the entrepreneurial climate, which allowed assessment of regions' positions in relation to one another. A ranking greater than 100 suggests that the situation is rather favourable, whereas a ranking below 100 suggests the opposite.[10]

As Table 30.3 shows, the majority of Russia's regions scored favourably (above 100) for the three top listed indicators, namely, financial situation, transactions costs and

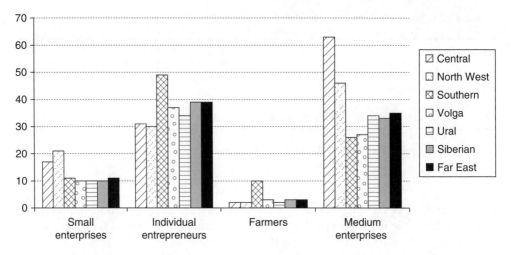

Note: SMEs are defined according to the standard EU employment size criterion.

Source: RCSME (2006).

Figure 30.2   Density of different types of SMEs per thousand of economically active population, by federal districts, 2005 (in physical units)

state support to SMEs, which seems to indicate that these three issues are not the main hindrances facing small entrepreneurs (OPORA Russia, 2006).

Specifically, with regards to the financial situation, more than half of the respondents characterized it as 'relatively favourable' and 'stable' in terms of the adequacy of financial resources to sustain business but, it is important to note, not enough to grow a business[11] (ibid.). This finding suggests that Russian entrepreneurs have learned to adapt and function within the existing 'restrictive' conditions relying on personal savings. About 54 percent of the respondents agreed that it was impossible to secure a bank loan. Most of these entrepreneurs still largely pursue a survival-oriented strategy which hampers further business development and growth. In addition, widespread corruption may prevent businesses from growing above a threshold level, as a means to avoid expropriation by officials, especially tax administrators (Barkhatova, 2000) and also to avoid engaging in 'illegal' practices (Aidis and Adachi, 2007). Sadly, many local authorities continue to use their power to extract funds from entrepreneurs treating them as a source of 'informal' income rather than viewing them as important sources of regional development.

In general, the poor quality of legislation, its weak enforcement, and lack of trust in courts are among the primary characteristics of inadequate legal conditions for entrepreneurial development (see also Aidis et al., 2008). In Russia, the OPORA survey data suggests the entrepreneurs search for other methods of protecting their interests and rights rather than appealing to courts. When asked what were their chances of winning their case in the court against administrative or municipal authorities, only 7 percent of the respondents were confident about a positive outcome.

Table 30.3   Evaluation of the entrepreneurial climate in Russia

Aspect of entrepreneurial climate	Brief description	Average value of the index for all regions	Number of regions with an index over 100
Financial situation	An entrepreneur's self-assessment of financial situation of the business	124.5	71
Transaction costs	Assessment of the costs related to dealing with authorities, including business regulation and corruption-related expenses	114.3	68
State support for small entrepreneurs	Assessment of the degree of state support to SMEs	113.2	57
Business motivation	Assessment of the conditions of business for SME and outlook, including business objectives, and financial results	93.5	27
Level of security	Assessment of the risk level of interaction with the authorities and criminal milieu	68.7	7
State of competitive environment	Market entry barriers	75.8	3
Access to property resources	Assessment of the accessibility of production space	55.3	3
Legal conditions	Adequacy of availability of legal (judicial) protection	47.6	0

Source: OPORA Russia (2006).

4.   Internationalization of entrepreneurs and SMEs: drivers and roadblocks

Only 13.1 percent of Russian SMEs are exporting, either directly or indirectly, according to the European Bank for Reconstruction and Development's Business Environment and Enterprise Performance Survey in 2005. This percentage is far below that of other transition countries in Central Europe, though it falls within a similar range with other Western CIS countries (see Figure 30.3).

This outcome may be partially explained by the negative impact of the appreciation of the rouble driven by revenue from oil and gas exports (that is, a form of the Dutch Disease). But a much greater portion of this situation is attributed to the weak institutional environment in Russia. Direct bureaucratic barriers on exporting are one of the two most serious barriers identified characterizing Russia's business environment (alongside licensing requirements) as found in the World Bank's (2007) 'Doing Business 2008' survey. On this dimension Russia ranks a dismal 155 out of 178 countries. In particular, this ranking is attributed to the high cost of exporting, which measures the fees associated with completing the procedures to export goods, including administrative fees for customs clearance and technical control, terminal handling charges and inland transport.[12]

Tovstiga et al. (2004) identify the internal institutional weakness of the Russian business environment as the key factor constraining Russian entrepreneurs from

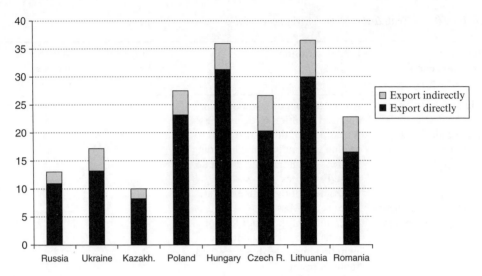

Source: EBRD-World Bank (2005), *Business Environment and Enterprise Performance Survey*, authors' calculations.

Figure 30.3   Percentage of small and medium enterprises exporting

internationalizing their operations. The authors also present two additional factors that limit Russian entrepreneurs from entering international markets: insufficient competences and differences in culture and business practices. Technologically advanced sectors could play an important role in exports, yet, Russia's base of active researchers has diminished significantly as throughout the 1990s scientists have left in search of higher wages and better working conditions. In addition, even those researchers who stayed and attempted to set up their own business often lacked the business skills needed to develop a successful business. In general, the inheritance of Soviet legacies ranging from the isolation of the Soviet economy from market mechanisms, to the development of negative practices such as a general acceptance of corruption, did not equip Russian entrepreneurs with adequate skills and understanding of how to succeed in the international business environment.

5.   Conclusion

Overall, despite numerous policy announcements oriented towards entrepreneurial development, entrepreneurs in Russia face a hostile business environment characterized by the weak rule of law and widespread corruption. As formal structures in Russia fail, they are complemented by informal networks, which form 'intangible assets' for certain well-connected entrepreneurs that allow them to overcome environmental barriers (Aidis et al., 2008). However, though some businesses learn to cope, the lack of a level playing field for businesses in general seriously distorts the development of a business environment. The crucial issue is not the existence and number of SMEs, but rather the fact that most of them have either no incentive to grow or are restricted in doing so given that if they are successful they face a serious risk of expropriation or forced takeover by those better connected to the intertwined economic and political structures of power.

Notes

1. Equivalent of self-employed.
2. The adoption of either a simplified tax system or a single tax is subject to meeting certain criteria set in the Tax Code. In essence, both the UNS and ENVD regimes introduce a single tax that replaces a number of other taxes.
3. Imputed income is the base yield – a conditional monthly income set for certain types of business activities by the federal law – multiplied by a physical indicator, characterizing a certain type of entrepreneurial activity (for example, parking area in square meters in the case of parking services).
4. The value of base yield needs to be multiplied by a corrective coefficient to allow for the differences in business conditions.
5. OPORA is Russia's NGO representing small and medium-sized enterprises.
6. The corrective coefficient is currently set between 0.005 and 1 that by all means should only decrease the single tax, given that the value of base yield is multiplied by this coefficient. Prior to the 2003 tax reform, the coefficient could have both a 'decreasing' and 'increasing' power. However, we anticipate that local authorities may pursue differential policies for SMEs, so that enterprises, which are eligible for a similar treatment in terms of the corrective coefficient in theory, may pay different tax rates in reality. This may explain the respondents' answers.
7. See the Resolution of the Council of Ministers No. 249 (22 April 2005 with additions and amendments as of 23 February 2007).
8. Within the Soviet Union, entrepreneurs were considered 'exploitative capitalists' and 'enemies of the state'. Even though the new economic system in Russia is based on private ownership and entrepreneurship, these negative entrepreneurship stereotypes continue to persist amongst the general population.
9. As of 1 January 2005, only 2.7 out of 4.8 million entrepreneurs re-registered their businesses. The vast majority of the rest, were in essence 'dead' and were taken off the register upon the completion of the re-registration.
10. For more detail on the methodology used by OPORA's experts and the results of the survey see OPORA Russia (2006).
11. See also Aidis and Adachi (2007).
12. Note that this measure excludes tariffs.

References

Aidis, R. and Y. Adachi (2007), 'Russia: firm entry and survival barriers', *Economic Systems*, **31**, 391–411.
Aidis, R., S. Estrin, and T. Mickiewicz (2008), 'Institutions and entrepreneurship development in Russia: a comparative perspective', *Journal of Business Venturing*, **23**(6), 656–72.
Barkhatova, N. (2000), 'Russian small business, authorities and the state', *Europe–Asia Studies*, **52**, 657–76.
Broadman, H. (2002) 'Unleashing Russia's business potential: lessons from the regions for building market institutions', *World Bank Discussion Paper*, No. 434, Washington, DC: World Bank.
Buccellato, T. and T. Mickiewicz (2008), 'Oil and gas: a blessing for few – hydrocarbons and within-region inequality in Russia', Centre for the Study of Economic and Social Change in Europe, Working Paper No. 80.
EBRD-World Bank (2005), *Business Environment and Enterprise Performance Survey (BEEPS)*, http://www.ebrd.com/country/sector/econo/surveys/beeps.htm (accessed 11 March 2009).
Gel'man, V. (2004), 'Introduction: the politics of local government in Russia: a framework for analysis', in A.B. Evans Jr and V. Gel'man (eds), *The Politics of Local Government in Russia*, Lanham, MD: Rowman & Littlefield.
Gerry, C., E. Nivorozhkin and J. Rigg (2008), 'The great divide: "Ruralisation" of poverty in Russia', *Cambridge Journal of Economics*, **32**(4), 593–607.
Glaeser, E., J. Scheinkman and A. Shleifer (2003), 'The injustice of inequality', *Journal of Monetary Economics*, **50**, 199–222.
OECD (2000), 'The development of entrepreneurship and enterprises in Russia: political principles and recommendations', http://www.rcsme.ru//libArt.asp?id=3520&r_id=129&l_id=1 (accessed 3 March 2008).
OPORA Russia (2006), 'Report on the results of all-Russian study: the conditions and factors affecting the development of small entrepreneurship in the regions of the Russian Federation', http://www.opora.ru (accessed 16 March 2008).
Radaev, V. (2003), 'The development of small entrepreneurship in Russia', in McIntyre and Dallago (eds) *SMEs in Transitional Economies*, Basingstoke: Palgrave, pp. 114–33.
RCSME (2006), 'The analysis of the role of SMEs in Russia', http://www.rcsme.ru/libArt.asp?id=4827 (accessed 3 March 2008).

RCSME (2007), 'The non-bank microfinance developments in Russia, 2003–05', http://www.rcsme.ru/libArt. asp?id=4811 (accessed 3 March 2008).

Russian Federation Federal Law (1995), 'On State Support of Small Enterprises in the Russian Federation', No. 88-FZ (14 June 1995), The Collection of Legislation of the Russian Federation, 1995, No. 25, art. 2343.

Russian Federation Federal Law (2007), 'On Development of Small and Medium Entrepreneurship in Russian Federation', No. 209-FZ (24 July 2007), published in *Rossiiskaya Gazeta*, 31 July 2007.

Taxation Code of the Russian Federation, No.117-FZ, Part II (5 August 2000 with additions and amendments as of 4 December 2007), The Collection of Legislation of the Russian Federation, 2000, No. 32, art. 3340.

Tovstiga, G., P. Den Hamer, V. Popova, I. Efimov, S. Moskalev and I. Bortnik (2004), 'Preparing Russian small innovative enterprises for international competitiveness: a scoping study', *Journal of International Entrepreneurship*, **2**, 89–108.

World Bank (2007), *Doing Business 2008*, Washington, DC: World Bank, http://www.doingbusiness.org/ documents/FullReport/2008/DB08_Full_Report.pdf (accessed 11 March 2009).

Zlobin, N., D. Skripichnikov, N. Smirnov, A. Terent'ev, O. Shestoperov, and A. Shestoperov (2005), 'A study of the impact of special tax regimes on SME development from 1 January 2003 and elaboration of suggestions for further improvement of the situation', http://www.rcsme.ru/libArt.asp?id=4646 (accessed 3 March 2008).

31 Saudi Arabia

Tim Rogmans

1 Introduction to Saudi Arabia

The Kingdom of Saudi Arabia was founded in 1932 and has been ruled by King Saud and his descendants since then. Saudi Arabia has a population of 27.6 million, including an expatriate workforce of nearly 6 million. The country's population is young and growing at a rapid rate of 3 percent per annum, with 38.2 percent of people being under 15 years of age. This makes education and tacking unemployment a major challenge, both today and in the next decade when millions of young people will enter the labor force.

Saudi Arabia holds approximately 25 percent of the world's proven oil reserves and is rich in other natural resources such as natural gas, iron ore, gold and copper. In order to reduce dependence on oil and to provide economic opportunities for its young population, Saudi Arabia has embarked on a major economic diversification and liberalization drive. Saudi Arabia joined the World Trade Organization (WTO) during 2005 and liberalized key economic sectors during the years preceding membership. Previously monopolistic sectors such as banking, insurance, telecommunications and real estate have now opened up to domestic and foreign competition.

With a per capita gross domestic product (GDP) of US$13 800, Saudi Arabia is a middle-income country. The economy is growing rapidly at a rate of between 4 and 5 percent per annum, owing to population growth, economic liberalization, foreign direct investment (FDI) and the construction of major economic cities across the country. Liberalization and growth are now beginning to get a momentum of their own. A booming real estate market is stimulating sectors such as construction and cement. The development of the petrochemicals sector, based on government support and the exploitation of a significant feedstock cost advantage, has resulted in SABIC becoming a global leader in petrochemicals. The encouragement of religious tourism is boosting growth in the construction, hotel and travel industries. The government is supporting the positive investment climate through its own investments in infrastructure, including roads, airports and a rail network. All these developments in turn are boosting the corporate banking sector and help to grow the local stock market. At the same time, Saudi consumers are catching up with their peers in other Gulf Cooperation Council (GCC) states in terms of consumption of products such as mobile telephony, Internet use, banking services and insurance. In short, the economy is growing and diversifying quickly, even though the share of oil in GDP remains in the 40–50 percent range.

The rapid growth in Saudi demand has been accompanied by an equally rapid growth in supply in many sectors of the economy. There has been a steady increase in the number of banks, both foreign owned and domestic. Insurance was traditionally the domain of the National Company for Co-operative Insurance (NCCI) and of brokers acting on behalf of foreign companies. Today, over 40 companies have obtained licenses to offer insurance products. The number of mobile phone operators has grown to three and competition on fixed telephony has been introduced. Concurrently, the stock market has grown in depth as a result of a steady stream of new initial public offerings (IPOs).

A major challenge for the government is to provide adequate employment opportunities for the young and rapidly growing population. Major government initiatives designed to increase employment opportunities include the construction of six economic cities in different parts of the country. These massive projects can be seen as government-led developments of clusters in a variety of industries, including petrochemicals, steel, glass, transport and health. Another key policy is that of Saudization of the workforce, imposing quotas on companies regarding the employment of nationals (minimum of 30 percent of the workforce) and supporting the development of the Saudi workforce through education and training. In this context, promoting entrepreneurship is another key opportunity to promote participation in the workforce.

Foreign direct investment is actively encouraged. In 2000, the Saudi Arabian General Investment Authority (SAGIA) was set up to facilitate foreign investment. Since the establishment of SAGIA, annual FDI inflows have increased tenfold. However, FDI is still relatively low compared to the size of the economy and is expected to continue to grow.

Finally, the government is investing massively in education at all levels. The latest manifestation is the King Abdullah University of Science and Technology (KAUST) which is scheduled to be opened on the Red Sea coast in September 2009 and benefits from a multi-billion dollar endowment.

Regionally, Saudi Arabia is committed to economic integration with the other GCC member states. In January 2008 the GCC single market was announced. The GCC states are still officially working toward a single currency by 2010, although many commentators doubt whether this goal will be realized by the announced date. Saudi Arabia, like its Gulf neighbors, has pegged its currency to the US dollar. With the decline in both the value of the dollar and US interest rates, Saudi authorities have had to decrease interest rates to maintain the dollar peg. As a result, inflation has been increasing and speculation is intensifying as to when Saudi Arabia will revalue or possibly float its currency.

Politically, the country's large geographic size and large population enhance its influence in the region and beyond. Saudi Arabia's importance is reinforced by the role the country plays in the Islamic world, being the birthplace of the prophet Muhammed and the home of the holy cities Mecca and Medina. Religious tourism continues to increase rapidly, supported by large investments in property and infrastructure in the western part of the country.

On the whole, the Saudi economy is characterized by rapidly growing demand and supply, with many sectors still dominated by large local companies despite increasing competition from multinationals. The main sectors where SMEs play a significant role are agriculture and construction. The share of oil in GDP remains high, despite rapid growth in other sectors of the economy.

2 Government policy on SMEs and entrepreneurship
Saudi Arabia operates as a quasi-market economy with the state playing a key role in managing economic activity. As the recipient of the country's oil revenues, the state has a major influence on economic affairs, not only through regulation but also through its expenditure and investment activities.

The government's eighth five-year plan (2005–09) is the first plan with a number of specific targets and objectives, within the framework of a long-term development strategy for the country. Overall economic objectives include the raising of the standard of living and improving the quality of life. This objective includes the specific aim of doubling per capita GDP between 2004 and 2024, which, given anticipated population growth rates, implies an annual real GDP growth rate of 6.6 percent.

The desired growth in GDP and living standards is to come to a large extent from growth in the private sector. Economic targets for the period 2004–09 include the increase of the contribution of the private sector from 54.6 percent of GDP to 57.5 percent of GDP and increasing private investment expenditure at an annual rate of 10.4 percent. Employment in the private sector is set to increase by 2.2 percent per year.

In order to reach these objectives, the government aims to improve the overall investment climate. Regarding SMEs in particular, the plan explicitly recognizes the role SMEs play in economic development. Small and medium enterprises are credited with attracting foreign investment, promoting non-oil exports and contributing effectively to a more balanced distribution of activities in different regions. The plan identifies the main obstacles to reaching development goals through SME activity as the time-consuming procedures in setting up a business and difficulties in obtaining funds from financial institutions. Other constraints on SME activity listed in the five-year plan include the lack of skilled labor and efficient management. The government recognizes that these obstacles need to be addressed and a number of policies are designed to improve the situation.

Government policies include technical support and training in order to meet the labor requirements of SMEs through the Resources Development Fund. The Fund has been active in organizing training to enhance critical business skills of the young Saudi population, for example through a program to develop business and information technology (IT) skills in cooperation with IBM . Another key initiative is the establishment of specialized centers by the Saudi Council of Chambers of Commerce and Industry that aim to support entrepreneurs.

The government also recognizes that access to capital can be an obstacle to the growth of entrepreneurship. A number of specialized financial institutions have been set up by the government to facilitate the availability of finance to entrepreneurs. The Saudi Industrial Development Fund offers loans and consultancy support to investors in Saudi industry. The Fund has established a special facility of US$50 million as a credit guarantee scheme with the aim of facilitating the availability of funds to SMEs. The Saudi Arabia Agricultural Bank (established 1963) provides interest-free loans to farmers in order to buy machinery, agricultural equipment and other supplies. The Real Estate Development Fund (established 1974) provides loans for homes for Saudi citizens and loans for investment purposes. The Public Investment Fund (established 1971) provides financing for commercial projects for which the private sector lacks sufficient capital or knowledge.

Another key government institution in the Saudi economy is the Saudi Arabian General Investment Authority (SAGIA). The Authority was set up to promote foreign direct investment into Saudi Arabia by providing information, investment services and a single window for administrative procedures to foreign investors. Its mission is 'to create a pro-business environment, provide comprehensive services to investors and foster investment opportunities in energy, transportation and knowledge based industries'.

Table 31.1   How easy is it in Saudi Arabia?

Ease of . . .	2008 rank	2007 rank	Change in rank
Starting a business	23	33	+ 10
Dealing with licenses	36	159	+ 123
Employing workers	47	46	−1
Registering property	40	31	−9
Getting credit	48	62	+14
Protecting investors	50	48	−2
Paying taxes	7	6	−1
Trading across borders	33	45	+12
Enforcing contracts	136	135	−1
Closing a business	79	88	+9

The Authority's activities have been extended to include support for domestic business, including SMEs. It has centers in each region of the country, in which it provides free consulting, support services and information on investment opportunities. In 2006, SAGIA, in partnership with Bahrain-based Venture Capital Bank and investment house Global Emerging Markets, established a US$100 million venture capital investment company. The bank's chief executive officer (CEO) Abdullatif Mohammed Janahi, commented: 'Despite the strategic importance of venture capital and SMEs to the growth of the economy, very few financial institutions and other funding sources in Saudi Arabia have focused on such opportunities' (*Arab News*, 2006).

In addition to finance from government-sponsored institutions, the number of domestic and foreign banks has been increasing. Banks are encouraged by the government to provide loans to SMEs and many see this as a growth sector. The stock market has deepened significantly over the past decade, with a large number of successful IPOs in various industries, thereby providing an exit route for successful entrepreneurs and venture capitalists. Finally, a growing number of private equity funds have been setting up operations in the GCC region and are looking for opportunities to invest in growing and under-capitalized business.

The results of the government policies on SMEs and entrepreneurship are to some extent reflected in the country's scores in the 'Doing Business' rankings, compiled by the World Bank and the International Finance Corporation (2008). The key measures from this survey are given in Table 31.1.

Out of a total of 178 countries, Saudi Arabia ranks above the global average on many of the key dimensions of relevance to entrepreneurs. The tax environment is very favorable to business, due to the country's oil revenues which result in massive budget surpluses for the government. In line with other countries in the region there are no taxes on personal income or corporate profits except for the Zakat, the charitable contribution that everyone is obliged to make under Islamic law.

In terms of the procedures, time and cost required to start a business, the country ranks better than its regional peers and worse than the average of Organisation for Economic Co-operation and Development (OECD) countries. One key advantage for Saudi entrepreneurs is that there is no minimum paid-up capital for a new enterprise, but of course this possibility is also open to entrepreneurs in many other countries if they register as sole traders. In several cases the data needs to be interpreted with great care. For example, dealing with licenses has improved greatly according to the survey. However, it appears that the improvement is based on a single example of obtaining licenses required to build a warehouse and it is not clear to what extent this improvement is generalizable across the economy. On the whole, there is still considerable effort to be made in streamlining documentation procedures. Another area where the data can mislead relates to the topic of registering property. Although it is true that the act of registering one's property is relatively easy, at the same time some reports estimate that ownership of 20 percent of the nation's land is disputed. Many people who bought land found out later that others have claims to the same property. In this sense, the country's poor performance in enforcing contracts is more relevant than the ease of registering property.

3   The economic and sociocultural environment for entrepreneurship

Given the rapid economic growth and the government's liberalization and diversification drive, the economic environment for entrepreneurship is very positive. The sociocultural environment is more difficult to analyse given the absence of research carried out on this topic in Saudi Arabia.

The growth of the Saudi economy, results in increased demands for good and services and an unprecedented availability of funds for investment. This positive economic environment for entrepreneurs is balanced by some structural changes in the economy which make life more difficult for SMEs. As a consequence of entry into the WTO, the country is opening up to foreign competition. Foreign players investing in Saudi Arabia are usually large multinationals with sizable financial resources, economies of scale, major brands and strong marketing skills. This new competition makes it more difficult for SMEs to flourish and grow. At the same time, strong domestic companies have been acquiring smaller players to gain scale in order to face up to foreign competition. As a result, several key sectors which have traditionally been breeding grounds for SMEs are now becoming more concentrated. Such sectors include construction, property development, agriculture and retail. Therefore, without specific incentives from the government, SMEs face an uphill battle against the market power of a handful of dominant players in each industry.

The negative side of the rapid economic growth, the currency peg to the dollar and the associated low interest rate environment is that inflation is running high at around 10 percent per annum. The inflationary environment affects SMEs in particular since they lack the pricing power to make up for the increases in their input prices.

With respect to the entrepreneurial culture, the available evidence suggests that the environment for entrepreneurs is not very supportive. In 2007, Intel's chairman Craig Barrett cited progress on his company's venture capital initiative in the region was slow due to the lack of a strong entrepreneurial culture in the region. Saudi Arabia in particular is a conservative country and it takes time for people to adapt to an economic environment in which entrepreneurial behavior is accepted and rewarded.

One major obstacle to the growth of SMEs is the severe skills shortage in many areas that are critical to entrepreneurs, particularly in the fields of general management, accounting and marketing. Although management education is expanding quickly, there is no evidence of university courses specifically targeted to potential entrepreneurs. The local Chambers of Commerce do provide some training for entrepreneurs, but much more is needed to unleash the entrepreneurial spirit of the population and provide the confidence and skills for young people to set up a company.

Female entrepreneurs face additional obstacles in terms of the professions they can enter and the ways in which they can operate. Although female participation in education is increasing, this has yet to be translated into greater participation among women in entrepreneurial activity.

In a rare article on entrepreneurship in the region, Florence Eid concludes that throughout the Middle East North Africa region governments must 'promote the creation of parallel educational programs to cultivate entrepreneurial skills at all levels of society' (2006: 115). Given the region's oil wealth, she concludes that it is not the availability of funds itself that is an obstacle but rather the 'channels that link finance with promising entrepreneurs' (ibid.).

Given this lack of both an entrepreneurial tradition and an entrepreneurial infrastructure, the role of incubators in encouraging and facilitating start-ups is potentially very great. Besides the support provided by the regional Chambers of Commerce, the main organization of note that provides such support is the Centennial Fund. Established in 2005, the Centennial Fund is the Saudi Arabian chapter of the Youth Business International organization, which supports young people in becoming entrepreneurs. By concentrating its efforts on young people outside the big cities, the organization aims to help those most in need of support. The Fund's main services include mentoring during the process of developing business plans and during the first three years of the company's existence, as well as the provision of interest free loans of up to US$53 000. In addition, the Fund provides access to other services such as training, consulting, IT and telecommunications. During 2007, the Fund supported over 400 entrepreneurs in setting up a business. Although this number is impressive in absolute terms, the need to help a far larger group of entrepreneurs of all ages clearly exists.

In order to make such support as effective as possible, more research into the attitudes of Saudi citizens to risk taking is needed to better understand the sociocultural environment. In the neighboring United Arab Emirates, the Global Entrepreneurship Monitor study (GEM) (Preiss and McCrohan, 2006) found that fear of failure is a major obstacle to entrepreneurial activity among the Emirati population. The consequences of failure are multifaceted. First, failure has the potential to place the family under unwanted scrutiny and lead to loss of face within their community. Furthermore, the consequences of insolvency and bankruptcy are punishing and onerous. As a result, the fear of failure overpowers the desire to even attempt the creation of a new venture, which by its very nature has higher risk than a career in a corporate entity. In addition, the appeal of a government position with all its attenuated career prospects and retirement benefits often appeal more than attempting a risk-oriented venture.

It would be useful to investigate to what extent this or other factors play a role in Saudi Arabia in order to determine which support policies are likely to have the greatest positive impact on local entrepreneurship. In fact, research into these topics has been earmarked as a priority by the Centennial Fund, which planned to carry out the first Global Entrepreneurship Monitor study in the country.

Attitudes to risk may have matured with the recent boom and bust of the stock market. The Saudi stock market is dominated by retail investors with short time horizons. Initially, many Saudi Arabian citizens were attracted to stock market investments during 2004 and 2005, especially since the spiraling prices led to perceptions there was no real risk involved. The severe stock market correction of 2006 has made many people experience risk in a hands-on way. Although no research has been done on the topic, these experiences may encourage people to try to improve their chances of success by investing in their own businesses rather than in quoted companies.

4   Internationalization of entrepreneurs and SMEs: drivers and roadblocks

There is very little evidence of internationalization of Saudi Arabian entrepreneurs. Around 90 percent of Saudi Arabia's exports of US\$204.5 billion (2006) are petroleum related. Although there are a number of large Saudi firms that are expanding internationally with significant success, it is debatable whether these can be called entrepreneurial ventures, given their size, length of experience and government ties. For example, SABIC has developed from a national champion in the petrochemicals field to one of the top chemical companies in the world. Similarly, Prince Alwaleed bin Talal has expanded his investments from a domestic base to a global portfolio of investments. The actively managed companies in his portfolio, such as Kingdom Hotels, expand aggressively across the globe. These companies can help to motivate managers in other companies to internationalize, but they are quite far removed from the positions of individual entrepreneurs who may be looking for role models.

For SMEs, it is clear that the home market is relatively large and flourishing, thereby providing plenty of domestic opportunity. Many companies still operate within only one region of the country, as is the case with nearly all cement companies and many construction firms. The need to expand abroad is therefore less than for entrepreneurs from smaller countries in the region, for example from neighbouring Oman or Qatar.

Regarding potential obstacles to internationalization, the data from the 'Doing Business' report provides some insight. The score for the number of documents required to export and the number of days needed to complete the export of goods are both better than the average scores for the region, but worse than the average score for OECD countries. The cost to export a container is in line with the regional and OECD average. On the whole, it is clear that export procedures could be somewhat simplified. However, these procedures do not appear to constitute a major impediment to the internationalization of SMEs, especially compared to regional competitors.

The noted lack of management and marketing skills is probably a bigger obstacle for companies looking to expand nationally, regionally or globally. Although business education is gaining in prominence, nearly all university courses are in Arabic, thereby creating a strong need for English language training to enable SMEs to capture international opportunities. Saudi Arabian students who have studied abroad often find more attractive opportunities at large and established companies or in government.

A logical first step on the road to internationalization for Saudi Arabian firms is to export and operate in countries that form part of the Gulf Cooperation Council (GCC). The GCC includes Saudi Arabia, Oman, Qatar, Bahrain, Kuwait and the United Arab Emirates among its members. Although the GCC Common Market was announced for 1 January 2008 and monetary union is still officially planned for 2010, many barriers remain to doing business within the region. Still, the GCC does provide a springboard for Saudi companies wanting to internationalize step by step. The countries share a common language, common religion and have some cultural similarities. The shared dollar peg also removes the day-to-day exchange rate risk of trading. Hence it is no surprise that many SMEs start to internationalize by exporting to neighboring GCC members and never move beyond.

5   Conclusions

Saudi Arabia has a huge need for entrepreneurs and at the same time offers unprecedented potential. Entrepreneurs are needed to diversify the economy, provide the population with goods and services, and provide employment opportunities to the country's rapidly growing labor force. The millions of young people entering their twenties can no longer rely on the government to provide jobs. Although employment in both the industrial and service sectors will grow, this will be not nearly enough to absorb the growth of the labor force. Only a large and vibrant entrepreneurial class will be able to provide attractive employment opportunities and support the growth towards a more knowledge-based economy.

The government has realized the importance of promoting entrepreneurship, but much remains to be done. The majority of support provided by the government is for private enterprise in general rather than for SMEs in particular. Given the industrialization strategy the country has chosen, many of the business opportunities will naturally be for large enterprises. However, the people considering entrepreneurship and the SME sector are the ones who need most support.

Entrepreneurship in the Kingdom of Saudi Arabia is an under-researched topic. Given the importance the government attached to economic growth and job creation, further research could help to identify the specific barriers to entrepreneurship and innovation in the country. On this basis, government policy could be further targeted to those policy measures and activities with the highest expected impact.

References

Arab News (2006), '$100 million venture capital investment firm planned in Saudi', 21 February.
Eid, Florence (2006), 'Recasting job creation strategies in developing regions: A role for entrepreneurial finance', *Journal of Entrepreneurship*, **15**, 115.
Preiss, Kenneth and Declan McCrohan (2006), 'Mohammed Bin Rashid Establishment For Young Business Leaders – GEM United Arab Emirates: entrepreneurship in the United Arab Emirates in 2006', College of Business Sciences, Zayed University, Vol. 1. No. 1. Abu Dhabi: Zayed University.
World Bank and the International Finance Corporation (2008), 'Doing business', www.doingbusiness.org (accessed 2 January 2008).

32 Singapore
Wee-Liang Tan and So-Jin Yoo

1. Introduction

Perched on an island spanning some 699 sq. km. with a resident population of 3.6 million, it is inconceivable that Singapore could be one of Asia's leading economies. In 2007 it had a gross domestic product (GDP) of S$243 168.8 and a per capita GDP of S$52 994. It ranks first as the most cost-competitive place for business in the KPMG Competitive Alternatives Study 2006, as the world's easiest place to do business in the World Bank report: 'Doing Business 2007: How to Reform' (www.edb.gov.sg) and seventh in World Competitiveness Report 2007 (http://www.gcr.weforum.org). Entrepreneurs featured in its economic development, together with multinational corporations. Entrepreneurship continues to remain an important part of Singapore's competitiveness, especially as she strives to be a global hub with an external wing to its economy.

Entrepreneurs in the private sector contributed to the development of Singapore's economy in the colonial days under British rule. With self-government in 1959, public sector entrepreneurship played a greater role (Tsao and Low, 1990). The advent of Singapore's first recession in 1986 brought to the fore the need for local entrepreneurship. In a master plan for economic restructuring, the Economic Committee charting Singapore's new economic directions placed emphasis on the development of entrepreneurship and local enterprises (Singapore Economic Committee, 1986). Until the recession, the emphasis had solely been on the attraction of foreign multinationals, with local enterprises playing second fiddle as subcontractors for these multinational companies. With this realization, a small and medium enterprise (SME) Master Plan was issued in 1987 to develop a multi-agency network tasked with developing and implementing the entrepreneurship infrastructure for Singapore (Tan et al., 2000). The second SME master plan (SME 21) was issued in 2001 with policy measures being laid to help SMEs fully embrace the knowledge-based economy and their structural issues such as weak entrepreneurial culture, insufficient management know-how and professionalism, shortage of professional and technical manpower, insufficient use of technology, outmoded and unproductive methods of operation, limited ability to tap economies of scale and a small domestic market.

With the policy measures introduced by both SME master plans, the SME community has become a key pillar of Singapore's economy, contributing 42 percent of the GDP, and employing more than half of the workforce. As a group, the top 500 SMEs have increased total turnover by 30 percent to S$13.5 billion and almost doubled net profits to S$630 million during 2002–07. It is hoped that Singapore SMEs will be a source of entrepreneurship and innovation, a base of strong supporting industries and strategic partners for foreign SMEs and MNCs and manufacturers of high value-added products, and global providers of professional services in the future.

2.   Government assistance

The development of the Singapore government's policies towards the small and medium-sized enterprises (SMEs) today can be traced back to Singapore's independence since the mid-1960s when Singapore's position as a regional entrepôt was threatened by the rapid developments of the competing ports of her neighbors. Singapore was then a largely untrained small population of 1.6 million lacking natural resources. Singapore then decided to leapfrog the industrialization process by focusing on a production-based economy. Singapore induced foreign direct investments attracting foreign multinational corporations (MNCs) to make huge capital investments locally through the building of factories to support manufacturing activities. Education at all levels, particularly technical education, had to be established so that trained manpower could support the export manufacturing activities of the foreign MNCs. As history shows, Singapore's industrialization strategy was successful.

Although the successful gearing up of the workforce met the labor requirements of the MNCs, the government policies seemingly neglected the growth of the local SMEs. More than two decades since the mid-1980s Singapore has experienced rapid industrialization which enabled the country to establish a niche in the world economy as a cost-effective international manufacturing center. In order to move the economy onto a higher plane of development, the government, through the Economic Development Board (EDB), wanted to develop Singapore into a major node in global business and a complete business center.

In order to allow Singapore's economy to encompass the full spectrum of business activities – from research and development to design and product development, production, marketing, distribution, finance and international business management – the promotion of local SMEs became increasingly important. Thus, instead of focusing purely on export manufacturing, the development of the local enterprises became a key component of the Singapore's strategy to develop the services and manufacturing sectors as the twin engines of growth.

The key feature of the first SME Master Plan was the formation of a multi-agency network. The agencies are formed by the public and private sectors including government agencies, chambers of commerce, financial institutions, venture capitalists and tertiary institutions. The SME 21 master plan furthers prior achievements, extending and refining the measures and incentives to the context of the new economy.

The lead agency for SME development is Standards, Productivity and Innovation Board [SPRING Singapore]. SPRING Singapore created the First Stop that any SME could call for assistance. This first stop has been augmented by the launch of EnterpriseOne, which stands for 'One Network for Enterprises'. The portal at www.business.gov.sg is a government-wide initiative managed by SPRING in partnership with business chambers and industry associations. It aims to enhance SMEs' access to business information, Government e-services from more than 30 agencies, and advisory and consultative services.[1]

In terms of task assistance, SPRING Singapore has its focus on championing enterprise formation and growth – through its network of valued relationships and resources – to nurture a host of dynamic and innovative Singapore enterprises.[2] Besides lending assistance to local enterprises with the preparation for quality certification and the provision of third-verification services, SPRING works with its partners to strengthen the business

Table 32.1   Financing options for SMEs

Loan	Characteristics
Factoring loan	SMEs can apply for a factoring loan if they have trade debts
Fixed asset loan	Long-term loans for buying fixed assets such as land, buildings, fixtures, heavy equipment and industrial machinery.
Hire purchase loan	To be used for vehicles, furniture, computers, equipment and industrial machinery.
Trade financing and insurance	A combination of loans, letters of credit and insurance is possible.
Working capital loan	This short-term loan helps to improve cash flow quickly.

infrastructure, review rules and regulations to cut red tape, and facilitate better access for enterprises to financing and other resources such as land and labor. The resources it provides come in the form of tax incentives, double taxation relief, investment allowances, overseas investment relief and the conferring of the pioneer status to local companies. The SME Development Survey in 2005 reflected a dramatic turnaround when 48 percent of SMEs indicated that it is now easier to get funding for their business. With more options available today, SMEs are also moving away from the traditional financing options such as overdrafts. The latest SME Development Survey showed an upward trend of companies accessing term loans.[3] Government loan schemes such as the Micro Loan Programme and Local Enterprise Finance Scheme (LEFS) managed by SPRING Singapore have been helpful to SMEs. The former offers very small businesses an unsecured loan of up to $50 000 which is useful for funding daily operations and upgrading equipment. The LEFS on the other hand, is a fixed interest rate loan of up to S$15 million to help larger, expanding SMEs. From 2004 to 2008 SPRING has extended some S$3 billion in loans to 12 400 SMEs under LEFS, and S$326 million to more than 9000 micro enterprises under the Micro Loan Programme. In order to stimulate bank financing during the last economic downturn, SPRING bore 80 percent of the default risk for both schemes. The risk is shared equally by SPRING and partner financial institutions. Table 32.1 shows the range of other financing options available to SMEs. Other startup financing schemes are available but, because of space constraints, the reader is referred to information available on the SPRING Singapore website (www.spring.gov.sg).

The Infocomm Development Authority (IDA) has several assistance schemes available aiming to provide the necessary infocomm infrastructure and technology standards, and to promote the adoption of infocomm technology in SMEs. The infocomm Enterprise Programme (iEP) is a sector-wide partnership programme assisting infocomm SMEs in developing their capabilities and intellectual property (IP) to implement and deliver large-scale, sector-wide projects.[4] Through participation in the iEP Programme, infocomm SMEs can enhance their capabilities to undertake large-scale, sector-wide infocomm projects by creating new IP and gaining increased recognition.

SPRING Singapore also provides consultancy services to SMEs by working closely with industry associations and chambers of commerce to jointly set up centers to provide convenient and informative channel for SMEs to obtain professional advice and consultation on business and operational issues. Examples include the SPRING Design Advisory, the SPRING Management Guidance Centre and the SPRING Diagnostic Center. The Enterprise Development Centre at the Singapore Manufacturers' Federation (EDC@ SMa) allows SMEs to assess their performance, identify areas for improvement and benchmark their performance against a global standard all in one location.[5] The new EDC@SMa will also provide various consultancy services at affordable rates. In the area of financial advisory services, SMEs looking at financing their entry into new markets or corporate finance requirements for initial public offering (IPO) listing can enjoy the expertise of a chief financial officer at a fraction of the cost of hiring one. Besides the above, EDC@SMa will also provide consultancy services to meet the unique needs of the manufacturing community. Consultancy services available include risk-based safety management, energy consumption management, and manufacturing automation management.

The Agency for Science Technology and Research (A*STAR) fosters scientific research and the exploitation of technology through incubator units. Similarly, the Jurong Town Coporation (JTC) continues to provide industrial space and incubator space as well. The government agency responsible for internationalization of SMEs and the incentives available are discussed in section 4.

3.   Sociocultural environment

Face and shame of failure
Entrepreneurship literature reveals general agreement that entrepreneurship flourishes where environmental conditions are most favorable. The environmental factors important to the decision to start a business include examples of entrepreneurial action, knowledge about entrepreneurship, societal attitudes towards entrepreneurship, salary and taxation levels, availability of venture capital, availability of personnel and supporting services, accessibility of customers, accessibility to universities, opportunities to take advantage of interim consulting and general economic conditions. These environmental factors can be categorized as sociocultural factors, economic factors, governmental factors, and individual differences.

In a study of the effect of sociocultural factors on entrepreneurship intentions across 13 countries including Singapore, it is found that at the cultural level, social status of entrepreneurs and possible shame from a business failure were better indicators of interest in entrepreneurship in East Asian rather than in Anglo countries (Begley and Tan, 2001). First, the findings indicated that the greater the social status accorded entrepreneurs, the greater the likelihood that there would be interest in starting a business. Second, the shame of failure was anticipated to have an opposite effect. In East Asian countries, including Singapore, face featured in that, unlike in the Anglo-Saxon countries where shame associated with failure did not negatively correlate with entrepreneurship intention, the shame associated with failure did influence intentions negatively. Hence, in Singapore the higher the shame associated with failure, the less likely individuals tended to engage in start-ups.

Since the time the research was conducted, much has been done in Singapore to address the issue of failure. At all levels of society there have been efforts to change the sociocultural perceptions of business failure. The laws with respect to bankruptcy have also changed to remove the draconian measures involving shame and the reluctance to permit bankrupts to be reinstated in society. A new award (Phoenix Award) was created to recognize businessmen who had failed but rebuilt their businesses or new businesses. Television programs have brought to the fore of attention the stories of entrepreneurs.

These developments, together with the economic conditions in the late 1990s after the Asian financial crisis, have encouraged greater interest on the part of the younger generation to consider entrepreneurship. The 2006 Global Entrepreneurship Monitor Singapore Report indicates that starting a business is perceived as a good career choice by 48.2 percent of Singaporeans (Wong et al., 2007). Efforts have also been made to encourage the development of entrepreneurial talent at the tertiary institutions. Funds have been channeled to the institutions of higher learning to be used as seed capital for interesting ventures. The aim of the financing is not the return on investment, although if they prove to be successful it would be welcomed, but to provide opportunities for experimentation. Not all applications are successful but the presence of this funding has inspired new student start-ups under the Entrepreneurship Talent Development Fund. According to the 2006 GEM Singapore Report (Wong et al., 2007), the adult population in Singapore has less positive attitudes towards entrepreneurship than those from the 22 GEM 2006 OECD nations. In 2006, 65.6 percent as compared to 61.5 percent in 2005 perceived that fear of failure was not a deterrent for business start-ups. This percentage is on par with the 65 percent average for all 22 GEM OECD nations. While the attitudes were positive and the social status of entrepreneurs was high (54.1 percent of Singaporeans believed that new business success was accorded with high status), the intention to start was still low at 11.8 percent (expects to start a business within next three years) with a high of 17 percent in 2005.

Social capital
Like many other countries in Asia, most of the SMEs are family-based businesses, predominantly Chinese in ethnicity, reflecting the population demographics in Singapore where 77 percent are Chinese and are involved in various industries like food, transport, traveling, retailing and clothing. Singapore's other races are also represented among the SMEs from the Malay and Indian ethnicities. A study by the Asian Productivity Organization (Tan, 2006) found that social capital played an important role in the ways that businesses operated. As part of a second phase to the research for the Asian Productivity Organization,[6] Singapore SMEs capitalize on their social capital to advance their businesses including business ventures overseas. This social capital takes the form of family members, business networks, trust and business norms within the businesses. The SMEs capitalized on their social capital to extend the businesses and to professionalize. They were not entrenched or hindered in any way by the social capital. The research examined whether social capital assisted or hindered productivity in the firms. The networks and trust within the family firms and their business associates enabled the firms to grow. Social capital will be a key ingredient in entrepreneurship in Singapore.

4. Internationalization of Singapore SMEs
In the early colonial days prior to independence, Singapore SMEs in an economy that began as primarily a port were engaged in import and export in trade.

Internationalization in the more complex forms such as the establishment of wholly owned subsidiaries abroad would have occurred in the regional countries either close to home like in Malaysia or where there were family ties in Indonesia or in Hong Kong. The reliance on branches of the family can be seen in the growth of businesses like Eu Yang Sang, which began in Malaysia, later extended into Singapore, was restructured and headquartered in Singapore with branches in Hong Kong. The overseas units were started by family members and a later son from a subsequent generation, Richard, took over control of the business. These forms of internationalization required resources and involved risk. It was usually in the purview of larger businesses.

Internationalization can take a number of other forms as well. Small and medium enterprises have long-term cooperative arrangements involving supply or procurement of goods. After all, most Singapore businesses are engaged in trade, and the extension of their goods and services to overseas markets is natural when faced with saturation of the relative small domestic markets. Others sourced for their goods or services in the neighboring countries where the costs of production are lower or where trades disappeared from Singapore with rapid industrialization. Yet, some began manufacturing in partnership or alliances with others. However, there was no public policy to encourage local enterprises to venture abroad until the big push in 1994.

Establishing Singapore's external wing
The impetus for SMEs to venture abroad came in a big way from the Singapore government. In 1993, the Singapore government convened a regionalization forum to explore the need for, the means needed, and the measures required for Singapore businesses to extend Singapore's external wing of its economy. The forum led to the introduction of tax incentives, assistance programs and innovative measures to assist Singapore businesses to go regional. Tax incentives took the form of tax credits for selected international activities and participation in international exhibitions and trade missions. Training programs and research initiatives were established to further the regionalization effort. Business missions were arranged by the government agencies to facilitate cross border investments. International conferences were held in Singapore aimed at promoting business matching, which was arranged at special events overseas. In addition to the face-to-face business matching, virtual business matching was made possible over the Internet to assist firms to venture overseas through strategic alliances via the Partner Singapore portal which is currently accessible at the website of the lead agency, International Enterprise Singapore (IE Singapore). The IE Singapore website has links to resources under the headings: Venture Abroad Guide, Market Info, Industry Info, Business Resources, Trade Statistics, Networking Platforms, and so on (see http://www.iesingapore.gov.sg/). Current government incentives take the form of grants, loans, tax incentives and equity financing (see Table 32.2). A perusal of the schemes available demonstrates the multi-agency approach adopted in Singapore.

Initially the focus was on regional economies. Since then local enterprises have been encouraged to go further afield – to go global. The Singapore government's strategy is to leverage on globalization by positioning Singapore as a global SME and entrepreneurship hub. To this end it seeks to develop a pro-business environment where enterprises can succeed in launching and developing their business operations seamlessly, upgrading their capabilities and business innovation levels, and expanding their operations beyond Singapore.

In addition to the programs helping SMEs to equip with the knowledge, skills and

Table 32.2   Internationalization incentives

Grants	
International Business Fellowship (IBF) Programme. Manpower development grants available to defray the costs of training a potential employee or sending executives for business-related training/attachment in the Asian region	International Enterprise Singapore [IE (Singapore)]
International Partners Programme (iPartners). Financial assistance to support the forming of strategic alliances among Singapore-based companies to penetrate overseas markets	IE (Singapore)
Internationalization Road-mapping Programme (IRP). Grants of up to S$300 000 to engage consultants to develop strategic internationalization plans and roadmaps	IE (Singapore)
Malaysia Singapore Third Country Business Development Fund (MSBF). A grant for Singaporean and Malaysian companies to collaborate in feasibility studies and joint missions to third countries	IE (Singapore)
Market Development Scheme (MDS). Travel grants of up to S$20 000 a year to market 'Made-by-Singapore' movies, television programmes and digital content at overseas trade fairs and missions	Media Development Authority of Singapore (MDA)
Promotion of Singapore Design Overseas Partnership Programme (OPP). Design companies can obtain a grant for taking part in prestigious international design events.	Design Singapore Council
Tax incentives	
Double Deduction (DD) for Overseas Investment Development Expenditure. Tax breaks for investment in overseas markets	IE (Singapore)
Double Tax Deduction (DTD) for Market Development, Master Franchising and Master Intellectual Property Licensing	IE (Singapore)
Overseas Enterprise Incentive (OEI). Approved overseas investment projects enjoy tax exemption on qualifying income for up to 10 years	IE (Singapore)
Double Tax Deduction (DTD) for Inbound Tourism Promotion. Tax breaks for participating in tourism trade fairs and missions overseas	Singapore Tourism Board (STB)
Double Tax Deduction (DTD) for Local Trade Exhibitions. Tax breaks for participation in international tourism trade fairs held in Singapore.	STB
Equity financing	
Enterprise Fund. Funds to grow overseas business or venture. S$1–3 million in equity funding available under the Enterprise Fund	IE (Singapore)
Scheme for Co-investment in Exportable Content (SCREEN). Co-investment projects in television, film, animation, games and publishing projects involving two or more parties, including international partners	MDA
Loans	
Internationalization Finance (IF) Scheme. Need funds to expand overseas? Get a loan of up to S$15 million to buy fixed assets and finance your overseas projects or orders	IE (Singapore)

Sources: Websites of the Singapore government agencies: Design Council Singapore (www.designsingapore. org); International Enterprise Singapore (www.iesingapore.gov.sg); Media Development Authority of Singapore (www.mda.gov.sg); Singapore Tourism Board (www.stb.gov.sg); and SPRING (www.spring.gov. sg), accessed 18 March 2007.

capability to venture overseas, to provide the financial resources needed, and to link them to prospective partners, the Singapore government has sought to develop its external economy by creating Singapore-style industrial and science parks overseas. These efforts came under Singapore's Regionalization 2000 program, through which Singapore taps the dynamism of other Asia-Pacific economies by establishing Singapore-styled business environments in the industrial parks. Embarking on this strategy allows the Singapore government to identify and develop provinces and sites in the region, and to use these Singapore-developed sites as locations to access resources and markets. The intent is to derive complementary benefits for Singapore firms and the host countries. These parks enabled Singapore to invest and build strategic linkages with the regions. Singapore can lend its core competencies in infrastructural and management to its neighbors aiding their process. Singapore can also help SMEs relocate to these parks and capitalize on resources available in the regions allowing the relocation of resource-dependent activities overseas.

The Singapore government has also assisted SMEs in opening doors through the extensive network of bilateral Free Trade Agreements (FTAs) and strong links within Association of South East Asian Nations (ASEAN). With China, Singapore has bilateral trade and economic ties under the Joint Council for Bilateral Cooperation (JCBC), which was established in 2005. With India, Singapore and India entered a Comprehensive Economic Cooperation Agreement (CECA). Under the CECA, preferential tariff rates are available to Singapore SMEs. The Middle East is another region that Singapore has facilitated business through high-level engagements and trade missions.

These efforts have impressed Singapore SMEs to consider international expansion as a key growth strategy. According to the 2004 SME Development Survey by DP Information Group, a third of SMEs surveyed have identified international expansion as a key growth strategy, compared with just 18 percent in 2003 (DP Information, 2004).[7] They have ventured beyond the conventional and popular markets in the ASEAN and China, and have forayed into Central Asia, Eastern Europe and Latin America. An example is Food Empire Holdings, a producer and distributor of food and beverage products such as finger food, seafood, and candy. It has three manufacturing plants located in Asia and representative and liaison offices in 12 countries. Its products are sold under its own brands like FesAroma, Klassno and Zinties, and can be found in more than 50 countries, including Russia, Kazakhstan, Turkey, and Bahrain.

There still remains significant potential for SMEs to expand their businesses overseas. The 2006 SME Development Survey report by DP Information Group revealed that the proportion of SME respondents who had revenues originating from outside Singapore fell from 69 percent in 2005, to 59 percent in 2006. It also points to the challenges that SMEs face in venturing overseas. The report noted that the respondents identified the top challenges they faced as the presence of strong overseas competition, a lack of overseas business knowledge and contacts, and a lack of external funds and manpower for overseas expansions. Small and medium enterprises could avail themselves of the IE Singapore's International Partners' program to form international alliances with other Singapore-based companies. Research has shown that although Singapore SMEs are Asian, similarities in culture do not necessarily ensure successful cooperation (Zutshi and Tan, 2008).

5. Conclusions

Entrepreneurship will continue to feature in Singapore's economy and all the more so as the nation seeks to be a global hub. The government's policy initiatives on entrepreneurship and internationalization have focused on the creation of the enterprise eco-systems to sustain both endeavors at home and abroad. While extending one's infrastructure overseas is difficult, Singapore has made headway with its projects in the science parks, industrial parks and ports. With these inducements and support in place, it behoves the SMEs to reach out and venture forth.

Notes

1. Speech by Mr Lim Hng Kiang, Minister for Trade and Industry during the Committee of Supply Debate on Monday, 6 March 2006.
2. SPRING Singapore, http://www.spring.gov.sg/ (accessed 18 March 2007).
3. SPRING Singapore, Stories of Enterprise Today, Mar/Apr 2007, http://www.spring.gov.sg/, (accessed 18 March 2007).
4. IDA Singapore, http://www.ida.gov.sg/ (accessed 18 March 2007).
5. SPRING Singapore Press Release, SPRING Singapore and the Singapore Manufacturers' Federation launch Singapore's second Enterprise Development Centre, Reference No : NR/28/2005, 27 October 2005
6. See Tan (2006, 2008).
7. Speech by Mr Lim Hng Kiang, Minister for Trade and Industry at the 18th Annual (2005) Singapore 1000 and SME500 Awards on 18 January 2005 at the Grand Ballroom, Ritz Carlton Millenia Singapore at 7.30pm.

References

Begley, T. and W.L. Tan (2001), 'The socio-cultural environment for entrepreneurship: a comparison between East Asian and Anglo countries', *Journal of International Business Studies*, **32**(3), 537–54.
DP Information (2004), *SME Development Survey: Report*, Singapore: DP Information Network Pte Ltd.
Lee, Tsao Yuan and Linda Low (eds) (1990), *Local Entrepreneurship in Singapore: Private and State*, Singapore: Times Academic Press for IPS.
Singapore Economic Committee (1986), 'The Singapore economy: new directions', report of the Economic Committee, Ministry of Trade and Industry, Singapore.
Tan, T.M., W.L. Tan and J.E. Young (2000), 'Entrepreneurial infrastructure in Singapore: developing a model and mapping participation', *Journal of Entrepreneurship*, **9**(1), 1–33.
Tan, W.L. (ed.) (2006), *Social Capital in Asia: An Exploratory Study*, Tokyo: Asian Productivity Organization.
Tan, W.L. (ed.) (2008), *Social Capital and Business Transformation in Asia*, Tokyo: Asian Productivity Organization.
Wong, P.K., L. Lee and Y.P. Ho (2007), *Global Entrepreneurship Monitor 2006 Singapore Report*. Singapore: NUS Entrepreneurship Centre.
Zutshi, R. and W.L. Tan (2008), 'Impact of culture on "partner selection criteria" in East Asian international joint ventures, *International Entrepreneurship and Management Journal*, DOI:10.1007/s11365-008-0076-1.

33 South Korea
Ed Hopkins and Siri Terjesen

Introduction

The Republic of Korea (South Korea) shares the Korean Peninsula with the Democratic People's Republic of Korea (North Korea). North and South Korea are separated by the Demilitarized Zone (DMZ), a 4 kilometre-wide strip at the thirty-eighth parallel. South Korea has a population of 49 million (twenty-fourth largest country in the world) and a gross domestic product (GDP) of US$1.28 trillion (thirteenth largest in the world, third largest in Asia). South Korea's capital, Seoul, is populated by 23 million residents, making it the world's second largest metropolitan area, behind Tokyo. Korea's other major cities are Busan (3.6 million), Incheon (2.6 million), Daegu (2.5 million), Gwangju (1.4 million), Daejeon (1.4 million) and Ulsan (1.1 million).

South Korea is one of the four Asian 'tiger' or 'dragon' economies described as such for their high rate of growth and industrialization since the 1960s, led by an export-driven model of economic development. South Korea has a strong presence in oil, steel, automobile, shipbuilding and science and technology industries, including information technology, electronics, semiconductors, computers and mobile telephones.

While nearly half (47 percent) of South Koreans report no religious preference, more than a quarter are Christian (29 percent) and about 23 percent are Buddhist. South Korea also has an avid sporting culture, with some of the most popular sports being Taekwondo and athletics. Korea hosted several international mega-sporting events including the Summer Olympic Games (1988), FIFA World Cup (2002), ultrarunning's IAU World 100 km (2006) and cycling's Tour de Korea (2007).

Koreans have inhabited the area since the Lower Paleolithic era. The nation was first unified during the seventh century, and in 1392 General Yi Song-gye started the Yi dynasty which ruled until the Japanese abolished the Korean monarchy in 1910. Throughout all the Yi dynasty, Korea maintained a tributary relationship with China. In 1876, Korea was forced to sign one-sided commercial treaties with China, Japan, and other nations. Britain, France, Germany, Japan, Russia and the United States invested heavily in the Korean economy and in 1894 Korean peasants revolted against the foreign influence. The revolt was suppressed, resulting in a heavy Japanese military presence on the peninsula. Following its victories in the Sino-Japanese War (1894–95) and the Russo-Japanese War (1905), Japan annexed Korea in 1910.

From 1910 until the end of World War II (WWII), Korea was a colony of Japan. During this time, the Korean barter system was replaced by the Japanese Yen, the Korean monarchy was separated from the state, civil law was codified, and discrimination against commoners was outlawed. Japan controlled Korea's finances, public services, natural resources, and 40 percent of Korea's land area.

In 1919, 2 million Koreans revolted due to Japanese discrimination. Koreans felt that Japan had been using their educational system as a tool to indoctrinate the theory of Korean inferiority and to deny Korea a national identity. Koreans felt that they were being robbed of their identity as they were forbidden to speak their own language and to use Korean names. The Japanese invested heavily in irrigation on the peninsula and Koreans often starved while the rice was shipped back to Japan. Japan maintained as much control over manufacturing in Korea as it did in the agricultural economy. The number of Japanese companies in Korea increased from 109 in 1911 to 1237 in 1929 with all large-scale firms under Japanese control.

In 1930 nearly one-quarter of all Korean factory products went to Japan. That number increased to as much as half by 1940. During this time the northern half of the peninsula focused on industrial production for Japan, while the southern half of the peninsula continued agricultural production traditions.

Japanese control of Korea continued following the Manchurian Incident (1931–37) and industrialization increased. During WWII there was a 50:50 ratio of light to heavy goods from Korean factories, a drastic change from the 80:20 ratio of 1930. The number of factories, hydroelectric plants, and railroad mileage were all increased in order to optimize the Japanese gain from Korean mineral resources and rice supply.

After the Allied victory in WWII, the Korean Peninsula was divided into two separate zones of control along the thirty-eighth parallel. The Soviets maintained control of northern Korea and formed the Democratic People's Republic of Korea (North Korea), while the United States took control of the south. In August 1948, the Republic of Korea (South Korea) was formed. Communist Russia influenced North Korea, as the United States influenced South Korea and, in 1950, North Korea invaded South Korea in hopes of creating a unified communist state.

The Korean War lasted from 1950 to 1953. The United States and United Nations forces fought alongside South Korea to defend them from North Korean attacks supported by the Soviet Union and China. An armistice was signed in 1953. Since the war, South Korea has experienced rapid economic growth with per capita income rising to roughly 14 times the level of that of North Korea.

In 1997 the Asian financial crisis drastically changed the South Korean economy, resulting in sizable bankruptices and government reforms. By 1999 one of the largest bankruptcies in history occurred when the chaebol, Daewoo, collapsed under 80 billion won of debts. Weaknesses in the South Korean economy, such as high-debt-to-equity ratios and high levels of borrowing from foreign countries were also exposed. Between 1995 and 2003, nearly half of the 30 largest chaebols in South Korea collapsed.

Government policy on small and medium enterprises and entrepreneurship
In the years following the Korean War, the United States supplied about two-thirds of the rehabilitation aid in order to implement an import substitution policy. Following a military coup in 1961, a policy of increased industrialization was established. This acceleration also led to laws protecting and encouraging entrepreneurship in the country. A key piece of this new legislation was the Small and Medium Industry Bank Act (1961). This legislation allowed the Industrial Bank of Korea to make loans to smaller entrepreneurs. In 1962, the first of several five-year economic development plans began. As one of the goals was to maximize growth and export volume, Korea created a command economy where wages were set low and interest rates were subsidized.

The Second and Third Five-Year Plans (1967–76) focused on export promotion rather than import substitution. The plans devalued the won and gave select firms subsidized interest rates below the market-clearing point. Firms specializing in export-oriented borrowing were given special subsidized loans. These methods allowed for more capital-intensive, rather than labor-intensive, methods of production. The excess supply of labor kept wages low. These steps led to smaller companies being forced out of the market, and the Korean chaebols were created. During the Vietnam War, Korean firms contracted with the United States army and firms in other nations.

From 1974 to 1981 South Korea passed several important economic acts and South Korea enacted its Fourth Five-Year Plan (1977–1981). Entrepreneurs were granted guarantees for liabilities by the Credit Gurantee Funds Act (1974), and cooperation between large and small firms was promoted by the Sub-Contracting System Promotion Act (1975). In 1980, the Small and Medium Industries Promotion Corporation Act was passed to benefit entreprenuers. Also, in 1981 the Procurement Facilitating Act specified the conditions of government procurements from entrepreneurs. The goal of this act was to allow smaller firms to sell to the state collectively, via cooperatives. The intent of the Fourth Five-Year Plan was to increase exports of a few key industries namely heavy industry and chemicals. As a result, a small number of highly diversified mega-conglomerates dominated the South Korean economy.

During the 1980s, South Korean workers earned roughly US$50 for a 72-hour week. However, after the labor dispute in 1989, wages were substantially raised. In 1989, salaries were 45 percent higher than in 1987 and from 1986 to 1989 automotive industry wages increased 80 percent. Economic policy acts passed including the Policy to Support Promising Small and Medium-scale Enterprises (1983), the Mutual Assistance Fund act (1984), and the Production Research Institute Act (1988). This legislation helped entrepreneurs and SME owners to obtain low-interest loans, product development, and technology transfers.

In the 1990s, over 50 percent of South Korea's gross national product (GNP) came from only five chaebols, and Korean government policy shifted to the promotion of SMEs and entrepreneurial firms. The government used tools such as capital assistance including low-cost loans and research and development (R&D) incentives to promote this.

The 1993–1997 Five-year Plan called for the reduction of government intervention in the economy, the lowering of entry barriers and the deregulation of business activities. In 1997, trading enterprises had their registration qualifications abolished. In 1998, the South Korean government established the Corporate Restructuring Fund valued at US$1.2 billion. Seventy percent of the fund was designated for small and medium firms and the top five chaebols were denied access to the fund.

The annual Global Entrepreneurship Monitor (GEM) tracks rates of entrepreneurial activity in over 50 countries around the globe. The GEM's Total Entrepreneurial Activity (TEA) rate captures the percentage of the adult population (18–64 years of age) who are currently trying to start a business or actively managing a young firm (less than 42 months old). Korea's average TEA rate is approximately 15 percent, one of the highest in the world (only Chile, India and Thailand had higher rates in 2002). Approximately 9 percent of Korea's population are motivated by opportunity (voluntarily pursuing as the best alternative) while 4.5 percent of the population are motivated by necessity (no other suitable work available). Korea's male:female ratio of entrepreneurs is 2.3:1 – based on 20.5 percent of adult Korean men being involved in entrepreneurial activity compared to just 8.8 percent of their female counterparts. The GEM reports that Korea has the world's highest percentage of domestic capital investment as a percentage of GDP: 6.3 percent, with the majority of this being informal investment (providing funds to other entrepreneurs).The GEM also tracks Firm Entrepreneurial Activity (FEA) which examines entrepreneurship within existing firms, finding 4 percent of the Korean population are involved in entrepreneurial firms, the second highest percentage in the world (China is 6 percent and the next highest is Mexico at 2.8 percent). Entrepreneurial firms comprise 22 percent of Korea's total population of firms and employ 29 percent of the adult population.

Environment for entrepreneurship and the state of small business
Although South Korea is known for its large-firm chaebol structure, SMEs play an important role. Small and medium enterprises comprise 95 percent of all businesses in South Korea. Using an index base of 100 in 1991, South Korean SMEs grew to 132.2 by 1999. Approximately one in every 20 South Koreans manages a small to medium enterprise. Nearly 80 percent of private sector employment in South Korea comes from SMEs. That is a significantly higher percentage than the 60 percent average of other Asia-Pacific Economic Cooperation Conference (APEC) nations. South Korean firms are small and typically employ only three to four people.

Overall, South Korea has put in practice sound policies on SMEs since the mid-1990s. This framework and the existence of SMEs help explain South Korea's ability to survive the Asian economic crisis of the late 1990s. However, there was a sharp decrease in the amount of bank funds available to SMEs following the 1997 crisis. In fact, in 1998 the level of bank funds available was only 18 percent of the 1995 level.

Internationalization of entrepreneurs and SMEs
In 2002, SMEs accounted for 42.9 percent of all South Korean exports. Overall, SME export growth has increased from an index level of 100 in 1995 to 157 in 2001.

The current expanding, global economy is a burden for many SMEs, due mostly to the smaller scale on which they operate, compared to chaebols. Still there is a great opportunity for growth in the global environment and possibly the most important characteristics of small to medium enterprises that can better enable them to overcome these challenges is their level of innovation.

Conclusion
In Korea, entrepreneurs have grown to become large, world-class conglomerates such as Samsung, Hyundai, and LG (which now comprise 30 percent of the country's GDP). Although Korea has one of the highest rates of entrepreneurial activity, the country still faces some barriers to entrepreneurship such as only 15 percent of the adult population see good opportunities to start a business (GEM, 2002) and 43 percent of the adult population report that fear of failure would prevent them from starting a business. Meanwhile, many Koreans are employed in entrepreneurial activities in existing firms. In both new and established firms, Koreans are actively engaged in streamlining bureaucracy, exchanging information and encouraging collaboration.

South Korea's economic and entrepreneurial future looks bright. The country currently boasts the third largest foreign investment market in Asia, with 12 000 foreign firms. The government's aim is to develop Seoul as the dominant business and financial hub in Northeast Asia and has set a goal to increase foreign investment from 10 percent to 20 percent by 2009. Korea has taken important steps to enforce intellectual property rights and has one of the world's highest rates of mobile phone and Internet penetration. The government has taken steps to provide over US$90 billion to recapitalize banks and secure commitment to international accounting standards. The Korean government has also lifted restrictions on mergers and acquisitions, and enabled foreign firms to undertake a range of financial services. Furthermore, the Korean government has committed to viewing foreign companies as allies and to harmonize Korean standards to international standards.

Acknowledgements
An initial draft of this chapter was prepared by Ed Hopkins. Parts of this chapter are based on Léo-Paul Dana's *Asian Models of Entrepreneurship* (2007).

References
Dana, Leo-Paul (2007), *Asian Models of Entrepreneurship – from the Indian Union and the Kingdom of Nepal to the Japanese Archipelago: Context, Policy and Practice*, Singapore and London: World Scientific.
Global Entrepreneurship Monitor (GEM) (2002), *Global Entrepreneurship Monitor 2002 Summary Report*, 30 November.

34 Sri Lanka

Sudatta Ranasinghe and Jay Weerawardena

1 Introduction

Sri Lanka is an island nation with a population of 19.8 million of which over 70 percent live in the rural areas. The recorded growth of population in Sri Lanka had been 1.1 percent at the end of 2006. Since gaining independence from British rule in 1948, the successive governments elected within the democratic political framework of the Westminster model have followed a set of welfare policies that incorporated free health care, free education and other measures of income redistribution. Thus, the country has been able to achieve an adult literacy rate of 94 percent and life expectancy and infant mortality rates comparable with advanced countries. Sri Lanka has also reached a per capita income level of US$1350 and a gross domestic product (GDP) growth rate of 7 percent by 2006. Although the country faced the adverse consequences of a serious political conflict during the past three decades due to the armed struggle launched by the separatist Tamil guerrillas, the economy had demonstrated a high degree of resilience evident from the continued growth of the GDP, which had averaged around 5 percent during the past five years.

The economic liberalization policy introduced as far back as 1978 has had far-reaching effects on the economy and the society. The outward-oriented economic policies vigorously pursued by successive governments have brought in a significant volume of export-oriented investments both foreign and local. There has also been a corresponding growth of the small and medium enterprise (SME) sector activities. However, in terms of the global competitiveness rankings reported by the World Economic Forum, Sri Lanka has not performed well compared to several other developing countries.

In this chapter the findings of a recent study of seven medium-size Sri Lankan export firms are presented. The chapter examines aspects of entrepreneurship and business strategy, dynamic capabilities and innovation in the process of internationalization of the case study firms. The firms covered in the study belonged to different industry segments such as ceramic tableware, value-added tea, organic tea, value-added rubber products, Ayurvedic medicinal products and handloom garments. In-depth interviews with the chief executive officers (CEOs) and senior managers of the firms as well as field visits by the research team provided the data required for the study.

2 Government policy on SMEs and entrepreneurship in Sri Lanka

Small and medium enterprises have been recognized as a means of increasing productivity and employment and as a vehicle of channeling entrepreneurial, management and technological skills to rural areas. Successive governments have provided policy and institutional support for the SME sector including credit facilities through state banks as well as management and entrepreneurial skills development programs provided through various government and non-governmental organizations. Technological support has been made available to SMEs through the Industrial Development Board, Industrial

Technology Institute and the Small and Medium Enterprise Developers Project in Sri Lanka. The SMEs that have entered the global market have been provided assistance through the Export Development Board. The government of Sri Lanka has also granted tax concessions to different types of SMEs. Although government policies have encouraged SMEs, it has been observed that the growth and sustainability of SMEs have faced various problems due to poor status of policy implementation and the conflicting nature of policies.

3   The environment of entrepreneurship and the state of small business in Sri Lanka
There are SMEs of different shades comprising urban and rural enterprises, those in export business, those catering to the local markets and producers of intermediary and final goods. According to The Task Force for SME Sector Development Programme (2005) the small enterprises that employed less than 30 persons accounted for 85 percent of the total number of establishments, and the medium enterprises that employed 30–150 persons accounted for little over 10 percent. The large enterprises which employed over 150 persons had accounted for 4 percent of the total. The contribution of large enterprises to value addition had been estimated at 80 percent, while the small and medium enterprises have contributed 5 and 15 percent respectively to value addition.

Studies have found that sustainability of SMEs has been affected due to reasons such as lack of entrepreneurial and managerial skills, threat of cheap imports and the inefficiency in the implementation of public sector support services. It has been observed that as compared with large-scale enterprises the SMEs are at a disadvantage due to their inadequate capacity to integrate competitively with the market mechanism (Abeyratne, 2005). Though several ministries and institutions in the public sector are involved with services that cater to the SMEs, studies have revealed that small and medium entrepreneurs face difficulties in obtaining the desired services on time from these institutions.

As there is no recognized institutional mechanism for monitoring the performance of SMEs at national or regional level, the survival and growth of SMEs has depended largely on the capacity of individual entrepreneurs to handle business-related problems. It has been found that in the context of the open economy only a limited number of SMEs have been able to face the competition from cheap imports. Studies have also suggested that government policies have been more favorable towards big businesses. The absence of credible and comprehensive databases required to obtain an in-depth understanding of SME problems and their performance, to feed the policy-making process, is recognized as a notable deficiency that has not been addressed as yet.

4   Internationalization of entrepreneurs and SMEs in Sri Lanka
Entering the international arena of business is a goal of a highly ambitious SME entrepreneur. Due to lack of a credible database on SME operations in Sri Lanka it is not possible to gauge how many SME entrepreneurs finally reach the goal of entering the international market. Among the few who have made it, the majority belongs to the category of 'gradually globalizing' entrepreneurs or those who enter the global market after having established their business on a firm footing in the local market. There is also a group of entrepreneurs who have developed a new product or started manufacturing an existing product targeting the international market. Of these, some have succeeded

in establishing a foothold in overseas markets with the assistance of a reliable partner. These entrepreneurs, classified as 'born global entrepreneurs', are small in number.

In the following sections we present findings based on a study of a selected number of cases carried out in two stages during 2004 and 2007. The study covered a total of 11 export firms of which four belonged to large-scale manufacturing firms in terms of the capital invested, volume of turnover and the number of employees. Though these case study firms provided valuable insights into the process of globalization of indigenous businesses, they were excluded from the analysis as these firms did not come within the classification of SMEs. Thus, for the purpose of the present study we have considered the data gathered from the remaining seven firms, which belong to the large category of SME enterprises in terms of the number employed.

A feature common to the seven case study firms was that they have been born as a result of the founder's entrepreneurial ambition to venture into a new business based on his or her accumulated knowledge and the wealth of experience. Table 34.1 gives a picture of the seven case study firms in terms of products and markets, core competencies, strategy, and management style and organizational structure.

Entrepreneurial characteristics and internationalization strategy
Among the sampled case studies three firms, namely, Hettigoda Industries, Samson Rubber Products, and Barbara Sansoni Fabrics, belonged to the gradually globalizing category and the remaining four belonged to the born global category. The leaders of the seven firms demonstrated the entrepreneurial drive to identify market opportunities and fulfill them with products that had special or unique value-adding features. As observed by Balakrishnan et al. (1999), the behavioral orientation of SME entrepreneurs is characterized by personal resourcefulness, achievement orientation, strategic vision, opportunity seeking and innovativeness. The leaders of the case study firms demonstrated these behavioral characteristics to a considerable extent and it was evident that they used these characteristics to overcome the environmental constraints which affect the performance and growth of businesses.

In developing and marketing the products the entrepreneurs of the case study firms depended initially on their own knowledge as well as experience accumulated over a long period of time. The case study firms that were engaged in manufacturing one or more products invested a significant part of the generated income on research and development (R&D), which helped in quality improvement, process improvement and development of new products. In addition to learning from internal R&D activities, the leaders learned from the markets as well as from overseas partners with whom they networked. The learning from both R&D-based internal sources and the market-related external sources such as trade fairs, agents and distributors, gave the entrepreneurs new insights into products and markets, enabling them to adjust and adapt the products as well as marketing strategies leading to sustainable competitive advantage.

In some cases the leader's ability to envision the future and introduce a totally new product using his or her expertise was found to have triggered new lines of business. For example, the Chairman of the Hettigoda Industries, who was an Ayurvedic physician, had the vision of developing and exporting traditional Ayurvedic medicines in ready-to-use form (as capsules, tablets, ointments, and so on). He succeeded in this venture after several years of experimentation or trial and error learning. Currently the firm exports

Table 34.1   *Case study firms in perspective*

Name of the firm and location	Products	Market	Core competencies	Strategy	Management approach and organization structure
Royal Fernwood Porcelain Ltd Kosgama (about 30 Kms away from Colombo)	Porcelain tableware	Mainly export market	Product design and marketing, R&D based product and process improvement, and quality assurance	Design variation and product differentiation, process innovation for cost reduction, networking and partnering, employee involvement	Owner managed and functionally differentiated structure with teamwork
Imperial Tea Exports Ltd Colombo	Value-added tea	Export market	Branding, marketing, quality assurance	Marketing of value-added tea through a network of partners abroad, focus on building the 'Impra' brand in the Eastern European market	Owner managed, teamwork-based structure with operational flexibility
Bio Foods Ltd, Kandy, the capital of the hill country	Organic tea and spices	Export market	R&D capability, product innovation, quality assurance, managing multiple organic farming units, supply chain management	Fair trading-based marketing of organic food products through foreign partners, product innovation, supply of raw material through empowered small farmer organizations, capacity building of raw material suppliers	SOFA (Small Organic Farmer Association) make decisions under expert guidance of the owner and the team

Company	Product	Market	Capabilities	Strategy	Structure
Hettigoda Industries Ltd Colombo	Ayurvedic medicinal products	Domestic and export markets	R&D capability, product innovation, quality assurance, branding and marketing	Conversion of indigenous knowledge in to value-added and ready-to-use medicinal products	Family-run business with functionally differentiated structure
Samson Rubber Products Ltd Colombo	Bicycle tyres and other rubber products	Domestic and export markets	R&D capability, product design, quality assurance, and marketing	Collaborating with foreign partners in product design and development as well as marketing	Owner-managed business with functional managers taking decisions in consultation with the Chairman
Micro Cells Ltd Colombo	Industrial rubber carpets	Export market	R&D capability, product design and quality assurance, and cost control	Ensure consistent supply of a quality product to selected buyers who maintain long-term relationships	Owner-managed business with a functionally differentiated structure
Barbara Sansoni Fabrics Ltd, Colombo	Handloom dresses and heritage artifacts	Domestic and export markets	Color mixing and design of fabrics, sustainable quality, branding and marketing	Niche marketing of handloom products under 'Barefoot' brand using a network of domestic handloom weavers	Family-run business with a simple and less differentiated structure

several Ayurvedic medicinal products to Europe and Japan. The Chairman also took the initiative to diversify his business by establishing an Ayurvedic healthcare facility and a tourist hotel that provided traditional Ayurvedic healthcare services.

The Chairman of Bio Foods Limited, who had been a research scientist at the Tea Research Institute, had the vision of developing organic green tea as well as organic health foods for the export market. He invented new machinery capable of producing organic green tea and developed the technology required to manufacture organic food products according to international standards. He also introduced a strategy to ensure continuous supply of quality raw material based on the fair-trading concept. At present the company enjoys a sustainable competitive advantage in the European market for organic food products such as organic tea and spices, and has networked with foreign partners and over 2000 small farmer families. These farmers, who are members of the Small Organic Farmer Association (SOFA), maintain a close link with Bio Foods Limited and are active in producing raw materials required for manufacturing organic food products. The pattern of international market entry displayed by this firm, in particular, the speed of market entry, conforms to those of born global firms (Weerawardena et al., 2007). Like any other born global, from its inception it viewed the world as its market.

The case study firms that entered the global market gradually appear to have taken moderate risks compared with their born global counterparts, who have taken greater risks in terms of developing new products as well as marketing those products. As indicated in Table 34.1, both types of firms acquired the capability to manage their business risks by developing firm-level core competencies that were in harmony with the business strategies pursued. The core competencies acquired over time (for example, R&D capability and marketing capability) appear to have insulated the firms against certain risks associated with product quality and design as well as marketing.

Born globals in the sample displayed a higher degree of innovativeness compared to their gradually globalizing counterparts. For example, the capacity to control costs through process innovation and improvements has enabled Royal Fernwood Porcelain Limited, a born global firm, to compete on price as well as quality in international markets. Bio Foods Limited which operated in a quality-conscious and highly competitive food industry in Europe developed an internal quality control system known as Critical Control Points (CCP), which has been applied to ensure consistent quality standards in the manufacturing of organic food products. The company also acquired the capability to ensure consistent quality of organic raw material through farm-level agriculture extension and quality assurance service.

The strategies adopted by the entrepreneurs reflect their unique adjustment to the emerging trends in the market. It was clear that apart from the learning from market intelligence as well as internal R&D activities, the entrepreneurs have been guided by their own judgment and intuition in developing the business strategies. The strategies outlined in Table 34.1 have helped the entrepreneurs to remain focused on their goals while sustaining the capacity to compete. As revealed by the data, the strategy of partnering with selected foreign buyers assisted almost all the case study firms to stabilize their businesses in overseas markets. In some cases (for example, Samson Rubber Products, Imperial Tea Exports and Bio Foods Limited) the foreign partners shared to a certain extent the entrepreneurial risk of introducing new products in foreign markets.

Innovation of products as well as processes using R&D-based knowledge as well as market intelligence was a core strategy adopted by most of the case study firms. This is particularly evident among born globals. For example, Bio Foods Limited invested about 35 percent of the profits annually on R&D and was able to introduce two or three new products in each year. The company was able to test market the new products with the assistance of its partner in Germany. A similar strategy was adopted by Samson Rubber Products Limited. It was revealed that Imperial Tea Exports Limited had depended on its foreign partners in building the 'Impra' brand.

Networking with raw material suppliers, overseas buyers and others who possessed the know-how and specific skills was a common strategy followed by the case study firms. For example, Bio Foods Limited networked with suppliers of organic raw material and a few foreign buyers recognized as partners. In the case of Samson Rubber Products, Micro Cells, Imperial Tea Exports, and Royal Fernwood Porcelain, the CEOs attributed the market success to the supportive role played by the foreign partners. Similarly the prior network relationships with the Russian market helped Imperial Tea Exports with its accelerated market entry. In the case of Hettigoda Industries, the strategy of networking with traditional Ayurvedic physicians contributed significantly towards development of several new products. The effectiveness of the networking strategy was found to be dependent on mutual trust and sharing of benefits.

Adopting a flexible approach to management creating space for introducing changes where necessary was a feature shared by the case study firms. Management innovation was also an important aspect of strategy adopted by some of the entrepreneurs. For example, the Chairman of Bio Foods adopted the strategy of combining fair-trading practice with the empowered farmer organizations by providing to the farmer organizations a few years of guidance and training on organic farming and quality assurance. This strategy appears to have paid rich dividends to both the farmers as well as the company. The CEO of Royal Fernwood Porcelain Ltd introduced quality circles, which created opportunities for the employees to participate in plant-level decision-making. The Chairman of Hettigoda Industries created opportunities for the floor-level workers to rise up to the level of director in the company.

In general, all the sampled firms displayed varying degrees of entrepreneurship in terms of innovativeness, proactiveness and risk-taking propensity (Covin and Slevin, 1986). However we found that born global firms, compared to their gradually globalizing counterparts, displayed a higher degree of entrepreneurship. Using the overseas market exposure and the network relationships they had developed in their prior employment, they exploited profitable market opportunities by developing innovative niche market focused products. In terms of risk-taking, whilst demonstrating a tendency to take higher risks, they also adopted risk-minimizing strategies such as extensive learning from markets. Here again, the prior market knowledge of born global firms had given them a competitive edge.

We found that sampled firms displayed somewhat unique behavioral characteristics in the way they led their firms. We believe that these characteristics should be understood in relation to the cultural context within which the Sri Lankan entrepreneurs operate. In terms of Hofstede's (1980) notion of cultural differences, Sri Lanka is a collectivist society with feminine values like caring for one another, rather than being concerned with accomplishing individual goals. Sri Lankan business organizations, similar to their Asian counterparts, display a higher power distance. Within this backdrop, the leaders of case study firms, in addition to displaying entrepreneurial characteristics of innovativeness, proactiveness and risk-taking, displayed the characteristics of transformational leaders in terms of visioning into the future, competency-building among their employees as well as the members of networks, changing products and processes, and building and empowering teams. It was evident that the leaders of some of the case study firms were following the model of 'leading from the front', which characterized leaders' active involvement in every important aspect of the business. These entrepreneurs were actively involved in directing R&D work, product design, quality assurance and maintaining relationships with the customers as well as the networks.

The leaders of case study firms displayed leadership characteristics somewhat unique in the Sri Lankan context. These entrepreneurs adopted behavioural tendencies that inspired the employees as well as those in the business networks. The findings show that some of the leaders were paternalistic in their approach towards the employees. The paternalistic tendency was characterized by their caring attitude to employees and the actions taken to ensure future security of the employees. This approach to managing people has been extremely effective, particularly in the context of higher power distance existing in such organizations. In return the leaders expected employees to be loyal and committed to the company. The organization culture of the case study firms promoted values such as commitment to quality, customer service and discipline among the employees. Almost all the leaders of case study firms maintained an 'open door' policy in their dealings with employees. They also promoted employee involvement in solving business-related problems, particularly in the direction of quality improvement and enhancing customer service.

One also observed that certain management practices adopted by the case study firms were blended with the indigenous culture. Particularly the practices such as opening savings accounts for the employees, providing subsidized meals, and attending to the welfare of the families of the employees, adopted by some of the case study firms reflected the features of the traditional familial organization identified by Gupta (1999) as a manifestation of the symbiosis between cultural values and business practices in the Asian context. Though these management practices characterize a paternalistic approach, the study found that they contributed towards building employee loyalty and commitment towards the organizations.

Conclusion
The findings of the present study provide valuable insights into the role of SME entrepreneurs in creating conditions necessary for innovation and acquisition of competitive capabilities. The tendency among the entrepreneurs of Sri Lankan case study firms to think strategically, integrate internal as well as external learning, and build core competencies led to innovation enabling the firms to gain competitive advantage in the global market. The findings suggest that the approach adopted by the leaders of 'born global' firms was different from 'gradually globalizing firms'. The leaders of 'born global' firms were more inclined towards substantial innovation in the context of globalization. These leaders attempted to minimize the risks involved with internationalization by combining their experience and competencies with the ability to network. In contrast, the leaders of gradually globalizing firms entered the export market at a later stage and were found to be oriented towards incremental innovation and moderate risk-taking.

The findings suggest that several important characteristics of the leaders contributed towards building competitive capabilities of the case study firms. The ability of the leaders to think strategically enabled the firms to focus on acquiring dynamic capabilities to respond to the changing conditions in the market. It was evident that the leaders of case study firms, particularly those of the born-global type, were effective in integrating market-based external learning, network-based relational learning and R&D-based internal learning for introducing product and process innovations. This tendency had helped these firms to acquire a greater capacity to sustain their competitive capability.

The findings suggest that the dynamic capability view of competitive advantage suggested in the literature (Prahalad and Hamel, 1990; Ranasinghe and Weerawardena, 2003; Teece et al., 1997; Weerawardena, 2003) fits well in the case of those firms that developed internal capability to innovate products and processes as well as management practices in order to take advantage of the changing market conditions. The leaders of these firms took a proactive stance and invested in technology development, human resources development and other projects that increased the firm's capability to reduce costs.

The findings suggested that some of the entrepreneurs were able to combine paternalism with achievement orientation, which had helped in sustaining employee involvement in the process of learning and innovation. The ability of the leaders to create achievement-oriented organizational culture supported by employee development and motivation played a key role in increasing the firm's capability to face the challenges posed by the international markets.

Overall we observe that the case study firms gradually built up their capabilities to achieve growth and sustainability through commitment and hard work of the business leaders and their employees and partners. The behaviour of these entrepreneurs is comparable to their international counterparts in terms of their entrepreneurial characteristics, particularly with regard to international market opportunity-seeking behaviour. The leaders of case study firms displayed somewhat unique behavioural characteristics which were a combination of the conventional entrepreneurial characteristics suggested in the literature, that is, innovativeness, proactiveness and risk-taking, and a supportive and caring leadership pattern which was strongly rooted in the Sri Lankan national culture. The leaders of case study firms have adopted leadership and managerial styles that facilitated greater trust and commitment among the employees as well as others who partnered with them. Overall, we find that entrepreneurial leadership characterized by strategic thinking, networking, capacity building and creating an achievement culture is a necessary pre-condition for effective integration of SMEs with the international market where organizational learning and innovation play a critical role in ensuring competitiveness. The study findings suggest that, to the extent that a firm is able to integrate its learning from different sources, the firm acquires dynamic capability which leads to innovation and competitive advantage. Thus, we conclude that strategic entrepreneurial leadership is a key antecedent of growth and sustainability of SMEs.

References

Abeyratne, S. (2005), 'Small and medium enterprises in Sri Lanka: integrating the SME sector with the market', Regional Convention on Policy Reforms for SME Development in SAARC Countries, Colombo, Sri Lanka, 25–7 November 2005.

Balakrishnan, S., K. Gopakumar and R.N. Kanungo (1999), 'Entrepreneurship development: concept and context', in Henry S.R. Kao, Durganand Sinha and Bernhard Wilpert (eds), *Management and Cultural Values – The Indigenization of Organizations in Asia*, New Delhi: Sage Publications.
Covin, J.G. and D.P. Slevin (1986), 'The development and testing of an organizational level entrepreneurship scale', *Frontiers of Entrepreneurship*, Wellesley, MA: Babson College.
Gupta, R.K. (1999), 'The truly familial work organization: extending the organizational boundary to include employees' families in the Indian context', in Henry S.R. Kao, Durganand Sinha and Bernhard Wilpert (eds), *Management and Cultural Values – The Indigenization of Organizations in Asia*, New Delhi: Sage Publications.
Hofstede, G.H. (1980), *Culture's Consequence, International Differences in Work-related Values*, Beverly Hills, CA: Sage Publications.
Knoll, L. (2004), 'Beyond cultural differences "intercultural" co-operation in a German/Sri Lankan development project', *Internationales Asienforum*, **35**(3–4), 295–306.
Prahalad, C.K. and G. Hamel (1990), 'The core competence of the corporation', *Harvard Business Review*, May–June, 79–91.
Ranasinghe, S. and J. Weerawardena (2003), 'The role of leadership in innovation and competitiveness of export firms: a Sri Lankan perspective', *Sri Lankan Journal of Management*, **8**(3&4), Colombo, Postgraduate Institute of Management, 103–25.
The Task Force for SME Development Programme (2005), Ministry of Internal Trade and Enterprise Development, Colombo, Sri Lanka.
Teece, D.J., G. Pisano and A. Shuen (1997), 'Dynamic capabilities and strategic management', *Strategic Management Journal*, **18**(7), 509–33.
Weerawardena, J., Mort. Sullivan, P. Liesch and G. Knight (2007), 'Conceptualizing accelerated internationalization in the born global firm: a dynamic capabilities perspective', *Journal of World Business*, **42**, 294–306.
Weerawardena, J. (2003), 'The role of marketing capability in innovation based competitive strategy', *Journal of Strategic Marketing*, **11**(1), 15–35.

35 Syria
Wafica A. Ghoul

Introduction

The Republic of Syria has a surface area of 185 180 km², and a population of 21 million growing at an average rate of 2.2 percent (2008 estimate). Damascus is the capital. Arabic is the official language. Syria's main resources are petroleum, natural gas, phosphates, chrome, iron, manganese ores, asphalt, rock salt, marble and gypsum.

Syria's gross domestic product (GDP) is around US$41 billion. In 2007 the economy grew by an estimated 5 percent mostly thanks to the rise in oil prices, expatriates' remittances, tourists' receipts and growing foreign investments. Foreign direct investment rose in 2007 to US$778 million, an increase of 30 percent on 2006. Foreign direct investments originate mostly from Russia, Iran and some of the Gulf Arab countries, while Western companies remain rather cautious due to the political turmoil in the Middle East region and sanctions against Syria.

Recent data show that the sectors of the economy are agriculture 23.6 percent, industry 27.5 percent, and services 48.9 percent of GDP (2007 estimates). In 2007 inflation was estimated at 7 percent, and public debt was 37.8 percent of GDP.

Syria has 2.4 billion barrels of proven oil reserves, hence it has recently benefited from the rise in oil prices, however it became a net oil importer of oil-related products in 2006 according to a May 2007 statement by Muhammad Hussein, the Minister of Finance who was quoted by Oxford Business Group. The same publication reported that 'in 2003, oil accounted for 47 percent of exports, 20 percent of GDP and 51 percent of government revenues. By 2007, these figures had dropped to 28 percent of exports, 20 percent of GDP and 49 percent of government revenues' www.oxfordbusinessgroup.com. Consequently, the government has plans to switch to natural gas as a source of energy with the help of some small independent companies; its gas reserves are estimated to be 240 billion cubic meters (www.banqueaudi.com/syria).

The government has been aiming to create a social market economy, that gets the best of both worlds: the stability which comes with socialism and the vitality of an open market. Economic reforms have been underway to accomplish several goals which include lowering lending interest rates, opening private banks, consolidating multiple exchange rates, phasing out government subsidies on some items, particularly gasoline and cement, and establishing the Damascus Stock Exchange by 2009.

Syria is currently in a state of transition as the government makes an effort to open its market, reduce state control, increase foreign investment, and diversify the economy in the face of dwindling oil reserves by promoting various sectors such as financial services, tourism, and industry, in an effort to compete in the global marketplace. Unfortunately this is happening at a difficult time with skyrocketing food and oil prices around the globe.

Syria is a lower-middle income developing country; the International Monetary Fund (IMF) reports an annual per capita income of US$1176. The unemployment rate is around 9 percent. More than 50 percent of the population is under 20 years of age, which presents a challenge since about 200 000 people enter the job market annually, a situation which forces the government to invest more heavily in education.

In 2006, Syria's labour force was estimated at 5.7 million, 20 percent of which are women. In terms of labor force distribution agriculture employs 19.2 percent of Syrians, services 66.3 percent, and industry 14.5 percent (2006 estimates)

The public sector suffers from over-employment; it employs more than 25 percent of the total labor force, with an average salary of US$200 per month. Critics opine that the public sector suffers from a high cost of production and low efficiency. There is a general belief that public sector employees resort to accepting bribes or taking additional employment in order to afford a reasonable standard of living.

Oxford Group (2008) quoted Safi Shujaa, the Director of the Syrian Economic Centre, who criticized economic reforms as being inequitable:

> According to some economists, 70 percent of gross domestic product goes to only 30 percent of Syrians . . . In the past incomes were supplemented by government support, but now as we move towards a free market, government support is being squeezed and society is becoming more privatized.

It is worth mentioning that about 11.9 percent of the Syrian population lives below the poverty line (2006 estimates).

Syria has been a member of the Greater Arab Free Trade Agreement (GAFTA) since 2005; GAFTA eliminates customs duties between Arab states. In 2007 Syria signed a free trade agreement with Turkey. Syria has also signed a free trade agreement with Iran. Syria has been preparing for World Trade Organization (WTO) accession since 2001, and the government has been making serious efforts for its system's compliance with WTO standards.

The Syrian currency is the Pound, with US$1 = 51.9 Pounds; it is currently pegged to the US dollar, with news of an expected abandonment of this peg in favor of a peg to an IMF basket of currencies (Special Drawing Rights – SDRs). Special Drawing Rights holdings are 44 percent in US dollar, 34 percent in euros, 11 percent in pounds Sterling and 11 percent in Japanese Yen. From 1 January 2007, the Central Bank became responsible for setting the daily exchange rate for commercial and non-commercial transactions. The Syrian Pound is not a fully convertible currency; there are government-imposed limits on the quantity of foreign currency that can be exchanged for Syrian Pounds. Syria continues to 'enjoy' a fairly prevalent black market for currency exchange.

Challenges which constrain the economy include insufficient economic reforms, declining oil reserves which will turn Syria into a net importer of oil by 2010, a demanding population growth rate which increases unemployment and inflation pressures and contributes to food shortages, rising poverty and widening budget deficits.

Other factors which currently limit economic growth include intense regional political uncertainties, water pollution, insufficient water supplies, as well as rapid industrial expansion.

According to country risk rankings by Euromoney, Syria improved its global risk positioning from 138 in September 2005 to 124 in March 2007, an improvement of 14 places in 18 months, mostly thanks to lower political risk, better economic performance, and improving debt indicators.

Policy on SMEs and entrepreneurship in Syria

Businesses face a rigid legal framework in Syria; there have been some efforts to improve the business environment, but it is a very slow change process, especially since politicians meddle and interfere in the enforcement of regulations. Just like other third world countries, it is a common practice to use bribes to get around administrative hurdles. The Syrian government has launched an extensive process of reform, which aims to develop business-friendly legislation. Improvements include lowering the barriers which face importers, facilitating licenses for foreign investments particularly for Arabs. Law No. 32 was enacted in 2007 to allow foreign ownership, and the latest introduction of Investment Law No. 10 is considered the basis of the government's interest in developing the private sector.

Syrian people are entrepreneurs by nature; many of them have historically immigrated to South America where they continue to provide the commercial drive for many regions of the continent. The International Labor Organization, reports that small and medium enterprises (SMEs) both public and private employ 88 percent of the labor force in Syria, with private SMEs getting the lion's share of the workforce.

The various methods of small business financing in Syria include government subsidized small loans, micro-loans and non-government financing programs. Access to capital remains a serious problem especially for start-ups, which is a common complaint around the globe. Additional challenges face start-up entrepreneurs; for example in the information and technology sector these include 'a lack of business maturity, a lack of trust in business people, and lack of proper legislation to protect IP rights', in the words of Rima Shaban, ITC Incubator Director of SCS (Syrian Computer Society) who spoke at The Sixth MENAinc workshop (2008).

In 2004 the government signed the Euro-Mediterranean Charter for Enterprise agreement, thus committing itself to promoting entrepreneurship and competitiveness.

The government currently has a five-year plan (2006–10) underway. Its main objectives include accelerating growth, creating employment opportunities, reducing poverty, opening the market to foreign investments, reducing bureaucracy and red tape, and encouraging entrepreneurship by helping start-ups through the efforts of various ministries such as the Ministry for Labor and Social Affairs.

The European Commission in collaboration with the Syrian government has been funding and supporting a Small and Medium Enterprises Support Program (SSP) in Syria, whose objectives include promoting the private sector in Syria with the help of the recently created Syrian Enterprise Business Centre (SEBC). The SEBC's website (www.sebcsyria.com), reports that 'SEBC is a private foundation created under the Syrian Associations and Private Institutions Law and presidential decree 1330'. The SSP aims to provide support, technical assistance, export development services, and financial advice to SMEs. The program hopes to improve access to information on export market opportunities, strengthen SME support institutions, and formulate policies to strengthen and support the private sector. The expected results from this endeavor include an improvement in the efficiency and competitiveness of SMEs, and development of local consultancy business so that development services are enhanced. Another important result would be improving and facilitating SMEs' access to and choice of medium- and long-term capital for SMEs.

Several non-governmental organizations in Syria are getting involved in supporting innovation and private enterprises. The following are some of the initiatives:

- Since 2000, the European Investment Bank (EIB) in close coordination with the European Commission has been providing technical and financial assistance through the SME Fund which provides funding to Syrian SMEs through local banks. During the period 2000–07, loans exceeded 1 billion euros in a number of sectors, including the industry, services, infrastructure, tourism, environmental protection, health and education sectors.
- The SHABAB program (Trust for Development) aims to promote entrepreneurship among young people by educating and training them to develop their entrepreneurial spirit.
- BIDAYA was established as an organization which aims to mentor and assist young 'would be' entrepreneurs 'who have a business idea but are unable to find help to become entrepreneurs. They provide seed funding and advice from a business mentor for three years to enable the young entrepreneur realize their dream'. This program was initiated by SYEA (Syrian Young Entrepreneurs Association) whose members provide mentoring to start-ups created by young business.
- SKILLS (Superior Knowledge by Intensive Labor Learning Schemes). The Syrian Enterprise and Business Centre (SEBC)/SME Support Program launched SKILLS which is an initiative co-organized by the European Training Foundation (ETF). Its goal is to serve as an addition, rather than being alternative, to traditional higher education in developing the skills of young people.

According to the SEBC website:

> most institutions and companies are experiencing serious shortages of skilled labor. Many promising, young individuals are ill-equipped to enter the labor market due to the lack of appropriate guidance and capacity building. Even those who manage to find employment discover that the information they have received is theoretical and needs to be complemented by practical skills to satisfy the requirements of their employers.

The environment for entrepreneurship & the state of small business in Syria
According to a report on Arab competitiveness prepared by the World Economic Forum in 2006, Syria's rank was 12 out of 13 Arab countries, and 84 out of 138 countries, with a higher rank being worse. Syria's weaknesses were in the areas of market efficiency (rank 114), technological readiness (109), innovation (99th), higher education and training (96). However, Syria had a better standing in the area of primary education and health (45), and macroeconomic criteria (61). Figure 35.1 shows that starting a business is not easy in Syria. Figure 35.2 shows that doing business is also challenging. Figure 35.3 reveals that the obtaining of credit can also be problematic.

Rami Alasadi (2007) reports that Syria has a centralized economy, a fact which hampers the growth of the private sector, and slows down the expansion of the small business environment in Syria. The government is waking up to the disadvantages of this system, and has been working towards decentralization which is essential if Syria has ambitions to turn into a market economy. One mechanism to accomplish that objective would be supporting the development of the small business sector. According to Alasadi 'the Syrian economy has witnessed a noticeable contribution of the SME sector towards reducing the unemployment rate'. He reports that the Syrian private sector creates 30 000 jobs annually mainly in SMEs, compared to 200 000 created by the government, of which

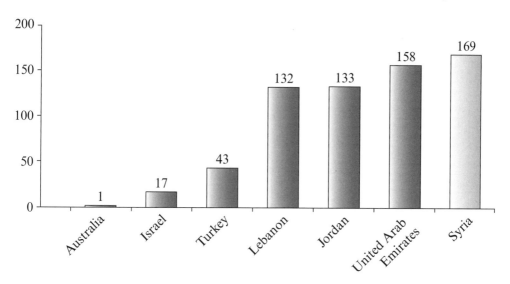

Source: World Bank (2008).

Figure 35.1   Starting a business – global rank

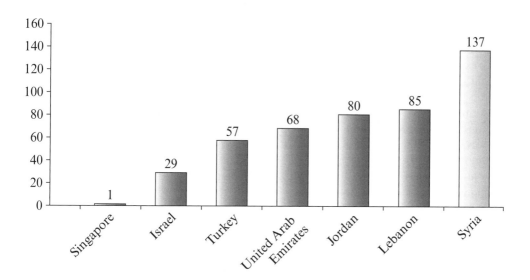

Source: World Bank (2008).

Figure 35.2   Ease of doing business – global rank

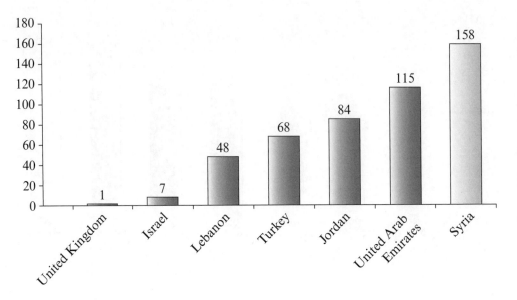

Source: World Bank (2008).

Figure 35.3   Getting credit – global rank

90000 are in the public sector. The implementation of Investment Promotion Laws has facilitated job creation by SMEs.

In an effort to improve the business environment, some of the recent government initiatives have attempted to foster private entrepreneurship; promote market mechanisms; open the economy to the outside world, in addition to modernizing and liberalizing the financial system. A draft law on competition aims to enhance fair competition between the public and private sectors. The government has also taken steps towards simplifying business procedures and lowering the administrative costs of starting a business. However, significant business risks continue to keep potential entrepreneurship ventures away. For instance, Syria's banking system suffers from rigidity and bureaucracy. As a case in point we discuss the Industrial Bank which is state owned; its main purpose, as its name indicates, is providing funding for industrial development. However, it suffers from a shortage of funds and tends to focus on lending to public sector concerns.

A new and recent phenomenon is the emergence of private banks which may ease the small business funding problem; however their ability to provide medium- and long-term financing is constrained by regulations and the shortage of long-term savings instruments. To make things worse, Syria does not really have a stock market, which eliminates the option of taking a company public as a source of financing operations. Syria is in the process of setting up a stock exchange.

Recent reforms have included lowering the tax rates for businesses as well as individuals, a simplification of the tax collection system, and reducing import tariffs.

According to an IMF report (2006):

> tax incentives (such as tax holidays and export promotion incentives) that favor one type of activity over another should be eliminated. To encourage investment, the law could provide for

a low single corporate income tax rate (say of no more than 25 percent) and a generous system of depreciation allowances, which might include an initial investment allowance or an investment tax credit. Incentives already granted should be grandfathered.

Let us discuss the difficulties which are encountered when doing business in Syria by looking at a study that was conducted by the International Finance Corporation (IFC), which is a member of the World Bank Group. The IFC conducts an annual survey that ranks 178 economies on the ease of doing business within each country. The survey ranks economies from 1 to 178, with a rank of 1 being best. The rank of a given country is determined through the examination of 10 indicators which evaluate the ease of doing business, the time, cost, and complexity of meeting government requirements when starting a business. These rankings indicate the impact of regulations on businesses; they can be used to identify bottlenecks which might be constraining business investment, productivity and growth.

In the 2008 survey, Syria had a rank of 137 out of 178 economies in the category of the ease of doing business, which was lower than the year before. It ranked 169 in starting a business, 86 in dealing with licenses, and 171 in enforcing contracts. Major indicators show the insufficiency of reforms to attract domestic and foreign direct investment.

Reforms in Syria during 2008 on 10 different fronts were non-existent except in the area of paying taxes. In addition, the indicator which measures the ease of starting a business suffered a negative impact or a setback from the 2008 reforms or lack thereof.

Internationalization of entrepreneurs and SMEs from Syria
Figure 35.4 reports on Syrian internationalization. It appears that the Syrian government is intent on helping enterprises to expand beyond the country's borders mainly through facilitating exports, signing free trade agreements, as well as easing the restrictions on

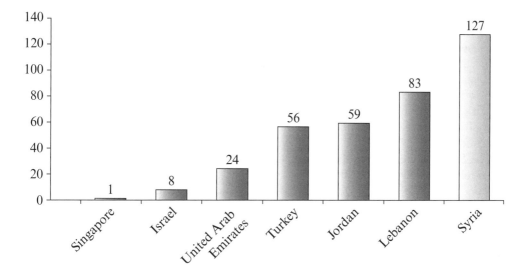

Figure 35.4   Trading across borders – global rank

foreign investments, with the expectation that Syrian ventures will be treated favorably by foreign governments. Syria ranks 127 in the area of trading across borders, compared to last year's rank of 119, which is a deterioration.

What follows is information about Syria's international trade as reported by the CIA Fact Book.

- Current account balance: –US$2.181 billion (2007 est.)
- Exports: US$10.58 billion free on board (f.o.b) (2007 est.)
- Exports – commodities: crude oil, minerals, petroleum products, fruits and vegetables, cotton fiber, textiles, clothing, meat and live animals, wheat
- Exports – partners: Iraq 27.4 percent, Germany 12.1 percent, Lebanon 9.5 percent, Italy 6.6 percent, Egypt 5.3 percent, Saudi Arabia 4.8 percent (2006)
- Imports: US$12.38 billion f.o.b. (2007 est.)
- Imports – commodities: machinery and transport equipment, electric power machinery, food and livestock, metal and metal products, chemicals and chemical products, plastics, yarn, paper
- Imports – partners: Saudi Arabia 12.3 percent, China 7.9 percent, Egypt 6.2 percent, UAE 6 percent, Italy 4.8 percent, Ukraine 4.8 percent, Germany 4.8 percent, Iran 4.5 percent (2006).

Since 2005 Syrian exports to Arab countries have been taking place under the umbrella of the GAFTA which eliminates customs duties between Arab states. In 2007 Syria signed a free trade agreement with Turkey.

The objectives of the Syrian Enterprise and Business Centre include increasing the Syrian private sector's competitiveness in the local and international markets, as well as assisting Syrian private sector enterprises which seek access to international markets.

As far as exporting to Europe is concerned, a 1977 European Union (EU)–Syria Cooperation Agreement gave Syrian exports access privileges to the EU market, on a non-reciprocal basis, particularly for industrial goods. Syria also benefits from reduced tariffs and quantitative ceilings for specific products thanks to the EU General Preferential System (GSP).

Another support system for Syrian exporters comes from an online Export Helpdesk which supplies information about the EU and the member states' import requirements, 'as well as internal taxes, establish whether a particular EU market is worth targeting or not, find trading partners and contacts within the EU'.

The Syrian Enterprise and Business Centre (SEBC) has prepared a Syrian Export Directory 7 (SED7), in cooperation with the Federation of Syrian Chambers of Commerce (FSCC). The Syrian Export Directory includes more than 600 Syrian exporters, in addition to useful information which is relevant to exports.

Conclusion

Syria is currently suffering from economic blockades, sanctions, isolation imposed by some Arab and Western states, and extreme political turmoil because it is surrounded by four countries which are in the middle of military struggles. Syria is making some progress towards improving the business environment for entrepreneurship; however more economic reforms are needed particularly as far as bureaucracy, corruption, transparency and disclosure are concerned.

In the next few years we would like to explore the impact of the escalation of turmoil or, hopefully, the peace process in the Middle East region on the pace of development of entrepreneurial activity in Syria.

References

Alasadi, Rami (2007), 'Critical analysis and modelling of small business performance (case study: Syria)', *Journal of Asia Entrepreneurship and Sustainability*, September, http://findarticles.com/p/articles/mi_qa5499/is_200709/ai_n21301961?tag=content;coll (accessed 12 March 2009).

CIA Fact Book, https://www.cia.gov/library/publications/the-world-factbook/geos/sy.html (accessed 24 July 2008).

Eid, F. and Saliba, J., 'Pantera Middle East – North Africa Region Research Presentation', 2nd Quarter 2008 Report.

Export Helpdesk, http://exporthelp.europa.eu (accessed 11 March 2009).

http://www.fedcommsyr.org/economy.html, Federation of Syrian Chambers of Commerce, accessed 12 March 2009.

http://www.sebcsyria.com/web2008/art.php?art_id=1366 (accessed 24 July 2008).

International Monetary Fund (IMF) (2006), 'Syrian Arab Republic – 2006 Article IV Consultation – Staff Report; and Public Information Notice on the Executive Board Discussion', http://www.imfbookstore.org/ProdDetails.asp?ID=ISRYEA20060012PG=12Type=BL661_14_FULL (accessed 12 March 2009).

Oxford Group (2008), 'Syria: committed to Reform' 13 May, oxfordgroup.com.

Street, Richard (2007), 'Why does Syria need entrepreneurs?', February, Damascus edition of *FOWARD on Entrepreneurship*, http://www.fw_magazine.com/ (accessed 23 July 2003).

The Doing Business project 2008, http://www.doingbusiness.org/EconomyRankings/, (accessed 28 July 2008).

The Sixth MENAinc workshop (2008), 'Entrepreneurship Development and Promotion of Innovation in MENA Countries through Cooperation between Business Incubators' June 3–5, 2008, in Damascus, Syria.

The Syria report website, 'New cooperation EU – Syria at a glance', http://www.syria_report.com (accessed 24 July 2008).

'The Village Business Incubator Project: Implemented by the Fund for Integrated Rural Development of Syria (FIRDOS)', www.vbi-lattakia.org/english/supported_entrepreneurs/services/norma_style.html (accessed 12 March 2009).

World Bank (2008), 'Doing Business 2008: comparing regulation in 178 economies', Washington, DC: World Bank Publications.

World Economic Forum (2006), 'The Global Competitiveness Report 2006, http://www.weforum.org/pdf/Global_Competitiveness_Reports/Reports/Chapters/Tables.pdf (accessed 12 March 2009).

www. banqueaudi.comSyria economic report (accessed 24 July 2008).

www.oxfordbusinessgroup.com/publication.asp?country=6, (accessed 24 July 2008).

36 Taiwan
Hung-bin Ding and Hsi-mei Chung

Introduction
In the last three decades, the Taiwanese economy has moved quickly from labor-intensive activities to technological innovation and the ability to understand customers around the world. Much of Taiwan's past success has been attributed to the small and medium enterprises (SMEs) and the emergence of the 'black-hand' technicians (Wu and Huang, 2003). They are specialists of narrow tasks such as operating certain types of machines. These technician-entrepreneur ventures are the backbone of the post-war Taiwanese economy and the driving force of high economic growth in the 1970s and 1980s. A signature character of black-hand entrepreneurs is their strong sense of cost management and excellent manufacturing capability. Although many of these business ventures are profitable – some even grow to become large enterprises – very few such ventures develop capabilities in corporate research and development (R&D) and marketing. In the era of fast industrial growth, entrepreneurial successes of many black-hand entrepreneurs motivate more black-hands to pursue entrepreneurial opportunities.

However, the increasing importance of technology-intensive industries such as semiconductor and information technology (IT) in Taiwan, and the emergence of China and other low-cost economies in the 1980s, have brought significant challenges to the business model building on cost saving and manufacturing excellence. The Taiwanese government and entrepreneurs have made great efforts to build an enabling environment for entrepreneurship in the last 15 years. In this chapter, we review these recent developments, followed by a brief discussion on their impact on internationalization entrepreneurial activities.

Government policy on SMEs and entrepreneurship in Taiwan
The Taiwanese government plays a central role in developing the national entrepreneurial environment. On one hand, governmental agencies perform effectively to coordinate the fragmented structure of industrial resources to facilitate the creation of high-technology (high-tech) industrial clusters (Ouyang, 2006). Conversely, the small business policies such as small business innovation research (SBIR) grants and women's entrepreneurship initiatives aim to reduce the barrier of new venture initiation, among others.

Industrial policy
Much of Taiwan's recent economic successes in developing globally competitive semiconductor and IT industries are believed to be associated to a series of public policy (Ouyang, 2006). In addition to the provision of tax incentives, many researchers have credited the Taiwanese government with the establishment of the Industrial Technology Research Institute (ITRI), a not-for-profit organization endowed by a one-time government fund, and the Hsinchu Science and Technology Park. The Institute has three main charges. First, ITRI is a bridge to state-of-art engineering research and the Taiwanese

manufacturers. This well-staffed organization assesses, imports, and disseminates the latest development in engineering research to Taiwan. Previous research has highlighted the effect of interpersonal ties between individuals in Silicon Valley and Hsinchu in the transfer of technical and managerial knowledge (Saxenian and Hsu, 2001). Second, ITRI is a corporate R&D center at the national level. It receives research grants from the government and contracts from the private sector to find solutions for technical challenges and to develop prototypes of new products. Third, ITRI is also charged with commercializing the results of government-supported projects through licensing, spin-off, and entrepreneurship (Simon, 1996). Many new ventures founded by former ITRI researchers find a home in the adjacent Hsinchu Science and Technology Park. The creation of ITRI and the Science Park enabled the emergence and later the thriving of semiconductor and IT industries (Ding and Abetti, 2002).

The geographical closeness between ITRI and the Science Park also facilitates the development of inter-organizational networking among technology entrepreneurs. From a social structural point of view, ITRI occupies a central position in the endogenous high-tech industry network, as many high-tech entrepreneurs and their R&D staff are former ITRI scientists or engineers. In addition to ITRI, major Taiwan-based multinational technology corporations have also experienced similar network development activities from their former employees. For example, Stan Shih, the founder of Acer Computer, and his colleagues are the driving forces for the new spin-offs in the development of the personal computer (PC) industry.

As the cost advantage of Taiwanese manufacturers has eroded in recent years, many endogenous semiconductor and IT companies have relocated to China and Southeast Asian countries to continue taking advantage of low-cost production. The Taiwanese government is turning to biotechnology and digital contents industries as new industry targets. The Hsinchu Science and Technology Park, along with two more recently established science parks, serve as a base for nurturing high-technology companies with great growth potential. Attempting to replicate the success with semiconductor and IT industries, the Taiwanese government has also created new research organizations to provide much needed knowledge infrastructure for the nascent biotechnology industry and to serve as hubs of a knowledge network (Chung and Wu, 2006).

Small business innovation research and other policy initiatives
In addition to industrial policy, the Taiwanese government has also launched many national and regional initiatives to encourage business ownership. Some of the long-term programs, such as the SME Credit Guarantee Fund in 1974, played a vital role in assisting technician businesses and other business owners (Wu and Huang, 2003). Building on the previous successes, the government introduced a few new SME initiatives to help nascent entrepreneurs to overcome entrepreneurial challenges in the twenty-first century. The most notable among these new programs are SBIR and the women's entrepreneurship initiative.

The SBIR program was launched in 1998. The objective of SBIR is to assist small technology start-ups in pursuing innovative industrial research. The SBIR program funded more than 1700 proposals from 1999 to 2006. The result of a recent assessment shows that SBIR grant winners have grown in average size, revenue, R&D expenditure, and R&D staff between 2001 and 2005 (Table 36.1).

Table 36.1   Post-grant performance of small business innovation research (SBIR) recipients

	Average no. of employees	Average revenue	Average R&D expenditure	Average no. of R&D staff
2001 (or year of grant approval)	135 322	43	9 317	10
2005	217 233	56	15 170	13
Growth rate	60.5%	31.7%	62.8%	20.3%

Source: Data retrieved 1 October 2007 from the Small Business Innovation Research website, http://www.sbir.org.tw/result/analysis.asp.

Women business owners historically received only 30 percent of government-sponsored start-up funds. Male business owners and nascent entrepreneurs are four times as likely as women entrepreneurs to participate in government-sponsored business training seminars and other information sessions (Tsai et al., 2003). The women's entrepreneurship initiative was launched in 2000 to close the gap between male and women entrepreneurs. More than 7000 women business owners and nascent entrepreneurs have participated in the seminars offered by a national women's entrepreneurship program between 2000 and 2006 (National Youth Commission, 2005).

The economic and socio-cultural environment for entrepreneurship and the state of small business in Taiwan

Human and intellectual capital
Investment in R&D activities contributes to the development of intellectual capital (Frantzen, 2000). From 1960 to 2000, the higher education system and endogenous R&D activities were of central importance to the development of Taiwanese economy (Lin, 2003) and entrepreneurial activities (Ding and Abetti, 2002).

Building on past success, the Taiwanese government and the private sector have made major strides in enhancing the quality of human and intellectual capitals. Major investment and expansions have been dedicated to its higher education system and domestic research and development activities since the mid-1990s. The expanded capacity of higher education institutions contributes to develop a better labor force for current and future industrial needs. In 2006, more than 464 000 full-time undergraduate students majored in science and technology, up from 164 000 in 1997 (Ministry of Education, 2007). This increase in college and university enrollment is mainly attributed to the recent effort to expand the capacity of the higher education system on the island state (see Table 36.2). In general, the expansion of higher education contributes to a major shift of labor quality in Taiwan. As the higher education system produces more college graduates, the supply of black-hand technicians declines.

In addition to the direct impact on the quality of labor supply, along with the increased R&D expenditure, a sizable higher education system in the twenty-first century also has profound influence in the development of science and technology. Universities hire new faculty members to fill the vacancies created from program expansions. More graduate degree programs have been offered, as well-staffed universities are increasingly capable of

Table 36.2   The expansion of the higher education system in Taiwan*

	1997	2002	2003	2004	2005	2006
No. of colleges and universities	78	139	143	145	145	147
Graduate student enrollment (000)	49	122	144	160	176	192
Undergraduate student enrollment (000)	374	771	838	895	938	966
No. of full-time faculty members in four-year colleges	23 729	41 412	43 050	44 787	45 818	46 926

Source: *Calculated by the authors based on data downloaded from the Ministry of Education. Data retrieved 1 October 2007 from http://english.moe.gov.tw/ct.asp?xItem=946&ctNode=1184&mp=1.

developing graduate courses and supervising graduate students. As shown in Table 36.2, the number of full-time faculty members with highest degrees in their fields of study in Taiwanese colleges and universities has grown from about 23 500 to almost 47 000 from 1997 to 2007. Meanwhile, the establishment of new universities and colleges, along with the expansion of the existing ones, brings significant growth to the number of college graduates (Table 36.2). As regards R&D investment, the gross expenditure on research and development activities has grown from US$6 billion in 1995 to nearly US$15 billion dollars in 2004 (Rausch, 2007). The increasing enrollment on domestic graduate programs has effectively retained young talent in Taiwan and reduced the problem of brain drain (Johnson, 2000) to Western countries and Japan. The improved staffing situation, increased graduate school enrollment, and relatively sufficient funding enable researchers to be more committed to research and development than before. As higher education institutions are the locus of both basic and applied research activities in Taiwan, academic innovations are likely to lead to successful commercialization or to aid the improvement of existing products/services.

Culture and social capital
Many studies have labeled the strong orientation to collectivism in the broadly defined Chinese societies (that is, China, Hong Kong, and Taiwan) as Confucianism. One such doctrine is the strong group identification with interpersonal ties. The economies of Confucian culture highly value the importance and harmony of family. This cultural doctrine is instrumental to two common practices in Taiwanese society. The first is the broad boundary of family. Distant relatives who do not share a common household, grandparents, or last name are, however, considered part of family in Taiwanese society. The implication of far-reaching family networks is that members of the network are obliged to behave as expected by the rest of the family (Skoggard, 1996).

The second common practice is the application of family concept to non-family social relationships. For example, Acer Inc. is known for its quasi-family apprenticeship in which junior engineers and managers are treated as family members of the chief executive officer (CEO) and senior managers. According to Bartlett and St. George's (1999) observation, this practice:

> created a close-knit culture, where coworkers treated each other like family and the norm was to do whatever was necessary for the greater good of the company . . . But, it was a very

Table 36.3   Overview of venture capital industry in Taiwan

	2001	2002	2003	2004	2005
Total venture funds	199	217	240	259	268
No. of fund management firms	79	86	93	101	105
Total no. of investment	6957	7560	8719	9782	10295
No. of new investment in year	614	603	1159	1063	513
New fund invested in year (NT$100 million)	81.5	117.4	165.4	152.7	108.6
Ranking in World Competitiveness Yearbook*	14	9	2	4	6
No. of new VCs founded in year	7	18	23	15	NA

Note: * International Institute for Management Development, *World Competitive Yearbook 2001–05.*

Source: Taiwan Venture Capital Association, retrieved 1 October 2007 from http://www.tvca.org.tw/english/Index_En.htm.

> demanding 'family' and . . . the patriarch, Stan Shih worked hard to combat complacency by creating a constant sense of crisis . . . As long as the managers took responsibility for their actions – acted as responsible older sons and daughters – they had the freedom to make decisions . . .

The compounded effect of broad family boundary and quasi-family relationships creates a broad network of personal relationships for nascent entrepreneurs. The interpersonal relationships are one's social capital, which allow an individual to gain access to resources not available internally (Portes, 1998). Such social capital is critical in the initial stage of entrepreneurial enterprises. The family ties or the quasi-family ties not only provide trustworthy relationships in communication or knowledge transfer, but also an important source for financial support. Previous research on the Taiwanese society and economic activities has documented the role of interpersonal relationships in enabling nascent entrepreneurs to exploit entrepreneurial opportunities (Hsiung, 1996). Relationship-based financing, including seeking funds from expanded families and friends, is the primary source of new venture financing in the Taiwanese society (Kao, 1999). Additionally, SME entrepreneurs usually rely on family ties to support the managerial and financial requirement in the initial stage (Kao, 1999). Family and friends provide trustworthy relationships and social capital that reduces cost and improves communication in the initial stage of a new business venture.

Venture capital (VC) industry
The successes in semiconductor and IT industries provide a fertile ground for the endogenous VC industry. From 1996 to 2004, the Taiwanese VC industry has invested about US$6 billion dollars in more than 10000 new ventures (Taiwan Venture Capital Association, 2005: 48). The venture capital industry in Taiwan has become one of the largest in the world in 20 years, and it is a central player in new venture financing (Table 36.3). The VC investment in Taiwan is ranked fourteenth in the World Competitive yearbook of 2001. Despite the tightened regulation on new venture fund incorporation and the abolishment of a long-held 20 percent tax credit for investing in venture funds in 2001, the number of VC funds continues to grow (Table 36.3).

There are about 1200 publicly traded companies in the Taiwanese stock market. Venture Capital backed firms account for about 30 percent of these public companies (Taiwan Venture Capital Association, 2005: 160). New ventures in semiconductor and IT hardware industries are historically the favorite target of investment for Taiwanese VCs. However, as these industries approach maturity, fund managers have started to direct their attentions to other emerging industries backed by the government. For example, the funds invested to biotechnology, software, and e-business have grown by 30.5 percent, 143.7 percent, and 337.3 percent respectively, from 2004 to 2005 (Taiwan Venture Capital Association, 2007).

Internationalization of entrepreneurs and SMEs from Taiwan: drivers and roadblocks
The pursuit of business opportunities and knowledge are two major motivators of SME and technology venture internationalization. Since the 1960s, the entrepreneurial drive for growth opportunities beyond the limited domestic market has motivated Taiwanese entrepreneurs to seek international business opportunities. Much of the past economic success of Taiwan builds on such opportunity-driven internationalization. The prevalence of black-hand entrepreneurs is instrumental to the emergence and growth of small and medium manufacturers. These SMEs' expertise in cost reduction and process improvement enable them to secure OEM contracts with world-class manufacturers in Europe, Japan, and the United States (Wu and Hsu, 2001).

In the last two decades, technology entrepreneurs have demonstrated strong interests in knowledge accumulation through internationalization. Many Taiwanese firms develop and accumulate their technological competence by learning from globally competitive firms through long-term original equipment manufacturer (OEM) contracts. The long-term contract allows systematic and regular knowledge transfer between Taiwanese firms and their international collaborators (Wu and Hsu, 2001). Although these knowledge transfers focus mostly on areas such as manufacturing and quality management, new knowledge gradually enhances the recipient firms' absorptive capacity, opening their international vision and developing their capabilities in monitoring and coping with world changes (Ding and Abetti, 2002).

The pursuits of overseas business opportunities and knowledge sources continue to shape the environment of new venture internationalization in the first decade of the twenty-first century. In our opinion, there are three major driving forces behind the increasing internationalization of entrepreneurship in Taiwan. First, the formation and development of multinational supply chain and the internationalization of manufacturing activities in China, and other emerging economies, provide an infrastructure for nascent entrepreneurs. Such infrastructure has two implications for entrepreneurial opportunity identification and exploitation. First, this infrastructure lowers the cost of new venture initiation. It enables entrepreneurs to focus on the core activity of their business (for example, R&D, design, and marketing) while outsourcing supply chain management and manufacturing to low-cost countries. Second, the internationalized supply chain and manufacturing activities are sources of potential entrepreneurial opportunities. A complex network consisting of multinational manufacturers offers many opportunities for minor improvements or incremental innovations. The growing number of international expatriates following the establishment of overseas factories (Liu et al., 1998) also creates new business opportunities for international human resource services. In short, the formation of a well-developed supply chain infrastructure creates new opportunities for international entrepreneurship.

The second driving force is the government. Despite its effectiveness in commercialization, Taiwan trails the US and a few Western economies in original technological innovation and basic research. The Taiwanese government's initiatives are designed to develop new industries by importing and localizing new technology for commercialization. Government programs and government-sponsored organizations such as ITRI and university research projects serve domestic entrepreneurs as the boundary-spanner. Although the Taiwanese government has an uneven track record in new industry development (Liu, 1998), there is little controversy about the prominent role of the government in bridging domestic and international technology communities (Ding and Abetti, 2002).

The third driving force is the success of semiconductor and IT industries. The technical and market leadership of Taiwanese firms in these two industries are attractive to international talents. The high-paying jobs also help to mitigate the problem of brain drain by attracting many overseas Taiwanese engineers and managers back to their birthplace. In addition, the ascendance of Taiwanese firms in these two industries put Taiwan on the map for international R&D joint ventures. A recently announced joint R&D agreement between IBM and Taiwan-based Mediatek exemplifies the critical role of Taiwanese firms in the global semiconductor industry (Reuters, 2007).

However, the effectiveness of these driving forces is limited by three major factors. The first factor is the lack of marketing capabilities in international markets. Although they have long been applauded for their performance in supply chain management and incremental innovations, most of the Taiwanese firms lack brand recognition to customers outside of Taiwan. Many Taiwanese manufacturers minimize the operations of brand products to avoid conflict of interest with their OEM/original design manufacturer (ODM) clients. As OEM/ODM requires little marketing capability, with few exceptions, marketing and branding activities have been underinvested by Taiwanese firms in the past. Recent government programs to publicize the top Taiwanese brands and the launch of the 'Branding Taiwan' initiative are examples to encourage business owners to engage in market learning.

Second, Taiwanese entrepreneurs have relatively little experience in developing and managing multinational corporations. As R&D, marketing, and other business functions become increasingly internationalized, Taiwanese firms must learn to cope with more internationally diverse staff, market, and associated regulatory and cultural differences. Acer's failed attempt to enter the US and Canadian personal computer market in the 1990s illustrates the difficulty in overcoming the challenges of managing a multinational corporation (Bartlett and St. George, 1999).

The third factor is the concentration of VC investment and manager expertise in domestic high-technology ventures. About 80–90 percent of Taiwanese VC investment went to domestic and Silicon Valley companies between 2000 and 2005 (Taiwan Venture Capital Association, 2005). Although venture capitalists specialize in ventures of select industries or geographically close ventures (Sahlman, 1990), high emphasis on domestic and Silicon Valley high-tech ventures gives VCs little incentive to develop competence in evaluating and developing ventures based in other promising geographical locations. In addition, the growing homogeneity of the Taiwanese venture capital industry makes it less likely to bring in the best talents and corporate contacts from their extensive international network to help fund recipients pursue internationalization.

Conclusion

In the last quarter of the twentieth century, Taiwan has emerged as a major partner in the global supply chain and later a lead player in semiconductor and IT industries. These achievements are instrumental to the development of new foundation for entrepreneurial activities. Facing the challenges from the emerging economies, the Taiwanese government and entrepreneurs have begun to pursue new opportunities building on this new foundation. The impact and effectiveness of such a shift of focus is worth exploring for policy makers and academic researchers.

References

Bartlett, C.A. and St. George, A. (1999), 'Acer America: development of the Aspire', Harvard Business School Multimedia/Video Case 301–109.

Chung, H.M., and R.T. Wu (2006), 'The challenges of duplicating the Taiwan's semi-conductor industry experience in bio-technological industry: a network theory viewpoint', paper presented at the 12th Asia Pacific Management Conference (APMC).

Ding, H.B. and P.A. Abetti (2002), 'The entrepreneurial success of Taiwan: synergy between social capital and institutional support', in Gary Libecap (ed.), *Advances in the Study of Entrepreneurship, Innovation, and Economic Growth*, Greenwich, CT: JAI Press, pp. 91–124.

Frantzen, D. (2000), 'R&D, human capital and international technology spillovers: a cross-country analysis', *Scandinavian Journal of Economics*, **102**(1), 57–75.

Hsiung, P.-C. (1996), *Living Rooms as Factories: Class, Gender, and the Satellite Factory System in Taiwan, Phildelphia*, PA: Temple University Press.

International Institute for Management Development (2001), *World Competitiveness Yearbook 2001*, Lausanne: IMD.

International Institute for Management Development (2002), *World Competitiveness Yearbook 2002*, Lausanne: IMD.

International Institute for Management Development (2003), *World Competitiveness Yearbook 2003*, Lausanne: IMD.

International Institute for Management Development (2004), *World Competitiveness Yearbook 2004*, Lausanne: IMD.

International Institute for Management Development (2005), *World Competitiveness Yearbook 2005*, Lausanne: IMD.

Johnson, J.M. (2000), 'Graduate education reform in Europe, Asia, and the Americas and international mobility of scientists and engineers', *Proceedings of an NSF Workshop*, Arlington, VA: National Science Foundation, Division of Science Resources Studies.

Kao, C.H. (1999), *The Boss's Wife: The Economic Activity and the Social Meanings of the Boss's Wife in the Small-to-Medium Enterprises in Taiwan*, Taipei, Taiwan: Linkingbooks. (In Chinese.)

Lin, T.-C. (2003), 'Education, technical progress, and economic growth: the case of Taiwan', *Economics of Education Review*, **22**(2), 213–20.

Liu, S.J. (1998), 'Industrial development and structural adaptation in Taiwan: some issues of learned entrepreneurship', *IEEE Transactions on Engineering Management*, **45**(4), 338–48.

Liu, S.-J., F.-L. Huang and Q.-H. Chen (1998), 'International development of Taiwan's information industry: An empirical study on human resource strategy of overseas subsidiaries', *TEEE Transactions on Engineering Management*, **45**(3), 296–310.

Ministry of Education (2007), http://www.edu.tw/EDU_WEB/EDU_MGT/STATISTICS/EDU7220001/data/serial/u.xls?FILEID=130550&UNITID=139&CAPTION=%A4j%B1M%B0%7C%AE%D5%B7%A7%AAp%B2%CE%ADp (accessed 19 August 2007).

National Youth Commission (2005), 'Statistics on participants in the Wild Geese program in previous years', http://english.nyc.gov.tw/content_link.php?page2=4&act=info&sn=4&page=4 (accessed 1 October 2007).

Ouyang, H.S. (2006), 'Agency problem, institutions, and technology policy: explaining Taiwan's semiconductor industry development', *Research Policy*, **36**, 1314–28.

Portes, A. (1998), 'Social capital: its origins and applications in modern sociology', *American Review of Sociology*, **24**, 1–24.

Rausch, L. (2007), 'Asia's rising science and technology strength: comparative indicators for Asia, the European Union, and the United States', National Science Foundation.

Reuters (2007), 'IBM and Taiwan's Mediatek launch chip R&D project', http://www.reuters.com/article/technologyNews/idUSTP4000320071022 (accessed 22 October 2007).

Sahlman, W. (1990), 'The structure and governance of venture capital organizations', *Journal of Financial Economics*, **27**, 473–521.

Saxenian, A., and J.-Y. Hsu (2001), 'The Silicon Valley-Hsinchu connection: technical communities and industrial upgrading', *Industrial and Corporate Change*, **10**(4), 893–920.

Simon, D. (1996), 'Charting Taiwan's technological future: the impact of globalization and regionalization', *The China Quarterly*, **148**, 1196–223.

Skoggard, I.A. (1996), *The Indigenous Dynamics in Taiwan's Postwar Development*, Armonk, NY: M.E. Sharpe.

Taiwan Venture Capital Association (2005), *TVCA 2005 Yearbook*, Taipei, Taiwan: Taiwan Venture Capital Association.

Taiwan Venture Capital Association (2007), 'Venture capital as a policy tool', http://www.tvca.org.tw/english/Index_En.htm (accessed 1 October 2007).

Tsai, S.L., C.T. Wen and M. Rice (2003), 'The influence of government policies on women entrepreneurship in Taiwan', paper presented in the 48th World Conference – International Council for Small Business, Belfast, Northern Ireland, 15–18 June 2003.

Wu, R.-I. and C.-C. Huang (2003), 'Entrepreneurship in Taiwan: turning point to restart', paper presented at the Global Forum – Entrepreneurship in Asia: 4th U.S.–Japan Dialogue, 16 April. Available from the Maureen and Mike Mansfield Foundation.

Wu, S. and F.B. Hsu (2001), 'Toward a knowledge-based view of OEM relationship building: sharing of industrial experiences in Taiwan', *International Journal of Technology Management*, **22**(5/6), 503–24.

37 Tajikistan[1]
Léo-Paul Dana

Introduction

Tajikistan, the poorest of the five Central Asian republics, covers an area of 143 100 square kilometres, making it the smallest of the five formerly Soviet Central Asian republics. It is landlocked – surrounded by Afghanistan, China, the Kyrgyz Republic, and Uzbekistan. Until 1930, the Tajik language was written using Arabic script. It used the Roman alphabet from 1930 to 1940, and Cyrillic from 1940 to 1992. Today, the Tajik language once again uses Arabic characters. There have been several changes in government since independence, in 1991. Economic development in Tajikistan was delayed by the 1992–97 civil war, between the government and the Islamic-led United Tajik Opposition. Of the 15 formerly Soviet republics, Tajikistan has the lowest per capita gross domestic product (GDP). According to the Economist Intelligence Unit, the black market in Tajikistan exceeds 57 percent of true GDP. In contrast to other transitional economies where small business thrives in the informal sector, Tajik entrepreneurs perceive the covert sector as a most interesting alternative for economic activity.

Surrounded today by Turkic neighbours, the Tajiks – people of Persian descent – have been in Central Asia long before the tenth century invasions by the Turkics. Between 1918 and 1924, Tajikistan was part of the Turkestan Soviet Socialist Republic. In 1924 – when the Uzbek Soviet Socialist Republic was carved out of Turkestan – Tajikistan became the Tajik Autonomous Soviet Socialist Republic, within the Uzbek Soviet Socialist Republic. On 5 December 1929, this Tajik region emerged as the Tajik Soviet Socialist Republic – a constituent republic of the USSR. It remained, nevertheless, controlled by Moscow, and its capital city Dushanbe became known as Stalinabad. Central planning forced out traditional mixed farming – which had supported self-sufficiency – and instead imposed specialization in cotton, to the benefit of the Russian economy.

During its years as a constituent of the Soviet Union, the Tajik Soviet Socialist Republic had the highest population growth rate of any republic in the USSR, and the second lowest per capita GDP in the union. The capital city, Dushanbe, was the base from which the Soviets invaded Afghanistan in 1979.

Occupation by the Soviet army was actually good for the Tajiks inasmuch as it controlled inter-regional tension within the Tajik Soviet Socialist Republic. In the same way that India was kept united under the British, or Yugoslavia under Tito, the Soviets maintained peace within each of its republics. Tight control by the Soviets postponed ethnic conflict among Tajiks. When Tajikistan became independent, however, inter-regional tension resulted in civil war and economic collapse.

In the economic realm, reforms were meaningless as former communist officials were reluctant to let go of their power. In 1991, Tajikistan tried to adopt the Russian rouble as its own domestic currency, but the instability and unpredictability of Moscow's economic policies resulted in a serious monetary crisis. Workers and pensioners were unpaid for months.

On 9 September 1991, the former Tajik Soviet Socialist Republic gained its independence, becoming the Republic of Tajikistan, known locally as Jumkhurii Tojikistan. Immediately after independence, *The Economist* correctly predicted a potential for trouble in the region, and Tajikistan fell into turmoil as it experienced several changes of government.

The Islamic opposition, legalized in 1991, took power in a 1992 coup, but the Islamic Renaissance Party, as it was known, was essentially ousted and outlawed. Meanwhile, civil war ravaged the country. A state of emergency was imposed in January 1993. The United Nations mediated peace talks between the government and its opponents, which agreed to a cease-fire in 1994. Yet, the conflict continued, despite the deployment of Russian troops throughout the country.

Industrial production shrank by 31 percent in 1994, while the population's rate of growth – in spite of emigration – continued to be 3 percent, the highest in Central Asia, and four times that in the nearby Republic of Kazakhstan. A new constitution was adopted on 6 November 1994, but a variety of factors prevented any significant reform, a prerequisite to the establishment of an entrepreneurial class. The Tajikistani rouble replaced Russian currency on 10 May 1995, making Tajikistan the last country outside Russia to abandon the Russian rouble.

By 1996, increasing tension and the continuation of shootings strained the environment for any form of legitimate entrepreneurial activity. A cease-fire was agreed to on 23 December 1996. After the 27 June 1997 peace agreement was signed, 5000 fighters of the opposition were integrated into the Tajik army. Yet, fighting resumed in November 1998.

On 27 February 2000, Tajikistan held its first multi-party parliamentary elections. However, international monitors reported that it fell short of minimum standards. As the national currency rapidly lost its value, the somoni was introduced on 30 October 2000. The new unit was defined as worth 1000 Tajikistani roubles. Not surprisingly, the economy has a significant covert sector.

Government policy
Transition to a market economy, in Tajikistan, was delayed by civil war. The combined effect of civil war, the loss of Soviet subsidies and the breakdown of Soviet distribution channels, resulted in the collapse of the Tajik economy. For years, the nation relied on humanitarian assistance for subsistence. Uzbekistan has been a major contributor, but fearing a spill-over of civil unrest, religious fervour and military conflict, this country often closed its border with Tajikistan, and disrupted fuel supplies.

This economic situation in Tajikistan is ironic, given that the republic is particularly endowed with a variety of natural resources, including antimony, coal, lead, mercury, petroleum, tungsten, uranium and zinc. In addition, it has significant potential for hydroelectric power; national efforts have been directed toward this option, but not in a way to maximize its potential. An aluminium plant, some obsolete small-scale factories involved in food processing, and other light industry are among the few signs of formal business activity in this country.

Increasing pressure is being placed on this nation, as the population exceeds 6 million people, with a labour force of about 2 million. The nation has failed to become self-sufficient and a low standard of living persists. This problem is worsened by the fact that women continue to bear an average of five children – compared to three in the neigh-bouring Kyrgyz Republic – and there is no system set up for the youth to grow into. A remarkable 43 percent of Tajikistan's population is under 15 years old; this is 6 percent more than is the case in the Kyrgyz Republic, and 12 percent more than the figures for Kazakhstan.

Numerous constraints in Tajikistan discourage legal forms of entrepreneurial activ-ity. Continued hostilities between ethnic groups contribute to a variety of problems, including strains on the environment, infrastructure inadequacies and the lack of impor-tance given to basic education. Among the relevant issues are: over-utilization of water, increasing pollution, excessive use of pesticides, inadequately developed and poorly maintained communication networks, chronic fuel shortages, worsening international relations, border conflicts and low attendance at school. In contrast, covert economic activities are quite promising due to their accessibility and uncontrolled channels of distribution. The lack of trust in the unstable currency has allowed the barter system to thrive over a modern cash economy. Cognitive innovation is necessary, as payments in kind require a different notion of measurability than do cash payments. Different ele-ments enter the equation and this changes social relations.

Some entrepreneurs see tourism as an opportunity to collect a fast dollar. However, it should be noted that in contrast to neighbouring Uzbekistan, which benefits from tour-ists visiting ancient centres of the Silk Road network, Tajikistan has almost no tourism. Concerns include inadequate sanitary facilities as well as security. Fuel shortages aggra-vate the situation, as people coming into the country are unsure about if and when they can get out. Nevertheless, a very big attraction in Tajikistan is the world's largest population of wild Marco Polo sheep. These animals have horns up to 6 feet long, and hunters from Germany and the United States have been paying US$18 000 for a kill. A problem, here, is that experts estimate that there are only 8000 adult Marco Polo sheep left.

Despite the so-called peace, the environment is still perceived as risky for investments. Instead, Tajikistan has become a major centre for the distribution of illicit drugs to Europe and to Canada, as well as to the United States. Policy-makers – riding in expen-sive limousines – claim that they lack the funds to chlorinate the water supply of the republic.

The environment for entrepreneurship and the state of small business
Enterprise is hindered by the general lack of infrastructure. Communications are poorly developed and the system is badly maintained. Fewer than one in ten people in Tajikistan has a telephone, and entire towns are excluded from the national network. This can be a difficult barrier when conducting business. Also plagued is the transporta-tion system. The entire country has only 480 kilometres – fewer than 300 miles – of rail track in common carrier service and the bus service is practically non-existent. During the summer, motor traffic is disrupted by fuel shortages, and during the winter, roads are blocked by snow and are seldom cleared. There are few petrol stations; along major highways, drivers purchase gasoline in bottles, from entrepreneurs who operate at the micro-enterprise level, but this is only when fuel is available.

The economy in Tajikistan is largely agricultural; half of the labour force works on farms, producing cotton, fruits and vegetables. Grapevines are grown not only for the grapes but also for the leaves, which are used in a variety of dishes. Farming is very labour intensive; one can observe literally hundreds of women hunched over, working in fields.

The agricultural sector has severe limitations, as only 6 percent of the land is arable. Tajikistan is part of the basin of the Aral Sea, and this region is suffering from severe over-utilization of water; and increasing levels of soil salinity are a problem. Furthermore, industrial pollution and the excessive use of pesticides have contaminated much of the soil. Cattle, goats and sheep are raised, but meadow and pasture cover less than one-quarter of the land, and animals are forced to graze on the shoulders of motorways. The country has no forest and the Pamir Mountains have semi-arid to polar weather.

Cotton is officially the number one crop, but only because the former USSR imposed its production. In fact, the land in Tajikistan is not ideal for this labour-intensive crop. Furthermore, the development of secondary industries – such as textiles – has not been an attractive option. Instead, there has been a significant rise in the cultivation of cannabis and opium poppies, both of which are less labour-intensive and much more profitable than is the case with cotton. In the north-west of the republic, near Lake Dushakha, heroin poppies appear to be the principal cash crop.

Internationalization
The geographic location of Tajikistan could be an important asset in itself. In neighbouring Uzbekistan, a snow-covered mountain range separates the capital city, Tashkent, from Kokand – in the Fergana Valley – and points north; therefore, Uzbek buses link towns in Uzbekistan, via Tajikistan. This provides transportation within Tajikistan, and business to Tajik entrepreneurs along the way. However, even after the 1994 cease-fire, border closings 'for security reasons' were disruptive to business. Fear of being knifed or hurt by homemade bombs are real concerns for the few people who happen to pass through. The town of Hudzand, alone, has the potential of making Tajikistan an international silk centre. However, entrepreneurs engaged in import/export operations are concerned about border closings and international disputes. Tajikistan's boundaries – both with China and with the Kyrgyz Republic – are in dispute. In 1996, the border with Afghanistan was the site of numerous killings. Better relations with one's neighbours might be more conducive to cross-border entrepreneurial activity.

As for inter-continental links, in 1994, Tajik Air leased a Boeing 747 from United Air Lines, and introduced air service between Europe and Tajikistan. This might have helped entrepreneurs in the short run, but the choice of aircraft was not a wise one, as the 747 – even with a low payload – consumed much jet fuel, and Tajikistan was experiencing fuel shortages. Moreover, the passenger capacity of this particular aircraft was much higher than the demand for seats. The national airline finally collapsed. More recently, Tajikistan International Airlines launched service as far west as London's Heathrow Airport; British Airways agreed to be the handling agent.

Toward the future
In contrast to the other peoples of Central Asia who are of Altaic stock, the Tajiks are racially Indo-European, and Mediterranean features are common. While the other republics of the region speak Turkic languages, the Tajik tongue is related to Farsi. A difference with possibly greater implications is that while Kazakhstan, Turkmenistan,

Uzbekistan and the Kyrgyz Republic have been looking at Turkey as a role model, Tajikistan has leaned more towards Iran. Whereas Turkey has been striving to improve its economic well-being, Iran concentrated first on strengthening religious ideals. This is manifested by such acts such as the funding, by Iran, of the major mosque in Dushanbe. However, emphasis swayed away from religion, in May 1997, when the Iranians elected Mohammed Khatami, a moderate leader.

At the time of the 1989 census – the last conducted in the USSR – 62.3 percent of the population of Tajikistan was Tajik, 23.5 percent Uzbek, and 7.6 percent Russian. The Tajiks are predominantly Sunni Muslims. Within Tajikistan is the Badakhshan Autonomous Province, whose inhabitants are predominantly of the Ismaili sect of Shi'ite Islam – with no mosques. These people claim to be descendants of people who were subjects of Alexander the Great. Their sect is led by the Aga Khan.

Two-thirds of the population in Tajikistan are Tajik, one-quarter is Uzbek, and the balance is comprised of Russians, Jews, and other ethnic groups. Lately, many of the minorities – including the Russians – have been feeling insecure, and some have moved away, contributing to Tajikistan's net emigration rate. As an illustration, membership at the Dushanbe synagogue fell from 20000 in 1989 to 10000 in 1993.

Tajikistan today is the victim of the historically rooted regional animosities which climaxed into serious civil war as people from the Hissar, Kulyab and Leninabad regions of this country have been resented by others who have felt relatively deprived in the political arena. Young (1971) suggested that entrepreneurship occurs when an ethnic group with low status is denied access to mainstream society, but only when resources are available. In Tajikistan, the politically deprived are also economically deprived.

Tajikistan is pluralistic, with a shared core universe, and different partial universes coexisting with the lack of mutual accommodation. The perpetuation of hostilities, despite the official cease-fire, has worsened the general economic situation. Kazakhstan, the Kyrgyz Republic, Russia and Uzbekistan have agreed to defend the Afghan–Tajik border. Yet, ethnic violence from within the country has threatened the sustainable existence of the Tajik people. Professionally trained mercenaries from Afghanistan, Iran and Pakistan were among those fighting inside Tajikistan.

The mountain region of Gorno-Badakshan is an Islamic rebel bastion within Tajikistan, but beyond the control of the Tajik government. Anarchy reigns here, contributing to the thriving of opium merchants who, from here, travel west into Europe and beyond. The road from Khorog, at the Afghan–Tajik border, is among many routes travelled by hardy nomads transporting illicit cargoes. Border guards are seemingly turning a blind eye to gift-bearing 'merchants' engaged in such covert entrepreneurial activities.

The move to a market economy is process driven. It requires people to understand the dynamics of free enterprise. However, due to considerable communist influence in the past, many Tajiks are not familiar with 'normal' business practices in a market economy. The Tajik concept of enterprise is not the same as that in the West, and management is not seen the same way. Under the old regime, there were no managers in the Western sense, but rather highly influential industrial bureaucrats. They did not manage; instead, they received orders from superior functionaries and simply executed the instructions. Consequently, people are still waiting for directives. Many are waiting for foreigners to initiate new ventures. Meanwhile, engaging in covert activities is providing an overwhelming source of hard currency, this to the detriment of engaging in legal entrepreneurial behaviour such as that found in internal, informal and formal categories of economic activity.

Whereas independence from Moscow has enabled entrepreneurs in some newly independent countries to enter better economic times, for Tajikistan, secession has not contributed to legitimate entrepreneurship. Instead, Tajiks perceive perestroika as having caused a loss of job security, and independence has resulted in a loss of subsidies and distribution channels. Furthermore, the departure of the Soviets helped rekindle ethnic and regional tensions. Aside from trading in illegal drugs and/or hunting endangered species, Tajiks see little opportunity for entrepreneurial activity in their new country.

Acknowledgement

Kind thanks to Gulnoza Saidazimova for reviewing the first draft of this chapter.

Note

1. This chapter is largely based on Dana (2002), containing information obtained from: the Ministry of Agriculture, Dushanbe; the Ministry of Culture and Innovation, Dushanbe; the Ministry of Commerce and Material Resources, Dushanbe; the Ministry of Economy and Foreign Economic Relations, Dushanbe; and the United Nations Military Observers Team.

References

Dana, Léo-Paul (2002), *When Economies Change Paths: Models of Transition in China, the Central Asian Republics, Myanmar, and the Nations of Former Indochine Française*, Singapore, London and Hong Kong: World Scientific.

Young, Frank W. (1971), 'A macrosocialized interpretation of entrepreneurship', in Peter Kilby (ed), *Entrepreneurship and Economic Development*, New York: Free Press, pp. 139–50.

38 Thailand

Scott A. Hipsher

Introduction

Thailand is located in central Southeast Asia (SEA) and has a land mass approximately equal to that of Spain (Leppart, 1996) while having a population estimated at slightly over 65 million (Thailand Facts and Figures, 2007), which is up from 55.84 million in 1990 (Asian Development Bank, 2007). Life expectancy in the country has risen sharply in recent years; in the 1970s life expectancy was only 58 years while today it is over 70 for men and nearly 75 for women (Somjai, 2003; Thailand Facts and Figures, 2007).

There is no concensus amongst historians on the exact origins of the Thai people and their culture, but it is generally assumed the original home of the ancestors of the Thai people was somewhere in present-day China (Jumsai, 2001: 8–15; Syamananda, 1993: 6–7). Apparently, the ancestors of the present-day Thais migrated to Nanchao, which is located in the present-day Yunnan Province of China, and later began to move south and west where they set up various kingdoms in present-day Burma, Laos, and Thailand, beginning over a thousand years ago in locations where the Mons and Khmers were already living and had established political institutions (Syamananda, 1993: 10–14).

One of the earliest kingdoms thought of as Thai was the Kingdom of Lannathai, which was located in present-day Northern Thailand. This kingdom came into its own in the thirteenth century under King Mengrai (Jumsai, 2001: 31–41). Shortly afterwards, the kingdom that is considered the forerunner of modern day Thailand, Sukhotai, was founded in 1238 when the Thais drove the Khmer governor out of the region (Jumsai, 2001: 26; Syamananda, 1993: 20). The most famous king of the Sukhotai period, and one of the most famous kings in all of Thai history, was King Ramkamhaeng in whose reign the Thai system of writing was created and whose reign is remembered from the stone inscriptions glorifying his rule (Jumsai, 2001: 81; Syamananda, 1993: 24). Eventually, the Kingdom of Sukhotai began a period of decline and was therefore swallowed up by the growing power of the Thai Kingdom of Ayutthaya in the early fifteenth century (Syamananda, 1993: 31).

The founding of the Kingdom of Ayutthaya in 1350 has historically been credited to King Ramathibodi; and the kingdom apparently stood on the same location as a previous Khmer settlement (Jumsai, 2001, 28; Syamananda, 1993, 32). Ayutthaya was the ancient capital of the Thai people until the city was devastated by the Burmese in 1767 (Syamananda, 1993: 91). After the Burmese army withdrew, Taksin of Thonburi united the Thai people and drove out the remaining Burmese and built a new Thai Kingdom. However, it has been claimed that he went insane and he was executed before founding a lasting dynasty (Syamananda, 1993: 93–9). The throne was then offered to Somdech Chao Phya Mahakasetsuek, who started the current Chakri dynasty (named after the title Chao Phya Chakri the first king previously held). The first king of the current dynasty is also referred to as King Ramatibodi, Pra Buddha Yodfachulaloke, and Rama I with each successive king also being referred to by the title Rama; the current king, the beloved King Bhumibol Adulyadej, is also referred to as Rama IV (Syamananda, 1993). The change from being an absolute monarchy to a constitutional monarchy occurred in 1932 (Syamananda, 1993: 162) but the move towards becoming a democratic country has been more of an evolutionary process rather than the result of any single event.

Politics in Thailand in recent times has been a very complex, divisive and messy affair. 'Following the 1932 revolution that imposed limits on the monarchy, Thai politics has been dominated for a half century by the military and bureaucratic elite. Changes of government were effected primarily by means of a long series of mostly bloodless coups' (A brief history of modern Thai politics, 2007). Politics in Thailand has always been more about personalities than issues and today's political parties are much more closely associated with the personality of their leaders as opposed to their stances on political issues.

Thailand began what appeared to be the start of becoming a true democracy in May 1992 when Chuan Leekpai of the Democrat Party became the elected leader of the country after the previous military regime lost its legitimacy in the minds of the Thai people and was forced out. Chavalit Youngchaiyudh's New Aspiration Party won the 1996 election but the Asian financial crisis brought a quick return of Chuan Leekpai to the job of Prime Minister. The political climate in Thailand changed quite dramatically with the election of the telecommunications tycoon, Thaksin Shinawatra and his Thai Rak Thai Party in 2001. With the heavy support of rural voters in the north and northeast, Thaksin and his party won a landslide reelection victory in 2005 (A brief history of modern Thai politics, 2007).

However, despite overwhelming support by the electorate, Thaksin Shinawatra proved to be a divisive figure. The Prime Minster was heavily criticized by his political opponents for his authoritarian manner, misuse of office for private gains and populist policies. While remaining widely popular in rural Thailand, the Prime Minister began finding many powerful figures, especially amongst the wealthy elites of Bangkok, were becoming political opponents. In a political maneuver to attempt to silence his critics, Thaksin Shinawatra called for snap elections in 2006. However, before the new elections took place, in which Thaksin and the Thai Rak Thai party were expected to easily win, a bloodless coup occurred on the night of 19 September 2006 led by General Sonthi Boonyaratglin; although speculation continues to this day about whether General Sonthi was acting on his own or other powerful figures were actually behind the takeover of power. This was the seventeenth coup since the abolition of the absolute monarchy in 1932. The stated aims of this most recent coup were the removal of influence of Thaksin Shinawatra from politics, to end corruption, bring about stability and unite the country (Charoensin-o-larn, 2007).

Subsequently to the military takeover of the country, the political divisions remain, violence in the south has continued, the economy has underperformed in comparison to regional neighbors, no court has found former Prime Minister Thaksin or any members of his inner circle guilty of corruption, and a pro-Thaksin party won the 2008 election that has returned the country to a state of a democracy. Neither this latest nor previous coups provide compelling support for the idea that military dictators rule the country better than elected officials.

Although Thailand has now held elections and a new government has been formed (Post Reporters, 2008), the political divisions between supporters of Thaksin, mostly rural, and the opponents of Thaksin, led by the old guard elites, continue and whether Thailand is now firmly on the road to continued democracy or the country can expect yet another military-led coup is unclear. There are also uncertainties about who is actually running the country. Samak Sundaravej was elected Prime Minister under the People Power Party (PPP) banner, but since the PPP is made up primarily of former Thai Rak Thai officials, openly aligned itself with former Prime Minister Thaksin Shinawatra, and many PPP officials had been frequent travelers to Hong Kong, which is where the former prime minister had previously set up residence, there is speculation Thaksin Shinawatra is the person who is actually running the PPP and the current political process in Thailand (Hengkietisal, 2008). At the time of writing, Thaksin Shinawatra has returned to Thailand with the expressed intent of clearing his name and fighting the legal charges against him. The drama continues and many twists and turns in the story can be expected. While the complexity, uncertainty, and personalities associated with the current political situation in Thailand provide a good deal of entertainment value for political observers of the country, the political situation in the country may be having a negative effect on the nation's economic performance

Thailand's economy
Taking a longer term view, Thailand's economic performance has been somewhat impressive. Thailand has a fairly well developed infrastructure, a mostly free-market economy and pro-investment government policies, which have led to sustained economic growth over recent decades. The gross domestic product (GDP) per capita, using the Purchasing Power Index, was estimated to be around US$9200 in 2006 with unemployment being around 1.6 percent in 2007 (Thailand Facts and Figures, 2007). The agricultural sector employs approximately 40 percent of the country's workforce, with over 15 percent of the workforce in manufacturing and the majority of the remaining working in various service industries (Asian Development Bank, 2007).

A shorter-term view of the economic performance is not quite as positive. In recent years, the Thai economy has underperformed in comparison to other economies in Southeast Asia. Thailand has had or is expected to have GDP growth of 4.5 percent, 5 percent, 4.3 percent and 4.6 percent in the years 2005 through 2008 in comparison to the SEA average of 5.1 percent, 5.4 percent, 5.7 percent and 5.8 percent for the same years (Thailand Facts and Figures, 2007). According to the most recent data, agriculture contributes 10.7 percent to the national GDP while the industrial and service sectors contribute 44.6 percent and 44.7 percent respectively. Thailand's trade balance returned to positive in 2006 after two years of the country running a negative trade balance. (Asian Development Bank, 2007).

Thailand's recovery from the 1997 Asian economic crisis 'demonstrates the resilience of its market-based economy' (Warr, 2005: 386). However, there remain some fundamental weaknesses. Vannukul (2002) identified seven fundamental causes of the economic crisis of 1997 in Thailand: cronyism, weak organization, misuse of resources, corrupt politics, poor employment policy, lack of reform, and the lack of transparency. Consensus in the business community in Thailand is that not all of these weaknesses have been adequately addressed.

Entrepreneurship in Thailand
The actions and attitudes of governments affect the development of private enterprises (Carter and Wilson, 2006). A generally consistent pro-business environment has

allowed the entrepreneurial spirit to continue to be a major force in modern Thai life (Dana, 2007). Moreover, there is a large informal entrepreneurial sector of the economy (Paulson and Townsend, 2005: 34)

Officially, the government has actively promoted the setting up of business activities since the 1960s. Examples of programs designed to stimulate the development of entrepreneurial activities include setting up the Board of Investment (BOI) which provided promotional and tax incentives to small and medium-sized enterprises, setting up the Market for Alternative Investment (MAI) for firms which did not meet the requirements to be listed on the Stock Exchange of Thailand (SET), the creation of the Industrial Estate Authority and providing advisory services to existing and potential entrepreneurs (Somjai, 2003). Nevertheless, business owners continue to complain of excessive bureaucracy and red tape. Successive Thai governments have promoted and generally welcomed foreign investment, but the Foreign Business Act of 1999 places substantial limitations on the activities of foreign owned business in the kingdom.

Entrepreneurs are typically motivated by factors in addition to financial gain to create new business activities. Pinfold (2001) discovered New Zealand entrepreneurs were motivated by a number of factors which included expectation of financial rewards, personal development and independence. Newbert (2003) believed entrepreneurs often had both selfish and altruistic motives for starting new businesses. Newbert felt entrepreneurs were often aware of the benefits to society, such as creating an increase in employment opportunities and providing valuable services to the community that came as a result of their efforts. Newbert felt a desire to benefit others while gaining financial rewards was a motivating factor driving entrepreneurs to create new businesses. Choo and Wong (2006) reported in the results of their study that in Singapore the top five motivators to start a new business were challenge, realization of dreams, taking advantage of creative talents, to be one's own boss, and having an interesting job, all of which can be more easily classified as lifestyle motivators rather than economic motivators. Choo and Wong found financial considerations were important considerations when deciding to become an entrepreneur, but their results suggest lifestyle factors were equally if not more important than financial factors in making the decision. Lifestyle and other non-economic factors appear to also play a crucial role in the decision-making process of Thai entrepreneurs (Hatcher and Terjesen, 2007).

Entrepreneurship in Thailand has some common features with entrepreneurship in other locations as well as having some differences. Thomas and Mueller (2000) reported there are some universal traits found in entrepreneurs in different locations, but also there are some distinct variations of the traits found in entrepreneurs in different cultural contexts. In Western countries, entrepreneurship is often associated with risk-taking, independence and desire to achieve. However, this association is built on the assumption that quality and secure paid employment is available. In a Western context, entrepreneurs are often thought of as individuals who have forgone financial security in order to take a chance (Shahidi and Smagulova, 2007). On the other hand, in Asia and other parts of the world entrepreneurship can be a method to increase financial security.

Therefore the motivations, characteristics and behaviors of entrepreneurs in Asia and Thailand may not always meet the expectations of Western business personnel or business academics who have been conditioned to expect business owners to display a specific set of motivations, characteristics and behaviors. Moy et al. (2003) reported that in a study in Hong Kong, it was found the perceptions of students of entrepreneurship as a career were quite positive and were distinctly different from the patterns found in studies of students in Western countries. In studies conducted in Western countries, the desire to become an entrepreneur is often associated with being a bit of an 'outsider' and being non-conventional. However in Asia, those possessing the desire to start their own business possessed attitudes that would be considered more conventional and they had more positive attitudes towards their existing circumstances than has been reported of individuals with a desire to become entrepreneurs found in studies in Western contexts.

Entrepreneurship in the West is usually considered to be a path towards independence, in Asia, starting a business is often associated with becoming part of an interdependent business network (Bjerke, 2000). Entrepreneurship in the Western context is often primarily an individualistic affair, with few firms being passed from generation to generation (Fairlie and Robb, 2007), and decisions are usually made to maximize benefits for the individual owner. However, in Asia, the focus in entrepreneurship often shifts from the individual to the family (Shapiro et al., 2003). In Asian family-owned businesses, decisions are not always made because they will bring in the most income and other benefits to the owner of the firm in the short term, but both the tangible and intangible benefits that multiple generations of the family will receive are taken into account.

Thailand, like much of Asia, is dominated by the existence of family-owned firms (Suehiro and Wailerdsak, 2004). This prevalence of family-owned firms affects the entrepreneurial environment to a considerable extent. Many entrepreneurs in Thailand are second or later generation entrepreneurs who have taken over family businesses. These second and later generation entrepreneurs in Asia are known to have different qualities than first-generation entrepreneurs (Chung and Yuen, 2003). In addition, the career advancement opportunities for outsiders in family-owned firms is limited, resulting in non-family paid employees seeking out their own entrepreneurial opportunities in order to have an opportunity for advancement. Furthermore, in family-owned firms in Thailand where there are few government-enforced workforce legal protections, an employee's career is often subject to the arbitrary decision making of the owner of the firm and therefore becoming an entrepreneur is often a path to increased financial and professional security.

Thomas and Mueller (2000) reported entrepreneurs in the USA displayed an internal locus of control, high levels of energy and were risk takers. These traits may be necessary as modern developed economies present many barriers to entry for potential entrepreneurs (Helms, 2003; Imai and Kawagoe, 2000). However, in Thailand, it is often push factors as opposed to orthodox pull factors (Dana, 1997) that drive people to become independent business owners (Kalantaridis and Labrianidis, 2004; Kristiansen, 2002; Pitamber, 2000). It appears many small-scale entrepreneurs in Thailand are primarily motivated by push factors due to lack of paid employment opportunities as opposed to seeking wealth, independence, status or other pull factors (Paulson and Townsend, 2005).

Using official statistics of entrepreneurs in Thailand can be very misleading. Only comparatively large-scale businesses are officially registered and the amount of unrecorded business activity is significant. Paulson and Townsend (2005) studied entrepreneurial behavior in provinces outside Bangkok in Thailand and found most small-scale entrepreneurs used their own savings or other informal sources to fund the creation of a new business. They also reported many of the new businesses required extremely low amounts of start-up capital, very rarely employed non-family members, and it was quite common for entrepreneurial activities to be used as a supplement to working for wages. The authors also found no correlation between wealth and likelihood of starting a business; the entrepreneurship spirit in Thailand crosses social status divisions. It is likely that entrepreneurs in Thailand starting larger-scale businesses in Thailand are primarily motivated by pull factors and have some of the characteristics associated with entrepreneurship in more developed Asian countries. On the other hand, it is likely most small-scale entrepreneurs (especially in rural areas) are mostly driven by push factors and share many characteristics with entrepreneurs in developing areas of the world.

An interesting aspect of entrepreneurship in Thailand is the comparatively extremely high percentage of women who are entrepreneurs (Hatcher and Terjesen, 2007). In addition, Hatcher and Terjesen reported Thailand has one of the highest rates of entrepreneurial participation, for both men and women, in the world. The authors found a number of factors that contributed to Thailand having such a high percentage of women entrepreneurs, such as the supplementary nature of much of the business activities conducted by women towards family income and a cultural environment that allows women to have a variety of different roles within society. Both empirical evidence and personal observation indicates that Thailand is filled with people, both men and women, with an entrepreneurial orientation.

Internationalization of Thai SMEs: roadblocks and incentives
Although the Thai government has made some efforts to promote the internationalization of Thai SMEs, examples include the efforts of the Department of Export Promotion and the One Tambun (Village) One Product (OTOP) Project, there have been limited moves by Thai SMEs to enter foreign markets. The size of the Thai economy in relation to most of Thailand's neighbours provides limited incentives to seek new markets. Andersson et al. (2004) found small firms in more dynamic industries were more likely than SMEs in less dynamic industries to internationalize operations and, as most Thai SME's are in more traditional industries, there are limited intangible benefits to be gained from internationalizing operations. The majority of SMEs in Thailand are family owned and family ownership has been found to be negatively correlated with internationalization of operations (Fernandez and Nieto, 2005). Family ownership of firms in SEA has been shown to be associated with being averse to risky strategies, such as being involved in internationalization (Carney and Gedailovic, 2003). The types of industry and ownership structures of most Thai SMEs do not provide the circumstances typically found to correlate with large-scale internationalization of Thai SMEs.

However, as Thailand's neighbors begin to grow economically and trade barriers are lowered, Thai SMEs and entrepreneurs are seeking new opportunities in neighboring countries. In studying Thai-owned SMEs in Cambodia, it was found many of these enterprises were not extensions of existing Thai SMEs but were first businesses for the Thai entrepreneurs. These 'Born Foreign' firms were created because of new opportunities and the lower barriers to entry found in Cambodia as compared to the barriers found in the more mature economy of Thailand (Hipsher, 2008).

Conclusion

Some Thai entrepreneurs share many characteristics with entrepreneurs in other locations. Most large-scale entrepreneurs in the country are mostly ethnic Chinese (Somjai, 2003) and are often part of 'overseas Chinese business networks' (Hipsher, et al., 2007). Thai-Chinese entrepreneurs share many characteristics with other ethnic Chinese entrepreneurs, which includes being more likely to invest in enterprises that are not capital intensive and being less likely to begin truly innovative companies in comparison to Western entrepreneurs (Hipsher et al., 2007). Most of these ethnic-Chinese larger-scale entrepreneurs appear to be primarily affected by pull factors to become entrepreneurs.

On the other hand, many of the smaller-scale entrepreneurs in the country appear to be driven more by push than pull factors into starting small businesses and many of these smaller-scale entrepreneurs share some characteristics with smaller-scale entrepreneurs in lesser developed nations. Finally, there is a very strong streak of independence that is part of the Thai national character which seems to influence both large-scale and small-scale entrepreneurs to start new business ventures resulting in a very large and active entrepreneurial segment of society.

References

A brief history of modern Thai politics (2007), *The Nation*, 7 February, 2008 edn.

Andersson, S., J. Gabrielsson and I. Wictor, (2004), 'International activities in small firms: examining factors influencing the export growth of small firms', *Canadian Journal of Administrative Science*, **21**(1), 22–34.

Asian Development Bank (2007), *Key Indicators 2007 (Vol. 38)*, Manila: Asian Development Bank.

Bjerke, B.V. (2000), 'A typified, culture-based, interpretation of management of SMEs in Southeast Asia', *Asia Pacific Journal of Management*, **17**(1), 103–32.

Carney, M. and E. Gedailovic (2003), 'Strategic innovation and the administrative heritage of East Asian family business groups', *Asia Pacific Journal of Management*, **20**(1), 5–26.

Carter. S. and W. Wilson (2006), 'Don't blame the entrepreneur, blame government: the centrality of the government in enterprise development; lessons from enterprise failure in Zimbabwe', *Journal of Enterprising Culture*, **14**(1), 65–84.

Charoensin-o-larn, C. (2007), 'Military coup and democracy in Thailand', paper delivered at the Thailand Update Conference 2007 at the Australian National University, 31 August.

Choo, S. and M. Wong, (2006), 'Entrepreneurial intention: triggers and barriers to new venture creation in Singapore', *Singapore Management Review*, **28**(2), 47–64.

Chung, W.C. and P.K. Yuen (2003), 'Management succession: a case for Chinese family-owned business', *Management Decision*, **41**(7), 643–55.

Dana, L.P. (1997), 'The origins of self-employment', *Canadian Journal of Administrative Sciences* **14**(1), 99–104.

Dana, L.P. (2007), *Asian Models of Entrepreneurship – From the Indian Union and the Kingdom of Nepal to the Japanese Archipelago: Context, Policy and Practice*, Singapore and London: World Scientific.

Fairlie, R.W. and A. Robb (2007), 'Families, human capital, and small business: evidence from the characteristics of business owners' survey', *Industrial and Labor Relations Review*, **60**(2), 225–45.

Fernandez, Z. and M. Nieto (2005), 'Internationalization strategy of small and medium-sized family businesses: Some influential factors', *Family Business Review*, **18**(1), 77–89.

Hatcher, C. and S. Terjesen (2007), 'Towards a new theory of entrepreneurship in culture and gender: a grounded study of Thailand's most successful female entrepreneurs', Fourth AGSE International Entrepreneurship Research Exchange, 6–9 February, Brisbane, Australia.

Helms, M.M. (2003), 'The challenge of entrepreneurship in a developed economy: the problematic case of Japan', *Journal of Development Entrepreneurship*, **8**(3), 247–63.

Hengkietisal, K. (2008), 'PPP must step carefully', *Bangkok Post*, 26 January, s. 1, 10.

Hipsher, S.A. (2008), 'Born Foreign firms in Cambodia: exploration of mode of entry decisions of firms originating from the Greater Mekong Sub-region', *International Journal of Emerging Markets*, **3**(1), 104–15.

Hipsher, S.A., S. Hansanti and S. Pomsuwan (2007), *The Nature of Asian Firms: An Evolutionary Perspective*, Oxford: Chandos.

Imai, Y. and M. Kawagoe (2000), 'Business start-ups in Japan: problems and policies', *Oxford Review of Economic Policy*, **16**(2), 114–23.

Jumsai, M. (2001), *History of Thailand and Cambodia*, Bangkok: Chalermnit.
Kalantaridis, C. and L. Labrianidis (2004), 'Rural entrepreneurs in Russia and the Ukraine: origins, motivations, and institutional change', *Journal of Economic Issues*, **38**(3), 659–81.
Kristiansen, S. (2002), 'Individual perception of business contexts: The case of small scale entrepreneurs in Tanzania', *Journal of Development Entrepreneurship*, **7**(3), 283–304.
Leppart, P. (1996), *Doing Business with Thailand*, Fremont, CA: Jain.
Moy, J, W.M. Vivienne and P.C. Wright (2003), 'Perceptions of entrepreneurship as a career: views of young people in Hong Kong', *Equal Opportunities International*, **22**(4), 16–40.
Newbert, S.L. (2003), 'Realizing the spirit and impact of Adam Smith's capitalism through entrepreneurship', *Journal of Business Ethics*, **46**(3), 251–61.
Paulson, A.L. and R.M. Townsend (2005), 'Financial constraints and entrepreneurship: Evidence from the Thai financial crisis', *Economic Perspectives*, 3rd quarter, 34–48.
Pinfold, J.F. (2001), 'The expectations of new business founders: the New Zealand case', *Journal of Small Business Management*, **39**(3), 279–85.
Pitamber, S. (2000), 'Accessing financial resources and entrepreneurial motivations amongst the female informal sector micro-entrepreneurs in Sudan', *Ahfad Journal*, **17**(1), 4–21.
Post Reporters (2008), 'Cabinet sworn in', *Bangkok Post*, 7 February, 2008 edn.
Shahidi, M. and A. Smagulova (2007), 'The challenges of entrepreneurship in dynamic society', *Central Asia Business*, **1**(1), 34–46.
Shapiro, D.M., E. Gedaijlovis and C. Erdener (2003), The Chinese family firm as a multinational enterprise, *International Journal of Organizational Analysis*, **11**(2), 105–22.
Somjai, P. (2003), 'Entrepreneurship in Thailand', paper presented at the Entrepreneurship in Asia: 4th U.S.–Japan Dialogue, 26 April, Hong Kong.
Suehiro, A. and N. Wailerdsak (2004), 'Family business in Thailand: its management, governance, and future challenges', *ASEAN Economic Bulletin*, **21**(1), 81–93.
Syamananda, R. (1993), *A History of Thailand*, Bangkok: Thai Watana Panich.
Thailand Facts and Figures (2007), *Bangkok Post 2007 Year-End Economic Review*, Bangkok: Post Publishing.
Thomas, A.S. and S.L. Mueller (2000), 'A case for comparative entrepreneurship: assessing the relevance of culture', *Journal of International Business Studies*, **31**(2), 287–301.
Vannukul, V. (2002), 'Thailand's economic crisis of 1997: continuation and possible cure: a case study', Doctoral dissertation, Capella University (3075324).
Warr, P. (2005), 'Thailand's paradoxical recovery', *Southeast Asian Affairs 2005*, **31**, 385–404.

39 Timor-Leste
Mats Lundahl and Fredrik Sjöholm

Introduction to Timor-Leste

Timor-Leste – one of the poorest countries in Asia, with a GDP per capita of US$366 in 2004 (UNDP, 2006: 10) – became a sovereign nation in 2002, after the end of almost 25 years of Indonesian occupation in 1999. During the first four years of independence growth rates were barely sufficient to keep pace with a population that increases with 3 percent per annum (Lundahl and Sjöholm, 2006: 16), in a country with 40 percent of the population living in poverty (Lundahl and Sjöholm, 2005: 13). During 2004, however, it became clear that Timor-Leste was on the threshold of substantial revenues from large oil deposits in the Timor Sea. The future looked reasonably bright in the medium term.

This would soon change. Dissatisfaction had spread in certain army circles. In February 2006, a cycle of violence was begun. This culminated with the fall of the government of Mari Alkatiri and the establishment of a potential guerrilla force near Dili under the leadership of Major Alfredo Reinado. Some 133 000 people had to leave their homes, and refugee camps grew up everywhere (Lundahl and Sjöholm, 2007: 29). In 2007, the Timorese went to the polls for presidential and parliamentary elections. President Xanana Gusmão and Prime Minister José Ramos Horta swapped jobs and the country got a new government, based on a potentially fragile four-party coalition.

Reinado was killed when he led an attempt to kill the president in February 2008, but the refugee problem remains unsolved. It was hoped that Timor-Leste would develop quickly with a committed leadership and strong foreign assistance. These expectations have not been met and the road to prosperity may be both long and rocky. Timor-Leste suffers from a structural weakness. Employment rests heavily on subsistence agriculture and the oil sector only serves to bring in revenue. The modern sector consists of trade-related activities serving the international community in the capital and the public administration. Productivity is so low in the non-service sector that it cannot compete with services or imports.

Government policy on enterprises and entrepreneurship in Timor-Leste

The Timor-Leste constitution envisages a leading role for the private sector within a market economy (Ministry of Development and Environment et al., 2004: vii). Overall, however, Timor-Leste ranked 168 out of 178 countries on the Ease of Doing Business Index computed by the World Bank (World Bank and IFC, 2007: 2). The country has a long way to go. The state cannot create employment alone (*Semanário*, 2008). What has the government of Timor-Leste done then to promote entrepreneurship?

In 1999, a multi-agency Joint Assessment Mission addressed issues like 'restarting the flow of goods and services, transportation, payments system, procurement, currency exchange, claims on deposits in Indonesian banks, micro-credit, taxes and customs' (Ministry of Development and Environment et al., 2004: 1). Foreign banks were allowed to operate, interim leasing systems were introduced, business registration was regulated, a system for taxation of personal corporate income was introduced and the US dollar was adopted as the currency of Timor-Leste. In 2001 'inertia in the production of laws and regulations relating to issues such as bankruptcy, leasing, contracts, land, non-bank financial institutions, cooperatives, NGOs [non-government organizations], collateral, loan foreclosure and insurance, and others did not allow much progress to be made in the private sector regulatory framework'. In 2003–04, a petroleum tax law and a petroleum mining code were drafted. The corporate tax was reduced from 40 to 30 percent (Ministry of Development and Environment et al., 2004: 1–2).

In 2005 one domestic and one foreign investment law were passed. These make possible tax deductions for employment of Timorese nationals and for tax and duty exemptions for inputs of various kinds. The minimum investment required is twenty times higher for foreign than for domestic firms. This discriminates against foreign investment. The tax deduction for employment discriminates against firms with few workers. Regulations are overly complex. The two laws should be merged into a single, simplified, one (IFC and ADB, 2007: 48). Two supporting agencies have been created: Trade Invest Timor-Leste (TITL), to attract foreign investment and promote exports, and a domestic Instituto Apoio Desenvovimento (IADE) (World Bank, 2006: 10–12).

Implementation of existing laws also leaves a lot to be desired (World Bank, 2006: 2):

> laws and regulations . . . are not being adequately administered. . . . the court system . . . has devoted hardly any time at all since 1999 to commercial dispute resolution, debt collection or other civil cases. [. . .] Getting approvals from Government departments . . . is a problem, capacity in the civil service is very thin, there are bottlenecks caused by the centralization of decision making at higher levels, and there have been anecdotal reports of corruption . . .

As new laws and regulations come into force, the strain on the government institutions increases, in a situation where trained and experienced personnel capable of exercising sound judgment is lacking.

The environment for entrepreneurship and the state of small business in Timor-Leste
Entrepreneurship may be defined in different ways (Hébert and Link, 1989; Wennekers and Thurik, 1999). According to the more ambitious definitions (for example, Schumpeter, 1961), entrepreneurship means discovery or creation of novel combinations of production factors. At the opposite end of the spectrum (for example, Kirzner, 1973) it simply amounts to taking advantage of unused profit opportunities in the market, without making any innovative contributions. In the case of Timor-Leste any reasonable definition must be close to the latter end of the scale: engaging in routine business activities, setting up an enterprise. This is the definition used throughout our discussion.

In 2004, the vast majority of urban enterprises were very small: more than half of the informal establishments were one-man ventures, and only 0.4 percent had more than 10 workers. Among the formal enterprises over 72 percent had less than 10 workers, and only 0.4 percent had more than 50 (Das and O'Keefe, 2007). Around 45 percent of the formal and some 90 percent of the informal urban enterprises had a turnover of less than US$5000 (IFC and ADB, 2007: 49). The urban establishments were concentrated mainly in trade, construction and services. Manufacturing accounted for only 2.5 percent of the formal enterprises. Trade dominated all size categories. Timorese enterprises are mainly home operations (Das and O'Keefe, 2007).

Institutional obstacles

Anyone doing formal business in Timor-Leste faces a number of institutional obstacles. The country ranks low on most indices computed in the Doing Business project of the World Bank (World Bank and IFC, 2007). Setting up a business is costly. The average number of days required is 82, which ranks the country at 140 of 178. Recently, however, the time for issuing business activities registration and licensing certificates has been cut from 30 days to between three and five days (Gusmão, 2007: 6).

Enforcing a contract in court takes on average 1800 days, involves 51 procedures and costs more than 163 percent of the value of the claim. Timor ranks at the very bottom: 178 (World Bank and IFC, 2007). The country lacks a civil code and a supreme court, and, until recently, a cadre of domestic judges. All of them failed the examination in Portuguese and had to be sent on a two-and-a-half-year course. Private investors 'regard the court system as practically non-functional and since legal certainty is one of the major criteria upon which investment decisions are made, this weakness is a major deterrent to private investment in the country' (World Bank, 2006: 18).

The recent violence has not improved the situation. In January 2007, the prosecution caseload amounted to 1658, significantly more than at the end of 2005, 985, but still not as much as the 2700 in January 2005. The judicial system rested on international personnel until the first Timorese who had completed their course work were reappointed in mid-2006 (World Bank, 2007: 3).

Weaknesses are not found only in the courts. No alternative dispute resolution mechanisms that could act as substitutes for court decisions exist. The few lawyers who were active in 2005 also had to undergo Portuguese training before they were allowed to continue their work. Timor-Leste furthermore lacks an approved accounting system and there is no certification of accountants and auditors (World Bank, 2006, 9).

Investor protection against insiders is weak under Timorese law (rank 122). The protection index covers issues related to the approval and disclosure of proposed transactions to the shareholders and the public at large, the ability of investors to hold directors and board members liable for damage and so on. Overall, Timor-Leste receives a score of 4 on a scale ranging from 0 (worst) to 10.

Property rights are chaotic. The land and property laws do not address the basic weakness: the absence of reliable land titles. Hence land cannot be used as collateral. Also, Timor-Leste ranks at the very bottom when it comes to the Registering Property indicator (number of procedures, duration in number of days and cost in percentage of the property value) (World Bank and IFC, 2007). The 'complexity and incompleteness of the legal and regulatory framework and the lack of capacity in the Land and Property Department' makes it futile to attempt registration (World Bank, 2006: 15).

Unfortunately, this situation can be expected to continue (World Bank, 2006: 15):

> Although preparatory work on a land titling system has been underway . . . for several years, the requirements are still complex and full implementation will depend on the resolution of conflicts over titles . . . These include traditional land ownership structures dating back centuries, changes effected during the Portuguese and Indonesian occupations, the enforced uprooting

of large sections of the population in 1999 [and 2006–07], and decisions taken during the UN [United Nations] transitional administration and under the rule of the present independent government. These uncertainties can be expected to continue until a new land titling system is fully designed and implemented. This will depend in turn on the completion of a cadastre, but progress on this so far has been very limited.

Foreign trade is cumbersome, especially the preparation of six and seven different documents for exports and imports, which requires 16 days. Customs clearance, controls, handling, and so on brings the total time to 25 and 26 days, respectively, at a total cost of close to US$1000 in both cases. Altogether this places the country at rank 78, worldwide, on the Doing Business index (World Bank and IFC, 2007).

Dealing with taxes is easier. Timor-Leste is in position 62, with no more than 15 payments per year, 640 hours to complete the various tax statements and a total tax rate of 28.3 percent on profits (World Bank and IFC, 2007). In the near future, the profit tax rate will be lowered to 10 percent.

Wages and labor
Wages are high in Dili (Das and O'Keefe, 2007: 25). The minimum wage is comparable to that of Uruguay in the 1990s, a country with a per capita income of US$6600 against 472 for Timor-Leste and 7.6 years of schooling on average, against 4.6 for Timor. The monthly minimum wage in West Nusa Tenggara in Indonesia in 2003 was less than half the figure for Timor-Leste (US$85).

More important, however, is the actual wage level. Around one-fourth of the urban workers earn less than the minimum wage (Das, 2004: 5), so the latter is not binding – which presumably goes for most potential competitor countries as well. On the other hand, in 2001 the monthly *average* wage in urban areas was US$150. In 2004, it was US$158. Given the 4–10 percent inflation rate in 2001–04, the real wage hence seems to have declined (Das and O'Keefe, 2007: 23, 25). The wage level is closely related to the demand emanating from the expatriate community in Dili. The 1999–2002 period saw a quadrupling of wages, driven by 15000 foreign experts and by the relatively high wage level in the public sector (considerably higher than in Indonesia) (World Bank, 2002: 18). The subsequent withdrawal of foreign personnel should thus have resulted in downward pressure on the wage level. In which direction the future lies will very much depend on the extent of continued international presence.

Wages have to be related to employee skills. In 2004, formal employers reported various kinds of deficiencies among their personnel. When asked which skills they considered would become important during the next two years, they listed customer handling, driving, problem solving as well as advanced computer skills, technical and practical skills, literacy, numeracy, communication and foreign languages. Some 40 percent of the enterprises provide some training, possibly because they do not value the formal training institutions highly (Das and O'Keefe, 2007: 27–9).

Still, at least at present, the workforce does not appear to be a serious constraint to enterprise growth in Timor-Leste. Less than 15 percent of the formal and less than 2.5 percent of the informal employers reported problems finding appropriate workers (Das and O'Keefe, 2007, 21). This statement, however, has to be interpreted with care, since it does not reveal what prospective entrepreneurs think.

Timor-Leste is in the middle range when it comes to hiring and firing: number 73 of

178, with a rigidity of employment index of 34 (maximum 100) (difficulty of hiring and firing and rigidity of work hours), zero non-wage labor costs and a firing wage cost of 17 weeks (World Bank and IFC, 2007).

Infrastructure

The infrastructure in Timor-Leste is deficient. Destruction was extreme in 1999. Thus, 85 percent of the telecommunications structures, the airfield in Dili and much of the electricity-producing capacity were destroyed (Lundahl and Sjöholm, 2005: 6). All has not been replaced.

The lack of roads make transport costly and segments an already small market into even smaller parts. The existing road network is about 1400 kilometers (IFC and ADB, 2007: 64). Country people have to walk for an average of two hours to reach the nearest market (UNDP, 2006: 29). Only 30 percent of the major roads are decent; most second-ary roads are in dismal shape (Ministry of Agriculture, Forestry and Fisheries, 2004: 2). During the rainy season many roads become impassable.

Timor-Leste has only one international airport, Dili, with a single daily flight to Indonesia and one to Australia. No regular domestic airline exists. The capacity of the port in Dili, which handles most international transports, is low and the goods-clearing process slow. The domestic ferry network is rudimentary (UNDP, 2006: 18).

Only 20 percent of all households (more than half in Dili) have access to electricity. The cost is very high mainly because power generation to a large extent depends on imported fuel. However, the government subsidizes electricity. Lack of maintenance and spare parts means that the existing power plants cannot use all of their capacity. Extensive bypassing of meters encourages waste and causes peak hour shortfalls. Since 2007, however, the Comoro Power Station has increased the supply capacity signifi-cantly (IFC and ADB, 2007: 43–5).

Telecommunications and information technology (IT) services are in short and expen-sive supply. Only about 5 percent of the population have access to telecommunications in the form of fixed telephone lines, mobile service or the Internet, and computer access is almost non-existent. A major reason seems to be the monopoly held by Timor Telecom (IFC and ADB, 2007: 59–60).

Credit

Access to finance is a major problem for Timorese enterprises. The country ranks as low as 170 out of 178 on the Doing Business index (World Bank and IFC, 2007) and there is strong excess demand for credit (Conroy, 2006: 6):

> bank credit . . . reach[ed] almost 22 percent of non-oil GDP early in 2005. This was only half the proportion for all 'low-income' countries . . . The system was intermediating 87 percent of the deposits to domestic lending. Together with evidence of excess demand, this suggests the need for expanded savings mobilization to bring Timor-Leste up to a more appropriate level of financial depth.
>
> [. . .] the great majority of the population remains untouched by formal financial services.

The activities of the country's three commercial banks are limited (Conroy, 2006). The Australia and New Zealand Banking Group (ANZ) is basically a non-lending institu-tion. The Caixa Geral de Depósitos (CGD) (Portuguese) is more active, with over 85 percent of all bank credit in Timor-Leste. It has offices in several provincial towns. It is the main provider of commercial bank credits to small-scale and micro enterprises, mainly for construction – households rebuilding homes (40 percent of the total) – and to the 'trade and finance' sector (less than 20 percent). The state-owned Indonesian Bank Mandiri (10–12 percent of total bank credit) concentrates mainly on trade with Indonesia and on Indonesian interests in Timor-Leste, but it has also extended credit to the largest Timorese microlending institute. The remaining 2 percent or so comes from the Instituçáo de Microfinanças de Timor-Leste (IMfTL), a quasi-bank with a limited license. '[O]verall the banking system provides negligible finance for agriculture, industry or tourism' (Conroy, 2006: 33).

The commercial banks reach very few entrepreneurs, and hardly any small businesses at all. These have to turn to the microlending institutions. The latter have formed the Association of Microfinance Institutions in Timor-Leste (AMFITIL). The activities of its largest member, IMfTL, include weekly group loans mainly to women, daily repayment loans to market vendors, some seasonal crop lending and somewhat larger 'business' loans. Delinquency rates (30 days or more overdue) have been high, possibly as high as 25 percent on average. Eighty percent of the IMfTL activities, however, consist of loans secured by borrower salaries, many of whom presumably have used the funds for micro enterprises (Conroy, 2006: 38–44).

The most important pure microfinance institution is Moris Rasik, with some 7000 borrowers in late 2004 and a low 3.6 percent portfolio at risk. It also provides credits of up to US$1000 to borrowers who have successfully serviced at least four progressively larger loans. Altogether, the AMFITIL lenders for which data are available (some three-fourths) served 19 200 borrowers in 2004. No microfinance institution is yet financially sustainable. The sector depends on support from international NGOs (Conroy, 2006: 42, 28).

Overall, in Timor-Leste, enterprises on all levels, except perhaps the few largest ones which may use cross-border arrangements, experience problems obtaining investment and working capital. The 2004 enterprise survey identified access to capital as the most important constraint to entrepreneurial development (Das and O'Keefe, 2007: 19–20). Around 85 percent of all formal and informal enterprises had relied on personal funds for start-up capital and less than 7 percent had obtained bank loans. More than 60 percent of the formal and 81 percent of the informal enterprises also reported financial constraints as the most important barrier to expansion.

Internationalization
The internationalization of entrepreneurship in Timor-Leste has been slow, and inward instead of outward. The main achievements have been the production sharing contract with Australia for the Bayu Undan oil field and two agreements, also with Australia, which will make possible the development of the Greater Sunrise oil field, the Timor Telecom venture, and the three commercial banks. Trade Invest Timor-Leste has signed a few letters of intent with potential overseas investors, a fisheries project and an oil refinery, among others, and more projects may be underway (World Bank, 2006: 11), but in practice little has happened. The oil sector will not contribute with employment or spillover effects into the rest of the Timorese economy, since it is located outside the country's *terra firma*.

The fact that the country's two different investment laws favor domestic companies does not help. Nor do the awkward export/import procedures, and the same argument may be advanced for all the other factors dealt with here, with the possible exception of credit, where foreign companies may have a competitive edge not being dependent on Timorese facilities.

In one sense, the main internationalization effects stem from the presence of the international community, but such ventures are often temporary. Hotels and restaurants easily close. Whenever political and social conditions get to the point where international presence is no longer required, demand will contract, and unless other business opportunities have by then been developed, the urban economy finds itself at the end of a temporary bubble. The sustainable internationalization of entrepreneurship in Timor-Leste lies in the probably not so near future.

Conclusions

The business environment in Timor-Leste ranks low from an international perspective. The economy suffered severe destruction as the Indonesians withdrew in 1999 and reconstruction had to begin almost from scratch. The vast majority of the population depends on subsistence agriculture, and the modern sector consists of little else than the state bureaucracy and service establishments catering to the international community in Dili. Businesses are usually very small. Most are informal.

The business environment of Timor-Leste is not conducive to entrepreneurship. The political and social situation has recently been turbulent. Business legislation is incomplete and implementation is deficient. The courts are overburdened with criminal cases and bureaucrats lack experience. Setting up a business, enforcing contracts and exporting or importing are expensive and time-consuming. Investor protection is weak and property rights are chaotic. Urban wages are high, transportation is bad, power is expensive and telecommunications are deficient. The main problem for prospective entrepreneurs, however, is credit. Setting up a business requires personal funds. The country has only three commercial banks. One does no lending. The microfinance movement is not yet viable. Overall, the credit market is characterized by excess demand. The development of a sustainable modern sector will require both time and effort. Meanwhile, agriculture will have to continue to absorb the additions to the labor force, as it has done in the past.

References

Conroy, John (2006), *Timor-Leste Access to Finance for Investment and Working Capital*, Report No. 37736, Washington, DC: World Bank.

Das, Maitreyi Bordia (2004), *The Labor Market Impact of Minimum Wage Policy: The Case of Timor-Leste in Comparative Perspective*, 26 June, Washington, DC: World Bank.

Das, Maitreyi Bordia and Philip O'Keefe (2007), 'Enterprises, workers and skills in urban Timor-Leste', World Bank Policy Research Working Paper 4177, March. Washington, DC

Gusmão, Xanana (2007), *Speech by His Excellency the Prime Minister Kay Rala Xanana Gusmão at the Presentation of the Bill on the State Budget for 2008 at the National Parliament*, 18 December, Dili: Democratic Republic of Timor-Leste, National Parliament

Hébert, Robert and Albert N. Link (1989), 'In search of the meaning of entrepreneurship', *Small Business Economics*, **1**, 39–49.

International Finance Corporation and Asian Development Bank (IFC and ADB) (2007), *Economic and Social Development Brief*, August, Dili.

Kirzner, Israel M. (1973), *Competition and Entrepreneurship*, Chicago, IL: Chicago University Press.

Lundahl, Mats and Fredrik Sjöholm (2005), *Poverty and Development in Timor-Leste*, Country Economic Report 2005:3, Stockholm: Sida.

Lundahl, Mats and Fredrik Sjöholm (2006), *Economic Development in Timor-Leste 2000–2005*, Country Economic Report 2006:4, Stockholm: Sida.

Lundahl, Mats and Fredrik Sjöholm (2007), *A Year of Turmoil: Timor-Leste 2006–2007*, Country Economic Report 2007:5, Stockholm: Sida.

Ministry of Agriculture, Forestry and Fisheries (2004), *National Food Security Policy for Timor-Leste*, Dili.

Ministry of Development and Environment, Ministry of Agriculture, Forestry and Fisheries, Ministry of Transport, Communications and Public Works, Ministry of Planning and Finance, Ministry of Justice, Secretariat of Trade and Industry, Secretariat of Labor and Solidarity, Banking and Payments Authority and Timor Sea Office (2004), *Private Sector Development. Priorities and Proposed Sector Investment Program*, September, Dili.

Schumpeter, Joseph A. (1961), *The Theory of Economic Development*, Oxford: Oxford University Press.

Semánario (2008), 'PM Xanana Gusmão: "O estado e o sector privado têm que andar juntos"', 19 January.

United Nations Development Programme (UNDP) (2006), *The Path Out of Poverty. Integrated Rural Development. Timor-Leste Human Development Report 2006*, Dili: United Nations Development Programme.

Wennekers, Sander and A. Roy Thurik (1999), 'Linking entrepreneurship and economic growth', *Small Business Entrepreneurship*, **13**, 27–55.

World Bank (2002), *East Timor. Policy Challenges for a New Nation*, May, Washington, DC: World Bank.

World Bank (2006), *Timor-Leste. The Business Regulatory Environment*, Report No. 37978, Washington, DC: World Bank.

World Bank (2007), *Timor-Leste: CSP Mission – February and March 2007*, Draft, 1 June, Washington, DC: World Bank.

World Bank and International Finance Corporation (IFC) (2007), *Doing Business 2008 Timor-Leste*, www.doingbusiness.org (accessed 22 January 2008).

40 Turkey
Serkan Yalcin

Introduction to Turkey

Turkey, or Republic of Turkey, is an Eastern Mediterranean or Eurasian country located at the crossroads of Europe and Asia. Turkey covers 814 578 sq km and borders Georgia, Armenia, Azerbaijan, Iran, Iraq, Syria, the Mediterranean Sea, the Aegean Sea, Greece, Bulgaria, and Black Sea. Turkish culture is mixed with Western and Eastern themes. Being culturally strong and economically influential in the region stretching from Europe to Russia, Middle East, and Central Asia, Turkey has always had a strategic geopolitical power (Shaw and Shaw, 1977).

Turkey was established in 1923 upon the collapse of the Great Ottoman Empire, established in 1299. Turkey is now a democratic, secular, and social state governed by the rule of law and has accepted the principle of the separation of powers: legislative power, executive power, and judicial power (Ministry of Culture and Tourism, 2007). From 1923 to 1980 the Turkish economy was based on a state-controlled economy. In the early years, the economic policies were implemented by State Economic Enterprises (SEE) to pursue economic growth and import substitution. These SEEs were successful in realizing various large-scale investments until 1960s. After the 1960s, industries became highly capital-intensive and required scale economies, therefore foreign exchange requirements increased substantially. Afterwards, SEEs became inefficient because of a sudden increase in oil prices and the inflation rate (Sogut, 1997).

Towards the end of the 1970s, the gap between imports and exports substantially enlarged and thus the budget deficit increased and the inflation rate rose significantly. These gaps were financed by foreign debts and reserves. But, this led to increases in foreign debts, damages in the structure of the foreign debts, and decreases in foreign currency reserves. The Turkish government facing such economic fluctuations put into effect (by the Undersecretariat of the Prime Ministry for Foreign Trade) a new economic program known as the 24 January 1980 economic decisions. With these decisions, Turkey launched a new and liberal trade and economic regime which envisaged restructuring the economy, expanding exports, decreasing inflation, and encouraging privatization. With the implementation of the program, inflation decreased, gross domestic product (GDP) increased, the financial system was liberalized, and trade became more open (Ertugrul and Selcuk, 2001).

After 1980, economic and political changes followed by growth in the economy have made Turkey an important emerging market. Turkey is now classified in the top-10 list of the world's emerging markets, together with China, Hong Kong, Taiwan, South Korea, Indonesia, India, South Africa, Mexico, Brazil, and Argentina (Garten, 1996). Also, Turkey is included in the Group of 20 (G-20) countries, which includes the world's major industrialized and emerging markets (g20.org). Turkey is also the world's seventeenth largest economy and the sixth largest of the European Union (EU) and was the thirteenth most attractive foreign investment location in 2006 (The Turkish Prime Ministry,

2007). Turkey has a population of around 72 million people and its GDP per capita is US$5041 as of 2006 (Undersecretariat of Treasury, 2007).

Turkish foreign policy has always favored Western orientation, as evidenced by Turkey's close connection with Europe. Turkey's main trading partners are the EU (approximately half of imports and exports), the US, and Russia. Political instability during 1990s prevented many foreign investors from investing in Turkey and thus the volume of foreign investments was low. However, Turkey achieved political stability in the early 2000s and was able to attract over US$8 billions of foreign investments in 2005; various large-scale privatizations, strong and stable growth, and structural changes in banking, retail, and telecommunication sectors also facilitated foreign investments in Turkey (Undersecretariat of Treasury, 2007). Turkey applied to the EU to be a member in 1959; it became an associate member in 1963 and applied to be a full member in 1987. Turkey and the EU signed a customs union agreement in 1995. Negotiations to become a full EU member are still in progress (Secretariat General for European Union Affairs, 2007). After the fall of the Soviet Union, Turkey constructed strong political and economic relations with the newly independent Turkic Republics that have historical and cultural ties with Turkey. This allowed Turkey to extend its influence toward the East as well (Bal, 2004).

Government policy on SMEs and entrepreneurship in Turkey

In Turkey, governmental establishment for small and medium enterprises (SMEs) is as follows. The *State Planning Organization* (SPO) provides long-term and annual development programmes for SMEs and acts as a coordinator between public and private organizations to implement SME policies by supervising and adjusting policies. The *Ministry of Industry and Trade* outlines SME policies; the Small and Medium Industry Development Organization (KOSGEB) is the unit within the Ministry responsible for implementing SME policies. The KOSGEB supports SME development and growth and provides technical, informational, training, financial, and managerial support. The *Undersecretariat of Treasury* provides state funds. The *Undersecretariat of Foreign Trade* sets up policies and programs to enhance SMEs creation.

In addition to these institutions, there are other institutions instrumental in implementing SME policies and supporting SMEs. These are the Union of Chambers of Commerce, Industry, Maritime Trade and Commodity Exchanges of Turkey (TOBB), and the Confederation of Tradesmen and Artisans of Turkey (TESK), Halk Bank, the Union of Credit and Guarantee Cooperatives for Tradesmen and Artisans of Turkey (TESKOMB), and the Credit Guarantee Fund Inc. (KGF).

The Turkish government has been paying very close attention to SMEs since 1960s. With the liberalization movements in 1980, interest in SMEs has increased and the Turkish government established SEGEM (the Industrial Training and Development Centre) and later the KOSGEB in 1990. The customs union agreement with, and membership application to, the EU put competitive pressures on Turkish SMEs as they need to compete with EU companies. However, the current state of Turkish SMEs is not so favorable; thus, Turkish SMEs are not yet ready to compete with EU companies. Turkish SMEs need support to increase their competitiveness in product design and development, technology, production planning, modernization, renovation, quality standards, and scale economies; they also need market and financing information such as competitor analysis, demand, pricing, marketing, foreign financing, venture capital, and loans (OECD, 2004; SPO, 2007).

The related governmental policy on these support and development needs was the SME Strategy and Action Plan (No. 2003/57) first established in 2003 and later revised. Comparing European SMEs with their Turkish counterparts, we see big differences in terms of competitiveness, scale, capital, technology, infrastructure, education, and entrepreneurial will. This justifies such a thorough national SME strategy. In addition to creating and implementing a national SME strategy in line with the SME policy requirements set out by the EU, the SME Strategy and Action Plan also aims to increase Turkish SMEs productivity, international competitiveness, and contribution to the economy and the national employment. The plan envisages such strategic areas as growth of entrepreneurship, integration of SMEs to international markets, improvement of business and institutional environments, and enhancement of technological and innovative capability (SPO, 2007).

The economic and socio-cultural environment for entrepreneurship and the state of small business in Turkey

State of small businesses in Turkey
The KOSGEB defines small enterprises as those having 1–50 workers and medium-sized enterprises as those having 51–150 workers; the Ministry of Treasury, on the other hand, has a broader definition in that micro, small, and medium-sized enterprises are defined as those having 1–9, 10–49, and 50–250 workers, respectively. Small and medium enterprises make up a major part of the Turkish economy and account for a large proportion of national employment; SMEs account for 99.8 percent of the total number of enterprises, 77 percent of total employment, 38 percent of capital investment, 26 percent of value added, 10 percent of exports, and 5 percent of bank credit. Therefore, while SMEs dominate the economy in terms of employment, they evidently operate with comparatively little capital, generate relatively low levels of value added, and receive only a marginal share of the funds mobilized by the banking sector. A very large share of SMEs is in trade and crafts sectors and only a small share of SMEs is in the manufacturing sector (OECD, 2004; SPO, 2007).

The small size of Turkish SMEs and their relatively modest contribution to national output are noticeable in international comparisons. For example, the percentage of SMEs with fewer than 100 workers is higher in Turkey than in many other OECD countries and most Turkish SMEs have fewer than 10 employees. While micro-enterprises account for 95 percent of Turkish businesses and 34 percent of Turkey's jobs, they account for a 7.8 percent of production, whereas in Italy, France, and Portugal, where such firms are proportionately fewer and employ fewer people, their contribution to total output ranges from 11 to 15 percent (OECD, 2004; SPO 2007).

Some major challenges and problems that Turkish SMEs face are as follows. Competition with EU companies requires Turkish SMEs to be innovative, but Turkish SMEs are not innovative and this is a big challenge. Demirbas (2006) found four types of barriers to innovation in Turkey: formal barriers (government research and development policy, instability on tax policies), informal barriers (corruption, informal economy, cultural attitudes), environmental barriers (perceived economic risks, high cost of innovation, lack of finance), and skill barriers (lack of qualified personnel, information on markets and technology). Kozan et al. (2006) also reported that lack of know-how and lack of financing negatively influence resource aggregation intentions of SMEs.

Economic and socio-cultural environment
There have recently been major changes in the economic environment such as declining interest rates, economic stability, privatizations, tax reforms, deregulations, abolishment of anticompetitive barriers, reduction in the number of monopolies, agricultural reforms, and the EU-related structural and legal changes. In addition, public sector employment became more and more difficult for people. These may encourage entrepreneurship. However, TUSIAD (2002) and Cetindamar (2005) indicated that Turkey has a high level of entrepreneurship culture compared to other developing countries.

Although the economic environment in Turkey has favourable features towards entrepreneurship, personal and cultural factors are perhaps more influential as individual behaviour is heavily affected by personal and cultural features as well. How people think of entrepreneurship is important and may reflect national entrepreneurship capacity. Perceptions about entrepreneurship include willingness and perceived ability to become an entrepreneur (Davidsson, 1991). These are affected by individual traits, environmental factors (cultural, economic, and political), and opportunity perception (Shane, 2003). Dana (2000) indicated that traditional values are also important in Turkey and in part affect business. Many companies in Turkey are family owned and in such businesses, loyalty to the extended family serves as a springboard to launch new enterprises.

We need to look at cultural characteristics of Turkey to understand the impact of culture on entrepreneurship. Historically, private initiative has never been a long-standing feature of the Turks. The Ottoman Empire, of which Turkey was a part, did not have much tradition of a powerful and indigenous entrepreneurial class as business activity was the stronghold of non-Muslim minorities (Richards and Waterbury, 1990). Therefore, we see a cultural heritage which is not conducive to entrepreneurship. Although Turkish population is young and culturally diverse, entrepreneurship in Turkey may be considered necessity based (GEM, 2001). Another important feature of Turkish SMEs is that firms and owners are highly dependent on state agencies and, as a result, they delegate little to employees and find it difficult to develop long-term commitments with business partners and competitors. Such a structure and unstable state policies inhibit entrepreneurial development in Turkey (Cetindamar, 2005).

Schwartz (1994) stated that Turkish people are high on conservatism, hierarchy, and egalitarian commitment, but low on affective and intellectual autonomy and mastery. Aycan et al. (2000) indicated that paternalistic orientation is also pervasive among Turkish people. Although young and educated urban population scores quite high on individualism, competitiveness, and autonomy, qualities like collectivism, hierarchy, power-distance, and conservative attitudes are common, especially for people from rural and lower socio-economical level districts. Hofstede's measures on Turkey indicate high collectivism and avoidance of uncertainty. Collectivism and uncertainty avoidance are negatively related to traits such as internal locus of control, risk-taking, and innovativeness, some key indicators of entrepreneurship (Mueller and Thomas, 2000). Figure 40.1 shows scores of selected countries with respect to

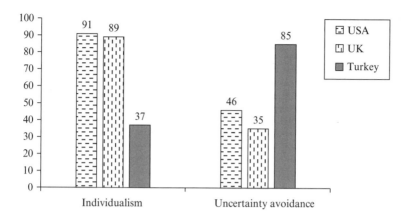

Source: Based on Hofstede (2001).

Figure 40.1   Culture dimensions

individualism-collectivism and uncertainty avoidance cultural dimensions in the Hofstede's framework.

The US and the UK have higher levels of entrepreneurial activity than Turkey; low collectivism and low uncertainty avoidance of these Western countries may justify this to a certain extent. Therefore, here we see the negative impact of culture on entrepreneurship in Turkey. Other differences between Turkish entrepreneurs and SMEs and their foreign counterparts include size (Turkish SMEs are smaller), financing availability and cost of capital (Turkish SMEs have more limited resources and higher cost of capital), and high share of rural entrepreneurship (in Turkey) (Coskun, 2004).

With respect to entrepreneurial motivations in Turkey, obtaining income and independence were reported to be entrepreneurial motivations in GEM (2007); Turan and Kara (2007) found that freedom to make decisions, the chance of achieving a relatively higher financial gain, and some environmental factors are important entrepreneurial motivations in Turkey.

With respect to geographical dispersion of entrepreneurship in Turkey, Istanbul has always been the trade and international entrepreneurship centre for over 2000 years (Dana, 2000); Ankara and Izmir follow Istanbul. In recent years, other cities (Kayseri, Gaziantep, Denizli, Kocaeli, Bursa, Konya) have become more competitive in both domestic and export-oriented trade. Turan and Kara (2007) reported the existence of the craftsmen and the opportunistic entrepreneurs in Turkey. The former consists of mostly male entrepreneurs with some college education who left their previous jobs to start their own business, whereas the latter consists of a larger number of female entrepreneurs who left their jobs to start their own business but who were mainly motivated to entrepreneurship due to layoff.

In sum, although the economic environment supports and encourages entrepreneurship and new venture creation, Turkish culture and personal characteristics of especially middle-aged and old people are not conducive to entrepreneurship. Education together with a strong governmental support policy may stimulate the level of entrepreneurship in Turkey.

Table 40.1　Major Turkish export items (US$ billion)

Chapters	2005	2006	2007
Motor vehicles and trailers	10.22	12.7	17.1
Manufacture of basic metals	6.89	9.33	12.3
Apparel	9.92	10.2	11.8
Textiles	8.74	9.26	10.8
Machinery	4.86	6.00	8.00
Food products and beverages	4.27	4.34	5.16
Petroleum products	2.52	3.40	4.92
Manufacture of fabricated metal products	2.68	3.35	4.25

Source:　Ministry of Treasury.

Table 40.2　Turkish export destinations (US$ billion)

Countries	2003	Share (%)	2004	Share (%)
1　Germany	7485	15.8	8743	13.9
2　United Kingdom	3670	7.8	5540	8.8
3　USA	3752	7.9	4832	7.7
4　Italy	3193	6.8	4625	7.3
5　Netherlands	1526	3.2	2134	3.4
6　France	2826	6.0	3668	5.8
7　Spain	1789	3.8	2616	4.2
8　Iraq	829	1.8	1815	2.9
9　Russian Federation	1368	2.9	1859	2.9
10　U.A.E.	703	1.5	1139	1.8

Source:　Ministry of Treasury.

Internationalization of entrepreneurs and SMEs from Turkey: drivers and roadblocks

Turkish trade and investments in overseas markets concentrate on Europe and the CIS countries. Dana (2000) indicated that pan-Turkic trade between Turkey and the CIS countries is on the rise. In 1992, Turkey began to establish relationships with the CIS countries and joined the Black Sea Economic Cooperation. Tables 40.1, 40.2 and 40.3 show Turkish exports.

Yalcin (2006, 2007) reported that in the CIS markets, Turkish companies compete with Russian companies and the competition is in the SMEs category; large-scale investments in this region generally focus on oil and energy sectors by American and British companies. Although internationalization of Turkish SMEs is mostly in the form of direct investment in the CIS markets, export mode is adopted towards the European markets as seen from Table 40.2.

Figure 40.1 shows the international orientation of early-stage entrepreneurs in the world. We can say that although the level of early international orientation of Turkish entrepreneurs is low compared to some high-income countries, Turkish entrepreneurs in their region (Eastern Europe and Central Asia) have high levels of international

Table 40.3   Sectoral breakdown of Turkish exports in Europe (US$ billion)

Year	Agriculture		Textile and clothing		Iron and steel		Chapter 84, 85 and 87*		Industrial products (other)		Total
	Value	Shr. (%)	Value	Shr. (%)	Value	Shr. (%)	Value	Shr. (%)	Value	Shr. (%)	Value
2003	1 896	8.1	8 991	38.3	1 363	5.8	6 794	29.0	4 413	18.8	23 457
2004	2 433	7.9	10 198	33.3	2 285	7.5	10 275	33.5	5 457	17.8	30 648

Note: * 87 Some vehicles, 85 Electrical machinery, 84 Nuclear reactors, and machinery.

Source: Ministry of Treasury.

orientation. High import needs of European markets and the high production potential of Turkey may be some drivers of increased Turkish exports towards European markets. With regard to the CIS region, smooth competition in the region in many industries (Kaynak et al., 2006) and geographical and cultural distance advantages of Turkey are other drivers of internationalization.

Perhaps the biggest roadblock for Turkish SMEs in their internationalization is their low level of technical and innovative ability. Turkish SMEs do relatively well in the CIS markets, but not in the European market. Customs union with the EU strongly influences international competition in the Turkish market and especially SMEs. In addition, if Turkey becomes a member of the EU, it will have to directly compete with innovative and competitive European companies. However, Turkish SMEs are not yet ready for this as they are weak in technical ability and innovation. Appropriate governmental policies, education, and investment in research and development may help Turkish SMEs to overcome this innovation challenge. For instance, the sharp increase in new-venture growth and international competitiveness of the Turkish clothing industry since 1980 illustrates a good case for successful SMEs' internationalization: government policies designed to encourage exports have inspired entrepreneurship and new-venture development, particularly among the segments of the population that have not had a family connection to the industry. Informal ties, such as friends and family, also played a significant role in information acquisition among new firm owners, particularly in terms of seeking information about technological developments, suppliers, and foreign markets (Riddle and Gillespie, 2003). However, the production process in the clothing industry is mainly domestic; therefore, it is under pressure of low-cost apparel producers of the East. Though not common among SMEs, offshoring, albeit partial, as indicated by Dana et al. (2007), may provide some cost and thus competitive advantages to Turkish producers over their Eastern rivals.

Conclusion
Turkey has many favourable endowments with respect to both domestic and international entrepreneurship: some of those are the young and educated population, many natural resources, a strategic location, governmental policies, and bilateral trade agreements facilitating overseas expansion. On the other hand, some problems (financing,

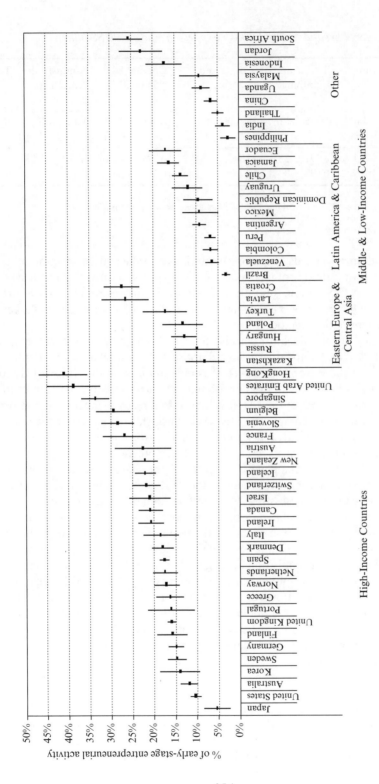

Source: GEM (2007: 39).

Figure 40.2 International orientation of early-stage entrepreneurs

technical inability, know-how) inherent in developing countries as well as a culture relatively inappropriate to entrepreneurship undermine entrepreneurship and SMEs' development in Turkey. Turkey opened its doors to international markets in 1980 and has had many political and economic crises that hindered entrepreneurial and SME development as well as foreign investments.

There are two important policy challenges with respect to entrepreneurship and SMEs in Turkey. First, is to create an environment or culture that will educate and encourage people towards becoming entrepreneurs; education can play an important role in changing individual's perception and minimizing fear of failure. Entrepreneurship in Turkey needs to be proactive (opportunity-seeking) rather than reactive (need based). The second challenge is to increase the competitiveness level of SMEs through creating more innovative SMEs. This requires investments in research and development, and an appropriate government strategy.

There are various research areas with respect to entrepreneurship in Turkey waiting for rigorous academic inquiries; Cetindamar (2005) indicated that entrepreneurship is not much researched in Turkey. With the economic integration, even micro enterprises may want to, or may be forced to, internationalize their operations; an analysis to forecast the effects of economic integration on domestic and international entrepreneurship in Turkey can enlarge entrepreneurial scholarship as well as provide useful managerial and policy recommendations. In addition, another appropriate study would be an extensive analysis of entrepreneurial motivations, personal values, cultural characteristics, and institutional environment in Turkey. Revealing the hidden interactions among these can provide insights into one of the key questions of entrepreneurship 'why do people become entrepreneurs?' and help us understand cultural features affecting entrepreneurship. These findings may also help shape government policies to create an entrepreneurial culture.

References

Aycan, Z., R. Kanungo, M. Mendonca, K. Yu, J. Deller, G. Stahl and A. Kurshiel (2000), 'Impact of culture on human resource management practices: a ten country comparison', *Applied Psychology: An International Review*, **49**, 192–220.

Bal, Idris (eds) (2004), *Turkish Foreign Policy in Post Cold War Era*, Boca Raton, FL: Brown Walker Press.

Cetindamar, D. (2005), 'Policy issues for Turkish entrepreneurs', *International Journal of Entrepreneurship and Innovation Management*, **5**(3/4), 187–205.

Coskun, A. (2004), 'Motors of innovation and development. Organization for Economic Cooperation and Development', *The OECD Observer*, **243**(May), 48–9.

Dana, L.P. (2000), *Economies of the Eastern Mediterranean Region: Economic Miracles in the Making*, NJ: World Scientific.

Dana, L.P., R. Hamilton and B. Pauwels (2007), 'Evaluating offshore and domestic production in the apparel industry: the small firm's perspective', *Journal of International Entrepreneurship*, **5**(3/4), 47–63.

Davidsson, P. (1991), 'Continued entrepreneurship: ability, need, and opportunity as determinants of small firm growth', *Journal of Business Venturing*, **6**(6), 405–29.

Demirbas, D. (2006), 'New institutional economy and innovation barriers: a microeconometric evidence', *The Business Review*, **5**(2), 82.

Ertugrul, A. and F. Selcuk (2001), 'A brief account of Turkish economy, 1980–2000', *Russian and East European Finance and Trade*, **36**(7), 6–30.

Garten, J.E. (1996), 'The big emerging markets', *The Columbia Journal of World Business*, **31**(2), 6–31.

GEM (2001), *Global Entrepreneurship Monitor: Executive Report*, London: GEM.

GEM (2007), *Global Entrepreneurship Monitor: Executive Report*, London: GEM.

Hofstede, G. (2001), *Culture's Consequences: Comparing Values, Behaviors, Institutions, and Organizations*, Thousand Oaks, CA: Sage Publications.

Kaynak, E., S. Yalcin and E. Tatoglu (2006), 'A comparative study of foreign direct investment activities in Georgia and Kyrgyz Republic', *Multinational Business Review*, **14**(3), 29–52.

Kozan, K., D. Oksoy and O. Ozsoy (2006), 'Growth plans of small businesses in Turkey: individual and environmental influences', *Journal of Small Business Management*, **44**(1), 114–29.

Ministry of Culture and Tourism (2007), http://www.tourismturkey.org/factsforvisitors.htm (accessed 19 October 2007).

Mueller, S. and A. Thomas (2000), 'Culture and entrepreneurial potential: a nine country study of locus of control and innovativeness', *Journal of Business Venturing*, **16**, 51–75.

OECD (2004), *Small and Medium-sized Enterprises in Turkey: Issues and Policies*, Paris: Organization for Economic Co-operation and Development.

Richards, A. and J. Waterbury (1990), *A Political Economy of the Middle East: State, Class, and Economic Development*, Boulder, CO: Westview Press.

Riddle, L. and K. Gillespie (2003), 'Information sources for new ventures in the Turkish clothing export industry', *Small Business Economics*, **20**(1), 105–20.

Schwartz, S. (1994), 'Beyond individualism/collectivism: new dimensions of values', in H.C.C.U. Kim Kagitcibasi (ed.), *Individualism and Collectivism: A Theory Application and Methods*, Newbury Park, CA: Sage Publications, pp. 85–119.

Secretariat General for European Union Affairs (2007), 'Chronology of Turkey–EU relations', http://www.abgs.gov.tr/index.php?p=112&l=2 (accessed 2 October 2007).

Shane, S. (2003), *A General Theory of Entrepreneurship: The Individual-Opportunity Nexus*, New Horizons entrepreneurship series, Cheltenham, UK and Northampton, MA, USA: Edward Elgar Publishing.

Shaw, Stanford and Ezel Shaw (1977), *History of the Ottoman Empire and Modern Turkey*, Cambridge: Cambridge University Press.

Sogut, Mehmet (1997), 'Experience in promotion of SMEs in Turkey', Financial Policies to Promote SMEs Conference, Southeast European Cooperative Initiative (SECI) Project Group, 24 April, Bucharest.

SPO (2007), 'SME Strategy and Action Plan 2007–2009', State Planning Organization, http://ekutup.dpt.gov.tr/esnaf/kobi/strateji/2007.pdf (accessed 11 February 2008).

The Turkish Prime Ministry (2007), 'The Investment Support and Promotion Agency of Turkey', http://www.invest.gov.tr (accessed 8 February 2008).

Turan, M. and A. Kara (2007), 'An exploratory study of characteristics and attributes of Turkish entrepreneurs: a cross-country comparison to Irish entrepreneurs', *Journal of International Entrepreneurship*, **5**, 25–46.

TUSIAD (2002), 'Entrepreneurship in Turkey', www.tusiad.org/turkish/rapor/girisimcilik/girisimcilik.pdf (accessed 9 February 2008).

Undersecretariat of Treasury (2007), http://www.hazine.gov.tr/english/forinvest.htm (accessed 14 November 2007).

Yalcin, S. (2006), 'Turkish investments in Georgia and Azerbaijan: recent trends and future prospects', *Caucaz Euronews*, 9 March, www.caucaz.com (accessed 17 September 2006).

Yalcin, S. (2007), 'Foreign direct investment in Caucasus and Central Asia: a comparative analysis of sectoral patterns and source countries', *Central Eurasian Studies Review*, **6**(1/2), 13–15.

41 Turkmenistan[1]
Gerard McElwee

1. Introduction

The Republic of Turkmenistan has a population of 5 million with a life expectancy of 59 for men and 68 for women. It covers an area of 488 100 square kilometres, bordering Afghanistan, Iran, Kazakhstan, Uzbekistan and the Caspian Sea. Turkmenistan is rich in energy, with 3 trillion cubic metres of natural gas – the fifth largest reserve in the world, after Russia, the United States and Iran. In addition, Turkmenistan has 700 million tonnes of oil reserves, and the world's third largest sulphur deposits. Turkmenistan is also among the 10 largest cotton producers in the world. Despite these riches, the people of Turkmenistan have remained generally poor. Under Soviet rule, poverty was blamed on the fact that the republic was required to sell its gas and cotton to Russia at artificially low prices.

Even after independence, the environment for enterprise in Turkmenistan has not been conducive for the creation of widespread prosperity. O'Driscoll et al. found more government intervention in this country, than anywhere else in Central Asia; they noted, 'Corruption is a major impediment, and the Economist Intelligence Unit reports that any thorough reform is unlikely for political reasons' (2001: 368). It is still impoverished, and since independence from the Soviet Union in 1991 has remained largely closed to the outside world.

It is effectively a one-party state, that party being the Democratic Party of Turkmenistan led by the late president Saparmurat Niyazov until his death in December 2006.

Although Turkmenistan is largely covered by desert, agriculture provides a significant proportion of the nation's employment opportunities accounting for almost half of its national gross domestic product (GDP). Much agriculture relies on irrigation.

The Turkmen government has an absolute monopoly of the media.

The majority of the population live below the poverty line, with conditions particularly bad in rural areas. Turkmens witnessed a steep declines in wages and in health, education and other public service provision, following the collapse of the Soviet Union.

2. Government policy on small and medium enterprises and entrepreneurship

Under central planning from Moscow the Turkmen economy was focused on cotton. Since the economy has changed paths, oil has become increasingly important.

A new constitution was adopted on 18 May 1992. Joint ventures became a popular means to combine capitalist ideas with local enterprise. In 1993, the Daykhanbank – a local state-owned bank specialized in agricultural projects – joined forces with the largest bank in Turkey – the state-owned Ziraat Bank – to create the Turkmen-Turkish Joint Stock Commercial Bank.

A cautious programme of limited privatization was launched on 1 June 1994; also in 1994, the national currency, the manta, was devalued. In May 1995, a railroad was opened between Iran and Turkmenistan; this provided Central Asia with a link to the

Indian Ocean cutting travel time between Europe and Southeast Asia by several days. In December 1995, President Niyazov launched the President's Programme for Social and Economic Development in Turkmenistan. As recommended by the International Monetary Fund (IMF), key objectives of this reform programme included the implementation of market reforms making the manat internally convertible and restructuring the economy with a focus on controlling the expansion of credit. The government subsequently announced more ambitious privatization plans, and the service sector was privatized.

3.   The environment for entrepreneurship and the state of small business
Presidential decrees have the power to restructure joint stock commercial banks into state banks, and the banking sector was restructured during the late twentieth century. In December 1998 presidential decrees, three major banks were declared state banks with narrowly defined scopes of activities. In January 1999 the number of banks operating in Turkmenistan was reduced from 67 to 13. Fifty-two peasant commercial banks became branches of the Daykhanbank. Other state banks include the State Commercial Investbank, the Turkmenbank and the Vnesheconombank – the State Bank for Foreign Economic Affairs of Turkmenistan – which was given the monopoly for all foreign exchange operations involving the government. State firms in Turkmenistan have been ordered to conduct business only with state banks. There are no official statistics for the number of SMEs and annual start-ups, but it appears that there is a move to support enterprise development.

4.   Internationalization of entrepreneurs and SMEs
Turkmenistan approached entrepreneurship issues with caution. It allowed the creation of 6000 small-scale firms in 1992, but delayed auction sales of mid-size and larger businesses.

In 1993, the Cabinet of Ministers founded a joint venture with the Khal Bank of Turkey, two state-owned Turkmen banks and private firms in Turkmenistan. The result was the International Joint Stock Bank for Reconstruction, Development and Promotion of Entrepreneurship. However, individuals interviewed by the author have doubts as to how effectively entrepreneurship was promoted. It appears, nevertheless, that the Rossiysky Credit Bank – Russian Turkmen Joint Stock Bank – provides consulting services that assist entrepreneurs.

The Rossiysky Credit Bank also provides a match-making service, providing opportunities for export. Interviewees claim, however, that opportunities were curtailed when recent legislation restricted access to foreign exchange to certain persons. Respondents also told the author that high inflation rendered business plans useless. According to O'Driscoll et al. (2001), annual inflation averaged 77.41 percent between 1991 and 1999.

Since 1995, the Small and Medium Enterprise Development Agency – a joint venture between the European Union and the Government of Turkmenistan – has been providing entrepreneurs with information on business law, taxation and related matters.

Initially it may be inferred that entrepreneurship is facilitated in Turkmenistan but in actuality, entrepreneurs in Turkmenistan face considerable regulation. Article 1 of the Law on Entrepreneurial Activity provides a definition: 'Entrepreneurship is initiative; independent activity of citizens aimed at obtaining profit or income and carried out on one's own behalf, at one's own risk and on one's own property liability of legal entity – enterprise.' Article 3 specifies that it 'is prohibited to carry out entrepreneurial activity without registration'. Article 9 states that an individual may apply for registration of a sole proprietorship – without creating a legal entity – and this be done by local executive bodies at the place of activity of an entrepreneur in the order determined by the Cabinet of Ministers. Registration may be refused, in which case the law allows appeal, in court. However, of all the individuals interviewed by the author, appeals seem to have helped none. When registration of an entrepreneur is permitted without the creation of a legal entity, the sole proprietor cannot hire labour. In order to have employees a firm must be registered – as detailed by Article 26 of the Law of Turkmenistan on Enterprises – with Commissions formed at khyakimliks of velayats and Ashgabat. Several businessmen complained to the author about the high cost of registration.

Article 9 also rules on the registration of entrepreneurial activity with the establishment of a legal entity, in accordance with the elaborate Law of Turkmenistan on Enterprises. Section III of the Law on Entrepreneurial Activity elaborates on regulations pertaining to entrepreneurs.

The Law of Turkmenistan on Enterprises is equally detailed. Article 17 of the Law of Turkmenistan on Enterprises states that the list of output – for sale at state prices – is determined by the Cabinet of Ministers of Turkmenistan, by agreement with an enterprise. An informer told the author, however, that an enterprise might not really have the option to disagree.

Article 21 of Law of Turkmenistan on Enterprises states that an enterprise is obliged to take action to improve labour conditions. One interviewee told the author, 'In order to be a successful entrepreneur you must first be a lawyer, or able to buy the law'.

Most of the self-employed, in Turkmenistan, operate micro-enterprises and these are often informal. Street vending is common. Vendors – dressed in colourful scarves and mismatched clothing – line the sides of dirt roads in hope of selling their fruit and vegetables. Mothers supervise their children with regard to sales techniques. Each vendor has a couple of colourful plastic buckets filled with produce. They offer, for sale, cherries, onions, peppers, plums, potatoes, and tomatoes depending on what is in season. As potential buyers approach, sellers inch closer to listen to the sales techniques, and anticipate the outcome.

5. Conclusions

Turkmenistan is said to have great potential. It is rich in fuel, and its weather allows for a long growing season. Its cotton is considered among the best in the world. Furthermore, its location puts it at the crossroads of Europe and Southeast Asia. Also in its favour is the fact that the Turkmenistan Internet domain '.tm' is very popular around the world, and this provides significant export revenues – an uncommon export!

Nevertheless, enterprise is stifled. Much entrepreneurial activity occurs at the margins and the incentives to enterprise creation are limited. Over-bureaucratic requirements are a strain to owner-managers with limited resources. The multiplicity of local, profit and property taxes further deters legitimate entrepreneurship. Frequently changing regulations and tax laws limit entrepreneurial expansion. As concluded by O'Driscoll et al., 'The legal reforms necessary for development of a market economy have not been put in place' (2001: 368).

Whereas foreign direct investment appears to be encouraged, the legislation to business start-up appears restrictive. This needs to be addressed in order to ensure the prosperity of the Turkmenistan economy.

Note
1.   This chapter builds on information published in Dana (2002).

References

Dana, L.P. (2002), *When Economies Change Paths: Models of Transition in China, the Central Asian Republics, Myanmar, and the Nations of Former Indochine Française*, Singapore, London and Hong Kong: World Scientific.
O'Driscoll, Gerald P., Kim R. Holmes and Melanie Kirkpatrick (2001), *2001 Index of Economic Freedom*, New York: The Wall Street Journal.

42 United Arab Emirates
Mervyn J. Morris

Introduction

The United Arab Emirates (UAE) is part of the geographic region known as the Middle East. With a land mass of 82 000 square kilometres, predominantly desert and mountains it is bordered by Oman, Saudi Arabia and the Arabian Gulf.[1] The UAE is strategically located due to its proximity to other oil rich Middle Eastern countries such as Kuwait, Iraq, Iran, and Saudi Arabia. The UAE was formed from a federation of seven emirates[2] (Abu Dhabi, Dubai, Sharjah, Ras Al Khaimah, Ajman, Fujuriah, and Um Al Quain) in December 1971 (Ras Al Khaimah did not join the federation until 1972) (Heard-bey, 2004: 370). Abu Dhabi is the political capital, and the richest emirate; while Dubai is the commercial centre. The majority of the population of the various Emirates live along the coast line as sources of fresh water often heavily influenced the site of different settlements. Unlike some near neighbours (Iran and Iraq) the UAE has not undergone any significant political instability since it was formed in 1971. Due to early British influences the UAE has had very strong political and economic ties with first Britain, and, more recently, the United States of America (Rugh, 2007). Until the economic production of oil in the early 1960s the separate Emirates had survived on a mixture of primary industry (dates), farming (goats and camels), pearling and subsidies from Britain (Davidson, 2005: 3; Hvidt, 2007: 565) Along with near neighbours Kuwait, Bahrain, Oman, Qatar and Saudi Arabia, the UAE is part of the Gulf Cooperation Council (GCC), a trading bloc (Hellyer, 2001: 166–8).

While the country is a federation, and the Federal government has control of national issues such as defence, foreign policy, immigration, labour and social affairs, education, health, a great deal of power remains with the governments of each emirate (UAE Interact, 2007a: 39). Each Emirate enacts its own regulations in relation to business issues. At each Emirate level the ruler of the Emirate (either the Sheik or the Crown Prince) oversees a variety of Emirate-specific government bodies with significant autonomy from the Federal level. (Davidson, 2005: 188–200) The country is a moderate, and probably the most liberal, Islamic country in the Middle East (Davidson, 2007). The country has never been subjected to any terrorist or terrorist related attacks, although some members of 9/11 group came from one of the northern emirates (Davidson, 2007: 83). Until the commercial production of oil in the early 1960s economic and social development was sporadic.

The oil price hikes of the 1970s added further impetus to the overall development of the country. Oil prices in 1973 increased from US$5 per barrel to US$41 per barrel, then dropped back to US$32 in 1978 before it rose to US$67 per barrel. The final price increase was in 1982, to US$68 per barrel. The price fell rapidly until it reached US$20 per barrel in 1986, and prices have fluctuated ever since (WTRG Economics, 2006).[3] With the increasing revenue being gained from oil production, the Federation was transformed, and continues to be transformed, albeit somewhat unevenly between the different Emirates. However, the dependence upon oil revenues has been lessened, particularly in Dubai where oil revenues have been replaced with a variety of other commercial activities concentrating on non-oil manufacturing and service sectors.

More recently economic growth in the UAE has seen real gross domestic product (GDP) growth rates of 11.8 percent in 2003 and 7.4 percent in 2004, with a GDP per capita of $US25 000 (UAE Interact, 2007a: 79).[4] Gross domestic product has been projected to continue growing, with an estimated growth rate of 9.7 percent for 2006; and projected growth rates of 8 percent and 6.9 percent for 2007 and 2008 respectively (*Gulf News*, 2007a). While much of this growth can be attributed to rising oil prices the governments of Abu Dhabi and Dubai have been working to lessen the reliance on oil revenues (UAE Interact, 2007a: 79) although each emirate has been pursuing differing strategies (Davidson, 2007). Currently, oil revenues consist of 36 percent of GDP (UAE Interact, 2007a: 71), with by far the greatest proportion going to the Federal government in Abu Dhabi.

The UAE economy has been 'inspected' by international economic institutions on a regular basis, generally receiving good reports on economic developments. For example the International Monetary Fund (IMF) found that 'economic growth has been impressive' (2006: 1) and has resulted in the UAE being ranked 32 out of 125 world economies, making it the highest among the Gulf Cooperation Council (*Khaleeji Times*, 2006). The government of the UAE has concentrated on a number of other key economic areas – aviation, port facilities, tourism, finance and telecommunications (Al Abed et al., 2006: 37). The IMF, during visits in 2005 and 2006, were satisfied overall with the directions and development of the UAE economy. A number of areas were of concern to the IMF (reducing the size of the public sector, tightening up financial regulations for stock exchanges and banks) but generally there were no major economic problems highlighted. The accelerated rate of economic growth has placed significant pressure on the supply of human resources needed to meet the expansionary demands of the public and private sectors.

Historically the UAE has not had a labour force in sufficient numbers, or with the necessary skills, to meet the needs of the public and private sectors. The UAE solved these shortages by using imported labour (expatriate labour). As recently as 1968 when the total population was estimated at 180 226, of this figure 68 485 were expatriates.[5] By 1975, after the first significant oil price rises, when the first census was carried out, this total had increased to 558 000, of which nationals represented 202 000 and expatriates 356 000 (Davidson, 2005: 145; Centre for Labour Market Research and Information, 2005: 9). As the UAE economy has grown so the demand for labour has increased. These circumstances of economic development and labour shortages combined to lead to expatriate labour becoming a key component of the overall economic development of the UAE. As the most recent census reveals, the total population of the UAE is 3.8 million; of this number 824 921 (20 percent) are nationals, with the balance being made up of expatriates from a variety of developed and developing countries (Ministry of Economy, 2006). While the UAE has always used a certain number of expatriates to bolster their workforce, the current social and economic dependence on expatriates has become very significant. Expatriates now dominate many areas of the economy of the UAE and can be found in managerial, professional, technical and unskilled positions. The Federal government has had to attempt to balance the needs of the national workforce, with the needs of the employers. One way the government does this is through controlling the issuing of work visas.[6] While at the same time controlling the supply of expatriate labour, the government has introduced a policy of Emiratization in an attempt to stimulate the demand for national labour. A number of areas have been targeted by the Federal government (financial services sector and trade); through the use of limited quotas; or reserving specific occupations for nationals – for example, public relations officers, human resource managers, and some secretarial positions. These attempts at increasing the numbers of nationals in the private sector workforce have had a limited degree of success but nationals seem to still display overwhelming preference for work in the public sector (88 percent; UAE Interact, 2007a: 217). While there are significant numbers of jobs created every year, paradoxically there are Emirati who are unable to find employment. The most recent data for Emirati unemployment is 15 percent (Hanouz and Yousef, 2007: 34). Despite the best efforts of the Federal government and its attempts to Emiratize[7] the workforce, success has been limited. One of the reasons attributed for this by Davidson (2005) and Preiss (2007) has been an oil-dependency culture which has meant Emirati males do not necessarily have to work.

   Prior to the discovery of oil and commercial exploitation in 1960s the country was basically a subsistence economy. Although oil exploration was first started in 1930s it was not until 1963 that oil began to be exploited in commercial quantities (UAE Interact, 2007a: 16). With the initial oil revenues, economic progress was steady rather than spectacular, and very uneven throughout the emirates. With the oil price hikes of the 1970s, the rulers of Dubai and Abu Dhabi had access to significant sources of revenue to undertake more rapid social and economic development. Fortunately for the remaining members of the Federation, the significant oil price rises took place after Federation in 1971 and instead of oil revenues being 'hoarded' by Abu Dhabi, the riches were shared with the other Emirates, either by direct subsidy or used for the funding of local projects. It is currently estimated that the UAE has 9.6 percent of the world's total oil reserves; this ranks the UAE with the fifth largest reserves in size in the world (UAE Interact, 2007a: 117). While the figures refer to the UAE, the oil reserves are actually in, and controlled, by the emirate of Abu Dhabi.

Government policy on SMEs and entrepreneurship in the United Arab Emirates
'Economic development is considered one of the most urgent priorities and goals for the United Arab Emirates' (Ministry of Economy, 2006: 3). In pursuing these goals, government policy has had to balance the need for economic development with the need for ensuring such development does not disadvantage the national population. The governments at both the Federal and Emirates levels have attempted to strike this balance by using two strategies. First, the Federal Companies Law requires that any business (irrespective of the nature of the business) be 51 per cent owned by a local (Federal Companies Law, Article 22).[8] While there is little solid evidence, strong anecdotal evidence would suggest that the national owners often simply collect a 'fee' from the manager of the business and have no involvement whatsoever in the running of the business. The second strategy is possible as the Federal Companies Law (Article 2) does not apply to free trade zones (FTZ) set up in and by the individual Emirates. This Federal legislative provision allows the Emirates governments to circumvent the ownership issue by designating trade free zones within the Emirate which then allows the establishment

and development of 100-percent foreign-owned companies. In 2007 there were approximately 36 FTZ and Special Economic Zones already in operation or planned (Wilson, 2007: 200). Of all the Emirates, Dubai especially has made significant use of this facility, establishing its first free trade zone in 1975, the Port of Jebel Ali (Davidson, 2007: 39). One of the consequences of this approach is that many of the more dynamic entrepreneurial businesses tend to be found in the free trade zones, while the majority of very small businesses (less than 10 employees) and the different types of service industries, can be found outside the zones.[9]

Taken together, the Federal government, and the governments of the various Emirates tend not to differentiate between SMEs and multinationals. While there are some concessions available to SMEs established by nationals, generally all businesses, irrespective of size, face a level playing field. One policy which has demonstrated a clear measure of support for the establishment of entrepreneurial activities is the willingness of the governments of the different Emirates to assist the development and establishment of business activities. Currently, there are no Federal corporate or income taxes and no sales taxes (Ministry of Economy, 2006: 3). Companies established in FTZs are free to repatriate capital and profits, and there are no currency restrictions (UAE Interact, 2007a: 77). The only Federal law which imposes taxes on businesses is a 5 percent import duty. This does not mean there is a *laissez-faire* approach to businesses in the UAE. There are provisions and regulations enacted by the different emirates which restrict the behaviour of businesses which, according to Preiss (2007: 69), have not been supportive of entrepreneurial activity. Governments at all levels are taking steps to reduce the regulations and time taken to establish a business in the UAE.

There is no federal government policy in relation to assistance schemes for entrepreneurs and small business enterprises generally. Rather there is a smattering of assistance schemes at the Emirates level designed to assist nationals in establishing and developing their own businesses.

Overall there is no unified Federal government policy in relation to entrepreneurs and small business enterprises. There are regulations that govern what businesses can do at both a Federal and an Emirate level. The major policy of the UAE governments at all levels has been to actively encourage the establishment and development of most kinds of businesses. The individual emirates will enact their policies in different ways. Any decisions in this regard are left to the governments of individual emirates (UAE Interact, 2007a: 92)

The economic and socio-cultural environment for entrepreneurship and the state of small business in the United Arab Emirates

> The UAE Government is focused on creating an environment that is investor friendly, limited in its bureaucracy, and fast in the processing of licences and other requirements. (UAE Ministry of Economy, 10/2006)

Hvidt (2007: 573) supports this general statement in relation to Dubai, arguing that the 'strong pro-business environment upheld by the ruler . . . facilitates policy formulation . . . in an atmosphere of consent between both parties [that is, government and business]'.

If one were to examine the results of the 2006 Global Entrepreneurship Monitor (GEM) (Bosma and Harding, 2007) one could come to the conclusion that the environment within the UAE does not encourage the formation and development of SMEs and an entrepreneurial culture within the country. The GEM survey indicates that in terms of GDP per capita 2006, in Purchasing Price Parities (PPP), the early-stage entrepreneurial activity rate was around 4 percent (Bosma and Harding, 2007: 13). In terms of rankings, this placed the UAE with the fourth lowest level of early-stage entrepreneurial activity by country, with only Belgium, Japan, Sweden, and Italy having lower rates. Wilson (2007: 200) agrees, pointing out that while the UAE has 'very good public institutions, infrastructure, and technological readiness' there is a distinct lack of innovation and entrepreneurship. The GDP growth rates seem to indicate that there is a significant level of economic activity, but not within entrepreneurial and small business sectors.

As was demonstrated in the previous section, the overall environment is certainly conducive to business in general. Infrastructure projects are constantly being developed (for example, every Emirate has a port facility; all Emirates have at least one international airport (Dubai is currently building a second)); and with the absence of any railways, road transport networks are extensive and well maintained. For example, Abu Dhabi plans to invest over Dh555 billion in the coming five years in the construction sector (Dh320 billion), development and expansion of tourism (Dh120 billion), power and water (Dh35 billion) and oil (Dh80 billion)(UAE Interact, 2007a: 77).

Another aspect to the environment is that some of the most significant and most prominent entrepreneurs are actually the governments of the Emirates (Davidson, 2007: 41; Hvidt, 2007: 571; UAE Interact, 2007a: 41). Companies are owned, either directly or indirectly by the governments of the different emirates (UAE Interact, 2007a: 103–4). For example, more than 90 percent of the lucrative oil production is owned by the Abu Dhabi government (UAE Interact, 2007a: 117); Emirates Airlines are owned by the Dubai government; one of the largest property development companies in Dubai, Emaar, has very close connections to the Dubai government (Davidson, 2007, 41).

Another feature of entrepreneurial activity in the Emirates is, as Hvidt (2007) demonstrates in relation to Dubai, the line dividing the public and private sectors is continually blurred – the government and business leaders are often the same people, or at least from the same kinship group (Hvidt, 2007: 571). Governments facilitate economic activity which is taken advantage of by companies owned by government leaders and their intimates (in relation to Dubai; see Hvidt, 2007: 570).

Wilson (2007: 200) examined the 'most problematic factors for doing business' in the UAE and what was notable was that there was not any single outstanding dominant factor. Instead there were a number of factors, the majority of which averaged around 16 percent of responses. For example, at 16.5 percent was restrictive labour regulations; an inadequately educated workforce 15.9 percent, poor work ethic among Emiratis 13.7 percent and inflation 13.6 percent were also main areas for concern.[10] Inflation appears to be becoming a major concern generally for the Emirates. According to the IMF, inflation grew from an annual average of 3 percent in 2001/03 to over 10 percent in 2005 (UAE Interact, 2007a: 79). The Abu Dhabi government is considering what actions to take as inflation is adding to the growing cost of doing business (*Gulf News*, 2007b).

Internationalization of entrepreneurs and SMEs from the United Arab Emirates: drivers and roadblocks
There is little evidence that entrepreneurs or SMEs have internationalized to any extent, even within the limited geographic area of the Middle East. Certainly, there are UAE companies which compete with other larger companies on the international stage (for example, RAK Ceramics is one of the largest providers of tiles and porcelain in the world; Emirates Airlines is a major international airline (UAE Interact, 2007a: 144)); and there are some signs that other investment companies are expanding their horizons (UAE Interact, 2007a: 76, 136), but there is little direct evidence of entrepreneurs doing so. There is anecdotal evidence again that would suggest that a number (how many is pure speculation) are increasingly doing business with China, particular in the areas of home furnishings, but this is on the import side, rather than the export side. There is a thriving re-export economy and aluminum and cement are important export products, but these are generally owned by large trading companies or are a part of government-owned companies. Not surprisingly, the petroleum sector accounts for 75 percent of total UAE exports (UAE Interact, 2007b) with 69 percent of 2005 exports going to Asia (Japan 28 percent; Korea 15 percent) (Wilson, 2007: 200).

Conclusion
The UAE continues to change at a significant rate. The rate and quality of economic and social growth that has occurred since the significant rises in the price of oil has propelled the UAE into a position of prominence in the Middle East area. Much of this growth can be attributed to the pro-business attitudes at all levels of government. There is certainly every reason to believe that the UAE governments will continue to encourage, and support, the development of entrepreneurs (both nationals and expatriates) in this most dynamic of countries. There is, however, one area in need of much closer examination and of direct interest to entrepreneurship researchers. Early entrepreneurial activity is extremely low (ranking the fourth worst in the 2006 GEM study) yet economic growth has been consistently strong. How and why this growth is occurring due to the absence of strong entrepreneurial activity is certainly worth pursuing.

Notes
1. Outside the Middle East, this body of water is known as the Persian Gulf. However, since the overthrow of the Shah of Persia in 1979 it is generally referred to in the Middle East as the Arabian Gulf.
2. It should be noted that the name of the largest city in an Emirate is also the name of the Emirate. For example, Abu Dhabi is the political capital of the UAE and also the name of the Emirate. This can, at times, create some confusion but usually context provides the differentiation.
3. The prices are expressed in 2006 US dollars.
4. The accuracy of data generally for the Middle East is an issue continually raised by such bodies as the International Monetary Fund; the World Bank; and, most recently the World Economic Forum – see Hanouz and Yousef (2007: 4).
5. Nationals, also known as locals or Emiratis, are those who hold citizenship of the UAE and thus have a 'special' status vis-à-vis expatriates.
6. No expatriate can legally work in the UAE without the employing organization obtaining a work visa for the prospective employee.
7. As a matter of policy, the Federal government is attempting to reduce the level of unemployment among nationals by following a path towards Emiratization, with nationals replacing expatriates in the workforce.
8. This law is currently under review as UAE's commitments to the World Trade Organization. However,

it is proposed that the revised law exclude SMEs – thus allowing nationals to maintain their 51 percent equity capital for companies outside FTZs (Minister of Economy, 2007).
9. By necessity, this oversimplifies the situation. As a general rule it holds, but there are many larger businesses that have been established outside FTZ. Often these much larger businesses will take the form of trading companies, and have agency agreements with multinational companies; for example, all the major car manufacturers have agency agreements with trading companies registered in the UAE and headed by a national.
10. It is difficult to understand the reasons for the first two comments in relation to labour market issues, given the liberal government attitude towards labour market issues. And when one takes into account that 88 percent of nationals work in the public sector (UAE Interact, 2007a: 217) the responses are even more difficult to understand.

References

Al Abed, Ibrahim, Paula Vine, Peter Hellyer and Peter Vine (eds) (2006), *UAE at a Glance*, London: Trident Press.
Bosma, Niels and Rebecca Harding, (2007), *Global Entrepreneurship Monitor: GEM 2006 Results*, Wellesley, MA: Babson College and London: London Business School.
Centre for Labour Market Research and Information (2005), *Human Resources Report 2005*, Dubai: UAE Ministry of Information and Culture.
Davidson, Christopher M. (2005), *The United Arab Emirates: A Study in Survival*, Boulder, CO: Rienner.
Davidson, Chistopher (2007), 'The Emirates of Abu Dhabi and Dubai: contrasting roles in the international system', *Asian Affairs*, 37/1, 33–48.
Gulf News (2007a), 'Gulf economies', www.gulfnews.com/images/07/08/09, (accessed 8 August 2007).
Gulf News (2007b) 'Abu Dhabi plans policy actions to contain inflation', 6 August 2007, http://archives.gulfnews.com/business/Economy/10144687, (accessed 7 August 2007).
Hanouz, Margareta D. and Tarick Yousef (2007), 'Accessing competitiveness in the Arab World: strategies for sustaining the growth momentum', http://www.weforum.org/pdf/Globalcompetitivenessreports/Reports (accessed 12 April 2007).
Heard-Bey, Frauke (2004), *From Trucial States to United Arab Emirates*, Dubai: Motivate Publishing.
Hellyer, Peter (2001), 'The evolution of UAE foreign policy', in Al Abed, Ibrahim and Peter Hellyer, *United Arab Emirates: A New Perspective*, London: Trident Press, pp. 161–78.
Hvidt, Martin (2007), 'Public-private ties and their contribution to development: the case of Dubai', *Middle Eastern Studies*, 43/4, 557–77.
International Monetary Fund Executive Board, (2006), *Article IV – Consultation with the United Arab Emirates*, 12/7, Public Information No. 06/76.
Khaleej Times (2006), 'UAE's economy is most competitive among Gulf states', 27 September, http://corp.gulfinthemedia.com (accessed 28 September 2006).
Ministry of Economy (2006), *The Annual Economic and Social Report 2005,* October, http://www.economy.ae/min/index.jsp (accessed 27 July 2007)
Minister of Economy (2007), quoted in *Gulf News*, 'SMEs exempt from Companies Law change', 21 March, http://archive.gulfnews.com/business/Economy/10112690 (accessed 22 March 2007).
Preiss, Kenneth (2007), 'GEM Global Summary 2006: United Arab Emirates', in Niels Bosma and Rebecca Harding, *Global Entrepreneurship Monitor: GEM 2006 Results*, Wellesley, MA: Babson College and London: London Business School, p. 69.
Rugh, Andrea B. (2007), *The Political Culture of Leadership in the United Arab Emirates*, New York: Palgrave Macmillan.
UAE Ministry of Economy (2006), 'The annual social and economic report 2005', http://economy.ae/min/index.jsp (accessed 27 July 2007).
UAE Interact (2007a), *United Arab Yearbook*, http://uaeinteract.com/docs (accessed 26 July 2007).
UAE Interact (2007b), 'UAE's economic fortunes rising', 8 July, http://uaeinteract.com/docs/UAEs_economicfortunes_rising/26057.htm (accessed 26 July 2007).
Wilson, Kenneth (2007), 'Reforms need to continue to sustain growth momentum', in World Economic Forum, *Global Competitiveness Reports*, http://:www.worldforum.org/pdf/Global_competitivenessreports/Reports (accessed 12 April 2007).
WTRG Economics (2006) 'Crude oil prices – 1947–Sept 2006', http://www.wtrg.com/oil_graphs/oil price1947.gif (accessed 23 August 2007).

43 Uzbekistan

Gulnoza S. Saidazimova

Introduction to Uzbekistan
The Uzbek language used Arabic script until 1929, and the Roman alphabet from 1929 until 1940 – when Stalin imposed Cyrillic. In 1994, the state began to phase out the use of Cyrillic (Dana, 2002).

Independent since 31 August 1991, the Republic of Uzbekistan covers 447 400 square kilometres, bordering Afghanistan, Kazakhstan, the Kyrgyz Republic, Tajikistan, Turkmenistan, and the Aral Sea. Uzbekistan is slightly smaller than Sweden and is one of the world's two double-locked countries.[1] In January 2000, Uzbek border guards entered Kazakhstan and unilaterally extended their country by marking out a 60-kilometre stretch.

With over 27 million people, Uzbekistan is the most populous country in Central Asia. More than 60 percent of them live in rural areas. Agriculture and industries processing agricultural products (primarily those related to cotton and foods) have constantly contributed about 35 percent of the country's gross domestic product (GDP). It relies heavily on cotton production as the major source of export revenues. Other major export earners include gold, natural gas, and oil (CIA, 'The World FactBook').

Uzbek President Islam Karimov said the country's GDP grew by 9.5 percent in 2007 (*UzA*, 2008). Independent sources cite some 8.1 percent of GDP growth in 2007 (CIA, 'The World FactBook') and say the growth is likely to stay high – at around 7.3 percent in 2008-09 (EIU. 2007). The growth has been high mostly due to exports of gas, cotton, gold, and other natural resources that currently enjoy high prices in the world markets.

Uzbekistan is the world's fourth largest cotton producer and second-largest exporter of cotton, which in 2005 accounted for approximately 20 percent of the country's exports after reaching 39 percent in the late 1990s. (Library of Congress. 2007).

Uzbekistan was a major source of cotton fibre in the Soviet Union, supplying raw cotton fibre to be processed in the Russian part of the country. After the collapse of the Soviet empire, Uzbekistan found itself in a situation when it had to sell raw cotton to Russia. The government announced development of textile industry as priority. However, at present, cotton is still sold abroad after being harvested, and a very limited amount is processed in the country.

Uzbekistan's cotton industry has been under attack since October 2007 due to a wide use of child labour in cotton harvesting. Uzbek authorities deny the allegation. However, a number of prominent companies, like Britain's Marks & Spencer, Tesco, Swedish retail giant H&M, Finland's Marimekko, and Estonia's Krenholm said they would boycott Uzbek cotton (Saidazimova. 2008).

The country also possesses enormous opportunities and potential in the area of gold mining: Uzbekistan had the world's sixth largest reserves of gold and ranked ninth in world production in 2005 (Library of Congress. 2007).

It is the second largest among 15 former Soviet republics and the group's biggest per-capita producer of gold. The gold-mining industry is among the most attractive in Uzbekistan for foreign investors (*RFE/RL*, 2007). Annual production estimated at 80 to 85 tons accounts for 10 to 20 percent of export earnings (Library of Congress. 2007).

Uzbekistan is the only country in Central Asia self-sufficient in food and energy (Library of Congress. 2007). It sits on huge fossil-fuel reserves selling gas mostly to Russia and neighbouring countries. Russia's gas state monopoly Gazprom re-exports Uzbek gas further to Europe at higher rates. Gas reserves satisfy all domestic needs and are an important export product, while oil resources can only meet the needs of domestic consumption if they are managed well.

In March 2008, Uzbekistan along with Kazakhstan and Turkmenistan agreed to sell gas to Russia at a 'European rate' starting January 2009 (Reuters, 2008). That will lead to an increase in revenues. In turn, the Uzbek government is likely to see fewer incentives to change its economic policy and conduct genuine market reforms.

The total mineral and raw-material potential of the country is estimated at some US$3.5 trillion. Uzbekistan is among the top ten on a list of global producers of copper and resource uranium. Other significant products of agriculture are silk, fruits and vegetables, cow's milk, and beef. (Library of Congress. 2007).

Uzbekistan gained independence in 1991 after the collapse of the Soviet Union. Following independence in September 1991, the government announced its plan to dismantle the Soviet-style command economy. However, in fact the system remained nearly untouched retaining many elements of Soviet economic planning including subsidies and tight controls on production and prices.

Economic policy remains under state control, the government has strictly limited foreign direct investment, and little privatization occurred aside from small enterprises. While aware of the need to improve the investment climate, the government still sponsors measures that often increase, not decrease, its control over business decisions.

Independent international economic institutions often criticize the Uzbek government for reluctance to conduct genuine market reforms. The European Bank for Reconstruction and Development (EBRD) held its 2003 annual meeting of the board of governors in Tashkent. Prior to the meeting, which became a subject of criticism of international and Uzbek human rights groups, the EBRD set benchmarks for Uzbekistan to meet in terms of economic liberalization as well as political freedoms. The EBRD ceased lending to the Uzbek government in 2004, citing slow reforms and human rights violations.

The country's relations with another international financial institution – the World Bank – have not been smooth either: in 2004, the World Bank announced it would stop making new loans to Uzbekistan as part of anti-corruption drive by the global lender (World Bank. 2006). Transparency International, an anti-graft group, rates Uzbekistan among the world's most corrupt countries, while economists have blamed government policies for keeping much of the ex-Soviet state in poverty. A sharp increase in the inequality of income distribution has hurt the lower ranks of society since independence. (CIA, The World FactBook).

Authoritarian President Islam Karimov, who has ruled the country since 1989, re-ran for the top post in December 2007 polls and won amid an absence of real political opponents. Karimov's victory paved the way for further political and economic stagnation in 2008 and beyond.

Western investment is likely to continue to be discouraged by the poor business environment and human rights concerns. A recent assessment of the London-based Economist Intelligence Unit describes the political risk in Uzbekistan as extremely high, especially for Western investments (*RFE/RL*, 2007). Uzbek authorities have accused US and other foreign companies operating in Uzbekistan of violating Uzbek tax laws and have frozen their assets (CIA, 'The World FactBook').

Meanwhile, Russia, China, and Southeast Asian countries are getting used to the environment. Russian businesses have shown increased interest in Uzbekistan, especially in the mining, telecommunications, and energy sectors (CIA, 'The World FactBook'). Russian and Asian investments in the oil and gas sector and in manufacturing will nevertheless provide an impetus to GDP growth.

Uzbekistan joined the Russia-led Eurasian Economic Community (EurASEC) and the Collective Security Treaty Organization (CSTO). It is also full member of the Shanghai Cooperation Organization dominated by Russia and China. In November 2005, Karimov and Russian President Vladimir Putin signed an unprecedented 'alliance' treaty, which also includes provisions for economic and business cooperation.

Independent experts agree that the overall economy is in decline (Library of Congress, 2007). However, Uzbekistan is highly likely to maintain large surpluses on its current account due to high commodity prices in the world markets. That reduces the Uzbek government's incentive for serious reforms.

It is important to note that informal economic activity accounts for between one-third and one-half of Uzbekistan's output (Library of Congress, 2007). Most of it is in the area of small and medium enterprises (SMEs). As is pointed out in the next section, the government has been reluctant to legalize informal economic businesses and instead has tried to eliminate them.

Amid high unemployment and poverty, a significant number of the Uzbekistani workforce has sought employment – in most cases illegal – abroad, notably in neighbouring Russia and Kazakhstan. An October 2007 report by the International Fund for Agricultural Development noted that Uzbeks abroad inject about US$2.9 billion into their country's economy – representing about 17 percent of GDP in 2006 (IFAD, 2007).

Uzbek officials put the unemployment rate at 0.7 percent, but actual unemployment is believed to be about 6 percent and underemployment – 20 percent of a labor force of 14.3 million (Library of Congress, 2007).

Uzbekistan also faces a number of very serious environmental problems. The most pressing is the crisis in the Aral Sea region, where poor water management over an extended period of time in Uzbekistan and its neighboring states, has resulted in the shrinkage of the sea and its contamination by agricultural chemicals. This is now adversely affecting economic activity and the health of the population (World Bank, 'Uzbekistan Country Brief').

Government policy on SMEs and entrepreneurship in Uzbekistan

The major economic challenge the country faced after becoming independent following the 1991 collapse of the Soviet Union was transformation of the centralized Soviet-planned economy into a market-based economy. President Karimov proclaimed this goal as a priority for Uzbekistan. The Uzbek government also identified development of medium- and small-size entrepreneurship as one of the sectors that should give impetus to transition toward market economy.

The government set the ambitious goal of increasing the share of SMEs in the GDP to 52 percent by 2010. President Karimov stated a few years ago that in 2000 the share of SMEs reached 31 percent of the country's GDP – a significant growth comparing to just 1.5 percent in 1991 after the collapse of the Soviet Union. In a well-known January 2003 speech, President Karimov stated that private sector development was vital for economic development of Uzbekistan and it should be supported through strengthening private property rights (Suhir, 2004).

The share of SMEs in the country's gross domestic product has been growing in recent years. In the early 2000s, the country saw development of small private enterprises, such as retail stores, restaurants, and computer technology. These contributed to the increase of share of services in national GDP. However, as the government continued to restrict consumer goods imports and licensing for retail commerce, many small-scale traders – both legitimate and black market – were forced to flee to neighbouring countries, which reduced the availability of consumer goods.

One independent source has pointed out that the share of small businesses in Uzbekistan's industrial sector was only 9 per cent in 2007 compared to some 90 per cent in developed market economies (Kurpayanidi, 2007). According to the Uzbek government statistics, 6.8 million people were involved in SMEs by July 2006 (data of the State Committee on Statistics, quoted by Kurpayanidi, 2007).

In 2005, the labor force was estimated at 14.3 million people, of whom 44 percent working in agriculture, 36 percent in services, and 20 percent in industry and manufacturing (Library of Congress, 2007).

The state interference into entrepreneurial activity remains great. Shuttle trade has developed in Uzbekistan since the collapse of the Soviet Union. However, it remained an unofficial sector of a 'gray economy' despite giving jobs to thousands of Uzbeks (Suhir, 2004). The Uzbek government failed to legalize it. Rather, it chose to eliminate it but the strategy proved ineffective as the sector gives jobs to many in the country where unemployment was rampant. In recent years, tactics toward the illegal shuttle trade as well as other activities within the 'gray economy' seem to have changed. Shuttle traders are forced to do business with partners abroad with mediation of companies that are controlled by President Karimov's elder daughter Gulnara Karimova, a well-known businesswoman herself (personal interviews with several shuttle traders in Tashkent in summer–autumn, 2007).

In recent years, Uzbekistan has passed several laws related to the promotion of SMEs. One of the most important was the May 2000 'Law on guarantees of freedom of entrepreneurial activity'.[2] However, the government has failed to go beyond its positive rhetoric and conduct real steps that create favorable conditions for SMEs. One independent source gives this data: the number of SMEs dropped in June 2001 to 15 000 from 40 000 in January 2001 (Suhir, 2004).

In 2004, a new law on private enterprises came into force. As the government officials said, the new legislation ended the period of double taxation for private businesses as well as their registration. The new law also changed the formal way of defining small businesses (Economy of Uzbekistan). Independent observers have said that the change in the definition of small business was in fact aimed at technically increasing the share of SMEs in GDP.

At present, most SMEs do not work in those sectors of economy the government defined as priority sectors, such as financial services, and tourism (Suvankulov, interview) along with traditional spheres of trade and catering. Entrepreneurs work mostly in retail, small services and catering, although international experts say agribusiness, manufacturing, and services should become priority sectors (IFC, 2008).

National legislation remains obscure for many local entrepreneurs who often lack knowledge and information regarding the legislation. In a survey conducted by the International Financial Corporation (IFC) in 2004, only 41 percent of Uzbek entrepreneurs said they had sufficient knowledge of national legislation regarding inspections (IFC, 2006). Procedures set by the government to regulate entrepreneurial activity, including inspections, reporting, permits, registration and tax administration, were too lengthy, complicated and often contradicted one another. The IFC's report also noted that according to the 2004 survey, more than half of inspections resulted in negative consequences for companies.[3]

The Uzbek government has said the necessary changes in national legislation have been under way during the whole period of transition. So, as response to the IFC's above-mentioned findings, the presidential decree on 'improvement of the system of legal protection of business entities' was passed in June 2005.[4]

The majority of SMEs do not receive any loans from banks – mostly due to difficulties in obtaining such loans, high requirements in providing security, and so on. However, many Uzbek entrepreneurs admit they have never applied for loans – either due to lack of awareness about such possibilities or expectations that they would have to bribe too many banking officials and would end up paying more for the loan (private interviews with entrepreneurs in Tashkent in summer–autumn 2007).

With assistance from the international organizations and financial institutions, the Uzbek government announced its plan to develop infrastructure for SMEs. In 2005, the government set up a specialized bank 'MicrocreditBank' to satisfy needs for financing SMEs. At present, 14 leasing companies and 18 commercial banks are said to render leasing services in the country. There are said to be 37 credit unions operating in Uzbekistan and offering financial services for the SME sector. Since 2002, credit unions in Uzbekistan created 12 000 jobs and provided entrepreneurs with simplified access to financing.

The government also said industrial clusters must be developed in the country. The Ministry of Foreign Economic Relations, Investment and Trade is promoting a 'Localization Program' in regions of Uzbekistan to produce goods equaled to nearly US$ 1.4 million.

The environment for entrepreneurship and the state of small business in Uzbekistan
Unlike some other former Soviet republics (namely, Russia, Ukraine and Moldova), Uzbekistan has not seen the emergence of a new economic elite after the collapse of the Soviet Union. Communist Party nomenklatura turned into a new nationalist elite and fully monopolized both politics and economics. It also has had a full control over the process of privatization (Gurevich, 2002).

The government tightly controls the cotton industry – the biggest source of cash crop. State-controlled companies buy cotton from farmers at fixed prices that are usually significantly lower than the world rates. Farmers are prevented from selling the harvest abroad at better prices.

Some examples of successful micro-enterprises include those related to the sale of candy, clothes, fruit, and farm animals. Successful small enterprises include those related to the sale of Uzbek handicrafts, and the operation of greenhouses, restaurants, and hotels. Other examples are bakeries, and household construction and renovation businesses. Successful medium enterprises include those related to the production of soft drinks and dairy products. (Tookey, 2002)

Many international organizations actively assist the development of SMEs in Uzbekistan. Those groups include the United States Agency for International Development, the Asian Development Bank, the United Nations Development Programme, the EBRD, the Organization for Security and Cooperation in Europe, and the International Financial Corporation. Their programmes usually focus on developing micro-credit sources, and providing SME training for entrepreneurs (Tookey, 2002). The IFC, which recently opened a private equity fund for Central Asia and the Caucasus, identified agribusiness, manufacturing, and services as 'vital for sustainable development and job creation in Central Asia' (IFC, 2008). Uzbekistan's SMEs often lack start-up capital and have limited access to capital markets.

Factors that will help Uzbekistan as it seeks to develop SMEs include its well-educated population and nearly 100-percent literacy rate. Many young Uzbekistanis have a tremendous desire to establish their own business. A significant number of entrepreneurs have good ideas and they are willing to work hard to develop a business.

The country's banking system remains underdeveloped with bank management as well as supervising government institutions, including the Central Bank, controlling the bank accounts of SMEs and limiting their access to their own accounts by numerous requests on purposes of withdrawals, and so on.

In 2003, the government accepted Article VIII obligations under the International Monetary Fund (IMF), providing for full currency convertibility. However, strict currency controls and tightening of borders have lessened the effects of convertibility and also led to some shortages that have further stifled economic activity. The Central Bank often delays or restricts convertibility, especially for consumer goods. The National Bank of Uzbekistan remains the key provider of both domestic and foreign loans.

The lack of own capital and borrowed funds prevents many SMEs from buying advanced technology abroad. That is a reason behind a small share of producing companies among SMEs. Small and medium enterprises have to operate amid an unreliable legal system as well as underdeveloped infrastructure, such as lack of services regarding insurance, audit, consulting, and others.

Internationalization of entrepreneurs and SMEs from Uzbekistan
Uzbekistan remains a closed country where all political, economic as well as business contacts with the outside world are strictly controlled by the government. While there are examples of international ties of the big Uzbek corporations, SMEs do not seem to have found their way to international markets. The government has repeatedly declared that internationalization of big corporations is a priority of its economic policies.

Foreign activities of the big-caliber corporations, like UzDaewooAuto (automobile production; export mainly to Russia and other former Soviet republics), TAPO (Tashkent Aviation plant producing Ilyushin aircrafts together with Russia) and few others have taken place under the watchful eye of President Karimov.

Internationalization of SMEs is hindered partly by the government's control of foreign currency exchange rate. The situation changed five years ago when the local currency was not freely convertible and multiple exchange rates existed. The introduction of a convertible currency in late 2003 improved the business climate.

However, SMEs are not able to convert their revenues freely and in amounts they want to. If entrepreneurs do need to convert their revenues, they are required to complete numerous documents to prove the need for foreign currency. They also have to often bribe bank officials.

Strict customs control remains another hurdle in the development of SMEs in Uzbekistan. Entrepreneurs have to collect many documents to prove that the commodities they bring from foreign countries are legal. Otherwise, imported goods are confiscated as contraband. A practice of confiscation, including that of private land plots, is rampant in Uzbekistan. It is seen as a way of patching the holes in a state budget that lacks constant flow of taxes due to an inefficient taxation system as well as high levels of corruption.

Conclusion
Uzbekistan has seen economic growth in recent years. It was mostly due to high world prices for commodities like gold, cotton, and hydrocarbon resources that make up the biggest part of the country's export. As long as the growth in prices continues for those commodities in world markets, the Uzbek authorities will see little incentive to change current policies of strong government control of the economy and continuing state interference in the activities of SMEs.

The government also has no motivation to change the current situation as regards the high level of corruption and nepotism, as most government officials often own and/or control businesses in Uzbekistan.

More than half of the country's population are youth. Unemployment is high, and poverty rampant. The largest part of the population, which lives mostly in rural areas, could be involved in agriculture as well as services. In this situation, the best strategy would be to develop medium- and small-size entrepreneurship to create jobs.

Many Uzbek men and women have fled the country in search of jobs elsewhere. Local human rights activists say the number of Uzbeks working both legally and illegally abroad could be as high as 7 million people (Ikramov, 2007). They work mainly in Russia, Kazakhstan, South Korea, Thailand, India, the United Arab Emirates, as well as the countries of Europe and North America.

Stability, both economic and political, may be maintained for the next few years. But in the long term the government will have no other option but to liberalize economy. Development of SMEs must be at the core of the liberalization.

As the Uzbek government identifies electricity, mining (gold, copper, gas) and processing industries (textile and garment, wood processing, agro-processing and beverage industries) as industries with comparative advantage, the government should prioritize development and direct support of SMEs in those sectors. Because approximately 44 percent of the Uzbek population is involved in agriculture, SMEs can benefit the agricultural sector, which in turn will increase the country's export potential.

Small and medium enterprises will play a significant role in promoting social stability, in giving citizens an ownership interest in their communities, in contributing to the economic prosperity of the country, and in helping Uzbekistan to compete in the world markets.

Notes

1. The other double-locked country is Liechtenstein.
2. This law is comprehensive and is meant to provide a solid legal basis for SMEs, addressing all aspects of SME creation, development, and legal protection. For example, Article 8 details the rights of entrepreneurs, including the right to sell products at prices the entrepreneurs determine, and the right to engage in foreign trade. Article 34 is meant to eliminate unnecessary government involvement in entrepreneurial activity, while Article 39 mandates that state inspections of SMEs should be reasonable and not disruptive of SME activity.
3. They came in forms of various sanctions, both official – fines, repeated inspections, suspension of all operations on the company's bank accounts, and so on – and those not envisioned by the law (unofficial payments, or bribes). In 2004, inspections resulted in official sanctions for 37 percent of respondents. A half of those firms paid fines of an average of 230 000 sums (approximately US$225). Another 36 percent of the respondents had to make unofficial payments as a result of inspections. During an inspection, an entrepreneur interacts directly with the inspector on the issues of the economic entity's compliance with the requirements set out in the legislation. However, as the inspection procedure is vague and poorly regulated, entrepreneurs often do not know which requirements the controlling body has the right to inspect.

    The research revealed that the mechanism for appealing the actions and decisions of the inspectors, which is said to provide for effective protection of the rights and legal interests of entrepreneurs and reduce the abuse of authority by government officials, was not functioning properly in Uzbekistan. Thus, only 3 percent of the respondents appealed the actions of controlling bodies. Only 39 percent of them were successful.
4. According to the decree, the following measures could only be applied to business entities by a court order: cessation of operations; suspension of operations on bank accounts excluding revealed cases of unlawful legalization of income acquired from criminal activity and the financing of terrorism; suspension of activities excluding the cases of suspension for the period of no more than 10 working days in connection to the prevention of emergencies, epidemics and other real threats to life and health of people; transfer of objects of violations of law to state ownership.

References

CIA, 'The World FactBook – Uzbekistan', https://www.cia.gov/library/publications/the-world-factbook/geos/uz.html (accessed 15 March 2009).

Dana, Leo-Paul (2002), *When Economies Change Paths: Models of Transition in China, the Central Asian Republics, Myanmar, and the Nations of Former Indochine Française*, Singapore, London and Hong Kong: World Scientific.

Economist Intelligence Unit (EIU) (2007), http://eiu.ecnext.com/coms2/browsetype_viewcountry_%60 Uzbekistan%60 (accessed 15 March 2009).

Economy of Uzbekistan, official information, www.panasia.ru.

Gurevich, Leonid (2002) President of BISAM Central Asia, *Evrazia*, No. 3.

IFAD (2007), 'Sending money home: worldwide remittances flows to developing countries', http://www.ifad.org/events/remittances/maps/index.htm (accessed 15 March 2009).

IFC (2006), Fourth Annual Survey on Business Environment of Uzbekistan, January 2006, http://www.press-service.uz/en/gsection.scm?groupId=5203&contentId=16608 (accessed February 2008).

IFC (2008), 'Private equity fund investment supports small and medium businesses in Central Asia', 4 March, http://www.ifc.org/ifcext/media.nsf/content/SelectedPressRelease?OpenDocument&UNID=2E203588D09 DDF668525740200597538 (accessed 15 March 2009).

Ikramor, Surat (2007), personal interview with Surat Ikramov, the head of the Tashkent-based human rights organization, Center for Human Rights Initiatives, conducted in late 2007.

Kurpayanidi, Konstantin (2007), 'What hinders small business development in Uzbekistan?' paper presented at the 14th International Conference at the Moscow State University, 11–14 April.

Library of Congress (2007), 'Country profile. Uzbekistan, February 2007', Library of Congress, Federal Research Division, http://lcweb2.loc.gov/frd/cs/profiles/Uzbekistan.pdf (accessed 15 March 2009).

Reuters (2008), 'Kazakhstan sees 70 pct gas price rise from 2009', 18 March, www.reuters.org (accessed 15 March 2009).

RFE/RL (2007), 'U.S. business ventures provide valuable lessons', 15 August, www.rferl.org (accessed 15 March 2009).

Saidazimova, Gulnoza (2008), 'Uzbekistan: cotton industry targeted by child-labor activists', *RFE/RL*, 19 January, http://www.rferl.org (accessed 15 March 2009).

Suhir, Yelena (2004), 'Good intentions and sad consequences: how excessive regulation hinders development of Uzbekistan', Center for International Private Enterprise (affiliate of the US Chamber of Commerce), 29 January, www.cipe.org (accessed 15 March 2009).

Suvankulov, Farruh, Uzbek Finance Ministry official, interview for CIS Research Network Economic, Education and Research Consortium, www.eerc.ru

Tookey, Douglas L. (2002), 'Challenges to small and medium enterprise development in Uzbekistan', *The Central Asia and Caucasus Analyst*, 27 March, http://www.cacianalyst.org/?q=node/138) (accessed 15 March 2009).

UzA (2008), 'Uzbekistan's GDP increases by 9.5 per cent in 2007', 9 February.

World Bank (2006), 'World Bank halts new lending to Uzbekistan', 16 March, http://www.noticias.info/Archi vo/2006/200603/20060316/20060316_155865.shtm (accessed 15 March 2009).

World Bank, 'Uzbekistan country brief', http://lnweb18.worldbank.org/ECA/eca.nsf/Countries/Uzbekistan/85 5279F327EA2C6685256C3C0071D5E1?OpenDocument. (accessed 15 March 2009).

44 Vietnam
Mai Thi Thanh Thai and Narendra M. Agrawal

1   Introduction to Vietnam

The entire national economy of Vietnam had a long period of inertia when it implemented a centrally planned economic system modeled after that of the Communist bloc. Its annual growth rate stopped at 0.4 percent while the population grew more than 2.3 percent per year, causing severe shortages in essential consumer goods and a trade deficit, with imports being four to five times greater than exports and hyperinflation which peaked at 774.7 percent in 1986 (CGVSF, 2006). This compelled Vietnam to start *doi moi* – literally means renovation – in 1986. Without overthrowing the socialist establishment, the *doi moi* involved ushering in entrepreneurship as a complement to state enterprises, rather than as a replacement of Marxist ideals (Dana, 1994).

By the early 1990s, remarkable policy improvements had been made and it was only then that a considerable amount of financial assistance began to flow into Vietnam in a sustained way, although Vietnam no longer enjoyed economic aid from the Soviet bloc, which collapsed in 1991. Since then Vietnam has achieved striking economic growth. Its gross domestic product (GDP) real growth rate peaked at 9.5 percent in 1995 and has consistently been among the highest in the world over recent years (Table 44.1).

Vietnam has also taken active steps to integrate into the world economy by normalizing its diplomatic relationship with the United States in 1994, which led to a bilateral trade agreement, joining the Association of Southeast Asian Nations in 1995, joining the Asia-Pacific Economic Co-operation Forum in 1998, and joining the World Trade Organization in 2007. This international economic integration process has increasingly been exposing Vietnamese small and medium enterprises (SMEs) to opportunities and threats in the international market. As a result, its exports grew much faster than its GDP and have been the highest in the dynamic East Asian region as well as the world as a whole (Phan et al., 2003). The total value of exports and imports in 2006 amounted to over 10 times that of 1986 (Figure 44.1) when Vietnam started implementing its open-door policies. Its indices of both imports and exports steadily rose on steep slopes over the past 20 years (Figure 44.2).

Table 44.1   GDP real growth rate from 1987 to 2010

1987	1988	1989	1990	1991	1992	1993	1994	1995	1996	1997	1998
3.9%	5.0%	8.5%	5.1%	6.0%	8.6%	8.1%	8.8%	9.5%	9.3%	8.2%	5.8%

1999	2000	2001	2002	2003	2004	2005	2006	2007	2008	2009	2010
4.8%	6.8%	6.9%	7.0%	7.3%	7.8%	8.4%	8.2%	8.5%	8.5%	8.7%	8.5%

Sources: Compiled from ADB (2007), BMI (2007), Chong (2002), GSO (2007) and UNCTAD (2007).

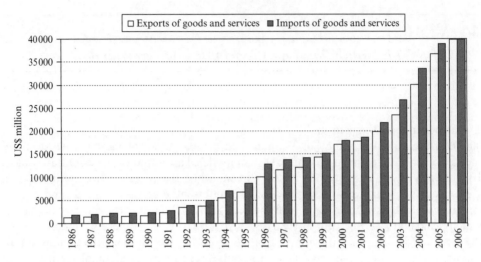

Sources: Compiled from GSO (2007) and UNCTAD (2007).

Figure 44.1   Volume of exports and imports from 1986 to 2006

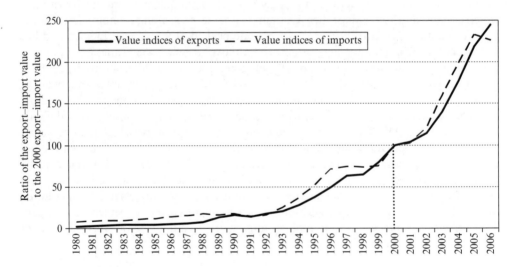

Source: Compiled from UNCTAD (2007).

Figure 44.2   Export–import indices from 1980 to 2006

2   Government policy on SMEs and entrepreneurship in Vietnam

Recognizing the importance of SMEs in Vietnam, the government of Vietnam has issued various decrees to promote development of small businesses in certain industries and called for international donors and loans to run SME support programs. It has also established a system of institutional support for SME development (Figure 44.3).

The Ministry of Planning and Investment has completed its national SME development

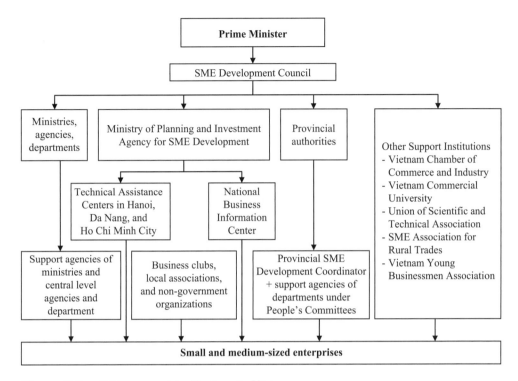

Figure 44.3   SME support institutions in Vietnam

policy 2006–2010 as part of Vietnam's five-year socio-economic development plan. Its stated objective is to 'push up the rate of SME development, create a healthy competitive environment, improve the competitiveness of the enterprises and the nation, encourage the SMEs to play a role in employment generation and income increment' (ASMED, 2006: 47). According to the plan, the government will keep on developing the regulatory framework and ensuring its stability, reduce the costs of SMEs' start-up, simplify business regulations, continue tax and banking reform, encourage an effective market on both demand and supply sides, encourage the involvement of the SMEs in inter-lines, inter-regions and inter-firm cooperation between them and higher education and research institutions, and so on.

3   The environment for entrepreneurship and the state of small business in Vietnam

Since 2000, the new Enterprise Law has made it easier and faster for businesses to register by clarifying procedures, eliminating certain difficult requirements, and requiring relevant agencies to process paperwork within a more reasonable timeframe. As a result, the number of new business registrations jumped dramatically (Figure 44.4). In just four years from 2000 to 2003, the number was already quadruple that of the 10-year period from 1990 to 1999 (Le, 2004). Remarkably, 99.6 percent of the 160 752 new business registrations between 2000 and 2005 were private enterprises (ASMED, 2007). Today, small and medium-sized enterprises have grown considerably and have played an overwhelmingly important role in Vietnam. Accounting for over 99 percent of all enterprises

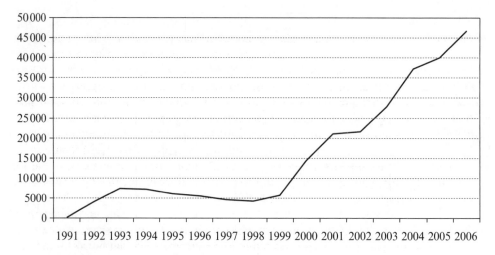

Sources: Compiled from Le (2004) and ASMED (2007).

Figure 44.4   Number of new business registrations from 1991 to 2006

in Vietnam (ASMED, 2007), they are the key to significant new employment creation and renewed economic growth. Given the ongoing SME support programs by both the Vietnamese government and international organizations, it is reasonable to expect that the number of SMEs will continue to grow, and so will their contribution to the Vietnamese economy.

Although most SMEs show some appreciation for the government's effort to liberalize the market, especially land reforms and some reduction in foreign currency control, they feel that the government has not pushed it far enough for SMEs to benefit from. They complain that the unstable policy environment puts them in a position to be reactive rather than proactive in making plans for their international activities unless they have insider information. They also deplore the government's system of tax control and public administration that preclude many international opportunities. Private firms are further tied because the government gives state-run enterprises better access to government loans, contracts, and land rights so that they have more power to implement their inter-nationalization strategies. Moreover, local authorities have tried to implement their own regulations and restrictions on private enterprises. Meanwhile government programs designed to support SMEs are ineffective. Most of the firms that we interviewed have no interest in such programs at all. Managers of the firms that have ever tried to approach the government for support said that they have received nothing useful.

Furthermore, weak law enforcement is seen by the interviewed managers to be among the most serious problems they have to face. To deal with domestic businesses they could use 'private ordering', that is, relying on social norms and using non-government forces to solve conflicts, but it does not work when handling international problems. While foreign businesses bank on the legal system to do business, Vietnamese SMEs are so accustomed to using relationships, that they are prone to accept international contracts that may have provisions to place them in a weaker position in front of the court.

The fact that Vietnam's financial system is underdeveloped makes it impossible for

SME managers to implement several strategies they wish to deploy. For example, many of the managers we interviewed want to embark on e-commerce but it is not possible for them to receive credit card payments online unless they have a bank account abroad. Despite reforms in the banking and financial sector, many private SMEs consider obtaining investment capital from financial institutions 'a mission impossible' because of its overly complicated appraisal procedures and strict collateral requirements.

Vietnamese SME managers have a general impression that the ongoing international economic integration would bring about changes, both good and bad, for the economy as a whole thanks to the government's propaganda campaigns. However, most managers of small private firms we interviewed claim not to know what it would really mean to their businesses. In fact, they do not have any clear expectations about the effects of continuing internationalization nor do they predict any notable changes in the way they conduct their business in the foreseeable future. This may be explained by the fact that they have been operating in market niches that are unattractive for larger firms both at home and abroad. On the other hand, managers of medium-sized private firms are working on adapting their internationalization strategies to take advantage of what globalization has to offer and be prepared for challenges it brings about. They believe that the government is going to have to reduce favoritism to the state-owned sector much further and those who have been successful thanks to close relationship with government contacts will be put on a level playing field with other firms. That fact deeply worries managers of many state-owned SMEs, whose comparative advantages lie in the preferred treatment from the government. Being faced with this seemingly irreversible trend, state-owned SMEs are trying to restructure their business in order to survive.

4 Internationalization of entrepreneurs and SMEs from Vietnam
This section presents the result of our qualitative study on 35 internationalizing Vietnamese SMEs that operate in different industries and are located in various parts of Vietnam from the North to the South. Since our chapter is the first paper to explore the phenomenon of Vietnamese SMEs' internationalization from the firms' perspective, it is necessary to validate our findings with further quantitative studies to ensure the generalizability of our proposed theory.

For Vietnamese SMEs, internationalization is only one of many strategies to satisfy their goals. Almost all of the 35 studied firms have engaged in multiple industries, many of which are not even related. This is even more so for trading companies. The reason why they have been able to hop between industries lies in their opportunistic-mindedness and tendency to avoid business lines that require high fixed costs for low liquid assets. And all interviewed managers are quite vocal about flexibility being the key to success.

If a firm runs business in different industries, it may internationalize in one but remains domestic in another. Figure 44.5 depicts the rationales behind Vietnamese SMEs' decision to internationalize in a particular industry.

At the point of decision-making, a firm may be positioned in any of the seven situations depicted in Figure 44.5. The characteristics of each situation are determined by the presence or absence of any of the three dimensions – desire, ability, and industry – which are described below.

In dimension D (whose characteristics are shared by situations 1, 2, 6, and 7), internationalization is what the firm and/or its managers desire. For example: the firm is

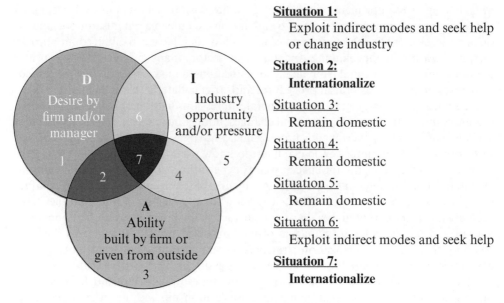

Situation 1:
    Exploit indirect modes and seek help
    or change industry

Situation 2:
    Internationalize

Situation 3:
    Remain domestic

Situation 4:
    Remain domestic

Situation 5:
    Remain domestic

Situation 6:
    Exploit indirect modes and seek help

Situation 7:
    Internationalize

Figure 44.5   To internationalize or not to internationalize

assigned by the Vietnamese government to promote exports or is delegated by the government to import materials for certain industries (this is often the case for state-owned enterprises); it wants to team up with foreigners in one or all of its business lines to learn how they do business as a way to build its competitive edge; it wants to diversify risks; its manager wants to satisfy his or her personal goal of proving he or she is capable of managing an international firm; its manager wants to live abroad; and so on. In short, the desire may be for the sake of reaching the firm's organizational goals or just the manager's personal goals.

In dimension A (whose characteristics are shared by situations 2, 3, 4, and 7), the firm is able to internationalize because it already has or is able to mobilize the required resources and capability or its environment enables it to internationalize. For example: the firm that employs handicapped people receives support from international charity organizations who assist it both in cash and in kind by buying its output; the government acts as a bridge between the firm and its potential partners; the government gives the firm a quota (which other firms do not have); and so on.

In dimension I (whose characteristics are shared by situations 4, 5, 6, and 7), the structure and attributes of the industry cause the firm's decision makers to think that there are opportunities and/or pressure for the firm to internationalize. The concept opportunity should be understood as possibility for the firm to make profits while the concept pressure should be understood as hardship the firm must endure if it does not internationalize. For example: the industry is in maturity and/or a decline stage whereby some firms in developed countries need to cut costs by outsourcing to countries like Vietnam, which has abundant national resources and cheap labor cost; the degree of internationalization of the industry is high; demand and price are higher abroad than in Vietnam; demand in Vietnam is too low because of consumer preference and/or income; and so on. The opportunity/pressure is what the firm's decision makers perceive and does not necessarily reflect the actual situation of the industry. How accurate their perception is depends on the quality of the information channels to which the firm's decision makers have access and their international management capacity.

In situation 1, the firm and/or its manager wants to embark on internationalization. The firm, however, does not see any opportunity in this industry nor is it able to internationalize in this industry. If its inability comes from within, that is, it does not yet have the needed resources and capability to do so, the manager will actively seek partnership and/or lobby government officials or anyone in power to help. It may even engage in a new industry so long as it creates an opportunity for the firm to go international. If the inability is caused by the government's policy to designate certain state-owned enterprises (SOEs) to engage in import/export in certain industries, the firm exploits indirect modes such as selling exported goods to or buying imported goods from these designated SOEs, and so on. However, this strategy is temporary since the firm will jump to direct internationalization (situation 2 or situation 7) when such a barrier is removed. For instance, before December 1998 it was almost impossible for private firms to obtain export quotas directly because the application procedures were reportedly cumbersome and costly, while private firms could only get small quota allocation if their application ever succeeded. The firms that could export directly were often the ones that bought a quota from state enterprises. Since this practice was considered illegal, they got around this by having the state-owned firms subcontract quota items to the private firms with the output still officially recorded as having originated from the state-owned firms. After the government had issued regulations for auctioning export quotas to assure that export quotas are allocated to the best performing enterprises, private firms started exporting directly. Nevertheless, it is still difficult for private firms to get export quotas if they do not have 'insiders' with strong connections with the Ministry of Trade and the Ministry of Industry.

In situation 2, the firm internationalizes because it wants to and has the ability to do so even though the managers see that industry pressure is light and opportunity is restricted. If there exists no opportunity in this industry, its managers will actively seek opportunities in another industry. For the firm to be able to do so, short-term profits for survival may not be critical. This is often the case of SOEs, whose financial standing is protected by the government.

In situation 3, the firm remains a purely domestic operation in this industry. The firm's managers do not want their firm to internationalize and they do not look for any foreign business opportunity or feel the pressure to go international. If this indifference is caused only by the firm's failure to identify opportunities, public propaganda and availability of the right information can quickly change their opinion. If the managers get the information, they will quickly change their attitude towards internationalization. In this case, availability of quality information and encouragement from seeing a successful experience by other firms can create significant impacts. If the indifference comes from the manager's prejudice and low risk tolerance, the situation remains the same for longer. But the firm may change its position when there is a change in the composition of the management board.

In situation 4, the firm chooses to stay domestic in its own industry. Although the firm has the capacity to internationalize, its managers are not interested in doing so.

There can be a number of reasons for the managers to remain aloof. The key decision makers may fear uncertainty and failure, which can damage their reputation and economic remuneration. In this case, seeing successful experience by peers can change their opinion. The firm may earn more profits from engaging in other industries, so if there is pressure in this industry the managers will just simply abandon the industry for another one. Or the managers may sense that leading their firm to internationalization will force them to compromise certain personal gains. In this case, the managers will try to avoid internationalization as much as they can.

In situation 5, the firm and its managers do not desire to internationalize nor does the firm have the necessary resources and capability to do so. Therefore, it remains solely domestic in this industry if the pressure is perceived to be low, or changes industry if otherwise. To be enticed to internationalize, the firm must be given encouragement and assistance from outside. In other words, the firm is reactive and even when it decides to internationalize, it does so with low managerial commitment.

In situation 6, the firm and/or its managers covet internationalization for the firm has spotted an opportunity or they perceive the industry pressure big enough to necessitate internationalization. However, it is unable to do so because of its inability to mobilize the needed resources and capability. Therefore, the firm chooses to ambush others in the same industry and exploit indirect modes. When given help either by the government or by people in the firm's networks, it will quickly spring to the international market. In the meantime, its managers are active in seeking help.

Finally, situation 7 is when the firm is most motivated to internationalize. If its perception of the opportunities that internationalization in that given industry is correct, then it is most likely to succeed. Therefore, quality information is the key for the firm to develop winning internationalization strategies.

Firms that chose to internationalize at inception are those placed in situation 7 (Figure 44.5) where all three dimensions of desire, ability, and industry meet at the time of its birth. If not endowed with such favorable conditions, the firms will internationalize later when its position enters situation 7 or situation 2. In the latter position, the firm may not identify any opportunity to make real profits or feel industry pressure to internationalize, but it still embarks on internationalization for reasons not related to firm's profits. Therefore, internationalization is possible in situation 2 only when short-term profits for survival is not an immediate concern.

The duration of each strategy implementation is not predetermined. The firms changed their strategies when the situation required. It appears that Vietnamese SMEs change their strategies quite often because of two major reasons. First, international business is new to Vietnamese SME managers and they are still learning how to do business in the international market. Changes in their cognitive ability coupled with availability of new information cause changes in their perception about the industry's opportunity/pressure and their ability to internationalize. Second, the external environment is changing quickly due to Vietnam's international economic integration process.

Before deciding on an international operation mode, the interviewed managers analyze several alternatives against their business situations. The chosen mode reflects the managers' optimal personal goal fulfillment with assurance of some organization goal achievement and feasibility. Nevertheless, their analysis is informal and still hinges on intuition rather than formal feasibility study because they are relatively inexperienced and have to make a decision with limited or no quality information input. Hence, the most frequently used strategy-making method is based on trial and error within their acceptable level of risks. This explains why their international operation does not follow a predetermined pattern; rather it exhibits an intermittent pattern of progress, pause, and retreat or continuity contingent to their situation.

One noticeable characteristic of the studied firms is that they do not stick with a product/service line or stay in just one industry. The interviewed managers share the view that they need to be flexible to capture good opportunities that the market has to offer. In fact, many of them run multiple unrelated business lines. They acknowledge that if they stay with one line of products/services or in one industry for long they will be able to develop a learning curve and build a bigger network in that specific industry. However, they do not do so because it is too costly for them, given their internal constraints, while they have to count on short-term profits to survive. Therefore, when they spot a more lucrative line of products/services, they divert the resources used for the existing line(s) to embark on the more profitable one. When the market of the abandoned product/service lines becomes lucrative again, the managers re-adopt these lines. As for traders, the sunk cost of changing product lines is minimal. Vietnamese small producers do not have high sunk costs either, because they concentrate on low-technology sectors.

The choice of market is driven by demand and price factors. Psychic distance concept does not apply to Vietnamese SMEs. They do not care if a country is psychically close or distant as long as the market price is good. This is perhaps caused by lack of international experience, which causes them not to include hidden costs in their estimation. Furthermore, their lack of systematic market analysis skills causes them to use the current market price as a decisive indicator of market conditions. However, a current market price cannot be used to predict future shifts in demand and supply. Therefore, it is no surprise that they change markets frequently.

On the other hand, Vietnam's political situation and the government's policy can preclude Vietnamese SMEs' access to certain markets. For example, before Vietnam and the United States signed their bilateral trade agreement, Vietnamese SMEs could not enter this market even though they wanted to. Quota is another strong determinant. If they fail to get an export quota for a certain product, which are often won by large firms, they cannot ship the goods out of Vietnam's border even though they have orders from foreign customers.

5 Conclusions

Vietnamese SMEs' internationalization is a dynamic process of continual proactive and reactive adaptation to situational changes to achieve the firms' organizational goals or to satisfy their managers' personal goals. That explains why they internationalize at one time but de-internationalize at another if engaging in international activities does not yield instant desired results. How they internationalize is determined by a combination of internal and external factors. Since these factors may remain the same for some time and then change, the firms' internationalization strategies are fixed or altered accordingly. Therefore, their internationalization path follows sporadic patterns in terms of duration, operation mode, product, and market. These findings have several implications for policy makers and Vietnamese SME managers.

Policy makers can shape Vietnamese SMEs' behavior in the international market by altering their business situations with policy changes. If policy makers want to encourage Vietnamese SMEs to engage in outward internationalization, they should come up with measures to make outward modes more profitable than inward modes, by reducing their foreign market search and marketing costs. To help upgrade the firms' competitiveness in the international market, business education should highlight the practical benefits of working with business plans and give entrepreneurs training in the field of business planning and risk management.

In order to correctly identify situational changes and understand what the changes mean to their business so that they can adapt to and benefit from the changes, Vietnamese SMEs should actively seek more information inputs from multiple sources, improve their analytic skills by continual training, and formalize their business processes. Indeed, the biggest lesson drawn by internationalizing Vietnamese SMEs is that professionalism and unity are the key to success.

References

ADB (2007), *Asian Development Outlook 2007 Update*, Manila: Asian Development Bank.
ASMED (2006), *Small and Medium Enterprise Development: 5 Year Plan 2006–2010*, Agency for SME Development, Vietnam's Ministry of Planning and Investment.
ASMED (2007), 'SMEs in Vietnam', Agency for SME Development, Vietnam's Ministry of Planning and Investment, http://www.business.gov.vn (accessed 27 November 2007).
BMI (2007), *Country Report: Vietnam Business Forecast Report Q4 2007*, London: Business Monitor International.
CGVSF (2006), 'Economy', Consulate General of Vietnam in San Francisco, http://www.vietnamconsulate-sf.org/economic-e.html (accessed 16 February 2006).
Chong, L.C. (2002), *Business Environment and Opportunities in Vietnam: Ho Chi Minh City and its Surrounding Region*, St Gallen: St Gallen Business Books & Tools.
Dana, L.P. (1994), 'A Marxist mini-dragon? Entrepreneurship in today's Vietnam', *Journal of Small Business Management*, **32**(2), 95–102.
GSO (2007), 'Statistical data' [Số liệu thống kê], General Statistics Office of Vietnam, http://www.gso.gov.vn (accessed 5 January 2008).
Le, D.D. (2004), 'Enterprise Law and the Development of the Domestic Private Sector in Vietnam', Proceeding of International Policy Conference on Transitional Economies. United Nations Development Programme, Hanoi, Vietnam, 31 May–1 June.
Phan, M.N., T.P.A. Nguyen and T.N. Phan (2003), 'Exports and long-run growth in Vietnam, 1975–2001' *ASEAN Economic Bulletin*, **20**(3), 211–32.
UNCTAD (2007), *UNCTAD Handbook of Statistics 2006–2007*, Geneva, Switzerland: United Nations Conference on Trade and Development.

45 Doing business in Asia[1]
Ilan Alon, Wenxian Zhang and Bob Moore

Asia includes rich Muslim nations such as Saudia Arabia; less wealthy Muslim countries such as Indonesia and Malaysia; transitional economies, including China, Kazakhstan, the Kyrgyz Republic, Tajikistan, Turkmenistan, Uzbekistan, Cambodia, Laos, and Vietnam (see Dana, 2002); the Newly Industrialized Economies – Singapore, South Korea, and Taiwan, and mature industrialized economies such as Japan (see Dana, 1999; 2007). Some of Asia's economies were formerly British or French; others were Ottoman (Dana, 2000).

It is, therefore, difficult to speak in generalities about all of these markets at the same time since historical, cultural and economic differences may mask the realities of the marketplace and varied human conditions (Cragg, 1993). As such we shall focus in our examination below on a number of important markets in more detail to show how the differences are manifested. Specifically, China is now by some measures the second largest economy in the world and a transitional economy that is changing the value systems and the economic well-being of its neighbors. Japan, on the other hand, is another special case study since the country has an aggressive history with its neighbors and a strong nationalist sentiment. We provide herein as a case study a comparison between these two great nations. Cultural factors are also very important in the formation of living conditions and economic growth. We provide another case study that examines the cultural values of Asia that have led to risky behaviors and the Asian financial crisis.

It would be a mistake to look at East Asia and the Pacific Rim in isolation in order to engage in the global economy. It is for this reason this book makes an important contribution that allows readers to compare various cultural and political underpinnings of business across Asia. Also for this reason, we include a short case study that contrasts Japanese management principles with those in the United States of America.

Geography and demographics

Geographic regions
Our discussion focuses mainly on the countries of the western edge of the Pacific Rim. This is an area that includes some of the world's most diverse populations and economies.

The eastern portion of the Eurasian land mass could be thought of as a subcontinent in itself that slopes downward to the east and south from the great uplifted massif of Tibet. From Tibet (which is an autonomous region within the People's Republic of China), and from the parallel mountain ranges that lie just to its east, emerge many of the great and famous rivers of China and Southeast Asia, including the Huang He (Yellow River), the Yangtze, and the Mekong. China's western region includes not only Tibet but also the autonomous region of Xinjiang and the provinces of Qinghai and Gansu. These areas are all dominated by lofty mountains and vast deserts, while the eastern half of China is both more humid and less mountainous. The north central region of China, through which the Yellow River flows, also receives relatively little rainfall and has for millennia been plagued by occasional droughts. This area is thought of as the cradle of Chinese civilization, since it was here that the earliest dynasties first emerged (Murowchick, 1994). China, which is about the same size as the United States, is also similar to the US in that it includes a variety of energy, mineral and other natural resources.

Vietnam, which borders China on the south, was a part of the Chinese empire for about 1000 years. The Vietnamese view their successful rebellion from the Chinese as an indication of their love of independence, and they view their history in general as a series of struggles against powerful invaders, including the Chinese, the Mongols, the French, the Japanese and the Americans. Its climate is largely tropical and subtropical.

The climates of Korea and Japan are similar to neighboring regions of northeastern China (which in turn is similar to the northeastern US) with some ameliorating effects in Japan due to the influence of the surrounding oceans. Summers in Japan, however, can be surprisingly humid, reminding some visitors of the summer climates of Miami or New Orleans.

Peoples
The total population of China (including the People's Republic and the Republic of China, or Taiwan), Japan, Korea (North and South), Vietnam, and Australia is over 1.5 billion or roughly one-fourth of the world's entire population. The giant among these Pacific Rim nations is, of course, China, whose current population of 1.3 billion accounts for over 80 percent of the Pacific Rim's total. China's great size, combined with its rapidly developing economy, makes it a power to be reckoned with in the twenty-first century (*Atlas of the World*, 2004).

China is also the most ethnically diverse of the western Pacific Rim countries. When picturing the people of China, most observers think automatically of the Han people, the majority population whose name is derived from the Han dynasty, a contemporary of the Roman Empire. The Han people dominate China today and have done so since the fall of the Qing dynasty in 1911, a dynasty whose rulers were Manchus, not Han Chinese. Mao Zedong, Deng Xiaoping, Jiang Zemin and Hu Jintao, the four most prominent leaders of the People's Republic, have all been Han Chinese. So are those Chinese who have made an impression in the West, including Bruce Lee, Jackie Chan and Yao Ming.

The Han Chinese, accounting for about 1.2 billion of China's total population, are themselves diverse. The largest group consists of the Mandarin speakers who populate northern, northeastern and central China. But also significant are the Cantonese who live mainly in Hong Kong and Guangdong province. Other significant Han Chinese groups are the Hakka and the Min who are the majority population on Taiwan, where they are often referred to as Taiwanese. These various Han groups are distinguished most importantly by the forms of Chinese that they speak. All of these so-called 'dialects' of Chinese are mutually unintelligible. In other words, a Mandarin speaker from Beijing cannot understand the Cantonese spoken by a Hong Kong Chinese, who, in turn, cannot understand the Taiwanese spoken by someone from Taibei (Taipei). The two forces that hold the Han Chinese together, are their use of a character-based writing system (which allows them to read and understand each other, even when they cannot do so by talking) and a powerful sense of pride in China as an enduring civilization which, according the claims of the Han Chinese themselves, has roots that are 5000 years old.

The non-Han Chinese on the mainland are divided into 55 ethnic groups or nationalities according to the government of the People's Republic. The best known of these are the Mongols, the Manchus, the Tibetans and the Uighurs. Within the latter two groups some resistance against Han domination has occurred, and the Beijing government is extremely sensitive about the issue of ethnic relations with them. Since the Uighurs are Muslims, a few of their anti-Han members have made their way to Afghanistan where they underwent training under the auspices of al-Qaeda.

The southwestern provinces of Yunnan and Guangxi are home to dozens of other ethnic minorities, some of whom overlap the borders of Vietnam, Laos and other Southeast Asian countries. Some of the better-known groups from this extremely varied area are the Zhuang, Miao, and Dai (Harrell, 2001).

Where China is marked by ethnic diversity, Japan is characterized by homogeneity. The vast majority of the Japanese speak more or less the same language (with certain definite regional dialect variations) and identify themselves as descendants of an ancestry dating back thousands of years. The very small minority populations are the Ryukyu Islanders (including the Okinawans), the Ainu of the extreme north, and the immigrant populations of Korean and Chinese. There is also a group of Japanese known as the burakumin that has traditionally suffered discrimination from the majority population (Hendry, 2003).

Korea is even more ethnically homogeneous than Japan, the main distinctions today being those stemming from the isolation between north and south that began as World War II ended. The northern half of the Korean peninsula is occupied by the isolated Democratic People's Republic of Korea currently ruled by the dictator Kim Jong-il. The south is known as the Republic of Korea and has been ruled by democratically elected leaders since the late 1980s.

Vietnam, unified after a long, bitter war against first the French and then the US, is, like China dominated by a single majority population, the Vietnamese. Like China, Vietnam also has a large number of mountain-based minority groups, indeed some of the same groups found in southwestern China also live in the mountains of Vietnam.

Cultural themes and patterns
An all too common mistake Westerners make in considering the people of East Asia is to overemphasize the similarities shared among them. Japan, for example, is at least as different from China, culturally speaking, as Finland is from Greece. Yet, being aware of cultural diversity should not blind us to broadly shared themes. Australia and New Zealand, of course, have their own distinct cultural features, but these, resembling in many basic ways those of North America and Western Europe, will not be considered in the same detail as those of Asia proper.

One underlying theme applicable to China, Japan, Vietnam and the Koreas, is that of the Confucian family ideal. In any society, East or West, the family occupies a place of honor and is a powerful shaper of ordinary lives. But one feature of the Confucian-influenced family that makes East Asia different from the West is the emphasis on hierarchy that favors the old over the young, and males over females. This hierarchical pattern is also reflected in the wider society. No modern East Asian country has been led by anyone younger than 50 years of age, nor by a woman of any age. Large corporations tend to be similarly dominated at their highest levels by men of late middle age or older. Both of these biases – favoring age and favoring males – are not written in stone, and, particularly in an energized economy like that of China, it is quite within the realm of possibility that a young Bill Gates or even a 'Belinda' Gates may rise to prominence in the near future.

In East Asia, family loyalty is talked about more than it is in the West, and the talk is supported by real behavior in many cases. For example, adolescent children who are university-bound expect much more input from their parents on what universities and what majors to select than do their Western counterparts. And, a university graduate's first job often comes by virtue of parental activation of social connections or, what in China is called *guanxi*. In general there is a strong expectation that one's relatives will extend themselves on one's behalf.

Another feature distinguishing the East Asian family systems is the deeply rooted sense that religion itself is largely a matter of tending to family interests. It has long been thought in these societies that ancestors continue to oversee the behavior of their descendants and that they can actually have an effect on their descendants' lives. Though this notion has been strongly discouraged in communist-dominated societies, it continues to live on, particularly among those of modest education.

Other Confucian-based values that have an impact on the economies of East Asia are its emphasis on the value of education and its glorification of harmony and *ren* or 'human-heartedness'. Harmony and human-heartedness (sometimes translated as benevolence), help shape the way business is done in East Asia, as will be discussed further below.

This Confucian, family-focused religion is supplemented, and in some ways contradicted by other religious traditions, such as Buddhism, Daoism, and Shinto. Catholicism established a strong foothold in Vietnam during the French colonial era, and both Catholic and Protestant churches have made significant inroads among South Koreans. The People's Republic of China is also seeing an increase in the number of Christian converts, a somewhat surprising development given the long Chinese tradition of seeing Christian missionaries as instruments of imperialism.

These religions, and other lesser ones, serve to provide adherents with a sense of spiritual purpose that is not strictly confined to family interests and, in the case of Buddhism, to offer practical rituals for dealing with the deaths of family members. East Asia differs from the West in that most people do not divide themselves into mutually exclusive religious groupings but rather approach religious ideologies as a kind of spiritual smorgasbord. It is typical, for example, for East Asians to visit temples of various different religions throughout their lives – Buddhist, Taoist, ancestral – without feeling a need to commit entirely to a single religion.

In Australia and New Zealand, the significance of family is similar to that found in other Western countries. Though family is important, the contradictory value of individualism, particularly with reference to the need for young people to show they can 'stand on their own two feet', weakens the family attachment factor to some extent.

Political factors
The political systems of the Western Pacific are extraordinarily diverse. Australia has a system of government that combines the parliamentary features of the United Kingdom

with the federalism of the US and Canada. As in the other English-speaking democracies, governments tend to be broadly pro-business, seeing the promotion of commerce as the key to prosperity.

The democracies of Japan and South Korea are in some ways similar to that of Australia and other Western nations. Japan differs from Australia and the Western model in that political parties and factions, allied with specific economic interests and segments of the bureaucracy, tend to be unusually stable. The Liberal Democratic Party (LDP), for example, has enjoyed about 50 years of all but uninterrupted power. This is at least partly due to the family-based model of strong group loyalty and respect for seniors, both of which ensure that shifts in personnel are relatively rare. Thus, a tightly woven, loyalty-based pyramid of power in the LDP parallels similar structures in the bureaucracies it controls and the corporate networks it serves, and on whom it relies for funds (Hendry, 2003). The stability and generally business-friendly world that 'Japan, Inc.' has created has proven its worth given the decades of prosperity it has yielded.

The other side of this coin is the rigidity of a system that would clearly benefit from some shaking up. For example, banks that loaned money to companies run by 'old friends' or cronies during the boom years of the 1980s, found themselves since the collapse of the bubble in 1990, faced with staggering debts, many of which will never be paid off. Japan, between 1955 and 1990, illustrated the tremendous power of an economy organized around the principles of loyalty and seniority. Since 1990 the lesson is more along the lines of the limits to the benefits of such a 'personalized' economic system. Some companies are responding to this by backing away from the long-held guarantee of lifetime employment for all loyal workers.

South Korea, with an elected president and National Assembly, has followed Japan into the liberal democratic world, albeit somewhat belatedly. Where Japan had an essentially democratic system in place immediately following the end of the American Occupation in 1950, South Korea continued as a dictatorship until the late 1980s. Today, as one of East Asia's rising economic powers, it features some of the same qualities that characterize Japan. In fact, South Korea, which nurtures a longstanding sense of rivalry with its island neighbor (which in history often resulted in war), has, in its efforts to catch up with Japan, followed many of the latter's political, economic and technological leads.

North Korea has been ruled by father and son dictators, Kim Il-song and Kim Jong-il, since the end of World War II. It is so impoverished and inaccessible to the West that it is of little interest to those seeking economic opportunities. This may change in the near future if South Korea's efforts at developing a stronger relationship with the north bear fruit.

North Korea aside, China is politically the most dramatic and problematic country in East Asia. Following a long civil war between two dictatorial camps, the Communists under Mao Zedong, and the Nationalists under Chiang Kai-shek, the People's Republic was declared by the former in Beijing on 1 October 1949. The Nationalists fled to the island province of Taiwan where, under the authority of Chiang's Nationalist Party (KMT), they established the last refuge of the Republic of China. To this day the People's Republic (PRC) and the Republic of China (ROC) stand in opposition to each other across the Taiwan Straits.

Change is in the air, however, though given the delicacy of this adversarial relationship, any change is likely to raise hackles and increase tension depending on which side benefits from it. The Republic of China, commonly referred to as Taiwan, has gradually evolved a relatively democratic system of government, more or less in tandem with the similar process taking place simultaneously in South Korea. As a conservative dictatorship Taiwan had always supported commercial and technological ventures, and it has enjoyed a level of prosperity for decades unusual in this part of the world.

In the meantime the PRC was intensely hostile to capitalism and the inequality that characterizes developing economies, and consequently prohibited the development of China's resources for the better part of three decades. Since the death of the communist dictator Mao Zedong in 1976, China has opened itself to trade, investment, technological innovation and various forms of international cooperation. The result is the looming power that is China today, a nation virtually assured of becoming the world's largest economy within the next few decades.

A major problem facing China is its continuing lack of democracy and the openness and freedom of expression typical of more liberal societies. The current ruling party, which continues to call itself the Chinese Communist Party, is in fact, free of any Marxist ideology. It governs a population that remains docile only insofar as prosperity continues to grow. In fact, this has been described as the 'deal' that China's 'communist' rulers have made with the populace: in exchange for stability and increasing prosperity, the public will accept the rule of a self-serving and undemocratic government (Alon, 2003b).

Hong Kong remains a unique geopolitical entity, following its return to China in 1997. It had been a British colony since the nineteenth century, and under the colonial authorities it managed to develop a level of prosperity rivaling that of the much larger island of Taiwan. Its proximity to China and the advantages of travel for its citizens afforded by its connection to the British government gave Hong Kong the leverage required to establish itself as a remarkable economic engine. Though smaller than a typical US county, Hong Kong became a center of shipping, banking and manufacturing that no city in China proper could rival. Though the government of the PRC sees Shanghai as superseding Hong Kong as a center of finance, Hong Kong will continue to be a regional force to be reckoned with. Until 2047 it is, according to the treaty of 1997, supposed to be allowed to run its own internal affairs with minimal interference from Beijing.

Vietnam has followed a path that resembles the PRC just as South Korea followed a path blazed by Japan. In 1986, after years of communist-controlled economic stagnation, Vietnam threw off its doctrinaire Marxist program in favor of *doi-moi* or broad economic reform. The result has been a burst of economic activity and a general improvement in living standards that promises to continue upward in the future. As in China, however, Vietnam's government has not been as friendly to liberal democratic reform as it has been to economic reform, and clashes between the rising expectations of its citizens and the rigidity of the governing authorities can be expected in the future as well (Chang, 2001).

Patterns of social interaction
Westerner travelers have been instructed often enough that Middle Easterners, Africans, Latin Americans and various other ethnic and national groups do not appreciate 'the direct approach' in business dealings. Indeed this lesson has been offered so often that

it is time for us (Westerners) to recognize a basic truth: these various peoples with their preference for indirectness are not the peculiar ones; we are. For historical reasons that may include, among other things, the growth of science and technology and the stark brutality of competitive capitalism in the West, we have developed a 'bottom line' approach to business dealings that encourages us to cut to the chase in our negotiating style. But most of the world sees this approach as denigrating the essential value of the person.

There may be wisdom in the notion that a breakneck race for practical payoffs, when it devalues the essential worthiness of our humanity, is a race toward moral oblivion. But, whether a given American or Australian traveler to East Asia buys this idea or not, it is important that it be kept in mind.

A corollary of the emphasis on the dignity of the person is the Asian interest in maintaining 'face'. Face is not an entirely alien concept for Westerners. It is best thought of as a heightened focus on the sensitivity of reputation. Both Westerners and Asians dislike being disrespected or looked down on, so we both understand something about face. What makes China, Japan and other Confucian-influenced countries different from the West is the principle that makes sensitivity to the other person's dignity so acute that sometimes obvious truths are disregarded in favor of polite fictions. 'Telling it like it is' is not valued in Asia the way it is in many American contexts (Moore, 1988).

This sensitivity to the dignity and sensitivity of the other person is also reflected in a general reluctance to say no directly to a request. If, after making a request, one is told, 'That might not be convenient', one should read this as definite 'no' couched in face-saving terms. In a social context where people are disinclined to simply refuse requests, polite excuses abound. One making a request may be told, for example, that the request cannot be met because the person with authority has gone to Tokyo or is otherwise unavailable. It may be, in fact, that the person offering this excuse may have more influence on the decision to fulfill your request than he or she is ready to admit. Do not push the issue, however. A more productive strategy is to continue the friendly relationship with the individual or institution concerned, and if this relationship develops smoothly, requests and opportunities for access are likely to blossom.

A corollary of the Asian (and Latin American, and so on) idea that the human connection supersedes in importance the pragmatic one is the idea that the best business relations are built on trust. Americans doing business in Japan, for example, have often been surprised at the thinness of Japanese contracts. While the American may see a simple, one-page contract as an invitation to future lawsuits, the Japanese negotiator is likely to see the 20-page American contract as an expression of distrust. To get a sense of this, imagine the response of the woman who, upon being proposed to by her kneeling suitor is told, 'Before I show you the ring, would you mind signing this prenuptial agreement?'

A business deal is not a marriage proposal, but in East Asia, the best business deals are thought to be based (like good marriages) on well-established foundations of mutual understanding and trust. For this reason, patience is a powerful virtue in doing business in Asia. The long-term cultivation of good relations between investors and entrepreneurs is the norm, and it is advisable, when initiating business dealings to plan for a series of meetings, dinners and conversations that do not culminate in the signing of any agreements. In fact, they may not seem to culminate in anything, but if good feelings are being established and reinforced in such interactions, very important things are being accomplished indeed. In China particularly, business relationships are often developed over leisurely banquets in which dish after dish is brought to the table, and cup after cup of white liquor is downed. A bit of pleasant inebriation is itself sometimes seen as an indicator of friendliness and trust.

Along with the idea of simple practical matters being best embedded in complex human relationships, is the idea that getting anything important done requires a connection with someone in a key position. In China this is reflected in the widely used term '*guanxi*' which literally means, simply, 'connection'. Guanxi reflects the value placed on human relationships in that guanxi networks are those in which individuals respond readily to people with whom they have developed some kind of relationship, while sometimes disregarding the needs of those with whom no such relationship has been established.

The connections themselves can be natural, as through relatives or old college classmates, or they can be the result of intentional cultivation, as when gifts and services are offered to someone whose influence or help is sought (Young, 1994). In the latter cases the cultivation of guanxi can evolve into simple corruption, a problem that plagues China, Vietnam, and, to a lesser extent, Japan and South Korea more than it does North America or Western Europe. The emphasis on the importance of human relations can be a two-sided sword.

The governments of China and other Asian countries occasionally pursue anti-corruption campaigns. These are sometimes designed to clean up economic messes in which illegal favor trading has got seriously and disruptively out of hand. At other times they reflect an internal governmental power shift in which one faction or guanxi network has gained the upper hand against a rival faction, and is using anti-corruption as a convenient excuse to attack or eliminate the competition.

Cases like those of Enron and Halliburton will remind us that corruption is not strictly an Asian problem, but, given the great emphasis placed on the importance of responding to the needs of one's friends and kinsmen in Asia's 'human-centered' moral systems, corruption finds more fertile ground than it does in Western societies where the practical, cut-and-dried approach to business dealings is often preferred.

Business conduct and characteristics
As in many other parts of the world, professional attire is essential for formal business gatherings in Asian countries, which includes a shirt, tie, jacket and trousers for men, and business dress for women. For social gathering and entertaining, it is recommended that you dress conservatively; then let your Asian counterparts set the tone. At the first meeting, a few phrases of greetings in native tones will be greatly appreciated by local people. Although business meetings may be conducted in English, the key decision-makers of the hosting organization may not have sufficient foreign language skills or prefer to communicate in native language. So instead of relying on a translator provided by the host, it is highly desirable to have someone on your side with ample language and cultural knowledge of the hosting country. Before your departure or first thing upon arrival, have your business cards translated into the native language on the reverse side, and make sure you bring plenty of them. Your official title and decision-making authority should be clearly stated. When attending business meetings, punctuality is expected; and at the initial gathering, a business card should be given and received with both hands, in a manner that the person receiving it can read without turning the card.

A polite handshake and a slight bow are the greeting customs in Asian countries. Unlike the generally outgoing and straightforward Westerners, Chinese, Japanese, and Koreans pride themselves on holding their emotions inside. Unless where long-term relationship has already been developed, it is extremely rare to see people embrace in public. In East Asian countries, family name traditionally precedes the given name. However, some people will switch the order of their names when dealing with Westerners. To avoid confusion, it is always advisable to ask how to address someone. People with formal titles should be addressed accordingly along with family names. Although many Asian nations have experienced some degrees of democratic reforms, in corporate culture you will find that most Asians still have a high regard for rank and seniority, as such the highest-ranking members of the company will always be introduced first.

Dining and entertaining is a major part of business culture in Asian countries, especially in East Asia. Deals may be reached during the course of a meal. As most Asians place a great emphasis on formality, it is best to wait for the host to gesture where you should sit, and be prepared to make a short speech and exchange toasts. Although on average Asians consume less alcohol-based beverages annually, several rounds of liquor toasts are not uncommon at business banquets. Some even regard the heavy-drinking 'bottom-up' style as a way to fast-forward the personal and business relationships. However, one needs to be careful in retaining control of the situation, and it is acceptable to politely refuse alcoholic drinks citing health or other reasons. If you are not familiar with dinning etiquette, it is best to just 'go with the flow'. However, even during informal conversations, try to avoid sensitive issues such as politics, religion and human rights, and be aware that some questions of strictly personal nature from Westerners' perspective may be asked by your Asian counterparts.

In Asian business culture, gift exchange signifies the establishment of a relationship. Therefore gifts of reasonable value are considered a normal part of business interactions. Expensive gifts should be avoided. They not only create significant obligations, but may also be violations of anti-corruption legislation of the hosting country. The appropriate gifts should be representative of your company, or your city and country, and be sure to indicate it is only a small token of appreciation for their assistance during your visit.

Entering the global marketplace

Case study: China versus Japan: who will trump Asia?

> China is a sleeping giant. Let her lie and sleep for when she awakens she will tremble the world.
> (Napoleon Bonaparte)

Napoleon's visionary statement about China resounds nearly two centuries later. Today, the debate is less whether or when China will awaken, but how to come to grips with this new global reality. The sleeping dragon has awakened, and is jockeying for position in the global political economy.

Is China a threat or an opportunity to Japan? The answer is of course: yes! China is both a threat and an opportunity to Japan. The answer also depends in part on who is asking this question. The relationship between China and Japan is multidimensional,

Table 45.1   Basic statistics on Japanese and Chinese domestic and international economy

	Japan	China
Population (million)	127	1 284
Population growth	0.2	0.9
GDP (US$ billion, market exchange rate)	3 973	1 266
GDP (US$ billion, PPP)	3 398	6 033
GDP per head (market exchange rate)	31 270	986
GDP per head (PPP)	26 739	4 698
Labor costs per hour (US$)	20.49	0.80
Foreign exchange reserves ($million)	663 289	291 128
Real domestic demand growth	0.2	8.3
Inflation	−0.4	−0.4
Current account balance/GDP	2.6	2.3
FDI inflows/GDP	0.2	3.9
Major exports	Transport equipment, electrical machinery	Clothing, computers
Major imports	Machinery equipment, fuels	Electrical equipment, fuels

Note: Growth = 1998–2002 in %.

Source: Alon (2005).

requiring an examination that cuts across the economic, political and social spectrums. This case study examines the dynamics of Sino-Japanese economic and socio-political engagements in a global context, provides evidence from statistics and experts, and suggests policy responses to enhance cooperative bilateral relations.

Basic statistics on the Japanese and Chinese domestic and international economy are shown in Table 45.1. After decades of astonishing economic growth during the Cold War period, Japan has taken pride in being an economic miracle and becoming the second largest economy in the world. According to Professor Toshihiko Kinoshita of Waseda University, 'Japan's glorious decades from the 1960 to the 1980s, have been followed by a lost decade from the 1990s to 2002 during which time China rose to economic prominence'. Still, according to the gross domestic product (GDP) statistics measured in current market exchange rates, Japan's economy is more than triple the size of that of China. 'Japan remains a 1st ranked Sumo, a real Yokozuna,' says Mr Kevin Newman, Senior Manager with Nathan Associates Inc., who has previously worked with the Japanese Ministry of Home Affairs, the World Bank, the United Nations (UN) and other international development agencies. He adds that although battered by 15 years of deflation and economic stagnation, Japan is recovering. The country has changed drastically, for the better, and an economic map of its per capita wealth, global investment, and value-added goods could demonstrate its present and future strengths as well as its long-term competitive advantage. Indeed, as can be seen from Table 45.1, Japan trumps China in its per capita income using market exchange rates by a factor of 32 and using purchasing power by a much smaller yet substantial factor of 5.7. And despite China's tenfold larger population, Japan's total foreign reserves are more than double those of China.

Of course this economic story is incomplete. Chinese economic prowess looms large and is growing. This strength is manifested in economic and political terms in the global arena. While Japan is the second largest economy based on GDP, China's economic size in terms of GDP measured by purchasing power parity (PPP) is much larger than that of Japan and second only to the United States of America. In Japan, a given dollar can buy 85 percent of the same goods it can buy in the United States. In contrast, a given dollar in China can buy about 4.77 times more things than in the United States. When measuring on a purchasing power parity basis, Japan is about 5.57 times more expensive and, thus, an adjustment to its GDP is needed for a meaningful comparison.

China's population is about 10 times larger than that of Japan. The top 10 percent of the population in China earns approximately US$14 519 per person in PPP terms, which is on par with the incomes of the individuals in the industrialized countries. Thus, the top 10 percent of China make up a target market that is equivalent in size and purchasing power to a developed market.

China has several other economic advantages over Japan: a substantially higher growth rate in real domestic demand, a much lower cost of labor, and foreign investment inflows that rival no other in the world, including the United States of America. For businesses, the size of the market coupled with its robust growth rate means higher per capita disposable income and larger markets, while an inexpensive labor force and investment inflows create a fertile environment for production.

According to Professor Kinoshita, 'Japan can co-prosper with China since the two countries have different cost structures and complementary industries and products'. Basing his findings on research by C.H. Kwan, a Senior Fellow of the Research Institute of Economy, Trade and Industry, Kinoshita noted that Japan has the most complementary market to China in Asia (Indonesia's was most competitive to China). However, the ratio of Japanese goods competing with Chinese goods exported to the United States has grown from 3 percent in 1990 to 21 percent in 2002.

The economic interdependence between Japan and China cannot be ignored. Accounting for 14.9 percent of China's total exports, Japan is the third largest market for Chinese goods and services, following the US and Hong Kong, China's own administrative region. Conversely, China buys more from Japan than any other country, about 18.1 percent of its total imports. From the Japanese perspective, China is Japan's second largest export customer and second largest import supplier after the US, with 9.6 percent and 13.0 percent of exports and imports respectively. According to Shane Frecklington, Manager of the American Chamber of Commerce in Shanghai, Japan is the second largest investor in China with 8 percent of total investment. 'This investment has been critical to the supply chain of Japanese export industries, which have assembly and construction factories in China,' claims Renfield Kuroda, Vice President of Deutsche Bank. For China, foreign direct investments in general contribute 20 percent of the GDP, 50 percent of total exports, 10 percent of the urban workforce, and 16 percent of taxes collected. Such symbiotic relationship conveys a great deal regarding the opportunities of this long-term partnership.

China and Japan share an economic space. If one country falters, it will affect the other adversely. If one prospers, the other can piggyback. Both countries face similar problems for which they can seek joint solutions: both countries are in the process of deregulating and liberalizing sectors of their respective economies, and both need to overhaul their banking systems. In other ways, too, the two economies have complementary needs. While the Japanese economy is sluggish, the Chinese economy is overheating; while the Japanese are experiencing asset price deflation, the Chinese are experiencing asset price inflation. The two countries can benefit greatly from multi-layered cooperation to synergistically solve each other's economic problems and benefit from their respective strengths and know-how.

According to Allen Kupetz, President of Kpartnerz and a former US State Department economic official in Korea, 'the current interdependence of Japan and China will end within a decade. Chinese firms, now dependent on Japanese companies for product design and manufacturing expertise, will soon design more of their own products and move up the food chain in terms of their ability to manufacture higher-end components'. He adds that

> Japan to remain competitive must continue to outsource manufacturing to China to lower cost and expand sales within China, exactly as most US firms are doing today. But the much larger US consumer spending power and growing trade deficit will give the US more leverage over China in trying to lessen the effects of the asymmetrical bilateral relationship. The Japanese will not be able to do this to the same extent because the Chinese would be much more willing to lose market share within Japan.

This is clearly a threat.

Not everyone is convinced that China will remain the economic superpower everybody takes for granted. According to Mr Newman,

> China is simply an amalgamation of provinces, hinterlands, and different ethnic groups that now must be forged to achieve national economic integration. Dissent and regional rivalries will increasingly become rife, if not causing major disruptions. China cannot pollute unabated and discriminate with a heavy-hand forever.

He continues that China's history is marked by 'arrogance, belligerence and then dramatic downfalls', and, 'without a solid local governmental administrative and wealth distribution policy'. An unstable China is very worrisome. Mr Newman is not alone in his view. A recent controversial (banned in China) book by Gordon G. Chang (2001), *The Coming Collapse of China*, echoes some of the same arguments. Salient among Chang's arguments are that people are discontent, the state-owned enterprises are dying, information is not controllable, industrial policies reward the inept, Chinese banks are failing, the World Trade Organization (WTO) accession will trigger collapse, and ideology and politics will restrain progress.

While the prospects for economic relations are promising, at least in the short term, and the two countries are experiencing deepening economic connection, these are stifled by increasing potential for political conflicts. For example, Japan's actions during WWII, and in particular the Nanjing Massacre (1937–38) have never been adequately addressed by the Japanese leadership. Frequent visits by the political elite of Japan to the Yasukuni shrine understandably angers the Chinese, who see it as proof that Japan refuses to renounce its militarist past. Even worse, according to Mr Renfield Kuroda, Vice President of Deutsche Bank, 'when the president of Fuji Xerox made a comment that the Prime Minister's visits to Yasukuni were bad for business, right-wingers threw a Molotov cocktail at his house and drove their trucks around his neighborhood blaring right-wing songs at 200 decibels'. A visit to the Yasukuni shrine war museum reveals a much different, if not conflicting, interpretation of Japanese war history. The Chinese have not forgotten or forgiven the harsh Japanese occupation of China and its experimentation with chemical and biological weapons on Chinese soil and people. The bitter past and the present indignation have precluded Japan from winning infrastructure development bids such as the high-speed rails connecting Beijing and Shanghai and Olympics-related infrastructure development – an area of expertise for which Japan is globally renowned.

China, however, can carry some of the blame as well. The ominous political tension between China and Taiwan, the US, and its neighbors (including Australia) may force Japan to take sides and to jeopardize the economic relations thus far built. China's figures on defense spending are believed to be understated, fast rising, and comparable to Japan's. But Japan can only use its military for collective self-defense. Recent US overtures to Japan by the Bush administration could be aimed at turning Japan into a military ally, similar to Britain, by allowing Japan to revise its constitution for a more activist role. The Chinese in the meantime are posturing in the South China Sea, making occasional naval incursions into Japan's waters, and building oil-drilling platforms dangerously close to Japanese territory. In turn, Japanese right-wing politicians lash out at the Chinese; and the Chinese allow (perhaps even encourage) popular anger towards the Japanese. This type of contentious political environment is certainly a threat to bilateral relationships.

To say that China violates intellectual property rights, including those of Japan, is axiomatic. The Chinese have benefited by copying the Japanese economic development model, its industries, and its products. 'China and the other developing nations do not understand the intellectual property right issues. They will continue copying. They do not see anything wrong in doing so,' said Mr K. Sam Tabucci, Japanese representative to Florida and Special Advisor to the Urban Land Institute. By some estimates, piracy accounts for 92 percent of all software used on the mainland, and China accounts for two-thirds of counterfeit goods worldwide. A legal environment that does not conform to international intellectual property protection standards can threaten investment relations and encourage unjust expropriation of Japanese knowledge-based resources. As a member of the WTO, Japan can enforce intellectual property rights through international courts, though the legal maneuvering will not forestall active entrepreneurial property-rights' violations in China for the foreseeable future.

Given the opportunities and threats that China poses, how should Japan respond? According to K. Sam Tabuchi, Japan should copy the US economic model, moving away from its traditional manufacturing focus to advanced and service industries. According to Mr Tabuchi, the leadership in Japan is old fashioned, focusing on past glory and missing the point that the economist Schumpeter championed long ago – creative destruction must happen for an economy to cope with changing global conditions. This can help solve some of the economic threats of China. According to Kim Beng Phar, from the Asian Center for Media Studies, at the Star, Kuala Lumpur, Malaysia: on the political level 'talks about China and Japan tend to focus single-mindedly on the highest tier of governmental relations'. What may be more useful in the future is the creation of a multi-layered engagement that promotes dialogue across and between the following nine levels:

1. Government-to-government relations
2. Think tanks to think tanks
3. Universities to universities
4. Cultural organizations to cultural organizations
5. Company to company
6. Tourism agencies to tourism agencies
7. Non-governmental organizations to non-governmental organizations
8. Religious organizations to religious organizations
9. Media organizations to media organizations.

While no solution can be a panacea for the economic and socio-political threats that China imposes, the Japanese people, government, and businesses must face the reality and enigma that is China. Engaging China productively requires internal assessment, willingness to change, and behaviors that will encourage China to cooperate using relationships, diplomacy, patience, and restraint. A sincere apology for the Nanjing Massacre is an example of such needed diplomacy. China's premier Wen recently quoted an old Chinese saying in a meeting in Laos: 'Let him who tied a bell on the tiger take it off.' Each country must do its part to take the bell off, release the tensions, and make sure no new bells get hung on the tiger.

Currencies and exchange rates

Case study: how cultural factors led to risky market conditions and the 1997 Asian economic crisis
While a large body of literature lays the blame for the 1997 Asian economic crisis on external factors, such as Japan's recession, speculative foreign investors, and non-stringent international bank credit, a body of literature examining the cultural factors is emerging. The purpose of this case is to examine the internal antecedents to the Asian crisis by focusing on region-specific cultural conditions leading to the crisis. Important cultural factors of collectivism, authoritarianism, and power-distance that led to precarious and risky financial practices are explored.

In July 1997 the Asian economic crisis burst to life when Thailand could not maintain its currency exchange rate. The crisis spread throughout Asia with a profound impact on local and global economies (Roubini, 1999). Previously an area of unprecedented and sustained growth, the crisis hit South Korea, Thailand, Indonesia, Malaysia, and the Philippines hardest (hereafter referred to as 'crisis Asia'). Within several months, the flight of foreign investment, declining currency values, crashing stock markets, large layoffs, contracting GDPs, bank closures and consolidations, and rising prices of staples afflicted the region severely. Furthermore, the area experienced an overall rise in lending rates, inflation, debt repayment problems, and cutbacks on mega projects.

Cultural factors   Joel Kotkin, senior fellow at the Institute for Public Policy at Pepperdine University, explained that culture forms a basis for most of what happens in economic progress and that a 'cultural virus' shapes most of what societies do, how they do it in politics, economics, and other areas (Lohr, 1998). This supports an emergent body of literature pointing towards cultural factors that produced antecedent conditions that allowed the economic crisis to happen. Collectivism, authoritarianism, power-distance (status and hierarchal considerations) were cultural considerations of the morally hazardous antecedent conditions that led to the Asian economic crisis.

Asian values may have brought Asian countries to the major leagues of the global economy, but they did not adopt Western norms in transparency and democracy issues that could have helped them avoid and prevent the pitfalls (Gardels, 1998). Singapore Senior Minister Lee Kuan Yew and others have said the Asian governments and business community had taken on a type of 'hubris' and lack of humility uncharacteristic of Asians (Hitchcock, 1998).

Media in those nations (many of them government controlled) often touted the Asian model – as good as Western business acumen but with Asian values that encouraged long-term planning, stability, and a togetherness Westerners should envy. Senior Minister Lee has said that 'these different values have made for fast growth' (*Time International*, 1998: 24), yet the question is still how could stewards of the Asian tigers' growth become so blind to the growing crisis and so unable to stem the turning tide? The answers may lie in three crucial areas of intercultural communication: collectivism, authoritarianism, and power-distance (status and hierarchal considerations).

Collectivism   Cultures differ in their members' orientation towards the group and the individual. A 1994 Center for Strategic and International Studies survey of 100 respected observers of Southeast Asia revealed that Asians rated orderly society, group harmony, and respect for authority as highest priorities. These were the lowest rated priorities among Americans who rated freedom of expression and resolving conflict through open debate as highest. While the Asian ideals of hard work, respect for learning, collectivism, and lack of individualism brought them unparalleled growth, many analysts now believe that these cultural factors led to the abuses of collusion, lack of transparency, poor banking practices, and corruption that precipitated large weaknesses in many of these countries' economies and continue to forestall recovery (Hitchcock, 1998). Lohr (1998) proposed that this collective ideology, specifically a high work ethic, a respect for family, and a deference to government authority was characteristic of Asian values and called it a type of Protestant work ethic without the Western reverence for individualism.

The cultural phenomenon of a collective, familistic and guanxi (personal connections) form of capitalism allowed government and business collusion, corruption and competition-thwarting to exist (Gardels, 1998). The desire for group harmony among economic agents and members of a society increased the 'moral hazard' – banks and conglomerates who feel little need to act fiscally responsible if they believe that a government will bail out the well connected. Zaman (1998) asserts that even the International Monetary Fund (IMF) failed to warn the world financial markets about Asia's impending collapse to 'assure continued cooperation and working relations with the governments concerned!' (p. 38).

An editorial in *The Economist* (1998) stated that:

> this problem of moral hazard is all too familiar to central bankers. To promote safe lending in the long term, some risk must be left with depositors, and far more (it is to be hoped) with owners, but not so much to make them vulnerable to short-term instability. A trade off must be

struck, involving guarantees of one kind or another on one side and regulation to curb excessive risk taking. (p. 13)

The tendency to ignore regulation and bankruptcy laws as a leading cause of the economic crisis was reified in collectivism.

Walker (1998) pointed out that the modern business practice of debt protection, liquidation, and bankruptcy so commonly utilized in the West were largely unused in Asia because Asians tend to favor reconstruction and compromise in line with Confucian tradition which can stave off insolvency for only so long. According to Hitchcock (1998), to confront an insolvency issue head on is a Western concept, yet the Asian collectivist practice of indirectness and avoiding public embarrassments by not airing dirty laundry in public led to the moral hazard of bailouts that contributed to the lack of market correction that precipitated the crash.

Combined with the cultural practice of 'special' relationships among favored clients for awarding contracts and a lack of oversight (Hitchcock, 1998), collectivism and power-distance (hierarchal considerations and status) precluded the public from asking for transparency even when faced with overwhelming evidence of mismanagement, corruption, and years of insolvency. Perhaps liberalization in transparency practices would have led to stabilization since market correction would have occurred sooner, avoiding such a large boom and bust cycle. This is a concept that former Japanese Prime Minister Kiichi Miyazawa has been recommending for his country saying that 'Transparency is a must . . . (this) means sometimes a brutal confrontation, which is not really part of our culture' (Hitchcock, 1998: 1), a view echoed by former dissident and current South Korean President Kim Dae Jung. Corruption that comes from the collectivist desire for group harmony affects a country's economy 'by injecting private preferences into public dealings. It cheats members of one group – taxpayers, shareholders or Sunday supplement readers – and distributes the spoils to a privileged group' (*The Economist*, 1999: 19). Furthermore, developing economies from Indonesia to Russia have been severely hurt by 'a corrupt form of capitalism which diverted resources from economically well founded enterprises to those that were merely well-connected' (ibid. 22).

In order to ensure collective welfare and harmony, East Asian nations developed their economies through (1) modernization of agriculture, (2) promotion of labor-based technologies, (3) increases in literacy, education, science, and technology, (4) industrial policy offering protection to infant industries and, (5) liberalization of trade and capital flows (Zaman, 1998). These investments, however, were often in industries in which these Asian countries had no comparative advantage (for example, Indonesia's aircraft manufacturing) and necessitated large government support to compete globally.

It later became clear that many of these policies were implemented to enrich select families, companies, and influential figures, a prominent feature of authoritarian governments and the Asian value of 'guanxi' (personal connections). The emphasis on export promotion came at the expense of other industries, leading to sub-optimal allocation of resources. Zaman (1998) pointed out that Asian economic growth was led by rapid exports expansion financed by foreign direct and portfolio investment growth. This required high levels of borrowing and industrial investment in such export-oriented industries as auto, shipbuilding, steel, and consumer electronics. Industries tailored to accommodate domestic consumption were given secondary emphasis, thus helping sensitize Asian economies to external economic shocks.

Authoritarianism   To say that Asian culture philosophy is heavily devoted to strong authority (government, social, familial, or societal), paternalism, collectivism, and the desire for group harmony would be an understatement. On the surface, the belief in an elite ruling power provides for a measure of certainty and security. On the other hand, authoritarians that promote harmony often produce lax oversight which stems from the concept of keeping group harmony which comes from a strong belief in authoritarianism – a vicious cycle that came back to haunt crisis Asia economies. The respect for an 'elite' ruler ensured that even outrageous allegations against entrenched interests went unheeded.

In reality, Sicherman (1998) suggested that the often-touted 'Asian model' was an exaggeration of a benevolent autocracy characterized by a modern 'free' economy (with much less pain and risk than classic capitalism's 'creative destruction'). He explained that these types of governments are not strong enough to compel sacrifice for necessary market corrections nor popular enough to inspire sacrifice voluntarily. In other words, governments were not strong enough to take more out of a paycheck to put into an Employee's Provident Retirement Fund (which the government could then use for more investments) nor ask the citizenry to do so on their own.

This untenable situation, combined with a lack of restraint and preference for authoritarians, led to the reckless and irresponsible pursuit of profits and piled risks onto an already fragile financial structure (Zhou, 1998). One major factor which increased the external vulnerability of crisis Asia was the obvious willingness to borrow heavily and on risky terms, leading to high foreign denominated short-term debt which further exaggerated their external vulnerability – another vicious cycle that came back to haunt crisis Asian economies.

Alan Greenspan (1998) claimed that a high degree of debt to equity leverage was a symptom of excessive risk-taking and was aggravated by the fact that these assets were less liquid than the liabilities. He reported that while the average growth in real GDP between 1986 and 1996 of crisis Asia was 7.32 percent, the rate of credit growth was nearly 17 percent. Excessive borrowing was also evident in the non-financial sectors.

Early indicators of the financial crisis were the payment delays of leading industrial conglomerates in South Korea (Hanbo Steel in January 1997 and Sammi Steel in March 1997) and Thailand (Somprasong in March 1997). These warnings were dismissed by Michael Camdessus, Managing Director of the IMF (Hitchcock, 1998). External short-term debt ranged from just over 13 percent in the Philippines to nearly 33 percent in Thailand, with much of that debt in variable-rates and hard currency.

As debt began to accumulate, the financial bubble grew. Krugman (1998) suggested that financial intermediaries, whose liabilities were seen as having implicit government guarantees, drove up prices of risky projects making their financial integrity seem more stable than it really was. Each newly funded project became another step in a giant Ponzi (pyramid selling) scheme (Alon and Kellerman, 1999).

To a large degree, this financial bubble was hidden from the eyes of investors and regulators. The authoritarian governments in Asia had no interest in revealing the structural weaknesses in their economy. At the outset of the crisis, the 'official' South Korean bad loan rate was 6.1 percent of total loans outstanding, while Merrill Lynch figured that the rate was more like 15 percent, compared to the US rate of 1–2 percent (*The Economist*, 1997). *The Economist* also reported that at nine of the largest institutions, bad loans ranged from 94 percent to 376 percent of banks' capital and on 8 November 1997, the central bank had to pump 5 trillion won (US$1 billion) into the financial system to keep it afloat. Authoritarian societies, at least on the surface, appear stable because the authoritarians rarely have challenges to their perception of events. Prior to the economic crisis, dire predictions and warnings of financial turmoil often brought accusations of promoting disharmony and seditious attempts at destabilization. Malaysian Prime Minister Mahatir bin Mohammed's jailing of Deputy Prime Minister and Finance Minister Anwar Ibrahim in 1998 for sedition and sexual perversion is a prime example. When charges of nepotism and cronyism against Dr Mahatir began to surface at the ruling party's general assembly, he told delegates 'those who raise issues that may destabilize the party must be accountable for their actions' (*The New Straits Times*, 1998: 1). Despite denials of a gag order, the threat quelled dissent overnight.

Authoritarianism often presents a double-edged sword. When economies start to fail, denial and efforts to find scapegoats become a dominant public theme, whether or not anyone outside those countries believes even the most outrageous claims. First, the Thais 'blamed Americans upset with Thai policy toward Cambodia; the Koreans blamed Westerners who feared they could not compete with Koreans; the Malaysian Prime Minister blamed Jews' (Lewis, 1998: 36). Dr Mahatir blamed such 'rogue speculators' as George Soros saying 'All these countries have spent 40 years trying to build up their economies and a moron like Soros comes along' (Roubini, 1999). In reply, Soros called Mahatir a menace to his own country. Many Asian governments accused Western nations of trying to buy Asian assets at 'bargain' rates.

Serious reform efforts rarely succeed in authoritarian administrations. Periodic demagoguery associated with authoritarianism had severe repercussions as in Indonesia's periodic burning, looting, and killing members of the Chinese ethnic community whose 4 percent of the population allegedly controls half the economy.

Paternalistic, familial, and authoritarian governments tend to control the information about conditions leading up to, and after a crisis and this hurts efforts at correction. Cultures who prize authoritarianism in a belief that the leaders will provide for the people (in return for 'guanxi') may have to realize that as Gardels (1998) advocated, adopting Western norms of democracy in the form of individual responsibility, transparency, and accountability may have to be part of economic reform.

At first, the IMF insisted on Suharto's removal before approving Indonesia's initial US$43 billion loan because they knew that most of it would end up in the hands of government cronies – Suharto as the 'bagman' in a continuing siphoning off of Indonesia's resources. In reality, much of the progress in crisis Asia in the past decade, especially in South Korea and Thailand, was due simply to ongoing bailouts of conglomerates, especially after the Japanese real estate market collapse in the early 1990s.

Companies continued to speculate wildly, building monuments that had little to do with infrastructure and solid economic development. Would they have been so keen if they thought that their government would not bail them out? It took the installation of South Korea opposition leader Kim Dae Jung and revelations of massive insolvency for demoralized South Koreans to finally insist upon ending the chaebol bailouts – an unheard of cultural turnaround.

Is authoritarianism good or bad for a developing economy? According to Francis Fukuyama (1998), Professor of Public Policy at George Mason University

> In the absence of adequate feedback mechanisms and institutional controls on state power, it ends up being a matter of luck whether authoritarian institutions are turned toward the single-minded pursuit of investment and growth or become vehicles for padding the bank accounts of the politicians in charge. (p. 24)

Power-distance A third factor in cultural variability is what Dutch researcher Geert Hofstede calls the power-distance – the extent to which members of a culture adhere to unequal distributions of power, and the amount of respect accorded people's positions and status in a hierarchy. The United States, a low power-distance country, has laws designed to protect whistleblowers. On the other hand, high power-distance Asians who cause trouble for their superiors may find themselves circumvented or out of a job.

Power-distance is an extension of the direct versus indirect communication styles favored by North Americans and Asians, respectively (Gudykunst and Ting-Toomey, 1988), and accounted for a significant amount of lack of transparency throughout the years leading up to the economic crisis. Power-distance is also the degree to which society accepts inequality and considers social and business distance normal.

Asian countries are far more power-distant than Western nations and their political and economic institutions embody this value. High power-distance cultures are more hierarchal with strong dependence on authority. Therefore, these societies tend to form authoritarian governments characterized by long periods of stability followed by short and abrupt periods of upheavals (Hofstede, 1991). The 1997 crisis represents just such an upheaval after a long period of growth and stability in crisis Asia.

When state banks ran out of money to lend, government ministers, state bank higher-ups, well-connected business executives, and top loan officers encouraged risky short-term external borrowing – the very damaging practice that started the currency collapses. Who was going to argue with the Prime Minister's office, the Minister of Trade, the State Bank, or someone with close connections to them? Lohr (1998) pointed out that this form of 'crony capitalism' of patronage for well-connected business executives is now under great scrutiny and disrepute, not unlike the exploitative system of the American robber-barons in the late 1800s who finally received their punishment through divestiture. When faced with questions involving transparency on insolvency issues, the aforementioned Asian tendency of (1) respect for people in powerful positions, (2) to not confront directly and (3) to go carefully around to local press outlets, friends and associates of the target did not lend themselves to the full and accurate disclosure necessary to correct perilous situations. This lack of confrontation led to ten years of face-value government assurances until 2 July 1997 when the Central Bank of Thailand admitted publicly they were insolvent due to unpaid loans.

How bad was the fallout from power-distance related risky borrowing? In late July, word leaked out from *The Economist* that taxpayers' burden for insolvent banks was 800 million baht, one-sixth of the Thai GDP. In addition, both the exchange crisis, and later the debt crisis, were worsened by a reversal of capital flows from private sources.

Debt that was denominated in foreign currency, in particular, could not be paid off easily because of the declining purchasing powers of local currencies. This triggered a collapse in asset prices in the banking sector with non-performing loans in crisis Asia ranging from 20 percent in the Philippines to 75 percent in Indonesia, with an average of around 42 percent. Nearly all banks in Korea, Thailand, and Indonesia were insolvent by current international standards (Sweet, 1999).

Jardine Fleming, a Japanese investment company, estimated the Southeast Asian banks were carrying US$73 billion worth of bad loans, representing a staggering 13 percent of Southeast Asian GDP (compared with the 2–3 percent of the US GDP to solve the Savings and Loan crisis and 10–12 percent to solve Mexico's 1994 currency crisis). The Central Bank of New York estimated that the costs of the recent banking crisis of Korea, Thailand, Indonesia were 30 to 35 percent of their GDPs, twice as high as that of the Mexican crisis, and 10 times as high as that of the US Savings and Loan banking crisis of 1984 to 1989 (Sweet, 1999).

This cultural value of non-confrontation of elite people in powerful positions promoted some astounding latitude in fiscal practices. *The Economist* (1997) reported that Thailand's Central Bank allowed banks to claim that a secured loan was performing even if no interest had been paid for a year and that they were spending nearly 100 million baht (US$2.6 million) a month to stave off insolvency. The same lack of confrontation occurred in South Korea with Hanbo, a steel group, and KIA Motors, both of whom had been insolvent for a decade. By the middle of 1997, correction was impossible and the effect rippled instantly and throughout the region.

Culturally, there could not have been any public or private challenge. Putting one's faith in elites through power-distance values is risky business as seen in the robber baron era of America in the late 1800s or in the Savings and Loans scandals of the 1980s. In Asia, all of its industrial culture 'had been built on a faith in elites. Elites rather than markets had determined who got capital, and therefore who was allowed to succeed in business' (Lewis, 1998: 36). Thais and especially South Koreans went through an unprecedented re-examination of cultural values and faith in elite leaders culminating in National Humiliation Day, 3 December 1997 – the day the IMF gave the terms of their US$57 billion loan to Seoul.

Conclusion   Government officials and businesspeople throughout Asia have continually stated that Asian values brought them incredible economic progress over the years. Yet another set of values (absolute trust in leaders, tolerance of corruption, lack of confrontation) encouraged risky antecedent conditions that led to the economic crisis. Simultaneously, higher-ups spent considerable time avoiding responsibility which at first played well with the public.

On the cultural side, the contention of this chapter that collectivism, authoritarianism, and power-distance brought a false sense of security is well supported. It is too hard to ignore the connection between such corruption as continuing government support for insolvent industries (a type of 'Bailouts for Harmony') and the lack of effort at market correction. Too much respect for hierarchy led to a critical lack of transparency just when Asia needed it most.

According to Meuhring (1998) some of the solutions to Asian countries' economic woes include such economic practices as new codes of conduct governing fiscal transparency from G-7 and IMF. Some are cultural. The IMF has proposed a new 'tiered response' system including 'yellow card' warning system, perhaps an Asian face-saving way to motivate fiscal responsibility and, as in soccer, one last chance to correct destructive behavior.

The causes of the Asian economic crisis are economic (too much growth too fast, too much unsecured credit, too many unworthy ventures and leaders) and cultural (too much confidence in the leaders' grand visions, too little investigation of people and situations who needed scrutiny, and too much insistence on group harmony by the leaders). They provide lessons that Asian leaders will have to learn whether it takes IMF restrictions, full-scale reform movement, revolution, or merely making laws and economic practices by which they will have to stand resolutely.

By examining the suggested cultural factors investors can properly assess financial risks and will take measures to hedge and diversify. Asian governments should increase the level of individual responsibility, become more transparent, and democratize their political institutions to reduce the risk of financial collapse. These governments can ease the pain by helping re-employ resources in more productive industries in which they have a comparative advantage.

This study is just the start of what should be a lengthy examination into how Asian cultural values will change to overcome current problems and stabilize future economic conditions. Will they have to adopt 'Anglo-Saxon' norms as Gardels (1998) suggested or modify the 'familistic and guanxi' form of capitalism with which Asian culture is most comfortable?

While there is no lack of educated leaders and population who should be insisting on change, Zhou (1998) reiterated that Asian values and mores are products of thousands of years, and cannot be expected to change quickly and drastically. Walter Russel Mead (1998), senior fellow at the Council on Foreign Relations, said that in the old days, a handshake, customs, and family relationships were strong enough to build a modern social safety net, however, 'when modern cities spring up, you need courts of law, unions, and government oversight' (p. 38).

This cataclysm has already spurred on deep philosophical introspection that will encourage Asian countries to forge economies that are less prone to a wild roller-coaster ride so that they enjoy a lengthy boom without this spectacular and devastating bust. Though Zhou states that Asian values change slowly, in a force-field analysis something has to give – either the forces of change, the forces of resistance, or the standards by which struggle is measured.

In July 1999, one year after the lowest point of the crisis, the South Korean government-run banks forced the managers to sign an agreement to dismantle the Daewoo Group, the second largest chaebol in Korea – the first time a chaebol has been broken up and largely to pay for its estimated $49 billion debt (*Business Week*, 1999). *Business Week* regards this restructuring and asset sell off, notably in South Korea, as positive signs of a recovery and 'that Asia appears to be headed out of its economic slump' (p. 24).

Asians have been holding their breath over Japan and China because as they go, often so goes much of Asia. The principal cultural value seems to be worry; for as writer George Washington Lyon once wrote, worry is the interest paid by those who borrow trouble.

Case study: Japanese corporate management in transition: will it converge with the US?
Despite the economic slowdown of Japan in recent years, Japan is still the second largest economy in the world, based on its gross domestic product. Kono and Clegg (2001)

argue that the economic problems of Japan are based on its financial and bureaucratic systems and not on its managerial systems. They also argue that the Western business world can still learn much from Japanese management practices. Management systems in Japan have exhibited unparalleled dynamism throughout history and have been studied around the world.

Japan's economic influence over the past decades has led to substantial interest in Japanese management practices. Further, many ask 'will the Japanese management system become more like the one in the United States or will it remain a hybridized system of management embodying a mix of Eastern and Western cultural elements?' For example, some authors have contended that Japanese and Western approaches to corporate governance are converging (for instance, Simeon, 2001), while others have contended that, despite recent changes in Japanese management style, important differences continue to exist (for instance, Kono and Clegg, 2001).

In their book, *Trends in Japanese Management: Continuing Strengths, Current Problems, and Changing Priorities*, Kono and Clegg (2001) suggested that in the last decade significant changes have taken place in the Japanese system of management. Among them are: the empowerment of shareholders, the emphasis on value-added economic activities, the development of career paths and skill enhancement in young managers, the introduction of merit pay, the decentralization of decision-making, and the formation of alliances outside the boundaries of the traditional *keiretsu*. This suggests that Japanese management approaches are changing.

Masui and Kakabadse (2002) reported on the changes in the decision-making process that need to occur in Japanese companies. According to these writers, Japanese organizations need to overhaul their management systems including shareholders' meetings, introduce an officer system to reduce the number of board members, abandon the seniority system and identify young professionals at an early stage, and accept individual responsibility in decision-making. This suggests a need for change, rather than ongoing change. (One wonders also whether the authors are suggesting implanting a Western concept of management onto the Japanese corporate culture.)

In contrast to these views, there is evidence to suggest that management practices are unlikely to change, or will change only slowly:

● Japanese firms operate in a special cultural context, one that is based on complex rules, interpersonal relationships, a unique history, a homogeneous population, distinctive political, educational, and institutional systems, and a hierarchical structured culture (Nishiyama, 1999). To explain the unique nature of Japanese institutions, corporate networks, and management, Bhappu (2000) used an anthropological approach. Her research suggests that the Japanese management systems can be traced to the evolution of the Japanese family, and that social capital is instrumental in the development of political and business environments and the persistence of the Japanese management system

● Decision-making processes are quite different in Japanese organizations when compared to Western firms. Ala and Cordeiro (1999) wrote about the Japanese philosophy of *ringiseido*. According to this philosophy, participative decision-making is preferred utilizing opinions from multiple levels of management. The *ringi* decision-making process stimulates group harmony, conformity and togetherness, provides a feeling of participation and moral suasion for enforcing group compliance, and creates a sense of hierarchy and loyalty to the group. In contrast to Western management, where one person in control exerts strong influence over the direction of the company, the Japanese management system places limited responsibility on individual decision makers.

- Research and development (R&D) is another area in which Japanese companies differ from their Western counterparts. Using citation analysis in a cross-national study of a high-technology industry (flat-panel display), Spencer (2001) found that Japanese university research is less influential than Japanese corporate research as compared to the US, where university and corporate research showed a marginal difference. The Japanese seemed to be focused more on applied rather than basic research when compared with the United States. Matsushita, for example, has shifted toward applied research over the years. In 1984, 54 percent of its R&D was basic research, compared with 25 percent in 1995. Interestingly, much of the research in Matsushita has become contract based (Nathan, 1999).
- The applied orientation pervades the human resource development aspect as well. In an interview with Sony's Yoshihide Nakamura, Beamish (1999) reported that while Sony provides opportunities to their employees to pursue graduate education, the company prefers on-the-job training and development as a general guiding principle. Japanese management systems remain unique in that they focus on longer-term strategies, they emphasize human resource investment, and they balance shareholders' value with that of other stakeholders of the organization, such as employees, banks, suppliers, and customers (Kono and Clegg, 2001).

While the Japanese management system may adopt, and adapt, certain practices from the United States, and the United States may do the same with Japanese practices, it seems unlikely that management practices will converge. The evidence suggests that Japanese culture has been slow to change and that it has a pervasive and persistent impact on the political and economic institutions of Japan. These, in turn, have a pervasive and persistent impact on organizations and their management practices. Japan has been different and will likely remain different for the foreseeable future. It is important to recognize that Japanese organizations remain among the most competitive in the world, and much can be learnt from them on issues of human resource management, organizational structure, global management, and R&D development. The recent negative developments in the Japanese economy should not be used as a reason to dismiss the management systems and global strategies, which the Japanese employ.

Note

1. This chapter is based on Alon, Ilan, Robert Moore and Wenxian Zhang (2007), 'Doing business in East Asia and the Pacific Rim', in W. Schmidt, R. Conaway, S. Easton and W. Wardrope (eds), *Communicating Globally: Intercultural Communication and International Business*, Thousand Oaks, CA: Sage Publications.

References

Ala, M. and W.P. Cordeiro (1999), 'Can we learn management techniques for the Japanese ringi process?' *Business Forum*, **24**(1/2), 22–3.

Alon, I. (ed.) (2003a), *Chinese Culture, Organizational Behavior, and International Business Management*, Westport, CT: Praeger.

Alon, I., (ed.) (2003b), *Chinese Economic Transition and International Marketing Strategy*, Westport, CT: Praeger.

Alon, I. (2005), 'The meaning of China: a newly powerful neighbor has Japan in fear and fascination', *ACCJ Journal*, 29 July, 24–9, available at: http://www.accj.or.jp/doclib/journal/05_feature3_jul05.pdf.

Alon, I. and E. Kellerman (1999), 'Meltdown in Southeast Asia: internal antecedents in the 1997 Asian economic crisis', *Multinational Business Review*, 7(2), 1–12.

Ambler, T. and Morgen W. (2004), *Doing Business in China*, 2nd edn, London: RoutledgeCurzon.

Atlas of the World (2004), 12th edn, London: Oxford University Press.

Beamish, P.W. (1999), Sony's Yoshihide Nakamura on structure and decision making', *Academy of Management Executive*, 13(4), 12–16.

Bhappu, A.D. (2000), 'The Japanese family: an institutional logic for Japanese corporate networks and Japanese management', *Academy of Management Review*, 25(2), 409–15.

Business Week (1999), 'Asia: how real is its recovery?' 36(27), 24.

Chang, G.G. (2001), *The Coming Collapse of China*, London: Random House.

Cragg, C. (1993), *Hunting With the Tigers: Doing Business With Hong Kong, Indonesia, South Korea, Malaysia, The Philippines, Singapore, Taiwan, Thailand, and Vietnam*, Amsterdam and San Diego, CA: Pfeiffer and Company.

Dana, L.P. (1999), *Entrepreneurship in Pacific Asia: Past Present & Future*, Singapore, London and Hong Kong: World Scientific.

Dana, L.P. (2000), *Economies of the Eastern Mediterranean Region: Economic Miracles in the Making*, Singapore, London and Hong Kong: World Scientific.

Dana, L.P. (2002), *When Economies Change Paths: Models of Transition in China, the Central Asian Republics, Myanmar, and the Nations of Former Indochine Française*, Singapore, London and Hong Kong: World Scientific.

Dana, L.P. (2007), *Asian Models of Entrepreneurship – From the Indian Union and the Kingdom of Nepal to the Japanese Archipelago: Context, Policy and Practice*, Singapore and London: World Scientific.

Fukuyama, F. (1998), 'Asian values and the Asian crisis', *Commentary*, 105(2), 23–8.

Gardels, N. (1998), *Global Fusion: Asian Ideals and Anglo-Saxon Norms*, Washington DC: Center for Democratic Institutions.

Greenspan, A. (1998), *Testimony before the Committee on Banking and Financial Services*, Washington, DC: US House of Representatives, January 30.

Gudykunst, W.B. and S. Ting-Toomey (1988), *Culture and Interpersonal Communication*, Newbury Park, CA: Sage.

Harrell, S. (2001), *Ways of Being Ethnic in Southwest China*, Seattle, WA: University of Washington Press.

Hendry, J. (2003), *Understanding Japanese Society*, 3rd edn, London: Routledge.

Hitchcock, D. (1998), 'Asian crisis is cultural as well as economic', *Pacific Forum Center for Strategic International Studies PacNet*, no. 15, http://www.csis.org/media/csis/pubs/pac9815.pdf.

Hofstede, G. (1991), *Culture and Organizations: Software of the Mind*, London: McGraw-Hill.

Kono, T. and S. Clegg (2001), *Trends in Japanese Management: Continuing Strengths, Current Problems, and Changing Priorities*, New York: Palgrave.

Krugman, P. (1998), 'Saving Asia: it's time to get radical', *Fortune*, 138(5), 74–80.

Lewis, M. (1998), 'The biggest going out of business sale', *The New York Times Magazine*, 31 May, pp. 37–41, 53, 58–64, 68–69.

Lohr, S. (1998), 'Business, Asian style: a revaluing of values; some say market collapse shows democracy is key to growth, after all', *New York Times*, 7 February, p. B9, col. 2.

Masui, K. and A. Kakabadse, (2002), 'Introducing officer systems in Japanese companies', *Corporate Governance*, 2(1), 10–12.

Mead, W.R. (1998), 'Asia devalued', *The New York Times Magazine*, May 31, pp. 38–9.

Meuhring, K. (1998), 'The fire next time', *Institutional Investor, Inc.*, September, p. 74.

Moore, R. (1988), 'Face and networks in urban Hong Kong', *City and Society*, 2, 50–59.

Murowchick, R. (1994), *Cradles of Civilization: China*, Norman, OK: University of Oklahoma Press.

Nathan, R. (1999), 'Matsushita hopes Silicon Valley links can boost its R&D', *Research Technology Management*, 42(2), 4–6.

Nishiyama, K. (1999), *Doing Business in Japan: Successful Strategies for Intercultural Communication*, Honolulu: University of Hawaii Press.

Roubini, N. (1999), 'Chronology of the Asian currency crisis and its global contagion', *NYU Asian Crisis Compilation*, New York: New York University, p. 2.

Sicherman, H. (1998), *The Asian Panic, Round Two*. Washington, DC: Foreign Policy Research Institute.

Simeon, R. (2001), 'Top team characteristics and the business strategies of Japanese firms', *Corporate Governance*, **1**(2), 4–13.

Spencer, J.W. (2001), 'How relevant is university-based research to private high-technology firms? A United States–Japan comparison', *Academy of Management Journal*, **44**(2), 432–40.

Sweet, L. (1999), 'Prospects for emerging markets', paper presented at the Federal Reserve Bank, 39th Central Banking Seminar, New York City, New York, January 12.

The Economist (1997), 'How far is down?', **345**(8043), 19–21.

The Economist (1998), 'Leaders: kill or cure?', editorial, **346**(8050), 13–14.

The Economist (1999), 'Stop the rot', **350**(8102), 19, 22.

The New Straits Times (1998), 'Be responsible, UMNO delegates told', 18 June, p. 1.

Time International (1998), '"Asian values" the crisis: an interview with Lee Kuan Yew', **150**(29), 24.

Walker, S. (1998), 'Debt "culture", Asian insolvency regimes feel strain; diversity bankruptcy systems in the region are suddenly forced to deal with a huge debt crisis', *National Law Journal*, 20(36), C3, col. 1.

Young, L.W.L. (1994), *Crosstalk and Culture in Sino-American Communication*, Cambridge: Cambridge University Press.

Zaman, M.R. (1998), 'The causes and consequences of the 1997 crisis in financial markets of East Asia', *The Journal of Global Business*, Fall, 37–43.

Zhou, D.R. (1998), 'Charting the course at the edges of the economic storm', *Pacific Forum CSIS*, PacNet no. 41.

46 Drivers of international entrepreneurship in Asia
Vanessa Ratten, Léo-Paul Dana and Isabell M. Welpe

Introduction

The aim of this edited book was to provide a comparative view of different entrepreneurship practices taking place in Asia. The book has examined the internationalization of small and medium enterprises (SMEs), as well as entrepreneurship in Asia.

This vast Asian continent is a geographic area that has a diverse array of countries with different cultures and business practices. It is an important continent as almost three-fifths of the world's population live in Asia. Seven of the 10 most populous countries in the world are located in Asia (China, India, Indonesia, Russia, Pakistan, Bangladesh and Japan). China and India are considered global business powerhouses and many countries in Asia such as Singapore, Hong Kong and Thailand have experienced strong economic growth rates in the past decade.

The rapid rise of many economies in Asia has been the result of globalization that has increased the importance of international business. Countries in Asia are becoming reliant on trade with other countries as trade barriers such as language, time zones and government regulations have decreased. Countries are retracting from being self-contained and isolated to countries that are becoming more reliant on trade experienced with other countries. In addition, the increase in technology has led some countries in Asia to advance faster than others in terms of manufacturing and production. This had led to some Asian economies specializing in certain industries, which in turn has led to an increase in international trade based on production demand in these industries. As an example, in the car industry the specialization of a country in Asia on the manufacturing process has led to a collation of efforts to produce a car. For example, the car may be designed by engineers in Asia, assembled in South Korea and sold in China.

The structure of this chapter is as follows. First, we provide a background to the research examined in this book. Next, the literature on the internationalization process of SMEs is reviewed, followed by a discussion on international entrepreneurship in Asia. Three major propositions are developed that relate to policy of fostering international entrepreneurship in Asia. We discuss how the findings from the chapters in this book are linked to the propositions. Finally, implications for public policy planners and practitioners are explained, with future research directions discussed.

International entrepreneurship

Asia in the last decade has catapulted to global prominence in the international business world and in this book we contribute to advancing the state of knowledge of international entrepreneurship in Asia. Part of the strong growth rates and international activities of businesses in Asia is due to the reliance on international entrepreneurship. There are a multitude of definitions for international entrepreneurship that exist in the literature (Fillis, 2007). McDougall (1989) defined it as the international activities of new ventures. Wright and Ricks (1994) saw it as a firm-level business activity, which involved business across cross-national borders. McDougall and Oviatt (2000), in a widely accepted definition used by numerous scholars, viewed it as the combination of innovative, proactive and risk-seeking behavior that crosses national borders, and this definition is adopted in this chapter. The internet and decreased shipping costs have resulted in more international marketplace opportunities for Asian firms. Ruzzier et al. (2006: 477) state 'internationalization is a synonym for the geographic expansion of economic activities over a national country's border'.

Previously closed markets in Asia such as China have motivated more businesses to focus on Asia. The role of SMEs in establishing markets outside their home countries is important in future economic growth (Ruzzier et al., 2006). In the past SMEs restricted their business activities to their home country or close neighbors. Ruzzier et al. (2006: 478) define internationalization as 'SMEs outward movement of international operations'. Internationalization theories have their roots in the behavioural theory of the firm, which was proposed by Cyert and March (1963). Entrepreneurs have been described as the main variable in an SME's internationalization process (Miesenbock, 1988). The success of international entrepreneurship requires an innovation that can be introduced to world markets.

Table 46.1 depicts the international trade composition of Asia. Each country in Asia that we have included in this book is stated together with its population, gross domestic product (GDP) composition by sector, export partners and import partners. As seen in Table 46.1, Asia incorporates a number of very diverse countries in terms of population, GDP and international business activities in terms of export and import partners.

An important part of international entrepreneurship is national and institutional environments. These environmental structures influence how entrepreneurial a country and region are. The decrease in trade barriers around the world has driven the success of many Asian economies. As much business occurs across national borders there is an increased reliance on Asia in international trade. International entrepreneurship in Asia is thriving as businesses form part of a global network (Geursen and Dana, 2001). In Asia this means that more firms are utilizing interorganizational collaborations such as strategic alliances, clusters and networks to engage in international business activity. Many firms in Asia undertake one or more steps of the production process for products and services of firms engaged in international markets.

The Uppsala school or traditional view of internationalization suggests that a firm goes through a gradual process to become international (Johanson and Vahlne, 1977). This gradual process, also referred to as the stages approach, has been criticized as not all firms undergo the same process of internationalization. Competition for many firms is now global, which means many firms focus on the international market from their inception. The 'born global' approach to firm internationalization refers to when a firm starts exporting or servicing the international market as soon as they begin their business (Oviatt and McDougall, 1999). Time is now an important strategic weapon in a firm's internationalization and success rate (Stalk, 1988). Timing is an important distinguishing feature of firm internationalization behavior (Coviello and Jones, 2004).

Government policy on SMEs and entrepreneurship: a comparison
In the Asian context some firms have taken a gradual process to internationalization whilst others have taken the born global approach. Some countries in Asia such as

Table 46.1   International trade composition of Asia

Country	Population	Gross domestic product composition by sector	Exports partners	Imports partners
Afghanistan	32 738 376	Agriculture: 80% Industry: 10% Services: 10% (2004 est.)	India 22.8%, Pakistan 21.7%, US 15.2%, UK 6.5%, Finland 4.4% (2006)	Pakistan 37.9%, US 12%, Germany 7.2%, India 5.1% (2006)
Armenia	2 968 586	Agriculture: 17.2% Industry: 36.4% Services: 46.4% (2007 est.)	Germany 18.3%, Netherlands 14.1%, Belgium 13.3%, Russia 13.1%, Israel 7%, US 6.1%, Georgia 5.1%, Iran 4.9% (2006)	Russia 21.8%, Ukraine 7.8%, Belgium 7.6%, Turkmenistan 7.1%, Italy 6.1%, Germany 5.7%, Iran 5.7%, Israel 4.8%, US 4.5%, Georgia 4.1% (2006)
Azerbaijan	8 177 717	Agriculture: 6.2% Industry: 63.3% Services: 30.5% (2007 est.)	Italy 44.7%, Israel 10.7%, Turkey 6.1%, France 5.5%, Russia 5.4%, Iran 4.6%, Georgia 4.5% (2006)	Russia 22.4%, UK 8.6%, Germany 7.7%, Turkey 7.3%, Turkmenistan 7%, Ukraine 6%, China 4.2% (2006)
Bahrain	718 306	Agriculture: 0.3% Industry: 43.6% Services: 56% (2007 est.)	Saudi Arabia 3.2%, US 3%, Japan 2.3% (2006)	Saudi Arabia 37.6%, Japan 6.8%, US 6.2%, UK 6.2%, Germany 5.1%, UAE 4.2% (2006)
Bangladesh	153 546 901	Agriculture: 19% Industry: 28.7% Services: 52.3% (2007 est.)	US 25%, Germany 12.6%, UK 9.8%, France 5% (2006)	China 17.7%, India 12.5%, Kuwait 7.9%, Singapore 5.5%, Hong Kong 4.1% (2006)
Cambodia	14 241 640	Agriculture: 31% Industry: 26% Services: 43% (2007 est.)	US 53.3%, Hong Kong 15.2%, Germany 6.6%, UK 4.3% (2006)	Hong Kong 18.1%, China 17.5%, Thailand 13.9%, Taiwan 12.7%, Vietnam 9%, Singapore 5.3%, South Korea 4.9%, Japan 4.3% (2006)

Table 46.1 (continued)

Country	Population	Gross domestic product composition by sector	Exports partners	Imports partners
China	1 330 044 605	Agriculture: 11.3% Industry: 48.6% Services: 40.1% (2007 est.)	US 21%, Hong Kong 16%, Japan 9.5%, South Korea 4.6%, Germany 4.2% (2006)	Japan 14.6%, South Korea 11.3%, Taiwan 10.9%, US 7.5%, Germany 4.8% (2006)
China: Special Administrative Regions	7 018 636 (Hong Kong)	Agriculture: 0.1% Industry: 8.1% Services: 91.7% (2007 est.) (Hong Kong)	China 47%, US 15.1%, Japan 4.9% (2006) (Hong Kong)	China 45.9%, Japan 10.3%, Taiwan 7.5%, Singapore 6.3%, US 4.8%, South Korea 4.6% (2006) (Hong Kong)
	460 823 (Macau)	Agriculture: 0.1% Industry: 3.9% Services: 96% (2006 est.) (Macau)	US 44.1%, China 14.8%, Hong Kong 11.3%, Germany 7.3%, UK 4.1% (2006) (Macau)	China 45.2%, Hong Kong 10.2%, Japan 8.4%, US 5.5%, Singapore 4.1%, France 4% (2006) (Macau)
India	1 147 995 898	Agriculture: 17.6% Industry: 29.4% Services: 52.9% (2007 est.)	US 17%, UAE 8.3%, China 7.7%, UK 4.3% (2006)	China 8.7%, US 6%, Germany 4.6%, Singapore 4.6%, Australia 4% (2006)
Indonesia	237 512 355	Agriculture: 13.8% Industry: 46.7% Services: 39.4% (2007 est.)	Japan 19.4%, Singapore 11.8%, US 11.5%, China 7.7%, South Korea 6.4%, Taiwan 4.2% (2006)	Singapore 29.6%, China 11.2%, Japan 8.8%, South Korea 5.3%, Malaysia 4.8% (2006)
Israel	7 112 359	Agriculture: 2.7% Industry: 30.2% Services: 67.1%	US 34.9%, Belgium 7.5%, Hong Kong 5.8%	US 15.9%, Belgium 7.9%, Germany 6.2%, China 6.1%, Switzerland 5.1%, UK 4.7%, Italy 4.1% (2006)
Japan	127 288 419	Agriculture: 1.4% Industry: 26.5% Services: 72% (2007 est.)	US 22.8%, China 14.3%, South Korea 7.8%, Taiwan 6.8%, Hong Kong 5.6% (2006)	China 20.5%, US 12%, Saudi Arabia 6.4%, UAE 5.5%, Australia 4.8%, South Korea 4.7%, Indonesia 4.2% (2006)

Table 46.1   (continued)

Country	Population	Gross domestic product composition by sector	Exports partners	Imports partners
Jordan	6 198 677	Agriculture: 3.5% Industry: 10.3% Services: 86.2%	US 22.4%, Iraq 12.9%, India 8.3%, UAE 7.8%, Saudi Arabia 7.5%, Syria 4.9%	Saudi Arabia 21%, China 9.7%, Germany 7.5%, US 4.7%, Egypt 4.4% (2006)
Kazakhstan	15 340 533	Agriculture: 5.8% Industry: 39.4% Services: 54.8% (2007 est.)	Germany 12.4%, Russia 11.6%, China 10.9%, Italy 10.5%, France 7.6%, Romania 5% (2006)	Russia 36.4%, China 19.3%, Germany 7.4% (2006)
Kyrgyzstan	5 356 869	Agriculture: 55% Industry: 15% Services: 30% (2000 est.)	Switzerland 26.1%, Kazakhstan 20.4%, Russia 19.3%, Afghanistan 9.4%, China 4.8% (2006)	Russia 38.1%, China 14.4%, Kazakhstan 11.7%, US 5.7% (2006)
Laos	6 677 534	Agriculture: 41.3% Industry: 32.2% Services: 26.5% (2007 est.)	Thailand 42.1%, Vietnam 9.5%, China 4% (2006)	Thailand 68.8%, China 11.3%, Vietnam 5.6% (2006)
Lebanon	3 971 941	Agriculture: 5.1% Industry: 19% Services 75.9%	Syria 26.1%, UAE 12.2%, Saudi Arabia 5.8%, Switzerland 5.5%	Syria 12.3%, Italy 8.6%, France 8.4%, US 7.1%, China 5.9%, Germany 5.4%, Saudi Arabia 4.9% (2006)
Malaysia	25 274 133	Agriculture: 13% Industry: 36% Services: 51% (2005 est.)	US 18.8%, Singapore 15.4%, Japan 8.9%, China 7.2%, Thailand 5.3%, Hong Kong 4.9% (2006)	Japan 13.3%, US 12.6%, China 12.2%, Singapore 11.7%, Thailand 5.5%, Taiwan 5.5%, South Korea 5.4%, Germany 4.4% (2006)
Maldives	379 174	Agriculture: 16% Industry: 7% Services: 77% (2006 est.)	Thailand 33.1%, UK 14.3%, Sri Lanka 11.9%, Japan 10.3%, France 6.9%, Algeria 6.1% (2006)	Singapore 23.2%, UAE 15.8%, India 11.1%, Malaysia 7.9%, Thailand 6.9%, Sri Lanka 5.7% (2006)

Table 46.1   (continued)

Country	Population	Gross domestic product composition by sector	Exports partners	Imports partners
Mongolia	2 996 081	Agriculture: 18.8% Industry: 40.4% Services: 40.8% (2006)	China 71.8%, Canada 11.7%, US 7.3% (2006)	Russia 29.8%, China 29.5%, Japan 11.9% (2006)
Myanmar	47 758 181	Agriculture: 50% Industry: 17.6% Services: 32.4% (2007 est.)	Thailand 48.8%, India 12.7%, China 5.2%, Japan 5.2% (2006)	China 35.1%, Thailand 22.1%, Singapore 16.4%, Malaysia 4.8% (2006)
Oman	3 311 640	Agriculture: 2.2% Industry: 38.3% Services: 59.5%	China 23.2%, South Korea 19.2%, Japan 12.2%, Thailand 8.9%, South Africa 8.3%, UAE 6.5%, Taiwan 4.2%	UAE 19.7%, Japan 18%, US 7.5%, Germany 5.3%, India 4.2% (2006)
Pakistan	167 762 040	Agriculture: 19.6% Industry: 26.8% Services: 53.7% (2007 est.)	US 21%, UAE 9%, Afghanistan 7.7%, China 5.3%, UK 5.1% (2006)	China 13.8%, Saudi Arabia 10.5%, UAE 9.7%, US 6.5%, Japan 5.7%, Kuwait 4.7%, Germany 4.1% (2006)
Palestine (West Bank)	2 611 904	Agriculture: 8% Industry: 13% Services: 79%	Israel, Jordan, Gaza Strip (no statistics available)	Israel, Jordan, Gaza Strip (no statistics available)
Philippines	92 681 453	Agriculture: 13.7% Industry: 31.4% Services: 54.8% (2007 est.)	US 18.3%, Japan 16.5%, Netherlands 10.1%, China 9.8%, Hong Kong 7.8%, Singapore 7.3%, Malaysia 5.6%, Taiwan 4.3% (2006)	US 16.3%, Japan 13.6%, Singapore 8.5%, Taiwan 8%, China 7.1%, South Korea 6.2%, Saudi Arabia 5.8%, Malaysia 4.1%, Thailand 4.1%, Hong Kong 4% (2006)
Qatar	928 635	Agriculture: 0.1% Industry: 71.2% Services: 28.7%	Japan 50.1%, Singapore 12.4%, India 6.5%, Thailand 6.1%, UAE 5%	US 14.2%, Italy 11.5%, Japan 9.5%, France 8.4%, Germany 7.8%, UK 6.1%, UAE 5.5%, Saudi Arabia 4.6% (2006)

Table 46.1   (continued)

Country	Population	Gross domestic product composition by sector	Exports partners	Imports partners
Russia	140 702 094	Agriculture: 4.7% Industry: 39.1% Services: 56.2% (2007 est.)	Netherlands 12.3%, Italy 8.6%, Germany 8.4%, China 5.4%, Ukraine 5.1%, Turkey 4.9%, Switzerland 4.1% (2006)	Germany 13.9%, China 9.7%, Ukraine 7%, Japan 5.9%, South Korea 5.1%, US 4.8%, France 4.4%, Italy 4.3% (2006)
Saudi Arabia	28 161 417	Agriculture: 3% Industry: 65.9% Services: 31.1%	US 16.8%, Japan 16.1%, South Korea 10.3%, China 7.8%, Taiwan 4.8%	US 12.6%, China 9.3%, Germany 8.8%, Japan 8.1%, Italy 5.1%, UK 4.5%, South Korea 4.1% (2006)
Singapore	4 608 167	Agriculture: 0% Industry: 31.2% Services: 68.8% (2007 est.)	Malaysia 13.1%, US 10.2%, Hong Kong 10.1%, China 9.7%, Indonesia 9.2%, Japan 5.5%, Thailand 4.2% (2006)	Malaysia 13%, US 12.7%, China 11.4%, Japan 8.3%, Taiwan 6.4%, Indonesia 6.2%, South Korea 4.4% (2006)
South Korea	49 232 844	Agriculture: 3% Industry: 39.4% Services: 57.6%	China 22%, US 12.5%, Japan 7.1%, Hong Kong 5% (2007)	China 17.7%, Japan 16%, US 10.7%, Saudi Arabia 5.9%, UAE 4.2% (2007)
Sri Lanka	21 128 773	Agriculture: 16.5% Industry: 26.9% Services: 56.5% (2007 est.)	US 27.7%, UK 11.3%, India 9.3%, Belgium 4.8%, Germany 4% (2006)	India 19.6%, China 10.5%, Singapore 8.8%, Iran 5.7%, Malaysia 5.1%, Hong Kong 4.2%, Japan 4.1% (2006)
Syria	79 747 586	Agriculture: 19.2% Industry: 14.5% Services: 66.3%	Iraq 29.6%, Lebanon 9.8%, Germany 6.5%, Italy 7.9%, Egypt 5.5%, Saudi Arabia 5.1%, France 4.9%	Saudi Arabia 12.1%, China 9.1%, Egypt 6.2%, Italy 6.1%, UAE 5.9%, Ukraine 4.9% (2006)
Taiwan	22 920 946	Agriculture: 1.4% Industry: 27.5% Services: 71.1% (2007 est.)	China 24%, Hong Kong 15%, US 13.4%, Japan 6.7% (2007 est.)	Japan 21%, China 12.7%, US 12.2%, South Korea 7.1%, Saudi Arabia 4.6% (2007 est.)

Table 46.1 (continued)

Country	Population	Gross domestic product composition by sector	Exports partners	Imports partners
Tajikistan	7211884	Agriculture: 23.4% Industry: 30.4% Services: 46.1% (2007 est.)	Netherlands 40.7%, Turkey 31.7%, Iran 5.4%, Uzbekistan 4.8%, Russia 4.7% (2006)	Russia 24.6%, Kazakhstan 10.8%, Uzbekistan 10.2%, China 8.6%, Azerbaijan 8% (2006)
Thailand	65493298	Agriculture: 11.4% Industry: 43.9% Services: 44.7% (2007 est.)	US 15%, Japan 12.6%, China 9%, Singapore 6.4%, Hong Kong 5.5%, Malaysia 5.1% (2006)	Japan 19.9%, China 10.6%, US 7.5%, Malaysia 6.6%, UAE 5.5%, Singapore 4.4% (2006)
Timor	1108777	Agriculture: 32.2% Industry: 12.8% Services: 55% (2005)	US, Germany, Portugal, Australia, Indonesia (Percentages not listed)	Not listed
Turkey	71892807	Agriculture: 8.9% Industry 28.3% Services 62.8%	Germany 11.2%, UK 8.1%, Italy 7%, France 5.6%, Russia 4.4%, Spain 4.3%	Russia 13.8%, Germany 10.3%, China 7.8%, Italy 5.9%, US 4.8%, France 4.6% (2006)
Turkmenistan	5179571	Agriculture: 11.5% Industry: 40.8% Services: 47.7% (2007 est.)	Ukraine 47.5%, Iran 16.4%, Azerbaijan 5.3% (2006)	UAE 15.5%, Turkey 11.1%, Ukraine 9.1%, Russia 9%, Germany 7.7%, Iran 7.6%, China 6.4%, US 4.5% (2006)
United Arab Emirates	4621399	Agriculture: 1.8% Indusry: 59.3% Services 38.9%	Japan 23.4%, South Korea 10.3%, Thailand 5%, India 4.8%	China 13.1%, India 10.2%, US 8.9%, Japan 6.2%, Germany 6.1%, Italy 4.7% (2006)
Uzbekistan	28268440	Agriculture: 29.4% Industry: 33.1% Services: 37.4% (2007 est.)	Russia 23.8%, Poland 11.7%, China 10.4%, Turkey 7.7%, Kazakhstan 5.9%, Ukraine 4.7%, Bangladesh 4.3% (2006)	Russia 27.8%, South Korea 15.2%, China 10.4%, Kazakhstan 7.3%, Germany 7.1%, Ukraine 4.8%, Turkey 4.5% (2006)

Table 46.1   (continued)

Country	Population	Gross domestic product composition by sector	Exports partners	Imports partners
Vietnam	86 116 559	Agriculture: 19.5% Industry: 42.3% Services: 38.2% (2007 est.)	US 21.2%, Japan 12.3%, Australia 9.4%, China 5.7%, Germany 4.5% (2006)	China 17.6%, Singapore 12.9%, Taiwan 11.5%, Japan 9.8%, South Korea 8.4%, Thailand 7.3%, Malaysia 4.2% (2006)

Source: Adapted from statistics found on https://www.cia.gov/library/publications/the-world-factbook/index.html (accessed 30 June 2008).

Vietnam and Singapore have focused on the global marketplace as a means of achieving rapid economic growth. Thai in the chapter on Vietnam found that the country has recognized the importance of SMEs to their international economic growth rate by completing a national SME development policy that will reduce SME start-up costs and continue regulatory reforms in the banking sector. Tan and Yoo in the chapter on Singapore found that SMEs which are mostly involved in exporting to the international market contribute 42 percent of the GDP and provide a support for large industries. However, other countries such as Russia have limited international activities as they have focused on their domestic market. Aidis, Korosteleva and Mickiewicz found in the chapter on Russia that despite it being the world's largest country, entrepreneurship is relatively new. Previous research shows that the emerging economies are different from established economies (Dana et al., 2008; Ratten et al., 2007). Other countries in Asia are only recently trying to focus on international markets and Ali in the chapter on Bangladesh highlights how the country is dependent on foreign aids and this has limited the types of industries that SMEs operate in as they largely specialize in the export of primary products and garments. An important driver of internationalization of firms in Asia has been the small and medium enterprise (SME) sector, which accounts for approximately 99 percent of all businesses in Asia. Morris, in the chapter on the United Arab Emirates, found that the United Arab Emirates government does not distinguish between SMEs and large firms and there are no income taxes, which further encourages business owners to establish small businesses. Small and medium enterprises sometimes take time before they are successful in the international market as they lack international managerial experience (Dana, 2005). Saidazimova in the chapter on Uzbekistan found that SMEs in the country lack international experience because it is hard for SMEs to compete as it is ranked amongst the world's most corrupt countries. Moreover, as opposed to large firms, SMEs typically have fewer written internationalization strategies (Mannio et al., 2003).

Both informal and formal networks SMEs utilize in order to gain access to an international market. Yalcin in the chapter on Turkey found that there are a number of government institutions that promote entrepreneurship in SMEs by utilizing informal and formal networks and these include the Industrial Training and Development Centre. Often these networks provide resource efficiencies that enable a firm cheaper and easier access to a market (Butler and Hanson, 1991). In the chapter on Malaysia, Madichie and Seow found that resources in the form of the Market Development Grant promoted internationalization of SMEs by covering their overseas promotional costs. Resources can be coordinated through networks in order to facilitate collaboration with firms in other international markets. In the Taiwan chapter, Ding and Chung found that SMEs have benefited from small business innovative research grants that have encouraged international collaboration. Most SMEs have a decentralized decision-making authority that is based around coordination between individuals in a firm. In the Turkmenistan chapter, McElwee found that most self-employed individuals operate micro-enterprises, which often operate informally and have a decentralized organizational structure. Large firms also often have access to a greater pool of network resources (Dana et al., 1999). For example, Morris in the chapter on the United Arab Emirates found that entrepreneurship is fostered in large firms by Free Trade Zones, which allow 100 percent foreign ownership. Networks are important drivers of international entrepreneurship in Asia. Rogmans in the chapter on Saudi Arabia found that it has increased the number of insurance companies and companies offering initial public offerings (IPOs) through networks with other financial institutions. Some previous research has focused on social ties in the internationalization process of firms (for example, Ellis, 2000; Ellis and Pecotich, 2001; Harris and Wheeler, 2005) and on business ties (for example, Chetty and Wilson, 2003; Coviello, 2006; Yli-Renko et al., 2002). Coviello (2006: 714) highlights that 'networks are widely recognized as influential in the internationalization process'. Network theory is an important part of international entrepreneurship (Oviatt and McDougall, 2005). Network ties drive the internationalization process of firms (Sharma and Blomstermo, 2003). Networks are primarily composed of socially embedded ties (Hite and Hesterly, 2001). These social ties can also be the result of serendipitous events (Crick and Spence, 2005). A firm that is internationalizing has a strong focus on social elements (Coviello, 2006). Ghoul in the chapter on Syria found that the government is utilizing social initiatives such as the country being energy self-sufficient to encourage small independent companies to invest in natural gas as the country is highly dependent on their export of oil reserves. Networks can open doors for internationalizing SMEs by allowing access to contacts that have information on finance and distribution channels (Coviello, 2006). Western management has mastered the art and science of doing business in the firm-type sector. In Asia, many opportunities are to be found in the bazaar and in the state-controlled planned sectors. In the bazaar, the movement of raw materials, processing, distribution and sales are intertwined activities. The focus on relationships supersedes the products and services that are being exchanged. A sliding price system results in prices that are negotiated, reflecting not only the cost or perceived value of a good or service, but also negotiating skills, the relationship between the buyer and the seller, and possibly the time, as well. Also important is an understanding of the parallel sector. Thus, the first proposition is:

Asian country governments need to distinguish their international market policies to take into account the difference in network structure between SMEs and large firms.

The environment for entrepreneurship and the state of small business in different countries: why the differences across Asian nations?
This book has included chapters on entrepreneurship and small business in Asia. Many governments across Asia recognize the importance of entrepreneurship but the way individual governments in Asia promote and encourage entrepreneurship varies greatly. For example, Cambodia is re-establishing the entrepreneurship sector after the Khmer Rouge extinguished the small business sector. In China, the entrepreneurial small business sector exists in supplement to the socialist political system. The culture, history and economic situation of a country in Asia influences the degree of importance placed on entrepreneurship. In India, the information technology sector has risen to become a global powerhouse by utilizing overseas networks of Indian businesspeople. In addition, education and national industry priorities influence entrepreneurship. In Japan, small business complements the entrepreneurship of large corporations by being part of inter-firm linkages. The nature of a domestic market can help to explain a firm's internationalization process (Oviatt and McDougall, 1999). Yalcin in the chapter on Turkey found that in Turkey the billion-dollar investment by foreign companies has led to renewed interest in developing complementary industries by SMEs. A domestic market that is very competitive means that a firm needs to concentrate more on the international market. Ranasinghe and Weerawardena in the chaper on Sri Lanka found that more government support is required to increase the support available for SMEs to concentrate on international markets. One of the quickest ways for a firm to develop their business in a competitive domestic market is to move into international markets. Ghoul found in the chapter on Syria that industries are developing as a result of foreign direct investment from Russia and some of the Gulf Arab countries. However, in markets that have insufficient domestic competition for some firms this means that there is no incentive to be internationally active. Sabri found in the chapter on Palestine that multi-currency circulations makes it difficult for entrepreneurs to focus on the local economy so initial entrepreneurship is made possible by family savings. Prashantham found in the chapter on India that the macro environment has not always been conducive to international entrepreneurship but India has been successful in the software industry by concentrating on the strengths of the Indian economy such as low wage rates and a high English-speaking population. Firms are affected by international competition differently depending on the industry in which they are in. For example, Madichie and Seow in the chapter on Malaysia found that the Information Technology industry has been promoted through the National SME Development Blueprint Act. Usually service-orientated industries are more international. Tan and Yoo in the chapter on Singapore found that Singapore has achieved high economic growth rates through promoting foreign multinationals and recently placing emphasis on local entrepreneurship. Technology industries are also very international because of standardization worldwide of their products and services. Ding and Chung in the chapter on Taiwan found that the establishment of an Industrial Technology Research Institute by the government has facilitated the development of high tech industrial clusters. Furthermore, Ding and Chung found that Taiwan has been competitive worldwide in its technology industries due to its interpersonal ties between Taiwanese individuals and Silicon Valley entrepreneurs. Firms in the technology sector have the added advantage of being international as they can reduce the costs of research and development. Thai in the chapter on Vietnam found that the technology industry

needs further financial reform so that banking transactions are easier to do online. Hopkins and Terjesen in the chapter on South Korea found that entrepreneurship is increased by investment in technology and this is strengthened by the country having the highest percentage of domestic capital investment as a percentage of GDP. Small and medium enterprises in Asia achieve global market power by being able to compete both domestically and globally by focusing on where it is cheapest and most efficient to produce their products and services. By linking into a value chain network of global firms they can further internationalize their business activities. In an industry context often the usage of technology indicates how competitive the industry is (Almeida and Kogut, 1997). This leads to the second proposition:

The competitive intensity of an industry should be taken into account when governments in Asia are evaluating international policy attitudes.

Internationalization of entrepreneurs and SMEs: why the differences across Asian nations?

Much of the international entrepreneurship research has focused on Western markets, which is why this edited book has focused on Asia. Studying entrepreneurship in different countries is important as it allows investigation of the conditions and characteristics that encourage entrepreneurship (Thomas and Mueller, 2006). Ali in the chapter on Bangladesh found that the entrepreneurial culture in Bangladesh is hampered by the lack of encouragement by the government to offer tax incentives for people to create new businesses. Entrepreneurs in Asia have different traits that relate to their own culture and upbringing. In the chapter on Laos Dana and Barthmann found that in Laos traditionally business activities were not associated with high social status, which has meant that more women and the Chinese community have concentrated on entrepreneurship. Some governments in Asia have encouraged entrepreneurship as a way of fostering international growth. International entrepreneurship is a measure of economic progress. Ali in the chapter on Bangladesh found that in developing countries like Bangladesh the government is promoting entrepreneurship through the establishment of monetary funds for SMEs in the agriculture-based industry and information and communication technology (ICT) sector. Significant changes have occurred in Asia during the past decade in terms of technological, social and political factors, which have influenced the attitudes of SMEs towards international entrepreneurship. However, as McElwee found in the chapter on Turkmenistan, entrepreneurs face hardship because of the high level of regulation and registration requirements required of small businesses. Moreover, in the chapter on Mongolia Innes-Brown found that the government has been proactive in trying to create a favorable economic and legal environment for SMEs through the 'SMEs Development Programme'. Entrepreneurs from different backgrounds undertake entrepreneurship for a variety of reasons some of which are driven by their ambition and motives (Turan and Kara, 2007). International entrepreneurship is important in Asia as it allows SMEs to deal with environmental constraints such as lack of political or legal safeguards (Jones, 2000). In the chapter on Vietnam Thai found that entrepreneurs are still somewhat skeptical of the weak law enforcement that exists in the country and they still prefer doing business using relationships. Galang and Tiong-Aquino also found in the chapter on the Philippines that legislation such as the BMBE Act have helped to encourage SMEs to export. Shachmurove found in the chapter on Qatar that it has implemented a common law framework based on Western law in order to foster international entrepreneurship. Thus, international entrepreneurship in Asia is intrinsically linked to cultural, social and business factors (Turan and Kara, 2007).

Economies in Asia are at different stages of transition. Saidazimova in the chapter on Uzbekistan found that the country has a competitive advantage in the gold industry as it has the world's sixth largest reserve of gold but as it is in the transition stage from being a former Soviet republic it needs more entrepreneurship to take advantage of business opportunities. Countries such as Singapore and Hong Kong have high average income levels where as Myanmar, the Maldives and Bangladesh are amongst the poorest countries in the world. Thus, in highly government-controlled economies such as Myanmar it can be difficult to estimate international business activity. Ghoul also found in the chapter on Syria that some countries in Asia are in the transition stage from having a highly government-controlled market to having a more open economy. Moreover, in Asian countries where there are a lot of state-owned enterprises, such as China, there may be understated export statistics by firms. In countries like Myanmar there is also little incentive for domestic firms to enter the international market. In countries that are still transitioning from different political systems, like Cambodia and Vietnam, there may be criminal networks and corruption in the local government, which makes firms reluctant to state their real export rates. Moreover, Adam in the chapter on Indonesia found that the country is not as attractive as its Southeast Asian neighbors due to the high costs of doing business and the lack of industry incentives. Asian countries that have had a market economy have learnt the importance of the international market. By increasing a firm's knowledge about foreign markets they are more likely to learn about international opportunities (Zahra et al., 2001). Rogmans in the chapter on Saudi Arabia found that the country is transitioning to more of a knowledge-based economy through its multi-billion dollar funding of universities and five-year plans. A firm learns about the international market through their experiential knowledge of foreign markets (Eriksson et al., 1997). Therefore, as learning from experience is a critical component of a firm's internationalization process, each firm learns at a different rate. In the chapter on the Maldives, Welpe and Dana found that tourism is the biggest and largest industry in the country as firms have learnt to focus on the international market due to the Maldives' small population. Learning about international markets can be demonstrated by export rates (Ratten, 2006). Exporting firms typically have higher productivity rates than non-exporting firms (Melitz, 2003) and are more productive than non-exporting firms (Greenway, 2004). For example, Katzenstein, Gimmon, Benjamin and Friedberg in the chapter on Israel found that the success of Israel's technology-based industries is largely the result of the country having one of the highest rates of economic growth in the Western world. In Asia, governments need to encourage firms to have a proactive attitude to exporting. Hipsher in the chapter on Thailand found that pro-investment government policies that encourage foreign investment and an international outlook have contributed to Thailand's economic performance. Moreover, he found that the informal entrepreneurial sector in Thailand includes mostly SMEs and lifestyle factors play a role in the development of entrepreneurship. The legacy of previous government regimes in Asia means that it takes time for firms to focus more on international markets. Lundahl and Sjöholm in the chapter on Timor-Leste found that 40 percent of the population lives in poverty; it is important that government policies focus on the development of entrepreneurship in SMEs. They also found that as Timor-Leste ranks very low in terms of a World Bank survey of ease of doing business it is crucial that foreign investment is encouraged, particularly in the banking sector. Therefore, the third proposition is that:

Transition economies in Asia will go through different stages of international development than developed countries in Asia.

Implications for public policy analysts

The findings from each of the chapters in this book provide important contributions to the practice of international entrepreneurship. Thus, it is important for owners of SMEs and government policy analysts to understand the characteristics and dynamics of Asian entrepreneurs. Companies and investors from around the world see Asia as an extremely attractive market that can be complemented with many Western companies in terms of the business environment and relatively high percentage of educated young people who speak both English and their national language. This book contributes to the growing interest in Asia that attempts to understand the similarities and differences of Asia compared to other parts of the world.

   Different governments have designed a variety of programmes to promote the development of entrepreneurship. Much spending, however, is in vain, as entrepreneurship development programs alone are insufficient. Programs may be useful to those who know about them; often, those who could use them the most are unaware of their existence. Furthermore, policies which are not implemented fairly consequently fail to have the desired effect on society. In some economies, bribery, excessive taxation and regulation can inhibit entrepreneurship. Factors that could facilitate entrepreneurship include: education; reductions in barriers to entry; the reduction of excessive regulation, bureaucracy and corruption; flat taxes; and the freedom to compete. Also beneficial is a stable legal framework. In order to facilitate entrepreneurship in Asia, governments need to encourage people to invest and support SMEs. As SMEs incorporate a large percentage of businesses in Asia it is vital that governments create a friendly business environment that encourages people to innovate and focus on the global market. A way in which governments can do this is through education. Education about export markets in terms of taxes and tariff rates, legal rules and product specifications can help enormously businesses to extend their international market opportunities. Governments in Asia that lend money or finance educational programs about internationalization activities of firms need to have training about finance, tax and payroll issues. Governments can also promote micro-lending to entrepreneurs with limited finance in developing areas of Asia. Some microfinance programs in Asia such as Grameen Bank have had success by relying on trust and word of mouth that is characteristic of some Asian countries' culture.

   Governments can also promote entrepreneurship by lessening tax and regulation rates so that more time and energy goes into the production and export of both manufacturing and service industries. A priority for governments should be to determine the appropriate degree of regulation to enact and to enforce, such that the benefits to society exceed the costs of compliance. businesses. While some regulation is required to ensure order, excessive intervention is counter-productive. Where import duties are considerable, smuggling becomes popular – as is the case in Myanmar and in Vietnam. Even a culture supportive of entrepreneurship benefits from the optimal level of regulation and government intervention. Transition countries in Asia can also learn from developed countries in the region that have a stable legal framework that enables international competition to flourish. Some government intervention is required in Asia to promote entrepreneurship and new business activity. Countries with low levels of international business activity, such as Cambodia and Myanmar, can learn from the example of planned export activity that has been very successful in Asian countries like China, South Korea and Singapore. It appears that the optimal level of regulation and government intervention is culture-specific. Policy-makers should therefore keep in mind that the success of a policy or program in the West does not guarantee equal success elsewhere. For this reason, it is crucial to avoid trans-locating these from one environment to a different one. To be effective, policies and programs should be appropriate to the culture of a society. Policy-makers should be aware of the cultural attributes of different ethnic groups, and policy should take these differences into account.

Asian governments also need to invest more in infrastructure so that there is access to roads, railways and ports so they can transport goods around the world. While some countries in Asia, such as Japan, have very good public transport systems, other countries in Asia, such as Indonesia, need to invest in public transport and infrastructure to promote business activity. Policies that encourage foreign investment in infrastructure and education will enable countries in Asia to further strengthen their position in the world economy. The role of culture on government policies needs to be taken into account when discussing entrepreneurship issues in Asia. The level of government intervention is dependent on a country's culture so it is important that policies designed to promote entrepreneurship are developed on an individual basis rather than being transferred from one country in Asia to another. These entrepreneurial policies also need to take into account how broad participation in economic development can be encouraged. Initiatives can include increasing funding to agriculture thereby allowing some Asian countries to be self-sufficient and improving vocational education about how to start and successfully develop a small business. In order to facilitate more small business activity the legal environment of some Asian countries needs to be more transparent so that property rights are improved and there is further liberalization of trade. Further development of entrepreneurship can occur through improving foreign investment policies and the management of government expenditures linked to performance objectives such as the increase in export activity of local

Perhaps the most valuable advice one can give to public policy analysts is that the importance of cultural differences should not be underestimated. There is neither one Asian culture, nor one Asian model. Just because people live in the same region, it does not mean that they share the same views about entrepreneurship. This is further complicated in pluralistic societies, where unlike cultures each have their own implicit and explicit assumptions. Risk also varies with different types of pluralism. Melting pot pluralism – the situation prevailing when minorities adapt to a secular mainstream society – is stable. In contrast, when ethnic groups do not share a mainstream society, polarization can result in violence, as has been the case in Indonesia, Myanmar, and elsewhere. There is no consistency across nations.

Nor is there consistency across time, and public policy-makers and analysts should keep in mind that in some transitional economies – such as Myanmar – the newly emerging private sector lacks professional, financial and economic structure. Rules change frequently. What is legal today may be banned tomorrow, and vice versa. Also, the ownership of property is not clearly documented, and the liquidity of immoveable assets is often delayed. Where acquisition is not practical, foreign investors may enter markets via networks. Given that communist planners traditionally emphasized vertical integration, public policy analysts might find it necessary to explain how, in a market economy, synergy often comes from horizontal integration.

In each economy, the nature of entrepreneurship will evolve in time, but one should not expect entrepreneurship to converge across societies. There is no one formula for a 'best' policy to promote entrepreneurship. Entrepreneurship is embedded in society, and the latter is affected by historical experience and cultural values. To understand the global nature of entrepreneurship, we must move beyond a universal model or a Western model; entrepreneurship must be understood in the context of national development, and importantly, policy-makers should take note that to be relevant, policies must be culturally sensitive.

Implications for entrepreneurs
In Asia networks and relationships are very important for entrepreneurs who want to grow the international activities of their businesses. Both transactions and profits are a function of networks and relationships, and by emphasizing reciprocal preferential treatment more profitability can result for entrepreneurs. Thus, entrepreneurs in Asia and outside investors wanting to encourage Asian entrepreneurs need to foster their business contacts so that it is easier and more efficient for them to gain access to different segments of their supply chain.

The vast differences in people in Asia due to value systems, class structures and religion means that these differences need to be taken into account by businesses. Respect must be paid to minorities and immigrant entrepreneurs throughout Asia as well as to entrepreneurs choosing to establish their headquarters in their home countries. Throughout Asia there is more diversity than in other parts of the world due to government systems in place. Some political systems in Asia are democratic whilst others are totalitarian or communist in nature. Thus, entrepreneurs in Asia need to realize how the differences in political systems impact on their business activities and how they can work with government officials in Asia productively.

Entrepreneurs should also be aware that Asia is changing quickly and this depends on the country and political context. Thus, in some Asian countries that are changing political and legal structures, such as Afghanistan, entrepreneurs need to be aware that the legal rules may change. It also might be harder to establish businesses in these areas as there may be a lack of English-speaking individuals or people with international management experience. Most importantly for entrepreneurs is the realization that Asia is a number of diverse countries and there is no single standard approach to conducting business in Asia but rather it is dependent on the religious and cultural values of a country. For example, countries such as Myanmar have a newly emerging private sector that is still developing legal rules and the country in general has a lack of professionals with experience in international financial transactions. Entrepreneurs in transitioning countries like Myanmar need to realize that ownership of property is not clearly documented and that often selling property may take some time to occur.

Entrepreneurs in Asia should also realize that in some Asian countries business is conducted differently. In the West, most business activity takes place through the firm-type sector that operates generally in a competitive market environment. However, in Asia some business is conducted through the state-controlled planned sector or through the informal market economy of markets and bazaars. This means that relationships between businesspeople are often the focus of the transaction rather than the product or service being sold or bought. Therefore, for entrepreneurs to succeed they need to realize that negotiating skills are important as are an understanding of the parallel sector in terms of the distribution and production of materials being intertwined activities.

Implications for entrepreneurship educators
The findings of this book suggest that factors which facilitate entrepreneurship include cultural attitude. Culture is central in explaining the social acceptability and perceived utility of entrepreneurship. More education is required in Asia that focuses on both cultural values and technical content. In order to be successful globally, entrepreneurship educators should teach more about ethics and religion so more is known about doing business in Asia. Previously, most of the education for entrepreneurship educators has been at the managerial level with content about accounting and tax rates being taught. However, more education is required on how to sustain entrepreneurship for the long term and a good way to do this is to combine teachings on managerial content with more general education about culture, ethics and religion of Asian countries. In addition, as technology and the world economy is changing at a fast rate, there is often a mismatch between the skills people have in some Asian countries and what the demand is in the workforce. Therefore, based on the rate of privatization or downsizing of state-owned enterprises in Asia, the technical content of what is in demand by businesses needs to be taught so that more people can be hired in appropriate jobs that encourage entrepreneurship. Training is require to help managers in Asia to solve complex business matters that include transportation, planning and distribution.

Educators can also promote the acceptance of entrepreneurship in Asia by highlighting how it is a legitimate and honest path to economic independence. Whilst some entrepreneurial activity in Asia is illegitimate in terms of informal or covert activities, entrepreneurship that is legitimate can promote employment opportunities and gain funding from government bodies or non-governmental authorities that promote entrepreneurship in Asia. Educators who promote a culture in Asia of having an entrepreneurial spirit can enhance the environment for entrepreneurship that exists in Asia. Entrepreneurship educators can encourage people in Asia to become entrepreneurs by teaching them entrepreneurial characteristics like being innovative and risk taking in business. Where a vibrant entrepreneurial class is absent, this may be due to the public policy environment, or to the lack of inherent entrepreneurial characteristics. Where entrepreneurial spirit exists, new venture programs may further enhance the environment for entrepreneurship, as is the case in the United States. However, in a transitional society with little experience of legitimate entrepreneurship, education should first focus on encouraging an entrepreneurship-friendly ideology. In addition, economies within Asia that are in the transition stage that have little experience of legitimate entrepreneurship should focus on educating their population to be more entrepreneurially friendly in terms of ideology and culture. As the entrepreneurial spirit increases then this will foster further new venture programs that encourage more entrepreneurship.

Suggestions for future research

More cross-cultural research is needed within Asia. Future researchers may use this book as a first-stop guide to understanding the distinguishing characteristics of entrepreneurship in Asia. More cross-cultural research would enable more generalizable entrepreneurship theories that take into account different economies. Moreover, an understanding of how entrepreneurs differ by culture in Asia may provide much needed insights into how to encourage more international entrepreneurship. As Asia is such a diverse area of countries that differ in population, religion and social values, much more research on entrepreneurship needs to be undertaken.

Future researchers, public policy practitioners and entrepreneurs can use this book to compare and contrast different entrepreneurship policies in Asia. There is much information in this book that needs to be further analysed and utilized to examine international entrepreneurship in Asia. For example, as evident from the research reported in this book entrepreneurship in Asia is not the same in each country. There is no single best policy to promote entrepreneurship, nor is entrepreneurship coverging across Asia. Hence, as entrepreneurship is a function of a country's society, future research should examine in more detail how historical experience, culture and religion have affected entrepreneurship within different Asian countries. Countries within Asia such as Singapore and India that were once part of the British Empire can be compared to see how they have developed based on historical change. Future research should also move beyond characterizing all entrepreneurship around the world as the same and instead take into account cultural sensitivities that make each country in Asia unique.

While entrepreneurial activity has been prescribed as the remedy for poverty, experience shows that entrepreneurial activity creates problems of its own. Of what good is rapid transition if its adverse effects are uncontrolled? It is useful to look not only at the creation of wealth, but also at its distribution. Myanmar is an example of rich country with a population that is mostly poor. Class mobility, in such an environment, is often a function of access to bribes rather than productive creativity or economic innovation. It would be wrong to attempt to understand entrepreneurship or innovation in isolation. What must change and what need not? The answer depends upon historical context and current situation, as well as the result desired. A variety of models are means to achieve different results. This is where more research is needed.

More research is required on the illegitimate entrepreneurship that occurs within Asia and how entrepreneurship may not guarantee economic growth for a nation. Future policy analysts should research what they can do to encourage entrepreneurship that fosters increased standards of living for people and at the same time ensures that wealth and social issues are spread through a country instead of being concentrated in the hands of a small number of people. More research could also examine how Asia is different to other geographic areas such as Europe and North America. The role of organizations such as the European Union and how Asia can utilize some of the same policies to promote entrepreneurship needs to be researched further. Finally, this research could be expanded by using more than a single paper on each country. This would increase the validity and reliability of the results as more information about each country would be provided to the researcher. This could also allow for a more comprehensive coding form and matrix to be developed.

Conclusion

Entrepreneurship is constantly changing. The rapid success and changing nature of many countries in Asia means that it is important to understand how entrepreneurship is developing. There are a variety of different types of entrepreneurship in Asia such as corporate, social and family entrepreneurship that all encourage international entrepreneurship. To understand the global nature of entrepreneurship in Asia it is important to move beyond a universal model and to understand each Asian country's uniqueness. This edited book has discussed entrepreneurship in a variety of different countries in Asia. The chapters in this book demonstrate that government policy is instrumental in explaining international entrepreneurial activity. The majority of the countries had some form of policy in place that facilitated international trade, which portrays that governments are taking an active role in creating a better international entrepreneurship activity. We hope that further research will use this book as a guide to elaborate on entrepreneurship in Asia.

Acknowledgement

We thank Professor David Smallbone for his endless input and ideas.

References

Almeida, P. and B. Kogut (1997), 'The exploration of technological diversity and the geographic localization of innovation', *Small Business Economics*, **9**, 21–31.

Butler, J.E. and G.S. Hanson (1991), 'Network evolution, entrepreneurial success and regional development', *Entrepreneurship & Regional Development*, **3**, 1–16.

Chetty, S.K. and H.I.M. Wilson (2003), 'Collaborating with competitors to acquire resources', *International Business Review*, **12**(1), 61–81.

Coviello, N. (2006), 'The network dynamics of international new ventures', *Journal of International Business Studies*, **37**(1): 713–31.

Coviello, N.E. and M.V. Jones (2004), 'Methodological issues in international entrepreneurship research', *Journal of Business Venturing*, **19**, 485–508.

Crick, D. and M. Spence (2005), 'The internationalization of "high performing" UK high-tech SMEs: a study of planned and unplanned strategies', *International Business Review*, **14**(2), 167–85.

Cyert, R.M. and J.G. March (1963), *A Behavioural Theory of the Firm*, Englewood Cliffs, NJ: Prentice Hall.

Dana, L.-P. (2005), *When Economies Change Hands: A Survey of Entrepreneurship in the Emerging Markets of Europe from the Balkans to the Baltic States*, Binghamton: Haworth Press.

Dana, L.-P., H. Etemad and R.W. Wright (1999), 'The impact of globalization on SMEs', *Global Focus*, **11**(4), 93–105.

Dana, L.-P., I.M. Welpe, M. Han and V. Ratten (eds) (2008), *Handbook of Research on European Business and Entrepreneurship: Towards a Theory of Internationalization,* Cheltenham, UK and Northampton, MA, USA: Edward Elgar Publishing.

Ellis, P. (2000), 'Social ties and foreign market entry', *Journal of International Business Studies*, **31**(3), 443–69.

Ellis, P. and A. Pecotich (2001), 'Social factors influencing export initiatives in small and medium-sized enterprises', *Journal of Marketing Research*, **38**(1), 119–30.

Eriksson, K., J. Johanson, A. Majkgard and D. Sharma (1997), 'Experiential knowledge and cost in the internationalization process', *Journal of International Business*, **28**(2), 1–25.

Fillis, I. (2007), 'A methodology for researching international entrepreneurship in SMEs: a challenge to the status quo', *Journal of Small Business and Enterprise Development*, **14**(1), 118–35.

Geursen, G. and L.-P. Dana (2001), 'International entrepreneurship: the concept of intellectual internationalization', *Journal of Enterprising Culture*, **9**(3), 331–52.

Greenway, D. (2004), 'The assessment: firm-level adjustment to globalization', *Oxford Review of Economic Policy*, **20**(3), 335–40.

Harris, S. and C. Wheeler (2005), 'Entrepreneurs relationships for internationalization: functions, origins and strategies', *International Business Review*, **14**(2), 187–207.

Hite, J.M. and W.S. Hesterly (2001), 'The evolution of firm networks: from emergence to early growth of the firm', *Strategic Management Journal*, **22**(3), 275–86.

Johanson, J. and J.-E. Vahlne (1977) 'The internationalization process of the firm – a model of knowledge development and increasing foreign market commitments', *Journal of International Business Studies*, **8**(1), 23–32.

Jones, K. (2000), 'Psychodynamics, gender and reactionary entrepreneurship in metropolitan Sao Paulo, Brazil', *Women Management Review*, **15**(4), 207–15.

Mannio, P., E. Vaara and P. Yla-Anttila (2003), *Our Path Abroad. Exploring Post-War Internationalization of Finnish Corporations*, Helsinki: Taloustieto Oy.

McDougall, P.P. (1989), 'International versus domestic entrepreneurship: a comparison of new venture behavior and industry structure in the computer and communications industries', *Journal of Business Venturing*, **4**, 387–400.

McDougall, P.P. and B.M. Oviatt (2000), 'International entrepreneurship: the intersection of two research paths', *Academy of Management Journal*, **43**(5), 902–906.

Miesenbock, K.J. (1988), 'Small business and exporting: a literature review', *International Small Business Journal*, **6**(2), 42–61.

Melitz, M. (2003), 'The impact of trade on intraindustry reallocations and aggregate industry productivity', *Econometrica*, **71**, 1695–725.

Oviatt, B.M. and P.P. McDougall (1999), 'A framework for understanding accelerated international entrepreneurship', in R.W. Wright (ed), *International Entrepreneurship: Globalization of Emerging Businesses*, Stamford, CT: JAI Press, pp. 23–40.

Oviatt, B.M. and P.P. McDougall (2005), 'Defining international entrepreneurship and modeling the speed of internationalization', *Entrepreneurship Theory and Practice*, **29**(5), 537–53.

Ratten, V. (2006), 'Policy drivers of international entrepreneurship in Europe', *EuroMed Journal of Business*, **1**(2), 15–28.

Ratten, V., L. Dana, M. Han and I. Welpe (2007), 'The differences in international entrepreneurship in transition economies versus established economies in Europe.', *International Journal of Entrepreneurship and Small Business*, **4**(3), 361–79.

Ruzzier, M., R.D. Hisrich and B. Antoncic (2006), 'SME internationalization research: past, present and future', *Journal of Small Business and Enterprise Development*, **13**(4), 476–97.

Sharma, D.D. and A. Blomstermo (2003), 'The internationalization process of born globals: a network view', *International Business Review*, **12**(6), 739–53.

Stalk, G. (1988), 'Time – the next source of competitive advantage', *Harvard Business Review*, July–August, 41–51.

Thomas, A.S. and S.L. Mueller (2006), 'A case for comparative entrepreneurship: assessing the relevance of culture', *Journal of International Business Studies*, **31**(2), 287–99.

Turan, M. and A. Kara (2007), 'An exploratory study of characteristics and attributes of Turkish entrepreneurs: a cross-country comparison to Irish entrepreneurs', *Journal of International Entrepreneurship*, **5**, 25–46.

Wright, R.W. and D.A. Ricks (1994), 'Trends in international business research: twenty-five years later', *Journal of International Business Studies*, **25**, 687–701.

Yli-Renko, H., A. Autio and V. Tontti (2002), 'Social capital, knowledge and the international growth of technology-based new firms', *International Business Review*, **11**(3), 279–304.

Zahra, S., J. Hayton, J. Marcel and H. O'Neill (2001), 'Fostering entrepreneurship during international expansion: managing key challenges', *European Management Review*, **19**(4), 359–69.

Index